UNCOMMON READERS:
DENIS DONOGHUE, FRANK KERMODE,
GEORGE STEINER, AND
THE TRADITION OF THE COMMON READER

UNCOMMON READERS

Denis Donoghue, Frank Kermode, George Steiner, and the Tradition of the Common Reader

Christopher J. Knight

UNIVERSITY OF TORONTO PRESS

Toronto Buffalo London

© University of Toronto Press Incorporated 2003
Toronto Buffalo London
Printed in Canada

ISBN 0-8020-8798-1

∞

Printed on acid-free paper

National Library of Canada Cataloguing in Publication

Knight, Christopher J., 1952–
Uncommon readers : Denis Donoghue, Frank Kermode, George
Steiner, and the tradition of the common reader / Christopher J. Knight

Includes bibliographical references and index.
ISBN 0-8020-8798-1

1. Donoghue, Denis.   2. Kermode, Frank, 1919–   3. Steiner, George,
1929–   4. Criticism – History – 20th century.   5. Book reviewing –
History – 20th century.   I. Title.

PN74.K55 2003   801'.95'0922   C2003-903075-X

University of Toronto Press acknowledges the financial assistance to
its publishing program of the Canada Council for the Arts and the
Ontario Arts Council.

University of Toronto Press acknowledges the financial support for
its publishing activities of the Government of Canada through the
Book Publishing Industry Development Program (BPIDP).

For

Ian and Matthew

CONTENTS

ACKNOWLEDGMENTS

I began researching and writing *Uncommon Readers* while living and teaching in the American Midwest, continued while doing much the same in upstate New York, and finished, more or less, in Missoula, Montana. Now in Aberystwyth, Wales, I look back with great gratitude for the people (more numerous because of the moves) who supported me along the way. The nature of the support was, of course, various, and I could, if required, categorize it according to the familiar categories. But fearing that such might become too Byzantine, I wish to say simply that the following people come to mind when I think of the time spent writing this book: Bob Baker, John and Kathy Cassidy, Angus Collins, Jane and Randall Craig, Sarah E. Hapner, Charissa Jones, Candice L. Knight, Robert E. Knight and family, Michael Holquist, Barbara Lundin and family, Anne ('Ma') Mancini, Allyson N. May, Jill McConkey, Kristen Pederson, Barbara Porter, Jayne Rachman and family, Walter Reed, Jim Reiss, Suzie Ryan and family, Jim Sosnoski, Keith Tuma, Lois Welch, and the University of Toronto Press's two anonymous readers. The book is dedicated to my two young sons, Ian and Matthew, blessings far greater than my deserving. And, as always, my most profound gratitude goes to my parents, Robert and Rosemary Knight, for their constancy, generosity, and love.

ABBREVIATIONS

Donoghue Texts

AWM	*The Arts without Mystery*
BBB	'Bewitched, Bothered, and Bewildered'
BMT	*Being Modern Together*
CC	*Connoisseurs of Chaos*
ETE	*England, Their England*
FA	*Ferocious Alphabets*
JS	*Jonathan Swift*
OU	*The Ordinary Universe*
PGT	*The Pure Good of Theory*
RA	*Reading America*
SCD	'The Strange Case of Paul de Man'
SG	*The Sovereign Ghost*
TF	*Thieves of Fire*
UAT	'The Use and Abuse of Theory'
W	*Warrenpoint*
WI	*We Irish*

Kermode Texts

AFK	*Addressing Frank Kermode*, ed. Margaret Tudeau-Clayton and Martin Warner
AP	*An Appetite for Poetry*
AT	*The Art of Telling*
C	*Continuities*
CS	Interview with Imre Salusinszky, in *Criticism in Society*

GS	*The Genesis of Secrecy*
FOA	*Forms of Attention*
HV	*History and Value*
L	*D.H. Lawrence*
LGB	*The Literary Guide to the Bible*
NE	*Not Entitled*
PE	*Puzzles and Epiphanies*
PNH	*Poetry, Narrative, History*
SE	*The Sense of an Ending*
SSD	*Shakespeare, Spenser, Donne*
TC	*The Classic*
UE	*The Uses of Error*
WS	*Wallace Stevens*

Steiner Texts

A	*Antigones*
AB	*After Babel*
AC	'The Art of Criticism II'
AE	'Archives of Eden'
BC	*In Bluebeard's Castle*
DT	*The Death of Tragedy*
E	*Extraterritorial*
FF	'A Friend of a Friend'
GSR	*George Steiner: A Reader*
H	*Martin Heidegger*
LLM	'The Long Life of Metaphor: Shoah'
LRS	'Little-Read Schoolhouse'
LS	*Language and Silence*
MH	'Making a Homeland for the Mind'
OD	*On Difficulty*
OHT	'Our Homeland, the Text'
PSC	*The Portage to San Cristóbal of A.H.*
R	'The Remembrancer'
RGS	*Reading George Steiner*, ed. Nathan A. Scott, Jr, and Ronald A. Sharp
RP	*Real Presences*
RI	'The Responsibility of Intellectuals,' a discussion moderated by Robert Boyers

SR	*The Scandal of Revelation*
TD	*Tolstoy or Dostoevsky*
TGD	'Through That Glass Darkly'
TT	'Totem or Taboo'
UR	*The Uncommon Reader*
WOW	'Wording Our World'

UNCOMMON READERS:
DENIS DONOGHUE, FRANK KERMODE,
GEORGE STEINER, AND
THE TRADITION OF THE COMMON READER

A genuine interest in criticism is an achievement in creation.
– Marianne Moore

INTRODUCTION

Criticism and a Common Culture

In his 'Preface' to *Beyond Culture* (1965), Lionel Trilling defended his use of the pronoun 'we' against the charge that it was 'imprecise and indiscriminate.' One reviewer, writing in the *Times Literary Supplement*, said that it was not always clear as to whether the pronoun's antecedents meant Trilling's contemporaries, his countrymen or, more narrowly, New York intellectuals. Trilling, a bit disingenuously, sloughed off the reference to New York intellectuals by saying that he did not think that such a group would wish to have its views identified with his own. In fact, said Trilling, 'if I try to discern the range of my pronoun, I would say that it very likely does move among the entities of diverse size that the writer names.' While this, no doubt, placed him in a vexed relation to various factions, he was confident that there was enough continuity among these factions that the 'we' might stand. '[T]he assumption of cultural continuities,' said Trilling, 'is not easily put down.' True, there were differences between nations such as Great Britain and the United States, but 'the sense of the dissimilarities even between England and America must go along with the perception of what is similar or congruent in the cultures of the two nations, less in what they may be thought to derive from their respective pasts than in what they are in the process of choosing from the possibilities of the present.' Here, '[t]he differences are of rate and phase.' Nor does the situation change much even when we speak of nations less historically related than Britain and the United States: 'The same may be said of certain of the differences among other nations. One cannot be aware of the large sub-culture ... of youth, of those characteristics that are shared by the young of many lands, without giving credence to the supposition that a world-wide continuity of culture tends to come into being and that it is possible to make predications about it.'

In the interim, much has changed in the intellectual climate, and, globalization notwithstanding, Trilling's presumption that cultures are more or less alike is one of the things that has changed most radically. The present is a time of cultural politics, and this has had a profound consequence upon literary criticism. Nowadays, the first thing that a critic often does is to declare his or her 'subject position' (as in Leslie Heywood's 'from an engaged subject position that is above all personal').[1] For whom does he or she propose to speak? For which group? And what credentials, what right, does the writer have to speak for such? The questions arise not only in literary criticism but in intellectual and artistic culture in general. Can one not of African descent – e.g., Norman Jewison – propose making a film about Malcolm X? Can a non-Islamic critic – e.g., Bernard Lewis – speak to Islamic experience? Can a male theorist – e.g., Terry Eagleton – employ 'the language of feminist criticism'?[2] Can a female critic – e.g., Eve Kosofsky Sedgwick – speak to male homosexual desire? Can a woman play Hamlet and a man play Rosalind? And when the latter do (as in recent productions), how does this redefine our notions of gender and what is expected of us? These are the kinds of questions that we now ask and they are not uninteresting.[3] Not to ask them, to carry on as if matters such as gender, ethnicity, and religion have no importance, might even serve as evidence of a critic's naiveté or lack of candour. Still, these forms of criticism are often disturbingly deterministic, as a perusal of a recent Modern Language Association call for convention papers well illustrates. Here, when 'problematics' are not at issue – as in '[t]he problematics of defining Generation X' or '[t]he problematics of cross-cultural dialogue in international writing by women' – determinations are. Thus one panel proposes to discuss the '[w]ays in which citizenship and subjectivity determine each other,' a second panel, '[o]rality as a determining trope in figurations of lesbianism,' and a third panel, '[h]ow reprinting in Everyman's, Modern Library, RLS, and so on determines literary reputation.' Determinations are a difficult thing to avoid, and there is reason enough for thinking them part of the aesthetic equation. Yet to speak of a poem or painting only in terms of its most accessible determinants – what Hillis Miller calls 'the Three Fates of contemporary cultural studies: race, gender, and class' (*Topographies*, 201) – is to immure ourselves within a rather small circle. Thus while Trilling, so affirming of a common culture, may appear ingenuous to present-day critics, the ingenuousness may not be all one-sided. Trilling can, I suppose, be accused of a failure to notice the forces of difference, even though as a Jew living at mid-century, he experienced such forces powerfully enough.[4] But whatever the compensations of cultivating one's personal cultural identity, he felt that there were even more compensations to be had by taking up residence, whether expressly welcome or not, in the middle of things, where a fractious community's tensions and contradictions cannot be avoided but must be negotiated and, if possible, reconciled.

What we find and most value in Trilling – and it is my argument with respect to Denis Donoghue, Frank Kermode, and George Steiner as well – is a criticism characterized by a willingness to reside in contradictions, to review and to take responsibility for conveying a host of viewpoints, not all of which the critic finds congenial, but which nevertheless enhance the critic's own best sense that final determinations should be kept in abeyance as long as possible. It is a criticism that practises the principle of negative capability, not because it has given up the hope, in deconstructive fashion, that determinations are themselves unreachable, but because it believes that the finest determinations will be those that take into account as many avenues of discussion as possible. It is a stance, says Andrew Delbanco, that hoped for 'nothing less than a deepened awareness of the paradox of being human' ('Night Vision,' 39), and, says Morris Dickstein, that predicates itself on 'the sense that the genuinely discriminating mind, unlike the political or ideological mind, does not understand itself too quickly, and doesn't move easily from reflection to action' (*Double Agent*, 69). Trilling is valued not because he can be identified with either a subject or an ideological position, but because he assumes it his responsibility to be welcoming to a variety of positions and because he appears patient even with those whose insistence verges upon an affront. It is what leads Dickstein to write that 'Trilling's distinctive style is rarely noticed by commentators who try to give his work a strongly ideological character. When they cut through his rhetoric to the Archimedian point of his belief or commitment, they are cutting away nearly everything we are likely to value about him – not his certitudes, which were few, but his way of arriving at them; not his ideology, but the undulations of mind that ran counter to the fixities of ideology' (*Double Agent*, 78–9).

In Trilling, Delbanco and Dickstein both celebrate a more traditional form of critical play, be it Schillerian or Arnoldian.[5] That is, they like Trilling's readiness to deal with an array of critical possibilities, holding each up for inspection, so as to judge which is the most suitable. But the playing among possibilities is not imagined as endless. At some point, the play must end and determinations must be made. As Trilling would say, there is a 'method of comprehension' at work, facilitating and ordering the perceptions of difference and contradiction. It is a situation not unlike the one that Trilling himself locates in Austen: 'Jane Austen's irony is only secondarily a matter of tone. Primarily it is a method of comprehension. It perceives the world through an awareness of its contradictions, paradoxes, and anomalies. It is by no means detached.'[6] Nor is Trilling's criticism detached, even as it celebrates play.[7] This balancing of play and attachment is rather Arnoldian, particularly if by this phrase we keep in mind the still important essay 'The Function of Criticism' (1864), in which Arnold argued on behalf of the 'free play of the mind' (*The Portable Matthew Arnold*, 249) and encouraged a wide-ranging criticism resistant to fixed ideologies. He did so even whilst acknowledging that, among his countrymen, the opposite spirit prevailed. That is, to Arnold's eyes, available criticisms were less wide-ranging than territorial and sect-like, inevitably finding refuge in journals whose appeals were predetermined:

> [W]e have the *Edinburgh Review*, existing as an organ of the old Whigs, and for as much play of mind as may suit its being that; we have the *Quarterly Review*, existing as an organ of the Tories, and for as much play of mind as may suit its being that; we have the *British Quarterly Review*, existing as an organ of the political Dissenters, and for as much play of mind as may suit its being that; we have the *Times*, existing as an organ of the common, satisfied, well-to-do Englishman, and for as much play of mind as may suit its being that. And so on through all the various fractions, political and religious, of our society; every fraction has, as such, its organ of criticism, but the notion of combining all fractions in the common pleasure of a free disinterested play of mind meets with no favour. (249)

The situation propelled Arnold to recommend the virtue of critical disinterestedness. Arnold entertained no fantasies about critics foregoing interests. Interests were everywhere; they were inescapable. It was almost a given that critics, seeking confirmation and community, would move to embrace one practice or another. There was no fear, then, that interests would go unspoken for. As Arnold said, 'plenty of people will be sure to attach' political and practical importance to this or that idea (248), so whatever success a disinterested criticism might meet, it would always find itself offset by discussions of a more immediate sort. The tensions could not be expected to go away, for the intellectual coteries had almost a life of their own, and could be expected to go on making their influence felt. But the hope was that the more gifted would acknowledge the weakness of thinking by fraction, and aspire to a less partisan criticism, more prepared to weigh carefully a host of viewpoints with the purpose of enlarging the breadth of its own judgments. It was, in effect, a call for a criticism of the largest possible purview, the sort that would later lead T.S. Eliot, in 'The Perfect Critic,' to say that 'there is no method except to be very intelligent.' And which led Arnold himself to say that the object of criticism was 'simply to know the best that is known and thought in the world, and by in its turn making this known, to create a current of true and fresh ideas' (*The Portable Matthew Arnold*, 248–9). In essence, Arnold called for a criticism equal to the other arts, such as literature, music, and painting.

To the degree that the criticism of Trilling, like that of Arnold and Eliot, aligned itself with a stance of disinterestedness, wherein specialist needs were to be balanced by those more widely felt, it had its antecedents in the common reader tradition. The eighteenth century – with its mercantilism, emergent middle class, and increased general literacy – had fostered the notion of the common reader, that reader whose interests were less identified with any one profession than with the more general ambition to stay informed of events as they transpired on several fronts. It was the reader to whom Dr Johnson, in his 'Life of Gray,' famously appealed: 'I rejoice to concur with the common reader; for by the common sense of readers uncorrupted with literary prejudices, after all the refinements of subtlety and the dogmaticism of learning, must be finally decided all claims to poetical honours.' It was, also, the reader who stood ready for *The Spectator, The Tatler* and, Arnold's complaint notwithstanding, subsequent periodicals like the *Edinburgh Review* and the *Quarterly Review*.[8] Meanwhile, because no good writer works unmindful of audience, this common reader might well be credited with coercing those who would address it into a mode that bent in the direction of public concerns and a conversational style. Certainly, many fine writers wrote for the said periodicals – e.g., Addison, Steele, Hazlitt, Macaulay, Carlyle, Scott, Southey, and Arnold himself – and it would be a mistake to suggest that it was not until Arnold's call for a criticism both more informed and playful that the style moved into high gear. But we ourselves are prone to view matters this way, and are more likely to identity the high point of the tradition with talents closer to hand – with

writers such as Virginia Woolf, T.S. Eliot, William Empson, R.P. Blackmur, Allen Tate, Kenneth Burke, Edmund Wilson, Lionel Trilling, and
Irving Howe. And, in the present moment, with Denis Donoghue, Frank
Kermode, and George Steiner, for these three also clearly work in the
common reader tradition.

Writing for the leading literary periodicals – *Encounter,* the *New York
Review of Books,* the *London Review of Books,* the *New Republic, The New
Yorker,* the *Times Literary Supplement* – Donoghue, Kermode, and Steiner,
like their distinguished predecessors, are critics who bring to their
reviews less a position (though positions they have) than an acute intelligence, prepared to be provoked by the last book they have read and to
place it at the centre of a discussion that ripples outward. One might say
that they are generalists of unusual calibre but not if this means overlooking the fact that they also qualify as experts in one field or another –
Donoghue in Modern American, British, and Irish literatures and criticism; Kermode in Renaissance and Modern literature as well as hermeneutics; Steiner in Continental literature and theories of translation.
But as impressive as their specialist credentials are, they refuse the
retreat of a discipline's discourse and think it imperative that the
scholar find a way to engage the larger educated public in conversation.
Like Arnold and Trilling before them, they too put their faith 'in the
common pleasure of a free disinterested play of mind,' and stand
opposed to the cloistering of knowledge in dogmatism and a sectarian
language. This Arnoldian faith 'that the mind may be made the source
of great pleasure' is, one suspects, what first drew them to the study of
literature, for each considers literature, especially as it bespeaks, in
Steiner's words, 'the boundless possibilities of the imagined' (RP, 11),
the source of some of the mind's greatest pleasures. In its identification
with the imaginary, literature implies that while determinate judgments
must come, we do well to begin our investigations by attending to those
meanings that reside within the aesthetic experience, yet are not themselves the thing – the judgment – to which the artwork alludes or points.
Imagined and real events are both alike and different – alike in the
sense that they both call for determinations, different in the sense that
the pressures to make such are less immediate in the former than in the
latter. Yet if we have not already lived and thought in the realm of the
imaginary, we shall probably make bad determinations in that of
the real. The realms are, in this sense, inextricably connected. Or as
Donoghue, mindful of Arnold's brief for disinterestedness, writes:

The judgements we make of them [the arts] have the advantage of being disinterested, because the fact that their objects are imaginary removes them from our ordinary needs and desires. But this disinterestedness is challenged at every point, as in *King Lear* or *La Bohème*, by sympathies and revulsions which nearly break through the conventions by which the artistic events appear at all. It is easier to declare an object as imaginary than to feel an emotion as imaginary. So our judgements of a work of art are different, though not totally different, from those we make in ordinary life, where the parentheses are removed and we judge in terms of local interests and needs. The arts are at once real and unreal; and, in responding to them, we are at once detached and involved. Their significance, the way in which they become present to us, arises from that strange set of conditions. (AWM, 128)

The desire to make determinations, to make stands, to declare ourselves one sort of person or critic rather than another is difficult to suppress. Yet art and most certainly literature are constantly warning us of the dangers of premature judgment. As Kermode notes, 'While we seek our intimations of latent order we may omit to notice that our text has a manifest gratuitousness, a playfulness – we might add a blindness, a deafness, a forgetfulness – that tells against our scheme' (GSR, 17). Or as Steiner writes in *Antigones*, all our homecomings, our grand orderings, must be thought of as 'provisional':

To 'understand' a text in classical Greek, to 'understand' any text in any language as formally and conceptually dense as Sophocles' *Antigone*, is to oscillate between poles of immediacy and inaccessibility. If we read well, if we make ourselves answerable to the text intellectually, if we discipline our sensibility to scrupulous attentiveness, if, in the final analysis, we make of our reading an exercise of moral trust, rendering our own risks of feeling concordant to those of the poet (though on a more modest, secondary level), this oscillation will find points of stability. It will, more or less consciously, come to rest in a general sense of the shapes of meaning. It will align local detail with the landscape, with the 'tonic' conventions of the work as a whole. But such 'coming to rest' is always provisional. (201)

It is precisely because texts frustrate all our interpretative schemes, all our efforts to say *this*, rather than *that*, is what is most important, that the embrace of a single interpretative strategy often ends up looking regrettable, given time. It is not that a Marxist, feminist, or a New Historicist reading of, say, *Paradise Lost* has nothing new to add to our understanding of the epic text; it is rather that what gets said often proves so partial, as the critic isolates solely that evidence which certifies the case. All interpretations involve reductions of one sort or another, so maybe it is a mistake to make this an issue; still, there remains the sense that critics, when employing this or that theory, have a bad habit of seeming to care more about the theory than the poem or play, and thereby inevitably slight the ostensible object of study. It makes Kenneth Burke's directive that the critic 'use all there is to use' appear all the more sensible. Burke is a critic as well spoken of today as in his own day. Undoubtedly, there is a lesson in this, especially as Burke, like Empson, is praised by those who can hardly find anything else about which to agree. In any event, there is an attractiveness about the three critics' desire to think of literature as irreducible to this or that program, as encompassing all such programs and yet still having more to say. For them, literature is perhaps synonymous with this *more*, though saying exactly what this is is most difficult, and most likely impossible. Meanwhile, it is not surprising to find Kermode write, 'I was never tempted to declare myself a structuralist, or a post-structuralist, or even a narratologist or poetician,' the reason being that '[a] good part of the pleasure I derived from my profession had come from finding out what texts seemed to be saying as it were voluntarily, and in conveying this information to others; and I should have felt uneasy to join a party whose sole business it was to elicit what they were saying in spite of themselves' (AT, 5). It is also not surprising to find Donoghue criticize those practices that approach literature 'merely as illustrations of a theory already fixed,' so much so that it comes to appear 'the fate of the theory merely to be fulfilled and of the work of literature merely to gratify the theory' (UAT, xxxi).

Donoghue, Kermode, and Steiner are not resistant to theory and have made a point of saying so. Thus Donoghue, in *The Old Moderns*, writes, 'I hope that I have made it clear that I am not "against theory." Not to have a theory is to have someone else's' (89), while Kermode, in 'The State of Criticism,' writes, 'I hope I can claim to have been sympathetic [to critical theory]' (4).[9] Yet if they have not been resistant to theory, they have been resistant to those efforts, theoretical or otherwise, that seemed more likely to contract – either through a reduction of perspectives or through a commitment to a strictly materialist understanding – rather than to enlarge our notions of the aesthetic. For them, Trilling's phrase 'beyond culture' remains felicitous, especially if by this is meant the recognition of a sense of possibility, even of a culture, more encompassing than that which usually prevails. Trilling himself connected the ambition to the purposes of the modern writer, with his or her 'clear purpose of detaching the reader from the habits of thought and feeling that the larger culture imposes, of giving him a ground and a vantage point from which to judge and condemn, and perhaps revise, the culture that produced him' ('Preface' to *Beyond Culture*). It is an attractive notion for our critics because it does not rule out the possibility of a standard by which things may be judged. Rather, it stresses that the standard should be expressive of the largest possible compass – of culture not only as it is known, but also as it has been known and as it might be known. It is a notion that looks not only back to the achievements of the past but also forward to the utopian possibilities of the future. It is a criticism that would, if it could, judge things *sub specie aeternitatis*, always conscious of the fact that things as they are are but a shadow of how they might be in a more perfect universe. In short, it is a criticism that repeatedly reminds itself, in Ernst Bloch's wonderful phrase, that 'something's missing' (*The Utopian Function of Art and Literature*, 15). What this something is may be impossible to say, though the thought is that if we rule out explorations of a metaphysical and religious sort, we shall guarantee our failure to render it. This is not to say that Donoghue, Kermode, and Steiner are religious critics. They are not, at least not per se. Still, compared to most present-day critics, they are unusually attentive to the nexus between literature and motives or desires that may well be spoken of as religious – attentive to things in their fullest possible import. Of the three, only Donoghue admits to practising a religion, but together they seem joined by what Steiner, in *Real Presences* (1989), speaks of as 'a wager on transcendence': 'This wager – it is that of Descartes, of Kant and of every poet, artist, composer of whom we have explicit record – predicates the presence of a realness, of a "substantiation" (the theological reach of this word is obvious) within language and form. It supposes a passage, beyond the fictive or the purely pragmatic, from meaning to meaningfulness' (4).

In the following chapters, I wish to attend to the writings of Donoghue, Kermode, and Steiner in the light of some of the concerns already announced – i.e., the common reader, a nonpartisanship, and an enlarged culture – and some not yet announced. Each chapter is divided into four sections. The first section attends to the critic's work as it exemplifies the common reader tradition; the second attends to a particular interest with which the critic is closely associated. In the instance of

Donoghue, this is the imagination; of Kermode, the canon; and of Steiner, the theme of elegy, or of a postlapsarian culture. The chapters' third section attends to the critic's understanding of the relation between aesthetic and religious experience. Sometimes this relation is clearly avowed, as in Steiner; sometimes it is more vexed, as in Kermode. In all three critics, it remains nevertheless a pertinent subject. Finally, the chapters' fourth section attends to the critic's stance vis-à-vis the theoretical debates that have both so energized and divided the academy for a generation or more. Donoghue, Kermode, and Steiner are invariably pigeon-holed as conservative, anti-theory critics, but I find their relation to these debates more complicated and interesting than any thumbnail sketch might suggest. This should be evident from what I have hitherto said, for I value these critics for offering proof that criticism can borrow from critical methodologies without becoming ensnared in this or that methodology. At the same time, it should be said that, given their interests in seeing literature resist the critic's proprietary motives, Donoghue, Kermode, and Steiner are more drawn into debate with the insights of a theory like that of deconstruction (with its own more radical attachment to negative capability) than with, say, those theories that articulate a more material, even political, resolve. Yet even this point will require eventual qualification, for there are degrees of difference among the three critics on this matter, as on others.

At the moment, I wish simply to stress that Donoghue, Kermode, and Steiner are public critics, capable, in a time of specialization, of ranging widely without a noticeable loss of critical acumen, and more than capable of expressing themselves in a language befitting that of the literary artists whom they so admire. Their independence has come at a cost, however. For while we could benefit from more such critics, professionals have been loath to recognize their contributions. In fact, if we take anthologies of criticism and theory as reflective of what we value, it is striking, rues Ihab Hassan, how much they 'seem hospitable only to "isms." A school, ideology, or trend fits easily in their modular, prefabricated history of the moment. In vain, therefore, may we seek in those thick-spined books the names of Denis Donoghue, Leslie Fielder, Irving Howe, Alfred Kazin, Hugh Kenner, Richard Poirier, Roger Shattuck, Susan Sontag, [and] George Steiner' ('Confessions,' 11). It's true, for these names seldom appear in the standard anthologies, though there is reason to think that their work, as read in the pages of the *New York Review of Books*, the *London Review of Books*, *The New Yorker*, the *Partisan Review*, *Raritan*, *Salmagundi*, the *Times Literary Supplement*, the *New States-*

man, and the *Yale Review*, finds as many readers (professionals included) as that of more celebrated theorists. Or as Dickstein says in *Double Agent: The Critic and Society*, 'Though you wouldn't know it from current debates or recent histories, some of the best criticism of the postwar years can be found in collections of literary journalism' (xii–xiii). He has in mind not only those critics who move back and forth between the academic and public realm – he names Irving Howe, Alfred Kazin, Kermode, Donoghue, Helen Vendler, Christopher Ricks, and John Bayley – but also those more fully committed to the public sphere, among whom he includes the Americans Elizabeth Hartwick, Randall Jarrell, Pauline Kael, Wilfred Sheed, John Updike, Andrew Sarris, and Stanley Kaufmann. Thinking in more strictly British terms, Malcolm Bradbury writes: 'We have just a few large players – shall we say George Steiner, John Carey, Peter Kemp, Peter Ackroyd – who perform as public critics used to: as ideal proxies, ultimate intelligent judges and readers, displaying what we might surely expect of a critic: literary learning, comparative standards, a power of intelligent judgement, a primary belief in the worth of the literary arts' ('A Stern and Righteous Reader').

For Hassan, Dickstein, and Bradbury, culture's highest achievements connect to the aesthetic, and they value criticism to the extent that it celebrates the aesthetic and borrows some of its virtues, including stylistic finesse. They know that recent academic criticism has oriented the discussion of culture away from the aesthetic, but it has done so, they believe, at considerable cost, most notably in terms of its readability. Or as Hassan, grown weary with the matter, writes: 'With few exceptions, the prose conforms, repels. No ear to rhythm, no eye to image or variegated sight. And rarely, how rarely, is a conference paper ever praised or blamed for its style, the tone, tenor, texture of its mind. Only its "position," its rehearsed response, counts. Here, again, is resistance, resistance not only to style, literature incarnate, but also to the world's body, which our senses seek as if in love' ('Confessions,' 11–12). Critics who direct their attentions away from literature so that they may attend to the work of other critics or other cultural formations end up, suggest Hassan, Dickstein, and Bradbury, writing too much like philosophers or sociologists: 'Criticism has left the public arena for the closets of the university; and there it has become something else. Disliking judgment in the old sense, it has now become literary theory: tribalised, compartmentalised, heavy with professional discourses, a variant of philosophy subservient to all the fashionable ideologies' (Bradbury, 'A Stern and Righteous Reader'). And so, writes Giles Gunn, we find ourselves 'in the uncomfortable position of witnessing the displacement first of literature by criticism and now of criticism by itself in the direction of some newer hierophantic mode as yet unnamable' (*The Culture of Criticism*, 62).

Artist – Critic – Theorist

Dickstein, Hassan, Bradbury, and Gunn express a minority opinion, at least in the academy. 'If we take the position, itself a literary one, that how we say it is as important as what we say, then the contrast' between the public and the academic critic will, says Geoffrey Hartman, be worth attending (*Minor Prophecies*, 62). But he is not so sure that the 'position' is any longer viable, and he proposes the counterposition that a focusing on style may be a sign that the critic has nothing new to say or is unable to keep up with the 'entropic' mode of contemporary criticism. This criticism, says Hartman, calls into question the assumptions that style is too ready to mask: 'Theory ... is not just another style of discourse but raises the entire question of discourse-control to a level where our awareness of it becomes irreversible, and such antiself-consciousness devices as parody, sangfroid, or a stubborn emphasis on the practical side of things (kicking the stone) begin to appear stupid rather than commonsensical' (75). In *Minor Prophecies: The Literary Essay in the Culture Wars*, Hartman attacks Donoghue, Kermode, and Steiner's motives, and seeks to expose the Arnoldian critical project: 'Theory does not fertilize itself by mingling with the empirical. It exposes the fact (Arnold's "object as itself is") as the untrue – an abstract form of immediacy which can masquerade as the totalizing "thing itself" by concealing a figurative or rhetorical operation: a part for whole substitution or exemplification as freely chosen rather than mediated and highly intentional' (82). That a critic so sceptical of the empirical object should continue to employ concepts like truth or untruth seems odd, if not contradictory, but this is in keeping with Hartman's wilful misreading of Arnold, who, as both a poet and critic, is much more a friend of verbal play than this representation allows. But Arnold's notion of play is rather different from unending, anti-foundational play, and it is the latter which Hartman extols. The work of Wittgenstein, Heidegger, and Dewey is said to be 'exemplary' because '[e]ach began with a project to make philosophy "foundational," only to find the '"epistemological"' or '"Kantian"' project was no longer viable. The consequence is that their work can be construed as 'therapeutic rather than constructive, or, as Rorty also likes to say, "edifying" (in the secular sense of the adjective, that conveys the

German idea of *Bildung*) rather than systematic' (69). The new philosophy puts into question all our everyday assumptions, and thereby
requires a new critical style, one that is both more ratiocinative and sinu-
ous in its argument and more technical in its vocabulary (Hartman:
'Without specifying what makes theory theory, I will say that it is prose
with a noticeable proportion of technical terms' [75]). Whether criticism shall ever be able to return to the more limpid and stylized prose of
the common reader tradition is, says Hartman, uncertain. Too much
has changed, especially as we have schooled ourselves in philosophy's
critique of language. This shift, writes Hartman, 'threatens the decorum
of the conversational style, with its avoidance of explicit learning or
technical terms, and which goes back to the ideal of the "honest man"
(*honnête homme*) in France and to the Common Reader tradition in
England. It may be that this style can be restored, that the new philosophy, which puts all in doubt, will be absorbed into a prose as remarkably free of jargon as before' (47). But in the present moment, he
remains doubtful, as does Bradbury, who, unlike Hartman, mourns the
loss:

> The office of public critic has never been an easy one to execute. Still, until
> very recent times, it clearly existed. We knew we needed uncommon super-
> readers to serve us common readers. We counted on great figures, often
> both writers and critics, who seriously devoted themselves to the common
> pursuit of true judgement and the correction of taste; who set out to
> explore the limits of the imagination, and purify the language and think-
> ing of the tribe. Dryden, Johnson, Coleridge, Arnold, Sainte-Beuve all per-
> formed and elaborated the great and necessary office. So, in more
> modernist times, did Virginia Woolf, Pound, Eliot, and then Leavis,
> Edmund Wilson, Lionel Trilling. And behind them lay the great maga-
> zines, the reviews of critical surveillance: *Edinburgh* and *Quarterly*, *Criterion*
> and *Scrutiny*, *Dial* and *Partisan Review*.
>   Today it is largely over; we have almost entirely lost such figures and such
> magazine venues. We live – we're proud to do so – in a non-judgmental, an
> equalising, a leveling, a willingly and articulately self-dumbing age. We
> won't say elite; we're ideologically under-critical.[10]

With Hartman, meanwhile, one has the sense that not only are philosophy and art inseparable, but that philosophy calls all the shots. He
praises literary theory for having 'defended and elaborated the thesis
that art was more philosophical than philosophy in uncovering the illu-

sion of an unmediated action or speech' (85), a formulation that bestows praise on art with one hand, only to take it away with the other. That art and literature might have other purposes than uncovering this illusion is downplayed. So is the thought that they are not one with philosophy. It is difficult not to recall Eliot's more scrupulous discrimination in *The Use of Poetry and The Use of Criticism*: 'I believe that for a poet to be also a philosopher he would have to be virtually two men; I cannot think of any example of this thorough schizophrenia, nor can I see anything to be gained by it: the work is better performed inside two skulls than one' (90). Eliot was a rather fine philosopher himself (as his dissertation on F.H. Bradley testifies), so perhaps I should not press the point. Yet literary studies has so noticeably shifted away from literature itself and towards its theorization, that it seems not impertinent to ask whether current theorists, such as those spoken of by Hartman, are better thought of as literature's friends or foes? It is the question put by Mark Edmundson, in *Literature against Philosophy, Plato to Derrida: A Defence of Poetry,* wherein the author begins by reminding us that '[l]iterary criticism in the West begins with the wish that literature disappear. Plato's chief objection to Homer is that he exists' (1). Since then, literary criticism has seen better days, yet it seems to Edmundson that Plato's heirs are once more regnant, though even Plato, with his suspicion of art, would no doubt recoil from the readiness among some of his heirs to let baneful assertion substitute for argumentation, the way for instance John Beverley, in *Against Literature,* states that his 'animus against literature ... is due above all to literature's connection with the formation of the modern state and the conditions of maintaining and redefining capitalist hegemony, particularly in situations of colonial or neocolonial domination' (xiii), or the way in which music critics Sheila James Keuhl and Susan McClary confuse, respectively, rap music and Beethoven with rape; thus Keuhl's argument that 'Rap is really rape music' and McClary's that in the recapitulation of the first movement of Beethoven's Ninth Symphony, 'the carefully prepared cadence is frustrated, damning up energy which finally explodes in the throttling, murderous rage of a rapist incapable of attaining release.'[11]

But to return to my point, there has been a critical readiness of late to think of art, especially literature, less as a virtual space of intellectual play and more as a servant of a concept or politics. Artists themselves have been known to protest this turn of events, as when Saul Bellow writes:

Art – I refer to the real thing – finds it hard to subordinate itself to this civilization of concepts: the ideas that rule over us, that tell us with arbitrary authority what the universe is and what we human beings are. On the human question, usually without the conscious mental ability to oppose the dominant view, the imagination, subject to visions, cannot bring itself to agree. Visions and concepts disagree, and it is because of these disagreements that artists cannot be described as intellectuals. The divergence first manifests itself in differences of language, for the language of intellectuals is the common language of the cognitions, whereas the languages of art are individual. Their uniqueness is a guarantee that they are genuine. The speech of one artist is not interchangeable with the speech of another. ('Summations,' 170–1)

Or when Milan Kundera, responding to Theodor Adorno's readiness to interpret music in terms of political categories, writes: 'What irritates me in Adorno is his short-circuit method that, with a fearsome facility, links works of art to political (sociological) causes, consequences, or meanings; extremely nuanced ideas (Adorno's musicological knowledge is admirable) thereby lead to extremely impoverished conclusions; in fact, given that an era's political tendencies are always reducible to just two opposing tendencies, a work of art necessarily ends up being classified as either progressive or reactionary; and since reaction is evil, the inquisition can start the trial proceedings' (*Testaments Betrayed*, 91). These objections have mostly fallen on deaf ears. The drift of criticism away from particular works of art and towards theory is connected to the fact that criticism has become so much more identified with the university. It is a phenomenon whose history is measurable in decades. In *The Rise and Fall of the Man of Letters,* John Gross speaks of F.R. Leavis, in the 1930s, as the progenitor of a distinctly academic criticism, whatever his ambition to be a more public voice might have been.[12] Gerald Graff, in *Professing Literature: An Institutional History,* and Brian McCrea, in *Addison and Steele Are Dead: The English Department, Its Canon, and the Professionalization of Literary Criticism,* also see the 1930s as a pivotal decade, the first quoting John Crowe Ransom's remark, in 'Criticism, Inc.,' that '[s]trategy requires now ... that criticism receive its own charter of rights and function independently' (148); and the second quoting from the same 1938 essay the critic's contention 'that criticism no longer can be the work of "amateurs," that it "must become more scientific, or precise and systematic, and this means that it must be developed by the collective and sustained efforts of learned persons – which means that its proper seat is in the universities'" (182). Irving Howe, in his essay 'The Common Reader,' while not refuting such judgments, says that 'in the United States as late as the 1950s, many of the leading critics, both New and New York, continued to take seriously the idea of the common reader' (120). But that situation did not continue long after the fifties, for the fact was that the avenues by which a man or woman could make even a modest living by penning reviews and other more journalistic writings were quickly drying up, as other media, especially radio, television, and film, began to command more of the general public's attention. The consequences for literary culture were, thinks Howe, momentous. Looking back to mid-century, to the days of the *Partisan Review* and *Kenyon Review*, and to critics such as Clement Greenberg, Eric Bentley, James Agee, Randall Jarrell, Edmund Wilson, Philip Rahv, Lionel Trilling, Robert Fitzgerald, Marius Bewley, and Dwight Macdonald, he writes, 'It was then generally assumed that the line of great English critics, from Dr. Johnson and Hazlitt to Arnold and Eliot, had cultivated, as a matter of course, a certain journalistic bent (critics often *had* to be journalists) and that the migration of critics to the universities that began in the early 1950s, while a practical advantage, was still a somewhat uncomfortable development. Surely in the history of American literary life, this was a major turning point. The new circumstances of our economy made it close to impossible for a free-lance man (or woman) of letters to survive. And this change must be one of the major reasons for the shift in attitudes toward the common reader' (123).

It is true that today the common reader is just as likely to be disparaged as extolled, the way, for instance, Lisa Jardine (echoing Leavis's 1933 death notice: 'there is no Common Reader ...[;] the tradition is dead')[13] comments, 'There isn't a Common Reader any more. There are readers from overlapping circles. The Common Reader was a wonderful security blanket presence, namely that of the nicely self-educated, maybe grammar school boy. The Common Reader is a grammar school boy, I think, and he's no longer the unique reader. You can't address your classroom studies to that unique reader any more, so the strategies used in academic departments of literature have more to do with the diverse cultural backgrounds of their student population and with a lack of conviction on the part of many of us that we have any self-evident right to claim the priority of one tradition' (Kaplan and Rose, *The Canon and the Common Reader*, 377). Catherine Gallagher, reviewing books by Kermode and Karl Miller, writes, 'In such apparently serendipitous experiences of the mind turning round to face itself, even a theoretically inclined reader might become a Common Reader, the self-reflective entity of the humanist imagination. But the effect is momentary; the grandiose self-projection fades, and one is still faced with a century's-worth of challenges to the very person these essays continue to manufacture, the creature Michel Foucault called "that empirico-transcendental doublet, Man"' ('Fighting for the Common Reader,' 84).

While Jardine's and Gallagher's objections have merit, the fact that both critics so readily identify themselves with the university does connect, it appears, with a certain diffidence respecting not only the tradition but also creative artists themselves. For the common reader tradition, which has, since Dr Johnson, always imagined itself in service of not only the larger reading public but also the creative artist, now finds itself dismissed for the reason that it appears insufficiently solicitous to both university readers and theory. Both suggestions are debatable. In the first instance, we might merely take note of the fact that some of the more prominent writers now identified with the tradition – Jamaica Kincaid, Henry Louis Gates, Cornell West, Stephen Carter, Toni Morrison, Stanley Crouch, Patricia J. Williams, et al. – are people of colour, who, like their white colleagues, must suffer the accusation that their views represent little more than bourgeois, even Victorian, pieties.[14] Meanwhile, with regard to theory, if we take Gallagher's scenario seriously, we should have to admit that not only does theory trump the common reader but that it also trumps literature, itself very partial to 'that empirico-transcendental doublet, Man.' Some appear ready not only to concede this, but to celebrate it. Witness, again, the remarks of Beverley, or those of Tony Bennett in *Outside Literature*, where, in the chapter 'Really Useless "Knowledge": A Political Critique of Aesthetics,' he argues that 'from the point of view of its yield for a socialist politics, aesthetic discourse ... constitutes a really useless form of knowledge, and one which would be quite appropriately satirised, in William Corbett's terms, as "heddakashun"' (149). The argument is that either art, literature included, is irrelevant to the progressivist's project or it is pernicious, for the reason that its true motives are both hegemonic and universalist: 'Aesthetic discourse ... is the form taken by discourses of value which are hegemonic in ambition and, correspondingly, universalist in their prescriptive ambit and which have, as their zone of application, those practices nominated as artistic' (152). That Bennett's 'discourse,' like that of Gallagher and Beverley, has a hegemonic and universalist character of its own goes unremarked.

Historically, the study of literature, in the Anglo-American university, was something imported from outside. It began, says Robert Alter, 'among poets and writers outside the academy, only gradually making its way into the precincts of the university and even then not at first altering its culturally engaged character' ('Outside the Academy,' 15). Things were noticeably different on the Continent, where scholars made a much more concerted effort, from the turn of the twentieth century onward, to transform the study of literature into a science, a *Wissenschaft*, capable of commanding the respect of their most advanced colleagues: 'Thus the prominent Anglo-American critics from 1900 to 1950 – for example, Leavis, T.S. Eliot, Edmund Wilson, Lionel Trilling – produce essentially essayistic work, legislating, setting up evaluative hierarchies, and at their worst, attitudinising. The major Central and East European critics of this period – figures like Auerbach, Spitzer, Bakhtin, and Jan Mukarovsky – variously seek to describe literature as a historically-evoking system, adapting tools from linguistics, sociology and other disciplines, and sometimes orienting their work in a particular philosophic framework' (ibid.). But, thinks Alter, this picture has decidedly changed in the last decades, most obviously in the fact that 'in America and England' the trend has been towards 'the pervasive academisation of criticism' (ibid.). By this, he means a criticism noticeably driven by the needs of theory and method, as well as by politics. It is less the latter than the former that I wish to address, for it brings to the fore the distinction between criticism and theory that partly justifies this book, my argument being that Donoghue, Kermode, and Steiner, while not themselves averse to theory, are best understood as critics working in a space between literature and theory, and thereby exemplifying Edmundson's contention that '[o]ne way to conceive of criticism ... is as writing that plays itself out between certain philosophic and poetic tendencies' (*Literature Against Philosophy*, 116).

Trilling once spoke of 'the natural amity between literature and the criticism of literature' (*Literary Criticism*, 28), as a way of countering the pervasive sense that criticism and literature were more like adversaries. I, too, think that criticism and literature are, on the whole, compatible,[15] especially when the critic demonstrates not only the analytic talent that must be a part of any serious study but also a readiness to learn from literature, to be open to its ways of seeing, knowing that in the best instances the relation between critic and book is something like that of a conversation, albeit naturally slanted in the direction of the artist's creation. Or as Edmundson writes, genuine criticism demonstrates a readiness 'to be interrogated by great writing,' an understanding that while '[s]ome works we read,' others seem fully capable of reading and interpreting us (*Literature Against Philosophy*, 128). If criticism is understood this way, then the main difference between it and theory would be that criticism feels an obligation to individual works, and the specific ways in which they differentiate themselves from other such works, whereas theory is more prepared to slight this difference, in the hope of fostering a more general knowledge. Both pursuits have their reason for being, and they may even, like literature and criticism, be thought complementary. Still, it is often the case that individual readers, like communities, find their allegiances pulled in one direction more than another, the way an earlier generation of Anglo-American readers found itself drawn to criticism and the present generation finds itself drawn to theory. Here, one might wonder whether it even makes sense to think of British and American criticism as a single ('Anglo-American') entity.[16]

A 'Mid-Atlantic' Criticism

In his 1967 review of René Wellek's *A History of Modern Criticism, 1750–1950*, Denis Donoghue sets English criticism not only against German and French but also American criticism. Speaking to the difference, Donoghue remarks that Wellek's book, so firmly on the side of theory,[17] is

> very much an American book, incidentally. English criticism is a more casual affair, takes more for granted, trusts to luck and temper. An English critic is guided by hunches. His best work is one part theory to nine parts practice. To what theory does William Empson aspire? An American critic is much more exacting in definitions and theory. It is not sufficient for his purposes that a statement is interesting and true; it must exhibit a strenuous connection with other truths, and the interest is deemed to consist in the whole relation. So the American critic is happy in discussion of organic form, the Concrete Universal, 'irony as a principle of structure,' metaphor, the definition of imaginative unity. I am not sure these concerns are always fruitful, though I am regularly impressed by the mastery disclosed along the line. ('The Gay Science,' 82)

Since 1967, British criticism has become more hospitable to the theorists among its ranks, though not enough to make Donoghue's earlier distinction appear dated.[18] This said, it is not my intention to complete

the suggestion, and identify Donoghue, Kermode, and Steiner as specifically English critics. True, they exemplify some of the more attractive
aspects of this criticism, including sensitivity to style and a healthy scepticism.[19] Nevertheless, their relation to the British academy has been
almost as vexed as to its American counterpart. Donoghue is not a British critic at all, unless his growing up in Northern Ireland in circumstances that he, like so many Catholics, experienced as colonial, should
make him such. While he is not insistent about the matter, he has made
it clear, most notably in his memoir, *Warrenpoint* (1990), that his respect
for things English, its language included, is mixed with an element of
misgiving. Recalling his boyhood relation to the English language (his
first language, though he grew up also speaking Irish), he writes: 'The
problem with speaking English as a native in Warrenpoint was that I
knew it wasn't – or wasn't entirely – my language. I spoke it not with a
bad accent but with bad faith' (135). It is one reason why he has held to
his father's advice 'to live as if among aliens' (142), a fact that, as Alfred
Kazin observed, explains much about him: 'Donoghue has been formed
by living among strangers. First in Ireland and England, where he studied and taught; now in America, where he is Henry James Professor of
English and American Literature at New York University' ('Habits of
Home,' 44).

Much the same can be said of Kermode, who while growing up on the
Isle of Man was also made to feel 'that to be a Manx was to be ... exiled
from the life and language of the English' (NE, 5). Kermode's experience may not have been as vexed as Donoghue's; still, he has always felt,
circumstances notwithstanding, largely out of place, as if he were a 'one-
man disapora' (NE, 261). In fact, Kermode's own 1995 memoir, *Not
Entitled* (which, in its earlier pages, resembles *Warrenpoint*, a somber
retelling of a young boy's estrangement from the people and place –
provincial, poor, and grim – about him), is very much a story of alienation. First, there is the alienation, or just the self-removal, of the child,
who cultivates a 'secret life,' lived apart from the street life of the other
children: 'I began as a philosopher, an eye among the blind, though
naturally I did not reveal my vocation to my friends. There was a whole
society of children from whom such truths must be kept' (45; cf. Donoghue's description of his boyhood: 'Besides, I was a watcher: it was best
to stay at a distance and live an internal life with impunity' [W, 54]).
Then, there is the distancing of the young man, who leaves the Isle, first
to attend Liverpool University, and later to serve in the navy during wartime, and who, in time, comes to view his natural state as one of exile:

'The idea of living anywhere else can never have occurred to my parents. I'm not sure when I first entertained it, though after my own war was over I had long been quite sure I had to choose exile' (7). This is followed by an increasingly peripatetic adulthood, as Kermode moves, with or without family, from Manchester to Bristol to London to Cambridge to New York back to Cambridge, never staying in any one place so long that he comes to think of it as home, though hoping to arrive at such a place. Looking back over the years, Kermode writes:

> Once more the *métèque.* No doubt there have been times in my life when I felt easy, enjoyed the peace that must come from an assurance that one is in the right place – a peace so natural that it is not remarked at the time of its holding, when the question of belonging simply doesn't come up. But I've not known that benign ignorance since 1940 at least. Perhaps I never knew it. Even in the society of the friendly tenement we were but secondary citizens; even at school I was among seniors, perpetually young and negligible; and in the years at college in a strange country still, for all the thrills and all the fun, still a *métèque.* I have been too ready to abandon what is never more than a temporary environment, quick to move jobs, quick to resign, glad to abandon one exile for another. It seems always to have been so. (NE, 199)

It is a dispiriting condition, even as some very good things, especially in the way of critical insights, have followed from such. So, while I wish to argue that Donoghue, Kermode, and Steiner's critical appeal is connected to their experiences of dislocation, I am also mindful of the costs, especially for Kermode, whose rootlessness at one point, during the early 1970s, overtook him with all the force of an addiction: 'Throughout these years my private life was in a great muddle. It was even hard to say where I lived; it might be in Hampstead or Dulwich, Regent's Park or Golders Green or Battersea. Or, for that matter, Connecticut or Massachusetts, New York or New Hampshire. Yet it was the only period of my life when I felt, perhaps only imagined I felt, in charge of it, in the way drunken drivers feel in charge of their vehicles' (NE, 213). In any event, Kermode's embrace of the alien's role appears to explain much about him and his work. So when Donoghue calls him a 'mid-Atlantic' critic ('Anger and Dismay,' 16), it is not only because he knows of what he speaks, being one himself, but because he, like Kermode, understands the value of the location and means it as a term of praise. We have passed beyond the time when Eliot, himself a mid-

Atlantic critic, could innocently say that '[s]ince Byron and Landor, no Englishman appears to have profited much from living abroad.'

More so than either Donoghue or Kermode, Steiner has experienced first-hand what it means to be homeless, outside the protection of either community or law.[20] He was born in Paris in 1929, the son of Middle-European Jews who, in the mid-twenties, moved to Paris, with the hope of escaping the brunt of the political upheavals emanating from Germany. But Paris, in the 1930s, was not far enough away to feel safe from Europe's festering hatreds. In his interview with Nicolas Tredell, Steiner recounts that '[p]sychologically, my father had no doubt at all, from the late twenties on, that the catastrophe was coming, and among my earliest memories are those of Hitler's voice on the radio being picked up by my parents with a sense of absolute and terrible certainty. So I was educated under the pressure of trying to get ready to move. My father saying, on a Monday you start packing your steamer trunk and on a Tuesday your hand baggage, stuck with me before I quite understood it' (75). The family left Paris in 1940 for New York, aboard one of the last American passenger ships, but the indelible memories of a French citizenry prepared to sacrifice the Jews among them remain, including a boyhood memory of marchers shouting 'Death to the Jews!' The hate-filled event led to one of the most crucial lessons of Steiner's life, for after his mother had lowered the window blinds to block out the marchers, his father, just returned, demanded that the blinds be put up so that his son might be a witness to history in all its horror: 'Papa comes home and says, "Up with those shades!" and takes me by the hand to look outside. I was fascinated, of course; any child would be. And he says, "You must never be frightened; what you're looking at is called history." I think that sentence may have formed my whole life' (AC, 62).[21]

If that one sentence did not, in truth, form Steiner's whole life, his childhood experiences did go a long way towards making him first feel, and then live out, his apartness. This sense is especially conveyed in his fine memoir, *Errata: An Examined Life* (1998), with its painful recollections of 'Jew-hatred' in 1930s Austria and Paris (1), as well as later in New York: 'It must have been in late 1944 or early 1945 when, in a moment of conspiratorial imbecility, I whispered to a class-mate what my father had begun to infer as to the "final solution." I shall never forget her outcry and the way she sought to scratch my face' (31). Meanwhile, a life lived in New York was followed by one lived in Chicago, Boston, Oxford, London, Princeton, Stanford, Cambridge, Geneva, and, one suspects, other places as well. For Steiner, as for Kermode, places have

begun to blur: '[t]here have been in my existence far too many bellow-
ing cities' (161). But it is less the moving about that has left him feeling
so noticeably homeless (unless the *idea* of Europe be thought a home),
so much as the fact of the Holocaust, the fact that, in his time and place,
the majority of European Jews were unforgivably hounded to their
deaths. This fact, or history, has left Steiner himself indifferent, even
hostile, to conventional notions of patriotism: 'I detest, I abhor nationalism. I am at home wherever there is a typewriter. I regard flags, pass-
ports as dangerous trash' (AC, 61). Nor does he make an exception for
Israel, for he believes that during the last decades, it has acted less like a
city on a hill than as a later and smaller Bismarckian state: 'I've polemi-
cized against Zionism my whole life because I detest nationalism,
because I have a kind of racial snobbery. I'm a racist to the tip of my
fingers *in an ethical sense.* That is to say, for me the fact that a Jew has to
torture another human being, as they have in the Israeli secret police in
order to survive, is something I can't live with rationally' (AC, 72). Better it is for Jews to think of the earth itself as their homeland. He thinks
that others should do so as well, but he believes it almost a Jewish obligation to show the way: 'I believe we must learn to be guests of each other
to survive; that it is the peculiar, tragic, Jewish destiny to try to live this
very difficult business of feeling at home anywhere. I have been at home
in many, many lands' (AC, 61). In the end, he thinks of his life in the
most solitary of terms – 'Solitude is, surely, the test' (AC, 102) – and,
given his say, he would probably resist even the present study's grouping, flattering though it is.

   Still, there is much merit in grouping these critics together, even after
granting that whereas Donoghue and Kermode are firmly rooted in the
Anglo-American critical tradition, Steiner looks more to European
influences. What unites them all is not only their stubborn critical independence but the fact that they have each been 'formed by living
among strangers.' The latter matter has, I think, worked to their great
advantage as critics, though not everyone has thought so; that is, while
their transcultural perspective has helped them to escape the characteristic insularity of British criticism, the modishness of American criticism,
and, in Steiner's case, the Christian bias of European criticism, their
critical detachment has not always been appreciated. Thus, Donoghue is
rebuked by Graham Hough, in a 1968 review of *The Ordinary Universe,*
for letting Saul Bellow into the hall of discussible novelists: 'It occurs
to me that Denis Donoghue is not altogether an English reader. The
standard Anglo-American literary valuations are natural to him; and

perhaps he is right. But from my corner of the world Saul Bellow with his instant alienation and his oh-so-easy solutions hardly belongs in this company' ('Life & Substance,' 18). It was a way of saying that neither the Irish nor the Jews should think themselves too welcome. Steiner, it seems, was delivered much the same message in the 1960s, when his foreignness was made an issue within British academic circles. Later, in 'The Clans and Their World-Pictures' (1975), Donald Davie, sympathizing with Steiner, though not to the point of divorcing himself from the British 'we,' made an effort to explain how he and his colleagues viewed Steiner:

> the difficulty that some British readers have had in 'taking Steiner seriously' – a difficulty which he is aware of and resents, which he is still trying to remove by trying a new 'register,' a new style – surely derives, though I'm not sure he realizes it, from his trilingualism, a condition which he presents to us in this book [*After Babel*] as being, to all intents and purposes, innate. Though we can accept without demur his contentions that he is lexically, grammatically, and in deeper ways too, a native-speaker of each of his three languages – French, German, English – I think a consideration of his career as a writer (also, I would guess, as a public speaker) would show that *rhetorically* one of his languages, British English, is *not* native to him. But of course, once we move into the rhetorical dimension of language, we know no longer whether we are speaking of a style of speech or a style of thought; and so some people might want to say that Steiner, though he speaks and writes an English without gallicisms, none the less *thinks* like a Frenchman ... (98)

Why Steiner, who grew up in Paris and New York, should be faulted for not writing British English like a native remains unclear. One would think it sufficient that he writes so well. But, as this was the demand of the time, one understands why he thought it necessary to leave Cambridge for a teaching post in Geneva. One also understands why, in something like a Parthian shot, Steiner, in a letter to *The New Review*, should write: 'An unmistable thinness, corner-of-the-mouth sparsity, sour fastidiousness, have developed in the English, intellectual literary tone. The age is less one of anxiety than of envy, of hopeful malice. To borrow an image from a French children's story, the thin gray ones, the steely trimmers, hate the round warm ones. They deride the messiness of intense presence, intense feeling which they call "flamboyance." They come with tight lips and deflation.'[22] Decades later, in *Errata*, Steiner finds it impossible either to forget or forgive the way in which he was treated:

> This belief [that of Davie and his colleagues] was murmured to me with unctuous venom by elements in the English Faculty of Cambridge University during the 1960s. It has been a raucous shibboleth in racist, nationalist, and tribal ideologies and 'cleansing' programs since the nineteenth century. Only the native speaker can proclaim, at mystical depths, the *Blut und Boden*, the *terre et les morts* of the race or nation-state. In its modern guise, this claim goes back to Herder and the romantic nationalism unleashed by the French Revolution and the Napoleonic saga. Communal and personal coherence, the identity and historicity of the culture are inalienably bound to the genius of the language as it surges from the tenebrous well-spring of the ethnic source. No outsider, no courier or carrier of contraband between tongues, even where such portage occurs from earliest childhood and inside the same psyche, can wholly belong. (102)[23]

And so one finds oneself agreeing with Terry Eagleton (another outsider denied a full insider's status) when he writes: 'The departure of George Steiner from Cambridge to Geneva was an ominous symptom of English parochialism' (*Against the Grain*, 56).[24]

Kermode, just as notoriously, was also victimized by this parochialism, and likewise came to see the wisdom of leaving Cambridge, where he says 'a cauldron of unholy hates hissed all about me' (NE, 248), for an appointment abroad. I refer to the Colin MacCabe matter, wherein the refusal of the English faculty to make MacCabe's temporary lectureship permanent turned into a bloody debate about the place of post-structuralism criticism within the university, with Christopher Ricks leading those against its introduction and Kermode and Raymond Williams as the senior-most faculty in support of MacCabe and, in essence, a revivified curriculum. For Kermode the dispute was actually less about 'rival literary theories' than about 'the whole question of how literature should be taught' (NE, 255), his strongest sense being that the English faculty, through long-term neglect, had let its syllabus and mode of instruction fall into desuetude. 'To my alien eyes,' he writes, 'the faults in its system were obvious and even scandalous; to most of my new colleagues, my complaints arose out of mere disaffection, presumption, or ignorance of Cambridge ways' (NE, 250). Kermode's response was in keeping with a long-standing ambition to be mindful of present needs and purposes, especially as they appear relevant to the general well-being of literary study. It helps to explain his reaching out across the ocean, in his 1960 study of Wallace Stevens, when few of his British colleagues knew of the poet's existence or were even prepared to acknowledge the general worthiness of American literary contributions; it also helps to explain his leadership role in the acclaimed theory seminar, based at London University, in the late 1960s and early 1970s; and it helps to explain his repeated assumption of foreign appointments, be they at Harvard, Columbia, Yale, Dartmouth, Houston, or elsewhere. The point is, Kermode has always sought to escape the complacencies that mar academic thinking, including versions of Little Englandism. Addressing the European Society for the Study of English in 1993, Kermode said,

> It can hardly be denied that two or three generations ago our studies were confidently, even unthinkingly, insular. At this distance it seems almost incredible that we weren't even certain whether we should admit 'American literature' to our courses. Yet it was more than anything else 'modernist' American literature, once the academics began to take it seriously, that compelled attention to other works not in our native canon, as Eliot directed us to Dante and to French poetry, Pound, more expansively, to Provençal, and early Italian literature, to Chinese and Japanese, and, incidentally, back to the Greek and Latin classics ... which had provided the matrix of English literary studies but had been increasingly neglected as the volume of work perceived as necessary to the study of native literature grew so enormous. After a while it became impossible to take very seriously a literary scholar who regarded Dostoevsky, Kafka, Proust, as irrelevant to his concerns. ('The Future of the English Literary Canon,' 9)[25]

In Britain and Ireland, Kermode and Donoghue have well-deserved reputations for championing the study of American literature; and Steiner, of European literature. They have, in this sense, been progressive forces, a fact that has, as noted, often put off more traditional scholars. Things are, however, somewhat different on the other side of the Atlantic, for if the British and Irish academies have been beset by insularity, the American academy is beset by modishness. Generally, this has not worked to Donoghue, Kermode, and Steiner's advantage, for their cultural and historical memories reach too far back for them to be much swayed by this year's intellectual fashion. They have each been publishing serious, independent criticism since the 1950s, and in this time have seen come and go the New Criticism, myth criticism, structuralism, deconstruction, first-, second- and third-wave feminist criticism, and several other methodologies geared to making the critic's work appear more professional. At times, one suspects, with Patrick Parrinder, that what we are really seeing is the working out of market forces: 'The academic "market-leaders" of theory ... have shown remarkable dexterity in refurbishing their product-lines, launching new brightly packaged intellectual models and consigning yesterday's theories to the remainder shop.'[26] At other times, it is as if literary study has surrendered itself to carnivalization. '[A]esthetic theory over the past twenty years,' writes Wendy Steiner, 'reminds me of a shooting gallery. Up pops a duck, only to be shot down and replaced by a new duck bearing a certain resemblance. Formalism, structuralism, semiotics, Marxism, feminism, the New Historicism – the approaches keep penetrating their little murders, transforming ducks who have barely shed their down into dead ducks piling up in English departments' (*The Scandal of Pleasure,* 6). Yet this said, earlier versions of critical theory actually did confer more respect upon the work of our three critics than have more recent methodologies. George Steiner, for instance, was asked by *New Literary History,* in the 1980s, to be one of its respondents to the question of what role literary theory should assume in the university. And the editors of *Critical Inquiry* once upon a time took what they called 'a dispute between a Manxman and an Irishman' ('Kermode and Donoghue' [March 1975]: 701) seriously enough to give quite a number of pages to seeing the conflict mediated, if not quite resolved. The dispute, which perhaps seems less such today, involved Kermode's and Donoghue's different way of reading Ford Madox Ford's *The Good Soldier,* with Kermode arguing that the novel stood as a testimony to the fact that 'the illusion of the single right reading is possible no longer' and Donoghue replying that 'there is only one story, and the reader is provoked into finding it, piecing it together with the doubtful aid of a narrator who, having survived the events, has time on his hand' ('A Reply to Frank Kermode,' 118). As the editors said at the time, 'the issue of "the single right reading" has been filling our pages'; and it seemed to them that the 'Kermode–Donoghue debate' nicely situated the discussion 'on a middle ground between the many who are willing, as Kermode is not, to cut all moorings with what he calls "naive consumption" of single readings imposed by authors, and those, who, unlike Donoghue, resist all ambiguities' ('Kermode and Donoghue,' 700). At the time, Kermode's interest in the way that a classic text could, over time, elicit an almost infinite number of distinct readings provoked more contentious responses than

Donoghue's gentle upbraiding. In her 1979–80 Charles Eliot Norton lectures, at Harvard University, Dame Helen Gardner, in what David Sexton calls her 'dippy attack' ('Kermode as compère,' 19), singled out Kermode as a monstrous relativist, who believes 'that because we cannot know everything, we cannot know anything; that the only alternative to certainty is total ignorance' (*In Defence of the Imagination*, 118).[27] Other attacks on American soil, this time from Americans, came from E.D. Hirsch ('I am especially troubled by Kermode's uncritical modernism [i.e., his view that the latest ideas are the most interesting], and his certainty that it is naïve to seek the correct, or definitive, interpretation of any text' ['Carnal Knowledge,' 18]), Hugh Kenner (who dismissed Kermode as 'England's grooviest general-purpose critic' [*A Sinking Island*, 40]) and Gerald Graff, who found Kermode's 'defense of interpretative conventions as a set of shared fictions ... finally indistinguishable from a kind of post-structuralist view which is too sophisticated, wise and weary to believe even in nihilism. Like Jacques Derrida, Kermode is not so presumptuous as to think he can break free from the ideological fictions whose bankruptcy he has exposed' (review of Kermode, *The Genesis of Secrecy*, 31).

A Criticism of Meaning in a Land of Value

More recent American responses to Donoghue, Kermode, and Steiner's work have tended to identify it as conservative. For instance, Nina Auerbach, reviewing Kermode's *An Appetite for Poetry* (1989), wrote: 'Today's universities are segmented into opposing critical camps. I fear most of my colleagues will notice only this polemical prologue to the book, skimming it to dismiss it as "conservative"' ('Roasting the Academics,' 12). She was no doubt right, as she was when she follows with the remark: 'It would be a pity, though, to reduce Mr. Kermode's passionate, intricate argument to a label, for at heart it is a defense of an eccentricity criticism is abandoning' (ibid.). Where Auerbach sees 'eccentricity,' however, others might see a penchant for critical independence, a refusal to accept, on faith, the tenets of any one camp. It is true, however, that those aligning themselves with one critical camp or another are less likely to appreciate not only Kermode's, but also Donoghue's and Steiner's, work. There may be many reasons for this, though a single crucial difference between the three critics and their more theory-oriented American counterparts is that while Kermode, Donoghue, and Steiner remain committed to the notion that humans do best to direct their lives towards some larger notion of temporal completion, be it religious or mythic, their counterparts are generally more committed to notions of open-ended spatialization. This difference has, of late, become more stark, with critics like W.J.T. Mitchell arguing that 'recent American criticism' has welcomed 'a shift in emphasis from *meaning* to *value*' ('The Good, the Bad, and the Ugly,' 63), wherein 'meaning' speaks of judgments understood in the light of more permanent truths, and 'value' speaks of those that exist in continual flux, with little, or any, hope of overcoming their contingency. Or as Barbara Herrnstein Smith, in her chapter 'Truth/Value,' writes: 'What appears to be needed, and is perhaps emerging, is a total and appropriately elaborated reformulation, and, in particular, one in which the various fundamentally problematic explanatory structures involving duplicative transmission, correspondence, equivalence, and recovery are replaced by an account of the dynamics of various types of *consequential interaction*' (*Contingencies of Value*, 95).

Actually, this division between meaning and value goes at least as far back as the Joseph Frank–Frank Kermode debate over spatial form that appeared in the pages of *Critical Inquiry* in 1977–8. In his essay, 'Spatial Form: An Answer to Critics,' Frank offered a lengthy attack against Kermode, for the reason that his work, especially in *The Sense of an Ending* (1967), emphasizes temporal relations at the expense of spatial relations. Frank, however, found solace in the fact that Kermode's argument appeared to refute itself: 'One of Kermode's essential aims, in *The Sense of an Ending*, was precisely to argue in favor of continuity and to reject the schismatic notion that a clean break with the past was either desirable or possible. It seems to me that he succeeded better than he knew, and that in polemicizing with "spatial form" he merely perpetuates a schism which in the deeper thrust of his own ideas has done much to reveal as nugatory and obsolete' (251). Frank's keenness to point out the logical inconsistency of Kermode's argument had, no doubt, something to do with his own dream of 'a unified theory of literary structures' (251), as well as his conviction that 'it is time that English critics overcame their provincialism' (249). Kermode himself was not so attached to the notion of theoretical harmony, though he thought that Frank's making him the representative of English critics might be taken as a slur by many of his colleagues. More seriously, he said that he was not against what Frank referred to as spatial form, but that his own interests were really focused elsewhere. Still, he wanted to make it clear that as far as he was concerned, spatial and temporal forms are inextricably linked:

The dynamics of understanding have to be thought of in terms of provi-sional assessments, selections of what Dilthey called *Eindruckspunkten*, and a general assumption of followability, which enable one to reach the end not with a mass of unprocessed information held in suspense but with a sense, not of course fully formed and not of course incorrigible, of what the end will be. The assumption of followability corresponds to the assumption that the sentence will be well formed. When we have the whole thing before us we shall not be surprised to discover that the consonance of its parts is not exactly as we predicted it, though we did predict it a consonance and could not have read it otherwise. It is this consonance, corrected from our preun-derstood version of it, that gets called 'spatial form.' But reading is less like making a map than like navigating entirely by dead reckoning; a knowl-edge of wind and tide can help; but only the end gives us an accurate fix. (581)

In truth, neither Frank nor Kermode wished to divorce the spatial and the temporal, but their emphases were quite different, with Frank focus-ing on the importance of the former and Kermode on the latter. Mean-while, when Kermode says at the end of the essay that literature has an implicit relation to immanence and eschatology (588),[28] he could easily be speaking for Donoghue and Steiner, each of whom has expressed similar views. For instance, Donoghue, in *The Arts without Mystery* (1983), writes of 'the imminence of a revelation which does not occur, the veil that continues to tremble, forever still to be enjoyed: it is a ques-tion of tense, in which the present leans from itself toward a future indefinitely proposed and postponed' (92); and Steiner, in *Real Pres-ences*, writes: 'It is the lucid intensity of its meeting with death that gener-ates in aesthetic forms that statement of vitality, of life-presence, which distinguishes serious thought and feeling from the trivial and opportu-nistic' (141).

Certitudes elude Kermode, Donoghue, and Steiner, as they elude most men and women; still, their hopes are pointed in the direction where the disparate strands of experience come together and find explanation. One might well, as Steiner does in 'Two Suppers,' speak of such in relation either to '*Logos*, the ultimate "One Truth" (Plotinus after Plato) or the Word, that Word that is and is with God in *John*' (46), though the more crucial matter is that a sense of purpose is intuited in the world – what Kermode speaks of as the 'divine plot'[29] – and one tries to be responsive to it. By contrast, American theorists are generally more prepared to live, as the title of Jay Clayton's book puts it, among

The Pleasures of Babel, thinking that perhaps 'the punishment of Babel has gotten bad press,' that there are, in fact, 'substantial pleasures to be found in the land of Babel and that these pleasures may ultimately benefit the nation' (viii). In a similar spirit, Regenia Gagnier argues that only the truly unprogressive – for instance, the 'hysterical' Joseph Conrad ('A Critique of Practical Aesthetics,' 271) – are made anxious about a life lived without clear direction or purpose:

> Anyone who has moved in progressive or Leftist circles – and here I include feminist circles – has witnessed the demoralizing case of the wannabe progressive who is incapable of operating in conditions of uncertainty, risk, or vulnerability; incapable of living without authoritarian or hierarchical structures; incapable, in short, of living with change. Since risk, vulnerability, and instability are the inevitable conditions of progressivism, this psychological incapacity, no matter how fervent the conscious commitment, throws the wannabe Leftist perpetually into contradiction between her emotional needs and her abstract desires. Due to the nature of nurture as we have known it, some people are psychologically incapable of living with freedom. (ibid.)

These 'wannabes' yearn not only for values, but for meaning (for something to give definition to their progress). It is the cause of their failing, and Gagnier, tough-mindedly, has neither sympathy nor respect for them. The age of meaning is over, and if one cannot manipulate the age of values to one's advantage, well, too bad. This heaven has only so much room, so its proprietors do well to be choosy. The key test, says Peter Brooks, is the ability to employ 'a rhetoric of virtue' ('Aesthetics and Ideology,' 157) coupled with an ability to keep hidden, especially from one's colleagues and students, all instances of false consciousness. There is a lot of posturing involved, obviously, and one might object, notes Brooks, that '[t]he terms in which the choice is posed create a kind of academic melodrama, of the disempowered professional wimp versus the macho resistance hero. Even if we want to align ourselves with the latter, and want to refuse definitively the notion of the critic as a genteel belated Victorian preaching sweetness and light, we may find that this version of the choice both plays into the hands of our enemies, and seriously undermines our ability to speak of literature with any particular qualifications for doing so' (158).

One also wonders about the 'freedom' proffered here, and whether the substitution of banausic values for the more consolatory values traditionally associated with both art and religion is such a great thing. 'We rarely,' Gagnier writes, 'make monistic claims for The Good, The True, or The Beautiful, but if we are not cowards we do insist that we know when we are confronted with evil, with lies, and with ugliness' ('Critique of Practical Aesthetics,' 281). How do they know? What is their standard? And what gives them the backbone to speak against evil when everyone else is cowering before its physical force? Gagnier does not have an answer, unless such banal tautologies that 'pain and poverty ... are bad,' and 'a government that ignores pain and poverty lies' (ibid.) are such. Yet just as, says Stanley Fish, 'there is always someone to the left of anybody' (*Professional Correctness*, 69), there is always someone more tough-minded, and Barbara Herrnstein Smith makes Gagnier, with her talk of pain and poverty, seem like a contemporary Major Barbara. The contrast naturally brings out Smith's kinship with Andrew Undershaft: 'society cannot be saved until either the Professors of Greek take to making gunpowder, or else the makers of gunpowder become Professors of Greek.' Like the Shaw character, Smith believes that the rules of business are also those of life, and sympathy is wasted upon those who refuse to understand this: 'All value is radically contingent, being neither a fixed attribute, an inherent quality, or an objective property of things but, rather, an effect of multiple, continuously changing, and continuously interacting variables or, to put this another way, the product of the dynamics of a system, specifically an *economic* system. It is readily granted, of course, that it is in relation to such a system that commodities such as gold, bread, and paperback editions of *Moby-Dick* acquire the value indicated by their market price' (*Contingencies of Value*, 30).

Smith's thesis seems less compelling as proof that '[a]ll value is radically contingent' than as a testimony to her own belief that all value is reducible to economic value: 'Like its price in the marketplace, the value of an entity to an individual subject is *also* the product of the dynamics of an economic system' (ibid.). That the 'business of America is business' is evident enough, though less evident is why so many American intellectuals should wish to acquiesce to this formulation. It does not save them. And one can still imagine how things might stand otherwise. But remarkably few do wish to imagine things otherwise, preferring to think, with W.J.T. Mitchell, that

Meaning ... is something like money in the economy of the professional humanities: the value of a text is proportional to the number of interpretations it can sustain. 'Priceless' works of genius, canonical masterpieces, can generate a theoretically infinite surplus of meanings. Difficult, cryptic, and highly allegorical texts provide an additional surplus of what might be called 'mystery-value,' the special mystique that attaches to hidden riches and buried treasure. The shift of critical attention to the value of meaning is not likely to put interpretation out of business, but it is likely to make that business a matter of self-conscious critical concern, if only by fostering inquiry into the meaning of value. ('The Good, the Bad, and the Ugly,' 63–4)[30]

When has the question of meaning not been 'a matter of self-conscious critical concern'? And why do Smith and Mitchell think that now that they have shown how easy it is to analogize to coin the things about which we care, that we must all do likewise? Even if we grant the real possibility that all value is contingent, what is there to celebrate about the making of everything commensurable to everything else?[31] For whom is this thought to be a good thing? Perhaps only those whose system of value betrays no vile anachronisms, for in practice this new ethic of commensurability favours the well-to-do and the au courant. 'It tacitly assumes,' writes Brooks, 'a place of privilege – within contemporary American academia, of all places – from which it proffers its discourse' ('Aesthetics and Ideology,' 164). The ethic is not especially hospitable to critics like Donoghue, Kermode, and Steiner, if only because their critical assumptions predicate a meaning above value. The critical difference between such assumptions is on view in the controversy provoked by Kermode's 1995 review of Marjorie Garber's *Vice Versa*. Kermode took exception to Garber's readiness to view everything as commensurable with everything else, so that it becomes a typical practice to discuss Henry James in relation to Ricki Lake or *Remembrance of Things Past* in relation to *Dynasty* and *Quantum Leap*. Not only is the high brought low, but the difference between them is refused. Category is imagined as a false construct; and bisexuality is imagined as the proof of this, as 'a category that undoes category' ('Beyond Category, 6). Put off by the evident rhetorical ploy, Kermode retorted: 'So the rowdy, assertive babble about definitions and categories, and the odd suggestion that if I weren't handicapped in some way or surfeited I too would be some sort of bi, mildly irritates me. I am what I am: let her, let him, be what they are; I wouldn't dream of inquiring' ('Beyond Category,' 7).

The review, appearing as it did in the *New York Times Book Review*, provided the American academy with its weekly scandal, and led to a virtual attack on Kermode's character by James Kincaid and Garber herself. The first accused him of writing a 'bumptious review' employing 'old-boy prose' and 'moldy commonplaces' lifted from 'the grave' by a critic with a discernibly 'uninquiring mind' (Letter, 23). The second accused him of writing in a 'spirit of Olympian entitlement,' which 'for all its genteel and world-weary tone, is as "agitated" and "strident" as anything that he dismisses. But the agitation of retired professors passes for "*gravitas*," whereas the lives and writings of gay men, lesbians and bi-sexuals are disdained as "fashion" and "trendiness." Two words in Ker-mode's review may be taken as emblematic of the whole: "approve" and "deplore." We are here in the Church of St. Frank, where moral judg-ments permit the true believer to avoid any semblance of thought' (Let-ter, 23). Once again, it was evidence that when the academy divides itself into camps, wishing to stand in the middle may prove dangerous to one's health. Or as Valentine Cunningham, at the time of the Cam-bridge débâcle, said about Kermode's inclination to be a mediator: 'And of course no side ... is ever particularly grateful to the middle man' ('The Ethical Backlash,' 790).

It is worth noting that it is not the 'lives and writings of gay, men, lesbians and bisexuals' that Kermode – or Steiner and Donoghue – disdains. For one, Steiner long ago, in *Bluebeard's Castle* (1971), offered a brief foreshadowing of Garber's thesis:

> The typologies of women's liberation, of the new politically, socially osten-tatious homosexuality (notably in the United States) and of 'unisex' point to a deep reordering or disordering of long-established frontiers. 'So loosly disally'd,' in Milton's telling phrase, men and women are not only maneu-vering in a neutral terrain of indistinction, but exchanging roles – sartori-ally, psychologically, in regard to economic and erotic functions which were formerly set apart.
>
> Again, a general rubric suggests itself. A common formlessness or search for new forms has all but undermined classic age-lines, sexual divisions, class structures, and hierarchic gradients of mind and power. We are caught in a Brownian movement at every vital, molecular level of individua-tion and society. And if I may carry the analogy one step further, the mem-branes through which social energies are current are now permeable and nonselective. (82–3)

Donoghue, meanwhile, is the father of the eminent lesbian novelist Emma Donoghue; and his pride in her and what she has accomplished has been readily apparent. Nevertheless, Donoghue, like Kermode, is less willing to think of artists according to such categories, thinking it wiser to resist the reductions that ensue. Hence Donoghue's objection to Andrew Sullivan's attempt to characterize homosexuals as people not only especially attuned to matters of form and style, but also as a familiar type: 'I don't think Mr. Sullivan is prudent in offering a characterization of "the homosexual" at all: it merely adds a type, ostensibly stable, to the stock of types already in the hands of sociologists' ('The Politics of Homosexuality,' 26). In short, these critics, committed to the middle way, wish not to be asked to choose between the aesthetic and the political, though this is exactly what progressives demand. Or as John Guillory notes, '[t]he effect of an openly progressive critique of aesthetics is to position the "aesthetic" and the "political" as the discursive antithesis of current critical thought, and thus to enjoin a choice between them' (*Cultural Capital*, 273). Forced to choose, Donoghue, Kermode, and Steiner will always come down on the side of the aesthetic, believing with Milan Kundera that when politics obtrudes itself into art's domain, there are only two possible positions, and they are both extreme. It is better, then, to ignore the demand and to return to one's work, the study of literature. But it is not so easy, for the opposing critique's implicit claim is that literature is either indiscernible as a bounded field or, granting its existence, irrelevant to, or counterproductive regarding, present-day concerns and needs. Cary Nelson writes: 'In this historical context, ... it is potentially a powerful and dangerous seduction to offer students literariness as something they can identify with, as a subject position they can occupy, while constructing it as an ideology that transcends such passing material trivialities as racial injustice.'[32] And while one might well wish to ignore the claims, thinking them mistaken, it is difficult to work against the grain of disciplinary opinion.

True, there is a strangeness about a discipline – literary study – setting itself in opposition to what it does, or has long done. It calls forth the image of lemmings marching to the sea. Still, many who work in literature departments have become convinced that the work they and their predecessors have traditionally done is too narrowly focused and has, in the words of Ben Agger, even contributed 'to overall domination by refusing a view of totality desperately needed in this stage of world capitalism, sexism and racism.'[33] It should be better, it is said, to open the discipline up to the study of those things, or texts, which cannot be considered literature in any traditional sense, but whose study should make us somehow less divorced from the world. This, then, is the rationale for cultural studies, which, says Patrick Brantlinger, 'aims to overcome the disabling fragmentation of knowledge within the disciplinary structure of the university, and ... also to overcome the fragmentation and alienation in the larger society which that structure mirrors.'[34] That alienation is an inescapable characteristic of human existence, a consequence of the world's extraordinary diversity and otherness, seems not to count for very much here, for the ambition is to offer 'a unified map of knowledge.'[35] It is a Faustian ambition, but cultural studies is nothing if not ambitious. This would be fine, if literary study – cultural studies' spawning ground – were itself a minnow-size thing, offering its practitioners plenty of time to fish in other streams, but it is not; and no one ever truly masters the discipline, especially if one thinks of it – as one well might – as entailing the literature not only of one's own culture but also the literatures (preferably not in translation) of neighbouring cultures. To read, as Donoghue, Kermode, and Steiner give evidence of doing, not only Anglophone literature but also that written in Latin, French, and German is a too-rare thing, and this ability, or something like it, might be thought an objective preceding that of pursuits recognizably outside the realm of literature. Geoffrey Hartman once objected that 'the trouble with Anglo-American formalism was that it was never formalist enough';[36] likewise, it might be objected that literary study, rather than being thought too exacting in its demands, has not been exacting enough. It is not that the realm of literature does not intersect the realms of mass media, politics, sociology, and so forth; it is rather that if, as in Garber, one starts making one or more of these other realms the overriding object of one's attention, there soon comes a point when one is no longer a student of literature but of something else. Or as Fish, in his worthy defence of literary study, *Professional Correctness*, puts the matter:

> Still, one might say, even if cultural studies must fail of its aspiration to reveal the deep causal structure of things, it *can* do something; it can produce a new object, another text. But that text – which Brantlinger calls the cultural text – has no epistemological or ontological superiority over the texts (of literature, history, law, etc.) it displaces. That is, it is not a larger text or a more inclusive text; it is just a *different* text, with its own emphases, details, and meanings of other texts. The cultural text, if it comes into view, will not provide a deeper apprehension of the literary text or the legal text; rather it will erase them even in the act of referring to them, for the references will always be produced from *its* angle of inter-

est, not theirs. If cultural studies tells us to look elsewhere to find the meaning of the literary text, I say that if you look elsewhere, you will see something else. (79)

This sense of things is at the heart of the Kermode-Garber dispute; for Kermode thinks that Garber, hired by Harvard's English Department to teach Shakespeare, should assume it her responsibility not only to cultivate an expert knowledge of, in this instance, Shakespeare, but also to do her best, through teaching and scholarship, to see that this same work (literary and critical) is transmitted to later generations. Like Fish, Kermode celebrates professionalism – or more precisely an aspect of it, that of the hard-working cleric whose labours, though rarely hailed, help to preserve in the cultural memory literary texts that might otherwise soon be lost to history. To some, this celebration may seem a contradictory position to hold, for Kermode has also assumed it his responsibility to speak to a more general public. In short, he practises both the role of insider and outsider; and the argument could be made, as it is by Diane Middlebrook, that this is also what Garber does: 'Ms. Garber employs a resourcefully public (as opposed to hieratically academic) language in her exposition of current thinking about these interesting subjects. Kermode can usually be counted on to appreciate such a gift' (Letter, 23). Garber, too, claims something like this when, defending her mixing of the literary with the popular, she writes, 'But Shakespeare himself was "popular culture" in his time' (23). Nevertheless, there is a real difference between what Kermode (like Donoghue and Steiner) and Garber do; for while it is true that they both straddle the fence separating insiders from outsiders, one of them thinks that he has, in fact, something important to convey to those outside, and the other is no longer quite so sure, and has even taken to wondering whether she might not prefer to live with the others, outside. If Garber's diminishing allegiance were only hers alone, the matter would not merit our attention. But it is not; and there is reason for thinking, as Kermode does, that Garber's book is testimony of a quite serious division, or crisis, in the profession. It is, writes Kermode, 'a sign of the academic times' ('Beyond Category,' 6), or as John Guillory, writing more broadly, notes: 'it is unquestionably the case that the several recent crises of the literary canon – its "opening" to philosophical works, to works by minorities, and now to popular and mass cultural works – amounts to a terminal crisis, more than sufficient evidence of the urgent need to reconceptualize the object of literary study' (*Cultural Capital*, 265).

'Irascible Loners'

One would like to think that Guillory is mistaken, that he is an alarmist, and that the only thing literary study truly needs to do is to take its own subject more seriously. Doing so, however, would probably necessitate the taking down of the departmental big tent – sheltering interests as disparate as literature, composition, creative writing, critical theory, cultural studies, film, gender studies, mass media, journalism, technical writing, computer 'literacy,' and so forth – and allowing English to become more like Classics, which is to say hamstrung by the knowledge that one's place in the university is dependent on sufferance. And we know that this is not going to transpire – not at a time when every university department has been forced to fight to hold on to its share of the budgetary pie, itself increasingly eaten up by administrative costs. And not at a time when the prevailing sentiment is that all those students aspiring to places in the corporate realm can succeed perfectly well without coursework in literature and the other humanities. In fact, in a recent survey of American *school teachers*, fewer than one-quarter thought that literature constituted an essential discipline, relegating it an even lower priority than civics and computers, though it beat out gym. The point is, we are witnessing, writes Guillory, 'the hegemony of that technobureaucratic organization of intellectual life which has rendered the literary curriculum socially marginal by transforming the university into the institution designed to produce a new class of technical/ managerial specialists possessed of purely technical/managerial knowledge' (261). If this, in fact, is the university's purpose, then the university really has no strong interest in departments of literature; and to the degree that it has been supportive of theory, it has, thinks Guillory, much to do with the sense that theory, unlike literature, is more at home in a world where the first rule is that knowledge must be systematized; and the second rule is that there must be recognizable experts who attract disciples, bringing further recognition to the institution. All of this may or may not be true, for it has its own too-systematic character. Yet it may be thought another reason why Donoghue, Kermode, and Steiner have garnered less attention for their work than others far less talented. They are simply too independent, too attentive to the sort of questions that remain unhoused in recent theory; and as their attentions are focused elsewhere, they appear less cultivating of disciples and less prepared, in Fish's revealing metaphor, to play the professional 'game': 'The name for this is professionalization, a form of organization in which membership is acquired by a course of special training whose end is the production of persons who recognize one another not because they regularly meet at the same ceremonial occasions (unless one equates an MLA meeting with the Elizabethan court), but because they perform the same "moves" in the same "game."' (*Professional Correctness*, 32)

That professionalism – or this version of it – now has, in literary study, the upper hand is clear; ones see evidence of this everywhere one looks, in the plethora of graduate programs, in the multitude of methodologies, in the bevy of acolytes, in the spate of specialized journals and seminars, and so forth. For better or worse, the study of literature has gone corporate; and if one does not wish to be left out, one needs to get with the program. There is little, or no, space for those lacking a corporate identification card. This has not always been so; and even now, one might wonder whether literature has truly benefited from all this attention, for so much of the latter has seemed displaced. Donald Davie, in his iconoclastic mood, has remarked: 'For those critics who aim above all at "professionalism" are only reflecting, in their own chosen sphere, the assumption that underlies School of Business Management, and the big corporations that recruit from them: the assumption that many minds systematically trained and collaborating will always outstrip one mind, self-trained, proceeding on its own with dedication and flair. (How much more Dryden could have achieved in criticism if he had been enlisted in an organization that would have required him to collaborate with John Dennis and Nahum Tate!)' ('Criticism and the Academy,' 176).[37] This view is also congenial to our three critics. Donoghue, in rebuttal to René Wellek's inclination to make theorists toe the line, writes: 'The problem is that critics are not willing to write criticism. Or criticism is always flying off to become something else; autobiography (Sainte-Beuve), history (Carlyle), psychology (De Sanctis), philosophy (Mill), morality (Ruskin), sociology (Taine), theology (Dallas), propaganda (Brandes), philosophy of history (Nietzsche). Critics will not learn their trade. The easy way out is to let each man go his own way. If the mind is good enough, the way is likely to be vivid' ('The Gay Science,' 81).

There is no doubt that Donoghue, Kermode, and Steiner's minds are 'good enough'; even as they have been repeatedly slurred with the new epithet 'conservative,' that term which, like 'elitist,' 'formalist,' and 'humanist,' functions, writes Hassan, 'as obloquy, dismissal, massive deterrence, triumphant demystification (I have found you out!). The label suffices, no argument required; for the accused, seppuka is expected' (*Rumors of Change*, 172). Still, what Kazin says of Donoghue – 'He is so much more intelligent than most academic critics' ('Habits of Home,' 46) – might as easily be said of Kermode or Steiner; and has, in fact, been said numerous times. They possess three of the finest minds in literary criticism, and if they have not, like a Fredric Jameson or a Stephen Greenblatt, been identified with any of the more emergent methodologies, it is because they really are independent critics, reluctant to force their views into conformity with others, preferring to write what they think true rather than what will earn them credit in the corporation. One will never hear them say anything like what one critic recently said of William Gaddis's novels – 'As postmodern texts, Gaddis's novels are ideologically sound' (Commes, *Ethics of Indeterminacy*, 2) – for they abjure litmus tests and party oaths. They are not stupid; they know the name of the 'game' has swerved in the direction of 'classroom advocacy,' 'coalitions,' 'collaborative criticism,' 'discourse communities,' 'networking,' 'power bases,' 'identity politics,' 'postmodern praxis,' and so forth; but they are not game players, and seem prepared to live with the consequences. They may work, or have worked, in universities, but they are not strictly academic critics; rather, they are the sort mentioned by Davie when he writes: 'There exist, here and there, critics worth listening to. Mostly, the state of the labor market being what it is, these few will turn out to hold a post in some college or university. But they are not "academic critics" in the sense I have written of. On the contrary, it will be found in almost every case that "the profession," so far as it takes note of them, looks on them askance as unpredictable and often irascible loners' ('Criticism and the Academy,' 176–7). That Donoghue, Kermode, and Steiner are loners, I have said; that the profession looks on them askance, I think has also been made clear. But they have also been praised – highly – by some of our most important minds, including John Banville, Kenneth Burke, Harold Bloom, Valentine Cunningham, Donald Davie, Ihab Hassan, Alfred Kazin, Michael Wood, Edward Said, John Updike, and Hayden White; and given the choice between being looked at askance by the profession and being praised by the likes of Burke ('[a]ny text that deserves some measure of appreciation can consider itself lucky if Denis Donoghue chooses to write about it' [Rev. of *The Sovereign Ghost*, 29]), Bloom (Kermode is 'the best living English critic' [*The Western Canon*, 3]), or Said ('Steiner is without peer in rendering and reflecting on patterns and motifs in modern ... culture' ['Himself Observed,' 244]), no thoughtful critic would need to think twice.

Still, one might ask what is so appealing about Donoghue, Kermode, and Steiner's critical independence? What insights can be found in their work that cannot be found in that of more aligned critics? There might be several answers, but I wish to emphasize two. The first relates to the fact that a commitment to a specific methodology, or theory, often has the unhappy consequence of both reigning in the sorts of things one reads and what one says about them. When the theory is sacrosanct, one becomes more cautious about exposing it to potential disharmony. In this respect, theory is quite unlike literature, which, says Edmundson, has historically been associated with 'the urge to prolifer-ate narrative, to spread before the reader a vast array of incidents that, while they may have much to teach, resist being housed under any given sign or system of signs' (*Literature Against Philosophy*, 14). Theory is meant to be taught, to be disseminated; and while literature can also be taught, its impulse to teach is complicated by its impulse to please, to offer imaginative pleasure. Nor, in doing either of these things, does it feel the same obligation, as theory, towards showing itself consistent with other texts. Poems, plays, and novels succeed best when they are recognized as individual achievements. So while literature finds some welcome in the university, its source of inspiration is more often else-where. This is, again, much less true of theory, which is really most at home in the university, and would probably expire outside its walls. Here, theory does not simply require readers; it requires disciples, and these are best found in the academy, the way, for instance, Paul de Man's classroom became a petri dish for culturing disciples, even as he was speaking of his disinterest in such. At his memorial service, Bar-bara Johnson noted: 'He never sought followers; people followed him in droves. He was ironic toward discipleship; the country is dotted with his disciples.'[38] Disciples require not a thousand readings of a thousand dif-ferent texts, but something more portable that can be applied as equally well to one text as to another, the way de Man's theory of deconstruc-tion suggested that every text was a variation on the same text. Or as de Man wrote in *Allegories of Reading*, after applying his theory to a passage from *Swann's Way*: 'The whole of literature would respond in similar fashion, although the techniques and the patterns would have to vary considerably, of course, from author to author. But there is absolutely no reason why analyses of the kind here suggested for Proust would not be applicable, with proper modifications of technique, to Milton or to Hölderlin. This will in fact be the task of literary criticism in the coming years' (16–17). Not only does the last sentence make us suspicious regarding de Man's professed disinterest in disciples, but the larger passage also makes it clear how much de Man, like Wellek, is wedded to the notion of theory, to the practice that often makes literature, in its infinite variety, seem like an impertinence. For de Man, literature is best imagined as but a handful of texts, some poems by Hölderlin, Rilke, and Wordsworth, Proust's novel, some works by Rousseau and Nietzsche, and a few other things. Compare this sense of literature to that of Donoghue, Kermode, and Steiner, who, week after week, in the pages of the leading literary journals, open themselves up to literature in its largest and most irreducible sense, offering full-fledged readings of authors as unlike one another as Walter Pater and James Kelman (Donoghue), St Mark and Majorie Garber (Kermode), and Homer and Albert Einstein (Steiner). Writing about Donoghue, Michael Levenson observes that 'it is a measure of his engagement and stamina that he attempts to answer that question [how might we be better readers?] not with a clinching theory, but with a hundred book reviews' ('Let us Advert,' 13). It is said in praise, and the same can be said of Kermode and Steiner, also in praise. They would be better theorists if only they were not such fine and scrupulous readers. Yet there is no regret.

Nor does one regret that by virtue of their outsider status, Donoghue, Kermode, and Steiner are free to raise questions that the academy, in its sophistication, thinks beneath it. I refer to the questions that arise out of the longing of human beings for their lives to make sense, to suggest and retain meaning, and somehow be understood in relation to first and last things. These are less social or political than existential and religious questions. They are not the sort that academics wish to be found asking, for fear of being dismissed as one of Gagnier's wannabes. Here, the academy finds its representative moment in Hartman's praise of de Man for offering 'no sublime moments, only perplexed readings,' a response that should, in truth, elicit, says Wendy Steiner, 'only a sigh,' especially when we admit that '[p]erplexity is the commonest effect of criticism, sublimity its rarest achievement' (*The Scandal of Pleasure*, 206–7). The sigh is seldom heard, though it is uncertain whether this is because its motivating emotion is never felt or because, though felt, it gets repressed. One would prefer to think the latter, though it is difficult to know. The result, writes Kazin, is that '[w]hat you don't find among literary scholars just now is any understanding of serious religious belief' ('Habits of Home,' 45), though the statement is made in the acknowledgment that Donoghue is an exception. Kermode and Steiner are also exceptions, even as their relation to religious belief is, unlike

Donoghue's, either agnostic (Kermode) or tenuous (Steiner). Still, what Robert Alter says about Steiner might, with greater qualification, also be said of Kermode:

> What informs his enterprise ... is a large vision of literature and history that deserves serious reflection. Perhaps the best way to understand the nature of that vision is to recognize that he has set himself the task – unique in contemporary criticism – of acting as a theological critic of literature and culture. I do not mean by this that he makes any clear-cut theistic assumptions of belief, but rather that he writes in the conviction that theology has asked the right questions: what are we to understand of the first and last things, creation and eschatology; what is the place of the human creature in the larger cosmic order; how do meaning and value emerge in a world that is constantly darkened with the threat of moral chaos; what purchase can the idea of redemption have in the stubbornly unredeemed realm of history? ('Against Messiness,' 23)

Alter is right. Such notions are deserving of reflection, and for this reason alone the work of Donoghue, Kermode, and Steiner – who are among the few literary critics asking such questions – merits attention. But their work, naturally, is so much more than this. It is rich in the quality of its critical discriminations, in its extraordinary range and learning, in its ethical good sense and appreciation for the virtue of measure, in its wisdom, and in its truly enthusiastic and loving responsiveness to literature, its acknowledged source of inspiration. This last point cannot be underestimated, for if among contemporary critics, these three are among the few whom, years from now, will continue to be read, it will be because what they have learned, and taken away, from literature has been less the order of an object lesson than of a style, of a sensitivity to words used well. Philosophy – what Swift called 'the lumber of the schools' – does not help one very much this way. And while the present impulse is to praise those critics who turn away from literature and towards philosophy, or theory, things must eventually right themselves. Donoghue, Kermode, and Steiner are three of the most masterful *writers* now working in criticism. Those who would disparage or dismiss their work, believing that style and substance can no longer co-exist, make a mistake. I do not think that Hartman, whose criticisms along this line were earlier discussed, makes this mistake, despite his readiness to place style under suspicion. In the end, the relation between criticism and art means too much to him, or, as he writes:

'Good critical writing does not judge or explain art in a coercive way; it evokes what Emerson called the alienated majesty of our own thoughts, thoughts neglected or rejected by us, and found again, here, in the restitutive work of the artist. We recognize in the artist, but also beyond him, our own potential genius. Criticism stages a recognition scene that speaks "of nothing more than what we are"' (*Minor Prophecies*, 14). Few critics offer this 'recognition scene' so well as Donoghue, Kermode, and Steiner; and in the following chapters, I wish, in terms earlier announced, to attend more fully to their work, with the hope of making this judgment more common.

Chapter One

DENIS DONOGHUE

The Common Reader

'From Dryden to Donoghue,' writes Geoffrey Hartman in *Minor Prophecies* (1991), 'this honesty, also called civility, is recognized as the characteristic of a critical style originating together with a mock-heroic savagery (think of Swift and Pope) whose major target is the same: enthusiasm, religious or secular, private or collective' (177). Hartman describes this style – i.e., the common reader – mostly to set it against more recent theoretical writings, and thereby to call attention to its shortcomings. He quotes Terry Eagleton to the effect that 'the honest style is anything but honest' and Fredric Jameson to the effect that the style represents 'an evasion of basic social facts' (178). Hartman then adds that the style, long considered a valuable addition to intellectual discourse, must now be recognized as akin to a 'teatotaling style' (64). Irrespective of its worth in 'Oxbridge,' the common reader style must be understood, from the American viewpoint, as 'stifl[ing] intellectual exchange' – 'a defensive mystique for which "dialectic" and even 'dialogue' (in Plato's or Gadamer's or Bakhtin's strong sense)' constitute 'threatening words' (66). It is not surprising, then, that Hartman – while granting Donoghue, Kermode, and Steiner's talent for translating difficult, abstract discussions into a more general idiom – wonders whether the effort does not do 'a disservice to language,' allowing some of the more important discursive elements to 'leak away' (67). Addressing himself specifically to Kermode and Steiner, Hartman writes 'that they are superb reviewers rather than originative thinkers: their vocation is the Arnoldian diffusion of ideas and not a radical revision or extension of knowledge' (ibid.).

In defence of Kermode and Steiner, as well as Donoghue, it might be said that they do not propose to offer a 'radical' rethinking of our knowledge. It is an important point, as well as the point of difference. Donoghue, Kermode, and Steiner are more wont to acknowledge their antecedents than to undermine them. They make no immodest claims for what they do, and they esteem it a privilege rather than an ignominy to participate in a critical discourse that has, in the past, offered a forum for such talents as Dryden, Johnson, Coleridge, Hazlitt, Emerson, James, Empson, Eliot, Woolf, Burke, Moore, Trilling, and others. It is the point of Donoghue's repeated reference to the passage in 'Tradition and the Individual Talent' wherein Eliot, responding to the objection that '[t]he dead writers are remote from us because we *know* so much more than they did,' replies, '[p]recisely, and they are that which we know' (40). It is also the point to Donoghue's allusion, in 'Newton's Other Law,' to the physicist's self-effacing explanation of his success as following from having planted his feet on the shoulders of giants.

To represent, as Hartman does, Steiner, Kermode, and Donoghue's criticism as inhabiting the subservient sphere of conceptual translation is to appear indifferent to style's genuine virtues, virtues that make it not merely an adorning addition but a substantive force. Or as Kenneth Burke, answering his own query ('Style for its own sake?'), writes: 'Decidedly, not at all. Style solely as the beneath-which-not, as the admonitory and hortatory act, as the example that would prod continually for its completion in all aspects of life, and so, in Eliot's phrase, "keep something alive," tiding us over a lean season.'[1] For Steiner, Kermode, and Donoghue, style does function this way, as the evidencing of a grace that does not necessarily originate with themselves, and thereby, as Donoghue writes, keeps '[f]aith, hope and charity' alive ('Kenneth Burke's Dangling Novel,' 84). Its work this way does not, however, come at the expense of critical judgment, nor have the critics' commitments to the common reader demonstratively undercut their ability to engage critical theory's more abstruse offerings. Hartman thinks otherwise, but he cannot quite will this style away. There are qualities about it – most notably its advocacy of moderation and dispassionate reasoning – that, try as he might, he cannot avoid valuing. Part of him wishes to see the common reader style, with its implicit linking of style with ethics, as no more than a mask for self-interested aggression. This part celebrates 'Derrida's rescue of style from its confusion with Greek *stulos*, column,' and the recovery of 'its links both with stiletto, a pointed weapon, and *stiglus* or *stigma* that emphasize cutting, pointing, branding' (*Minor*

Prophecies, 69). Another part of him, mindful of an earlier time in the twentieth century, when political conviction outpaced the forces of moderation, is made anxious by the increasing politicization of academic discourse, especially in the realm of cultural studies: 'Cultural criticism has become more complex and circumstantial than in the period between the World Wars, yet it still tends to see through texts rather than with them. And there are signs that new days of rage are upon us, on the part of those who are so much in touch with reality that they do not have to be in touch with language' (208).

Almost against his will, then, Hartman is forced to acknowledge the value of the common reader style: 'Despite some danger that the "friendship style" ... may degenerate into an anti-intellectual manner, a jargon of civility, it is crucial not to give up that public and conversational mode' (206). The reason relates to his discussion of the style's history, which he sees as arising in the seventeenth century with the growth of an educated middle class and continuing through the present day (in such forums as the *New York Review of Books* ['notorious for using Anglos' (62)],[2] the *New York Times Book Review*, the *Times Literary Supplement*, and the *London Review of Books*). The style, thinks Hartman, has tended to safeguard us against those inflammatory situations that have always been more numerous than many an American academic is prepared to acknowledge: 'The birth of the New Prose, moreover, acted as a moderating event at a time when the production of *news* became a potentially explosive spark, a rumor with slanderous or revolutionary or messianic force, aided by the spread of print as a popular medium. *The Spectator* newspaper extended the power of the familiar style; though it ostensibly brought news, it was really a form of antinews and tempered evangelical and enthusiastic flights' (177). As Hartman views matters, we are going to remain in need of this style's moderating influence. So he writes: 'Crossing from that period to ours, I want to suggest that as cultural history succumbs to cultural prophecy, this civil and critical prose grows in importance. The more pressure, the more it becomes a *style* as well as a medium, one that remains deliberately anti-inflammatory and resists futuristic generalizations of both the optimistic and the pessimistic kind' (ibid.).

In *Minor Prophecies*, then, *Hartman* begins by setting up an opposition between one style and another, yet if truth be told he gives evidence that the opposition cannot be held. It deconstructs itself, as he might say, though he does not. Rather, he leaves it to Donoghue, reviewing the book in the *New York Review of Books*, to say it for him: 'Hartman has set

up an opposition between two styles of criticism and between the ideological axioms on which each of them supposedly depends, but he is too
honorable to allow the invidious comparisons to stand' ('Critics at the
Top,' 54). It is a strikingly generous correction, for Donoghue is, more
than once, attacked by Hartman. 'Denis Donoghue,' Hartman snipes,
worries too much 'about creative critics inciting their disciplines to
dithyrambs instead of dissertations' (*Minor Prophecies*, 59). Donoghue
does not respond to the slight, as if to demonstrate that the common
reader style might entail interests other than the partisan. At the same
time, he rejects the argument that the style has no vigour, that it is the
embodiment of genteel 'teatotaling.' Hartman, writes Donoghue, 'can't
avoid presenting the' common reader style 'as that of a genteel tradition, and then we wonder where the gentility is to be found in Leavis,
Empson, Richards, G. Wilson Knight, and many other critics who supposedly embody it. In fact each of these critics puts genteel assumptions
under severe scrutiny' ('Critics at the Top,' 54). Donoghue is right
about this, and what he says about Leavis, Empson, and the others might
easily be said of his own work: it does not truckle to conventional expectations, whatever their points of origin. Or as Adam Phillips writes,
'With Donoghue, unlike many other critics, passion has not shrunk to
an obsession. His often brilliant readings have been reassuringly unpredictable; but his surprises are always framed by an underlying contention' ('Provocation,' 10). Part of this contention is that conviction that
the critic, in league with the artist, should assume something akin to an
adversarial stance towards society: 'My own understanding is that we
receive the arts most completely not when we pay lip service to them but
when the relation between art and society is mostly one of conflict and
suspicion, if not one of hostility' (AWM, 14).

Donoghue's stance has brought forth the charge that he speaks 'of an
antagonism between the arts and politics as if "the arts" were something
apart from politics, merely an aesthetic and not also a social practice'
(AWM, 14). The charge is not altogether unfair. Donoghue clearly
thinks that the artist stands apart from the culture at large, able to see
truths to which others remain blind: 'On the whole we try to include
the artist in the forms of our knowledge, but if he rejects our embrace
we know in some profound sense he is right, he knows he is not really
one of us' (AWM, 16). It is an essentially modernist stance, holding on to
the conviction that someone – i.e., the artist – might, in the larger
scheme of things, prove to be less implicated in the more pernicious
ways of the world. In truth, the stance is not all that different from Dono-

ghue's more postmodern critic. That is, both stances suggest the possibility of stepping back from the cultural matrix. Where they differ is in
the matter of who is thought best able to do so. In Donoghue's modernist formulation, it is clearly the artist; whereas, in the latter formulation,
it is the academic schooled in cultural criticism. Either way, a 'we versus
them' scenario is created, though the tones of each are different. In the
first, knowledge is looked upon as a positive fact; it is what the artist possesses and, in turn, offers to others of similar desire. Like the prophet
who offered the people parables 'because seeing they do not see, and
hearing they do not hear' (Matt.: 13.13), the artist is conceived as an
emissary capable of leading others to a truth that might otherwise
escape them. With knowledge imagined as a definite good, the only fear
is that there are too few genuine artists to deliver the good news.

Matters are somewhat different in the more patently academic criticism, for here knowledge itself comes under suspicion, and the artist,
rather than being instantly credited as the conveyor of good news, is
now imagined as implicated in the very matrix that has been judged suspect. There appears no way out. All are caught in the labyrinth of their
undoing, and whatever salvation might arrive comes not via the means
of knowledge and virtue but rather via the embrace of the monster
itself: power. In *Minor Prophecies*, Hartman, specifically speaking of new
historicism, poignantly expresses his own unhappiness regarding this
situation:

> [T]here *is* something remarkable in the new historicism: not its disclosure
> of some perfidious Western link between knowledge and power, but the
> movement's subversion of the claim that knowledge breeds sympathy, and
> so a tolerance of difference.
>
> It is knowledge more than power that stands accused of not leading to
> sympathy, or else perverting it subtly. Power after all is a fact that we live
> with; but that knowledge might transform the brute fact of power, that jus-
> tice, as a reflection of sympathetic inquiry, might modify the reliance on
> force, is a premise few are willing to abandon. (5)

Hartman articulates a fear shared by Donoghue, that 'a set of principles which would renew or establish a sense of value in what we read and
look at and hear' is missing (AWM, 122). The fear is not altogether
unwarranted, especially as there is a growing penchant among critics to
situate themselves in the flux of the moment, thinking it as not less real,
or unreal, than anything else. To conceive of things as other than they

present themselves requires imagination, requires perhaps the conviction, as Donoghue notes regarding Eliot, 'that the ordinary world, rich as it is in every other aspect, cannot provide a valid perspective upon itself and its processes' ('Eliot's "Marina,"' 372–3). When this is lacking, it is easy to assume that appearances – e.g., of achievement, of creativity, even of a self – are one with their objects. Donoghue notes the debonair coolness that distinguishes the postmodern sensibility from the modern. The modernist impulse to judge things by an enlarged, if not higher, standard,[3] an impulse that places one in an adversarial relation to society, gives way to another impulse, characterized by a greater readiness to accept things as they are, their ephemerality and inconsequentiality notwithstanding. Thus Donoghue writes that postmodernism

> has given up the adversary stance. It doesn't say, 'When in Rome, do as the Greeks,' but 'Do as the Romans, but with more flair and style.' Postmodernism has made peace with modernism's enemies. What are we supposed to find in Robert Venturi's architectural manifesto 'Learning From Las Vegas' is that anything goes with anything, and besides, a clash is just as good as its resolution ... Modernism's asserted distinction between high culture and popular culture is regarded as untenable, or in any case a lost cause not worth fighting for. Postmodernism recognizes that ideology has now secreted itself among the images we consume, and that it is no longer worth the effort to hold ideas separate from the daily practice of life to which they supposedly refer. The consumption of objects is already an ideology, and a successful one. ('The Promiscuous Cool of Postmodernism,' 37)

Temperamentally, Donoghue is comfortable neither with the consumerist side of postmodernism nor with the instantaneousness character of its enthusiasms and commitments. The common reader's scepticism towards enthusiasms (religious or secular), along with the style's commitment to moderation, thus serves Donoghue well. Yet what is it about the style that seems to warrant the conclusion? Once again, Hartman helps us by noting not only the style's debt to a confluence of styles already manifest in English literature, but also its relation to the open-ended nature of conversation. The style appeals 'to the symbiosis, rather than clash, of learned and vernacular traditions, a symbiosis that had previously characterized English poetry, even if the results were as different as Spenser and Shakespeare. The mingled style develops into the ideal of unaffected conversation, in which something is held in reserve and solicits reader or listener. It intends to provoke a reply rather than to dazzle, and it subordinates ingeniousness to the *ingenium* of natural wit' (65). When put this way, it seems odd that Hartman should divorce himself from the tradition of the common reader or, as he likes to call it, the 'friendship style.' Its attractions seem so manifest. Yet if Hartman thinks the style akin to a lost cause, Donoghue does not. He relishes the style, especially as it allies itself to the sonorities of the human voice. Initially a student of music, Donoghue has always been attentive to the way that body, voice, and breath work together to certify an individual's presence, to place speakers in relation to other speakers. Ideally, Donoghue thinks of this relation as one not only of conversation – speakers soliciting one another in a back-and-forth fashion – but also of communion: 'the crucial quality of voice is that it does not leave the speaker's body: hence, as Derrida has acknowledged, voice as pure expression is the only paradigm of a natural language. Breath, the rhythm of taking and expelling breath, represents the only understanding of presence, which persists not by staying in one unchanging form but by committing itself to a moving form as vulnerable as the heartbeat. Our bodily presence in the world is equally vulnerable. The aura which suffuses the idea of dialogue, conversation, communication, and communion arises from the sense of vulnerability in common. Communion is an attempt not to transcend the conditions in which we live upon our breathing, moment by moment, but to assent to them completely' (FA, 98).

The desire for communion is, perhaps, the governing force behind Donoghue's work. By communion, he means the reaching out not only to other people but also to the world's body – the plenitude of facts that make up our universe. The good critic will not be too shy to initiate the process, but it is understood that the process will only count for something if it entails, in Blackmur's phrase, a 'wooing both ways' (FA, 59). Reciprocity is at the heart of things, and Donoghue would frown upon any concept of communion, not to speak of the imagination, that did not involve a quality of back-and-forthness. He believes the world gives back sustenance to all those who wrestle with its objects, and from this conviction he develops a theory of the imagination (to be discussed in the next section). He also believes the critic's audience is crucial; and that mindful of it, critics do well to introduce an element of conversation into their prose. The critic must be aware that issues are generally resolvable in more than one way, and thus avoid moving too aggressively towards closure. In fact, by its nature, the conversational style is suspicious of closures, tending to judge them as premature. Truth is not discounted as an end, but it is imagined as residing on the horizon of our discussions, offering them direction and impetus but seldom unequivocal benediction. Thus the critic does well not to frame matters too definitively, for such will seldom resolve the discussion, though it might well end it by alienating one's interlocutors: 'One of the conventions of conversation is that neither party tries to make his statements definitive: a definitive statement would transcend the particular desires of conversation. The desires are not appeased: they are frustrated, humiliated, replaced by a totally different decorum, that of truth or adequacy. Completeness is not a property of conversation, except in principle as the cooperation of the two speakers. So it is considered vulgar for anyone in conversation to claim the last word' (FA, 44).

What the critic and communicant share is not truth but the desire for truth, the desire to hear someone else say, 'yes, I too think that a question worth asking and pursuing.' The question might be as concrete as relating to an author's poetics or as expansive as Plato's 'how should one live?' 'What makes a conversation memorable,' then, 'is the desire of each person to share experience with the other, giving and receiving. All that can be shared strictly speaking, is the desire: it is impossible to reach the experience. But the desire is enough to cause the reverberation to take place which we value in conversation' (43). This assumes that we are alike enough in our needs and desires to effect the exchange. Much recent criticism starts from the assumption that our differences are more worthy of attention than our sympathies, but Donoghue's own criticism does not. The most that one can perhaps say respecting the alternatives is that the jury is still out. This might simply be a way of saying that the matter comes down to one of choice. Do we want to believe that conversation is impossible except among those who already share our assumptions? Or do we want to hold out for the possibility that our shared humanity outweighs differences and makes conversation not only possible but imperative? It is as much a philosophical, as it is a literary, question; and it is not surprising – to pursue a brief excursus – to find such distinguished contemporary philosophers as Alasdair MacIntyre and Charles Taylor assuming opposing positions. MacIntyre, most notably in *After Virtue*, has well argued the first case, saying that '[t]here seems to be no rational way of securing moral agreement in our culture' (2), so disparate are the assumptions of the various discourse communities. Charles Taylor, most notably in *Sources of the Self*, has well argued the second case, saying that 'our normal understanding of self-realization presupposes that some things are important beyond the self, that there are some goods or purposes the furthering of which has significance for us and which hence can provide the significance a fulfilling life needs. A total and fully consistent subjectivism would tend towards emptiness: nothing would count as a fulfillment in a world in which literally nothing was important but self-fulfillment' (507).

The disagreement between MacIntyre and Taylor is, I suspect, as much one of tone as of substance. MacIntyre would agree with Taylor that there can be no important living if the subject and its community are taken as the final determinant of value. Yet while he believes this, MacIntyre sees the world turning away from this same understanding: 'We possess ... simulacra of morality, we continue to use many of the key expressions. But we have – very largely, if not entirely – lost our comprehension, both theoretical and practical, of morality' (*After Virtue*, 2). Taylor also acknowledges the conflictual character of recent discourses – 'Indeed, it is too simple to speak of a tension. We are in conflict, even confusion, about what it means to affirm ordinary life' (*Sources of the Self*, 23–4) – but rejects MacIntyre's pessimism, pressing forward the point that only through conversation with other selves do we work out our sense of our horizons and what it is that they demand of us. 'We first learn our languages of moral and spiritual discernment,' he says, 'by being brought into an ongoing conversation by those who bring us up' (35). It is specifically in the back-and-forthness of our conversations that we create objects – including a common telos – for one another: 'Here a crucial feature of conversation is relevant, that in talking about something you and I make it an object for us together, that is, not just an object for me which happens also to be one for you, even if we add that I know that it's an object for you, and you know, etc. The object is for us in a strong sense,' in the sense of '"public" or "common space"' (ibid.). MacIntyre, Taylor suggests, should not possess his own strong sense of telos if there were not others who helped sustain this conviction. It would not be impossible, but it would be unlikely. We need others to validate our sense of the good as much as we need them to validate our sense of, say, the meaning of left and right, or up and down. Thus Taylor argues, 'I can only learn what anger, love, anxiety, the aspiration to wholeness, etc., are through my and others' experience of these being objects for *us*, in some common space. This is the truth behind Wittgenstein's dictum that agreement in meanings involves agreement in judgements' (ibid.).

Donoghue's own position is closer to Taylor's, even as he has, on occasion, praised aspects of MacIntyre's work; and even as he has also expressed the worry that our readiness to investigate our differences might lead us to a point wherein we should have nothing to say to one another. Or if we, as members of the same constituency, did have something to say, it would, in all likelihood, appear redundant. While his worry this way can appear alarmist, he is perfectly aware of the problems with MacIntyre's position. Thus Donoghue argues that if we, like MacIntyre, accept the premise that conversations can seldom, if ever, cross borders, we give muscle to the condition that we say we abhor. It constitutes something like a bad faith argument. It makes more sense to side with our hopes, here allied with the imagination, than with our fears. Thus Donoghue, in rejection of MacIntyre's larger contention that the Western community is so divided within that intercommunication has become impossible, writes: 'If MacIntyre means what he says, he would have us believe that the privilege conventionally given to the imagination is specious. We normally say that the imagination is in the mind operating under conditions of freedom, freedom not absolute but sufficient for most human purposes. If I can imagine being different from myself, or from my sense of myself, I can enter with sympathy (or envy, of course) into the life of another person. That makes sympathy possible; if sympathy, then communication; if communication, then participation in a community. MacIntyre appears to say that this sequence is impossible because the first act in it, the imagining of difference, is impossible' ('What's Really Wrong,' 98).

Donoghue's whole sense of what he does as a critic revolves around the terms of conversation and imagination. The two are closely related. Together they speak not only of the possibility but also of the need for the individual – be one a critic, an artist, or simply a citizen – to engage in a reciprocating relation with the world and its inhabitants. This sense that our obligations are far-reaching helps to explain Donoghue's own commitment to the general reader. As he notes in the 'Introduction' to *Reading America* (1987), many of his writings have been intended for an audience whose interests were not those of the specialist: 'In several cases I was writing for a magazine – *The New York Times Book Review, The Times Literary Supplement, The New Statesman* – whose readers were, I trusted, interested in American literature but not at the cost of their other interests' (xi). His reasons here have to do with his own sense of himself as a generalist – 'I think of myself as a generalist, rather than a specialist' (PGT, 91) – as well as a desire to avoid pedantry, the academic's curse. While he also writes for audiences with more avowed professional interests, he continues to believe that 'the variety of such readerships' helps to protect him 'from the danger of being pedantic' (RA, xi). Beyond these considerations, it happens that the criticism that has most moved him – e.g., that of Blackmur, Burke, Eliot, James, Ransom, Trilling – has always addressed interests that were as much cultural as literary, or at least not easily confined within the sphere of a single discipline. He praises Matthew Arnold, for instance, for 'making available, more completely than anyone else, the role of the "general critic," the man who directs the force of his intelligence upon the common life and its manifestations. The general critic thinks his own business hardly worth minding except so far as it coincides with everyone's business. If he is a literary critic, it is because the formal complexity of literature protects him from the naïveté of thinking that he has understood the common life when he has merely registered its most vociferous forms' (ETE, 206). He also praises Arnold for promoting a more general literary criticism: 'It is chiefly because of Arnold that literary criticism has not become, to its impoverishment, entirely literary; that a general criticism is still practised by critics who nevertheless have a particular commitment to literature' (207). Books such as Leavis's *Education and the University*, Trilling's *The Liberal Imagination*, and Kenneth Burke's *Attitudes towards History* have been, he says, the happy consequence.

Much of Donoghue's own work functions as 'general criticism,' and apart from the review essays quite a number first took shape as public lectures, either in the setting of the university or as part of cultural programs such as those sponsored by the BBC. These include *Jonathan Swift*, the follow-up of lectures delivered at Cambridge University in the academic year 1965–6; *Thieves of Fire*, the text of the T.S. Eliot Memorial Lecture in 1972; *The Sovereign Ghost*, an outgrowth of the Ewing Lectures in 1971 and the W.P. Ker Memorial Lecture in 1974; *The Arts without Mystery*, the expansion of the Reith Lectures in 1982; *Ferocious Alphabets*, parts of which were first prepared for the BBC radio program 'Words'; *Being Modern Together*, the text of his Richard Ellmann Lectures in Modern Literature, offered in 1990; and *The Pure Good of Theory*, the text of the Bucknell Lectures in Literary Theory, first published in 1992. The format of the public lecture clearly makes different demands upon the critic than that of the scholarly book. Most notably, the audience is different: more varied in its interests and also more demanding about having its attention held or – as some might say – entertained. Not that audiences attending the Eliot or the Ellmann lectures do not come for reasons of edification; they do. Still, an audience of disparate intellectual interests makes extraordinary demands upon a lecturer to keep things interesting and moving along. It asks to be entreated as much by style as by substance. Donoghue is sensitive to these demands and has been responsive to them. He could not have garnered as many invitations as he has were he not up to the task.

Occasionally – as in the openings to *Ferocious Alphabets* (1981) and *The Arts without Mystery* (1983) – he has addressed the issue of audience directly, and what we find here is a critic keenly sensitive to the way an audience helps to determine what is said and how it is said. About the Reith Lectures for instance, a series of talks broadcast on BBC Radio 3 and 4, Donoghue speaks of the difficulty of having not one but two distinct audiences, for Radio 3 listeners are identified by their interests in classical music and matters more bookish, whereas Radio 4 listeners are identified by a more general interest in public events. At times, naturally, the Radio 3 and 4 listeners might have been one and the same, for the broadcasts went out on separate days of the week. In any event, Donoghue found the matter of audience a perplexing problem, leading him to rewrite the lectures more than he ordinarily might: 'Several drafts were required: it was hard to get the tone right, I was alluding to too many works of art which the audience would not necessarily have read, heard, or seen ... If I tried to make the necessary distinctions, would I still have an audience when I had made them?' (AWM, 8).

In his lectures for the BBC program 'Words,' the starting point for *Ferocious Alphabets*, Donoghue also had difficulty in finding the right tone. The difficulty followed from the fact that he wanted to talk about questions of language – questions to which his English audience might assume it had a certain proprietary relation – and the fact that he wished to challenge what he subsequently described as a 'gunboat linguistics still practiced by Dame Helen, Empson, Quirk, and other English scholars' (FA, 30). The matter of tone in this instance was made particularly fretful by the consciousness that he spoke as an outsider, an Irishman not above feeling 'resentment against the English, given a little provocation, and especially when the provocation touches upon unspoken matters of social class' (ibid.). It is a resentment that most Americans understand, and when Donoghue complains that the said English scholars 'seem to claim, by their style rather than overtly, that they represent what Arnold called "the tone of the center," which casts other people as provincial' (FA, 31), one senses that the audience for this remark is largely an American one; and one also begins to question further, to retreat from, Hartman's identification of Donoghue's prose with an Oxbridge style, a linkage that brushes over differences for the sake of the thesis.

Another thing to note in *Ferocious Alphabets*'s opening pages is Donoghue's expression of anxiety about bringing the listener into the discussion as quickly as possible. In his meta-commentary on the first BBC talk, he says: 'Note how anxious I was to seize the listener's attention with a grand piece of poetry. Frost seemed the right poet, since his poems are stirring precisely because of the range of experience imputed to his speakers. Note, too, how anxious I was to get the word *you* said immediately, to conjure a listener into existence and force him to stay with me: it would be bad manners to leave, once addressed so cordially. Linguists since Jesperson have called such words shifters, words explicated only by their contexts: such words as *I, you, here, tomorrow*. In my talk I used the shifter at once to establish a context: in other words, to gain and hold an audience' (FA, 22–3). The question of audience here merges with that of style; and it interesting to see how much attention Donoghue bestows upon the problem of capturing and holding an audience's attention. But this really is no surprise. Donoghue is a consummate stylist, and he would be less so if he did not think of what it would mean to employ lines from one poet, in this instance Robert Frost, rather than another, particularly when the objective is to introduce a subject as well as to retain an audience. Even the fact that Donoghue confesses his anxiety and allows us to see the behind-the-scenes thought processes is a stylistic move, designed to make the reader (the lecture audience now a memory) feel privy to the author's confidences. There has always been an especially intimate quality to Donoghue's prose. The reader is made to feel part of the discussion even though the author does all the real work. Partly this has to do with Donoghue's willingness, from time to time, to share what seem (and doubtless are) private opinions. There are, for instance, sprinkled throughout his work confessions of anxiety about the lectures; confessions of his youth in the memoir *Warrenpoint* (1990), and confessions (albeit few) regarding his religious faith. There are also numerous confessions of personal esteem, as when he remarks, 'I would enjoy a bit of wrestling with Kermode's prose at any time. He is one of the few critics who please while instructing' (ETE, 273). Or when, in a strange blend of criticism and praise, he says of Harold Bloom: 'Bloom rarely convinces me of anything, except that in a differently constituted world the beauty of his sentences or of the lives he quotes would make them true' ('The Sad Captain of Criticism,' 23–4).

The intimacy of Donoghue's style also follows from smaller things, such as the choice of personal pronouns. He likes to use 'I,' 'we,' and 'you,' but as he makes clear in *Ferocious Alphabets*, he can barely tolerate the use of 'one,' associating it, as he does, with English RP: 'Think of the several differences between saying "I," "we," and "one." Saying "I" implies a "you" addressed. Saying "we" adverts to a "they" as our shared horizon; it allows also for differences of sentiment between each of us who make up the "we." But saying "one" dissolves these differences, assumes a common purpose based on moral and aesthetic criteria, good taste, and so on. The stance of saying "one" is editorial; it eliminates the "they" of other people and rival judgments' (28).

In some ways, the less formal 'I' and 'you,' in the Irish and American context, accomplish what their counterparts do in the English context. Certainly in the United States, the use of 'we' and 'one' tends to go against the grain of our democratic sensibilities, where it is deemed almost improper to speak (even as I do so here) for anyone other than oneself. Morris Dickstein notes, for example, that 'Lionel Trilling was sometimes criticized for his use of the first-person plural' (*Double Agent*, 63). Dickstein, like Donoghue, reveres Trilling, so he is quick to defend him on this point, saying that 'at its frequent best his "we" spoke not for an in-group of the critic and his friends but for an acute sensibility attuned to the rhythms of the Zeitgeist and the nuances of the social mood' (ibid.). Donoghue also relishes the use of 'we' (as in *We Irish*),[4] believing, as noted, that the 'we' implies a 'they,' and helps clarify which side one stands on. I suspect many an American academic feels about his employment of 'we' the way he feels about the English academic's employment of 'one.' It is slightly annoying, particularly when it no longer appears evident that 'we' can divide the world into a society and its opposing selves. The world is more complicated than this, and there are too many diverse communities seeking to be heard for 'us' to employ too repeatedly the first-person plural. At least things stand this way in the United States. Elsewhere, as in Ireland, things, no doubt, stand differently. Donoghue's affection for 'we' is reflective of this difference. Still, even when allowing for this, my guess is that it remains difficult for the American academic not to possess reservations about sentences such as the following, the subject of which are those critics who first dismissed the arrival of artistic genius: 'We say that such critics are dogmatic, but we are irritated not by the dogma but by the will exercised in the pronouncement. Our standard reaction is who does he think he is?' (AWM, 56).[5] Donoghue's phrasing here raises concern about whether he himself is not too dogmatic. And then the American academic is also likely to ask, why must the critic or the artist always be a 'he'? Might not Donoghue evince greater sensitivity than the offer, in *The Arts without Mystery*, that 'the reader is invited to pronounce "him" and "his" as "her" if he or she wishes to do so' (13).

However, I began by saying that Donoghue's strategy with regard to personal pronouns made his style seem not less but more intimate, and, on the whole, I believe this. Thus, while his preference for 'we' might, from time to time, annoy the American reader, there remains the sense that it is capable of working as something that binds the author with his readers, the majority of whom are likely to share his opinions on literature and criticism. Then, more effectively than the employment of 'we,' there is Donoghue's equally frequent use of 'you,' which in its informality tends to assuage the American (if not the British) reader, for the reason of its inherent democratic colour. In saying all this, I am aware that I am making an issue of what (i.e., nationality) some might prefer not to think of as an issue at all. But it is an issue, especially given the fact that Donoghue is an Irishman who has divided his attention among the literatures of England, Ireland, and the United States (hence the three collected volumes of essays: *We Irish* [1986]; *Reading America* [1987] and *England, Their England* [1988]) and who has, for a generation, held a prominent position (the Henry James Chair at New York University) in the American academy. Meanwhile, I myself cannot help responding to his work as an American academic, even as I am aware that his British and Irish readers may find some things otherwise.

In fact, part of Donoghue's appeal for the American reader has much to do with his affection for our literature and criticism. Used to having British and European critics disparage things American, it is refreshing to be told by this critic that when his university classmates 'were reading F.R. Leavis and *Scrutiny*,' he 'was reading John Crowe Ransom, Cleanth Brooks, Kenneth Burke, R.P. Blackmur, Lionel Trilling, and Robert Penn Warren' (CC, 3). At a time when American critics repeatedly look to Europe for their inspiration, it remains refreshing to find Donoghue reminding us of what a fine homegrown critical tradition we have in the likes of Emerson, Thoreau, James, Eliot, Burke, Blackmur, Trilling, and others. Meanwhile, the same appreciation that Donoghue extends to our criticism, he also extends to our literature, particularly to the poetry of William Carlos Williams, Marianne Moore, T.S. Eliot, Wallace Stevens, James Merrill, and John Ashbery; the fiction of Herman Melville and Henry James; and the prose of Henry Adams. Altogether, it is a quite flattering picture of our literature and, by extension, our culture that Donoghue offers, even as he professes that there are times when he is not sure that he knows us at all – that is until he goes back and dips into, say, the poetry of Stevens and the connections are once again established: 'My relation to American literature, like my presence in the United States, is that of a "resident alien": I feel I hold a Green Card in both capacities. The literature is, I assume, an epitome of the society that has provoked it, and may be read on that understanding. I read it by spelling it, a little at a time. Sometimes – as on April 15, 1986 – the dreadful day of President Reagan's bombing attack on Benghazi and Tripoli – I'm sure I don't understand anything of America, and can only stare at it in dismay. But when I read Wallace Stevens's "The Course of a Particular," I feel not entirely blank about it' (RA, xi).

I mention, in a discussion of style, Donoghue's strong affection for American literature because it is part of the equation to which we as readers do, or do not, respond. It is not only a matter of substance, it is also a matter of style, demonstrating an awareness of audience that, in its turn, finds itself reflected in the critic's rhetorical gestures. At the same time, I do not mean to suggest that Donoghue's sensitivity to audience causes him to alter radically what he has to say. I do not think this the case. Audiences are disparate, but also much alike; and Donoghue's work has always been biased towards those interpretations that make sense whether one lives in Dublin, London, or New York. For him, the critic's first responsibility is towards the material. One's audience does not make a difference if the subject is approached dishonestly or is inherently uninteresting. This sense of things is for Donoghue something like a matter of principle. As he commented in his BBC 'Words' presentation: 'I suppose the moral of this talk is that if you don't know to whom you are talking or that you're talking to anyone, you try to make what you say intrinsically interesting. You may fail with the audience, but at least you have kept faith with the matter. Wallace Stevens, seeing members of his audience leave the room, retained at least the satisfaction of feeling that his relation to his theme was cordial' (FA, 24).

Yet, this said, Donoghue's prose seems particularly responsive to its readers. There is a sense that he invites response, and though his views have been fairly consistent over the years, it remains possible to find him modifying them in the light of public debate and further reading. Statements such as, 'But I have only recently come to understand the scope of the claim he [Bloom] is making for Romanticism,' are not uncommon ('The Sad Captain of Criticism,' 22). Modifications of judgment also occur. Donoghue's serial judgments of not only Bloom's work but also that of other notables such as Mikhail Bahktin, Roland Barthes, R.P. Blackmur, Kenneth Burke, Paul de Man, Jacques Derrida, J. Hillis Miller, Alasdair MacIntyre, and others are witness to his readiness to weigh contrary considerations and to rethink prior opinions. One who has read in 'A Criticism of One's Own' (1986) his harsh judgments regarding the editorial principles informing the *Norton Anthology of Literature by Women* may at first be surprised to hear him, in 'The Use and Abuse of Theory' (1992), dissociate himself from those colleagues who appear 'dismayed to find that the libraries have to find space not only for the *Norton Anthology of Literature by Women*, various collections of Black Writing, and the *Faber Book of Gay Short Stories*' (xxx). But it is not so unusual for him to speak well of what he has formerly spoken critically of. Perhaps the most notable instance here is the growing accommodation of those critics – e.g., Derrida, de Man, Miller, and Hartman – influenced by deconstruction. As he, in a 1992 interview, told Pauline Fletcher and Harold Schweizer: 'My relation to deconstruction for a time was indeed hostile, but has in fact become much less so. What I've written about Derrida, Paul de Man, and others in the last few years is much more appreciative than earlier stuff I published' (PGT, 92). And so, more recently, we find generous praise from Donoghue gracing the book jacket of Hartman's *The Fateful Question of Culture* (1997): 'Geoffrey Hartman is the only scholar-critic who could have written this book. Not because he has read everything but because he is gifted with unique largeness and generosity of mind. Other scholars have written about "literature after Auschwitz," but none has brought to this dire subject Hartman's combination of knowledge, thoughtfulness, scope, and scruple. The book is, in effect, his autobiography. It is immensely moving, a beautiful testament.'

The point to be stressed is Donoghue's esteem for conversation as a model for what the critic does. It is something different from that of communication, wherein the aim is for a message to pass from person A to person B. This helps to explain Donoghue's harsh judgment of I.A. Richards's work, for it was Richards's contention that even poetry itself basically boils down to a matter of communication. '[I]t is as a communicator,' Richards wrote in *Principles of Literary Criticism*, 'that it is most profitable to consider the artist' (26). But conversation elicits a response and does not predicate itself on an immediate or early resolution of the matter. Hence, Donoghue, distinguishing himself from Richards, writes: 'the best form of verbal communication is conversation and that conversation is radically different from communication ...; so different that I think of it as communion rather than communication. The crucial difference is that in conversation there is no unit; and even if there were, it would not be a message or signal to be delivered' (FA, 43). Here, Donoghue's discussion relates crucially to the point about style, for as he understands the matter, one way of talking about style is in terms of 'compensation.' That is, if we grant that communion, as goal, surpasses conversation, then writing is one of the most difficult things we do because 'it cannot be present in the sense in which the voice is present to itself within the body' (FA, 46). Speaking to others, we are required to listen as well to modify our gestures, both verbal and physical, in the light of the conversation's dynamics. But when we write, we do not have before us that audience (be it one person or many), the reactions of whom give us some guide respecting the effectiveness of our discourse. The consequence, says Donoghue, is that the writer needs to compensate for that loss. The way in which he or she does so manifests itself as a style: 'If communion is the true name of a writer's desire, we may expect him to make up for the lack of it. This would be an extreme version of the common case; since culture is in any event a compensation for the frustrations attendant upon biological life. In the present context the form of compensation may be called style. Styles of compensation are ways in which a writer proceeds with far more freedom than he can count on in daily social life' (ibid.).

In *Ferocious Alphabets*, Donoghue demonstrates his own acute sensitivity to the way in which notable critics have forged individual styles. In the middle section, prior to the discussion of epireading and graphireading, Donoghue pithily comments on the styles of several critics whom he judges as engaged by the problem of style as a compensation for an absent audience. He observes, for instance, how 'Ransom's prose is hardly even predicated upon a reader's existence' (FA, 54), evidenced by the critic's marshalling his sentences into something akin to an autonomous image or picture: 'The sentences are ordered to make a little picture, not a drama but a moral frame of reference occupied by two figures of different bearing. The interest of the picture is intrinsic, like the texture of the prose. The words on the page testify to a human speaker, but to one suspicious of urgency, especially the urgency by which a writer demands that a reader come hither and pay attention' (ibid.). Similarly, Donoghue observes, with respect to Blackmur, the seriousness of his theme and his approach to it, as well as the fact that Blackmur appears to resent 'the absence of conversation, debate, [and] argument,' elements which the writer needs to imagine almost as much as he or she needs to imagine a reader at all. The consequence is that we find, in Blackmur, a writer almost wrestling with himself, as he takes on the responsibility of acting for two, weighing one argument against another, testing them out, and seeing which is better: 'Blackmur makes space in which the possibilities are tempted to occur. In many paragraphs of an essay by Blackmur the argument is as clear and fresh as the air at Brighton, but to get not only the argument but its tone you have to trust his way with words, believing that he is serious and not merely eloquent. In extreme moments, his style doesn't seem to need the reader it presumes it lacks, the style appeases the desire as it runs ahead; it is unofficial, like a cadenza. There is always in his style a 'wooing both ways' between the argument and word; the style solicits the theme and his gypsy phrases make up in warmth for the cold and absence in their circumstances' (FA, 59).

To offer one more example, there is William Empson, whom Donoghue believes writes out of the conviction 'that the main thing common to people is that they are all lonely' (ibid., 74). Accordingly, for Empson, literature presents the attempt to overcome in some form that loneliness, to make a connection where the possibility of connection is thought unlikely. Still, Empson forges ahead, and the most notable feature of his work, believes Donoghue, is its talk-like quality, the product of a man, aware of his isolation, but trying to conjure up an interlocutor possessed of talents not unlike his own. In the later books, says Donoghue, Empson employs this conversational style almost 'outrageously, pretending that the author is having a quiet chat with a few friends, decent English agnostics free of piety, except piety in favor of England and agnosticism. His rhetoric says that if people are left to their own devices they will be decent and all they need is encouragement to keep going. The poems and the critical books alike imply that common sense is more intimate with sympathy than with knowledge and therefore we don't feel obliged to stop talking to one another when knowledge collides with ignorance, because sympathy keeps the thing going well enough' (FA, 75–6). It is something like this later style of Empson's, wherein it is understood that we are all good Englishmen and that common sense is the supreme virtue, that, as I noted earlier, Geoffrey Hartman equates with the 'friendship style.' As he sees the matter, the style has an artificial straightforwardness about it and is too concerned with good manners to be especially penetrative. Certainly, the style, like any other, is capable of having its more crucial elements – in this instance, lucidity and a receptivity to audience – transmogrified into something at odds with the original. This is Donoghue's own argument with respect to Empson's later style, which he sees as too characteristic of an eighteenth-century Tory. Meanwhile, it strikes me as unfair for Hartman, suspicious of the style to begin with, to jump to the conclusion that Donoghue's prose constitutes little more than a respect for good form: 'With a book like Denis Donoghue's *Ferocious Alphabets* we are, in terms of argument, not far from Maugham's summing up of the tradition he embodies. "To like good prose is an affair of good manners. It is, unlike verse, a civil art"' (64). For one, as noted, we can easily put too much stock in this putative gentility. Donoghue is a critic sensitive to, and respectful of, audience, but he hardly seems the embodiment of a genteel tradition, especially if what is meant by this is a critical mannerism. His prose has too much bite to be dismissed this way, and it is easy to suspect that it is the very quality of this bite in *Ferocious Alphabets* that results in the Hartman accusation. For another, Donoghue's prose is hardly straightforward, if what is meant by this is a criticism that is definite and delimiting. Rather, it makes more sense to identify Donoghue, as Morris Dickstein does, with a tradition of criticism that makes the breadth and the quality of a critic's thought its supreme test. Here, '[t]he test of a critic comes not in his ideas about art, and certainly not in his ideas about criticism, but in the depth and intimacy of his encounter with the work itself – not the work in isolation, but the work in its abundance or reference, richness of texture, complexity of thought and feeling' (*Double Agent*, 39).

Donoghue has, more than once, referred to Eliot's statement that in criticism 'the only method is to be very intelligent,' and while this criterion is notably generic, it is worth mentioning in the present context. There are two reasons for this. One, Donoghue himself holds it to be, more or less, true. As a literary critic, he professes to be less committed to any one thesis or theory than to the most full-fledged response to the work. If he subscribes to a doctrine, it is, he says, Burke's doctrine which tells the critic to 'use all there is to use' ('What Makes Life Worth Writing?,' 12). And then, two, for the reason that his work gives illustration of a mind that can only be described as very intelligent, never bereft of a further analogy or allusion to help clarify the subject at hand. One thing leads to another and the reader, invited along, is never quite sure where the critic's peregrinations will end up. In fact, we might apply Donoghue's description of plural form, offered in his book on Swift, as somewhat analogous to the way his own prose works. I say 'somewhat' for the description (of plural form) is meant to serve as a way into Swift's antic style. Still, a style wherein '[l]inear movement of thought ... seem[s] too easy, a distortion in the cause of simplicity' (JS, 18), might already be said to have a kinship with Donoghue's own. So do some of the style's other attributes, including its refusal to cater to the single-minded reader. Or as Donoghue, describing the style, writes: 'Like paradox, plural form is never single-minded: it takes wry pleasure in defeating single-minded readers, since defeat is its own error. The words of the page lead the reader in a dozen directions, lest he settle comfortably for one. So the movement from the first word to last is likely to be devious, elliptical, walking with a limp in circles drawn awry' (17–18).

In this same book on Swift, there is a passage that might serve as a demonstration of how plural Donoghue's prose can be. It is little more than a quarter of a paragraph, yet notice how Donoghue, in the discussion of a single text, *The Tale of the Tub*, seems almost effortlessly to connect this text to quite a number of other texts and events:

> In fact the [*Moriae*] *Encomium* [by Erasmus] is a Hall of Mirrors, often distorted mirrors which, receiving distortions, send further distortions on their distorted way. The final effect of the book, as of Swift's *Tale*, is to impede the arrogance of judgment: this is how Pride is tamed ... Again it is entirely proper, within the tradition of plural form which I would describe, that the author of the *Anatomy of Melancholy* is given as 'Democritus Junior' and that when we hunt him through byways and digressions we recall with increasing frustration his first warning, 'I would not willingly be known.' In *The Rehearsal Transpros'd* Marvell defends the King's Declaration of Indulgence to Non-Conformists, so he finds it convenient to write, in some parts, as if he were a court wit and in other parts, as if he were a sober spokesman for the Non-Conformists themselves. At one point he asks pardon for this breach of formal decorum, but clearly the breach was already commonplace. Horace had not prevented sixteenth- and seventeenth-century writers from shifting ground, within the work, as often as they wished. Indeed it might be argued that it was necessary to play fast and loose with *decorum personae* if the full possibilities of print culture were to be fulfilled. (13–14)

In a paragraph that begins with concrete allusions to Plato, Coleridge, *Gulliver's Travels* and Thomas More's *Utopia*, Donoghue follows with further concrete allusions to Erasmus, Burton, Marvell, Horace, Restoration politics, and McLuhan's theory of print culture. It is not Donoghue's purpose to show off his erudition, and his allusions never appear

gratuitous. Rather, his references reflect, in the best liberal arts tradition, that any single event has many valences; and that the critic, when
adept, will be able to contextualize the material in the light of numerous interests. In the present instance, Donoghue discusses *A Tale of the
Tub* not only in the context of a literary style (i.e., plural form) but also
in the context of the historical, philosophical, political, religious, and
technological interests that intersect at the point of the text. Donoghue
is not a New Critic, if by this one means someone exclusively attentive to
a literary tradition, and to the close, compartmentalized readings of its
texts. By this definition, Cleanth Brooks, John Ransom, and Robert
Penn Warren were probably not New Critics either, the point being that
New Criticism was never as reductive as recent descriptions would suggest. Yet it is not my ambition to identify Donoghue with a school, no
matter how flatteringly we might define it. Rather, I would take him at
his word and see him as a critic who, while wishing to make the study of
literature (i.e., American, English, and Irish) his first interest, also
wishes to 'use all there is to use.' His work is abundant to be sure, but
this practice, while it may run parallel to recent academic interests, is
reflective only of the sense that good criticism and scholarship have
always been, by their natures, interdisciplinary. In any event, his criticism has been characterized by an extraordinary learning, and if the
Eliot standard should be taken as the rule, few should fare as well as
Donoghue.

And yet if Donoghue's learning strengthens his appeal to the common reader and makes him a more effective generalist, there are in this
role dangers, of which he is aware. Specifically, he is afraid of slipping
into a situation where one begins to *use* literature for other purposes,
where it becomes not something worthy of attention in itself but a form
of illustration for other concerns. As he says in an interview, 'there's a
great temptation in being a generalist; one gets into the habit of merely
using literature as exemplification, and I think Arnold did that. When
he quotes a few lines from Chaucer or Dante, it's always with an exemplifying motive. I don't want to talk about literature as chiefly exemplifying something that's going on in society. I want to give literature more
space to move in, and not to be pressing upon it to disclose its character' (PGT, 91). Mostly, Donoghue has been successful. He may not
possess the scholarly temper of a Kermode (Donoghue: 'Kermode has
always been a scholar in his own right ... His spiritual home is the Warburg Institute, where the primacy of scholarship is taken for granted'
['Critics at the Top,' 54]). Still, his scholarship has always been impres-

sive. For him, it has been especially important that scholars get their facts right. It is not uncommon, even in a review essay, for Donoghue to take scholars to task for shoddy scholarship. For example, in 'Joyce's Many Lives,' a review of recent Joyce scholarship that appeared in the *New York Review*, Donoghue pointedly rebukes several scholars for their failure to distinguish between the author's fiction and life. Peter Costello and Brenda Maddox are depicted as irresponsible for the liberty they take with Joyce's 'made me a man' letter of 7 August 1909 to Nora Barnacle. The first, says Donoghue, reads 'Molly Bloom's account of an episode with Lt. Harvey Mulvey in Gibraltar' back into the few details surrounding Joyce and Nora's first date; and the second, again to lascivious effect, offers a seemingly eyewitness account of the couple's first sexual relation and, at the same time, 'claims to disclose "their own private feelings that first night at Ringsend"' (30). A more eminent critic, Paul de Man, is also criticized for misquoting, in a discussion of Yeats's 'Among School Children,' the poem's memorable last line as 'How can we tell the dancer from the dance?' ('The Limits of Language, 43). True, Donoghue has often shown an animus towards de Man, and this may largely explain the reprimand. But Donoghue's own explanation is credible: 'If I rebuke de Man for misquoting Yeats, it is not because I fear his influence. It is, rather, because I think a teacher should, when it is possible, get things right' (ibid.).[6]

For Donoghue, the matter has to do less with mistakes per se than the ethic they imply. That is, Donoghue has always treated the literary text as an exemplary form of otherness, demanding our acknowledgment and respect. In *The Ordinary Universe* (1968), he writes that '[t]he fact of "otherness" is a beautiful necessity that invites recognition; if the "I" turns back upon itself, it commits a breach of tact, falls from the condition of grace' (25–6). Like persons, literary texts demand recognition; and while Donoghue knows the difference between people and books, he is suspicious of those claiming that our obligations to the former can be made an excuse for our inattentiveness to the latter. Hence, he has been severe on those readers who appear to employ literature as if it were a means to some other end. Terry Eagleton, for instance, is criticized for being 'in literary theory in the sense in which we say of someone that he is in politics or in economics or in real estate.' That is, '[h]e is bent upon an ideological programme, and uses literature only as a means to a political end' ('The Use and Abuse of Theory,' xxxii). Fredric Jameson is likewise criticized: 'Jameson's reading of *Ulysses* ... is disabled by his insistence that literature will serve political cause'

('The Political Turn in Criticism,' 110). It is not that critics are not granted the right to prefer other things to literature. It is more a displeasure with those who profess an attentiveness to literature but then make it seem a secondary thing.

In the end, any discussion of style will, in relation to Donoghue's work, come back to the question of literature's otherness. There may be no inherent reason why we should attend to literature more than any other interest, except that literature is the receptacle of all those emotions and thoughts – and they are among the most important – which we find it often difficult to articulate to one another in the clear light of day. But once we make the commitment, Donoghue argues, we then find ourselves under several obligations. These include (but are not limited to) obligations to the literature and its readers. Also entailed is the subsequent obligation that we submit to a 'wooing both ways,' that we continually turn back to the literature, not to mine it for examples but in order to learn from it. Parallel to this is the obligation to be attentive to what others have to say about the literature. Again, the model is one of conversation, undertaken with the hope of communion. The literature is never separate from who we are, much as we ourselves are never separate from one another. If by saying this, we appear to endorse an interpretative model that values our common needs and desires over our differences, so be it. Or so I imagine Donoghue saying. It is why he prefers the role of the generalist. It gives him the opportunity to discover the similitudes that bind. True, he has written for publications as different as the *New York Review of Books*, the *Times Literary Supplement*, the *London Review of Books*, the *New York Times Book Review*, *The New Republic*, the *New Review*, *Encounter*, *Salmagundi*, *Sewanee Review*, *Magill*, *Hibernia*, *The Spectator*, *The Listener*, and the *Wilson Quarterly*. It is also true that the readers of these journals, as he notes, are 'more diverse than any description of them would suggest. The common reader, the educated public, the professional reader: these phrases imply a certain range of interests and sentiments, easy enough to assume in practice but difficult to specify' (WI, viii). Yet different as they are, Donoghue would like to imagine their differences as reconcilable. Thus, should he be asked to imagine an ideal reader, it would be 'one who moves with winning flexibility between these categories without committing himself to any of them' (ibid.). Again, it is the 'friendly style' regnant, and while some might think the style now obsolete, my own sense is that it still has its part to play and that Donoghue's public criticism makes this beautifully apparent.

The Imagination

In his 1971 book on Yeats, Donoghue wrote, 'The single article of faith that goes undisputed in the Babel of modern criticism is the primacy of the creative imagination' (*William Butler Yeats*, 132). The claim was not well timed. Post-structuralist criticism had just begun to make its influence felt, and it demonstrated a marked scepticism regarding this 'primacy of the creative imagination,' that which Kant spoke of as genius. In the *Critique of Judgement*, Kant had spoken of the imagination as something free, 'not taken as reproductive, as in its subjection to the laws of association, but as productive and exerting an activity of its own (as originator of arbitrary forms of possible intuitions)' (I, 86). While the imagination, in its apprehension of an object, might find its expression circumscribed by contingencies, in poetry the imagination would not be so dependent on circumstances outside of itself and would thereby be capable of 'enjoy[ing] free play' (I, 86). Like God, whom Kant speaks of as the 'supreme Artist' (II, 102), the poet might be understood as autonomous, capable of an originality discoverable not through exterior rules but by a turning inward to 'the innate mental aptitude (*ingenium*)' which constituted one's genius and '*through which* nature gives the rule to art' (I, 168). Yet there is a crucial difficulty, for in Kant's description, art is both what, in its freedom, distinguishes itself from nature at the same time that it is spoken of as the articulation of nature. Or as Derrida, in 'Economimesis,' his essay on the *Critique*, writes: 'What is art? Kant seems to begin by replying: art is not nature, thus subscribing to the inherited, ossified, simplified opposition between *tekné* and *physis*. On the side of nature is mechanical necessity; on the side of art, the play of freedom. In between them is a whole series of secondary determinations. But analogy annuls this opposition. It places under Nature's dictate what is most wildly free in the production of art. Genius is the locus of such a dictation – the means by which art receives its rules from nature. All propositions of an anti-mimetic cast, all condemnations leveled against imitation are undermined at this point. One must not imitate nature; but nature, assigning its rules to genius, folds itself, returns to itself, reflects itself through art' (4). In effect, Derrida argues that imagination is much more reproductive than Kant suggests. Its freedom is a contingent freedom, dependent on the very thing – nature – that it purports to elide. Imagination does not create something brand new, never having existed, but something that will be found to have been there already. In *The Archeology of the Frivolous*, Derrida writes: 'invention no more depends on imagination than imagination has the ability to create anything whatever. The fact is, production of the new – and imagination – are only productions: by analogical connection and repetition, they bring to light what, without being there, *will have been* there' (71).

The post-structuralist critique of the Romantic imagination and its genius made it difficult to use these terms with the same confidence as before. In his 1976 book *The Sovereign Ghost*, subtitled 'Studies in Imagination,' Donoghue acknowledged the change of climate. Responding to Wordsworth's claim that the imagination is 'the faculty which is perhaps the noblest of our nature,' Donoghue wrote: 'On the whole, this is no longer true, imagination is not one of our key terms. Very little energy is spent upon its use, or upon any other effort to distinguish among the faculties of our nature' (1). The tone is both chiding and mournful, for while Donoghue concedes that the imagination no longer counts as a privileged term, he thinks that something has been lost. The suggestion is that two things in particular have been lost: the concept itself and the *knowledge of* that loss. Those around him seem insensitive to the cost of their new concepts, a situation that provokes his ire, controlled though it be. It is a mood, or simply a tone of voice, familiar to his readers. It can be both attractive and disconcerting, depending on whether one thinks the occasion calls for rebuke. In any event, to return to the question of the imagination, in *The Sovereign Ghost*, Donoghue acknowledged that the terms of the discussion had changed – 'Only a wilful or nostalgic critic would now use Blake's term "genius" or "vision"' (2) – but still claimed that the discussion continued to be valuable.

The imagination and its relevance to the artist might be said to constitute the central theme of Donoghue's criticism. He has examined it explicitly – as in *The Ordinary Universe, Thieves of Fire*, and *The Sovereign Ghost* – and less explicitly in just about everything else that he has written. Even later, when the academy had generally tabled the discussion, Donoghue was not hesitant about trying to bring it back, as in *Ferocious Alphabets* (1981) when, critiquing the post-structuralist critics, he wrote: 'The conflict among the alphabets of criticism today turns upon the question of imagination. Graphireaders [i.e., post-structuralists] want to get along without acknowledging the creative imagination; because if they acknowledged it, they could not stop short of acknowledging a complex humanism of mind, consciousness, and genius. Is it still a question of Romanticism, then? Yes; but of Romanticism as a permanent category, not as something to be defined by renewing the old paper-war with Classicism' (210).

Donoghue was not necessarily alone in wishing to speak of Romanticism as something like a permanent category. Both de Man and Bloom might also be identified with the wish, if for different reasons. Yet the desire to keep open the discussion of the imagination (i.e., of Romanticism) neither meant that the imagination is an ahistorical concept nor that Donoghue's own understanding of it was not subject to change. In fact, if Donoghue's arguments on behalf of the imagination are to be taken seriously, it is important to have some sense of where they come in the larger discussion. Accordingly, I should like to do two things: 1) briefly to indicate Donoghue's understanding of the imagination when he first entered into the discussion; and 2) to examine, subsequent to that entry, Donoghue's own history in relation to the discussion.

In relation to the first proposal, if we look at Donoghue's book on Swift, the product of lectures given at Cambridge University in the mid-sixties, we see that his sense of the history of the imagination, in English and then later American literature, was not out of keeping with the judgments of either that time or since. That is, he judged the interest in the imagination as connected with that of Romanticism, and he judged the latter as a reaction to the materialism of Newton, Locke, Hume, and their like. Following Yeats's lead, Donoghue identifies Bishop Berkeley as instrumental in the formulation of an alternative to a materialist's explanation of things: 'Where Locke urged that the mind works as matter works and therefore can be construed in the same terms, Berkeley liberated the mind by denying the existence of material substance independent of perception. In Berkeley's system the mind was the imagination, answerable in the first instance to its own integrity and, behind that, to the law of Nature which is the will of God. So Berkeley attacked Locke and Newton in behalf of religion; Yeats gratefully accepted his arguments and used them in favour of poetry. If the primary act was the act of the imagination, and if the mind worked in accordance with its own powers and not at all by analogy with the operations of matter, then nothing more was needed for a complete poetry' (JS, 104–5).

If literature had to wait for Yeats to discover the importance of the imagination, there would have been, naturally enough, no Romantic literature to speak of. Donoghue accordingly makes mention of the other important texts that have helped form our understanding of the imagination. He speaks, for instance, of Thomas Warton's objection to Pope's poetry as living too readily in sunlight and of Addison's essay on the Pleasures of the Imagination. Here, he says '[t]he suggestion is that the effect of the whole light of Reason is to enforce the separation of man from Nature. The light of reconciliation is twilight, when the pleasures of the imagination are available without rational effort. Along with this, there is a new assumption, that the crucial events take place within the mind' (JS, 195). This 'new assumption' begins, says Donoghue, to take root in the mid-eighteenth century. It led to the replacement of politics by psychology as a main source of interest for the writer, a turnabout that first manifested itself in Edward Young's 'Night Thoughts' and then, some time later, in Blake, De Quincey, Coleridge, Shelley, Keats, and others. But it was in the pre-Romantic eighteenth century that the seeds for the split between reason and imagination, as well as between science and art, were first sown. The new psychology began to promulgate a new law, about which Donoghue writes: 'The new law reads: anything on which the imagination can work is legitimate. As Reason is supplanted by Imagination, it becomes natural to rescue the unconscious from Pope's denunciation, because sensations and associations come vividly from that source. When this is done, the split between Reason and Imagination is complete. Reason is handed over to the scientists, the merchants and the philosophers. Imagination is retained and promoted as the strictly creative power, the only power which can see things in all their variety' (JS, 196).

The price of this separation was high, for 'one of the disadvantages of the new psychology was that it eventually drove the poet from society altogether' (JS, 197). At the time this was written, Donoghue seemed, like most of his contemporaries, to accept the split, and to think that the artist took away the better half of the equation. That the artist was forced to think like an exile in his or her own land only enhanced the artist's specialness, along the line that the prophet remains unrecognized among his or her own people. In recent decades we have nevertheless begun to question the artist's presumed nobility. Forced to acknowledge that we should not wish to live in a polis ruled by a Yeats, Pound, and Lewis, we have generally begun to wonder whether too much has been conceded to the artist's 'genius,' and whether we might not examine their gifts with more scrutiny. Yet this is to rush ahead, when at present I wish only to chart Donoghue's initial understanding of the Romantic imagination. And here the point is that beginning in the middle of the eighteenth century, an interest in an interior life – in psychology and consciousness – appeared to push to the side an interest in the public realm. Then after Kant, this interest experienced a further magnification when it became part of intellectual lore that transcendental understanding was obtained not by looking outward but by looking, as the philosopher put it, 'to our *way of thinking*' (*Critique of Judgement*, I, 127). The mind was the home of the imagination, and the imagination was that which, by analogy, linked us to God: 'If Hume is right; if the missing relation between things cannot be perceived; perhaps it may be prescribed, derived from the character of the mind itself. What the imagination has joined together may not be put asunder. "The imagination is the will of things," Wallace Stevens said in our time; meaning that the imagination is the will, engaged upon certain tasks congenial to its nature. The first task is the prescription of relation. Man and Nature are related because man's need is great. That is the chief cause of the critical preoccupation with the nature of the imagination; because in the Kantian universe the imagination is God. Or rather, the only meaning to be ascribed to "God" is: the imagination' (JS, 124).

From Kant, says Donoghue, it is a very short step to Coleridge's statement concerning 'the primary IMAGINATION' in the thirteenth chapter of *Biographia Literaria*, wherein the poet compares the powers of the artist with that of God: 'The primary IMAGINATION I hold to be the living power and prime agent of all human perception, and as a repetition in the finite mind of the eternal act of creation in the infinite I AM.' As Donoghue says, there is not much difference between such a statement and that of Stevens's 'God and the imagination are one' (JS, 74). In both instances, the creative individual – i.e., the artist possessing an acute imagination – is described as having an autonomy modelled after God's own. The artist, here, is in effect a demi-god, presumed to fulfil a certain ambassadorial role between ordinary people and Divinity (or Its like). We ourselves may no longer grant the artist or anyone else such powers, but we do generally grant the tradition its prominence and acknowledge that its history has carried itself even to the edges of our own time. Thus it seems fair for Donoghue to claim, as he does elsewhere: 'From Kant, Hegel, Coleridge, and Hazlitt to Stevens and Valéry there is substantial agreement on the nature and scope of the imagination: the differences are matters of shading or emphasis' (SG, 39).

The Imagination: The Carvers

Donoghue has been more than a student of the imagination; he has also been one of its strongest proponents, making a case for a tradition that others might prefer to think concluded. As noted, he has made this case most expressly in *The Ordinary Universe*, *Thieves of Fire*, and *The Sovereign Ghost*; and I would like to recapitulate the arguments made before addressing the matter of whether we can still esteem the imagination as an important value. *The Ordinary Universe* in many ways might be thought closest to the author's heart, for it articulates a view of the imagination that puts the greatest emphasis on a 'wooing both ways.' The phrase, again, is Blackmur's and is one of Donoghue's favourites, probably because it expresses the author's own desire not to have a thing described via one pole or another, but rather as it finds its identity in the tension between the two. Later, Donoghue came to see *The Ordinary Universe* as a book in which he perhaps gave too much away to things themselves, as opposed to the ability of artists to shape them according to their own wants and needs. For instance, in *Thieves of Fire*, he noted that 'in a book called *The Ordinary Universe* I tried to set out a preference for certain writers whose works are conceived primarily from the carving side. But I found myself fending off the versatile giants, trying not to notice their presence, so that my carving writers would have all the show to themselves. It was as if, offering to say something about Christianity, I identified the faith with the temper of St. Francis of Assisi, and tried for the moment not to recognize the presence of St. Augustine' (28).

This was true enough, but what it does not say is how Franciscan is the author's own temperament. The imagination has always been Donoghue's main theme but he has been, at the same time, distrustful of it. He is especially distrustful of the peremptory imagination, with its celebration of the artistic self. In *The Ordinary Universe*, meanwhile, the imagination is his theme, but it is an imagination schooled in the practice of acknowledgment. By virtue of this, the reciprocal equation – signified by the phrase 'wooing both ways' – is already in place, for the imagination needs the world's objects to supply it with content just as those same objects need the imagination to rescue them from oblivion. Not that the objects necessarily care about being recognized this way, though they might. In any event, the theory of the imagination most satisfies our longing for personhood, for the sense that we are real and that our relations with the world, including other people, are not devoid of consequence. From this, one might conclude that personhood entails an action. It is not simply a given but involves our movement in relation to others (again things as well as people). They help to define who we are, and we do the same for them. It is not surprising then that Donoghue should find the following lines, from 'Notes Toward a Supreme Fiction,' 'perhaps the most beautiful in Stevens's entire work' (OU, 276):

> Two things of opposite natures seem to depend
> On one another, as a man depends
> On a woman, day on night, the imagined
> On the real ... (II, iv)[7]

The reason follows from the fact that the imagination and the real are conceived as interdependent: the one cannot exist without the other. This is not always the case in Stevens's poetry, and in *The Ordinary Universe*, Stevens often serves Donoghue as an example of a poet who appears too willing to make consciousness 'the centre of all human circles' (OU, 277). But in the present instance, Stevens's lines are just right for the sort of imagination that Donoghue esteems most valuable. Here, consciousness is viewed as 'an instrument in the service of something other than itself' (OU, 15), the way in which Marianne Moore's poems are said to be 'full of quotations because she has come upon many things which have only to be exhibited to be appreciated, and appreciation is poetic' (OU, 45). What particularly makes appreciation poetic is the conviction that the world is infused with a divine intention that only needs to be recognized for it to have positive consequences, to create positive value: 'I would argue that existence, being, and fact are valuable because they are sponsored by something properly if loosely called an intention, and by an intention properly if loosely called divine; what Buber calls "the speech of God articulated in things and events." In this sense fact is the locus of value, for without fact value cannot reside in the human condition at all' (OU, 61). It is a crucial point. For Donoghue, a major feature of the imagination is its identification with the means by which we not only meet *what is* but also *what is not*, at least palpably. The interest helps to explain Donoghue's appreciation of James's distinction (in the 'Preface' to *The American*) between the real and the romantic, the first identified with 'the things we cannot possibly *not* know,' and the second identified with 'the things that, with all the facilities in the world, all the wealth and all the courage and all the wit and all the adventure, we never *can* directly know; the things that can reach us only through the beautiful circuit and subterfuge of our thought and our desire' (RA, 135). The imagination, as Donoghue conceives it, puts us in relation to both these interests, and in *The Ordinary Universe* he praises James's fiction for the way it sets up 'a remarkably dynamic relation between the admitted claims of the two worlds, this world and the world elsewhere; it is the "ache of the actual," as James calls it, an ache of acknowledgement as well as an ache of dream' (OU, 77).

Donoghue speaks of 'resuscitating the relation between the tongue and the heart' (OU, 17), making it clear that for him the imagination speaks as much to the realm of desire as it does to that of fact. But the object of this desire is sought through fact rather than over it. This is why Donoghue feels uncomfortable with the form that Eliot's spirituality assumes, for it seems almost to call for the voiding of fact rather than its re-signification: 'It is a gruff dismissal, when all is said. And it points to the deepest embarrassment – or so I think – in Eliot's poetry; the feeling, in part, that all the declared values of human life are somehow illusory and, in part, that nevertheless God so loved the world that He gave up for its redemption His beloved Son' (OU, 262).[8] Better, thinks Donoghue, would it be to acknowledge the realm of fact, to admit its pull, and yet at the same time refuse an allegiance to it alone. This would not be a stance of dismissal but of renunciation, a different response altogether: 'It is difficult to propose the voiding of all human allegiances without implying that they are in any event meretricious. The idiom of renunciation is more hopeful, since the value of renunciation is all the greater if what is renounced is indisputably fine' (OU, 261). If a reader, unacquainted with scholastic axiology, should ask, why renounce that which is judged fine, the answer would be that such is given up in the hope of gaining something even finer.

As Donoghue understands things, the world is an attractive place, replete with the most extraordinary forms of pleasure and promise. Like Herbert, he too would say, 'I know the wayes of Pleasure, the sweet strains, / The lulling and the relishes of it' (OU, 264). So while he praises the value of renunciation, he does not assume the monastic path the only one worth travelling. Rather, Donoghue's preferred relation to the world is less one of renunciation than of assent, of a saying yes to the things he finds and then – like Marianne Moore, a poet whom he much admires – raising them up to a point of inspection and celebration, making it clear that he too is among the 'literalists of the imagination.' For Donoghue, the most cherished stance towards the world is reverence, a 'saying "yes" to the human situation, limited and finite as it is; it disposes us to respect persons, to value them, to find the human predicament full of hazard and therefore full of significance; [and] to find that moral choice is important and that life is possibility if not promise' (69). Life is lived in time, and time is the envoy of all those contingencies, both pleasing and painful, that 'thicken the plot' of our existence and give it the quality of *gravitas*.[9]

If 'the poet does well to assent to Time as one of the incorrigible but

valuable conditions of his art' (OU, 60), it is because our most important discoveries are made in time. Understood this way, the world has
about it a quality of facticity or presence that cannot be read in an
instant. To the attentive, the world admits discoveries, but they require
the percipient's acknowledgment that the world is not subject to his or
her will. These discoveries also entail a history, which then plays a crucial part in future discoveries. The author 'who commits himself to plot
and time assumes that the real is to be disclosed rather than invented,
that man is not God, that the human mind devising concepts is fallible
but not feeble. The corresponding epistemology holds that the real
exists "independent of how we think it," that "empirical reality does not
need to be assumed nor to be proved, but only to be acknowledged."
With these commitments a genial relation between Fact and Value
becomes feasible without the insinuation of a predatory Self' (OU, 60–
1). This represents one theory of our relation to the world, and while
Donoghue has investigated others, this is the one that, over time, he has
most abided.

In *The Ordinary Universe*, Donoghue tries to coerce his separate discussions on the writers Tomlinson, Hopkins, Eliot, Yeats, Williams, Stevens,
Pound, and others into those terms – e.g., fact, value, recognition,
acknowledgment – that he finds most congenial. Yet he also acknowledges that it is something of a losing battle, and that some of these writers (most notably Stevens) might actually be thought of as working
against the grain. For if his preferred model speaks of an artist discovering value in a world that is independent of his or her consciousness,
there remains the sense that some artists imagine their relation to the
world in more hubristic terms. They subscribe to the 'theory of Symbolism,' which contends 'that a man makes his own reality, that reality is
not there to be discovered and disclosed, [and] that the grammatical
relation of subject, verb, and object has nothing to do with the mind's
way of knowing and is therefore an arbitrary imposition' (OU, 60). The
practice almost makes consciousness an end in itself, and is as much a
consequence of the 'new psychology' that began to appear in the mid-
eighteenth century as is Romanticism itself. Yet if Donoghue, in *The
Ordinary Universe*, is receptive to Romanticism, at least to the extent that
it is willing to acknowledge fact, he is much less receptive to this particular branch of it, which again he equates with Symbolism. For one, Donoghue finds it an impertinence that the artist, assuming a deity-like
posture, should think the world depends on him or her. For another, he
finds that the cultivation of consciousness comes at the expense of the

highly valued tension between imagination and fact. Consciousness makes most sense when it is consciousness of something – that is, of something other than its own mechanism. Otherwise, it is likely to appear a banal gesture in the direction of purity, either as a language purified of its referents or of a morality purified of all the contingencies that make the formulations of morality necessary in the first place. Respecting the former instance, Donoghue writes: 'If you make language as independent as possible; if you think of it as a poor relation to music and hope to improve it by cultivating musical manners; you can never do this as thoroughly as the musicians, and you are unlikely to do much better than the Pure Poets' (OU, 128). Respecting the latter, he writes: 'aesthetic answers are often more coherent than moral answers; more coherent because "purer." Problems intolerable in morality are often understandable if we translate them into aesthetic terms' (OU, 179).

In sum, Donoghue chooses, in *The Ordinary Universe*, to chastise the peremptory imagination, seeing it as principally disengaged from all responsibility to reality and too willing to think of the latter as 'an object, an icon, a mobile floating free and pure in air' (OU, 128); and he chooses to praise that form of the imagination that prefers to welcome reality's recalcitrance and thereby makes a virtue out of a constraint. 'The *world* differs from the *word* in a thousand ways, all perhaps represented by the difference of one letter; but one letter is enough' (OU, 179).[10] World and word remain apart, even as it is the rightful ambition of the poet to place them in dialogue. What is attractive about dialogue is that each party is able to hold on to its quality of being other – is able to hold off the co-optation which threatens to conflate the difference that distinguishes, in this instance, world from word. It is in this light that Donoghue compares the ambitions of Stevens and Buber. In Stevens, Donoghue claims, the imagination is 'characteristically if not always' Narcissus. In Buber, however, 'a sense of reality increases our sense of the Otherness, the integrity, of each of its members,' even as 'in Stevens, it sets up another reality, in rivalry, because this new reality is "made" in the image of its maker' (OU, 277). So, finally, when Donoghue must choose an image which best represents the imagination in its most viable and welcome form, it is the image of the falcon, both riding and resisting the wind, found in Hopkins's poem 'The Windhover': 'It would be difficult to find a figure more lucid in suggesting the relation between the imagination and reality, when that relation is a mutual excellence. The bird flies of its own volition and yet it needs the sustenance and the opposition of the air, a happy meeting of necessity and freedom coming from a poet who was interested in such things. The continuity of the energy from line to line, from "striding" to "High," suggests the imagination going about its proper business. The poet's imagination is, like the bird, daring and self-contained but it needs the opposition of reality; and the air, like reality, is dense even when it is transparent' (OU, 87).

The Imagination: The Modellers

Donoghue must no sooner have finished *The Ordinary Universe* than he felt some pangs of misgiving. That is, judging by his next effort in the study of the imagination, *Thieves of Fire*, he must have felt somewhat the justice of Hartman's criticism of those critics who try to deflate the imaginative efforts of our most robust writers into the domestic space of the plain style: 'Yet just as logic tries to escape or purify rhetoric, so literary criticism too has tried to control words or else recall them to their direct, most referential function. It may seem strange to admit that the literary critic is often no friendlier to imaginative literature than the logician. In this self-deputized censor, the critic, there is love-hate rather than friendship' (*Minor Prophecies*, 58). In *The Ordinary Universe*, Donoghue did, in fact, play something like the role of the censor, refusing the more wilful claims of an Eliot or a Stevens. He admits as much in the passage quoted above, wherein he identifies his interest in *The Ordinary Universe* as more given to those writers (the Franciscans) who carve rather than model their work. The distinction between carvers and modellers is borrowed from sculpture. A carver is an artist 'concerned with the release of significance deemed already to exist, imprisoned in the stone' or world itself. A modeller is an artist who bestows upon the stone or world 'his own truth, or what he insists is his own truth' (TF, 27). The modeller is not always checking his or her vision with the populace to see if it approves. He or she is prepared to be more arbitrary – to insist on the vision regardless of market-place values. In this respect, the artist is like the God of *Paradise Lost*, arbitrary and wilful; and what Donoghue says about the critics in relation to this God might, keeping the Hartman criticism in mind, also be said more generally about the critic's relation to the artist: 'Those [critics] who go out of their way to make a case for God in *Paradise Lost* by somehow squaring his acts with the human idea of fair play are misguided, because the laws of fair dealings do not apply. The desire to make God just and reasonable in human terms is merely the desire to have him respect our common law. But God's law is statute law, arbitrary by definition' (TF, 41).

Donoghue knows that what he says of God can also be said (though not by him except by way of report) of the artist. Milton, Blake, Melville, and Lawrence are the writers Donoghue chooses to examine in *Thieves of Fire*, and each might, says he, be thought of as exemplifying a god-like ambition, or Promethean imagination. In Aeschylus's *Prometheus Bound*, Prometheus is the Titan who, defying Zeus's command, steals fire from Olympus and makes a gift of it to humankind. As punishment for this defiance, he is bound to a rock, where every day his liver is torn at by an eagle, until the day when Hercules releases him. Prometheus stands then 'in our minds as a notable gesture, a style of defiance, resistance brought to the end of the line; and since he has been a friend to man, we think him justified in everything, not least in the quality of his defeat' (TF, 33). This resistance, undertaken in an effort to enhance our freedom, also makes Prometheus a fitting symbol of a certain kind of writer who, esteeming his or her imaginative powers as self-engendered, chooses to use these powers assertively, so as to enlarge the territory of humankind's orbit and freedom. Like Milton's God, the Promethean author appears arbitrary and wilful, convinced that his or hers is the right way. This author gives little cognizance to more restrained articulations, suspecting they are but a pap proffered to make us more content with a lot clearly inadequate. 'The Promethean imagination is more deeply responsive to harsh themes than to genial themes, to the arbitrary than to the reasonable; it does not delight in the continuity of reasons, causes, effects, mediations between one hand and the other. It delights rather in an act of will, without any further ground in the nature of the case' (TF, 53). Wilful by its nature, the Promethean imagination, unlike that discussed in *The Ordinary Universe*, is much more like an action, a stance wherein the writer marches out to meet and take hold of the world. 'Sartre,' says Donoghue, 'has encouraged us to think of imagination as an act of consciousness. If we think of imagination in this way we free ourselves from the habit of thinking of images as little pictures in the mind: images are registered as acts of the mind, their content is their nature as acts, their force and direction. The Promethean imagination is in a special sense an act of the mind, because it seizes what it requires, it steals the divine fire' (TF, 52).

The act, however, is identified with consciousness, and though Donoghue, in *Thieves of Fire*, does not speak much better of this imaginative form than he did previously, he seeks to understand matters from the transgressor's viewpoint – to understand the writers' vaunting ambition, their attempt to rival God. The attempt is most marked, thinks Donoghue, in the temple of the imagination: 'We think imagination a wonderful power, unpredictable and diverse, and we are satisfied to call it divine and to ascribe to it an early association with transgression. A Promethean says of it that it is the most precious part of man, perhaps the only precious part, the only respect in which man's claim to superior character is tenable' (TF, 62). To be god-like, less prepared to acknowledge creation than to compete with it, is the pose struck by a Blake, Melville, or Lawrence. They seek to transmute the world into words, and words into symbols. For the Promethean author, the world appears barren until seized by the imagination. It is only through the author's investment in words – ordinary enough conduits between consciousness and nature – that experience begins to appear more attractive. It becomes symbolic, as the literary artist transmutes a lumpish world into something nobler. Prometheus's gift of consciousness thus 'made possible the imaginative enhancement of experience, the metaphorical distinction between what happens to us and what we make of the happening. That is to say, Prometheus provided men with consciousness as the transformational grammar of experience' (TF, 26). This consciousness was both good and bad: good in the sense that it spoke of artists' kinship with the divine; bad in the sense that they then used it to distance themselves from the same. Wrapped up in their new possession, they forgot to acknowledge its source. They forgot that this imagination was something stolen: '[t]he reflexiveness of mind, which is in one sense its glory, is in another a token of its criminality, its transgression at the source' (TF, 26).

For Donoghue, the Promethean imagination can never aspire to be more than a mixed blessing. It is 'dynamic if we want to praise it, and insistent if we distrust it' (TF, 20), and Donoghue still distrusts it. For him, it errs on the side of rebellion, of defiance. It prefers to promote itself over the objects of its attention, suggesting that it can only be trusted to the extent that its interests coincide with these objects. Otherwise, its hubris predominates: 'The Promethean imagination does not begin with any respect for "the Other": specific objects of attention are valued only in default of other objects, and there is a sense in which all objects are interchangeable. Or, to put it more precisely, the imagination does not allow objects to assert themselves or to hold out for their right. They have no right, except to be useful. No object is ever allowed to mark an outer limit of the Promethean imagination: on the contrary, limits are observed only to be transcended' (TF, 26–7).

'The Promethean poet,' says Donoghue, 'feels that the fate of the world depends upon him, he must not seek help or sign treaties' (TF, 77). It is a Byronic stance, which Donoghue can admire from a distance but not finally embrace. As a relation towards the world, it is too self-important and melodramatic. And in the author's grasping a deity's powers, it verges on the sacrilegious. 'Blake believes that the natural world may be redeemed by man's imagination, may be rendered human and therefore transfigured' (TF, 65), but Donoghue already believes the world blessed, and thus less in need of transfiguring than acknowledgment. Between the world and ourselves, there is an affinity that we need to enhance, not sunder. Yet in the end, the Promethean author sunders, and this leaves Donoghue troubled. The feeling does not go away.

The Imagination: Mind Plus Energy

In his next book upon the imagination, *The Sovereign Ghost*, Donoghue again admitted, as he had in *Thieves of Fire*, that his own most recent discussion left him dissatisfied. He had entered into the *Thieves of Fire* project with the purpose of placing himself in a more sympathetic relation to what he came to call the Promethean imagination, yet he never quite overcame his uneasiness about the alliance. Or, as he admitted in the new book's 'Preface,' 'In *Thieves of Fire* I looked somewhat nervously at certain writers whose imaginations are peremptory, strident in the presence of common experience and the received poetic forms' (SG, ix). If, in *The Ordinary Universe*, he had viewed the topic from the perspective of objects and in *Thieves of Fire* from that of subjects, in the *Sovereign Ghost* his plan was simply 'to deal with some of the questions raised by the imagination itself, its character and relations, the claims regularly made on its behalf, the problems it proposes' (ibid.). In a sense, the need followed from the fact that in intellectual culture the imagination had ceased to function as an operative term. In *The Ordinary Universe*, Donoghue could with some justice claim that '[t]his word, imagination, is one of three or four inescapable terms which we use in describing our engagement with litcrature' (OU, 86). But in the years intervening between that book and *The Sovereign Ghost*, the sense, in literary studies, of what was important had decidedly shifted, following from the influence of structuralist and post-structuralist theory. One may, said Donoghue, still 'find poets brooding upon the imagination, but they rarely

construe it as the essential power, the attribute in which man is most glo-
riously expressed. Power is still a crucial question, but glory is no longer
deemed interesting' (SG, 1). The tone is rueful, the tone Donoghue
tends to adopt when he feels as if he is swimming upstream, as he
undoubtedly was. This is not to say that Donoghue did not have a legitimate argument to make. I think he did. Still, it proved necessary for him
to change the accent of the discussion, to concede certain things which
he had not conceded before, and to try to translate his own term (i.e.,
imagination) into those terms (e.g., energy, mind) more palatable to his
contemporaries. Hence, we find him saying that '[e]nergy is the word
we need when we propose to translate imagination into modern terms;
we understand it, as we do not understand imagination, in its relation to
force' (SG, 25). The new term is Henry Adams's, and Donoghue's
employment of it is a momentary concession that our current discussions are by and large secular in tone, and thereby somewhat opposed
to imagination (with its religious overtones) on principle. The same
concession seemed evident in his employment of the term 'mind.' The
term had recently been resuscitated by Lionel Trilling in his 1972
Thomas Jefferson Lecture: *Mind in the Modern World*. And it is in *The Sovereign Ghost* that Donoghue noticeably begins to make use of Trilling
(who died in 1975) as an ally against a range of critics (e.g., anthropologists, deconstructionists, Freudians, Marxists, structuralists) who are, for
convenience sake, spoken of singularly 'as structuralists without distinguishing one from another or establishing the attribution in any individual case' (SG, 38). The reason, perhaps no more suasive then than now,
related to the author's interest in speaking to (and of course against)
'an intellectual spirit at large, nothing more than that' (ibid.). In any
event, he thought, not without reason, that if he could widen the discussion by bringing in 'mind,' the imagination's sibling, he might gain
greater ground for the imagination itself. Thus he tried to show that
there was no dispute between the imagination and mind, even as there
were differences, differences that only increased our respect for the
imagination:

> there is no inevitable quarrel between imagination and mind. There are
> indeed differences between them, each is a mood of the other and is
> moody in its own favour. The mind complains of imagination that it is way-
> ward, irresponsible, self-engrossed. Imagination complains of mind that it
> is totalitarian, it demands immediate obedience, imposes its categories
> upon existence with little thought for the nature of the experience, it is

premature in its orders and conclusions. Imagination regards mind as a
civil servant, a bureaucrat, illiberal in administrative zeal, too Roman for its
own good. If it comes to a choice between mind and that mindlessness
which Trilling indicates, the fashionable subversion of knowledge and
truth, then the choice is clear: I choose mind with all its limitations. But I
think imagination can be preserved as the grander term. (SG, 8–9)

In bringing Trilling into the discussion, Donoghue was obligated to
acknowledge the older critic's objections to the imagination. That is,
Trilling's purpose in invoking mind was to oppose it to what he thought
the real danger, the forces of irrationalism. In the sixties and seventies,
these forces appeared to him emergent. In the Jefferson Lecture, Trilling argued that '[i]n our day, it has become just possible to claim just
such credence for the idea that madness is a beneficent condition, to be
understood as the paradigm of authentic experience and cognition'
(quoted in RA, 181). As such, mind for Trilling was a principle more
identified with reason and a quotidian order than with imagination (as
formulated by the Romantics) and a transcendent order. Needing an
ally, Donoghue appears to grant some of the objections that mind
should raise against imagination, including the sense that it is too way-
ward and irresponsible. These are the objections that have always
dogged the imagination, and while they tend to diminish its importance, they do not dismiss it the way post-structuralism does. Hence
there was a logic in identifying imagination with the cause of mind. This
did not mean that Donoghue would shy away from pointing out mind's
limitations, from presenting it as the bureaucratic – and therefore inferior – partner to imagination's brave doings: 'Mind is the name we give
to the intellectual power which we call upon when we propose to deal
with the chaos of our experience merely by putting its constituents in
separate compartments; when our dealing with experience is strictly
administrative, the method of Ramist logic. We call upon imagination,
that is, upon the whole range of our intelligence, when we are prepared
to settle for nothing less than a continuous series of enhancements; *tempus* into *aevum*, fact into value, force into intellect, and the dualism of
word and deed into an Orphic unity' (SG, 222).

Though Donoghue makes concessions that appear to reduce imagination's importance, he is also forced – due to widespread scepticism –
to make greater claims for it than he might otherwise make. That is,
despite his own cautious history vis-à-vis the imagination in its more
peremptory form, he comes close in *The Sovereign Ghost* to urging this

form upon us. I say 'close,' for he really does not do so. Still, there is the sense that, as in the alliance negotiated with mind, it is better to combine and marshal forces. For instance, comparing imagination to perception, he writes of the former that it 'exercises its freedom by determining to what extent if at all it will yield to the weight or force of objects, and it is ready to surpass them if its freedom calls for such a show of violence' (45). Donoghue acknowledges that imagination in this form is peremptory, that it longs for omnipotence. But it comes more as an acknowledgment than as a charge, and to the extent that it is a charge, it is muted. In *The Sovereign Ghost*, then, Donoghue feels the need to make larger claims for the imagination, and to look less to Wordsworth than to Coleridge for a sense of how to proceed. He takes inspiration from Coleridge's brief on behalf of the artist who discerns a unity above the muster of everyday events, who cultivates not Fancy but Imagination. 'To emancipate the mind from the despotism of the eye,' writes Coleridge, 'is the first step towards its emancipation from the influences and intrusions of the senses, sensations and passions generally' (quoted in SG, 168). It is to move in a realm wherein forms possess greater credence than particulars, and wherein the superiority of one person over another is demonstrated by his or her 'greater power of abstraction' (SG, 168). Almost by definition, it shall be the artist who possesses this greater power, for it is the power of abstraction itself which determines one's status as an artist. Without such power, one is an ordinary person, there being no essential difference between the artist and this person except that the former maximizes the potential of the latter: 'As the artist is merely a special case of the ordinary man, his circumstances are bound to be exemplary and of general significance' (SG, 28). The circumstances are such – i.e., exemplary and significant – because the artist makes them so, wills a life that is different from that of others most notably in terms of the source of its inspiration. While it would be foolish not to acknowledge the importance of that source, it might also be foolish not to acknowledge that what is spoken of as the artist's will is the consequence of a choice, and a prior freedom. The imagination either speaks of a free act or of nothing at all.

Drawing on a tradition that includes Kant, Hegel, Coleridge, Hazlitt, Stevens, and Valéry, Donoghue speaks of the imagination as 'a free power,' the kind evidenced in Aristotle's statement in *De Anima* that 'imagining lies within our own power whenever we wish' (SG, 39). Most notably, he speaks of a freedom to respond to something transcendental, something that might be thought of as the source of our lives, and yet something that will seem as nothing unless we freely acknowledge it: 'The imagination is distinct from the will, but it is propelled by man's desire to create, to transcend himself, to surpass in his real experience that portion of it which is merely given ... As such, imagination is a form of man's spirituality' (ibid.). Following Coleridge's lead, Donoghue thinks it necessary to conceive of the imagination 'not only in relation to psychology but [also] in relation to theology' (SG, 24). Thus '[i]f you posit in man a creative faculty, it is easier to suppose for it a religious rather than a secular origin since the most plausible analogue for creativity is its "original" form, the divine act of creation. Chapter 14 of the *Biographia Literaria* is a haunted meditation on this analogue, the original act of creation and unity, the infinite I AM' (ibid.).

In the twentieth and twentieth-first centuries, the poet lives in a secular world. True, the vestiges of a prior, more religious dispensation are everywhere manifest, and the imagination is often identified as one such vestige. This was the gist of M.L. Abrams's argument in *Natural Supernatural*, wherein, as Donoghue points out, the Romantic imagination is spoken of as 'a late theology of the creative word, animated by religious belief or by a nostalgia brooding upon the effigies of belief and the ideal of a transparently true language' (SG, 24–5). Donoghue does not dispute the description, even as he would argue that theology remains among our most fruitful discourses. Yet wishing to be a good neighbour, he prefers the term 'imagination' rather than one that might more explicitly bespeak the religious tie: 'Let us say, then, that imagination is the secular name we apply to the soul when we wish to live peacefully with our neighbors. I cannot believe that the imagination is other than divine in its origins; but even if we leave that belief aside, or disagree upon it, we may agree that the imagination is a form of energy, demonstrable in its consequences if not in its nature, and that it strives to realise itself by living in the world. Like the soul, the imagination seeks to inhabit not only a human body but a human world. Even if the given world is regarded as a mere transit camp in a journey toward the abiding City of God, it is the only world available to us in the meantime' (SG, 29).

In the next section, I wish to examine more fully Donoghue's understanding of the relation between literature and theology. In the present space, I wish simply to make clear that there is a theological dimension to Donoghue's thinking about the imagination even as he is sensitive to the modern state's requirement that we make religion a private affair. (This is easier to do if one thinks of religion as less a public [e.g., per-

taining to a action] than a private matter, something that Enlightenment thinking encourages us – albeit not persuasively – to do.) Thus he
thinks the artist somewhat like the priest in that both deem it imperative
to put themselves in touch with those mysteries only explainable, most
likely, by reference to a Divine intention. He does not conflate the artist
with the priest, but he does think divination an essential component to
the work of each. While the world goes about its business, too preoccupied to take notice of things not directly before it, the artist and the
priest delve beneath the surface of events, searching out their meaning.
Art then is 'the inspired work of a few rare souls, adepts of a sacred mystery; that while common minds slide upon the surface of things, artists
search the depths' (SG, 32). The artist is not an ordinary person,
though the critic, responding to a countervailing pressure, concedes
that the artist's difference from his or her contemporaries is more one
of degree than kind. Or as Donoghue, taking his lead from Allen Tate,
writes: 'The poet differs from the rest of us only in degree, not in kind.
To speak of the poetic imagination is merely to name one of the human
possibilities and to deny that it is a freak of nature ... [A] poet's imagination differs from anyone else's only in degree and bearing. So the symbolic imagination is an extreme instance of something which is available
to everyone as an attitude to life, a particular response, a stance of
expectation' (SG, 86).

The imagination is available to all, and this makes it, in one sense,
quintessentially democratic. However, there is another sense in which
the imagination is opposed to the politics of democracy. For starters, the
imagination, while so available, is exactly what the majority appears to
lack. This is more true as societies structure their ends around the satisfaction of consumer desire as opposed to more traditional philosophical
or religious ends. 'Increasingly,' Donoghue writes, 'fundamental values
must be apprehended as living beneath or beyond the structure of
needs and drives which, in a consumer society, constitutes normal life.
These are values so alien to those of any actual society that they can be
sustained only in effigy as the virtualities of artistic form: this is the role
of form, to preserve as fundamental truths the values which are otherwise homeless. So it is that the artist has been driven into the position of
writing against time in the desperate hope of redeeming time' (SG,
224). If the imagination can be thought allied with values more genuine
than ersatz, it becomes imperative to resist those values that, while finding validation in the market place, continue to remain suspect. But the
problem of adjudication has become more difficult, for there has been

a tendency for Western democracies, led by the United States, to identify their interests with the market place. The artist who embraces the
Romantic theory of imagination is pressed aside, left alone with his or
her beliefs that there are values more profound than those on show, yet
plagued by the doubt that there may be none.[11]

The Imagination: An Ally of Form

In *The Sovereign Ghost*, Donoghue's argument for the imagination is still
being pitched in an aggressive form. The mood is not as confident as
that in *The Ordinary Universe* or *Thieves of Fire*, but it is still much more so
than anything we find in the later work, particularly *The Arts Without
Mystery* and *Being Modern Together*. For one, the artist is still seen as a
form of hero, as someone who, while familiar with the temptations of a
material culture, is nevertheless able to resist them and to hold faithful
to an ideal that is, in essence, otherworldly. It is a view not unlike that
offered by Theodor Adorno in his *Aesthetic Theory*, wherein he argues
that '[t]he artist must feel the presence of the empirical other in the
foreground of his own experience in order to be able to sublimate that
experience, thus freeing himself from his confinement to content while
at the same time saving the being-for-itself of art from slipping into outright indifference toward the world' (9). For Adorno, modern society is
that which art resists. If art did not, it should become too much like any
other object, whose value is determined by the buyer. Or as Adorno
writes: 'Art will live on only as long as it has the power to resist society. If
it refuses to objectify itself, it becomes a commodity. What it contributes
to society is not some directly communicable content but something
more mediate, i.e., resistance' (321).

For Adorno, art's resistance to society crucially connects to the matter
of form, for only such offers art an escape from the deadening contingencies of a material culture: 'The concept of form draws a qualitative
and antagonistic dividing-line between art and empirical life, the modern variety of which is denying art the right to exist. In this situation,
art's fortunes are tied to those of form: they will live or die together'
(205). Like Kant, Adorno thinks art's glory is tied to its purposelessness.
It may mean in an almost quasi-teleological sense, but it should not
effect a purpose: 'Works of art are purposeless in the sense of being
removed from the reality and from useless personal strategies of survival. It is precisely for this reason that we speak of "meaning" rather
than "purpose" in art, despite the patent affinities that exist between

meaning and the immanent teleology of purpose' (219). For Adorno, meaning speaks of something non-contingent and timeless. It speaks of art's relation to truth, the sense being that art is, in some way, emblematic of truth. Or rather, art is emblematic of truth to the extent that it is expressive of form. Form bridges the realm of the contingent and the non-contingent. With form, all reality's contradictory elements are elevated into a new synthesis, wherein a quality of suspension prevails. Now, these elements speak of something larger than themselves even as they provide implicit commentary on our mundanities: 'Form is the non-repressive synthesis of diffuse particulars; it preserves them in their diffuse, divergent and contradictory condition. Form therefore is the unfolding of truth. While form is thetic unity, it constantly suspends itself; its essential property seems to be that it interrupts its continuity by its other, just as it is the essential property of consistency to be inconsistent. In relation to its other, form succeeds in mitigating its strangeness while at the same time keeping it intact. This goes to show that form is the anti-barbaric dimension of art. Form ensures that art both shares in the process of civilization and criticizes it by its sheer existence' (207).

Donoghue makes occasional references to Adorno, but I am unaware of any specific reference to *Aesthetic Theory*. Rather, it is to another Frankfurt School critic, Herbert Marcuse, whom he goes for exactly this same purpose – i.e., to confirm his sense of form as still crucial to the discussion of art. The references to Marcuse do not appear until after *The Sovereign Ghost*. One of the earliest references occurs in *The Arts without Mystery*, wherein Donoghue, referring to *The Aesthetic Dimension*, quotes Marcuse to the effect that art constitutes an alternative reality that allows us to escape the realm of the cash-nexus, with all its oppressiveness. '[A]rt,' says Marcuse, 'creates the realm in which the subversion of experience proper to art becomes possible: the world formed by art is recognized as a reality which is suppressed and distorted in the given reality' (AWM, 68). This (part of a larger passage) leads Donoghue to say that Marcuse 'values art, as I do, for its power of contradiction, its protest against a narrow definition of reality and the prescription of its forms' (AWM, 68–9). Donoghue has continued, in subsequent years, to refer to this volume of Marcuse, particularly as the matter of form has become more central to his own understanding of what sets literature apart.[12]

In *The Sovereign Ghost*, the interest in form is not quite as explicit as it is in Donoghue's later work, but it is certainly there, and it is possible to argue that it is in this volume that the matter actually begins to pique his

interest. In a sense, the interest in form follows the interest in the imagination, for it is the place wherein the consequences of that faculty manifest themselves, in a sort of virtual space. The point is, the imagination is
a synthetical operation that reconciles things that, on the surface,
appear contrary. The imagination is, says Donoghue, 'that mental
power which finds unnecessary the strict separation of conscious and
unconscious life, of primary and secondary processes, in Freud's terminology; which deals with contradictions not by subordinating one to
another but by accommodating all within a larger perspective; and
which entertains feelings and motives before they have been assigned to
categories or organized into thoughts, attitudes, statements, values, or
commitments' (SG, 26). Ordinarily, these things (i.e., processes, contradictions, feelings, and so forth) seem more constitutive of daily life's
contingencies, contingencies that, some might argue, are as resistant to
form as vice versa. Critics like Pierre Bourdieu and Barbara Herrnstein
Smith are especially dismissive of the move towards some virtual space
wherein disinterest – or life within parentheses – is presumed to reign.
Bourdieu cannot but wonder whether the wide-scale embrace by academics of the Kantian values of detachment and art's purposelessness is
not a covert bid for distinction. He reminds his readers that while aesthetic theory has so often offered detachment, disinterestedness, and
indifference 'as the only way to recognize the work of art for what it is,
autonomous, *selbständig*, ... one ends up forgetting that they really mean
disinvestment, detachment, indifference, in other words, the refusal to
invest oneself and take things seriously' (*Distinction*, 34). Smith also
argues along these lines, esteeming the attempt to adjudicate value
according to some timeless standard as a lesson in avoidance: 'The
recurrent impulse and effort to define aesthetic value by contradistinction to all forms of utility or as the negation of all other nameable
sources of interest or forms of value – hedonic, practical, sentimental,
ornamental, historical, ideological, and so forth – is, in effect, to define
it out of existence; for when all such utilities, interests, and other particular sources of value have been subtracted, nothing remains. Or, to put
this in other terms: the 'essential value' of an artwork consists of everything from which it is usually distinguished' (*Contingencies of Value*, 33).

The Bourdieu and Smith arguments are impressive, and they make it
harder to claim disinterest on behalf of forms. Disinterest is itself an
interest. There is, however, no harm in saying this: that my desire to
ground my adjudications in something more embracing than either the
objects or my relation to them is expressive of an interest. That is exactly

what it is. That does not stop me from wishing to square my judgments against the largest possible set of circumstances that I can imagine, or against that set of circumstances that may exist (e.g., God) even as I myself cannot imagine what form such might take. Nor is there any reason to believe that this ambition fails to 'take things seriously' (Bourdieu, *Distinction*, 34) or that it equates itself with 'the negation of all ... nameable sources of interest or forms of value' (Smith, *Contingencies of Value*, 33). It is true that this ambition thinks less of those values that Smith believes inescapable: 'hedonic, practical, sentimental, ornamental, historical, ideological, and so forth' (ibid.). This does not mean that the question of value is dismissed. Rather, it means that one wants to investigate value by granting it the largest conceivable orbit. It is in this context that all other – and arguably lesser – values appear almost suspended, their estimations held in a parentheses of meaning until the dimension of the larger value is known. Of course, most activities do not require that we know for certain the dimension of this value. Their demands are circumscribed, and we meet them as they arise. With art or literature, the situation is – or may, at least, be conceived as – different. That is, we tend to think of art as virtual, as something offered less to instigate an immediate consequence than to allow us to examine a matter in its fullest import. Action may follow, but it will be an indirect consequence and after a time; and if it does follow, there always will appear something premature about it, at least when art and literature are conceived as they are by Donoghue: 'Auden was right: poetry makes nothing happen. Indeed, that is why it resents every attempt to translate its fictions out of themselves and into practice. The order it seeks is figurative, its unity is virtual, its energy uncommitted, so it is patient of any form of unity except those, if they are any such, which have no time or place for the perceiving, creative subject. Within the parentheses, the imagination is appropriately liberal, it can afford to be; its modifying power is exercised by having words attract to their orbit meanings over and beyond those required by the plot of the occasion' (SG, 23).

This conception puts Donoghue at odds with much current criticism, and the serious reader must, at times, wonder whether he has not hobbled himself with interests – i.e., the imagination, form – that have outlived their usefulness. In fact, there is a passage in *The Sovereign Ghost* wherein Donoghue, commenting on Trilling's tendency to promote certain terms (e.g., mind, reason, self, society), could almost be describing his own way of going about things: 'Trilling's rhetorical method is to surround his god term with a halo as a mark of its presence in history and an indication that he means to assert its continuing validity despite the fact that the time is unpropitious. Sometimes he argues directly and trenchantly in favour of his god term, sometimes he draws upon its ancestral reverberations in the hope that these will be enough, and sometimes he recites the holy word as if it had never been desecrated. There is always a temptation to assume that because a god term is holy to its celebrant it must be holy to everyone; a writer may make the mistake of thinking that he does not need to establish the sanctity of the word, that he has only to invoke it' (SG, 123).

Donoghue's respect for Trilling is great, yet his remarks are critical. The suggestion is that Trilling let his terms too often carry the discussion, forgetting that they were tropes in need of reification. The criticism is valid enough, but what strikes one, more than its validity or invalidity, is how much the criticism is also applicable to Donoghue's relation to the term 'imagination.' This term is also a trope in need of constant attestation, and yet Donoghue seems, at least until *The Sovereign Ghost*, to take its reality almost for granted. Even later, in *Ferocious Alphabets*, he will state, 'The imagination is real' (210), though at this point the assertion belies the fact that he himself has begun to wonder whether it truly is. While it is true that Donoghue has never relinquished his interest in the imagination, so that it continues to constitute for him a cardinal theme, there is a discernible difference in the way the theme is handled in the work after *The Sovereign Ghost*. Donoghue's relation to the term becomes more defensive, more cognizant that if the term is going to remain viable, he is going to have to take current conditions more into account. And by this, I refer not only to the shifting philosophies of the academy but also of the art world. As I have said, Donoghue's sense of the imagination has been crucially tied to his belief that the artist stands apart from society's disaffecting compromises, that the artist is a variant of the hero. In *The Sovereign Ghost*, he writes: 'Is the poet, then, privileged? Yes, in the sense that he, at least to a greater extent than anyone else, is master rather than victim of the public conventions, the sinister axioms of language, and is therefore undeceived. What he cannot do, he knows he cannot do' (227). Of course, it is still possible to believe this, and Donoghue still does believe it, though not so strongly. Notice, for instance, the concessionary tone of the following passage from *The Practice of Reading* (1998): 'Nothing is to be gained by positing a categorical discrepancy between individuals and society. Or by exaggerating the creative or inaugural character of the subject; even though it would be wicked to deride one's possession of an inner life and the soliloquies in which it may be expressed' (106).

The Imagination: The Non-Opposing Artist

There is, more generally, a problem, noticeable after the 1950s, when art movements like the New York School made their opposition to society a major tenet. Or after the triumph, in 1960s film, of the auteur, of the imagined Kantian-like genius of Antonioni, Bergman, Fellini, Godard, Kurosawa, Resnais, Rohmer, and Truffaut. The problem has to do with the fact that artists themselves are found to be taking a less opposing stance towards society. It is difficult to maintain a theory that extols the artist as apart from the mainstream when that same artist is offering Brillo boxes (Andy Warhol), Balantine beer cans (Jasper Johns), Las Vegas–inspired architecture (Robert Venturi and Denise Brown), Hollywood stills (Cindy Sherman), graffiti drawings (Keith Haring), pornographic photographs (Jeffrey Koons), and tongue-in-cheek quotations (Larry Rivers). Granted, things are not as simple as this. Not all artists have embraced middle-class, quotidian values. But enough has changed in the previous decades vis-à-vis the artist's relation to society so as to make the celebration of the imagination a more problematic affair. Two of Donoghue's later books – *The Arts without Mystery* and *Being Modern Together* (later included in *The Old Moderns*) – are especially responsive to this change. Or, as he writes in the first book: 'The problem now is that the relation between the arts and society has changed in ways which make many of these traditional critical enterprises redundant. There has been a change in the way artists see themselves, and the way in which society acknowledges them. The antagonism I mentioned between bourgeois and bohemian, duty and pleasure, constraint and freedom has been dissolved. Serious artists don't think of themselves as avant garde, on the subversive margin of society, driven there by capitalism and the corruption of the market. The division of society into middle-class liberals and the rest has lost its meaning' (AWM, 17).

What has most notably given way is the conviction that value exists independent of institutions: 'Thirty or forty years ago it was commonly assumed that there were higher values than those administered by our official institutions: government, law, the market, the banks' (AWM, 18). However, now one witnesses a greater willingness to define value in terms that are emphatically local. There may be no shortage of energy around, but it has no one direction. Even in the arts, one observes the

fact that no one form or movement is anywhere near capable, as in the
past, of commanding widespread allegiance. Our voices have become
disparate and multiple. While there are some attractive things about
this, it does make the desire for unified meanings more and more quixotic. If, as Donoghue argues, '[t]he crucial issue has to do with unity,
and with the work of art as the image of that unity' (AWM, 26), the current artistic climate can only elicit a sense of frustration and loss. The
frustration follows from the fact that the artifacts making claims for
attention are so multitudinous. No one person can even conceive of
making adequate adjudications respecting them. Or, as Donoghue
writes: 'What is the clearest and truest thing we can say about the arts in
modern societies? Answer: that they offer to one's attention millions of
images, their proliferation such that nobody could respond to them in
ten lifetimes. The one thing is clear is: they are too many' (AWM, 69).
This situation also undercuts our confidence that if one works hard
enough one can gradually acquire authority – i.e., the ability to discriminate between the false and the true. Instead, our discriminations seem
almost to be made for us, and we are left with the fear that our society,
complicated beyond the power of any individual to comprehend, runs
as if on automatic pilot: 'It could be argued that mass society is already
well on the way to fulfilling itself. Mechanisation, bureaucracy, the
increasing complexity of technology and scientific specialisation are, as
Chiaromonte says, typical phenomena of mass society today, "yet they
seem to vitiate the authority of the individual, as well as the democratic
power of the majority, in favour of an anonymous principle of organisa-
tion and discipline." If this is the case, the artist can't hope for any privileges from mass society, or even from the concession of a marginal
status' (AWM, 91).

There is much evidence for this view. Thus if the artist once felt
secure in the position of society's conscience – felt even with Shelley
that 'Poets are the unacknowledged legislators of the world' – he or she
no longer does, and is often grateful simply to be given a chance to
work. Mostly, the artist does not imagine that society cares much for
what he or she thinks about it. Contemporary society is happy to enter-
tain the arts, to exhibit them as luxurious goods, but it feels no compulsion to change its ways at the behest of its artists: 'Society never offers to
change itself or to take on any of the attributes of art; the invitation
always goes the other way. After all, the arts are not necessary; you can
keep body and soul together without them. But if they are not necessary,
society at least has to recognize that they are desirable and they can be

made to stand for luxuriousness otherwise unattainable. So they are brought into society as glamorous objects, conspicuous proof that the society that contains them is intrinsically fine' (AWM, 79). Donoghue's descriptions, though truculent, are an accurate report of a cultural shift that many others have also noticed: that art has become one relation among others and that no special privilege is granted it, at least not from elsewhere and seldom times from within. It is a point that Donoghue later picks up in his 1986 essay, 'The Promiscuous Cool of Postmodernism.' Here, he observes that even our artists appear content to reside in a world of images, no one of which is deemed more authentic or real than another: 'Instead of being assaulted and browbeaten by millions of historical images, each demanding some degree of attention, postmodern artists unruefully accept that proliferation is here to stay, and are promiscuously cool in their sense of it' (37). The desire for an original relation to the world – for the sense that art manifests a correlation not only to the world's parts but to its whole, to its truth – has given way to a 'cool acceptance of the belatedness of experience. There is no longing, as in modernism, to wipe the slate clean or to keep it safe for the inscription of one's chosen few images. Postmodern painting alludes, without disgust, to images already man-made: they are quotations from quotations' (ibid.). Compared to modernism, with its urgency and 'reputable exorbitance,' there is a marked complacency and fecklessness about contemporary art. Donoghue writes, 'There is a certain weightlessness in postmodernism that makes it possible for an artist to do anything he chooses, but doesn't suggest that he should try for anything in particular: like a game without rules' (ibid.).

In *The Arts without Mystery*, Donoghue notes how art has become more uncertain about its purposes, more the 'anxious object' spoken of by Harold Rosenberg. What is the case with society in general – that it 'doesn't know what is true, [so] it pretends to know it and settles for what is effective' (AWM, 80) – also appears the case with the artist. The criteria for what counts as significant art seem so fungible that no contemporary artist can be confident that the reputation that his or her work has garnered will last more than a brief moment. An exaggeration perhaps, though compared to the aesthetic standards of past epochs, the present standards are extraordinarily fickle: 'the difference between the nineteenth and the twentieth century in this regard is that in the nineteenth the work of art was still separable from the artist and it participated in forms and genres to which specific criteria applied. Bottle racks, snow shovels, and soup tins embody intentions and gestures to

which criteria don't apply. All you can do with an intention is to enter-
tain it. When Rosenberg said that it was no longer possible to say what a
work of art is or what is not a work of art, he meant that many works
offered as art no longer reveal in themselves the reasons why they are
such: they disable critical judgement by being arbitrary' (AWM, 99).

As a result, patrons begin to place their faith not so much in the art
object as in the name we attach to it. An object hardly exists unless we
can plug it into some recognizable category, as expressive not only of
this or that artist's work but also of a movement, be it abstract expres-
sionism, pop art, minimalism, neo-expressionism, new abstraction, new
realism, performance art, and so forth. The same applies to artists in
relation to such movements. For instance, think of how Jean-Michel
Basquiat's work acquired legitimacy by being identified with the new
realm of graffiti art. Evaluation becomes both arbitrary and conservative. That is, despite our aesthetic judgments' vagaries, there is something managerial about the way we go about sorting matters out. When
it comes to art, we may not know what is or is not true, yet we do know
what is or is not marketable, what is managerially effective. Donoghue
writes, 'The question of what is true has become unspeakable, but an air
of seriousness can still be achieved by switching from truth to effectiveness. When that word is used it's thought impertinent to ask what is
the nature of the effect. The main point about saying that someone
is effective is that it praises the means without reference to the end:
it's attached to images and gestures without saying anything about the
totality they serve' (AWM, 80).

We have, says Donoghue, become attached to labels. There may be no
reason why labels should prevent us from further examination, but
there are so many things calling out to be examined that it is easier to
deal with them as types. Types, or labels, make our relation to art and
the world more manageable; they can also make our critical discriminations more superficial, more apt to praise the familiar than to investigate that which might force us into an adversarial stance towards the
status quo, even that status quo which proclaims its newness: 'It's rare to
find a critical discrimination between one Action Painting and another.
The experience seems to begin and end with the recognition that the
work is, indeed, an Action Painting. There is nothing to prevent critical
discrimination from taking place. The label is not a veto. But the label
gives the viewer, if anything, too much, it pacifies him too soon. To see a
poem or a picture as fulfilling a category is to reach a premature sense
of it. Naming or labeling is important because it is the most effective

means of making something familiar, and familiarity comes too soon, the label imposes local clarity by ridding the work of its mystery and releasing the viewer from his hesitation' (AWM, 77).

What interests me here are not Donoghue's descriptions of what might be spoken of as contemporary, or postmodern, practice. The descriptions themselves are not that different from those offered by recent theorists. Instead, what does interest me is Donoghue's refusal to accept such practice as a given, and his insistence that art is still the best space available for us to imagine 'an alternative life,' even 'an adversary image if the official life is understood as enforced social practice' (AWM, 15). In the first instance, what holds Donoghue's allegiance to the arts is his sense that they, more than any other discipline (theology excepted), offer us the chance to imagine a world elsewhere, reflective of our utopian longings. He makes no mention of the work of Ernst Bloch (in later writings he does), yet Bloch's sense of the intimacy between the aesthetic and the utopian dimension is very much a part of Donoghue's own sense of things. I refer to the Bloch who reminds us that 'something's missing,' that 'each and every criticism of imperfection, incompleteness, intolerance, and impatience already without a doubt presupposes the conception of, and longing for, a possible perfection' (*Utopian Function of Art and Literature*, 15, 16), a perfection that resides not in the 'ideology' of any single epoch but in a realm cognizable only by that 'genius' capable of imagining the whole from the experience of the fragments: 'The surplus that genius engenders is much like something that has a continual impact, is valid and utopian: *ideological surplus arises according to the utopian function in the formation of ideology and above this ideology.* Thus, great art or great philosophy is not only its time manifested in images and ideas, but it is also the *journey of its time and the concerns of its time if it is anything at all,* manifested in images and ideas. From this vantage point of all times, it is that which is not yet fulfilled. It is from this element of utopia alone, which ultimately must be prepared in advance by the phenomenon of genius, that the continual impact of the surplus is derived and goes beyond the particular ideology of an epoch' (38).

Bloch's use of the term 'utopia' has its counterpart in Donoghue's term 'mystery.' In both instances, the term speaks of all the things that we do not know first-hand yet which inform everything else that we do. 'I would want,' writes Donoghue, 'a sense of the mystery of the work of art to pervade anyone's experience of it, at whatever degree of naïveté or initiation; and not as something to be dispelled by superior education or concentration of mind and purpose' (AWM, 44). For Donoghue, the concept retains its religious connotation: 'mystery is a truth offered only by divine revelation' (AWM, 24). In this sense, it is different from Bloch's use of the term 'utopia' and different as well from, say, Gilles Deleuze's term 'essence,' which Donoghue notes is 'a more acceptable term in Western philosophy' (ibid.). It is perhaps the quality of this difference that leads Terry Eagleton to argue 'that mystery is an authoritarian concept to use about the arts' (AWM, 22).

Donoghue does put his faith in an authority that supersedes the ordinary, yet he does not demand that others do the same, so much as to imagine why they might. Not everyone will agree with this assessment. One critic comments harshly upon Donoghue's 'Olympian condescension, of his being too damnably *tall* in his writing, so tall that he is too blandly in a position to pat every head or to pat any two heads together.'[13] And while I concede that Donoghue is susceptible to a magisterial tone, I do not find him irreclaimably, or even especially, authoritarian. In any event, when he writes that '[t]he artist and priest know that there are mysteries beyond anything that can be done with words, sound or forms' (AWM, 21), he makes clear that he thinks, much like Bloch, that there is space that transcends ideology's circumscriptions. Art, while not that space, nevertheless emulates it, at least in its best moments. This helps to explain, again, Donoghue's interest in the question of art's autonomy and virtuality. The interest does not demand that the art object abrogate its relations to other things. This would be 'absurd' (AWM, 27), and only the most naïve critic could think it a serious possibility. Rather, the interest speaks more to the desire not to see the art object *reduced* to its relations or parts. 'A valid claim,' argues Donoghue, 'means to say that the work of art cannot be reduced to its constituents; a novel cannot be reduced, for instance, to its story, plot, characters, and so forth. A sculpture cannot be reduced to the materials of which it is made. The autonomy of the work is embodied, there, in its precise form, its structure, however inadequately these terms may be construed' (ibid.). The art work, autonomously understood, is really a question not about less but about more, about its quality of surplus: 'The achieved work of art is present to itself, more fully at one with itself, than anything in the world which completes its meaning elsewhere, apart from its own form' (ibid.).

It is, again, a point that places Donoghue's work in congruence with Bloch's. Here, I am thinking of the philosopher's beautiful articulation of the way in which a utopian desire appears immanent in art itself:

The course of the world is still undecided, unended, and so is the depth in all aesthetic information: *this utopian element is the paradox in the aesthetic immanence. It is the most thoroughly immanent to itself.* The aesthetic imagination would have enough conception in the world without that potential for the fragment, more than any other apperception, but ultimately there would be no correlate. For the world itself, as it lies in malice, lies in incompleteness and in the experimental process away from malice. The figures that this process generates, the ciphers, the allegories, and the symbols, in which the process is so rich, are *altogether fragments, real-fragments themselves through which the process flows unevenly and through which the process proceeds dialectically toward further forms of fragments.* (153)

To say that a utopian element resides in art assumes that art, in Donoghue's words, 'testifies to some permanent feature of human life' (AWM, 100). Not everyone would agree, and the disagreement has of late become more pronounced. But Donoghue believes this;[14] and the belief helps to explain why he considers the relation between art and society to be less than friendly: 'My own understanding is that we receive the arts most completely not when we pay lip service to them but when the relation between art and society is mostly one of conflict and suspicion, if not one of hostility' (AWM, 14). The conflict locates itself in the fact that societies tend to be more responsive to immediate and pragmatic ends. The artist, like others, may often be the beneficiary of such practice; and yet he or she is also likely to want to explore that space in which 'the rigmarole of purposes and ends' appears not so explicit (AWM, 62). The artist, then, tends to be less involved in protecting our sense of reality than in enlarging it: 'Art does not confirm the reality we normally think we know and possess. In fact, art is permanently antagonistic to our sense of reality because it makes a space for those images which our sense of reality excludes' (AWM, 16). Art has not always been so antagonistic to society's purposes, as a simple allusion to Giotto or Palestrina might testify. Yet in the present, with the culture so aggressively material, Donoghue thinks that the artist has little choice but to take an antagonistic stance towards society, even if this entails causing bad feelings or hurt: 'There isn't much point in having the arts at all unless we have them with all their interrogative power. They are not cosy or ornamental ... If the arts don't hurt, why have them?' (AWM, 20–1).

In *The Arts without Mystery*, Donoghue argues that in a world increasingly administered – and thus defined – by politicians, the arts constitute one of the few remaining spaces in which independence seems obtainable. If he argues that the arts adopt 'an interrogative or subversive stance' vis-à-vis society, it is because he thinks it 'important that certain intuitions and sentiments be kept alive which are not, or at least not as a regular thing, maintained by those societies' (AWM, 42). Nevertheless, Donoghue's tone is more pessimistic than previously. The fact that contemporary artists appear to have worked out a compromise with society contributes to this mood. This situation is made more sobering when placed in the context of managed society's manifest indifference to our needs. It is almost as if the enemy has proven too strong, too capable of stifling complaint. As a consequence, '[t]he most popular arts these days are those which provide the most direct access to their experience' (AWM, 102) – that are the most at one with society's own values. For better or worse, the obligation that the artist make his or her work accord with a standard different and above quotidian experience has largely given way. Addressing himself to John Cage's music, which has 'room for everything and everyone,' Donoghue comments, 'You can't compare one thing with another while immersed in either. You have to hold them at arm's length, or at mind's length, to judge them' (AWM, 104–5). Otherwise, force will predominate. And as Donoghue looks around, this is what he sees, force, rather than mystery, predominating.

The Imagination: Unsettled by the Modern City

In *The Arts without Mystery*, Donoghue argued on the side of the imagination, but he also began, in his way, to concede that the prevailing forces were stacked against it. In *Being Modern Together*, he also suggests that recent artists have tended to betray the cause of modernism, if by this we mean an aesthetic which placed itself in opposition to all those forces that made light of the individual. He says that '[i]t is doubtful if any cultural deductions can be made on the basis of contemporary art, a proliferation of objects good, bad, and indifferent but so palpably compromised by the collaboration of corporate money, gallery-owners, dealers, agents, advertising, and the media that it can no longer be taken seriously as a cultural institution' (BMT, 52). Thinking this, Donoghue prefers to go to earlier artists, especially those identified with Romanticism and modernism, for sustenance. Still, he does not wish to give the game away, to suggest that the values he advocates, while available earlier, are now anachronistic. Thus while modern literature offers 'some indication of what a transformed culture would be' (BMT, 53), modernity itself represents more an attitude, yet available, than an historical moment: 'Modernity is not a fact of historical life or of chronology: it is not something that happened at a particular time. Nor is it a cause, such that everything else in its domain became a consequence. The name refers to a stance, an attitude, a choice. By definition, the invitation could be declined' (BMT, 69). Many contemporary artists have, in fact, declined the invitation. The painter David Salle, for instance, avers: 'I'm not interested in making a statement about alienation, or any of that nonsense.'[15] Donoghue, however, chooses not to decline the invitation, nor should he. An historical epoch is in its mood coercive, but it is never monologic. Main currents are subverted by alternative currents, and there is no reason to think that because the imagination – with its suggestion of interiority and creativity – has ceased to be a working concept for many that it can no longer be usefully appealed to. Donoghue, then, has reason, if not history, on his side when he, quoting Levinas, argues 'that interiority constitutes an order in which "what is no longer possible historically remains always possible"' (BMT, 71).

Still, the overall thesis of *Being Modern Together* has much to do with history – with the suggestion that the modern imagination is a response to certain historical formations. Donoghue wants to argue that the moderns' emphasis on interiority constituted a response to the urban crowd and its opacity. To support his thesis, he employs Poe's story 'The Man of the Crowd' as an emblematic witness: 'Finally it is a parable about the ambition of the human imagination to comprehend what it sees; and the opacity which, as in this case, thwarts it. The crowd is crucial to Poe's story and to Baudelaire's poems because it represents the conditions with which the modern imagination has to cope. The city streets are the places in which social enclosures are, for the time being, dismantled: attorneys are no longer enclosed with their kind but are exposed to the proximity of clerks, thieves, and other orders. The story is a parable of imagination and reality, of what Wallace Stevens called the violence within in its dealings with the violence without' (BMT, 9).

Much had changed since the English Romantics, looking out over a 'congenial landscape,' could imagine that the landscape itself 'was susceptible to the feelings it aroused' (BMT, 17). Much had even changed since Wordsworth, in *The Prelude*, could look through an urban crowd, determined 'not to be oppressed by it' (BMT, 3). What had particularly changed was the rise of the city, a palpable social formation that the artist could not entirely ignore, even if he or she had wanted to. Unlike the Lake District, the city was not notably welcoming to the artist, Whitman aside. It did not invite the imagination to make what it would of it, but instead set its own conditions. Noting the difference, Donoghue writes, 'Felicities of the mind, in the presence of a congenial landscape, might be too easily achieved to be significant. Perhaps it needed the much more problematic experience of a body confronting other bodies, crowded in a city street, to make the question of subject and object a real test' (BMT, 17). The city refused to confirm the artist's sense of his or her own self-worth, resulting in a friction. This friction, says Donoghue, helped to provoke modern literature: 'I want to suggest that a distinctive modern literature arose not from the development of cities as such, but from the experience of crowds on city streets; or rather, the friction between the individual mind and appearances – city streets, crowds, anonymity – over which it had little or no control' (BMT, 12).

Artists were not the only ones who felt the city to be a threat to their individuality. But they did, thinks Donoghue, feel the threat most acutely, almost to the point that their sense of alienation came to certify their positions as artists. If 'the crowd in city streets seemed to bring a threat of anonymity, the loss of differentiation,' not to everyone but to 'the most sensitive among them' (BMT, 25), it might follow, as it often did, that the artist should begin to adopt a dismissive stance towards all those – i.e., the crowd – who were not artists. Yet the crowd's members, says Donoghue, were not to blame for the situation of the cities, and artists' snobbery was an inadequate response. This said, the oppressiveness of the modern city with its anonymous crowds – Eliot: 'Unreal City, / Under the brown fog of a winter dawn, / A crowd flowed over London Bridge, so many, / I had not thought death had undone so many' – still remained a problem. Crowds easily became objects and objects, when numerous, had a power to oppress. The individual still clung to an image of itself as spirit rather than matter, yet if all the forces were marshalled on the side of the latter, the question arose as to 'how can subject, or spirit, resist that oppression? Or must it yield to it at every point?' (BMT, 29).

The tendency was for the artist not to meet this oppression head on, but to retreat from it, to seek an asylum in the realm of the mind and its creations. One wanted to get 'beyond culture' (to use Trilling's phrase), to get beyond unsatisfactory social practices, even as one did not know what might replace them. '[T]he writers we think of as being modern,' writes Donoghue, 'are those who at least contemplated the possibility of seceding from society and disavowing the predominantly social understanding of human life' (BMT, 33). Trilling, thinks Donoghue, offers the best description of this situation in *The Liberal Imagination*, wherein he speaks of the novel and its 'long dream of virtue in which the will, while never abating its strength and activity, learns to refuse to exercise itself upon the unworthy objects with which the social world tempts it, and either conceives its own right objects or becomes content with its own sense of potential force' (BMT, 34). It is a key passage for Donoghue, making clear why he thinks Trilling one of his most important allies. Both critics tend to view twentieth-century social practices as inadequate and frequently tawdry. The more distance put between such practices and oneself, the better off one is. The modern world is replete with 'unworthy objects,' a judgment arrived at either by comparing them to those in other times and places, or by comparing them to one's own internal sense of what might and might not constitute a worthy object. The latter is not dismissed as an option. Yes, the mind reflects its world, but it is also the home of conscience, 'the capacity by which we reflect upon our actions in the light of our sense of justice' (BMT, 53). Justice may be found in society, but it originates elsewhere. Thus an artist such as Eliot, says Donoghue, 'maintains the responsibility of individual consciousness and at the same time forces it to acknowledge, at every point, a higher perspective than its own' (BMT, 48). This higher perspective might refer simply to an enlarged sense of experience or, more grandly, to God's will. In any event, there was a strong sense among modern artists that the society's objects were best judged according to a standard found elsewhere.

Yet, it is not an artist but an economist, Georg Simmel, whom Donoghue mentions as offering the clearest explanation, in *The Philosophy of Money* (1900), as to why it became necessary historically to live in relation to oneself rather than to society's proffered objects. He quotes Simmel as saying, '[e]very day and from all sides the wealth of objective culture increases, but the individual mind can enrich the forms and contents of its own development only by distancing itself still further from that culture and developing its own at a much slower pace' (BMT, 37). Modern culture creates more and more objects, not *ex nihilo* exactly, yet almost so. People, meanwhile, need to protect themselves from the onslaught, or risk having their identities eclipsed. If they do so, they will begin to 'pursue their development as an inner drama, rather than as a willing engagement with the contents of the objective culture' (ibid.). This situation is not exactly at one with that of Trilling, for 'Simmel doesn't allow for the situation ... in which the will refuses to exercise itself upon any contents provided by the world' (BMT, 39). Donoghue likes this quality of refusal, especially the way it makes more emphatic the adversarial relation extant between the artist and social practice. He quotes, approvingly, Trilling's remark, made in the 1960s, that '[n]ever, in a secular society, has the inner life seemed of such moment as it does in our culture' (BMT, 51). He additionally approves, in respective discussions of Stevens and Yeats, of the notions of reverie and the gaze. The first 'is the act of mind which displaces attention, so far as possible, from the object to the mind itself, its own processes and reflections' (BMT, 40). The second, the gaze (the term is Yeats's), functions similarly. It speaks, says Donoghue, of 'the mind's attention to its own processes and not at all to objects: it is inward, or as we say, reflexive' (BMT, 41). It also speaks of a provocation: 'The reason why such a form of attention exists is that under certain provocations the mind recoils from external objects and desires the sensation of paying attention to itself alone' (ibid.).

Donoghue finds enough provocation in the modern world to explain why the artist should wish to withdraw into the precinct of the imagination. Still, this starts to raise some questions, for if in *The Ordinary Universe* Donoghue began by stressing the need 'to acknowledge a reality not yourself, not your Supreme Fiction, a reality independent of your consciousness' (129), he now appears almost tempted to forswear the outward obligation. Certainly, he speaks of the modern artist as doing something like this, for he writes of their rejection of 'a long-established tradition' with which his own work has been identified: 'But there is a long-established tradition which would go further and hold that we ought to feel responsible for things on the analogy of our responsibility toward other people. If we feel that things and people are the work of God, however different their scale of being, it becomes a more pressing matter to respect things somewhat as we respect people. One of the marks of the literature we think of as modern, however, is a rejection of such responsibility, a turning away from the things in front of us, as if they constituted chiefly an obstacle to our relation to ourselves' (BMT, 39).

The fear is that high culture should, for the modernist, become but a version of the pastoral, a version that, in Adam Phillips's words, 'can be made to look unassailable because of the apparent complexity and subtlety and depth of its inclusions. A strangely modern version of the pastoral, because it persuades us to forget that pastoral is what it is. At its worst it is a refuge for masquerading as a profound engagement' ('Bellow and *Ravelstein*,' 1). Donoghue himself does not actually forswear the

tradition that holds us responsible to things, and, as such, he is not necessarily guilty of succumbing to the temptation mentioned by Phillips.[16]
Nonetheless, one observes the shift in tone, reflected in the greater sympathy for the Stevensian imagination, the sort that urges poets, when
faced with society's objects, to create 'a wonderful instead' (BMT, 61).
Interiority is felt to be under threat from theorists such as Fredric Jameson, among others, and Donoghue feels compelled to make a case for it,
even if this means branding Jameson's arguments 'wicked' for denying
'individuals ... recourse to their inwardness' (BMT, 47).[17] Here, then,
'[d]egraded objects are often the occasion of undegraded feelings and
thoughts' (ibid.), and the artist, when not engaged in battle with society's practices, does well to 'revert to the dialogue of the mind with
itself' (BMT, 53). This dialogue need not be thought of as merely a prelude to action, but can be valuable in and of itself. In fact, the latter is a
more modern stance, and it is what makes Pater, rather than Arnold,
modern literature's true father: 'The reason why Pater, and not Arnold,
is the begetter of Modernity in English literature is that he showed how
thinking could be valued as an intrinsic satisfaction: it did not have to be
justified in relation to its consequence as action in the world' (BMT,
53). It is a strong statement, bespeaking a grave disenchantment with
the world, and making intellectual hermeticism seem more attractive.
Donoghue would not put the matter in these terms. 'My own prejudice
suggests that one's feeling of being "beyond culture" is a valuable sentiment, provided one acknowledges that it would be better still to be
within an enlarged or more diverse culture' (BMT, 17). Yet in Donoghue's later work the mood is darker, as if he no longer believes that artists possess either the will or the power to transform society for the
better, so that we should do better either to take whatever satisfactions
avail themselves in the mind finding interest in its own processes, its
own intensities, or place our faith in something else. In *Walter Pater*
(1995), Donoghue argues that Pater's 'supreme value is not form but
force, energy, the flow of mind among phenomena. He settles for mobility as the condition under which he has access to either subject or
object, and makes the best of every moment by making the most of it'
(53).

Literature and Religion

In her introduction to *The Pure Good of Theory* (1992), Pauline Fletcher
observes that Donoghue, in the later work, 'begins to sound remarkably

like Stevens, the ruefully wise Stevens of "Final Soliloquy of the Interior Paramour," for whom the imagination is at once pitifully inadequate, "a single thing, a single shawl / Wrapped tightly round us, since we are poor," and "a power, the miraculous influence." In this context the assertion that "God and the imagination are one" is just that, a desperate assertion, a lone candle to light the dark, and it is made tentatively, almost humbly, without the slightest Romantic swagger' (PGT, 10). Fletcher knows how different Stevens and Donoghue are, even on the point of the imagination. (Cf. Donoghue: 'If you can translate "God" as "the imagination" and effect the translation as swiftly as Stevens did, you are not spilling real blood or crying bitter tears' [*Adam's Curse*, 100].) Nevertheless, she thinks the poet can be said to celebrate the imagination 'because there is no God,' whereas the critic, finding his allies where he can, joins the poet in this celebration because he thinks the imagination 'the only guarantee ... we have left of our spiritual nature' (PGT, 10). She is right, as she is when she claims that what Donoghue 'is proposing goes far beyond the boundaries of literary criticism; it constitutes not only a metaphysics and politics of the imagination, but, by implication, a metaphysics and politics of the soul' (ibid.).

For Donoghue, there is a clear relation between literature and metaphysics. He does not deny that literature has a 'relation to historical, cultural, economic, and political considerations. Of course it does' (PGT, 90). However, these are not the considerations that most interest him. Literature may be inseparable from material culture, but it has also long been hospitable to that desire that attends as much to how things *ought* to be as to how they *are*. The two projects are themselves not separable, obviously. Those who view literature in terms of its 'historical, cultural, economic and political considerations' – i.e., as to how things *are* – almost always do so with a sense of how things *ought* to be. And those who view literature in terms of how things *ought* to be almost always do so by reference to how things *are*. It is, then, more a question of emphases than of radical disagreement, though I do not wish to negate the significance of emphases. They constitute a difference. In any event, Donoghue's thinking about literature usually entails an element of critique, which is not surprising given his contention that '[t]he only real justification for literature is that it provides us with ways of imagining what it would be like to be different' (PGT, 96); and that '[e]thics defines a space between what is and what ought to be. So does aesthetics' (PGT, 68–9). And when metaphysics turns into religion, with its notion of a community of men and women who deliberately choose to live aslant to the values of mainstream,[18] material culture, then the character of critique that enjoins art and religion becomes even more linking. Or as Donoghue, in *Adam's Curse: Reflections on Religion and Literature*, writes: 'Why "reflections on religion and literature"? Why religion; why literature; why, even more to the point, the pathos of "and," bringing into the same field of reference values that may not want to be familiarly associated? Each is a deviation, and increasingly a vagabond, a nomad, a critic. Religion deviates from the material ways of the world. Literature deviates from the orders of economics, law, and rationality, even though it is obliged to them and could not exist without the political economy it affects to deride. And "and" deviates from the old consanguinities that made the assertion of "and" unnecessary. No wonder the values are hated, all three' (13).

Hence, says Donoghue, there is some justice in our judging Henry James's Strether by the standard of Art, so long as one understands that the standard is itself ostensible, that it, in its turn, speaks of a larger acknowledgment: 'Art ... imposes the standard by which life is to be judged, but only because the standard is available and high. Indeed, I would argue that what distinguishes James's central fiction is a remarkably dynamic relation between the admitted claims of the two worlds, this world and the world elsewhere; it is "the ache of the actual," as James called it, an ache of acknowledgement as well as an ache of dream' (OU, 77). Should the artist refuse this acknowledgment, there would be no further reason to identify art either with the ethical or with that which is more encompassing. Whether one calls the latter the Law as Such or God makes a difference, yet not so great a difference as that separating those who do and do not grant the acknowledgment. In the first instance, the difference might be as wide as that between Stevens and Donoghue, in the second instance, as wide as that between these two and, say, Jeff Koons and Madonna.[19] There is nothing wrong with the latter if there is nothing wrong with narcissism. But there *is* something wrong with narcissism, for we seem to be obliged to extend our sympathies beyond the self, to enlarge 'our lives so that they are not wholly contained here and now' ('The Idea of a Christian Society,' 232). This is what Donoghue had in mind when, in an early book, *Jonathan Swift*, he spoke of the need for an artist to imagine experience in its largest dimension: 'Even if you do not claim for your imagination any divine powers, you may posit a mode of knowledge beyond the human range within which human experience may be tolerably understood. That is: you retain the idiom of knowledge, but you posit a mode of knowledge raised to the nth degree. More briefly; you say, if human perspectives are fallible, there is always God. If human perspectives are inevitably limited, God is what is not limited' (JS, 75).

Of course, belief in God must, in one sense, be understood as an imaginative act. That is, if one accepts the distinction, first proposed by Gabriel Marcel, between 'belief that' and 'belief in.' Or as Donoghue puts the matter: '"Belief that" is assent to a statement or proposition as true. The content of the belief is open to verification or disproof. "Belief in" is an act of testimony to the believer's manner of being; an act of faith or trust, a commitment of attestation. As such, it is not subject to confirmation or disproof. If I believe in God, the Father Almighty, Creator of Heaven and Earth, that belief can't be confirmed or denied: it is immune to the production of belief' ('Book of Books Books,' 48). Belief stated in this form is, however, not simply imaginative or fideistic.[20] As a Christian, Donoghue believes that God enters into the world through the Incarnation. It may be that '[t]he Kingdom of God is within you,' as Christ, sounding like a Kantian, said (OU, 93);[21] but it is also found without, 'in the animation of natural forms, the work of Creation, and the Incarnation' (SG, 134). The sacred, then, intersects secular history. 'A Christian believes that secular history participates in sacred history and will eventually be found to coincide with it' (RA, 130). Their coincidence or intersection is most strongly felt in the person of Christ. Here, God dramatically enters into human history, takes on its garb, feels its attachments and triumphs, but more importantly experiences its most profound forms of abandonment, humiliation, and suffering. The Crucifixion should be a tragedy except that a merciful God chooses to forgive men and women their deed; and to transmute a negative event into a positive. 'The Christian sense of history [counts] as significant because God sent his beloved Son to redeem mankind' (ibid.), and in this gesture, thinks Donoghue, proffered an invitation that the imaginative person will see a way to accept.

One may choose not to accept, for it is not a command but an invitation. It entails a freedom. But should a person say yes, he or she gives a portion of this freedom away, as he or she enters into a conversation with 'the force not oneself that makes for truth' (SG, 200). For Donoghue, 'conversation is the privileged form of language' (FA, 93); and it – along with its first component, speech – binds us to another (in this instance, God) whereupon obligations begin to accrue. In the Christian tradition, 'the primal creative principle is identified as the Word of God, God uttering Himself, ... either directly or through the World He created' (ibid.). A person is called upon not only to act but to listen: to hear God's voice as it speaks through the prophets, Christ, the Church, family and friends, nature, and so forth. In answer, one seeks a return to, or a communion with, this primal voice. One acknowledges the presence of Divinity throughout one's world; and one seeks out the Origin of that presence. In this world, a person does not expect to meet God face to face, but he or she does believe it possible to move closer to, or further away from, God; and one naturally desires the former over the latter. The occasion involves, as René Girard says elsewhere, a form of 'mimetic desire.' That is, 'what Jesus advocates *is* mimetic desire. Imitate me, and imitate the father through me, he says, so it's twice mimetic' ('Violence, Difference, Sacrifice,' 23).

Desire, originating out of need, is a governing force in Donoghue. 'God is the name of my desire,' he quotes Tolstoy as saying, though the discussion is about Lawrence, an author who 'makes us feel that nothing less than a theology of desire would do, a revelation in words for which the actual words on the page are mere tokens in passing' (TF, 116). Certainly, for Donoghue, words themselves appear not enough. If they do not direct us towards an originating voice – be it a person's or the Deity's – they fail us. This is why he attaches such importance not only to the Christian tradition that sees God as presencing Himself in the Word but also to the parallel philosophical tradition of *Logos*. 'Logocentricism is the assumption that the primal act, so far as human history is concerned, is one by which a divine power uttered itself and created the world in the mode of an utterance. In that tradition, alphabetic or phonetic writing is received as a transcript of speech: it is deemed to be preceded by the primary act within the terms of *logos*' (FA, 98). What we do, as interlocutors or readers, is to seek out the source of what is spoken or written. We presume a personal presence behind the words, and are not satisfied until we can prove to ourselves that we are not mistaken. This is something that we take almost for granted as interlocutors but less so as readers. Authors are seldom nearby and often dead. But Donoghue argues that the situations remain analogous, and he labels the reader's desire to reverse chronology as 'epireading, following the Greek *epos*, which means speech or utterance' (ibid.). In this tradition, the reader is often imagined as 'trying to find the secret of each text, like a message lodged in a bottle floating in the sea. But it would be more accurate to say that the object of discovery is not a message or a secret but a person. We read a poem not to enlighten ourselves but to verify the axiom of presence: we read to meet the other' (FA, 99).

Granted, we might very well read a poem for reasons that have nothing to do with the author – e.g., to enlighten ourselves. Yet Donoghue's point is well taken, that our interest in literature generally involves a fundamental desire to live beyond ourselves, to escape the loneliness of our condition. We ultimately desire communion less with another text than another person. And maybe not even another person but with God, especially if we should think that the latter is more discernible in those things, literature included, that manifest traits like generosity, grace, intelligence, measure, proportion, and wit. In any event, it is unlikely that we should need literature, this intermediary, if what is best about our selves did not so often reside within the shadows. In a sense, literature reminds us that all is not lost; that all are not fools; and that if our dealings with the world and its people should lead us to think so, it is only because we have not pursued the matter far enough: 'The normal conditions in which we meet one another are puerile. The advantage of literature is that it makes a more complete meeting possible; a statement not at all invalidated by the fact that in literature the other we meet is virtual rather than actual' (FA, 101).

This last point about virtuality constitutes something like a catch, however. It is what prevents us from ever knowing the other, not to mention God, completely. It is an important concept for Donoghue, having the same importance for his thought as that of the aporia for Derrida. In both instances, the desire to march towards the object of cognition finds itself deflected into an adjacent terrain, be it that of the symbol in Donoghue or that of *différance* in Derrida. In any event, for Donoghue, virtuality is a concept that he identifies with the fact that the art work, be it a poem or a sonata, is always in a state of suspension, wherein ultimate ambitions are found pending but never resolved. He grants that a work of art interacts with the world, both reflecting and shaping it, but there is another aspect of the work that he finds more interesting, perhaps because it is more singular: its ability to round itself off, to present itself as a thing unto itself. Form is at the heart of what makes one thing, and not another, art. In *The Pure Good of Theory*, where the problem of form is posited as crucial (even as Donoghue admits its difficulties), he writes: 'Suzanne Langer is right when she speaks of all artistic elements as "virtual, created for perception." It is difficult to say even as much as that without incurring a further charge of wanting to remove works of art from social, economic, and political consideration. In a sense, that is precisely what I want to do, if only to be able to say that a work of art is not an editorial or a letter to the Editor; it is a form, the trace of a symbolic act, and as a form it exists only to be perceived' (PGT, 66).

Donoghue's tone is almost polemical, yet one need not be against the study of art vis-à-vis its material conditions to appreciate the possibility that art might raise problems that are, *more or less*, its own. If we continue to use terms such as 'art,' 'literature,' and 'music,' we need to be able to say what distinguishes these from everything else, to be able to say when, or under what conditions, something ceases to be considered, say, a poem and becomes something else. True, our answers here will change from one epoch to the next, and from one community to another, and this makes it imperative that we not dismiss those investigations that address the problem of a work's material conditions. It is a weakness of Donoghue's criticism that on such matters he often lets his ire speak in the place of his judgments. Nevertheless, the question of what makes literature different from other disciplines remains worthy of investigation. It is, as noted earlier, the one that has most recently garnered Donoghue's attention, again particularly in relation to the matter of form: 'Literature is different from either a conversation or a discourse; it's a question of trying to see what the difference amounts to. That's why I think the issue of form is inescapable, and why I would now take any risk involved in being a formalist. We must somehow say what form means. That's why I value Marcuse's insistence on the formal value of art, that it is in its form that literature is revolutionary, not in its content. It is in its content having become form or having fulfilled itself as form' (PGT, 86–7).[22]

Form is one of those concepts considered central to the discussion of art though its definition remains elusive. It suggests qualities that are either mathematical or geometrical, and though it is easy enough to bring these qualities forward when discussing a Beethoven sonata or a Henri Moore sculpture, the matter becomes more problematic with, for instance, a Robert Rauschenberg 'combine' or a Jenny Holzer electronic billboard. But the question of form will not go away. It remains crucial to the definition of art, even as we tend to think of it as something that has been consigned to our conceptual attic.[23] Meanwhile, for Donoghue, form is most linked to the propensity of art to be virtual, to be present for perception alone. There is about art a not-yet quality. It instigates a process of perception or contemplation but it does not require action. In fact, action, as the consequence of reading a novel or viewing a picture, should almost always constitute a premature response, a refusal to take everything in. In this view, art encourages us to refrain from the desire to put things in their place, to dominate them. It is, as such, an ethic in its own way, one that both instructs us about the gap between things as they *are* and as they *ought* to be, and about the danger of believing that we require only a new politics, full of brave action, in order to close the gap. Politics measures itself against the compass of historical events, whereas art speaks, at least for Donoghue, of a possibility that exists aslant from historical time. It is in this light that he refers to Goethe, who, in a letter describing the relief of *Phigalia*, expressed the conviction that the energies surrounding the aesthetic project must, as Donoghue notes, 'be recognized as the emotions of hope, anticipation, and astonishment. The condition of art ... is probability, "but within the realm of probability the highest ideal must be supplied which does not otherwise appear"' (PGT, 63). Cultural materialists might seek to explain all things, art included, in the light of their historical contexts, but contexts – especially when we make the crucial acknowledgment that the future is part of any context – are always open-ended and thereby subject to change. We can never say exactly what a thing is or has been. We can, however, invest such a thing with our hopes and expectations, and this is what art, in Donoghue's formulation, does. It strives to say how things might be otherwise, how they might be better.

Art is the discipline most sensitive and responsive to the quality of things as they exist in abeyance. Other disciplines – e.g., history, politics, economics, medicine, etc. – cannot wait. They are caught up in the world of action, of doing things now. But art is less intertwined with action than contemplation, with the imagining not only of how things are and have been, but how they might be. Form is equated with the stepping away from the contingent. It may speak of an interest, but it does something more. It signals the 'reversal of human subjectivity[,] ... no longer defined in terms of an *in itself*, nor by a *for itself*,' but rather in terms of its adherence, in Socrates's words, to 'a pattern ... laid up in heaven.'[24] It is reflective of the artist's reaching beyond his or her partial experience to something much larger, something capable of encompassing and reconciling events that, looked at otherwise, might seem in conflict. And it is in this sense that art, through its identification with form, finds itself linked to matters such as autonomy and unity, matters that speak, perhaps, as much to the point of art's potential as anything else. 'If, as Pater thought, all the arts aspire to the conditions of music, it is because music, or at least certain kinds of music, testifies to the possibility of Deleuze's "unity of an immaterial sign and an entirely spiritual meaning"' (AWM, 24).

The music that Donoghue has in mind can be likened to that which moves Langer, whom he quotes, to say, 'All music creates an order of virtual time, in which its sonorous forms move in relation to each other – always and only to each other, for "nothing else exists there"' (BMT, 68). And yet, as the reference to Deleuze suggests, this order is always *in potentia*. Music may suggest an order that is timeless, but it does not itself escape time. In fact, music does not so much escape time as it '"makes time audible, and its forms and continuity sensible"' (AWM, 94).[25] Hence the point of disagreement that Donoghue articulates respecting Lévi-Strauss's statements on music: 'I don't understand Lévi-Strauss's saying that the time of the music was "transmuted" into a synchronic totality, if he means me to take seriously the spatial form he implies, or even if he has in mind that the music happens "simultaneously." The sonata didn't; it enacted a relation to time such that the themes, cadences, repetitions, and rhythms seemed to want to realize themselves in a time enhanced by that striving, and by the momentum of it. It was the difference between Chronos and Kairos, between mere passing time and time animated by value and power' (AWM, 93).

Understood this way, music, like art in general, is conceived as crucially intertwined with the question of time, but especially as time entails the quality of tense. Time speaks of what has been and what is. It also speaks of what is not yet, of what is in abeyance. In short, it speaks of a future, wherein what are now partial understandings may come to be more fully understood. Or may not – that is, the immanent meanings that we meet in the course of time may, even as they lead us forward into the future, hold on to their secrets beyond the point of time itself. This, I think, is the sense of Donoghue's reference to 'the imminence of a revelation which does not occur, the veil that continues to tremble, forever still to be enjoyed: it a question of tense, in which the present leans from itself toward a future indefinitely proposed and postponed' (AWM, 92). So if art is crucially intertwined with the question of time, it is because it is crucially intertwined with the question of immanent meanings, of the way in which things speak of a unity even as we fail to comprehend it. Not everyone will locate art here, but Donoghue does. And he knows, even as the company dwindles, that the tradition is too rich ever to die out. Not when one can, as he does, support the argument with the brilliance of, say, a Borges, when the latter writes: 'Music, states of happiness, mythology, faces belaboured by time, certain twilights and certain places try to tell us something, or have said something we should have missed, or are about to say something; this imminence of a revelation which does not occur is, perhaps, the aesthetic phenomenon' (ibid.).

For Donoghue, 'poetry is adequate only insofar as it beckons beyond itself' (AWM, 114). Particularly, as it beckons towards the realm of the inexpressible, that which, as Wittgenstein argued, functions as the ground for all that finds expression: 'What is inexpressible – what I find mysterious and am not able to express – is the background against which whatever I could express has its meaning' (AWM, 120). The realm of the inexpressible, of silence, becomes, in Donoghue's later work, especially identified with the notion of the Deity, as language becomes understood as a characteristically human effort to sort things out: 'Language is a change of natures, it changes every nature into human nature. God has to put up with the indignity' (*Adam's Curse*, 23). Language, even the language of the Bible, follows an anthropomorphic impulse, so that as soon as 'they [authors, both Biblical and more generally (Milton, for instance)] make God speak, they turn him into a person in the ordinary untheological sense. In speech, God is forced to give up the singularity of His silence and to move into a human world of discourse. There are no special words for God which can express the divinity without changing God into a man' (*Adam's Curse*, 22). So if poetry, or philosophy and religion for that matter, is going to beckon in the direction of the mysterious, it will need to take the symbolic dimension of its language more seriously than it has, of late, been wont to do. Certainly for Donoghue, the symbol remains a crucial component of poetic language, and while others, most notably de Man in *Allegories of Reading*, have sought to disinvest the symbol of its potency, of its power to suggest a world elsewhere,[26] Donoghue has continued to see symbolism as a more powerful force than allegory. For instance, in a review centring on de Man's criticism ('The Limits of Language'), Donoghue recalls it as

> a commonplace that writers from Kant, Goethe, and Coleridge to Yeats and Eliot set their minds astir upon notions of symbol and allegory. Usually they valued symbol over allegory because symbols held out the promise of organic unity – Unity of Being, in Yeats's phrase – and allegory was merely an instrument for conveying a moral lesson. Among many things Coleridge said about symbol, the most tangible is that it is characterized by 'the translucence of the Eternal through and in the Temporal' and that 'while it enunciates the whole, it abides itself as a living part in that Unity, of which it is the representative.' Allegory, a lesser thing, is 'but a translation of abstract notions into a picture-language which is itself nothing but an abstraction from objects of the senses.' (43)

In *William Butler Yeats*, Donoghue writes, 'Symbol redeems fact, because through symbol the imagination enters experience, as Christ redeemed fact in the Incarnation' (71). The allusion to the Incarnation is clearly pivotal to Donoghue's understanding of the symbol. For him, symbol guarantees 'the presence of the supernatural in the natural.'[27] It speaks of those moments – e.g., Wordsworth's 'spots of time' – when the world and our consciousness of it seem to exist in harmony. Mostly, our relation to the world bespeaks a certain friction. What we want and what the world allows are seldom the same thing. But there are times when the disharmony appears to give way, and we seem to stand in a relation of unusual sympathy vis-à-vis the world. The sympathy may be false, the product of our own imagining. Or it may be true. It is impossible to say. Yet for a long time, the romantic symbol has 'been understood as the sign of a possible, if intermittent and unforeseeable reconciliation between man and nature, the being of consciousness and natural being' (PGT, 42). And while a sceptic is apt to distrust this mood, there is no reason why others need follow suit. There is good reason not to – for it is to our benefit to believe the world not altogether hostile to our desires. Donoghue does not believe that it is hostile, and his reason for this connects with his 'belief in' the Incarnation. 'God's love for His creatures is revealed in the animation of natural forms, the works of creation, and the Incarnation' (SG, 134). Men and women are called upon to acknowledge and to accept this love, and, in effect, to reconcile themselves to their world.

For Donoghue, the romantic symbol is one way this reconciliation takes place. He has, as noted, not always been so friendly to the interest of symbolism, for though he has long believed that the imagination plays a crucial part in our ability to recognize the world's immanence, he has been uneasy about the ease with which the same interest converts theories of inspiration into theories of imagination. The problem is that what begins as a theological narrative ends up as an aesthetic narrative, wherein the artist inserts him- or herself into the space of the Divine. In *Thieves of Fire*, Donoghue wrote: 'Imagination is the secular equivalent of God as creator, including especially God as self-creator, in Coleridge's phrase "the infinite I AM." Theology becomes aesthetics; hence our questions about the nature of the imagination, and its relation to the activity of the senses' (50). It is, in his view, not a happy progress, and he should be hesitant to validate it except that, in his own day, intellectuals promoting religious narratives are forced to make allies. The arts have generally been kind to such quasi-theological values as the imagination and mystery. This, in turn, made it easier to conceive a kinship between

the aesthetic and religious realms. Like Kermode and Steiner, Donoghue continues to argue on behalf of this kinship, even as he deems the
religious the more important realm: 'Even in a world mostly secular, the
arts can make a space for our intuition of mystery, which isn't at all the
same thing as saying that the arts are a substitute for religion. There is
nothing in art or in our sense of art which corresponds to my belief in
God. In religion, our faith and love are directed beyond ourselves. In art,
faith doesn't arise' (AWM, 129). In making statements of this sort, Donoghue certainly takes a risk. Adam Phillips's remark, 'Donoghue's piety
grates on one's own' ('Provocation,' 9), reflects a common response
among educated readers. I, however, think the risk worth taking, and
admire the refusal to be politic, to repress one's religious beliefs because
one's colleagues think them anachronistic.

The most notable difference between art and religion, Donoghue
suggests, resides in their different claims with regard to redemption.
The claims made for art usually pertain to its capacity to make us sensitive to the existence of others, in addition to making us more respectful
of all that we do not know – i.e., respectful of the world's mystery. Less
often does one hear of salvific claims made on art's behalf, though in
The Pure Good of Theory Donoghue criticizes Hillis Miller for making, in a
discussion of James's *What Maisie Knew*, a claim of this sort: 'The book
exists for perception, not for obedience or disobedience. Miller is perhaps taking literally Matthew Arnold's notion that when we have abandoned religious belief, we may be still saved by great literature. It is not
true' (PGT, 82). And, in a more general sense, romanticism might be
construed as proffering a salvific claim of some sort, albeit vague. That
is, when the artist presumes to usurp the role of the priest, a new claim
is made for art akin to religion's claim of salvation, even if the claim
comes couched, as in Stevens's 'Sunday Morning,' in naturalistic terms:
'The sky will be much friendlier then than now. / A part of labor and a
part of pain, And next in glory to enduring love. / Not this dividing and
indifferent blue.'[28]

Donoghue, however, does not take art's salvific claim seriously. He
makes himself an ally of romanticism, but he does not wish to confuse
art with religion. The first is valued for its formal properties and for
its ability to spur us beyond ourselves; the second is valued for the
demands it makes upon our daily lives and for the hope of salvation
that it holds out. When Hillis Miller suggests that we find a way to 'emulate' Maisie's act of renunciation, Donoghue replies that this is too
great a confusion of an aesthetic with an ethical consideration. A reli-

gious narrative might demand our emulation but not a belletristic one: 'I would be willing to read the *New Testament* in that spirit, and to argue the parable of the sower and the fate of the seeds he sows, but that is because the words issue, I believe, from Christ, and have meaning upon his authority. We are not dealing with Henry James and his fictions' (PGT, 82). Clearly, Donoghue takes the Incarnation seriously. He believes Christ the Son of God, and this belief will always make art a subordinate interest. His adjudication is not meant as a slur upon art. Rather, it simply testifies to the acknowledgment that all things, art included, have their meaning in God. (Irenaeus: 'Nihil cavum neque sine signo apud Deum.') Others, like Kenneth Burke in *Permanence and Change*, might argue that meaning (in Donoghue's words) be built 'from the ground up, the ground being man as symbol-using animal' (ibid.), but Donoghue finds this insufficient: 'This is fine as far as it goes, but it doesn't go very far. And when is the fresh unity of purpose to emerge? And whose purpose will it be? And how will we prevent such a purpose from being a highly controversial linkage, just like the theological one?' (ibid.) Meanings will be contested whether we think of them as deriving from God or from men and women. There is no doubt about this. What Donoghue wants no part of, however, are those attempts (and he places Burke's efforts here) to foster a new homogeneity among peoples, wherein the values of cooperation, ingratiation, and persuasion are extolled at the expense of the real differences that distinguish one community from another. He grants that many of these differences (beliefs included) are as happenstance as the place of one's birth. He says that his own Catholicism – so intertwined with his criticism,[29] the subject of our interest – is fully the consequence of his having been born in Ireland: 'I would not be a Catholic but for the fact that I was born and brought up in a Catholic family in Ireland' (PGT, 100). Nevertheless, he wants to hold on to these differences, and is suspicious of attempts such as Burke's to translate the harm out of the Christian religion so as to make for a more congenial universalism: 'Being a Christian I should want the harm left in the Christian religion, and I should feel that Burke's program, however stylishly grounded upon the poetic metaphor, is feasible only if we all agree not to recall the divisive topics that he would translate out of dogmatic existence. And few of us could make or keep that promise. What life would be like in a Burkean condition of "pure" ingratiation I do not know. Most poems are better for a good deal of impurity. And my own life seems to need a great deal of argumentative impurity to make it feel substantial.

With that, we are back again in the gritty world of specific belief, specific commitment' (CC, 180).

Donoghue does not wish to blur the distinction between art and religion. He may have authored a book – *The Arts without Mystery* – that suggests, in Fletcher's words, that art is 'a spiritual prelude ... to a greater mystery' (PGT, 100), but when asked directly about the matter, he prefers to keep the realms separate: 'I would be suspicious of any attempt to approach religious conviction by way of an engagement with art' (ibid.). The suspicion has do with the specificity of his religious commitment. He grants that Christianity, like art, has much to do with questions of mystery and spirituality, but it starts off as a set of specific beliefs and practices, and if these are not cogent and suasive, no appeal to the spiritual is going to save them. Religion, like art, is best approached through its particulars, so it does not surprise to hear Donoghue speak of his commitment to Catholicism's doctrine and dogma: 'My relation to religion is doctrinal and dogmatic. I don't value my religious belief for the emotions it gives me, but because it enables me to believe in something that is independent of me. I acknowledge the doctrines of the Catholic Church because I believe them to be true. It is not because I feel good in their presence, or because they give me a further range of emotions' (ibid.).

It is unusual, these days, to hear an academic talk in terms of specific religious commitment. The academy fosters its own brand of ecumenicalism, professing support for all faiths so long as they remain cultural categories rather than doctrinal beliefs. Religions bereft of content are what the academy allows, but religions bereft of content are rather empty signifiers. What is the point of a religion if it does not commit one to particular practices? If it does not make a difference between the way one lives one's life and the way others do? One asks these questions knowing that the academy often conflates religious belief with intolerance, and that it deems the history of religions an inexhaustible display of persecution and conflict. In *Framing the Sign*, Jonathan Culler writes: 'The complicity of literary studies with religion today is a subject that has scarcely been broached but cries out for attention, not least because religion provides a legitimation for many reactionary or repressive forces in the United States and is arguably a greater danger today than ideological positions critics do spend their time attacking' (78). Among the sins committed in the name of religion – Culler has Christianity particularly in mind – are sexism, racism, and sadism, sins so overt and outrageous that Culler thinks it imperative that criticism make the unmasking of theistic beliefs one of its top priorities: 'The essential step is to take up the relation of our teaching and writing to religious discourse and to maintain a critical attitude when discussing religious themes – that is, not to assume that theistic beliefs deserve respect, any more than we would assume that sexist or racist beliefs deserve respect. This might involve us in comparing Christianity with other mythologies when we teach works imbued with religion, or making sadism and sexism of religious discourse an explicit object of discussion ...' (80).

Culler's remarks seem of a cloth with that same intolerance that he likes to locate elsewhere, as for instance in those 'arrogant' Catholics whose political manoeuverings, we are told, even Star Wars Republicans think beneath them (78).[30] Yet if Culler is more injurious than insightful, his point that the academy's lip service in the direction of religions means that they are not taken seriously is well taken: 'There has ... arisen in our day an assumption that one should not argue about religion. This is sometimes taken as evidence that we pay lip service to religion but grant it no importance' (77). Culler wants the academy to take religious beliefs seriously so as to expedite their expulsion from academic and normative discourse. I would prefer to see these beliefs taken seriously not because I think them all worthy and sensible – I do not – but because we owe it to ourselves to separate out those that are from those that are not, and to integrate the better of these into our normative values. One might say that this is what we already do, and this is, more or less, true. At the same time, especially in the United States, the segregation of the religious from mainstream culture – following the principle that separates church and state – has led to a discernible impoverishment, along the lines of another, formerly revered, political principle: separate but equal. The tendency is to think that only the excluded culture suffers, but the reality is that all experience a loss. Few would defend the quality of our public religious discourse. It is generally sentimental and insipid, when it is not bigoted and mean. Culler's own arguments testify to this, for despite his disparagement of religions, he gives no evidence of understanding them or why so many people are committed to one religion or another. Fools rush in where academics dare not go – one more fact testifying to the cultural inferiority of the United States vis-à-vis England: 'If religion has subsided in England, it has not in the United States; on the contrary, it has become a formidable public force' (77). The regret, thinks Culler, is that we have 'no American Monty Python[, ...] no vital tradition of anti-religious satire that would keep the sanctimonious in check' (77).[31]

Donoghue does not escape Culler's ire. Culler quotes Donoghue's criticism of Empson's attacks upon Christianity but not without slurring an entire religious community: '"the most tedious part of his mind," as Catholic Denis Donoghue smugly calls it' (76). Culler's apposition bespeaks its own smugness; and, in *Words Alone: The Poet T.S. Eliot,* Donoghue retorts: 'The implication, that only by being a Catholic could anyone find Empson's hatred of Christianity tedious, speaks all too clearly of a particular prejudice on Culler's part, which of course will not come in for any severe comment' (225). The suggestion is that 1) Culler, in the tradition of Empson, is a bigot; and 2) that the academy will not object to this behaviour, for it either believes what only Culler is careless enough to say, or it is indifferent. Again, Donoghue writes: 'It is now not only permissible but almost obligatory, in intellectual circles, to attack Christianity and to deride any Christian's faith – and the attack is regularly made by people who claim to be appalled by anti-Semitism. To hate Christianity is not deemed to reflect badly upon the hater' (233). Donoghue has a point, but so does Adam Kirsch when he writes that 'this equation misses the point. The intellectual revolt against Christianity in the West is a revolt from within, and is not stained with blood, as anti-Semitism has so terribly been' (17).

In *Words Alone,* Donoghue seeks to offer a measured appraisal of the charge of anti-Semitism that, in the 1990s, was repeatedly lodged against Eliot, most notably by Cynthia Ozick, in the pages of the *New Yorker,* and Anthony Julius, in *T.S. Eliot: Anti-Semitism and Literary Form* (1996), to the point it has become de rigueur to speak of Eliot as an anti-Semite. Donoghue is also interested in the accusation as it relates to the social criticism, especially in the tenth chapter devoted to Eliot's 1939 volume *The Idea of a Christian Society.* Donoghue does not think very highly of the volume – 'It is a difficult book to like' (*Words Alone,* 210) – nor of an earlier volume, *After Strange Gods* (1934). But he finds – prematurely I think – the fact that Eliot 'is still accused of anti-Semitism ... an injustice' (225), arguing that 'if we attend to the detail as well as to the broad outline of his social thought, even his most notorious utterances become understandable, if still contentious' (213). Donoghue makes the attempt to put an offending phrase such as 'free-thinking Jews' (from *After Strange Gods* [1994]) in a context more hospitable to Eliot, viewing the remark as of piece with Eliot's later expressed notion that what makes a Jew a Jew or a Christian a Christian is a discernible religious practice. Or as Eliot, in 1962, wrote: 'It seems to me that there should be close culture-contact between devout and practising Chris-

tians and devout and practising Jews. Much culture-contact in the past
has been within those neutral zones of culture in which religion can be
ignored, and between Jews and Gentiles both more or less emancipated
from their religious traditions' (216). Donoghue scores some successes
this way, and he is to be commended for attempting to set the authentic
philo-Semitic side of Eliot's thinking against the anti-Semitic utterances,
all of which, as Kirsch points out, 'date from before World War II' ('So
Elegant, So Intelligent,' 17), and might be thought of as reflective of 'a
common class prejudice or a questionable outgrowth of his theology,'
standing 'far from the center of Eliot's thought and art' (ibid.). But
there is also a rancorousness about Donoghue's defence of Eliot on this
score that proves self-defeating. Likewise there are too many scholastic
efforts to explain away lines such as those in 'Gerontion' ('And the jew
squats on the window-sill, the owner, / Spawned in some estaminet of
Antwerp') and 'Burbank with a Baedeker: Bleinstein with a Cigar': 'The
main issue is: who is speaking this poem? Is it Eliot in his own voice and
the person and on his own responsibility?' (*Words Alone*, 103). And it certainly seems a mistake, in a book ostensibly about Eliot, to let the discussion, however reasonable, drift into the area of Mideast politics: 'Israel
has shown that in war and peace it conducts itself in much the same
spirit as any other worldly nation and is just as ready as its opponents to
play rough and dirty' (225).

Yet to return to Donoghue's main point, it is to observe that what
Eliot, in *The Idea of a Christian Society*, offers should best be understood in
the light of the attempt to imagine what a Christian society might be like
if it should live according to its ideal of itself: 'Eliot does not analyze any
society that exists and thinks of itself as Christian. He asks, rather: what
is the end, the ultimate aim, of a Christian society, whether or not this
end is at all discernible in any existing society or any past society? What
would a Christian society be, if it were to come into being? And what
changes in a Christian's social attitudes would be required to bring it
about?' (219). Donoghue does not share Eliot's longing for a Christian
society – in present circumstances, how could he? how could anyone? –
but he does not mock the longing (expressed more than a half-century
ago) either. He realizes that the homogeneity of Eliot's proposed society
goes against the value of heterogeneity that we now honour, but this
does not make the proposal, considered as an abstraction, inconceivable. There are and have been states constructed around religious
beliefs, just as there are and have been states constructed around ethnic
or economic beliefs. The United States, for instance, is amazingly homo-

geneous with regard to its peoples' economic beliefs. There are certainly other beliefs that we speak of as if one, making it clear that heterogeneity does not cancel out homogeneity, or vice versa. Donoghue reproaches those readers who assume, like Blackmur, that '"a Christian state, a Christian education, a Christian philosophy, are as outmoded as the Christian astronomy which accompanied them when they flourished"' (222). The argument, says Donoghue, is a poor one, for it not only ignores the fact that millions of people still profess a Christian belief, it also ignores the fact that the church had in the end 'no real difficulty in surviving the passage of Ptolemaic astronomy. A Christian state is, theoretically, just as conceivable as a Jewish one or an Islamic one; a Christian education is still feasible, and a Christian philosophy is demonstrably available in more contemporary philosophers than one has time to read' (ibid.). But the argument, Donoghue reminds us, is being waged in the realm of the theoretical. Eliot's explicit model for *The Idea of a Christian Society* is Coleridge's *On the Constitution of the Church and State, According to the Idea of Each,* a work also reliant upon the notion of 'as if.' 'By *idea*,' Coleridge writes, 'I mean (in this instance) that conception of a thing which is not abstracted from any particular state, form, or mode, in which the thing may happen to exist at this or that time; nor yet generalized from any number or succession of such forms or modes; but which is given by the knowledge of *its ultimate aim*' (quoted in *Words Alone*, 218).

For Donoghue, the thrust of both Eliot's poetry and prose is to remind his reader that things should be understood in the light of their 'ultimate aim.' 'It was more typical of him to deal with each situation by bringing to bear upon it a higher perspective – religious, invariably – and a more demanding system of values' (216–17). Donoghue is aware of the risk entailed in this position, and he makes it clear that he thinks Eliot's interest in a world elsewhere made him too disinterested in the immediate political event, much the way that Kermode found him strangely disinterested in the Spanish Civil War,[32] and Steiner found him so with regard to the Holocaust.[33] At the same time, Donoghue has an interest in seeing things in the light of their idea or ultimate aim, and his meditations this way are what I find most interesting in the discussion. Here, in addition to the allusion to Coleridge, he alludes to the work of four philosophers. First, he refers to Socrates' statement (in response to Glaucon's asking where the ideal city might be found) that 'Perhaps it is laid up as a pattern in heaven, which he who desires may behold and, beholding, may set his own house in order' (219). Second, he refers to Kant's distinction between a concept and an idea ('which is independent of experience and has its source in reason' [220]). Third, he refers to Gilles Deleuze, who in his discussion of Kant (*Kant's Critical Philosophy*), writes that 'in order to find a middle term which makes possible the attribution of an *a priori* concept to *all* objects, reason can no longer look to another concept (even an *a priori* one) but must form *Ideas* which go beyond the possibility of experience' (quoted in *Words Alone*, 223). And then, lastly, he refers to a conversation with Robert Nozick, wherein it was said that 'the content of an ideal ... is not exhausted by the way or ways in which we manage to work it,' but 'also includes its realization by better people': 'When we try to pursue a philosophical ideal, Nozick remarked, we associate our lives with how the ideal would have worked out in other and better worlds or with how it might still work out in a better world. I interpret Nozick as saying that an idea, in Eliot's or Coleridge's or Plato's terms, might if nothing else enrich the reverberation of our lives. Or, especially in *The Idea of a Christian Society*, it might enforce upon us the scruple of attending to a daunting system of values' (224).

The idea proposes a reality that is not ours, but might be. It asks that we live our lives in response to it. It holds out a promise, fulfillable only in the future, if then. And it urges us to live our lives in the light of an understanding larger than either present or past material conditions can justify. Whether we do so or not depends, perhaps, upon the quality of our imaginations, upon whether we can conceive of a world better than the one in which we live. For Donoghue, this is where literature comes in, for it trains us to 'imagine the forms and shapes of being, other than her own' (224). It may be true that literature is not capable of saving us, that to think so is like, in Eliot's words, thinking 'that the wallpaper will save us when the walls have crumbled.' Nevertheless, literature – or the imaginative operations that it encourages – helps us to understand just what is at stake in the course of our decisions and acts; and it pushes us to consider not only how things are but also how they might be. Hence, to return to Blackmur's overlooking the conditional nature of Eliot's proposal, it would appear to disqualify the critic as a competent judge of the proposal: 'As an unbeliever, Blackmur could not imagine that some other readers, Christians perhaps, would find the contemplation of Eliot's idea of a Christian society a chastening or otherwise edifying experience. "Mr. Eliot's ideal of a Christian society – his idea of what is aimed at – cannot be realized in this world." [...] So much the worse, I would say' (230).

The Theory Debates

In 'The Use and Abuse of Theory,' Donoghue quotes Hillis Miller offering a definition of literary theory: 'I mean by "literary theory" the shift from the hermeneutical process of identifying the meaning of a work to a focus on the question of how that meaning is generated' (ibid.). Described this way, theory would refer to those critical practices that are less attentive to the art object than to the environments in which its meaning is 'produced.' So, rather than seeing the works as calling for a new response or theory – the way, says Donoghue, modernists works such as *The Waste Land, Ulysses, The Waves* and *The Cantos* did – contemporary critical practice begins in theory and attends to literary works afterwards, as a way of illustration. Or as Miller, in the same quotation, observes: 'Theory tends to become a primary means of access to the works read. These works now tend to be redefined as "examples" demonstrating the productive effectiveness of this or that theory. In such a situation, literary theory even tends to become a primary object for study in itself' (ibid.). As one might expect, the placement of theory before literature strikes Donoghue as an instance of placing the cart before the horse: 'Generally, it seems to me that Theory, far from being a primary means of access to the works read, becomes a primary means of endlessly postponing access to them. Or if works of literature are read, they are read merely as illustrations of a theory already fixed: it is the fate of the theory merely to be fulfilled, and of the work of literature merely to gratify the theory' (ibid.).

No doubt, Donoghue overstates the matter, for he differs from most contemporary literary academics in his view that literature's priority should be more acknowledged than questioned. Others have tended to question it, however, and it not clear that they should be denied the option. Granted, it is easy to think that literature's value is less contingent than inherent. Yet it is a hard case to make to those who do not start with the assumption, and most contemporary academics do not. Hence, writes Donoghue, the 'concentration "on the question of how that meaning is generated" keeps theorists busy; especially proponents of Marxism, Feminism, Minority Discourse, Cultural Studies, Deconstruction, New Historicism, and other schools of indictment' ('Bewitched, Bothered and Bewildered,' 46). That last phrase is, obviously, a slur, in keeping with Donoghue's statement, to a *Chronicle of Higher Education* reporter, that 'literary critics have become district attorneys,' followed by the rhetorical question: 'Once you've decided that

Shakespeare was a fascist pig, what then?' (10/13/93; A 17). Donoghue is a superb critic, yet there are reoccurring problems with tone, especially when the discussion turns to contemporary theoretical and critical practices. The difficulty may be a reflection of his passion for literature and his profound regret at witnessing a beloved discipline turn itself into something quite different. The critics whom Donoghue most esteems – e.g., James, Eliot, Blackmur, Burke, Empson, Kermode, Ransom, Tate – are those identified with the study of literature qua literature, sensitive to its inner workings, to its schemes and tropes, and to those authors who show themselves its masters. It is a magnificent tradition that he honours, and the only surprise is that there are not more critics, today, to do the same: to acknowledge the debt. This seems particularly surprising if one admits, as I think we must, that our passage from, say, New Criticism to present-day theory entailed less a repudiation than a need to complicate the question. Dickstein, for instance, writes: 'What finally signed the death warrant for the New Criticism was not its conceptual weaknesses but its practical triumphs. Like all successful movements, the New Criticism died when it was universally assimilated' (*Double Agent*, 38). Or as David Damrosch, reflecting upon the dissertations that graduate students now author, writes: 'To be sure, they're rejected the New Critical approach they were taught in college, but their feminist-deconstructionist dissertation is still a Jane Austen dissertation after all, and in fact it still incorporates New Critical methods of close reading. *Something* has changed, but much has not, if you compare their dissertations with the ones that their sponsors wrote thirty years before' (*We Scholars*, 64). The New Historicist or feminist critic is still expected to grasp the rhetorical dimension, even richness, of a literary text, and while the addition of more things to be responsible for makes the critic's job all the harder, the best critics manage to get the job done, sometimes brilliantly. Not surprising then is Paul de Man's acknowledgment of the continuity between New Criticism and theory and his statement that he did not mind the 'accusation' that his work represented an outgrowth of New Criticism: 'So, personally, I don't have a bad conscience when I'm being told that, to the extent that it is didactic, my work is academic or even, as it is used as a supreme insult, it is just more New Criticism. I can live with that very easily' (*Resistance to Theory*, 117).

Is Donoghue himself a New Critic? As said earlier, I do not think so, but it also depends on how the term is used. If by this, one means – to refer to the familiar stereotype – an academic pledged to the exegetical description of a self-enclosed literary work, then definitely not. Though he values close reading, his work seldom takes the form of this kind of specific literary analysis, and his prose is less academic than public. But if one enlists a more generous definition, the kind which should not only include the work of such critics as Blackmur, Brooks, Burke, Eliot, Empson, Ransom, and others, but also recognizes their brilliance and the desirability of pursuing this tradition, albeit mindful of all that is elsewhere new, then perhaps yes. De Man himself seems almost to offer such a definition in *Resistance to Theory* (1986), though ultimately it, too, with its references to gentility and repression, exists too much in the realm of parody. Nonetheless, in its suggestion of a cosmopolitan intelligence and wit, it remains an attractive definition, and one which (its other elements aside) Donoghue appears to embody: 'The perfect embodiment of the New Criticism remains, in many respects, the personality and the ideology of T.S. Eliot, a combination of original talent, traditional learning, verbal wit and moral earnestness, an Anglo-American blend of intellectual gentility not so repressed as not to afford tantalizing glimpses of darker psychic and political depths, but without breaking the surface of an ambivalent decorum that has its own complacencies and seductions. The normative principle of such a literary ambiance are cultural and ideological rather than theoretical, oriented towards the integrity of a social and historical self rather than towards the impersonal consistency that theory requires' (6).

This said, Donoghue has never spoken of himself as a New Critic, and this is as we would want it. A generalist, his commitments are to Irish, British, and American literatures, and while his work often returns to an examination of the modernist poets and to issues of theory, he is also at home in Shakespeare criticism and eighteenth-century literature. In fact, one of his books is, as noted, on Swift. In short, his purview is broad and his prose eloquent, and he fitfully takes his place at the end of a critical tradition that begins with Dr Johnson, and passes through Arnold, James, and Woolf, before finding itself practically institutionalized by the likes of Eliot, Burke, Ransom, Blackmur, Empson, Trilling, and others. In *The Pure Good of Theory*, Donoghue himself describes this history, noting that while Arnold, with his 'public style' and more general cultural interests, is the perfect begetter of much twentieth-century criticism, his interest in literature is rather unanalytical: '*Culture and Anarchy* is a choice example of what we call "critical theory" or "cultural criticism." It is not literary theory or literary criticism, if only because its relation to literature is occasional and opportunistic. Arnold's interest in

literature is not, as we used to say, an intrinsic interest; he is not interested in poems as exhibiting the play of language and mind. For him, literature is always exemplary and illustrative. When he quotes a phrase or
a few lines, it is because he wants to illustrate a particular sentiment or a
certain style or tone he thinks important for society at large' (PGT, 33).

Donoghue would prefer an Arnold more sensitive to literature's
nuances and less anxious to translate fundamentally religious concerns
into secular terms. Still, he values Arnold's achievement and sees it as
the forerunner of much that followed. Arnold may have been Henry
James's inferior as far as literary criticism goes, '[b]ut as a campaigner,
satirist, and polemicist, Arnold was supreme, and he made available to
later generations a public style in which nearly everything could be said
that had to be said' (PGT, 34). And yet, Donoghue thinks an Arnoldian
criticism would have only shown up badly had it been used in response
to this century's most visible modernist texts: the novels of Joyce,
Lawrence, and Woolf; the poetry of Eliot, Moore, Pound, and Williams.
It would have had nothing meaningful to say, for its refusal to take note
of poetic detail would have meant its overlooking the locus wherein
meaning most fully blossomed. Donoghue's point is well taken. It is difficult to see how an Arnoldian criticism would have constituted an adequate response to Anglo-American literary modernism. The vigour of
the style continued to be valued, yet 'Eliot's definition of wit, Cleanth
Brooks's dealing with irony, Empson's with ambiguity, Kenneth Burke's
with progression, and Blackmur's wooings of the sublime pointed the
reader toward more strenuous engagements with verbal detail than anything promised or threatened by Arnold' (PGT, 35). A new literature
demanded a new critical response, and the New Criticism, with its attention to the linguistic moment, rose to the occasion. Yet there is a follow-
up point that, at least in its suggested ramifications, is less well taken. If
New Criticism can be thought of as a response to a literature which had,
more or less, already set the terms in which a response might make
sense, it seems, says Donoghue, that the most recent epoch has felt no
comparable demands from its literature: 'No literature written in the
past forty years has called for a distinctive critical response; by this, I
mean a response such as was required to deal with the formal organization of *The Waste Land*, *Ulysses*, and *Finnegans Wake*. So far as I can judge,
critics no longer feel impelled to devise new procedures to deal with
current poems and novels. Nor do poets and novelists show much interest in the theory and practice of criticism' ('The Use and Abuse of
Theory,' xxx).

I have few quarrels with this view when strictly understood. That is, I mostly agree that our current critical practices are not reflective of demands made of us by our literature, though I can think of exceptions. But it is the suggestion that literary theory and criticism must function only in response to literature – that they are not welcome to bring their own interests to bear – that I think questionable. It is true that the forms of our literature have not changed dramatically from those of the modernist period, and have not therefore demanded a new manner of response. Yet other circumstances have changed, often quite radically. These include the dramatic increase in population and industrialization; the harm to the environment concurrent with this increase; the dramatic revolution in transportation and telecommunications; the transformation in our sense of selves as a consequence of this revolution; the globalization of the economy; the mass migrations and ethnic tensions that follow from this globalization; the threat of nuclear proliferation and mass destruction, and the large-scale anxiety and fear produced by this threat; and so forth. These events, while they have not provoked a significant amount of formal innovation in our literature, have been very much part of its themes; and it should not surprise that they have also influenced our critical concerns. Ours would be an irresponsible criticism if it did not take note of the world's major events and transformations. Fortunately, our criticism has been *responsive* this way, perhaps to a fault.

Certainly, Donoghue thinks that literary criticism errs by making its references too socio-political. Modernist literature demanded a new criticism, yet he does not see the need for current critical practices to change in the wake of transformed circumstances. As he sees it, literature should continue to be approached as literature, and his tendency is to be dismissive of those approaches that seek to expand our notion of literature to include interests that not too long ago were construed as extrinsic to the definition. It may be, as Donoghue claims, a 'contentious' matter to announce an interest in literature itself – i.e., an interest in what distinguishes literature as different from economics, history, and other discourses (PGT, 86). I myself think the interest worthy of investigation. At the same time, I would not insist, as Donoghue generally does, that critics devote their attention to this interest alone, assuming that they could say for certain what is, and is not, literature. Like Frank Kermode, Donoghue's hackles rise when critics venture to speak of literature in terms of its social occasions, even as he knows that literature is altogether marked by these occasions.[34] Thus, for instance, his one serious excursion into the field of feminist literary criticism, the 1986 essay 'A Criticism of One's Own,' is undercut by a peevishness that is itself a response to what he, rightly, thought was this criticism's subordination of literary merit to political and sociological interests. But its tone not withstanding, 'A Criticism of One's Own' is a valuable essay, not only for the fact that it shows Donoghue performing one of the most important functions of the generalist critic – the readiness to investigate areas outside one's safe zone of expertise – but also because Donoghue's criticisms, as always, are very perceptive, and in fact foreshadow statements that would later be made by feminist critics themselves.

Again, though, we first need to appreciate the effort made by Donoghue to read rather extensively in a field that is not his own. He, in fact, begins the essay – an omnibus review of mid-eighties feminist (mostly American) criticism, including Elaine Showalter's edited collection *The New Feminist Criticism*, Nina Auerbach's *Romantic Imprisonment*, and Caroll Smith-Rosenberg's *Disorderly Conduct* – by acknowledging his status as an outsider, albeit one anxious to learn more about an area of study that has obviously excited much attention and that has clear relevance to how literary study is conducted: 'I have been reading a good deal of feminist criticism and scholarship. Not all of it – I am sure I have missed many books and essays I should have read. But I have made an attempt to see what has been happening in feminist criticism since 1970, when Kate Millett's *Sexual Politics* ... was published' (30). By this point, feminist criticism had already gone through a few methodological waves, beginning with a version of image study – that is, an attention to how women were represented in British and American literature – and then moving on to what became known as gynocriticism, which focused more specifically on women's writing itself. Meanwhile, at this point, there was also French feminist theory, largely influenced by the post-structuralist work of Derrida and Lacan, to take note of. Today, one can find serious feminist criticisms of each of these methodologies – e.g., Jane Gallop speaks of the first wave as now generally regarded 'as juvenalia, of archival value at best' (*Around 1981*, 79); and Rita Felski has quite severe things to say about gynocriticism and French feminist theory – but in 1986 there was less self-scrutinizing. So it is unlikely that Donoghue's criticisms were much welcomed by those feminist critics who might have read the essay, published in the *New Republic*,[35] even as some of his views have since been embraced by insiders.

Actually, 'A Criticism of One's Own' begins with a restatement of Gail

Godwin's critical view of Sandra M. Gilbert and Susan Gubar's editorial principles in the *Norton Anthology of Literature by Women*, a view which, when published in the *Times Book Review*, earned her an extraordinary amount of obloquy from the feminist community, of which she thought herself a member. Godwin had criticized what she read as the editors' 'stated desire to document and connect female literary experience rather than present a showcase of the most distinguished writing by women in English from Julian of Norwich in the 14th century to the present day' (30). What Godwin had in mind were literary, rather than political or sociological, criteria, the kind 'by which it is agreed,' wrote Donoghue, 'that Yeats's "Among School Children" is a much better poem than his "The Lake Isle of Innisfree"' (30–1). Then going further, Donoghue wrote:

> If literary criticism were to have its way, *The Norton Anthology of Literature by Women* would be a textbook in sociology rather than in literature. But literary criticism has so often failed to define its way, so often failed to know what its way is, that one more failure won't amount to a scandal. It is common practice for courses in literature to roam into considerations of history, nationality, theology, and indeed sociology. Courses on 'the English novel' are rarely confined to a strict account of forms and genres. But teachers keep their consciences reasonably clear by choosing the best novels; or at least the novels that seem to be the best, according to the criteria of critical discrimination. True, these criteria are rarely defined, and teachers often rely upon a conventional or habitual notion of their deliverances. I suppose most teachers have a general sense of critical discrimination, like a passport; they don't carry it around, but they could produce it if they had to. (31)

Needless to say, Donoghue did not, on this occasion, think it necessary to produce his own critical passport. He has, as we know, a genuine scepticism towards such manifestations – that is, towards making one's critical practice subordinate to this or that theory. It was enough that the *Norton* editors were partial to texts expressive of a sociological dimension for him to question the anthology's value. In the editors' defence, it might be noted that they make it clear, in their prefatory remarks, that their principle of inclusion is not exclusively literary, but is also, in large part, documentary, a manner of approach that has become only more widespread in the intervening years: 'Together, these texts not only emphasize the vitality of women's literary history, they also allow us to trace a number of traditions within that history – the black, the regional, the lesbian, the working-class, and the native-American traditions – as well as to document the many ways in which women poets and fiction writers have confronted female experiences of creation and procreation, marriage and maternity, adolescence and aging, desire and death' (xxx). Yet even as one grants the immense importance of the *Norton Anthology of Literature By Women*'s publication, Donoghue (matters of tone aside) was not altogether wrong to wonder whether it was truly in the best interests of feminist critics to promote texts less considerate, in Felski's words, of 'the fact that literature also involves an organization of meaning as *form*, the cultural and aesthetic significance of which is necessarily shaped by its relation to existing literary traditions and conventions' (*Beyond Feminist Aesthetics*, 28–9). Without such criticism, one helps to encourage that situation wherein, writes Felski, Elaine 'Showalter passes a negative judgment on Virginia Woolf because the ironic, elusive quality of her writing cannot be reconciled with this prescriptive notion of women's writing as an expression of female experience' (29).

Beyond his questioning of American gynocriticism, Donoghue also expresses, in this same essay, his doubts with regard to feminist literary theory, of the sort identified with critics such as Luce Irigaray, Gayatri Chakravorty Spivak, and (though she is not mentioned) Hélène Cixous. He is especially sceptical regarding the thesis that 'there is no discourse but masculine discourse, that women are trapped in a syntax that is phallocratic and phallogocentric' ('A Criticism of One's Own,' 31), or, in the words of Irigaray: 'the articulation of the reality of my sex is impossible in discourse, and for a structural, eidetic reason. My sex is removed, at least as the property of a subject, from the predicative mechanism that assures discursive coherence. I can thus speak intelligently as sexualized male (whether I recognize this or not) or as asexualized' (32). For one, Donoghue notes, this sense of exclusion is something that has been felt by 'virtually every modern writer,' testified by the frequent claim 'that the words available to him or to her are somehow wrong' (ibid.). For another, the charge is too 'omnivorous,' amounting 'to an imputation of Original Sin, except that the official Original Sin was ascribed to the whole human race and this one is confined to men' (ibid.). It is, again, a point later given persuasive form by Felski, as when she writes in criticism of the notion that if discourse is essentially masculine, then women need to write in a way that is disruptive of traditional grammar and literary forms: 'The notion of a purely "feminine" writing is defended as a utopian moment within feminism by several commentators; *l'ecriture féminine* is to be understood as a liberating form of writing which cannot as yet even be fully imagined. It may well be the case that a utopian perspective constitutes a necessary inspiratory vision for feminism as an oppositional ideology. Nevertheless, this vision of an autonomous women's language and aesthetic also appears to generate intense anxiety; by claiming that women's writing must be radically *other* than anything which has gone before, feminism sets itself the hopeless task of generating a new aesthetic by means of a negation of the entirety of existing cultural and literary traditions' (*Beyond Feminist Aesthetics*, 43).

   To return to Donoghue, it is true that his hesitancy to jump on bandwagons has earned him the label, in theory circles, of a cultural conservative; nevertheless, his criticism has always been reflective of considered judgment, and one might just as well argue that his hesitancy to be a joiner has, in fact, given his criticism a more enduring character. So, if it is his conviction that while 'feminist critics and scholars' should be applauded for 'compelling attention to forgotten or ignored moments in the past,' they should also be rebuked for having 'matronized their writers,' setting 'them a list of themes, motifs, and situations amounting to one physiologically ordained predicament, and told them it is their destiny to annotate it' ('A Criticism of One's Own,' 34), one would not be surprised if this a version of what future generations of women writers and critics will end up thinking about their predecessors when they look back upon the 1970s and '80s. This said, it must again be stressed that Donoghue's interest in feminist criticism is but a brief footnote to his work, even in the domain that attempts to be responsive to contemporary critical theory. It might be that the violence of the response that this essay generated, especially Nancy K. Miller's excoriating 'Man on Feminism: A Criticism of His Own,' made the effort seem not worthwhile. If one has other interests, why stay about to be abused and accused, to be even tried and convicted (Miller: 'yes Denis, ... you really are guilty' [137]) for practising what Miller calls 'p.e.m. (phallocentric enforcement of meaning)' (139), as well as more general forms of 'phallogocentricism' [138]: 'Donoghue's language is inhabited by a metaphorics of the Law' (137). And while, at the time, most analysts would have judged Miller the winner in this contest, her essay has not worn well. It seems not only dated, but also – in its jargon, self-righteousness, and adolescent name-calling (e.g., 'The fight between the girls leaves the Daddies to their old struggles over ownership of the discourse. This is why we so often feel in presence of the Law'

[141]) – unprofessional. Some of us are now only beginning to see this.[36] It is to Donoghue's credit that he saw such work for what it was – a form of overstatement – and had the courage to say so. Meanwhile, whatever his reasons, Donoghue has, since his 1986 essay, foregone discussions of feminist criticism and has, instead, focused more on post-structuralist criticism.

Donoghue is not a post-structuralist, even as he is drawn to the sorts of question that critics such as Derrida, de Man, Hartman, and Miller address. Thus, while Donoghue has often placed himself in something like an adversarial relation to these critics, there is also the sense that, as other criticisms – e.g., minority discourse, Marxist, post-colonial, cultural studies, and so forth – begin to move to the theoretical forefront, they (Donoghue and the former Yale School critics) have become almost allied, by virtue of their common respect for close reading and for the same rich literary heritage that has been both the source for their endless permutations and their constant surprise. As noted earlier, Donoghue feels that 'whereas his relation to deconstruction for a time was indeed hostile,' it 'has in fact become much less so' (PGT, 92). Hence, interspersed among the criticisms of Derrida, de Man, and Miller, there are also quite flattering descriptions, reflective of his genuine respect for their abilities. Here, Derrida is spoken of as 'normally a careful, abstemious writer' (BBB, 51) and one of philosophy's most important thinkers ('if philosophy from Kant to Husserl and Derrida has indeed been a major achievement' [BMT, 70]); de Man is spoken of as 'one of the most formidable literary theorists in America, a remarkably forceful teacher, and an indelible presence in the lives of his many pupils and colleagues' ('The Strange Case,' 32); and Miller's reading of James's *What Maisie Knew* is spoken of as 'very acute' and as offering 'commentary [that] is, as one has come to expect, responsive and responsible' ('Critics at the Top,' 56; PGT, 78).

Despite the common interests, Donoghue has made his opposition to deconstructive criticism clear, and unlike his response, say, to feminist criticism, his critique has been developed. *Ferocious Alphabets*, for instance, the book which brought Donoghue the unhappy reputation as a conservative point man, remains a fine book. In fact, it seems a better book now than when it first came out, for then the whole discussion surrounding post-structuralist criticism was so charged that it was difficult to make proper discriminations. Now that the debate has subsided, it is less difficult to do so, and what impresses one about *Ferocious Alphabets* is how sensible it is. The distinction between epireading and graphireading is still heuristically sound; and while Donoghue's sections on Derrida and de Man are clearly oppositional and sceptical in tone, the thrust of their work does not seem misrepresented. The dispute between Donoghue and Derrida has never really been something that could be resolved via a further unpacking of their arguments, as if it were simply a matter of locating the points where logic falters. They do not disagree about the facts of the matter; they disagree about how one should respond once these facts are stated. For instance, Donoghue, in his various discussions of Derrida's work, repeatedly returns to a passage in *Writing and Difference* wherein the latter, in a discussion of Lévi-Strauss and Nietzsche, distinguishes between two different kinds of interpretation. The first, which Derrida identifies with Lévi-Strauss, 'seeks to decipher, dreams of deciphering a truth or an origin which escapes play and the order of the sign and which lives the necessity of interpretation as an exile' (FA, 165). The second, identified with Nietzsche, offers a stance 'which is no longer turned toward the origin, [but] affirms play and tries to pass beyond man and humanism; the name of man being the name of that being who, throughout the history of metaphysics or of ontotheology – in other words, throughout his entire history – has dreamed of full presence, the reassuring foundation, the origin and the end of play' (ibid.). In *Ferocious Alphabets*, Donoghue identifies the first form as epireading – 'it is turned toward speech, voice, a personal presence' (ibid.) – and the second as graphireading: 'it takes the text as a written thing, disowns the dream of presence, puts under erasure every term that offers itself as positive, and regards reading as an act by which we release ourselves from the oppression of an official significance beyond the reach of our play' (ibid.). He also identifies Derrida (whom he believes strongly influenced by Nietzsche) with the latter form, and himself with the former.[37] This is not because he is disdainful of play; he is not. Play is also a crucial term in Donoghue's vocabulary, especially as it connotes the artist's freedom to act against official narratives. When he thinks of play, Donoghue has thinkers such as Kant, Schiller, Gadamer, Winnicott, and Marcuse in mind (AWM, 66). Key documents include *The Critique of Judgement*, *On the Aesthetic Education of Man*, *Truth and Method*, and *The Aesthetic Dimension*. He most likes Schiller's claim, in the fifteenth letter, that 'Man plays only when he is in the full sense of the word a human being, and he is a perfect human being only when he plays' (AWM, 67). For Schiller play is intertwined with the aesthetic, and the aesthetic is defined as that activity which mimics the spontaneity of nature. The freedom is not absolute because the aesthetic exists vis-à-vis nature, but unlike reason, which must obey nature's rule, the aesthetic speaks of a capacity to hold things in abeyance, to explore the possibilities that the imagination holds out to it. 'When we remember,' Schiller writes, 'that it is precisely this freedom which is withheld from man by the one-sided constraint which nature imposes on his feelings, and by the exclusive legislation of reason in his thinking, we must regard the capacity which is restored to him in the aesthetic mood as the highest of all gifts, the gift of humanity itself' (ibid.).

For Donoghue, play speaks of art's capacity to imagine a story different from the official one, particularly as the latter, in the nineteenth and twentieth centuries, became identified with all that was 'deemed to be verifiable by scientific methods' (AWM, 68). But for Derrida, it speaks of something else. That is, claims Donoghue, Derrida's notion of play, while itself oppositional, is also linked to the notion of force. Derrida himself does not make this link, but it is, says Donoghue, implicit in the discussion, notably in *Writing and Difference*, wherein the philosopher's critique of structuralism – conceived 'as a relaxation, if not a lapse, of the attention given to force, which is the tension of force itself' (FA, 166) – employs the term (i.e., 'force') in a way that makes it seem synonymous with play. '[W]hat else can force be,' writes Donoghue, 'if not that endless play of the world which Derrida's later books exalt?' (ibid.). The suggestion that this play is endless is what most troubles Donoghue. He is not opposed to notions of postponement or deferral. His notion of the aesthetic is crucially intertwined with such, and his sense that the aesthetic and the ethical are related is also tied up with such notions: 'I would like to acknowledge that moral emphasis [in literature] by almost endlessly postponing its application. When I think of myself in some relation to aesthetic or formal experience, I still don't regard a work of literature as a free-floating object or as having no relation to historical, cultural, economic, and political considerations. Of course it does. But the difficulty, the point of embarrassment in the moral tradition, is precisely the point at which the moral decision is taken. The decision has to be taken, but I want to keep postponing it. There's nothing wrong with the moral emphasis unless it is premature, applied before it has to be' (PGT, 90). But if a notion of deferral is crucial to Donoghue's thinking, he differs from Derrida in believing that play takes place in relation to origin rather than with its back to it. Derrida himself does not believe the matter of origin or metaphysics escapable. Quite the opposite, for as he writes, 'There is no sense in doing without the concepts of metaphysics in order to shake metaphysics. We have no language – no syntax and no lexicon – which is foreign to this history; we can produce not a single destructive proposition which has not already had to slip into the form, the logic, and the implicit postulations of precisely what it seeks to contest' (*Writing and Difference*, 280–1). Yet in his readiness to regard origin as more like an absence than a presence, Derrida is clearly unlike Donoghue. The difference is made evident simply by the fact that Donoghue personalizes the matter: he speaks not of origin but of God. For Donoghue, God is also both absence and presence, but it is the presence which predominates. His relation is to God the Father, God the Son, and the Holy Spirit. God creates the world; His Son enters into the world; and the Holy Spirit abides as His continuing presence thereafter.

Put this way, there is a temptation to think of the difference between Donoghue and Derrida less in philosophical than theological terms. I wish to resist the temptation because it is ultimately too reductive. Still, some have wished, especially in the wake of Susan Handelman's book, *The Slayers of Moses*, to accent the Rabbinic nature of deconstruction. Hartman, for instance, writes: 'But just as there are two testaments, there are two modes of interpretation: Patristic, chiefly typological, and Rabbinic, which stands in a "negative" relation toward the Messianic event as a fulfillment of time and of the Word. The second mode has reemerged in recent thought but has not generally been recognized as having an affinity with a major Jewish tradition of exegesis (Midrash)' ('Minor Prophecies,' 152). By 'recent thought,' Hartman has deconstruction in mind. The link is the willingness to reside in textuality, to resist John's conflation of 'The Word' with 'God.' 'That a carpenter's son,' writes Hartman, 'should be the Messiah is a scandalous event not predictable by any soothsaying text,' 'the so-called Old Testament' (150). In this view, Christianity is a little too much like 'the latest realism': they both posit 'a realm of error made visible by haunting ideas of reference' (152). This, too, is Handelman's point. She sees Paul, for instance, as in effect stealing the letter from the Jews in order to abolish it – so that room might be made for the Spirit in the form of Christ. Here, 'Jesus becomes the predicate of all statements, the singular and ultimate referent, a referent beyond language entirely, whose appearance nullifies the written text – which is now considered as a long deviation, a detour, an exile' (*Slayers of Moses*, 88). As far as language is concerned, Christianity constitutes a 'semiological idolatry' (118), most fully exemplified by its doctrine of the Incarnation. The Incarnation, writes Handelman, is 'the bridge of an otherwise unfathomable abyss'

dividing language from truth (120). Attending specifically to Augustine's theory of signs, she writes: 'God descends into human language,
into human time and history: the word becomes flesh. And this doctrine
becomes the only possible escape from man's exile into language. Jesus
is the essential link between signifier and signified because with the doctrine of the incarnation, the substance and its representation are one
and the same' (120).

Derrida rejects the linkage. 'To love the Torah more than God,' he
approvingly quotes Levinas, '[is] protection against the madness of a
direct contact with the sacred' (quoted in *Slayers of Moses*, 171). But as
Handelman see him, he is a rebel from the Jewish Law as well. Unlike
Levinas, who 'writes a specifically post-Holocaust French Jewish philosophy' (*Slayers of Moses*, 172), wherein an absent God paradoxically makes
greater demands upon the Jewish people and their belief, Derrida wonders not whether the world is 'the effect of the "trace of God,"' but the
reverse: what if "God is the effect of the trace"' (173). Derrida is 'the
prodigal son, but unrepentant, enjoying his escapade' (175), the nature
of which is to promote 'a writing beyond the Book' (quoted in *Slayers of
Moses*, 174). This writing, unlike the rabbis', is virtually unmoored,
claiming independence both from God and Scripture. Derrida is, says
Handelman, a 'Jewish heretic hermeneutic,' whose transgression lies
not so much in the direction which it takes but in its boundlessness:
'Whereas Levinas claims that at some point there must be an unveiling
and redemption – though postponed, it must come – Derrida chooses
to stay in exile, to infinitely defer and differ – to play. Derrida will play in
the interval between book and book, play with the 'center,' and
decenter origin through writing. He will define the center as only a hole
... Derrida will have the last laugh on all pretenders to his new throne of
writing. No one can slay this new Moses. At any point, he can take
another detour, or choose to differ. Derrida's feigning the book is also a
feigning of philosophy, feigning seriousness, feigning play' (*Slayers of
Moses*, 174).

Handelman articulates Donoghue's own reservations regarding Derrida's earlier work: the sense, particularly in such texts as *Glas* and *Éper-
ons*, that he is too prepared to trivialize the question of meaning. For
Donoghue, interpretation postulates a truth which it seeks to know
and which governs the search. Play has a part in this equation, most
notably as it fends off premature conclusions and closures. This is quite
different than the sense it has in Derrida's equation, wherein meaning
seems more a function of play than play of meaning. The elements are

the same, but the emphases and tone are different. Donoghue's position resembles Levinas's in this respect; he knows the problems that attach to any discussion of ultimate meaning, yet feels that our needs are great, and accordingly resents the ironic, urbane detachment, even dismissiveness, locatable in the writings that first garnered Derrida's his reputation. As a Catholic, Donoghue takes seriously the Incarnation, the Word become Flesh, but, in the end, what sets him apart from Derrida is less a theological than a temperamental interest. Play for Schiller was a corrective; play for Derrida is a force; and the difference leans the latter in a direction that Donoghue finds ultimately dispiriting: 'I have an interest in making a link between play and force [in Derrida's work], because the trouble with the notion of play is the air of triviality which we can hardly remove from it. I am aware of serious contexts in which the concept of play is introduced: nevertheless, who doesn't find his morale sinking when something he cares about is compared with chess or bridge?' (FA, 166).[38]

Tone is also a problem, thinks Donoghue, in de Man's criticism. His work is not as playful as Derrida's; it does not 'resort, as a matter of habit, to Derrida's puns, his opportunistic etymologies, or indeed to Blanchot's heuristic repetitions' ('The Limits of Language,' 41). It is much more somber, and in the later work, the essays are 'so difficult, so ascetic in their refusal to take pleasure in literature, as to seem a mark of personal sanctity' (SCD, 32). Derrida and de Man 'seem different more than alike' (SCD, 34), yet Donoghue acknowledges the common interest in deconstruction. Donoghue credits Derrida as the theory's originating genius and de Man as its promoter, particularly in the classroom study of literary texts. De Man's own training, under Reuben Brower at Harvard, had been in the close reading of literature, and this history was not so much jettisoned as merged with the new philosophical interest, itself a variation on scepticism. In fact, Donoghue sees de Man as leaning towards deconstruction even before his 1966 introduction to Derrida. A crucial prior event was de Man's 'reading of Heidegger; or rather, with his reading of Heidegger's reading of Hölderlin' (ibid.). This introduced de Man to 'a philology that takes linguistic failure for granted' (ibid.), itself a definition for deconstruction.

Donoghue views de Man, 'even more insistently than Derrida,' as prescribing 'the stance Deconstruction should take. It should present itself as a form of reading designed to show that statements in a text necessarily give themselves away: whatever authority they claim is specious' ('The Limits of Language,' 41). Donoghue's estimation of de Man's work has, over time, become more admiring, but he has always been troubled by de Man's unwillingness to open himself to, or take risks in the presence of, a literary text. That is, Donoghue sees de Man's patented technique of unmasking an author's metaphorical illusions – be it Wordsworth's, Kant's, Proust's, or Yeats's – as akin to a refusal to countenance basic human longings, so often manifest in the language of poetic desire. For instance, Donoghue notes, when poets make use of the moon as a symbol for their emotional states, it is less because they confuse that object with something else than because they are as interested in similarity – in the discerning of those connective tissues that bind and unite – as they are in difference. When Wordsworth reports that 'the moon doth with delight look round her when the heavens are bare' and Sidney muses, 'With how sad steps, O Moon, thou climbst the skies!,' it should, says Donoghue, seem easy to feel 'that the apparent rift between one's consciousness and the world in which it finds itself has been, at least for the moment, transcended. Unity of experience is possible, at least for a brief interval between indifferences' (SCD, 35).

In a way, the disagreement between Donoghue and de Man comes down to a matter of a preference, one for unity, the other for difference. For Donoghue, unity represents something longed for. It is not met with so often, and when it is, it is usually against the backdrop of disorder. As such, unity and disorder, or resemblance and difference, exist in something like a permanent tension. Poetry, thinks Donoghue, has always been expressive of this tension, particularly through the vehicle of metaphor. He agrees with de Man's definition of metaphor as 'an exchange or substitution of properties on the basis of resemblance,' but cannot see why, to this, he adds 'by a proximity or an analogy so close and intimate that it allows the one to substitute for the other without revealing the difference necessarily introduced by the substitution' (SCD, 35–6). For Donoghue, this addition falsifies the matter. Some metaphors may work this way, but many more do not. Instead, they bring notice to the tension extant between similarity and difference: 'When Donne writes of parted lovers as a pair of compasses, with one foot fixed and the other in motion elsewhere, the resemblance and the difference are indeed sustained. But de Man, ignoring or putting aside such examples, suggested that in metaphor the mind wants to suppress differences and to enforce resemblance to the point of what he called "totalization" – total identity' (SCD, 36).

For Donoghue, the desire to bridge our disparate experiences through metaphor is a reasonable and worthy endeavour; and if the activity hints at a more encompassing unity, so much the better. It should be a comfort to think that the world holds together, that it makes sense, and even that it was meant to possess meaning. Yet it is precisely this comfort, thinks Donoghue, that de Man seems bent on doing without; and he cannot quite figure out why, for it seems, in its more familiar forms, harmless enough. De Man 'could not tolerate what he regarded as the mind's regression, through the recognition of resemblance, to the gratuitous satisfactions of unity. In the same way, he regarded the claim to know as "an unwarranted totalization of the claim to perceive and to feel"' (SCD, 36). But why speak of this as a 'totalization'? And why, when writing about other writers, does de Man so often stack the deck, suggesting that the writers have proposed an ultimacy more easily locatable in de Man's own descriptions? This is evident in de Man's critique of Proust: 'Yet, our reading of the Proust passage shows that *precisely* when the *highest* claims are being made for the *unifying power* of metaphor, these *very* images rely in fact on the *deceptive* use of *semi-automatic* grammatical patterns. The de-construction of metaphor and of all rhetorical patterns such as mimesis, paranomasis or personification that uses resemblance as a way to *disguise* differences, take us back to the *impersonal precision* of grammar of a semiology derived from grammatical patterns. Such a deconstruction puts into question a *whole series* of concepts that underlie the value of judgments of our critical discourse: the metaphors of *primacy*, of genetic history, and, *most* notably, of the *autonomous power* to will of the self' (quoted in FA, 181–2; italics added). That Proust, in *Remembrance of Things Past*, wished to celebrate the 'power of metaphor' stands to reason. He is a writer. This is what many writers do, or try to do. That his claims are vaunted and demand to be unmasked is itself not so certain, however, for it appears that the 'highest claims' come not from Proust but from de Man – that is, from de Man speaking for Proust. It is a classic case of prosopopoeia. And it forces one to wonder whether, as Donoghue argues, de Man's close readings are not 'strained' (SCD, 37). They seem to rely too much on a straw man, on the naive reader who cannot discern the difference between word and object. Or as Donoghue, quoting de Man, writes: 'there is no evidence that anyone, with the possible exception of Husserl, has ever wanted language to achieve "the absolute identity with itself that exists in the natural object." It is enough, for most readers, that poetic language is capable of coming into being over and over again: if it is always constitutive, always "positing," always summoning an absent thing as if it were not irrevocably absent, I can't see in that activity any appalling fault' (ibid.).

Donoghue likes the symbol for its suggestion of a unity that the world mostly masks; and de Man likes allegory for its deferral of this same suggestion. A crucial disagreement, it helps to explains why Donoghue, in his several responses to de Man's work, returns to two or three specific passages. One of these is the statement, offered in 'The Rhetoric of Temporality,' that 'Whereas the symbol postulates the possibility of an identity or identification, allegory designates primarily a distance in relation to its own origin, and, renouncing the nostalgia and the desire to coincide, it establishes its language in the void of this temporal difference. In doing so, it prevents the self from the illusory identification with the non-self, which is now fully, though painfully, recognized as a non-self' (quoted in PGT, 43; and in SCD, 35). For Donoghue, the passage shows that de Man has been influenced (as the latter acknowledged) by Walter Benjamin's *The Origins of German Tragic Drama.* Benjamin gives de Man precedent for favouring allegory over symbolism. Benjamin, says Donoghue, 'thought allegory worthier than symbolism, precisely because it didn't hold out any offer of the unity of experience: it had the decency to maintain the distance between the story being told and the historical and moral forces referred to, and to discourage the sentimental longing for unity' (SCD, 35). Put this way, de Man's esteem for allegory might be construed as simply a matter of temperament, which it in large part is. This said, allegory still remains essentially but one form of meaning, that which is 'held in abeyance till a moral or historical correlative completes it' (ibid.). As such, it speaks of a stance that must be thought congenial to Donoghue, and he says as much, for he has no adversion to allegory, especially when it is granted that it is one 'figurative procedure' among others (PGT, 44). Here, allegory is both like symbolism and different from it, but not opposed to it. What Donoghue finds difficult to understand is why de Man insists on the opposition. There is no opposition, no contradiction, unless one insists on identifying symbolism with an 'extreme form of idealism.' But why insist on this when neither past nor present usage compels it, and when one's next move shall be to decry the identification? It amounts, thinks Donoghue, to an act of bad faith. Such represents a cogent criticism, fostering the impression that de Man was as guilty as any Romantic of hypostasizing things. And perhaps more wilful. That is, if a Wordsworth or a Proust appears to ask more of their symbols than they can offer, the motive was mostly innocuous; they were led by their hopes. De Man, on the other hand, almost knowingly overstates matters, not for reasons of a hope but of an argument. True, one can put a great deal of hope in an argument as well, and I do not wish to cast aspersions on de Man's character. Too much of this has been done already. I admire the mature work, and the man through this. Still, the work often appears to force matters, and as the direction is towards undermining 'a whole series of concepts that underlie the value judgments' not only, as de Man says, 'of our critical discourse' but also of our non-critical discourse, a question might be posed with regard to motive (FA, 182). Donoghue does pose this question in 'The Strange Case of Paul de Man.' Here, he proposes something like a theory that takes into account the revelations respecting the wartime experiences and writings. He argues that de Man's critical preoccupation with totalization and its consequent misrepresentations has its source, perhaps, in the wartime experience. Donoghue speculates that de Man, taken in at first by the Nazi claims, must have later carried the memory of his collaboration not only as a painful statement of personal weakness but also as a cautious reminder regarding the danger of belief systems: 'But in 1940 and for about two years thereafter it seemed to him that he could seize the day, run to possess the future. It must have been a release for him, and a source of new-found conviction of unity, to feel that he was on the crest of the wave of history. The fact that he was wrong; and was proved wrong, threw him back upon his earlier divided state and made him for the rest of his life fixated upon the forms that division took: thereafter, he was obsessed with discrepancy, rupture, disconnection, and he refused every mitigation' (SCD, 36).

As theories go, it is noticeably schematic, yet not implausible. Indeed, it seems likely that the wartime episode must have been experienced by de Man as something like an admonishment against future professions of faith. That is, against premature professions, though after his wartime failing, such discriminations might have been more difficult to make. Professions of faith – e.g., political, intellectual, cultural, material, theological, etc. – are unavoidable, or so it would seem. The question is not whether one places one's faith in anything, but in what. Like anything else, faith entails discriminations. There are good choices and bad choices to be made. Donoghue thinks that de Man, in shrinking from any poetic gesture that evoked the desire for unity, made something akin to a poor choice, imprisoning himself in a realm – a '[s]uspended ignorance' – wherein all victories are Pyrrhic (FA, 185). It a view that Wendy Steiner, in *The Scandal of Pleasure* (1995), has also well expressed: 'Seduced briefly by the same Nazi aestheticism that attracted Heidegger, de Man kept interposing a barrier of theory against the allure of belief, closure, and beauty (as his followers, all the while idolized him). But if Heidegger succumbed to Nazism and Hölderlin, de Man's failure came in not succumbing, in not accepting the fact that a certain degree of abandon is essential to aesthetic experience. Steeled against the pleasure of art and thought, his criticism is an allegory of denial and deprivation' (206).

This helps to explain Donoghue's unhappiness with de Man's reading of the last stanza of Yeats's 'Among School Children,' one of those passages in de Man to which Donoghue repeatedly turns.[39] The Yeats stanza itself reads:

> O chestnut-tree, great-rooted blossomer,
> Are you the leaf, the blossom or the bole?
> O body swayed to music, O brightening glance,
> How can we know the dancer from the dance?

It is a stanza, de Man admits, in which '[it] might seem far-fetched or even perverse to find here anything but a splendid statement glorifying organic, natural form, its sensuous experience and fundamental unity' (*The Rhetoric of Romanticism*, 197). Certainly, critics, including Kermode in *The Romantic Image* (1957), have tended to read it as such, taking the stanza's questions as rhetorical – as urging us to believe apparent antinomies reconcilable in a larger unity. But de Man chooses to read it otherwise, as illustrating the rule of deconstruction: '*not* that sign and referent are so exquisitely fitted to each other that all difference between them is at times blotted out but, rather, since the two essentially different elements, sign and meaning, are so intricately intertwined in the imagined "presence" that the poem addresses, how can we possibly make the distinctions that would shelter us from the error of identifying what can be identified?' (*Allegories of Reading*, 11). It is a tortuous sentence, difficult to untangle. The long and short of it, says de Man, is the claim that a 'literal' reading of the stanza undoes a 'figurative' reading. Here, 'it turns out that the entire scheme set up by the first reading can be undermined, or deconstructed, in the terms of the second, in which the final line is read literally as meaning that, since the dancer and the dance are not the same, it might be useful, perhaps even desperately necessary – for the question can be given a ring of urgency, "Please tell me, how *can* I know the dancer from the dance" – to tell them apart' (11–12). De Man further states that we have 'two entirely coherent but entirely incompatible readings,' which 'have to engage each other in direct confrontation for the one reading is precisely the error denounced by the other and has to be undone by it' (12). The argument is forced, and to the degree that it appears true, it has much to do with de Man's propensity for tilting the table. Modifiers such as 'entirely' (used twice), 'direct,' and 'precisely' help create the sense that we have two antithetical readings, when what we have are two *different* readings, one of which (i.e., Kermode's) is, in fact, more persuasive than the other. The sensitive reader will acknowledge that the felt unity does not obliterate the difference between the dancer and the dance; but to say, with de Man, that it remains 'desperately necessary' to clarify this difference is to engage in hyperbole and to beg the question. A critic should demonstrate greater responsibility towards texts. That de Man, in this instance, does not, leads to a rebuke from Donoghue, to his saying that the literalist reading 'seems to me so alien to the tone of the entire last stanza that I can't believe de Man ever listened to the Yeatsian music. The fact that within a few pages he misquotes the questioning line as "How can we tell the dancer from the dance?" shows that he hasn't really read it' ('The Limits of Language,' 44). His anger vented, Donoghue concludes this same discussion with the fitting remark: 'Still, the entire essay on Yeats in *The Rhetoric of Romanticism* makes me hesitate, even in the interpretation of poems I know pretty well' (ibid.).

Of the three critics most identified with deconstruction – Derrida, de Man, and Miller – Donoghue seems most comfortable with Miller. This makes sense, for they both practise a criticism that makes the patient and close reading of a literary text into something of an ethic. There are few better ways to demonstrate respect, their criticism suggests, than by taking an author's work seriously. 'To be too subjective with what an artist has managed to make objective,' Robert Frost once observed, 'is to come on him presumptuously and render ungraceful what he in pain of his life had faith he had made graceful.' Thankfully, neither Donoghue nor Miller is presumptuous this way, and they each have repeatedly demonstrated the grace of reading the works of others carefully, as if much depended on it. Granted, they make their mistakes, and granted, Miller's deconstructive practice is predicated on the belief that mistakes, or misrepresentations, are part and parcel of reading. But they are, overall, attentive readers and masterful literary critics, and Donoghue does Miller the kindness of saying as much when, reviewing his work along with that of Geoffrey Hartman, Irving Howe, and Frank Kermode, he writes: 'There is a question of competence, of knowing what one is doing and being able to do it. T.S. Eliot once remarked that the best method in criticism is to be very intelligent. The four critics I have been reading are masters' ('Critics at the Top,' 56).

Donoghue has perhaps commented as much on Miller's work as he has on Derrida's and de Man's. The principal discussions are found in *The Pure Good of Theory*, the *New York Review* essays 'Critics at the Top' and 'Bewitched, Bothered and Bewildered,' the *TLS* review of *Topographies* ('Doing Things with Words') and, more parenthetically, in 'The Use and Abuse of Theory.' His admiration for Miller follows from the fact that he is one of the few prominent American critics who still not only believes in the value of close reading but also does it very well. Donoghue thinks, however, that Miller bows too easily to theoretical pressures, and he admonishes him for doing so even while praising him. He writes, for instance, that Miller 'remains a paid-up deconstructionist, but he has set about showing that his version of deconstructive practice, which he disarmingly calls "rhetorical criticism," is formidable not only as a method but as an ethic, a way of being critically honest. He does this by allowing his book to be arduous: no critic would take on such work for fun' (BBB, 46). If the dominant note is one of respect ('Miller is patient, perceptive – as we know him always to be' ['Critics at the Top,' 56]), Donoghue still cannot hide his sense of exasperation when reading Miller: 'I can only read Miller's books by haggling over them, wondering why he wants to make life so hard for his readers and why the only pleasure he allows them is the gratification of fighting a dour fight in a cause he regards as noble' (BBB, 48).

Donoghue and Miller esteem many of the same authors – James, Stevens, Hopkins, et al. – and values – e.g., reading, craft, character – but whereas Donoghue appears unembarrassed by such values, Miller has an almost insecure need to be on the cutting edge, even if this requires masking traditional conceptions regarding literature and its definition as radical, and reassuring critics on the left that 'so-called "deconstruction,"' with its penchant for ironizing political truisms, is nevertheless friendly 'to today's frontier work in cultural studies, women's studies, historicism, and minority discourses' (*Topographies*, 314). As a critic, Miller has a habit of obsequiously looking over his shoulder, of checking to see what others are doing, and of hoping not to displease. It is too bad, for at his best, he is a remarkable reader of literature, notably sensitive to its ethical, narrative, and rhetorical dimensions. But he cannot proceed without implanting his reading in some greater newness, be it critical, theoretical, or technological. As Donoghue points out, Miller likes to travel far to reach destinations that are near. About Miller's discussion of *What Maisie Knew* (in *Versions of Pygmalion*), Donoghue writes: 'Miller is very acute in showing how Maisie conjures into a semblance of existence certain ideal persons by comparison with whom she judges each of the characters surrounding her. Maisie's capacity to project these ideal persons is what James call her power of "wonder." The novel has to end when Maisie has outgrown this capacity; after that, as James says, there would have to be "another scale, another perspective, another horizon." Miller deals splendidly with these matters, but he needed no elaborate theory to achieve this result. His has always been a scruple that reads well by reading slowly' ('Critics at the Top,' 56).

Yet, in fairness to Miller, I am not sure that either Donoghue's criticism of him for reading Maisie's behaviour as exemplary, or the representation of his work as an assertion that 'every given or public ground is corrupt' (BBB, 48), is well taken. In the first instance, Donoghue, responding to Miller's asking whether or not we might do well to emulate Maisie's act of renunciation, writes: 'Miller is evidently asserting that an ethics of reading should replace an aesthetic of reading. I don't understand why. *What Maisie Knew* is a sequence of words, implying among many other things an imaginary sequence of acts and sufferances. Readers are certainly invited to participate in these sequences and to imagine their ramifications; but not further to obey the narrator or the author. To take the novel as an ethical *casus* and to pursue it as such, as a case in casuistry, is to read it omnivorously' (PGT, 81–2). In Miller's reading of *What Maisie Knew*, I do not find warrant for the claim that we are being asked 'to obey the narrator or the author,' or that we are '[t]o take the novel as an ethical *casus*.' Instead, we are urged to understand Maisie's act as exemplifying an ethical law difficult to articulate even as we acknowledge its claim upon us. Maisie's act is not identical with this law, nor is any statement to this effect made by either the narrator or the author. Still, there is the sense that all these things participate in, and give evidence of, a universal law; and that we should recognize them as such, even when we cannot reduce this understanding to a set of rules. For Miller, Maisie's '[r]enunciation expresses "symbolically" the impossibility of any adequate embodiment of the "universal." It expresses, moreover, the incommensurability between the demand made on the unique individual by the universal moral law and any expression of this demand that would convey it perspicuously to others – so I could, for example, make what Maisie does (or what James does) the known basis for my own doing' (*Versions of Pygmalion*, 70).

It is easy to feel unhappy with this formulation, for unlike an ethics grounded in theology, it is rather inexplicit in its terms. It is hard to feel as bound to something inanimate – i.e., 'the universal moral law' – as to a person or, more compellingly, to God. But these are not quite the reasons that Donoghue criticizes Miller, though he does mention the difference between our response to *What Maisie Knew* and the *New Testament* (PGT, 82). Rather, Donoghue seems, as said earlier, more keen on understanding a novel such as James's in terms of its virtuality rather than its ethical implication. 'The book,' he says, 'exists for perception, not for obedience or disobedience' (PGT, 82). But this overstates Miller's claim, and it is not clear why this novel, or any other, should not be examined in terms of its ethical import. Donoghue would not urge this, particularly as he has, under the influence of Levinas, been seeking to understand better the relation of ethics to aesthetics. Yet the thrust of his criticism of Miller here points this way.[40]

As should be evident from Miller's mention of the 'universal moral law,' his work does not propose that all our actions are groundless or, as Donoghue writes, that he 'needs Deconstruction ... to give him the bleak assurance that there are no given or stable grounds for a speech act' (BBB, 48). Rather, his work suggests that though there may be – in fact, are assumed to be – grounds for what we do and say, these remain difficult to articulate, and that there is a sense in which we know them as much by their effects as by anything else. Miller writes, 'The law, as Jacques Derrida puts it, gives itself without giving itself. It may only be confronted in its delegates or representatives or by its effects on us or on others. It is those that generate respect for the law' (*The Ethics of Reading*, 20). As in Christ's parables, the law resides in the text, even as it does not announce itself. Every action taken in the spirit of, say, the parables constitutes a further confirmation of the law itself. These actions become self-generating or, in Miller's terms, 'inaugural.' Donoghue takes umbrage here, thinking the description too Emersonian, too self-reliant. And perhaps he is right. Again, it is difficult to imagine placing ourselves in a long-term relation of obligation if we know the source of this obligation only via its effects. It has been done, yet it still remains difficult. We can see its dangers when such an ethic gets translated into a political program, as it invariably must. In *Illustration*, Miller translates it this way, and while his intentions are well meaning and democratic,

Donoghue finds him 'dangerously sanguine about those founders of modern states who take responsibility for their actions. In many cases it doesn't cost them anything. They have the satisfaction, and their victims pay the price' (BBB, 48). It is a good point.

In the end, Donoghue, while respecting the work of critics such as Derrida, de Man and Miller, finds deconstruction unpersuasive, 'an example of "going far to seek disquietude"' (SCD, 37). It is true that his initial hostility to deconstruction has been, over the years, noticeably modified, but he still feels uncomfortable with what remains a contemporary form of linguistic scepticism. Caution may be a virtue, but so is considered action, and deconstruction puts too much emphasis on the former and not enough on the latter: 'At best, Deconstruction may impose delay in one's acceptance of apparent meanings, and make one more scrupulous than one would otherwise be. In many respects it is like a metaphysical conceit, an obliquity by which we are forced to question how we see things when we think we see them straight. I can imagine how one might think deconstructively, at least on certain strenuous occasions, ... ; but I can't see how one could keep it up; on election day, one has to vote, putting further scruples aside' (ibid.).

Donoghue's responses to deconstruction have mostly taken the form of review essays. As noted earlier, he likes this form, and believes the good reviewer performs an essential and undervalued function. I agree with him, and the present book is a testimony to this. At the same time, Donoghue does not make the mistake of believing that review criticism is a substitute for more sustained scrutiny. Rather, it tends to invite such. So while Donoghue's responses to deconstruction (and to critical theory more generally) have been, on the whole, incisive, they have also tended to come back to a select group of concerns (e.g., Derrida's two forms of interpretation, or de Man's discussion of allegory versus symbolism). They give directions as to where a more detailed discussion might wish to start, and do not presume to have settled matters. It is the way things should be. And it explains his criticism of a fellow *New York Review* critic, Frederick Crews, when, in *The Critics Bear It Away*, the attack on critical theory is less measured than indiscriminate. It may be, says Donoghue, '[g]ood polemic, but it hardly even pretends to be fair. It doesn't do justice to Barthes, Derrida, or Foucault. Nor would it do justice to Miller, who never "makes a text mean anything or nothing according to whim." What each of these critics does with words is certainly open to debate. But Barthes, Derrida, and Foucault are writers so different from one another that it is unfair to line them up together for attack ... Besides, I doubt that charges as comprehensive as Crews's are now worth making. It's time for analysis of particular essays, paragraph by paragraph' (BBB, 51).

Where does this leave Donoghue in relation to critical theory? In both 'The Use and Abuse of Theory' and *The Pure Good of Theory*, Donoghue says that he is 'not, in the vulgar phrase, "against theory"' (PGT, 47), but that he would like to see theory, or what passes for it, as something more probing and less tendentious: 'It's not so much that I want to rescue literature from theory. I want to redefine theory. I would like to see theory becoming more speculative, much more experimental. I'd like to see it being written in much the way in which many poems are written, as an exploration among the possibilities of words. I don't want theory to be a function of an already determined politics' (PGT, 97). As things stand in the academy, he finds that theory tends to be equated with a set of pre-determined beliefs – i.e., a politics or an ideology. Beliefs per se are inescapable, but 'pre-determined' beliefs are something else, for they speak, particularly in criticism, of programmatic purposes. Meanwhile, he thinks the term 'theory' is being asked, as it doubtless is, to wear too many hats, and Donoghue suggests that we expand the vocabulary for purposes of clarification. Two terms that he would like to introduce into the discussion are 'belief(s)' and 'principle(s).' The first he discovered in Ralph Barton Perry's 1912 volume *Present Philosophical Tendencies*. The second was a familiar term for critics such as Richards, Burke, Empson and Tate. Donoghue himself would like to employ the term 'belief' to speak of those convictions which 'should change far more slowly than one's theory' (PGT, 48). And he would like to employ the term 'principle' to speak of the process that mediates between belief and specific applications. Theory itself would speak of the process which seeks to reformulate our governing concepts or beliefs. Thus, referring to Perry but also speaking on his own behalf, he writes: 'Now Perry's distinction between theory and belief seems to me a valuable one, and it implies that while changes in one's belief should be made slowly and reluctantly, one's theories should be sought in a comparatively light or debonair style, speculative, experimental, and daring. What we are witnessing today is belief (ideology) disguising itself as theory for immediate rhetorical advantage. I risk repeating myself by urging that we regard the work of theory as prolegomena toward the establishing of a concept – whatever the concept may be – and regard principles as finding their destiny in application of that concept and in the consequence of that application' (PGT, 49).

It is a sensible proposal, though unlikely to be acted upon. Things have almost a momentum of their own, and it is likely that we shall go on using the term 'theory' to describe a set of practices – beliefs and investigations included – until its inexactitude leaves us completely exhausted. There is some suggestion that this has already started to happen, and it is almost amusing to hear Stanley Fish, taking note of the fatigue, suggest that we should '[l]ook for more discussions about a new aestheticism' to begin emanating from the academy.[41] Whether that day comes or not, Donoghue shall continue to be, as he has long been, of the opinion that the best theory, literary or otherwise, will be that which emulates the practice of art and literature, especially when the latter identifies itself with the possibilities of play and the imagination. In both 'The Use and Abuse of Theory' and the *Pure Good of Theory*, Donoghue refers to Kant's definition, in *The Critique of Judgement*, of the aesthetic idea as 'that representation of the imagination which induces much thought, yet without the possibility of any definite thought whatever, i.e. *concept*, being adequate to it' (xxxv; 62). The suggestion is that until we have an understanding not only of art but of a theory adequate to art – i.e., a theory wherein we grant as much credence to possibility as we do to matrix – we shall be poor theorizers of anything. This too seems sensible, and constitutes a welcome suggestion from a very fine reviewer, critic, and theoretician.

Chapter Two

FRANK KERMODE

The Common Reader

In addressing the question of the common reader, Frank Kermode looks back to Dr Johnson, who in his 'Life of Gray' memorably wrote: 'By the common sense of readers uncorrupted with literary prejudices, after all the refinements of subtilty and the dogmatism of learning, must be finally decided all claim to poetical honours' (AP, 48). Johnson's reference was to a growing mass of middle-class readers, educated clerks, lawyers, merchants, physicians, their spouses and children, people who did a fair amount of reading, be it for reasons of business, edification, or pleasure. There usually was a reason, said Johnson, for '[p]eople in general do not willingly read, if they can have anything else to amuse them' (AP, 50). There was, nevertheless, an increasingly large number of readers who could not be defined as scholars, but who had a notable say about what did and did not survive as poetry or, more broadly, as literature. Though he did not say so, Johnson would not have included himself among this group – he was an *un*common reader – but he did, much like Kermode, acknowledge its presence and its right not to be patronized. It amounted, as it still does, to an ethical issue. Today, Kermode is in the forefront of those who think it imperative that a path be kept open between scholars, with their recondite interests, and the larger reading public. It is one reason why he esteems reviewing, thinking it 'as important as any other kind of literary criticism,' and that 'academics who think it an interference with graver matters need to give some thought to the whole question of the wider literary public on whose existence their own, with its mandarin privileges, must depend' (AP, 67).

This 'literary public' is somewhat different than in Dr Johnson's day. Certainly, films, radio, television, mass-market magazines, and the internet provide other amusements than the book or serious essay. The old common reader, never 'a person but a constituency,' is, sighs Kermode, now 'a pretty rotten borough' (AP, 49). We may continue to 'speak of the "general reader," but not very hopefully, and it is acknowledged that the kinds of people who constituted the Common Reader class have now thought of other things to do; the class is as nearly obsolete as "polite literature," which is what it once chose to read' (AP, 50). Yet if the old common reader is, more or less, dead, it still remains possible to speak of the common reader. Or rather, what Kermode speaks of as the new common reader. This person has attended a university and studied with accomplished scholars, but then has gone out into the professional world to make a living, or if he or she has remained in the academy, it is in a field other than literary study. This person, though not fully attentive to scholarly discussions, has nevertheless been introduced to them, and has a desire to stay somewhat abreast of their progress. Kermode writes, 'I have assumed that the modern Common Reader passes through a university. The number of people now teaching literature is probably greater than the total of critics who formerly existed throughout history, and they must have some effect on the millions of readers who frequent their classes' (AP, 56). He is undoubtedly right, and there is reason to believe that while the new common reader might have little time for the books of a Stephen Greenblatt, Terry Eagleton or, even, Kermode, he or she might be conversant with such periodicals as the *New York Review of Books*, the *London Review of Books*, the *Times Literary Supplement*, *The Nation*, *The New Statesman*, the *New York Times Review of Books*, and *The New Yorker*, periodicals in which serious writing and reviewing take place. These are themselves the descendants of 'the great nineteenth-century quarterlies,' in which 'long and lucid reviews of important books' were offered (AP, 53), but if the latter were 'bourgeois family reading,' the former are better described as 'dons writing for dons and their pupils' (ibid.).

The new common reader is, then, an invention of the academy: 'To be realistic ... , we have little to do with the oppressed, with the hapless victims of television and advertising, insofar as they constitute an inaccessible mass. We have to do with the new Common Reader, who has to be our creation, who will want to join us, as people who speak with the past and know something of reading as an art to be mastered' (AP, 58). Put this way, the project may strike some as a little too proselytizing, and

Paul de Man, in 'Blocking the Road,' once took Kermode to task for the zeal with which he sought (in the latter's words) 'to induce sufficient numbers of younger people to think as we do' (ibid.). De Man took particular note of Kermode's interest in the canon, and suggested that such an interest raised issues of religion and authority: 'What is at stake, in these recent debates, is not personalities or fashions but a very genuine and important issue: whether or not the teaching of literature, in the university, should be a substitution for or a complement to the teaching of religion' (190). As it relates to the common reader, the representation is not altogether unfair. For instance, in the essay 'The Common Reader,' from which I have been quoting, Kermode stresses the need to think of the common reader as making up a single community in need of authority, a description that is, in its way, churchly: It is true that "unified cultures" tend to be authoritarian, so the culture of the new Common Reader, however subtle and various, would need authority. There is something to be learned, perhaps, from the success of F.R. Leavis as a teacher: these books prescribed, those proscribed; a bold doctrine of minority culture, and the creation of an image of it that made the young want to join it. As Donald Davie, who underwent that influence, has recently remarked, it was at least as encouraging to be told what you should not read as what you should. There was a canon; and where there is a canon there is authority' (AP, 57).

I do not share de Man's belief that literature can bypass questions of canon – 'literature is noncanonical, the critique or, if you wish, the deconstruction of canonical models' ('Blocking the Road,' 191). Put this way, literature becomes synonymous with deconstructive practice; it becomes that quixotic thing that perpetually escapes definition. Yet while literature's definition assumes different shades of meaning from epoch to epoch, it really does not escape definition (however inexact); and in the post-Romantic era – so determining of both de Man's and Kermode's understanding of the concept – literature bespoke (as it still, for many, bespeaks) those discriminations that distinguished between memorable work (Pound's 'news that STAYS news') from yesterday's news. In doing so, it implied a notion of a canon, a notion that is manifest in practically everything that de Man, as a professional critic, wrote. Hölderlin, Kleist, Rousseau, Shelley, Wordsworth, Yeats – the focal subjects of de Man's writings – are generally conceived as eminently canonical, and as they are so, the question of canonicity is always near at hand. As for de Man's sense that Kermode's interest in literature was bound up with undeclared (perhaps because unacknowledged) religious interests, there is reason for thinking the connection real. Certainly, other critics – most notably William Empson, Edward Said, Majorie Garber – have taken similar notice of the connection; and even here, in relation to the notion of the common reader, one notes that for Kermode this person is imagined as residing in a community that seems also congregational. But what is true of Kermode is also, in a sense, true of de Man, so that even the question of pedagogy cannot be easily divorced from that of churchliness, though the churchliness assumes a different tone for each critic. It is what leads Kermode, in turn, to say of de Man that he 'really did think that there was a sort of clerisy – or that there ought to be such a thing – which read texts with the sort of intensity that he did. But we've got to have vulgarization, I fear – *haute vulgarization*, of course' (PNH, 85–6). Both de Man and Kermode require a clerisy, though de Man's is High Church and Kermode's Broad Church. De Man imagines his students as future scholars, whereas Kermode wants to take into account all those who shall not be such: 'academic literary criticism is ultimately dependent on the preservation of a class of readers, who nowadays, if at all "serious," have usually been through our classrooms, though they almost certainly do not read our books. That is why, like Lionel Trilling, I regard it as essential to "keep the road open" – to maintain, somehow, a style of talking about literature (in classroom and in literary journalism as well) which will preserve the reading public, and quite simply – literature (which we must presume to recognize) from destruction. I regard this as by far the most important single element in the task of university teachers of literature; it is nothing less than the preservation of what we give that name' (AFK, 103).

By 'keep[ing] the road open,' Kermode stresses the importance of the clerisy's talking in a language that the congregation can understand. His fear has been that literature faculties have been doing something else of late, especially as the profession's interests have moved further in the direction of theory. The problem is that the more specialized a discipline becomes, the more private becomes its language. Granted, other disciplines (e.g., biology, chemistry, physics) have managed to encourage very particular subdisciplines (e.g., embryology, thermochemistry, particle physics, etc.) and survive, even as their languages have become increasingly opaque to non-members. But Kermode thinks that with the study of literature, things might be different. Literary study has, in modern times, predicated itself on a broad-based support. Few studied literature in a scholarly fashion, but many read literature; and the encouragement of the latter has facilitated the pursuits of the former.

Things now are threatening to change. The profession, warns Kermode, has become less mindful of its obligation to teach literature, as this is aesthetically understood, preferring to teach theory, or any of the more specific programs (e.g., cultural studies) that currently find shelter beneath theory's umbrella. It is what leads Kermode to aver 'that if literary study becomes entirely a matter of theory – so that undergraduates are reading *Diacritics* and even publishing articles in *Diacritics*, which really show that what you need is a certain number of assumptions and methods, not a knowledge of literature at all – then we will lose the channels by which an informed faculty communicates with students. If you lose your students, if you can't think of any way of teaching students literature as opposed to teaching them theory, then you lose literature, because nobody else now really reads what we call literature, except people who've been taught how to read it at universities. So if you stop teaching them to read it, then you might as well give up having literary theories, because you've destroyed literature ...' (PNH, 84–5).

The statement, made in an interview, is reactive. It is the sort of response that led de Man to accuse Kermode of being 'avuncular': 'Parental guidance, it is clear, should keep the young sheltered from the hard porn of theory' ('Blocking the Road,' 190). If Kermode's stance is too worried, it still makes sense to stress literary scholars' obligation towards making their discipline accessible to the broad range of undergraduates. These students will, or will not, be the future's common readers, and how they are addressed in the classroom will help to determine the difference. To ignore their needs, to speak over their heads, and to forget that they will care little for literature's failings (i.e., its latent ideologies) if they have not been shown how to care for it in the first place, are strategies guaranteed to make things worse. Professors may 'read what they like and deconstruct or neo-historicise what they like, but in the classroom they should be on their honour to make people know books well enough to understand what it is to love them. If they fail in that, either because they despise the humbleness of the task or because they don't themselves love literature, they are failures and frauds' (AFK, 103).

The profession, thinks Kermode, has hurt itself by an 'arrogant or hectic spirit, to say nothing of the esoteric dialects' (CS, 59). His remark pertains not only to the classroom but also to the profession's dealings with the public at large. Again, it partly explains why he finds reviewing such an important endeavour; it is an attempt to speak not only to other scholars but also to an educated public (including scholars in other disciplines) that, it is hoped, takes an interest in literature and the discussions it provokes. He is afraid, however, that the time of profitable intercourse between the professoriate and this public might be no more: 'the time is long past when the Common Reader could expect to follow the discourses of theoretical professors, and we have a rather remarkable situation in which literary theorists would actually be offended if it were suggested that they had any obvious relation to common readers. They claim to be specialists, with no more obligation to common readers than theoretical physicists have. And so there is an ever-increasing supply of books classified as literary criticism which few people interested in literature, and not even all the professors, can read' (AP, 8). The criticism is not made of the professoriate as a whole but of its theorists. It is a rather indiscriminate dismissal, and while evidence, no doubt, might be easily come by, it appears too rash. De Man's reply to a similar dismissal is worth recalling: 'All this [Kermode's criticism of de Man's own work] is fine with me. I feel less tolerant, however, about the dismissal of all theoretical articles and first (that is, untenured) books as "very wretched ... a sort of desiccated rant." Is Frank Kermode certain that he has read all these unreadable articles and books and that he has given them, as the saying goes, a fair shake? Is he certain he has not overlooked some half-hidden grain among all this chaff that "dismays" and "repels" him?' ('Blocking the Road,' 190). The retort reminds us that books, like people, are generally best judged with their individuality in mind.

Kermode would likely grant the justice of the reply. Still, he has little patience for pretentiousness, and while theory is not the only home for such, it has been noticeably hospitable to what the critic thinks of as intellectual and stylistic excess. Over the years, Kermode has especially singled out the deconstructionists and the New Historicists as transgressors of normative scholarly practices, including that of offering one's argument and evidence clearly and straightforwardly. In 1983, for instance, Kermode spoke of deconstruction as 'the most frightening manifestation of the newer criticism,' which 'when deployed with a fervour no less evangelical than ludic, ... can be extremely dull' (ibid.). He allowed that Derrida 'is full of surprises and hardly ever dull' (AT, 5), but he appeared not to care for the philosopher's prose. Later, in the interview with Imre Salusinszky (1987), he said as much:

He's someone whom I find very attractive in all sorts of ways. I find the so-called 'ludic' element is very baffling to me, particularly when it spoils something, as I think it spoils, for example, the brilliant essay on Heidegger and Meyer Shapiro. It seems to me to be one of the things he does almost as an obligation, and I don't understand that. I sharply differ, not by conscious decision but by temperament, from this type of criticism; not just Derrida, but all those like him – Hillis Miller will go on worrying at some pun – because I have a great prejudice in favor of lucidity. I think that people ought to be able to understand what you're saying without getting involved in some pseudo-poetry or pseudo-crossword-puzzle. This is a very simple complaint, but it seems to me a serious one, and I think that in the end it will be a destructive one. (CS, 109)

As for the New Historicists, Kermode, whose historicist credentials are nonpareil, takes issue with them on behalf not only of methodology but also of style. Reviewing H. Aram Veeser's founding collection of essays, *The New Historicism*, Kermode criticizes most of the contributors for 'not *doing* New Historicism but only talking about it, often in prose that has taken on' a 'self-important semi-illiteracy' ('Talk about Doing,' 22). The New Historicist Majorie Levinson, writing in another venue (*Rethinking Historicism: Critical Essays in Romantic History*), comes in for particular attack: 'An Introduction by Marjorie Levinson is followed by a long essay from the same hand, with the consequence that nearly half the book is written in unacceptable prose and offers some opinions that will always remain pretty mysterious' (ibid.). George Hunter, a Kermode advocate, claims that 'cultural journalism has protected him from the inbred silliness of the academy' (AFK, 77). The reason has to do with style: the need to write with clarity for a miscellaneous audience, and the (related) requirement to address specific topics in measurable space, are disciplines that could have a salutary effect in many places' (ibid.). There is much sense in this, but there is another way to look at the matter, and that is as Geoffrey Hartman frames it: 'To view theory only in its effect on style, even as an effect of style, promotes it as a fashion, with rebelliousness and incivility as trademarks. Its claim to rigor could then be dismissed. Theory, however, is not just another style of discourse but raises the entire question of discourse-control to a level where our awareness of it becomes irreversible, and such antiself-consciousness devices as parody, sangfroid, or a stubborn emphasis on the practical side of things (kicking the stone) begin to appear stupid rather than commonsensical' (*Minor Prophecies*, 75).

Hartman is, at this moment, not specifically speaking of Kermode, so there is no clear insult. Yet he does identify Kermode, along with Donoghue and Steiner, as a practitioner of the 'conversational style'; and he thinks that though this helps to make Kermode an effective reviewer, it impairs the quality of his work: 'The critic who uses the conversational style because of its propriety may actually be doing a disservice to language. However difficult Blackmur, Burke, Heidegger, or Derrida may be, there is less entropy in them than in those who translate, with the best intentions, hazardous ideas or expressions into ordinary speech. Kermode's translative skill is great; one admires how rebarbative concepts from German hermeneutics or French semiotics steal into the English idiom, but something can leak away' (67). For Hartman, difficult ideas resist translation into a more public discourse. If the style of the theorists is difficult, it might be because the concepts themselves are difficult, and the language reflects their contours. Hartman thinks that those who employ the conversational style 'too often stifle intellectual exchange,' pressed as they are into defensive positions wherein '"dialectic" and even "dialogue" (in Plato's or Gadamer's or Bakhtin's strong sense) are threatening words' (66). To which Kermode, in a mood more barbed than teatotaling, replies that 'Here one needs to distinguish blanket condemnations of all terminological innovation from more limited objections to unnecessary or pretentious innovation – to the use of some tremendous piece of jargon for what might be well said in such a way that an intelligent amateur would know what one was talking about. For example, instead of "B learned a lot from A" the professional (a.k.a. Geoffrey Hartman) is tempted to say: "A was crucially propaedeutic to B." But the border between professionalism and bombast will always be hard to define' ('Theory and Truth,' 9).

Kermode thinks that theory must first test itself in practice, and is sceptical of those who claim the privilege of abstraction. Hence, his discomfort with such Marxist writers as Raymond Williams, Terry Eagleton, and Fredric Jameson: 'Williams has written a sort of treatise on Marxism and literature, as Eagleton has written a good many of them, but they always have the air, curiously enough, even more so than most recent criticism, I think, of detachment from real-life politics. They're very high-flown. Some of the things in Eagleton, as I've read him, are almost impossibly obscure ... Fred Jameson is another good example, an interesting fellow, but you hardly suspect that he's ever seen a worker' (PNH, 88). Furthermore, Kermode has a very different sense than does Hartman of the role of the critic. He thinks, he says, 'against much influential opinion, that literary criticism should not be wholly or even principally a matter of rigorous investigation into what criticism is and does.

Critics have a duty to interpret as well as to study the modes of fallacies or interpretative performance. They equally have a duty to evaluate, and to transmit interpretations of value (but not prescriptive valuations), as well as to make and study theory' (AP, 3). The critic, for Kermode, is a facilitator who helps the work find and hold an audience, principally by pointing to those places within it where value (an adjunct of meaning, for Kermode) may be found: 'If critics have any reason for existence, this is it; to give assurances of value, and to provide, somehow – perhaps anyhow – the means by which readers may be put into possession of the valuable book' (PE, 199).

Kermode's stance predicates an artist who has captured a truth beyond our ordinary understanding. Here, it well serves the critic, a lesser talent, to guide others to this truth, be it an aesthetic truth or of another sort (e.g., social, philosophical, etc.). It is a humble stance, which Kermode seems prepared to live with, so long as he can participate in the achievements of those more talented – more blessed with genius. For Hartman, it is, however, a too limited role: 'The dominance of review essay and expository article reflects in a general way the self-delimitation of practical criticism in America and England. Though these forms of commentary serve primary texts, they now claim to teach rather than preach. And to teach as unself-consciously as possible' (*Minor Prophecies*, 63). The suggestion, in Hartman's criticism, is that the work of the artist is not instructive or illuminative enough. Theorists can do better. They are more attuned to the fact 'that language has no "proper" meaning, and so must, yet cannot, be appropriated' (104). Artists, by contrast, seem less philosophically astute. Hartman does not say this, but it is the subtext of what he does say. It is what leads Giles Gunn to write that Hartman, among others, is of the mindset, if not the conviction, that 'the artist *as artist* is no longer centrally in touch with the most representative or seminal experience of our time and that this experience is no longer necessarily susceptible to being rendered in the more traditional fictive forms. In fact, there seems to be at work in literary culture an active belief to the contrary: that the only forms capable of fully and accurately rendering the ironic, disjunctive, self-contradictory character of contemporary experience are critical, recursive, ratiocinative, and highly self-reflexive, just because the characteristic experience of our time centers on the human mind itself as it moves in brilliant but sometimes fitful and ever more disbelieving steps toward the end of its own tether' (*The Culture of Criticism*, 61)

There is no reason why the artist, vis-à-vis the theorist, might not be found wanting. Romantic and modernist thought have placed the artist at the interpretative centre of experience, but this centrality is not a given. The position has, throughout history, also been occupied by other sorts (e.g., *philosophes*, scientists, theologians). Kermode still thinks of the artist as retaining a central interpretative role. In *Wallace Stevens* (1960), Kermode, following Stevens, writes that the poet 'saves the world out of poverty and "gives to life the supreme fictions without which we should be unable to conceive it." His words are literally the life of the world' (80). And in *Shakespeare, Spenser, Donne* (1971), he writes that Shakespeare is 'a major man,' 'a sacred book,' 'a source of order and civility' (153, 154). Order and civility also characterize Kermode's prose. Thinking that artists, both past and present, are worth caring about, he finds his motivation for writing in admiration. It is part of his virtue – and some would say his fault – that he chooses to decline membership in this school or that in order that he might, as disinterestedly as possible, bring attention to those texts that, together, constitute our cultural lifeblood. 'I was never tempted,' he wrote in *The Art of Telling* (1983), 'to declare myself a structuralist, or a post-structuralist, or even a narratologist or poetician' (AT, 5).

In the course of his career, Kermode has written hundreds of reviews – of fiction, poetry, drama, literary studies, and so forth – for a multitude of publications, especially *The Listener, Encounter,* the *New York Review of Books*, the *New York Times Book Review,* and the *London Review of Books*. The work has required genuine skill, an ability to write clearly to a specific audience – or audiences, for large circulation periodicals will have greater diversity among their readers: '[T]he reviewer obviously needs to think about the probable audience, the Sunday skimmer at one end of the scale, the person already interested enough in the subject to tackle a serious review-article at the other' (UE, ix). The work has also required a knowledge marked not only by depth but by breadth: 'A reviewer needs to know quite a bit about quite a number of things; and must be able to write prose that intelligent people can understand and enjoy. It follows almost infallibly that the reviewer will be somebody who writes other things besides reviews' (UE, ix). This last point has always been important for Kermode. More than once, he has noted the difference between reviewing as done, one, in Germany and, two, in the United States and the United Kingdom. In the former there is a real division 'between the reviewing of books, *Tageskritik,* and the study of literature in the universities, *Literaturwissenschaft*' (AP, 51). In the latter '*Tageskritik* is very often ... the work of the same hands that produce *Literaturwissenschaft*. The writers use a different tone, but are essentially academics; either they are talking to an audience that consists, approximately, of their former students (the new Common Readers), or they indulge themselves as wits or punsters. The dyer's hand is visible, though there may be attempts to conceal it; and it can hardly be denied that their aesthetic expectations, the general set of their interests, are very different from those of their audience, even in the posh Sunday papers' (AP, 53). Kermode knows that some on the left might think such work as compromised, a capitulation to a system endemically hostile to the interests of intellectuals: 'it is easy enough to see that to the New Left, the reviewers must seem to be passive instruments of a vicious system, contributors to "systematically distorted communication"' (ibid.). In fact, Catherine Gallagher, reviewing *An Appetite for Poetry* (1989), brings a very similar charge against Kermode's embrace of the common reader, thinking the latter nothing but 'the self-reflective entity of the humanist imagination,' and asking, 'Why does the Common Reader inspire such righteous rhetoric? Why is that keeping him alive on review essays seems tantamount to preserving cultural continuity, critical responsibility, individuality, and perhaps even a viable planet? The claims seem especially hyperbolic in Kermode's book, where the Common Reader is given no independent value or even a *modus vivendi* outside the activity of criticism itself' ('Fighting for the Common Reader,' 84). Yet when Gallagher tries to flesh out this reader's identity, the lucidity that Kermode brings to the discussion is – doubtless because the concept is, as Hartman might say, too entropic – not only noticeably absent, but also missed:

Who, then, is the Common Reader? The citizen side of a literary version of the citizen/bourgeois distinction, or the amateur side of an amateur/professional split? It would be more accurate to say that, as the review essay's creature, he is the person who registers and values that distinction. He is forever being solicited out of his particularity by the lure of the universal, yet he resists the delusion that he could actually inhabit such a place; he has learned from an Anglo-American tradition of poets ... that the particular is the habitation of the universal, and since it his particular calling to repeat this universal truth, it isn't at all surprising that he fiercely protects this idea of doubleness as the essence of humanity. We might call the Common Reader 'Man/man,' or perhaps simply '/', the slash itself. (ibid.)

The object of perhaps too many critiques of this sort (cf. Auerbach, Garber, Kincaid and, again, Hartman), Kermode can be forgiven if he starts to feel like 'the slash itself.' Still, the world is a fractious place, and Kermode does not expect to please everyone. So, while his stance has generally been that of a conciliator, he is fully aware of how quarrelsome academic debates have become, and how even peacemakers are readily denigrated. In *The Art of Telling*, he wrote, 'we do not lack doctrinaire and unconsidering people on both sides of the argument. My own inadequacy as a mediator has already been adequately demonstrated' (7).

Nevertheless, Kermode continues to believe moderation possible, and while Christopher Norris once criticized him for attempting to reconcile two positions, in the critical wars, that were 'beyond all reach of moderating judgment' (AT, 8), he thinks it imperative that he go 'on trying,' that he can do nothing less, for 'there is no possibility of retreat' (ibid.). Again, this helps explain why he thinks reviewing so important, for the forum requires a talent for moderation, an ability to adjudicate fairly among competing interests, and not to leave one or another party feeling abused. Over the years, Kermode has managed to perform this role brilliantly. It is, among other things, what provokes Salusinszky to observe that compared to other successful critics, Kermode 'seems to be one of the least interested in generating a "position" that will identify him as the author of his own books. He seems to enjoy dealing with the question *as* questions, visibly wondering about them and working them through' (*Criticism in Society*, 102). I think the statement true, and while there are times when Kermode, especially when reviewing the works of friends and colleagues, too plainly pulls his punches, even here there is an attempt in the direction of evenhandedness. For instance, reviewing *The Western Canon*, or Harold Bloom in all his obstreperousness, Kermode characteristically writes, 'And there is surely no doubt that even when the idiosyncratic judgments are discounted, this book says a great deal of what all who fear the consequences of the loss of the idea of canonicity must feel' ['Strange, Sublime, Uncanny, Anxious,' 9]). Kermode's tact here is a honed talent, and while it often irks readers on both the Left (mostly Americans) and Right (from whom one hears the accusation about 'kermode frozen glib-food'),[1] it (or the ethos underlying it) is at the heart of what makes Kermode such a fine reviewer.

Meanwhile, as committed as Kermode is to the task of reviewing, he is not unmindful of how ephemeral the review essay is thought to be; and he is not so virtuous that he does not give in, from time to time, to statements of misgiving as to how he has spent his professional life. This misgiving, part of a larger misgiving or melancholia, is noticeably expressed in the reminiscence 'My Formation,' wherein he recalls the influence of a Newcastle mentor, John Butt: 'I have a memory of him bent over proofs [of *R.E.S.*], wholly concentrated, in the weak light of a candle during power cut. He launched [Peter] Ure and myself on our careers as reviewers – which causes me to reflect that in thirty-odd years I have written several hundred reviews, an example I would strongly urge the young not to follow. It is, once one begins, all too easy. Somebody mentioned me to J.R. Ackerley at *The Listener,* and so was born the journalist who has wasted so much of my time' (UE, 404). This note of regret also carries with it the notion of soldiering on, of doing what is required of one, and might be understood as less plaintive than resigned. The tone again might prove irksome to some, for Kermode, over the decades, has been so wonderfully positioned to have his voice heard, a situation that most academics seldom, outside the classroom, get to experience. But the envied forum has naturally demanded an extraordinary amount of toil; and it is not surprising that Kermode should view what he does less as a privilege than an obligation, impressed upon everyone who thinks that living with, or within, a viable literary culture a genuine necessity. As he observes in a discussion of his own favourite reviewer, Edmund Wilson, '[g]ood reviewing in the weeklies and monthlies is ... an essential element in the hygiene of a literary culture' (C, 100); and when it is done well, others, scholars included, are likely to benefit.

It is tempting to wonder if Kermode might have written more books on the order of *The Sense of an Ending* (1967) and *The Genesis of Secrecy* (1979) had he not taken on so many responsibilities (e.g., co-editor of *Encounter*; editor of the Modern Masters series; presiding over the London seminar; working on the Arts Council; a principal member of the *London Review*'s editorial board; the visiting appointments) over the years, especially as a reviewer. Undoubtedly, he would have. But while this suggests a loss, my own sense is, as it is with Donoghue and Steiner, that not to have had the more public reviewer would have been a greater loss. We have no way of measuring the value that rank-and-file academicians, as well as the more attentive members of the reading public, attach to a familiar voice in their favourite literary reviews, but I think it is considerable. We can each probably draw up our own list of reviewers whose writings, serially read, mean as much to us as that of even justly admired novelists and poets. One can say this not only because the merit of this or that critic is truly distinctive, but also because of the continuity of the relation, the way in which over time this relation starts to seem more like an ongoing conversation. One could object that it is, in fact, a one-sided affair, yet because the critic, writing so often, is almost required to adjust to history's perturbations on stage, as it were, the loyal reader, more attentive to the critic's thinking things through, experiences something like what one knows best through good conversation, an intimacy of minds. Or so one likes to imagine, though it may be wrong to press the matter, for fear of insulting the very persons whom I wish to compliment. Still, I began by saying that not only is there no reason to regret the fact that Kermode has devoted so much time to reviewing, but that the perceived loss has actually been more like a gain. One also has the sense that Kermode, despite the occasional rueful remark, likewise feels this way.

Actually, despite the many accolades that Kermode has received – e.g., Harold Bloom: Kermode is 'the best living English critic' (*The Western Canon*, 3); Jonathan Arac: 'he is surely the best-known English critic of' his 'generation' ('Frank Kermode and Normal Criticism,' 218); David Lodge: 'Frank Kermode is the finest English critic of his generation' ('Confessions of a Literary Man,' 32); David Bromwich: 'one of the best-known, most widely and deeply learned ex-pounders of literature in our time' (*Politics by Other Means*, 13); John Sutherland: 'this country's most distinguished living literary critic'; Colin MacCabe: 'Frank Kermode is undoubtedly the greatest living scholar of his generation'; James Wood: '[as a Shakespearean,] Coleridge's worthy heir'; and so forth – I do not think that people truly realize how splendid a reviewer he is. When I say this, I do not mean in some lost time; I mean right now. Reviewing Kermode's collection *The Use of Error* (1991), Patrick Parrinder wrote, 'It's one unkind duty to say that he was a more influential reviewer in the 1960s than he is now, despite the excellence of much included here' ('Civil Service,' 45). In its most overt sense, Parrinder's remark is undoubtedly correct. In the 1960s, Kermode was a more influential reviewer than he is now. Not only did he, for a time, serve as co-editor of *Encounter*, but he was also expressing views more reflective of the prevailing intellectual climate. Yet if Parrinder means – and I am not sure that he does – that Kermode was not only a more influential but also a better reviewer then than now, I should seek, in turn, to suggest that the opposite is the case: that while Kermode hurts his reception with his too-oft repeated cavils against contemporary theory, he has been, in recent decades, one of the two or three finest reviewers working, and certainly the most prolific. As for the last matter, I imagine it has something to do with the fact that his retirement from teaching has freed up time for him to write, as well as the fact that the *London Review of Books*, which he helped start, has provided him with such a splendid space in which to present his work, including the autobiographical essays that, together, later formed his poignant memoir, *Not Entitled* (1995). As for the work's quality, it is so marvelously distinguished by learning, limpidity and wit that the predictable slips into mordancy do not interfere with the more general pleasure. Kermode has always been curmudgeonly, though now, when progressive criticism is locatable elsewhere, it has become more noticeable. This, again, is okay, so long as the reader also takes note of work's remarkable range – the non-stop reviewing of biographies, literary histories, literary criticism, novels, and poetry – and Kermode's unabating readiness to put himself in the service of the writer, even when that writer may have meant him less good than harm, as for instance Hartman in *Minor Prophecies*, about whose book Kermode writes: '*Minor Prophecies* is the best book this quite prolific author has produced for some time' ('Theory and Truth,' 9). That final 'for some time' represents, no doubt, Kermode's own sly revenge, for though he is a generous reviewer, he also knows when, and how, to use the barb. Often, these are witty in a quiet sort of way, as when, in his review of two books by Ann Douglas, he writes: 'Edna St Vincent Millay had so many lovers that they considered holding reunions'; 'Having taken the cultural lead America could now export what William Carlos Williams called its "rich regenerative violence" to the rest of the civilized world'; and, after a brief mention of William James, he describes Mary Baker Eddy as '[a]nother mind healer' ('The Spree,' 11).

Finally, I wish to pay tribute to the fact that Kermode is our finest disciplinary memoirist. He has been an active intellectual force for more than five decades, and he has, over this time, known or met many of the most accomplished artists and critics of the twentieth century's latter half. How many other critics are there who can, when reviewing Edmund Wilson's journals, say, 'I have known some of Edmund Wilson's friends, and usually find his appraisals of them both generous and shrewd' ('"I Shall Presently Be Extinguished,"' 11); or, when reviewing Diana Trilling's memoir, say, 'I ought to say that I write as one who regards Diana Trilling as a highly esteemed friend' ('The Trillings,' 160); or, when reviewing a biography of Angus Wilson, say, 'He [Wilson] was happy to help the less well endowed, me for example, with magisterial solutions to technical scholarly problems' ('Gaiety,' 3); or, lastly, when reviewing William Golding's final novel, 'He [Golding] once asked me if I was keeping up my Greek, and when I confessed that I wasn't, asked what I would do all day in retirement if I couldn't read Homer' ('The Guilt Laureate,' 14). Such remarks, while never obtrusive, are a characteristic feature of Kermode's later criticism; and they are simply one more reason why observations such as Parrinder's need to countered. Nonetheless, the profession's interest is now less in historical perspective and the hoped-for wisdom that comes with it, than in youth, energy, and force; and when it requires a memorist, it is more likely to turn to someone like Michael Eric Dyson, to whom, as a thirty-something cultural studies star, Random House proffered a six-figure advance for his memoir (McLillen, '"Hip-Hop Intellectural,"' A 6). It suggests a disheartening disjuncture of values, in need of a well-placed Kermodian barb.

Canons

Salusinszky has remarked that Kermode is a difficult critic to 'sum up' due to 'the extraordinary range of his interests, including Renaissance and seventeenth-century poetry, modern poetry, theories of narrative, and biblical poetics' (*Criticism in Society*, 100). It's true, and my decision to focus on his interest in canons reflects not only his very real interest in the matter but also a personal choice. I like the way he addresses the question; it has, prior to this, influenced my own thinking; and I find it a central concern in the later criticism, which is for me the richest. I am not the first person to notice how important the matter is to Kermode. Parrinder, in '"Secular Surrogates,"' has linked the attention to canons with Kermode's interest in interpretation and the institutionalization of literary study, seeing it as part of a critical triad. And de Man has taken note not only of how central the discussion is to Kermode's thought but also how it reflects the thought's religious tenor: 'The key term, obviously, is "canon," a term of religious connotation' ('Blocking the Road,' 190). Kermode himself thinks that canons can be secular as well as religious. Yet he readily admits that our notions of the literary canon have been much influenced by prior religious understandings: 'The word ["canon"] means "rod" or "rule" or "measure" and we all know, roughly, how it applies to the Old and New Testaments, or to Shakespeare' (AT, 172). Kermode is especially interested in the early Church's efforts to create a canon, and, like the scholar that he is, he is good at reconstructing the details of an ancient dispute: 'The canon seems to have begun to crystallise in reaction against an heretical attempt to impose a rigorously restricted list of sacred books on the church of the mid-century. Marcion rejected the whole of the Old Testament, accepted one gospel (Luke, much reduced) and added ten purged versions of Pauline letters to complete the canon ... In abolishing the Old Testament he was acting on a belief that its types and prophecies were false' (ibid.). Kermode describes Marcion as 'the first in a long line of protestant reformers,' confident in their ability to discern 'the original tradition ... in its purity' (AT, 173). Marcion's 'was the original canon' (ibid.), but it produced, as canons often do, a backlash: 'The counter-offensive had to include the provision of a canon more acceptable to the consensus of the Church. There is much dispute about the criteria employed. The Old Testament was defended, and out of a mass of gospels four were chosen as 'authentic' (the rejected included of course Marcion's). All this took time; and the idea of closing the canon more time, and was prompted by the threat of another heresy, namely Montanism, which used innumerable apocalyptic books. Thus was the canon achieved; and eventually the habit grew of thinking of it as two books, or two parts of one total, comprehensive book' (ibid.).

For Roman Catholics, the canon was not finally closed, notes Kermode, until 1546, with the Council of Trent. Among Protestants, the Lutherans continue to oppose the canon; and, more generally, '[i]t is among Protestant theologians that one notes a tendency at present to re-open the canon – and perhaps to admit the Gospel of St Thomas, discovered at Nag Hammadi in 1945' (ibid.). In offering this history, Kermode also takes note (to return to Parrinder's point) of the twined relation of canon with institution and interpretation: 'The desire to have a canon, more or less unchanging, and to protect it against charges of inauthenticity or low value ... is an aspect of the necessary conservatism of a learned institution' (AT, 173). Likewise, the 'decision as to canonicity depends upon a consensus that a book has the requisite qualities, the determination of which is, in part, a work of interpretation' (AT, 174). It is the nature of institutions to exert control over interpretations, even as interpretation is an ongoing process. The more conservative the institution, the greater, clearly, will be the control; and it has been a long-standing contention of Kermode's that the Church, as opposed to the academy, has, in effect, managed to freeze its canon, and to pressure its own interpreters into harmonizing their work with Church doctrine: 'Scrutiny of the gospels never ceased to be intense; but the attention they got was controlled by the desire of the institution to justify them as they were and find them harmonious' (ibid.). Only recently, as more secular scholars have focused on religious texts (thereby putting pressure upon clerical interpretations), has the Church begun to demonstrate some flexibility.

Kermode thinks the Church's understanding of canon too rigid, and he does not attempt to defend it. Yet as a model of an institution, the primary duty of which is to interpret texts, it remains an instructive analogue to the academy's own relation to texts. 'Self-perpetuating, hierarchical, authoritative, much concerned with questions of canon, and wont, as we are, to distinguish sharply between initiative and uninitiative readings,' academics cannot fail, he says, to be mindful of the prior model (AT, 172). Not all the academy's members think this way, nor should they. There has been, in years past, a marked effort to democratize the profession, and while few entirely dismiss notions of hierarchy and authority – English departments, after all, are an exemplification of such – many would like to see such things played down more. A strong reason for this is that there has been, for some time now (in the United States and, to a lesser degree, in Britain) a noticeable difference in the make-up (i.e., ethnicity, gender, class antecedents, religious commitments, etc.) of the senior and junior faculties, and an even more noticeable difference between the senior faculty and the larger student body. It is not clear that either the junior faculty or the students wish to follow where the senior faculty would lead. In fact, the opposite seems the case. Kermode knows this, yet still proceeds with what some dismiss as his 'quasi-theological' desire to proselytize among the young (Norris, 'Introduction,' 42). He does so with the conviction that the category 'literature' truly stands for something extraordinary and that those who accept this, and make it their goal to learn its contours and secrets, end up distinguishing themselves from others. This is not meant as a slur against these others, for they certainly have many other ways by which to set themselves apart. It is, nevertheless, meant as something akin to a profession of faith in what one, as a teacher of literature, does, and in what one studies, as well as a statement of hope regarding the possibility that others, especially among one's students, will also come to see the value of these things. It is hardly the stance of a radical relativist, and even while Kermode was often called this in his prime, I doubt that it was ever true. It is certainly not true in connection to his thinking on the canon, about which he – like Harold Bloom: 'All canons, including our currently fashionable counter-canon, are elitist' (*The Western Canon*, 37) – writes that in its study, there inevitably ensues 'a form of élitism – I suppose you have to say that – or "election," to use a more neutral term. I think that must be so, and just is empirically so. We all know this. Why do we fool ourselves about such things? What we do, to satisfy our consciences, is to behave in our studies as if we were, in this very limited sense, members of an elect, and behave in the classroom as if we wanted other people to become members of that elect. Whether we achieve it or not is doubtful; and under modern conditions, even in important universities like this one [Columbia], it becomes even more difficult to achieve than it used to be, simply because people are not prepared for it' (CS, 108).

For the elect, a canon is thought crucial, and Kermode does not seek to disguise the fact. It is the means by which a group perpetuates itself, by which it assumes the form of an institution. As such, 'canons are complicit with power' (HV, 115), though the goodness or badness of any one canon will depend not on this fact, but on what sort of institution it serves. The point is, a canon, like an institution, is not good or bad per se, but only becomes such in a context, wherein the ends which it serves are judged either favourably or not. This judgment can easily differ from party to party, and community to community; and the consequence is that the estimation of a canon's value is seldom final. Kermode knows this, for it is his argument, though he seems, at times, to forget the particularity of his own allegiances, and what this means in terms of canonical definition. That is, he seems hesitant to acknowledge that, in practice, there is no such thing as *the* canon. There are canons, yes, but it is much more difficult to say that there is *one* canon, either outside or inside the academy, that commands respect from all. Kermode does not exactly deny this, but he often confuses his own understanding of literature with the more ideal notion of *the* canon.[2] A British academic who has often taught in the United States, Kermode tends to equate the canon with British and U.S. literatures of a particular poetic slant. Here, the canon is understood to include Spenser, Shakespeare, Donne, Milton, Hawthorne, James, Lawrence, Eliot, Stevens, and others. It is that canon which, early in the twentieth century, replaced the classics, though its legitimacy has, of late, come under heavy attack. Few really dispute the importance of this canon's main figures, though when Kermode, discussing Yeats in *The Romantic Image* (1957), equates this same image with the body of a beautiful young woman – 'Proportion, movement, meaning, are not intellectual properties, but belong to that reality of the imagination which is a symbolic reality. The beauty of a woman, and particularly of a woman in movement, is the emblem of the work of art of Image' (54) – it is easy enough to understand why feminist critics, among others, would wish to readdress such a patronizing and patriarchal formulation. Equally, when in a discussion of John Donne, Kermode casually derides Roman Catholicism – 'Donne, then,

accepted the Church of England because it was truly Catholic ... He
wanted tradition but without its errors: Aquinas, but not the scholastic
nonsense; the Fathers, but not their mistakes' (SSD, 138) – it is easy
enough to understand why someone living across the Irish Sea might
think the terms of appreciation insulting, just as he or she might think
that Spenser's anti-Catholicism and Imperialist ambitions – 'It [the
supremacy of the Prerogative Courts coupled with conviction that the
King was above the law] was an important argument for Spenser
because as an Imperialist, which in a sense he was, he would clearly be
attracted by the notion of the Prerogative Courts. He himself, inciden-
tally, was an officer of the Court of Chancery in Ireland' (*English Renaissance Literature*, 11) – were not irrelevant critical concerns, including
that which Kermode speaks of as an 'incidental' matter. After all, if it is
true that 'an inheritance from Virgil would necessarily require the
[Renaissance] epic to have a political dimension' (ERL, 1), why should
our understanding of that dimension, when *The Faerie Queene* is being
discussed, be restricted to the way Imperialism looks to the conqueror?

I am quoting from Kermode's earlier work, where there is a greater
readiness to reside in the gender, religious, and political assumptions
of English historical culture. The later work demonstrates greater self-
consciousness regarding these assumptions, though not enough to impress Hermione Lee, who reviewing *Shakespeare's Language* (2000) in
The Observer, writes: 'You won't find discussions here of post-coloniality
or cultural history, gender or feminism, identity or hegemony. Instead,
Kermode deliberately reinstates the tradition of the dead white male
writer-critics who have paid most attention to Shakespeare's words:
Johnson, Coleridge, Hazlitt, de Quincey, Auden, Eliot and Empson'
('Will's Power'). Now a cliché, 'dead white male writer-critic' is employed by Lee less as a form of invective than as a reminder that in
seeing Shakespeare through the lens of a nativist critical response, Kermode ensures that his Shakespeare will be reflective of a cultural quies-
cence. And this will be further ensured by Kermode's insistence that the
discussion be restricted to Shakespeare's language: 'There are modern
attitudes to Shakespeare I particularly dislike: the worst of them maintains that the reputation of Shakespeare is fraudulent, the result of an
eighteenth-century nationalist or imperialist plot. A related notion,
almost equally presumptuous, is that to make sense of Shakespeare we
need first to see the plays as involved in the political discourse of his day
to a degree that has only now become intelligible. These and other ways
of taking Shakespeare down a peg seem, when you examine them, to be

interesting only as evidence of a recurring need to find something different to say, and to say it on topics that happen to interest the writer more
than Shakespeare's words, which are, as I say, only rarely invoked'
(*Shakespeare's Language*, viii). But even as Kermode seeks to restrict the
discussion to language, he ends up restricting it even more than he imagined. As Philip Hensher writes: 'Shakespeare's language isn't ... really the
subject of this book. Plenty of interesting books could be written on the
subject of the English language as manifested in Shakespeare; on his
characteristic syntactical structures, his grammatical innovations, pros-
ody and morphology. Plenty more could be written on the attitudes to
linguistic use evident in the plays and poems. Frank Kermode has written
quite an interesting book, but its interest in Shakespeare's language
more or less stops short at figures or rhetoric and semantics' ('Wild and
Whirling Words,' 28). One might wonder whether Kermode, in insisting
that our attentions be focused upon language in inherited canonical
texts, is not foreclosing a number of interesting discussions, including
those focused upon authors who do not quite fit into Spenser, Shakespeare, Donne, and Yeats's interests, if they be what Kermode says they
are. As such, we have reason for thinking that Kermode's canonical
authors, even when conjoined, tell a partial story about a reality that is
more complex and varied. Especially left out in the received tradition
were women and, more generally, people of divergent ethnic, class, and
religious identities. While these people often found, for reasons of
adverse circumstances, their opportunities to write comparatively limited, we now know, through the research of a new generation of scholars,
that they wrote more often and more eloquently than was previously
thought. Thinking that Kermode does not take this matter enough into
account, Nina Auerbach qualifies her endorsement of his notions of
both canon and institution by saying, 'But others, in the academy and
outside, might find themselves silenced. Those whose race, nationality,
class, temperament or gender exclude them from what Mr. Kermode
beautifully calls "the sense and the value of the inheritance" may feel as
unequivocally disinherited by this book as Mr. Kermode's postulated
common reader is by literary theory' ('Roasting the Academics,' 12).

Kermode might admit as much, but grudgingly. The reason has to do
with his conception of the literary canon – both as an imaginary ideal
and in practice – as singular and circumscribed. The canon has only so
much room; if a new writer is admitted, chances are a writer from an
earlier generation will him- or herself be displaced. That the more quotidian canon might develop subsets (e.g., African-American literature,

gay writers) or might even break into two or more parts, is not a notion he much countenances, though he would not deny it. Still, he should prefer to safeguard the fort: 'I think it's very important to do a certain amount of digging in and resisting, not out of enmity or disapproval of the aspirations of feminists and blacks, and so on – certainly not; but because this move is a great deal more destructive than the people who are making it imagine it to be. The fact is that you can't, paradoxically, have a canon unless you have a tradition of canon. You can't suddenly say, let's have a new canon. That's not the way canons work. You can't say out with Milton and in with ... Zora Neale Hurston. You can't do that. That's not the way canons are formed' (PNH, 76).

It is, no doubt, true that the canon, especially as it moves in the direction of an ideal, requires a notion of tradition; yet it is not equally clear that canons (i.e., the more local subsets) require this. Thus while some canons are obviously richer in tradition than others, in its simplest form, a canon is something like a list of recommended titles. If a reader, having found pleasure in the themes of, say, Edmund White, should wish to read more gay fiction, he or she would most likely inquire among friends about whom might be profitably read, and in a short time, this person would have a list of titles, a canon of sorts. This canon would not have the antecedents that Kermode has in mind when he speaks of tradition, but if the reader pursued the task with assiduity, he or she would find something akin to a genuine field. After a period of exploring, the reader might even formulate his or her own canon, one which this person could then attempt to convince others that it should be worth their while to read. If hitherto this reader were a Miltonist, it is possible that this new interest might undercut the prior commitment, yet not necessarily. The reader might find a way to reconcile such interests, to understand them as subsets of a larger literary interest. Or the reader might come to understand them as separate interests altogether, with the more recent interest as demanding, once again, a new canon. Should this happen, the reader would be an attendant to two canons, neither one of which he or she would likely refer to as *the* canon, though the notion of *the* canon might still be honoured. The canon itself is an imagined ideal, something exceeding the possibility of even the most tireless reader to grasp in anything but the most partial sense. Or as Bloom writes: 'No one has the authority to tell us what the Western Canon is, certainly not from about 1800 to the present day. It is not, cannot be, precisely the list I give, or that anyone else might give. If it were, that would make such a list a mere fetish, just another commodity' (*The Western Canon*, 37).

Even as Kermode often conflates practical and ideal notions of the canon, he would probably agree with such a distinction. His own distinction between the ecclesiastical and the literary canon offers some evidence this way, though not to the point that he appears extolling of more pluralistic conceptions of the canon. His thinking on the canon has been too much influenced by the Church, as well as by the writings of E.R. Curtius, for this to happen. In *The Art of Telling*, he in fact spoke of the Modern Language Association as something like the Church, permitting the presence of quasi-heretical movements ('There are sessions on Black literature, on neglected women writers, and the like; there are discussions of relatively avant-garde critical and theoretical movements which have certainly not won their appeal to the senior consensus' [179]), but ready to reign such in when things threaten to get out of hand: 'A few years ago the MLA suffered something that looked for a moment like a revolution; but it was only a saturnalian interlude ... , an episode of Misrule, tolerated because in the end reinforcing the stability of the institution. The boy bishops had their day, and the more usual, more authentically prelatical figures have resumed their places' (179). Things have changed a lot since: the boy (and girl) bishops are back. And Kermode, who was once the strongest advocate of literary study as akin to an institution, now, at the end of his career, seeks to go around the institutional bulwarks so as to speak directly to the common reader. The very first sentence of *Shakespeare's Language* reads: 'This book is addressed to a non-professional audience with an interest in Shakespeare that has not, I believe, been well served by modern critics' (vii). And while the book raises some doubts about the sincerity of this claim, it is clear that Kermode, who has also said that the book is 'not for horrid profs' (Burrow, 'Not for Horrid Profs,' 11), and who sets out not to 'pay much attention to what are nevertheless the prevailing modes of Shakespearean criticism' (ix), has experienced a noticeable apostatism. A generation ago, when Kermode was likening the Modern Language Association to the Church, this apostatism seemed anything but likely. Kermode was in the midst of formulating his notion of canon, and as the canon was – ever so circumspectly acknowledged – a political entity, it required a powerful, albeit liberal and enlightened, institutional force (i.e., the academy) to keep it viable and prospective. But while the academy and its offshoots might be likened to the Church, they were different not only because more modern, or enlightened, but also, thought Kermode, because the canon of the literary academy was soft whereas that of the Church was hard. The clerical canon is hard because it is moored to past revelation and report. Kermode would not exactly say that the Bible is closed, for it admits of unending interpretation, but the sense remains that it is something quite stable – so to the extent that it is open, it is not likely to force further revolutions in our thought.

On the other hand, the literary-academic canon is soft because literature itself seeks to be perpetually modern. Kermode here borrows an idea from de Man (who borrowed it from Nietzsche) that literature engenders history by its attempt to reach out and be true to life – i.e., to be modern. It never quite achieves this ambition, but the failure itself is what gets recorded as history, and is what engenders further attempts this way, as well as further history. De Man writes, 'Considered as a principle of life, modernity becomes a principle of origination and turns at once into a generative power that is itself historical. It becomes impossible to overcome history in the name of life or to forget the past in the name of modernity, because both are linked by a temporal chain that gives them a common destiny' (*Blindness and Insight*, 150). Or as Kermode says, 'all literary canons are soft ... because of the need of modernity. You see you've got to have the possibility of being modern without which literature may very well cease to interest. It could also cease to have a history, because if you're not modern you're repeating something else and its history will stop' (PNH, 75).

It seems that Kermode, again like de Man, thinks of literature as impelled by this phenomenological desire. It is perhaps this that urges him to conceive of it as constituent of a single canon. In his first book, *The Romantic Image*, Kermode argued that the image was both a 'radiant truth out of space and time' and the '"primary pigment of poetry"' (2, vii). The poet, bound to this image, experienced 'the necessary isolation or estrangement of men who can perceive it' (2). In his later writings, Kermode stepped back from this description of the aesthetic ambition, yet the desire for a truth that stands outside the bounds of space and time has always characterized his work. In *The Art of Telling*, Kermode writes that 'there are those who argue that the history of criticism is a history of error; but if we stay within the tradition, rather than seek to overthrow it, we shall have to say rather that it is a history of accommodations, of attempts to earn the privilege of access to that kingdom of the larger existence which is in our time the secular surrogate of another Kingdom whose horizon is no longer within our range' (31). The tone is decidedly more melancholy than that found in *The Romantic Image*, but there remains the sense of a unified being, which if it cannot exactly be known nevertheless requires us to seek it out. Or as Kermode writes in *A Genesis of Secrecy*, 'If there is one belief (however the facts resist it) that unites us all, from the evangelists to those who argue away inconvenient portions of their texts, and those who spin large plots to accommodate the discrepancies and dissonances into some larger scheme, it is this conviction that somehow, in some occult fashion, if we could only detect it, everything will be found to hang together' (AP, 72). (Twenty-one years later, Kermode can still be found speaking in these terms: 'We expect everything to hang together' [Interview with Katie Donovan].) The belief moves him to speak of 'the purpose of criticism,' one of the arts, as 'illumination' (AT, 5). It also moves him to say that '[w]e are all fulfillment men, *pleromatists*: we all seek the center that will allow the senses to rest, at any rate for one interpreter, at any rate for one moment' (GS, 72).

Practical circumstances make a 'single right reading' an impossible thing (AT, 102), but not because such is thought not to exist. If one's interpretative powers were great enough, one might experience 'the perception of a momentary radiance' (GS, 145), momentary for the reason that everything stands in the way of our seeing truth in its ultimate form. Kermode is idealistic enough to think that 'a perfect interpretation would, as Valéry said of pure reality, stop the heart' (FOA, 91), and realistic enough to think that such seldom occurs. Interpretation, in its most aspirant mode, is an attempt at re-cognition, an attempt to merge meaning with truth. Those interpretations that aspire to do less encourage the divorce of meaning and truth, and while they help us to see that a text 'has internal relationships independent of the coding procedures by which we may find it transparent upon a known world,' they forego 'the possibility of consensus, and of access to a single truth at the heart of thing' (GS, 122–3). In short, no one, says Kermode, alluding to Kafka's parable of the man before the Law, 'however special his point of vantage, can get past all those doorkeepers into the shrine of the single sense' (GS, 123). We are urged to acknowledge this more. But doing so forces us to reconceive the '[t]he pleasures of interpretation' as thereby 'linked to loss and disappointment, so that most of us will find the task too hard, or simply repugnant; and then, abandoning meaning, we slip back into the old comfortable fictions of transparency, the single sense, the truth' (ibid.), something different from that truth which makes its presence felt, but is never known.

There is no certitude that there is such a truth, and experience often compels us to think otherwise. Yet not all the time, and there are enough occasions when reality suggests that beneath the palimpsest of the quotidian things do somehow hang together. Kermode speaks of the importance of *Vorverständnis*, or the ability to understand something before we have been introduced to all its details: 'Even at the level of the sentence we have some ability to understand a statement before we have heard it all, or at any rate to follow it with a decent provisional sense of its outcome; and we can do this only because we bring to our interpretation of the sentence a pre-understanding of its totality. We may be wrong on detail, but not, as a rule, wholly wrong' (GS, 70).[3] This *Vorverständnis* is a form of intuition, something Kermode grants the value of in his discussion of divination ('Something, therefore, must happen, some intuition by which we break out of this situation – a leap, a *divination*, ... whereby we are enabled to understand both part and whole' [AP, 154]). Intuition has often been conceived as an important element of knowledge. In the *Critique of Judgement,* Kant writes that 'intuition is also a factor in knowledge, and a faculty of *complete spontaneity of intuition* would be a cognitive faculty distinct from sensibility and wholly independent of it. Hence it would be understanding in the widest sense of the term' (II, 62). More recently, Thomas Nagel, in a discussion of moral understanding, writes: 'To trust our intuitions, ... we need only believe that our ... understanding extends farther than our capacity to spell out the principles which underlie it. Intuition can be corrupted by customs, self-interest, or commitment to a theory, but it need not be' (*Quality and Partiality*, 7).

Keenly aware of those historical and social contingencies that make interpretation such a fool's game, Kermode nevertheless refuses to relinquish the dream of plenitude. Rather, like the rabbis' midrash, his work, 'with all its accommodations, updatings and euphemisms, still aspires to the condition of the impossible presence of the Word' (AT, 25). Meanwhile, because Kermode is ever mindful of this 'impossible presence,' he is especially prepared for viewing readings as either carnal or spiritual. Carnal readings are those that fail to see the figurative in the literal, that fail to see, in addition to what the text reveals, what it hides. 'Carnal readings are much the same. Spiritual readings are all different' (GS, 9). The reason is that whereas the former reading hankers to see things in black-and-white terms, the latter does not. It imagines the text as radiant with meaning, wherein every part has some significance with regard to the ultimate meaning: 'where enigmas are credibly thought to exist in a text, it is virtually impossible to maintain that some parts of it are certainly not enigmatic' (GS, 53). Texts are enigmatic, mysterious, but to the spiritual reader, this is not something that repels, but instead draws the person on with the hope of solving the puzzle. Why should this be so? Well, perhaps, because, as Kermode claims, 'it require[s] a more strenuous effort to believe that a narrative lacks coherence than to believe that somehow, if we could only find out, it doesn't' (GS, 53). Not everyone thinks this way. In fact, it would seem that only a minority experience the need to pursue texts back to their first sense. Kermode himself has a '"recuperative" temperament' (AT, 7), and his understanding of interpretation is much like those rabbis who thought 'that they must not interfere with the original sense in adding others, and also that in doing so they were not really adding at all, but merely working towards the restoration of the full original meaning, a plenum that human endeavour cannot ever hope to achieve' (AT, 25).

The desire for the 'original sense' leads not to a final resting place, but to more interpretations. That is, much like the concept of literature's perpetual modernity, the longing for something beyond or anterior to the text engenders, ironically, more texts. Instead of freeing oneself from an irksome situation, the hermeneut only makes the situation more so for those who follow. The temptation for the one who comes later will be to ignore the history of prior interpretation, and to aim for the thing-itself. The Protestant Reformation itself was in some measure about this, that is, the distrust of a history of interpretation combined with the sense that one might know the Gospels first-hand. Raised in the Anglican Low Church, Kermode is not dismissive of Protestant-like desires for original meanings. In his interview with Michael Payne, he recalls the canonical dispute between Brevard Childs and James Barr, the latter of whom argues 'that the vocation of biblical scholars is to see through, as it were, the mess that history has made of the books, to what actually happened in the first place' (PNH, 73). Kermode speaks of himself as 'a great admirer of Barr,' and of finding his view attractive. Still, he thinks, in the end, that Childs has the better argument; and that is to see the canon as text plus commentary, or the Gospels as part and parcel of their interpretative history: 'Childs's view is that the whole canon is the formation of historical evolution, which is really the same as the historical evolution of a single book; so there is perfect justification for not breaking the canon down into its constituents, and then breaking the constituents down into their constituents, but treating it as a whole, recognizing that all sorts of historical influences were brought to bear, sometimes irrelevantly, sometimes not' (ibid. 73).

If this is the case, thinks Kermode, then it would be fair to say that had a text – he mentions the Book of Ecclesiastes – not been included in the original canon, we would read it differently were it suddenly to be rediscovered. Our understanding of the text, no longer coloured by centuries of commentary and praise, would be so radically altered that we might easily say that we were talking about two separate texts. Here, Kermode has been much influenced by the work of John Barton, and, in the Payne interview, offers the idea as Barton's:

> Let's take a particular book, the Book of Ecclesiastes is the one he [Barton] takes. Supposing it had not got into the canon of the Jewish Bible, as it might not have done, because it could obviously be represented as an undesirable book in some ways. The Book of Revelation would be a parallel in the Christian canon. But supposing Ecclesiastes had not been included and had therefore disappeared from view, which it certainly would have done because of the rather strict Jewish tradition which kept the inside of the books in high profile and let the others go. Supposing instead it had been found at Qumran with certain of the other documents which had been totally lost and forgotten. Now, Barton says it wouldn't be the same book. It would be literally identical, or very close to being identical with the one that we have, but it still wouldn't be the same book because it had missed out on two thousand years of attention, and that makes all the difference. (PNH, 74)

The context in which a book is read makes a difference, and I would say with Kermode that it 'makes all the difference.' It is difficult to imagine that were we only now to discover the text of *Hamlet* that we would not attribute importance to it, even if we did not ascribe it to Shakespeare; but it is also hard to imagine that, after the Shoah, anyone reads *The Merchant of Venice* without being sensitive to the question of anti-Semitism. Contexts alter texts, and while Kermode is not alone in his longing for a single right reading, he is right to stress the importance of the interpretative history, the whole in which any text resides. The text is never distinct from this whole, and if the latter is identified with the canon, we see how it is that a book not yet considered part of the literary canon – e.g., William Gaddis's *J R* (1975) – is read quite differently, no matter how extraordinary it might be, than one that is. '[W]orks transmitted inside a canon are understood differently from those without, so that, if only in that sense, the canon, however assembled, forms an integral whole, the internal and external relations of which are both proper subjects of disinterested inquiry' (LGB, 608). This gives the canon the quality of a living organism, not so unlike the world itself: 'It remains quite difficult to think of the wholeness of a canon without associating the idea with the wholeness of an organism or the wholeness of a world' (LGB, 608).

For Kermode, the canon is understood as text plus commentary: 'If texts were all, canons would quickly cease to be of much interest. But it is pointless to think about canons without first thinking about commentary; the two go together, there is never the first without the second; without commentary canons would, as such, simply disappear' (AP, 15). This is why midrash, as a way of reading, has so interested him, for it is in the nature of this rabbinical practice to stress the additive nature of interpretation. As already noted, it is not that the rabbis forswore a commitment to the original sense of things; rather, for them, midrash has been a way of keeping that sense modern. 'By midrash the interpreter, either by rewriting the story or explaining it in a more acceptable sense, bridges the gap between an original and a modern audience' (GS, x). Like old narratives in general, Biblical stories age, and their value for modern audiences is always in need of restatement or reinterpretation. If we were required to understand such stories in the manner of our ancestors, we might well reject them out of hand. They would appear too foreign, and while a minority might choose to repress all modern considerations in their favour, the majority would choose otherwise. The stories thus need to be reinterpreted, not for the purpose of making hard truths less difficult, but so that the past and present can be put in touch with each other. This is, in large part, what midrash does. Yet if midrash starts to appear too attentive to historical circumstances – thereby lending support to the 'commonplace that Israel's God is a God of history' (Kugel, 'Two Introductions to Midrash,' 84) – we also need to take note of the fact that for the rabbinical commentator the Bible exists in a space that has, over time, become almost ahistorical. Or to put this another way, the Hebrew Bible, like other sacred books, seems almost to exist – despite its multitude of 'one-time events that, having happened, change things forever' (ibid.) – before history, a sense of things that only adds to its authoritative claim; and forces the rabbi to turn backward to the Bible, that place where God first spoke. James Kugel writes: 'For in midrash the Bible becomes ... a world unto itself. Midrashic exegesis is the way into that world; it does not seek to view present-day reality through biblical spectacles, neither to find referents to the daily life of the soul in biblical allegory. Instead it simply overwhelms the present; the Bible's time is important, while the present is not; and so it invites the reader to cross over into the enterable world of Scripture' (90).

Here, we have another sense of midrash: the desire not only to return to beginnings but to get things right. The word 'midrash,' Kermode writes, 'derives from *darash*, to probe or examine,' and this seems fitting, for the most pressing aim is 'to penetrate and reveal a secret sense; to show what is concealed in what is proclaimed' (GS, x). We might, then, best understand midrash in relation to *peshat*, defined as the plain sense of things. The two are 'an intrinsic plural; ... the play, might one say even gaiety, of the one is required to give a human sense to the inaccessible mystery of the other' (AP, 174). The point is, the plain sense is never that – plain. It is a figure for that part of experience which we would like to think of as discrete and discernible, but the moment we try to cognize it, we discover how much it is part of a larger whole, in this instance, midrash. The dilemma parallels the problem of the hermeneutic circle, wherein one needs 'to understand the whole to understand the parts, the parts to understand the whole' (TC, 76). *Peshat* cannot be understood apart from its relation to midrash, nor midrash apart from its relation to *peshat*. Midrash is always seeking to discover *peshat*, always trying to pull out the real from the world in which it hides. It is, says Kermode, the problem of interpretation itself: 'Interpretation may be regarded not as modern increments but rather as discoveries of original meanings hitherto hidden; so that, together with the written text, these interpretations constitute a total object of which the text is but a part or version: an Oral Torah, or Oral Tradition, preserved by an apostolic institution, equal in authority to and coeval with the written' (FOA, 75). This said, we should perhaps note that there have been other attempts, of late, to extend this relation of interpretation to text – which, as we can see, Kermode prefers to view in light of its quality of conflation – to the point that the text's priority to commentary finds itself called into question. David Stern, for instance, writes that 'Midrash ... touches upon literature not at that point where literature becomes exegesis but at what might be called its opposite conjunction, where exegesis turns into literature and comes to possess its own language and voice' (105). And Geoffrey Hartman and Sanford Budick, editors of the volume *Midrash and Literature*, write in their 'Introduction': 'By confronting the undecidability of textual meaning, this species of interpretation [i.e., midrash] does not paralyze itself. Instead its own activity is absorbed into the activity of the text, producing a continuum of intextual supplements, often in a spirit of high-serious play. And even when we encounter play of a seemingly outrageous kind we cannot dismiss it as merely self-indulgence, because the phenomena of intertexuality and supplementarity systematically achieve, to a remarkable degree, the very effacement of self' (xi). In an aside, Hartman and Budick admit that midrash's theological nature places 'significant constraints and restraints upon [its] freedom' (ibid.), but this is not something that they wish to dwell on, for the purpose of their volume is to connect midrash with that 'whole universe of allusive textuality (the history of writing itself, some say) which lately goes by the name of *intextuality*' (ibid.). However, not all their contributors – 'Reb Kermode' included (ibid.) – seek to go where they would lead, a fact that enhances the value of the volume.[4]

For Kermode, one of the most notable instances of midrash is not strictly speaking a Jewish text at all; it is the New Testament. That is, what strikes Kermode about the Gospels is how often they refer to the Hebrew Bible, as if they sought to rewrite it. And in a sense, they did seek to rewrite it, for if it seemed important not to disavow the tradition which produced Jesus (something that Marcion wished to do, later in the second century), it was going to be necessary to explain the relation of the Jewish Bible to the still unwritten stories pertaining to Jesus's life. One way to do this is to do as Matthew did, which was to grant the older 'text its sanctity and its perpetual force, but ... to assume[ ] that in an important sense it is not complete in itself' (LGB, 388). It was to see Jesus as the Christ, the fulfiller of Biblical prophecy. Here, the Hebrew Bible found its importance radically transformed. Now, instead of being read as the history of the Jewish people's relation to God, it found itself read, by the evolving Christian community, allegorically, as a prefiguring of future events. For Matthew, the 'event or saying foreshadowed in the old text is fulfilled in the new, and the new is therefore validated by it; but it also contains and transcends it. The relation of the new to the old is a typological relation; though the old was complete and invited no addition it must nevertheless be completed. It is as if history and story acquired a new and unexpected dimension' (ibid.). It is in this sense that Matthew's Gospel can be seen as 'an interpretation of the Jewish Bible' or, in short, as midrash (LGB, 401).

Understanding Matthew's Gospel in this light also helps to explain how it is that secrecy plays such an important part in interpretation. Matthew's interpretation of the Jewish Bible is an insider's reading. It offers a reading of that text which only those who are privy to a Christian viewpoint can see. Others, coming to this same Jewish Bible, would altogether miss the allegory of Christ's prefigurement. Seeing, they should not see; and hearing, they should not hear. They would, in this situation, be outsiders. In another situation, they might well be insiders, for interpretation does not create a permanent caste of insiders and outsiders, but moves people about depending on the secret. 'If we cannot agree about the nature of the secret, we are nevertheless compelled to agree that secrecy exists, the source of the interpreter's pleasures, but also of his necessary disappointment' (GS, xi). The disappointment comes when the secret, the plain sense, refuses to give up its truth. One seeks to say what it is, but ends up talking about everything that is not it, as when critics attempt to tell us what *literature* is. Disappointment, then, is part and parcel of the equation, though knowing this does not stop us from seeking out the secret. Rather, we seek to divine the narrative's meaning, that secret which, should we discern it, would guide us in our interpretation of the larger whole. It is true that the part cannot be understood without reference to the whole, nor the whole without reference to the part. Yet if we should stop here, we would find ourselves in a textual labyrinth. How do we escape such a bind? Kermode, looking back to Schleiermacher, stresses the need for divination, the reaching for an answer that is as much directed by intuition as anything else: 'To break out of this bind you have to perform an act of divination: that is, you have to bring something to the text that was not already in it. This intuitive leap must be the historical warrant for all theories which allow the interpreter to make his own productive contribution to the text' (AT, 203).

It is in the nature of divination that it highlights some aspects of the text and excludes others, much as the New Testament's reading of the Hebrew Bible suggested that great portions were better left in the shadows: 'that which is edifying [in the Hebrew Bible] is so only because it already conforms with the New Testament, and the unedifying has to be made edifying by figurative reading in New Testament terms' (AP, 179). If elements cannot be made to serve present purposes, there is a tendency to forget them. Exclusions are, in a sense, as much a part of the process of interpretation as inclusions. Faced with 'an indefinite measure of plurality' (AT, 73), interpreters do well to remember 'the importance of forgetting' (AT, 106). They repress some textual elements in favour of others, so that the text's potential openness does not undo them. We appear 'programmed to prefer fulfillment to disappointment, the closed to the open' (GS, 64). So, when confronted with the criticism of a Jonathan Culler – 'Closure ... testifies to the presence of an ideology' – Kermode responds that while the 'halt of free movement of senses within a text' might be thought 'a kind of wickedness,' 'it is our only means of reading until revolutionary new concepts of writing prevail' (GS, 71). It is a sound judgment, even as we feel, more than ever, the need to be attentive to those realities beyond our peripheries.

It is because we are each historically situated, because it is impossible for anyone to comprehend the larger truth of things, that, one, divination is necessary and, two, secrecy prevails. Frustrated by the penury of our lots, we seek to divine the way things stand as when seen by God. And so 'we tend to reserve our highest praise for those interpretations that seem most intuitive, most theory-free, seeming to proceed from some untrammeled divinatory impulse, having the gratuity, the fortuity of genius' (GS, 4). A materialist would think the whole project foolhardy, an attempt to make the world accord with one's most sentimental longings rather than with obdurate fact. Nor would this person's scepticism be allayed by that logic which converts absences into presences: 'the initiate assumes that the absence of some usual satisfactions, the disappointment of conventional expectations, connote the existence of other satisfactions, deeper and more difficult, inaccessible to those who see without perceiving and hear without understanding' (GS, 7). Aware of the pitfalls, Kermode prefers the spiritual to the carnal reading, for the latter appears passive before facts, whereas the former ventures to interpret facts in the light of the hope that the world possesses a structure and an order congruent with our desire. '[T]here is the *moment* of interpretation, the discovery or choice of what, after Dilthey, might be called an "impression-point." One may perceive in a life some moment that gives sense and structure to the whole, and it need not come at the end of the life; Dilthey cites the conversion of Augustine, which made sense of the apparently unrelated flux of events on which it supervened – it is a part with a relation of particular privilege to the whole' (GS, 16).

It is exactly this choice, or divination, that makes, however, for secrecy. When Augustine chooses to live his life one way rather than another, it is the consequence of an interpretation, one which will, in its outward signs, make sense only to those similarly committed, and appear mysteriously uncommunicative to all others. It is, thinks Kermode, the way of all divinations: they simultaneously both reveal and conceal. To the elect, they reveal a truth that will to others appear more like a delusion. Truth in this sense means an insight, even if momentary, of how the larger world holds together. For Kermode, the world, properly seen, bespeaks a radiance. This radiance, however, is not out there for all to see, for it shelters itself in reality's recesses. Even when it permits itself to be seen, the view is never complete. Just as our views of the world are always partial, what glimpses we are afforded of this splendour are themselves partial. They speak of our historical circumstance, 'though now that limitation is no longer thought of just as a limitation – it is the prerequisite of interpretation, each act of which is unique, one man on one stool, so to speak, seeing what no power can withhold from him, his glimpse of the radiance' (GS, 39–40).

It is divination that makes even this partial insight into the world's plain sense possible. Without this, we would always live suspended between part and whole, between *peshat* and midrash. For the most part, we do remain suspended, for the divining moment of radiance is the startling exception. Still, to the extent that the plain sense of things reveals itself, we become more confident that interpretations can be spoken of as true and false. 'The plain sense is hidden' (AP, 176), but this does not mean that it cannot be discerned. In fact, the driving ambition of interpretation is to discern, if not to discover, the plain sense. Mostly, however, interpretation will lead us astray; it will not bring us to the plain sense but to its simulacrum, that which looks like, or is mistaken for, it, but which is something else. The plain sense remains in its shelter, and mystery prevails. Interpretation, then, is not only the servant of clarity, but of mystery. '[W]ithout interpretation,' says Kermode, 'there would be no mystery' (GS, 126). And while nowadays, there is a rush to 'de-mystify' our understandings both of interpretation and experience at large, Kermode holds to the sense that there is something irreducible about the world that remains forever beyond our ken and also forever determinant, thus requiring our efforts to know it, to interpret it: 'We are unwilling to accept mystery, what cannot be reduced to other and more intelligible forms. Yet that is what we find here: something irreducible, therefore perpetually to be interpreted; not secrets to be found out one by one, but Secrecy' (GS, 143).

For Kermode, the Gospel parables, as texts, have always proven instructive. For one, there is Jesus's own explanation of his purposes, an explanation that, says Kermode, illustrates his own thesis about insiders and outsiders: 'When Jesus was asked to explain the purpose of his parables, he described them as stories *told to them without* – to outsiders – with the express purpose of concealing a mystery that was to be understood only by insiders' (GS, 2). It is not clear whether Jesus spoke in parables in order to conceal a mystery or to make it more manifest. Kermode points to the interpretative problems surrounding Mark 4: 11–12 ('To you [the disciples] has been given the secret of the kingdom of God, but for those outside everything is in parables; so that they may indeed see but not perceive, and may indeed hear but not understand; lest they should turn again, and be forgiven'). Here, in a passage adapted from Isaiah 6: 9–10, Mark seems to suggest that Jesus employed the parable to make more certain the present case, a multitude seeing without truly seeing, and hearing without truly hearing. Whether this is what Mark really meant to say or is a problem in translation (did Mark use *hina* [in order that] when he meant *hoti* [because]?) is uncertain. Our inclination is to want him to say something quite different, as in Matthew 13: 13: 'This is why I speak to them in parables, because seeing they do not see, and hearing they do not hear, nor do they understand.'[5] We prefer *hoti* to *hina*. Kermode, however, is not altogether satisfied with this substitution: 'One says the stories are obscure on purpose to damn the outsiders; the other, even if we state it in the toughest form the language will support, says that they are not necessarily impenetrable, but that outsiders, being what they are, will misunderstand them anyway' (GS, 32). This seems a forced reading, the sort that de Man sometimes offered when the purpose was to accent the 'vertiginous possibilities of referential aberration' (*Allegories*, 10).[6] In fact, one might observe a parallel between Kermode's notion of secrecy and de Man's notion of blindness as they relate to interpretation. In *Forms of Attention* (1985), Kermode writes, 'De Man gives *Blindness and Insight* a marvelous epigraph from Proust: "Cette perpetualle erreur, qui est précisément la vie ..." The blindness is vital and beneficent, for all interpretations are erroneous,' and then goes on to add, 'but some, in relation to their ultimate purpose, are good nevertheless, saying what they had not meant or more than they meant, and defeating time' (FOA, 91). This last note is pure Kermode, reflective of one who views the parable as not only illustrating the need for, and the limitation of, interpretation, but also as manifesting a truth that, though conveyed differently to outsiders and insiders, nevertheless remains one: 'Parable, it seems, may proclaim a truth as a herald does, and at the same time conceal truth like an oracle' (GS, 47).

This discussion is not irrelevant to Kermode's understanding of the canonical. For him, the canonical literary work, like a Gospel parable, does not yield its meaning easily, and while, like a sacred text, it hints of transcendent meanings, it does so darkly. The canonical text retains, over time, a mystery that more mundane texts do not. Interpreters come and go, yet there remain more things to be discovered and said about the text. In *Forms of Attention*, Kermode seeks to illustrate, in his chapters on Botticelli and *Hamlet*, that even the most often discussed canonical works yield, when pressed, new meanings. There is, not surprisingly, a temptation to think otherwise. Kermode himself prefaces his discussion of the Shakespeare drama with the question, 'If one allows the assumption that something new ought regularly to be said, how is one to say something new, and not manifestly absurd, about *Hamlet*?' (FOA, 31). And then, in his discussion of doubling, he goes ahead and opens the drama to new insights. That he can do so has everything to do with the fact – questions of interpretative communities aside – that the drama possesses both manifest and latent senses; and while the first are more readily understood, and the second are understood in time, the relations between the two seem unlimited. Assumptions of this sort are characteristically made about canonical texts, texts that share with the sacred at least this quality: that however a particular epoch or a particular community may define a proper mode of attention or a licit area of interest, there will always be something else and something different to say ... And this is what it means to call a book canonical' (FOA, 62).

Canonical texts, Kermode argues, have a quality of 'permanent value' or 'perpetual modernity' (ibid.). This sense of permanence is reinforced by the fact that such texts, by virtue of their canonical status, usually find their material form frozen, as scholars hasten to supply definitive texts. 'The process of selecting the canon may be very long but, once it is concluded, the inside works will normally be provided with the kinds of reading they require if they are to keep their immediacy to any moment; that is, to maintain their modernity. They quickly acquire immunity to textual alteration, so the necessary changes must all be interpretative' (FOA, 75). Canonical texts are read differently from other texts. The recipients of kind attention, their interpreters, by and large, seek to perpetuate their status, to find new evidence for their modernity, and thus their permanence. The motives are not all above suspicion, for scholars' identities are often intertwined with their subjects, and the Austen or Whitman scholar has a vested interest in seeing his or her artist praised. Readers and the institutions they serve are, then, part and parcel of the canonical equation, leading Kermode, at one point, to say that 'we need not histories of literature but histories of reading' (AT, 123). The point is that a canonical work would lose its sacramental status if those insiders (i.e., scholars) most sensitive to its hidden values should die off. 'It is clear that there is, in the canonical texts, a reserve of privileged senses which are accessible only to people who in some measure have the kind of training, and are supported by the authority, of the learned institution to which they belong. And even in the most disinterested forms of interpretation – those which depend on historical enquiry or editorial techniques – there is, practically always, some effect from a prior doctrinal commitment' (AT, 175). For Kermode, there is an extraordinary intimacy between a canonical work and its scholars, so that if the latter are placed under threat, so is the former. This helps to explain his past anger about the academy's generational war, for it was not only the old guard that was being threatened, it was also the canon itself, with all its secrets. In fact, Kermode seems to regard his own eventual demise as a less serious matter than that of the canon's conceivable demise – i.e., the canon which he and his contemporaries have made such an intimate part of their lives that they may rightly be thought to have a sort of proprietary relation to it. About the canon's would-be dismantlers, Kermode says they

> are quite unimpressed by the assertion, however vehement, that 'we' – the protectors of a canon they but not we regard as an enclosure of inert cultural monuments – *know*, as surely as we know anything at all, that certain poems, certain paintings, certain pieces of music can be confidently regarded as more valuable than others. For 'we' know these works with an intimacy their prejudices prevent them from acquiring and are experienced in the endless business of exploring them, a business in which our opponents have never joined, see no need to join, indeed would regard it as treachery to their cause to join. Hence the difficulty of entering into anything like a real discussion: one set of interpreters thinks it absurd to be called upon to explain that *Le Nozze di Figaro* is worthy of a form of attention that can safely be withheld from rap or rock, while the other scorns the very notion of listening attentively to an opera by a dead white male much admired by dead white males. ('Freedom and Interpretation,' 56)

Kermode knows that canonical choices entail elements of 'a prior doctrinal commitment,' but he wishes to extend the discussion of canonicity beyond the matter of whose interests are served. He is too dismissive of this latter question – the sort which, as Paul Lauter argues, might be formulated as 'what one reads' rather than 'how one reads' (*Canons and Contexts*, 158). He wants to imagine a canon as *also* existing apart from the cultural matrix, where it seems worthwhile to discuss the canonical in light of its enduring value and 'quasi-sacred status' (PNH,

31). For Kermode, there is a genuine link between religious and secular canons, and it has to do with the conviction that both are about secret meanings, requiring devoted investigation and hinting of transcendent purposes. Like John's Gospel, wherein 'he is always attending to his deepest purpose, which is the representation of the eternal in relation to the transient, of the manifestations of being in a world of becoming' (LGB, 453), the canonical work is best recognized by its aspirations to permanence. Or as Kermode writes, 'the only rule common to all inter- pretation ... is that the canonical work, so endlessly discussed, must be assumed to have permanent value' (FOA, 62). Many would now ques- tion this, yet it is central to Kermode's definition of the canonical, that work which 'is fixed in time but applicable to all time' and which 'has figural qualities not to be detected, save at an appropriate moment in the future' (FOA, 75).[7] Meanwhile, it is because the canonical work shares with the sacred a quality of guarded secrecy and mystery that the literary scholars' investigation of it resembles the manner in which reli- gious scholars have long investigated sacred texts. That is, in addition to attending to manifest meanings, Jews and Christians have long assumed 'that there were *secrets* in the text, and that they could be brought to light only by devoted research.' Accordingly, rabbis and clerics can be said to have 'anticipated ambitious secular commentary, which really became possible only when certain texts were granted a pseudo- canonical status' (PNH, 31). The texts Kermode has in mind include *Hamlet, Paradise Lost,* and *Ulysses.* About the last, he says that it 'has been expounded with a devotion that might well, even in its occasional excesses, be called religious. We are talking about a spiritual encyclope- dia' (AP, 211).

The search for occulted meanings has, argues Kermode, been very much part of modernism, of both its literature and criticism: 'Modern literature, and in its wake modern criticism, have been increasingly con- cerned with the double plot, occult and obvious, the plot of time and the plot of intimate structural relationships' (AP, 209). The interest has not been confined to writers and critics, for it has also been an interest of psychologists, anthropologists, mythographers, and others, but it probably has had its most notable and widespread successes in literary study. '[H]owever the matter is expressed, there are always ... two plots, and one of them is always deeper, darker, and more primitive than the other; for it escapes time, whereas its companion is always in time, con- cerned with things that happen, with the apparently unpredictable say- ings and doings of its agents, with anecdote and excess. And the value of

this plot depends on its fidelity to the first' (AP, 210). It is the intercon-
nectedness of the two that makes all the seemingly quotidian events in a
book such as *Ulysses* (not to speak of the world itself) relevant: 'The fact
is ... that when a book reaches the quasi-sacred status attained by *Ulysses*
we assume that everything we can find out about it is valuable, including
every possible parallel, whether intended or not; and whether we are
baffled or not by this magical view of the world' (AP, 214). Other critics
have suggested that we might image the book's relation to the world as
less metaphoric than metonymic, though doing so undercuts a book's
mystery, making it seem one contingent event among others. The sense
of things being invested with spiritual meaning gives way, for New His-
torcists and the like, to a more material description. Kermode, however,
prefers to understand the book as the shadow of something hidden; and
this, in turn, has consequences for what he understands as literary criticism's purposes. Thus, speaking of modern literary criticism (in effect,
his own practice), he writes: 'Literary criticism has tended toward what
has been called, figuratively, spatial interpretation, which means only
that books are considered not *sub specie temporis* but rather as what
Augustine thought of as images of eternity. It looks for secrets, for what
is not declared overtly, for the occult or secret plots in poems and narratives. Its interpretations complete what is already in principle complete
by revealing those hidden plots, the mysteries and the ground of the
mysteries' (AP, 221).

In the same essay, 'The Bible: Story and Plot,' Kermode acknowledges
that 'the great early-twentieth-century myth of the book as world, which
has taken so many different forms in modern creative and critical writing, may not survive for long into a future where information is pro-
cessed in disparate bits' (AP, 222). In truth, it probably has already given
way. This might help to explain why Kermode has lashed out at critics
such as Jonathan Culler and Houston Baker regarding their notion of
canonicity. For Culler, Baker, Lauter, and many current scholars, there is
a desire both to resist the canon and to enlarge it. The ambition is, perhaps, not as contradictory as it sounds. In any event, what unifies the
complex desire is a politics that seeks to be more welcoming of the university's increasingly diversified population. For Culler, the traditional
canon gave literature departments licence to monumentalize a group of
texts that were often axiologically at odds with the students' own, more
varied histories. 'The New Criticism succeeded as well as it did,' he
writes, 'because it could function as a way of making the literary heritage accessible to a growing and more diversified student body entering

universities. This model would lead one to expect literature departments to devote considerable energy to controlling the content of offerings ... It gives criticism the role of interpreting the canon, elucidating the "core" of knowledge to be conveyed' (*Framing the Sign*, 33). For Culler and others, the canon has been hitherto defined in terms that are crypto-religious and narrowly aesthetic. Culler, for one, has made it clear that he thinks the literary academy too ready 'to legitimize religious discourse and strengthen its political power rather than to foster a critique of religion and religious authoritarianism' (71). Others, including John Guillory, have argued that the canon, with its celebration of literary language, tends to homogenize what is read. Guillory writes that 'literary culture has aspired to canonical consensus, an illusion reinforced by the cognitive silence of the literary work, the silencing of difference. Very simply, canonical authors are made to *agree* with one another; the ambiguity of literary language means nothing less than the *univocity* of the canon' ('Ideology of Canon Formation,' 350). To defeat such practices, we are urged to read more non-canonical texts, for they, says Lauter, '*teach us* how to view experience through the prisms of gender, race, nationality, and other forms of marginalization' (*Canons and Contexts*, 161).

Guillory is something of an exception among such critics, for he, thinking the issue of representation more complex than it is generally given credit for, does not maintain that the reading of noncanonical texts will necessarily solve the problem of literature's deracination. Nor does he think that noncanonical texts have been excluded from the classroom. In fact, he believes that the noncanonical is already treated as a version – albeit sharper and more politically astute – of the canonical. This, he thinks, is not something that the promoters of the noncanonical truly wish to trumpet, for if avowed, it should undercut the institutional privileges that accrue to them as befitting their cutting-edge status. They have, in short, too much invested in their being understood as unfairly marginalized. Yet as Guillory writes: 'the most surprising aspect of the current legitimation crisis is the fact that the "noncanonical" is not what fails to appear in the classroom, but what, in the context of liberal pedagogy, *signifies exclusion*. The noncanonical is a newly constituted category of text production and reception, permitting certain authors and texts to be *taught* as noncanonical, to have the status of noncanonical works in the classroom. This effect is quite different from the effect of total absence, of nonrepresentation *tout court*' (*Cultural Capital*, 9). The noncanonical has become a more contemporary version of modernism's avant garde, except rather than a text's finding distinction in technical experimentation, it now finds its distinction by prominently addressing a set of social and politic themes, especially those involving issues of race, gender, and class. The noncanonical has also become something like a giant divider for separating progressives from reactionaries, it being understood that there is no middle ground. Again, Guillory writes: 'the social referents of inclusion and exclusion – the dominant or subordinate groups defined by race, gender, class, or national status – are now represented in the discourse of canon formation by two groups of authors and texts: the canonical and the noncanonical. It is only *as* canonical works that certain texts can be said to represent hegemonic social groups. Conversely, it is only *as* noncanonical works that certain other texts can truly represent socially subordinated groups' (*Cultural Capital,* 9). That both life and literature, if not academic politics, are much more complex than this binary allows, is the truth that generally goes unacknowledged.

Not that Kermode is taken in. He is aware of how even decent purposes can be corrupted by more selfish interests; and of how even a small group can make it appear that it has a proprietary hold on virtue, to the point that it not only gains more adherents but also makes all those who resist feel the weight of being ethical retreatists, whereupon they too acquiesce or, if not, they keep their resistance private:

> The political attack on literature considered as a belletristic canon imposed by unjust authority – often a theme, though an uneasy one, of Marxist criticism – has been greatly strengthened by our enhanced consciousness of sexist and racist injustice, and our wish to eliminate them: so that campaigns for women's canons, black canons, black women's canons, campaigns against white male dominance in literature as elsewhere, can be seen to reflect larger movement in public sentiment and public conscience. Political 'attacks on literature' and on canon can thus be prosecuted in the knowledge that those who oppose them need to explain how they can do so and still be credited with a measure of political purity; and they themselves may suffer some disturbance to their social conscience, or just feel irked at being called reactionary, or even fascist. This partly explains one central aspect of the present situation – the lack of any resolute resistance to the decanonization of literature now in rapid progress in the United States, and probably elsewhere – a process often accompanied, strangely enough at first sight, since it is the project of people who think canons wicked, by the construction of rival canons *de novo* with, of course,

no real pretense that their purpose is other than political and revolutionary. (AP, 23–4)

What upsets Kermode is his sense that many literary scholars have vacated the middle ground, either because they have failed to see that literature (as it is identified with notions of openness and irreducible meaning) is dependent on this ground, or because they no longer believe in literature's distinctiveness and importance. Or if they do so, it is more as a means to an end than as a proper end in its own right, qualified as this must be. Once again, then, it is as if Plato's heirs, with their suspicions of poetry, have obtained the upper hand, not simply in the managerial class and larger academy, where their forces have always been potent, but in literature faculties themselves; so whereas in the past, there have always been fine minds to stand up in poetry's defence, today there are fewer such individuals. Instead, when Kermode looks around, he sees too many colleagues trying to outdo one another in their discrediting of not only specific literary texts but even of the category itself, much in the spirit of Jane Gallop's contention that 'literature is ... one among various signifying practices rather than ... a privileged site of "culture"' (*Around 1981*, 243). Kermode objects – at times angrily – to literature's demotion and to the now familiar practice of caricaturing literature as 'some form of stupefying aesthetic ideology' (AP, 13). Not without reason, he thinks that the literature that has traditionally been taught in British and American classrooms – i.e., Chaucer, Shakespeare, Donne, Johnson, Coleridge, Austen, Dickens, George Eliot, Balzac, Dostoevsky, Dickinson, James, Woolf, Stevens and company – has a more profound sense of life's complexity than its disparagers are likely to grant. True, few women or minority authors have hitherto been judged canonical, and for this, the literary establishment must assume its share of responsibility. But there is also warrant to the argument that pre-modern social realities and values were unaccommodating to such authorial aspirations. Or as Guillory notes: 'By defining canonicity as determined by the social identity of the author, the current critique of the canon both discovers, and misrepresents, the obvious fact that the older the literature, the less likely it will be that texts by socially defined minorities exist in sufficient numbers to produce a "representative" canon' (*Cultural Capital*, 15).[8] It might also be noted that writing is generally a quite isolating and individualistic occupation, and that rather than seeing the writer as the spokesperson for his or her time and place, we might do just as well to see this person in the role of adversary (especially in post-Romantic writings); or if this is also too reductive, then at least as figuring in a more complicated and vexed relation to society than that of most of his or her contemporaries. So, to esteem Shakespeare as complicitous with a misogynist society (e.g., 'Shakespeare ... depicts gender relations only in the framework of... maintaining the dominance of males while publicly denouncing the empowerment of women ...'[9]) may constitute an instance of being too ready to place the blame of larger cultural injustices upon individual authors, especially when we grant the role played by these same authors in our own later enlightenment. As bad faith arguments, such readings might themselves be construed as ethically problematic. This is not to say that all attempts to situate authors in terms of their cultural contexts – wherein the contexts are especially understood as possessing ethical and political consequences – are misguided. The truth is otherwise. Yet to the extent that literary scholars assume, with Lauter, that 'it is in the realms of ethics and politics that the question of the canon must now be contested' (*Canons and Contexts*, 170), the more they put themselves in danger of self-righteousness. The goal might be worth the risk, and many clearly think so; but it seems equally worthwhile to contemplate the ethical implications of reducing, by means of a tabloid-like attention, Hawthorne to a misogynist, Melville to a wife-beater, Whitman to a racist, Conrad to an imperialist, Eliot to an anti-Semite, and Bellow to a racist. These are serious accusations, and while at times treated as such (as in Ricks's *T.S. Eliot and Prejudice*), there is also a noticeable inclination (as in Anthony Julius's *T.S. Eliot, Anti-Semitism and Literary Form*) to dismiss authors and their work out-of-hand, on the basis of markedly partial representations of their biographies and work. It is easier to dismiss Eliot as a reactionary (or, in the instance of Lyndall Gordon's biography, as a cad)[10] than to deal with the difficulties of the poems and plays. It is easier for Culler to display his bigotry (e.g., he urges us 'not to assume that theistic beliefs deserve respect, any more than we would assume that sexist or racist beliefs deserve respect' [*Framing the Sign*, 80]) than for him to say anything interesting about religion.

This last reference brings us back to Kermode's own particular wranglings over the canon, for he has made clear his dissatisfaction with Culler's notion of canon, saying that he 'has very little idea of what a canon is, merely identifying the term with a state of affairs which his own metanarrative or crisis-fiction (roughly, that of the revolutionary purge) requires him to deplore' (AP, 14). In *Framing the Sign*, the book that provokes Kermode's ire, Culler views canonical literature with suspicion, admitting it into the curriculum only on the understanding that it does not say what it wishes to say: 'This is a point that deserves emphasis, for there should be no question of avoiding canonical texts. They are often, as deconstructive readings of the great works of English and German romanticism have shown, the most powerful demystifiers of the ideologies they have been shown to promote' (32). It even makes sense, he says, to include such texts, for while more 'exotic texts from other traditions' might better deconstruct our cultural values, their 'strangeness' makes 'the reading of them a process of naturalization, a matter of fitting them to our own categories' (ibid.). That some of our cultural values, and the works in which they are transmitted, might be worth nurturing, as opposed to 'demystifying,' weighs little with Culler. 'Accepted forms of thought,' he writes, 'can take care of themselves' (53). Kermode's own point is that they do not 'take care of themselves,' but need to be studied, understood, and cared for; and then passed down to subsequent generations in the form of a tradition. Canons are, most importantly, about value; and value 'is the product of intergenerational transactions. So are institutions, and the canons with which they have a reciprocal relation. They can certainly change – canons, institutions, and values – but such changes are perforce a matter of intricate negotiations (conducted by acts of reading, talking, and writing) and rarely of abolitionist propaganda' (AP, 40).

Perhaps Kermode overstates the case, but he thinks not. 'There are very strong anti-canonical and rival-canonical arguments going on now,' he says in the Salusinszky interview (117). Then, referring to remarks made by Houston Baker, the prominent scholar of African-American literature, he goes further, saying that

> the man who writes this piece goes on to say that dismantling the canon is the prime object of this enterprise. Well, of course, deconstructors oddly don't deconstruct the canon: they have to have something in its place. But he wants to remove works from the canon, by which I think he really means the list of things studied in English departments, names he doesn't specify that have been foisted on to them, by white males, who tell half-truths about everything. We've got to get rid of them, and replace them with black women writers like Zora Neale Hurston and Toni Morrison. Taking it to its extreme, this really means that he thinks that English departments should stop teaching, say, Spenser – I don't know what he had in mind: it might have been Wordsworth, it might have been Dickens – and put in these other objects of attention instead. Then he ends by saying that the

purpose of this is, in the end, a political purpose, a revolutionary purpose. I can't sufficiently express my disagreement with such a view. (CS, 118)[11]

Baker, an ex–Modern Language Association president, hardly fits the model of a radical; and my own sense is that while the piece ('Literature') referred to by Kermode is jargony and poorly conceived (e.g., 'theoretical accounts of the cultural products of race and gender will help to undermine the half-truths that white males have established as constituting American culture as a whole' [12]), Baker was hardly saying more than that the literature curriculum needed to be more reflective of the country's cultural diversity. This would appear to be a good thing, and work still remains to be done towards this goal. There are, however, other ambitions that make Kermode more uneasy, including Baker's desire to see literary study as synonymous with 'literary theory,' for the reason that this theory is 'full of disruptive and deeply political potential,' a potential that 'Afro-American and feminist critics will' be best positioned to understand and to exploit. An enlightened politics will then lead the way in the 'reshaping of the literary canon,' leaving a host of unnamed British and Anglo-American male authors out in the cold, as room is cleared for such 'Afro-American women writers as Zora Neale Hurston, Sonia Sanchez, Gloria Naylor, and Toni Morrison' (13).

While one might criticize Baker for his ingenuous notion of representation,[12] for Kermode the problem is more connected with his apparent dismissal of literature as itself a value. Granted, literature has never been a pure discipline, and for Kermode's generation, there was even a readiness to imagine it as a subset of religious longings. Despite this, Kermode would argue that he and his contemporaries maintained a healthy respect for the notion of literature qua literature, and that this respect, among members of the following generation, has gone by the wayside. The latter generation's notion of literature, thinks Kermode, is too analogous to that maintained by Culler, when he writes 'that formerly the history of criticism was part of the history of literature ... , but that now the history of literature is part of the history of criticism. Specifically, the history of literature in our day depends on what happens in the critical communities in universities: what is canonized, what is explicated, what is articulated as a major problem for literature. One might ... suggest that today the literary avant-garde simply *is* literary theory and criticism' (*Framing the Sign*, 40). It is a view that Kermode, while mindful of the relation of interpretation to literary value, finds anathematic, for the reason that it so sanguinely contemplates the displacement of

literature by theory. With many younger scholars deserting the camp of
poetry for that of Plato, Kermode finds himself more driven to reach
out, in the space of his reviews, to those common readers who also
might be thought of as having something to say as to what is, and is not,
considered literature. If academics increasingly evince less interest in literature, except as illustration or, worse, an object of scorn, the hope is
that others (including those teaching and studying in the burgeoning
creative writing departments)[13] might assume a greater share of the
responsibility for keeping it alive. Still, Kermode is not very optimistic
this way, and – like Harold Bloom who, in *The Western Canon*, wrote:
'This book is not directed to academics, because only a small remnant
of them still read for the love of reading. What Johnson and Woolf after
him called the Common Reader still exists and possibly goes on welcoming suggestions of what might be read' (518) – he is particularly dismayed by the increasing indifference of academics towards literature:

> It is not really possible for me (and for the remnant to which I suppose I
> belong) to think that the values we give to (or, more boldly, that we *recog-
> nize* in) *Hamlet* or *Coriolanus* or the 'Horatian Ode' (considered, of course,
> as works, totalities, not simply stretches of text) are the product of our own
> brainwashed responses. They are instances of literary value. It is true that
> the capacity to recognize such value is sometimes hard to distinguish from
> its shadow, the trained but vacuous response, the stock cultural OK. But
> that is far from being a reason for giving up faith in the real thing. To do so
> might entail the destruction of literature, be its quantity ever so little, and
> the substitution of the kind of theory that may exhibit zeal and intelligence
> but abandons what Valéry calls poetry. (AP, 45)

For Kermode, literature has always been distinguished by it quality of
renewable energy, by the sense that, at its best, it escapes the critic's
ambition to delimit it according to the values of a specific place and
time. More recently, he has been stressing the need to direct our attentions to 'the rare experience of poetry,' 'something that we should all
know more and say more about' (AFK, 94), and something that he finds
in Stevens and Larkin. Here, poetry, in all its radiant gist, exists in that
'condition Wallace Stevens thought a poem might achieve, a sort of
August moment, a moment of illusory fixity, having the "Joy of such permanence, right ignorance / Of change still possible" – a sort ... of
momentary utmost' (AFK, 93). The hope is to articulate '"the the"'
(Stevens), something that he also finds in Larkin's 'Unfinished Poem'

(AFK, 94). '[T]he shock of encountering the true' leaves Kermode unprepared 'to believe that this "text" of Larkin's is distinguishable from an advertisement or a white paper or a newspaper report only because a small community of readers wants to "privilege" one kind of discourse over others' (AFK, 95). Poetry has its own forms and traditions, a situation no less true even when one concedes that such include other interests, many of which are not poetic per se but may be made so by being brought within a poem's compass. Poetry, like the literature of which it is a subset, is a discipline, related to other disciplines, and therefore interdisciplinary, but also having a certain self-integrity. This would appear a truism, but the recent rush to imagine things as interdisciplinary has left, thinks Kermode, many forgetful of poetry as poetry. And so he finds himself pressed to state that while it 'seems absurd to have to keep saying so, ... there is a valid experience of poetry, a response appropriate to the world as humanly apprehended' (ibid.).

To speak of poetry is, argues Kermode, to speak, first and foremost, of the poem qua poem, the poem in relation to other poems, and the poem in relation to the history of poetry. A critic can go further than this, and often does, but there soon comes a point when the interest has shifted away from the poem and towards something else, be it biography, criticism, history, religion, politics, and so forth, and it is best to acknowledge this when it happens, rather than to go on pretending that our discussion has as its object poetry: 'Perhaps we need a new poetic of a different sort from any of the current versions of "the science of literature," which offers so many ways of talking about poems or at any rate texts, but in such a manner as often to make it appear preferable not to do so. It is ominous that there should be a continuing and clamorous practice of criticism, of poetics, when it is not apparent that there is anything distinctly understood as a poem to be practiced on' (AFK, 94). If there is to be any chance that literature should survive as something that people seriously value, not as something ancillary but as something essential to the way that they understand the world and their places in it, then we will need, thinks Kermode, to shore up our collapsing notion of canonicity. Many, of late, have made it clear that they are no longer interested in literature qua literature, and thereby have no interest in discussing what does and does not merit canonical inclusion. They may be professors of literature, but their interests have drifted elsewhere, towards theory, history, gender studies, mass media, politics, the internet, and so forth. Viewed from a different perspective, their purposes may seem perfectly reasonable, but from the perspective of literary study, their purposes appear a threat to the discipline's future, and it is not certain that the academy has fully calibrated the future consequences. In the interim, academics move forward with their crusade to de-mystify the received canon, now often conceived as little more than a mass of 'lifeless texts.' The phrase is Culler's, and points to the way in which a distancing from literature is accompanied by a devaluation of the canonical, and perhaps even a growing failure to understand the nature of such. As we have seen, this is the accusation that Kermode makes against Culler; and before closing this section, I would like to recapitulate Kermode's reasons for rejecting Culler's conception, not because I wish to dwell upon whether or not Culler is guilty as charged, but because the reasons help to summarize Kermode's own conception of canon.

Thus, after remarking that Culler's conception of the canon is that it 'is made up of works written by white males, and should therefore be odious to all who care about the privations hitherto imposed on women and ethnic minorities' (AP, 13), Kermode goes on to offer five specific criticisms. First, despite wishes to the contrary, 'canons are formed by exclusions as well as inclusions' and will thereby entail hard choices as to what should or should not be included. Culler, he thinks, is too prepared to reside in the realm of the textual, wherein hierarchies of value do not apply. Second, 'canons are not, as Culler alleges, enclosures full of static monuments' (AP, 15). Rather, they are texts plus commentary, giving 'the contents of the canon a perpetual modernity' (ibid.). Third, 'without canon there would be no tradition ensuring what can be thought of as the special forms of attention elicited by canonical texts' (AP, 16). Here, canonical texts are conceived as those that always require that we return to the texts themselves for confirmation regarding their meaning. Fourth, 'there is, indeed, no ... necessary association between canons and political oppression' (AP, 17). In truth, the present literary canon was formed 'not in powerful institutions but in such establishments as the fledging University of London, where it was a substitute for the classics unavailable at Oxford or Cambridge to women, Jews, and dissenters'; and in the United States, it was an essential part of a curriculum designed 'to give immigrants a better command of English' (ibid.). Lastly, it is not true that canons are predicated on the notion of aesthetic totality. The relation of a text 'to a totality of texts' is always a problematic matter, and this 'is why interpretation is endless – why it can make sense to speak of texts as inexhaustible, and of the "great" texts as calling for continual institutional inquiry' (AP, 18).

It is not clear how well Kermode's notion of canon, despite the formidable intelligence that informs such, shall fare in the future. For one, it must be conceded that it is a rather conservative notion that does not fully acknowledge how rapidly the make-up (i.e., ethnic, economic, religious) of societies – in the United States, notably, but also throughout the parts of the world where English has planted its roots and become the vessel of literary cultures (e.g., India, Nigeria, Australia – are changing and that these changes always entail a transformation in cultural values. There is a growing sense that we should be talking as much about canons as the canon, yet Kermode's formulation, while not actually rejecting the point, gives greater weight to a singular literary canon. For another, it is not clear how much longer literature shall be able to retain its position as the primary cultural reflector and historian. Already, there is the sense that it is being displaced by the powerful new technologies of film, television, recorded music, and the internet. With reason, literary scholars might fear that unless they broaden their notion of literary culture, they could end up resembling antiquarians. I raise such points less in the spirit of objection to Kermode's formulation of canonicity than in the spirit of wanting to acknowledge just how in flux the whole matter is at present. Some matters we can will, and others almost seem to will us. Any devoted reader of Kermode will, most likely, share his sentiment that literary traditions be respected and that canonical changes should be the product of thoughtful debate. Nevertheless, the context in which we reside as readers can change without our concurrence; and when they do, they inevitably raise new questions respecting value, which, in literary terms, generally (though not always) implies canonical values. Kermode knows this; and he makes his arguments without ever assuming that his shall be the last word. Quite the opposite, for his point is that we continually need to reinterpret not only texts but our relations to them. In the discussion of the canon, Kermode has made an extraordinary contribution. For me, he often convinces as much by passion – bound up with an unquestionable love for literature – as by other means. That he convinces at all might, given the current mood of literary studies, seem itself surprising, even when one grants that his argument are unfailingly cogent, sensible, and wise. Yet whatever disadvantages present purposes burden him with, he continues to have all the best talents – Dante, Shakespeare, Donne, Milton, Johnson, Austen, Coleridge, Hawthorne, George Eliot, James, Stevens, Woolf, et al. – on his side.

Literature and Religion

In *The Use of Poetry and The Use of Criticism*, Eliot, taking note of nineteenth-century artists' encroachment upon religion's realm, even when religion itself was struggling to retain its own adherents, writes:

> The decay of religion, and the attrition of political institutions, left dubious frontiers upon which the poet encroached; and the annexations of the poet were legitimated by the critic. For a long time the poet is the priest: there are still, I believe, people who imagine that they draw religious aliment from Browning or Meredith. But the next stage is best exemplified by Matthew Arnold. Arnold was too temperate and reasonable a man to maintain exactly that religious instruction is best conveyed by poetry, and he himself had very little to convey; but he discovered a new formula: poetry is not religion, but it is a capital substitute for religion – not invalid port, which may lend itself to hypocrisy, but coffee without caffeine, and tea without tannin. The doctrine of Arnold was extended, if also somewhat travestied, in the doctrine of 'art for art's sake.' This creed might seem a reversion to the simpler faith of an earlier time, in which the poet was like a dentist, a man with a definite job. But it was really a hopeless admission of irresponsibility. The poetry of revolt and the poetry of retreat are not the same. (17)

It is a point also made by both Donoghue and Steiner. In *The Pure Good of Theory*, Donoghue, criticizing Hillis Miller's identification of *What Maisie Knew* with 'an ethical *casus*,' writes: 'The book exists for perception, not for obedience or disobedience. Miller is perhaps taking literally Matthew Arnold's notion that when we have abandoned religious belief, we may be still saved by great literature. It is not true' (82). And in 'The Good Books,' Steiner, reviewing Kermode and Robert Alter's *Literary Guide to the Bible* (1987), narrates, with the purpose of rejecting, the same history: 'Some hundred years ago Matthew Arnold foresaw just such a reversal [of religion and literature]. He prophesied that the truth of poetry would come to replace those of religious doctrine. More precisely Arnold recognized that the religious legacy in the West, both in the arts and in letters, would survive best where it became an object of aesthetic valuation – that the Psalms would endure as poetry and Chartres as supreme architecture' (94). The tradition would have us believe that '[w]here belief ebbs, beauty remains' (ibid.), but Steiner (at least in the present essay) does not believe it.

The Eliot, Donoghue, and Steiner statements remind us that while the religious and literary impulse may possess affinities, religion and literature are, in fact, two different things, serving two different purposes. If a religion is thought to be untenable, replacing it with literature shall not solve the problem. Such a move will, most likely, only end in disappointment. The three seem worth quoting, for the reason that Kermode's own understanding of literature, as other commentators have noted, has such a strong religious dimension to it, as if he were asking literature to assume the role which, it is thought, religion can no longer sustain. In his fine essay '"Secular Surrogates": Frank Kermode and the Idea of the Critic,' Patrick Parrinder, for instance, writes:

> A surrogate, from the Latin *surrogare*, was traditionally a deputy – specifically, the deputy appointed by a bishop. The qualities that literary texts and the institutions of literary study may be felt to 'share with the sacred'... have been a consistent theme of Kermode's writing in the last fifteen years, if not earlier. He has invoked the scriptural analogy for literary works as a means of reconciling, on the one hand, his powerful urge to be understood as the exponent of a distinctively modern sensibility and, on the other, his conservative attachment to historical and institutional continuities. For Kermode, modern literature and literary commentary are privileged both as a basis of intellectual power (it is taken for granted by Kermode and his fellow-editor in *The Literary Guide to the Bible*, for example, that a modern reading of the Bible would necessarily be a literary reading), and as a site and source of spiritual virtue. (AFK, 59)

Kermode has sought, throughout his career, to discourage statements of this sort. He has repeatedly spoken of himself as 'a secular critic' (GS, viii), as one who, while raised in the Anglican Church, has 'had nothing to do with the church since I was about 14' (CS, 110). When critics such as Empson and Said have spoken of his work as a form of 'religious criticism,' Kermode has bridled, as if the description were an accusation, which, in the mouths of Empson and Said, it was. About Empson's opinion of him, he says, 'He got me down as a neo-Christian long before, and he could never really quite forgive me for being that, as he thought. As so often, the judgment was a totally prejudiced one' (ibid.). And about Said's: 'I am willing to recognize Edward Said as a "secular" critic but not at the expense of being called a "religious" critic myself; that is simply a misunderstanding' (CS, 104).[14] Meanwhile, as to Parrinder's description, Kermode confesses:

I find myself wondering whether Patrick Parrinder ... can have been right after all to find in much of what I have written a displaced religiosity, the cult of a 'secular surrogate.' Perhaps my first response was a stock secularist reaction, a reflex prompted by a need to conceal a blush, a sense of having been found out. It must be possible that we are still in the mourning period for God, whose absence is our unacknowledged subject. However, if that is so it applies equally to us all. I was brought up in the Church of England and keep a faint absenteeist affection for it, but in fact (and this may be a sign of mourning) I have come to think of all religion as likely to be corrupting, and believe it important that we should be able to recognize this fact, if it is agreed to be one, while at the same time understanding to what an enormous degree we still live, think, and read under its shadow, as indeed the whole world does, though we are obliged as clerical sceptics to eschew violent fundamentalisms, false pieties, false consolations. (AFK, 105)

Neither here nor elsewhere does Kermode offer evidence to support the charge that 'all religion' is 'corrupting,' a statement that, the admonitory we 'recognize this fact' notwithstanding, is simply false. Unless it is his point to argue the truism that all things, criticism included, are capable of bad as well as good effects, but this seems unlikely. It is not to this offhand remark, however, that I wish to attend. Rather, I am more interested in Kermode's sense that we are in mourning for a dead God and the consequent sense that literature and its handmaiden, criticism, are fitting places to enact this mourning even as we recognize that 'since – not if, as in the original formulation – God is dead,' we must 'lack all hope of that kind of success, the success of salvation, access to the kingdom' that religious belief encouraged (AFK, 105). We live, says Kermode, at 'the end of the long-drawn-out Christian epoch' (L, 84), in an age that, for better or worse, has gone a long way towards desacralizing the world:

It is sometimes said to be a characteristic of our time that we undo the spiritual structures of our ancestors; whatever they sacralized we desacralize. They retreated from the evident unholiness of the world into images which stored up the strength of those moments when it seemed holy or terrible in a different way. They built in order to make space sacred, and in their rites they abolished the terrors of time, as spring kills winter and St. George the dragon. They made books which were compact of all the world and of all its history, syllabically inspired and, like nature itself, signed with the secret meanings of a god. We build to serve human functions, and not to make models of a divine world; cathedrals that were living bibles, churches proportioned as the music of the spheres. We live, more than any of our ancestors, in a time become linear and patternless. Our books inform or divert in a purely human sense. Where a book continues to be venerable, we attribute its power to different causes: we demythologize, find reasons in nature for its being as it is; we see it as figuring not the whole world of knowledge but dead men's knowledge of the world. It sinks into history, becomes the victim of our perspectival trick, falls under the rule of time. So we desacralize the world. (SSD, 153)

Kermode is clearly ambivalent about this process of desacralization. On the one hand, God is dead, and as 'clerical sceptics' we need to be honest about this. We cannot go on believing that the world evinces as much interest in our situation as we evince in its. '[I]t is much harder now than it was even quite recently to imagine a relation between the time of a life and the time of a world' (SE, 166). But if Kermode believes that 'for everybody, the origin and the end of the world [have] receded' (SE, 167), he also holds on to the hope that meaning, of an ennobling sort, can be salvaged from the ruins. It is one of the reasons why Kermode so embraced the work of Wallace Stevens, for in Stevens Kermode found a kindred spirit, one who, in *The Necessary Angel*, expressed the belief 'that in an age in which disbelief is so profoundly prevalent or, if not disbelief, indifference to questions of belief, poetry and painting, and the arts in general, are, in their measure, a compensation for what has been lost' (171). In *Wallace Stevens*, first published in 1960, Kermode quotes this sentence (83), and goes on to add that he is struck and, it seems, inspired by 'the huge burdens he [Stevens] places upon the arts as "sources of our present conception of reality"' (WS, 83). What is especially attractive about Stevens is the acceptance of the world's facts as lying '"in disconnexion, dead and spiritless"' (WS, 84) combined with the belief that the artist can do something about this. 'The imagination of the poet deals in the final uncertainties, the "confusion of the intelligence," by means of "the formulations of midnight" – and this places him in total contrast to the priests with their "ever-living subject"' (WS, 91). Where religion is felt to have floundered, poetry is proposed as an answer to our spiritual poverty: 'If it can take us out of poverty and into this content ['Notes toward a Supreme Fiction'], we may well say that "Poetry is a means of redemption"' (WS, 92). In the end, says Kermode, Stevens's subject may be thought of as 'living without God and finding it good, because of the survival of the power [to compose fictions] that once made Him suffice' (WS, 117).

The conviction that we must create fictions to stand in for the truths that have been found wanting is a major theme for Kermode, especially in *The Sense of an Ending* (1967). The book appeared six years after that on Stevens, and Kermode has remarked that it 'is, if possible, even more steeped in Stevens than the book on Stevens' (WS, vii). In a sense, what Kermode says about Stevens in relation to Vahinger and Nietzsche might similarly be said about Kermode in relation to Stevens, albeit with consequences not in poetry but in criticism: 'Stevens's brooding over Vahinger's theory of fictions, and also over Nietzsche, issued not in a theory of fiction but in poetry, though a poetry that repeatedly considered its own existence as a fiction with a problematic relation to reality, and also, it must be said, as a theory of fiction' (WS, xvii). Thus Kermode began the latter book by saying that he wished to speak 'not only about the persistence of fictions but about their truth, and also about their decay. There is the question, also, of our growing suspicious of fictions in general. But it seems that we still need them. Our poverty – to borrow that rich concept from Wallace Stevens – is great enough, in a world which is not our own, to necessitate a continuous preoccupation with the changing fiction' (SE, 4).

Fearful of finding himself hoodwinked, Kermode attempts, in *A Sense of an Ending*, to draw a firm distinction between good and bad fictions. Fictions are inescapable, but the clerical sceptic can, it is suggested, recognize the difference between those that he or she wills and those that amount to a belief in something like an absolute truth. The first are simply called fictions, following from the conviction that '[a]fter Nietzsche it was possible to say, as Stevens did, that the "final belief must be in a fiction"' (SE, 36). The second are called myths, following from the conviction that they are those beliefs to which we give uncritical credence: 'We have to distinguish between myths and fictions. Fictions can degenerate into myths whenever they are not unconsciously held to be fictive. In this sense anti-Semitism is a degenerate fiction, a myth; and *Lear* is a fiction. Myths operate within the diagrams of ritual, which presupposes total and adequate explanations of things as they are and were; it is a sequence of radically unchangeable gestures. Fictions are for finding things out, and they change as the needs of sense-making change. Myths are the agents of stability, fictions the agents of change. Myths call for absolute, fictions for conditional assent' (SE, 39). The distinction has its weaknesses, and if applied across the board should even lead us to the conclusion that Kermode's own theory was a myth, for its author submits to it as if it were a timeless condition. Most of us submit to one thing or another – e.g., e = mc^2 – as holding true over time, though we hardly wish to label every such belief a myth, with its suggestion of being untenable as fact. Nor does it seem valuable not to distinguish, as Kermode appears not to, between myths that are pernicious (e.g., anti-Semitism) and those that are not.[15] Repeatedly, he speaks of fictions 'regressing' to myth, suggesting that fictions are the myths we approve of, and myths the fictions that we do not. Meanwhile, Kermode leans towards the view that we can protect ourselves from being hoodwinked through 'clerical scepticism.' It is a seductive thought, but history makes it clear that not even intellectuals are immune to hoodwinking. Think, for instance, of Heidegger, Sartre, and de Man. Kermode admits that 'there must, even when we have achieved a modern degree of clerical scepticism, be some submission to the fictive patterns' (SE, 57), but does not let the admission truly register. The consequence is a theory that elevates things – e.g., literary fictions – that are thought as 'consciously false' over those that might, consciously or not, be found true: 'They [literary fictions] find out about the changing world on our behalf; they arrange our complementarities. They do this, for some of us, perhaps better than history, perhaps better than theology, largely because they are consciously false' (SE, 64).

For Kermode, religion is less a fiction than a myth. Fictions are disposable. When they prove false, we simply throw them, 'in Steven's figure, on to the "dump" – 'to sit among mattresses of the dead.' In this they resemble the fictions of science, mathematics, and law, and differ from those of theology only because religious fictions are harder to free from the mythical "deposit"' (SE, 40). That religious belief might be marked by reason as well as faith, by doubt as well as hope, and by an obligation to the present as well as to the past, almost seems not to matter. Instead, like their canons, religious institutions are viewed here as rigid and closed: 'One of the reasons why theological canons are difficult to defend is that knowledge has seemed to destroy many of the reasons for their being as they are; another is that very rigidity that was formerly a powerful protection. In thinking about canonicity in the history of the arts and literature, we have at once to reflect that our canons have never been impermeable; that our defenses of them are always more provisional than a church's would be; that we therefore have the advantage of being able to preserve the modernity of our choices without surrendering the right to add to them, even to exclude members of them, not by means of difficult administrative procedures but simply by continuing a conversation' (FOA, 78).

This is not a very flattering picture of religions, even when one grants that religions do place more emphasis on tradition and a spiritual truth. Here, religions resemble a little too much those fictions that have lost their explanatory force but have not been allowed to die, and so 'sink into myths and satisfy nobody but critics who lack the critic's first qualification, a scepticism, an interest in things as they are, in inhuman reality as well as in human justice' (SE, 64). Religions also are criticized for being institutions. That they are so would seem, radical fundamentalism notwithstanding, almost inescapable.[16] But the fact makes them blind to that which the clerical sceptic most surprisingly claims to see: 'things as they are.' Thus, Kermode writes of Lawrence 'peeling away of Christian and imperial sophistications to reach the valuable mystery beneath' (SSD, 31) and of Donne giving his faith to 'the *true*, not the *Roman*, Catholicism,' something that he found in the Church of England, happily 'divested of the Romanist accretions': 'Donne ... accepted the Church of England because it was truly Catholic. He rejoiced to discover a Reformed Church which cultivated the Fathers and was slow to come "to a final resolution" in "particulars." He wanted tradition but without its errors: Aquinas, but not the scholastic nonsense; the Fathers, but not their mistakes' (SSD, 138–9).

Kermode is a little bit like Donne in this respect: he wants belief but not if it involves an institution's accretions and errors, not if it comes at the cost of his clerical scepticism. For Kermode, as for Empson, whom he quotes, '"life involves maintaining oneself between contradictions that can't be solved by analysis"' ('William Empson'); and it is better to submit stoically to this governing fact than to profess belief in that which stands so contrary to one's notions of things as they are. And so he, too, turns his back on the more established religions, and gives his allegiance to a newer church, not that of a nation, England, but of an art and literature. Hence, Clara Park writes, that 'in an age in which the Sea of Faith has even further receded, it is finally, for him [Kermode] as for Arnold, art and literature that provide his articles of belief' ('Left-Handed Compliments,' 666). This seems true enough, as does Harold Fromm's claim that 'Kermode is a damaged child of an age of disbelief, whose writings seem to be expressions of desperation: a non-believer's need to believe, if only for a day, some system or structure (semiotics, canon formation, and the rest) that will serve to foster both practical action in the world and professional stature in the university. This whistling in the dark leads him through the kaleidoscopic theoretical fashions of his times. But unfortunately the strength derived from these fabrications seems very short-lived and even at its most puissant it does not really hoodwink their author, whose writings are sprinkled with disclaimers at the very moment of assertion' ('One Type of Ambiguity,' 624).

For Kermode, the difficulty of religious belief connects with the scientific events of the nineteenth century, key among these being Darwin's theory of evolution, something which, along with concurrent geological investigations, made it clear that our prior understanding of time entailed an extraordinary foreshortening. 'Fictional paradigms really belong to a world in which the relation of beginning and end is not too tenuous – a six days world, the tight world-scheme of Augustine, the limited time-scale of Ussher' (SE, 166). It has not, in fact, been that long a time since such notions seemed viable. 'The six-days world was still perfectly acceptable to intelligent contemporaries of Jane Austen'; and this is why the 'quite sudden and enormous lengthening of the scale of history has been far more worrying than the Copernican revolution' (SE, 166–7). The change is still felt in dramatic terms, as if what was believed in our great-grandparents' time could no longer be thought of as viable in our own. Unlike, say, the narrator of Graham Swift's *Ever After* ('I have dipped into Darwin ... It is hard to see in this sober stodge the bombshell which ... horrified Victorian society. Perhaps this proves Darwin's point. Species *adapt*. Yesterday's cataclysm is today's absorbed fact' [237]), Kermode thinks of himself as a child of that revolution, and continues to conceive of it as something that neither religion nor literature has, as yet, come to terms with: 'For literature this created problems we have not yet solved, though it is obviously relevant that the novel developed as the time of the world expanded, and that the facts are related' (SE, 167).

Literature has not solved the problem of expanded time, but it has made more accommodations, thinks Kermode, than religions. We live in a time of permanent crisis, a time when 'the End' has lost 'its downbeat, tonic-and-dominant finality,' leading us to think of it 'as immanent rather than imminent,' and 'to think in terms of crisis rather than temporal ends' (SE, 30). It is not that prior ages have not also experienced moods of crisis, for they have. 'Many of them felt as we do' (SE, 95), meaning that an age's anxiety about its relation to past and future is a common occurrence. But there seems to be a difference about our own relation to crisis, for it is as if such has become less a trait of our times than its overriding feature: 'It is commonplace that our times do in fact suffer a more rapid rate of change technologically, and consequently in the increase of social mobility, than any before us. There is nothing fictive about that, and its implications are clear in our own day-to-day lives. What is interesting, though, is the way in which this knowledge is related to apocalypse, so that a mere celebratory figure of social mobility, like *On the Road*, acquires apocalyptic overtones and establishes the language of an elect; and the way in which writers, that is to say, clerks, are willing to go along, arguing that this is a perpetual requirement; that the stage of transition, like the whole time in an earlier revolution, has become *endless*' (SE, 101).

We live, thinks Kermode, in the 'middest,' where origin and end have receded from view. This helps explain why, as he argues in *The Sense of an Ending*, we have been better served by our literature than our theology. The latter has been too preoccupied with the recognition of meaning, whereas the former has also shown itself capable of forging new meanings in line with the times. Like religion, literature once 'assumed that it was imitating an order' (SE, 167). Now, however, conscious of 'this protraction of time,' literature 'assumes that it has to create an order, unique and self-dependent, and possibly attainable only after a critical process that might be called "decreation"' (ibid.). 'Decreation' is a Stevens word (itself borrowed from Simone Weil), which the poet, in *The Necessary Angel*, made use of so as to stress the importance of rejecting past truths (largely religious) and forging our own: 'Modern reality is a reality of decreation, in which our revelations are not the revelations of belief, but the precious portents of our own powers. The greatest truth we could hope to discover ... is that man's truth is the final resolution of everything' (175). Stevens speaks like one who believes his decreations, his new truths, shall prove attractive to all. In modern times, many (with characters less handsome than Stevens's) have spoken with a similar confidence regarding their own decreations. Yet if History might be called to judge, it would appear that such confidence was often misplaced. Millions have suffered and died as a consequence of the stalwart decreationist, be his name Lenin, Stalin, Hitler, Mao, Pol Pot, Mobuto, or some other such tyrant. And while Stevens clearly had another kind of decreationist in mind, there is nothing to prevent the concept from being used to justify evil ambition. Fortunately, the decreative fictions of our artists have been, by comparison, rather innocent. Still, they have, from time to time, verged on the dangerous, as Kermode admits: 'It appears ... that modernist radicalism in art – breaking down of pseudo-traditions, the making new on a true understanding of the nature of the elements of art – this radicalism involves the creation of fictions which may be dangerous in the dispositions they breed towards the world. There is, for instance, the fantasy of an elect which will end the hegemony of bourgeois or *Massenmensch*, which will end democracy and all the "Bergsonian" attitudes to time or human psychology, all the mess which makes up a commonplace modern view of reality' (SE, 111).

Here, Kermode offers evidence that fictions, too, can be deadly, but then lets it go, preferring to hold on to the faith that even if the majority cannot be trusted to distinguish adequately between fictions and myths, clerical sceptics can. Except sometimes, as in the instance of Pound: 'Pound's radio talks were no doubt the work of a man who had lost some of the sense of reality; but above all they represented a failure of what I have called clerical scepticism, and a betrayal rather than a renovation of the tradition which, it is assumed, lies under threat of destruction by corrupt politics, economics, and language' (SE, 109). And in the instance of Wyndham Lewis, who 'was certainly anti-feminist, anti-Semitic, anti-democratic, and had ambivalent views on colour' (SE, 110). One then begins to wonder whether, in making such concessions, Kermode is not giving the game away. Are clerical skeptics really less prone to 'error' than everyone else? And if they are, what exactly is the reason? Kermode would, it seems, suggest that such people, with their manifest interest in art and literature, are less bound up in the quotidian frictions of politics and economics, and are thereby more disinterested. Even when the fictions of the modernists were eschatological, they remained 'innocent as ways of reordering the past and present of art, and prescribing for its future' (SE, 111). The Audenesque reason is that outside its own realm, poetry makes nothing happen. Yeats can write, 'Plato thought nature but a spume that plays / Upon a ghostly paradigm of things,' but 'to clear that paradigm of natural spume is one thing in poetry or in a theory of poetry; another when the encumbrances can be removed, the spume for ever blown away by a police and a civil service devoted to this final solution' (ibid.).

Kermode reiterated the argument in *History and Value* (1989), when discussing the writers of the Thirties: 'I don't hope to show that these writers were never deluded, never silly; nor that their courtship of the proletariat did not leave them into difficulties and out of their depths. But we should not allow our opinion of their politics to serve as a judgment on their art. Indeed one only has to say so out loud for the point to be over-obvious. If I were referring to the great moderns of the previous generation – to Yeats, Pound, Eliot – the remark would be thought a truism; yet that elementary wisdom doesn't at present come into play when we are talking about the Thirties' (62).

The argument is not as convincing as Kermode suggests. Granted, art is different from politics, and one of the things that most distinguishes it is its quality of considering things in abeyance, wherein immediate action is not required and would even be thought an infringement of art's purposes. This point was taken up in the last chapter, in the discussion of Donoghue's understanding of the aesthetic. Still, even as politics and aesthetics are judged as separate interests, this does not mean that they never intersect, nor that when they do, there is no alteration of values. One reading Pound, in his 1939 essay 'What Is Money For?,' praising Hitler for his stance 'against international finance and loan capital,' a stance shared with 'all men of good will,' and kept secret from the world only by the 'Jewspapers' which 'try now to obscure' it (*Selected Prose*, 269), would no doubt have a difficult time bracketing such views, in the hope of judging Pound's poetry, or perhaps even the essay itself, in strictly aesthetic terms. Granted, it should be a mistake (as I have hitherto argued) to reduce the sum of Pound's work to his rantings, but it should also be a mistake to pretend they were of account only to those interested in Pound's politics, as opposed to his art. Kermode's inclination to draw a line between literature and the 'silly' thinking of its author encourages the prejudice that literature is apolitical and that when it espouses views thought regressive or worse, we may discount the consequences for the reason that it never truly makes anything happen. The study of literature, writes Kermode in *An Appetite for Poetry*, makes us better readers but not better persons (57).

All of this raises some questions about the efficacy of those fictions that are partly meant to console us to the loss of religious belief, and also meant to be more responsive to our situation of crisis. As noted, for Kermode, in his Stevensian phase, literature seeks not so much to discover as to impose an order, and one of the most crucial ways of ordering our experiences is in terms of crisis: 'It has been my argument [in *The Sense of an Ending*] that there must be a link between the forms of literature and the other ways in which, to quote Erich Auerbach, "we try to give some kind of order and design to the past, the present and the future.' One of these ways is crisis' (93). Crisis is said to be less a fact than a trope, 'a way of thinking about one's moment, and not inherent in the moment itself' (SE, 101). Here, what we think reflects an apocalyptic sense of things, of feeling ourselves at the end of history but also feeling that this end, or epoch, shall have no end, that it is a transition to only more of the same. Kermode writes, 'This is the modern apotheosis of Joachism: the belief that one's own age is transitional between two major periods turns into a belief that the transition itself becomes an age, a *saeculum*. We strip the three-and-a-half years of the Beast, which was the original Johannine period glossed by Joachim, of all its "primitive" number associations, and are left with eternal transition, perpetual crisis' (ibid.).

In this situation, literature serves us better than religion because it is not as bound to the poles of origin and end, or to a preset notion of history. In a somewhat similar juxtaposition, Kermode, in *Poetry, Narrative, History* (1990), criticizes Marxists and feminists for presupposing 'something like a determinate and intelligible status for history,' something that might, he thinks, find its correction in Popper's thesis that '[a]lthough history has no meaning, we can give it a meaning' (49). What makes literature preferable to other such narratives is that it does not forget its fictiveness, its quality of being forever in abeyance, in transition from one meaning to another, never content to reside in one place for too long. Literature is, first and foremost, figurative, and therefore its stance towards the world is always somewhat playful and ironic, warding off those who would reify its fictions into something more mythic. Noting the difference between the way poetry and history work, Kermode, using as his example Marvell's 'Horatian Ode on Cromwell's Return from Ireland,' writes: 'The poem winds itself in and out of these attitudes [respecting Cromwell], its figuration often centripetal in respect of the ostensible theme; if it is deliberative, it also ironized its deliberations. It does not weigh the evidence like a newspaper leader which knows what side it will end on; it does not put the case for the beauty of an *ancien régime* like, say, Burke on Marie Antoinette; but it does not, either, speak for Fate against Justice, or for a Machiavellian *virtù*. It will not submit to doctrine or myth; its light strikes the myth and casts another shadow' (61). It is, in many ways, a quite eloquent and expressive way of characterizing the different purposes of poetry and history; and it proves instructive. Or at least until Kermode makes that final, implicit, identification of history with myth. The difficulty is that for Kermode, myths are by their very nature suspect things, premature reifications of a reality that is itself more slippery and aporetic than history or religion will allow. In praising literature, Kermode tends to caricature history and religion. Here, history, like religion, is conceived rather in the manner Hillis Miller describes it in *Hawthorne and History*, that is, as 'an endless series of disruptive happenings,' each naively repeating, 'in one way or another, the linguistic error of personifying the absent, the inanimate, or the dead' (125). History and religion come to resemble myths not because they lack a fictive component, but because their practitioners fail to recognize this same component, and make the mistake of believing that there is something more to both these narratives than their fictiveness. Now, not only might there be more to history and religion than seeing them as fictions allows; but we might also question whether historians and religious scholars have been entirely susceptible to the myth of 'total and adequate' explanation (SE, 39). No doubt, some, maybe even a majority, have been. Nevertheless, it is likely that the most astute have always thought it sensible to offset their desire for explanation against those contingencies that make such explanation elusive. This is a point that Valentine Cunningham, in *In the Reading Gaol*, makes quite forcefully with respect to the Judaeo-Christian tradition, noting how the two sides of interpretation (i.e., the desire for presence offset by the acknowledgment of textuality) 'are both located within' the tradition's 'idea of the text, the book, and reading,' to the point that one might well argue that 'deconstruction is utterly parasitic upon the Biblical' (393):

> the Judaeo-Christian tradition has never lost sight of this rupture [between writing and interpretation], 'a rupture within God as the origin of history,' and so within writing and interpretation, as articulated by the breaking of the tables of the Law. Alongside the idea of the revelatoriness of the Open Book, the Light of Scripture, the historicism and referentialism of the Word, alongside the claim to true teleology and to the reality of God and the real presence of Christ in the Writings, in history, and within the sacrament, there has always functioned a counterset of equally felt realities: the dark side of the Deity, the mystery of the absence of God and the averted divine face (the de-facing of God, as it were – the antithesis of prosopopoeia), the troubling silence of the heavens, the founding wilderness experience, the daunting caginess of hermeticism and closed meanings – indeed, the occasional but persistent sheer uninterpretability of the Scripture. (394)

As genuine as Kermode's interest is in religious narratives, he seldom grants this much, tending rather to reduce such narratives to a longing for 'a lost order of time,' one distinctly apart from 'the here and now'

(SE, 39). Despite the parallel he draws between religion and myth, and despite his view that the Bible is, before it is anything else, literature, Kermode appears reluctant to give up completely the idea that time is rectilinear, with a beginning and end, the latter of which reshapes our understanding of everything that comes before. The Bible, as Kermode observes, 'begins at the beginning ("In the beginning ...") and ends with a vision of the end ("Even so, come, Lord Jesus"); the first book is Genesis, the last Apocalypse'; and '[i]deally, it is a wholly concordant structure, the end is in harmony with the beginning, the middle with beginning and end' (SF, 6). But this is not the only way in which time can be imagined, and Kermode, believing that we live in a state of 'perpetual crisis' (SE, 28), would seemingly find a notion that stressed time's spatialization, its quality of *différance*, more congenial. But he does not. Difficult as it might be to think in terms of beginning and end, Kermode imagines it as something like a need: 'it seems ... that in "making sense" of the world we still feel a need, harder than ever to satisfy because of an accumulated scepticism, to experience that concordance of beginning, middle, and end which is the essence of our explanatory fictions, and especially when they belong to cultural traditions which treat historical time as primarily rectilinear rather than cyclic' (SE, 36). The satisfaction of ends is clear; they shape and bestow meaning on all that we do prior to their arrival. Yet why they should be thought as 'the essence of our explanatory fictions' appears unclear, especially when one of decreation's first legislative acts would be to abolish rectilinear time.

Kermode's understanding of time is heavily indebted to prior theological notions. He says as much, noting how his use of *chronos* and *kairos* 'is derived from the theologians' (SE, 46–7), and how the literary critics' interest in the uniting of the end to the quotidian has a similar derivation: 'The theologians revive typology, and are followed by the literary critics. We seek to repeat the performance of the New Testament, a book which rewrites and requires another book and achieves harmony with it rather than questioning its truth' (SE, 59). Of course, the Christian's conception that all things be understood in the light of the Second Coming – the End that reshapes all prior history – is but one notion of time. Neither the Greeks nor the Hebrews, notes Kermode, had such a notion, for the 'Greeks ... thought that even the gods could not change the past,' and the Hebrews 'had no word for *chronos*, and so no contrast between time which is simply "one damn thing after another" and time as concentrated in *kairoi*' (SE, 47–8). But while Kermode thinks that the End itself is a fiction – 'something we know does not exist, but which helps us to make sense of and to move in the world' (SE, 37) – he holds on to it as a means of ordering experience. He looks beyond the theological for a reason not to give it up, saying that '[b]iology and cultural adaptation require it,' that it 'is a fact of life and a fact of the imagination' (SE, 58). However, the biological, cultural, and imaginative demands appear less imperative than the nostalgia for meanings that have been denigrated but not entirely dismissed. This is, at any rate, how I read a passage like the following: 'As the theologians say, we "live from the End," even if the world should be endless. We need ends and *kairoi* and the *pleroma*, even now when the history of the world has so terribly and so untidily expanded its endless successiveness. We re-create the horizons we have abolished, the structures that have collapsed; and we do so in terms of the old patterns, adapting them to our new worlds' (ibid.).

Kermode's notion of time is dependent on previous religious notions: 'I have used the theologians and their treatment of apocalypse as a model of what we might expect to find not only in more literary treatments of the same radical fiction, but in the literary treatment of radical fictions in general' (SE, 28). But if he borrows such notions as *chronos, kairos, pleroma,* and *aevum* from the theologians, there is a crucial difference between his notion and that of the theologians. That is, if the theologians understand human time in relation to an Other (i.e., to God), Kermode's own understanding is more self-reflexive: 'Ends become a matter of images, figures for what does not exist except humanly' (SE, 58). Here, we are said to go forward in time in order both to meet and learn more about ourselves. 'We know that if we want to find out about ourselves,' we will need to 'avoid the regress into myth' (SE, 43), including the myth that postulates that History has a purpose, an ultimate End. A theologian would say that we exist in a relation of obligation to this End, and would no doubt be troubled by Kermode's claim that our fictions can be judged by reference only to that end which we ourselves project. Kermode acknowledges the objection, but his solution of the problem appears more like a restatement of it: 'I think we have to admit that the consciously false apocalypse of the Third Reich and the consciously false apocalypse of *King Lear* imply equally a recognition that it is ourselves we are encountering whenever we invent fictions. There may even be a real relation between certain kinds of effectiveness in literature and totalitarianism in politics. But although the fictions are alike ways of finding out about the human world, anti-Semitism is a fiction of escape which tells you nothing about death but projects it onto others; whereas *King Lear* is a fiction that inescapably involves an encounter with oneself, and the image of one's end' (SE, 38–9).

I am not sure that this distinction, like that between fiction and myth, would have, in any way, retarded the efforts of the death camps' overseers. Their future designs – or fictions – might have been numerous, but encountering their own ends was probably not high on their lists, no matter how anxious they were to dispatch others to their deaths. Nor is it clear that the most important lesson that our fictions can offer us is about 'oneself, and the image of one's end.' That is part of it, but if it is just this, with no reference outward, to the lives of others and to the larger world, it should seem too solipsistic. In *The Sense of an Ending*, Kermode is suspicious of the view, held by Wordsworth, that 'Nature never did betray / The heart that loved her' (37). It is spoken as an 'innocent theory,' though curious and touching (ibid.). What is more curious, however, is that Kermode creates a bridge between this view and the death camps. The explanation starts off by identifying the view, '[i]n its purely operational form' (ibid.), with the assumption that there is a real world by which we may adjudicate our theories. This is said to be 'the basis of the theoretical physicist's life' (ibid.), which, in turn, is followed by Kermode's suspect bridge: 'Naturally, the answers, like the questions, are purely human. "Nature is patient of interpretation in terms of laws that happen to interest us," as Whitehead remarked. But on the other hand you have the gas-chambers' (SE, 38). That 'other hand' does a lot of work here. This includes making an incredible logical leap, the essence of which is that since the scientist (or the poet with a love of nature) assumes that there is a *real* world to be known, this person is especially liable to treat his or her ideas about this world as if they were truths (i.e., myths) rather than fictions. And here, truths – representing the attempt to know a realm beyond ourselves – destroy; and fictions – representing one's 'encounter with oneself' – restore us, except if the fiction makers happen to be patently evil. Or as Kermode told Salusinszky, 'there is a very great difference between those benevolent or neutral fictions and the sort of fiction that is involved in anti-Semitism' (CS, 111). This last statement is true, but calling benevolent fictions one thing (i.e., fictions) and nasty fictions another (i.e., myths) does not help us all that much, especially when there is so little agreement about whose fictions are benevolent and whose are not. Nor does the invocation of the Shoah seem proper, for Kermode appears to be exploiting the murderous event for argumentative purposes that are themselves quite detached from the event, quite unprepared to front that particular horror.

In truth, Kermode's scheme offers less a world split between practitioners of fiction and of myth than a world of competing fictions. The fact is, people seldom think of their beliefs as 'consciously false'; and when they are ethically inclined, they tend to embrace practices that appear true not only in the context of immediate but also of distant and abstract circumstances. Does Kermode think the death camps a 'fiction,' as existing among the realm of the 'consciously false'? If so, there is a problem. If otherwise, there is also a problem, for then we find him, by his own definition, believing in a myth. The way out of the quandary is, perhaps, to acknowledge the contingency of value, allowing that the architects of the death camps believed they were engaged in something good, at the same time that a person does everything in his or her power to marshal an alternative consensus, and then to make the builders themselves experience the judgment of this consensus. Now, if this is done solely out of consideration of one's own needs, including the 'encounter with oneself,' then it should be easy to think the operation, if successful, an example of 'might makes right.' On the other hand, if this is done mindful of the needs of a wide range of others, even at the cost of considerable self-sacrifice, then it might be possible to think the operation a real good. Not an absolute good, for contingencies make such judgments virtually impossible. Still, it should seem a real good, something that the vast majority would like to imagine themselves as doing if they could put aside their self-interests and fears. The hope would be that such an action – e.g., the ship captain who, on a sinking ship, is the last to depart – might correspond with a good or a truth that transcends local value, even as there can never be any guarantee of this. There is only the hope and perhaps the faith that such is so, plus the sign manifest in the approval of the world and then of history.

To speak of hope and faith, instead of self-conscious fictions, is to raise once more the matter of religious belief. Kermode has always demonstrated an interest in the realm of the sacred, and he has, as noted, even been spoken of as a religious critic. I am referring not only to discussions by Said and de Man, but also by Christopher Norris, who (as Empson's self-appointed deputy) speaks of the work's 'quasi-theological dimension' ('Introduction,' 42), O.B. Hardison, who finds a 'quasi-religious tendency in Mr. Kermode's thought' ('Keeping the Canon Rolling,'), and various others. Such descriptions have always left him surprised, though they should not have, given his wont for speaking of literary texts as if they were sacred, demanding interpretation for the reason that they contain a truth that it is imperative we discern. Thus, speaking of Shakespeare, he writes, 'It is part of our literary holism – the device by which we try to maintain a semblance of the sacred in our literary lives – that we cannot treat him otherwise than as we treat the great books of our own time. And it is the mark of his perpetuity and patience that he can tolerate this treatment. Every age, so far at any rate, has been able to find in Shakespeare whatever it needed to maintain contact with him, considered as a focus of given, natural meaning, a source of order and civility. So far as we can see it is usually possible to discover in this presence that 'interior sensitization' of which theologians speak in relation to the Bible' (SSD, 153–4). The practice of reading secular texts, Shakespeare's included, as if they were sacred, raises certain questions. For one, if we understand that the source of a text's sacred, or special, status follows from its relation to 'given, natural meaning,' is there not the presumption that if we ourselves cannot say what this meaning is, we are, at least, capable of recognizing it when it is put before us? And whether we can, like Shakespeare, say what this meaning is, or simply recognize it when we see it, does this not place us back in the realm of Kermode's fallacy of mythic understanding? Do we not find a situation wherein our determinations regarding fiction depend on the myth of 'given, natural meaning'? If so, must we, then, not only 'distinguish between myths and fictions' (SE, 39), but also note their interdependence? It would seem so. Thus, if we accept the notion of a 'given, natural meaning' – the basis for a text's sacredness – we cannot really say that interpretation (including that of sacred texts) is infinite, though Kermode does move this way: 'one might almost say that it was a rediscovery of the apparently infinite possibilities of interpretation, and a new understanding of the necessary obsolescence of commentary, partly dependent on the grant of quasi-sacred status to secular texts, that impelled the secular scholars to look again at the originally sacred texts' (PNH, 31).

To speak of infinite interpretative possibilities, it is necessary first to posit an open universe, wherein things are in perpetual flight from any imaginable order. This itself is probably impossible to do, but Kermode does not make the attempt, for he tends, as we have seen, towards seeing things as somehow 'hang[ing] together' (GS, 72). He speaks of *certain* texts as semi-sacred, or canonical, not because they are fictions, related to nothing other than their own reflexive order, but because they appear immanent, as if they were emblematic of some larger order or truth. '[S]ome element of literary value is at least as-if immanent,' he says in *History and Value* (104), a conviction that, prior to this, encouraged him to speak of the *Aeneid* and *Genesis* as related by their quality of being end governed: 'Virgil and Genesis belong to our end-determined fictions; their stories are placed at what Dante calls the point where all times are present, *il punto a cui tutti li tempi son presenti*; or within the shadow of it. It gives each moment its fullness. And although for us the End has perhaps lost its naïve *imminence*, its shadow still lies on the crisis of our fictions; we may speak of it as *immanent*' (SE, 6).

If it is true that our literature is still to be read in the light of 'the End,' then it would appear not only that some texts are more canonical than others, but also that some are more sacred. The sacredness of a text would follow not only from its immanence – its speaking, without speaking, of a determining End – but also from its speaking (in a way that texts that are merely literary do not) spiritual truths. One distinguishes *Genesis* from *The Aeneid*, the *Gospel of St. John* from *Finnegans Wake*. Here, interpretations are not thought infinite, but as reined in by the End of which Kermode speaks. The interpretations that come closest to the truth will be, if this is identified with Divinity, the most sacred, or, if not, the most scientific. Literary texts may reflect this truth, but they seldom make it their exclusive ambition. Otherwise, they would be considered sacred or scientific texts. The point is, literature operates according to 'a different reality principle' not only from those myths that, says Kermode, Northrop Frye wants to merge it with, but also from those sacred texts that he himself would merge it with (C, 120). Literature's focus pertains 'to *this* time' (ibid.), to the ways in which people live their day-to-day lives, sometimes mindful of the ends that shape their existence and sometimes not. Canonical literature has, more times than not, been attuned to the question of ends, even while its main thrust might be said to lie elsewhere. In his later work, Kermode glosses over this distinction, but it still requires attention. Literary and sacred texts are responsive to different purposes, and while Kermode imagines the Classic as a subset of the sacred, and Scripture as a subset of the literary, it is best to be mindful of the differences. In this vein, Cunningham writes:

> Borges well appreciates ... that the secular literary Classic, however subject to repeated interpretation, usually fails to rise to the provoking hermeneutical density of the Bible. Homer can be said to have nodded at times; the Holy Spirit, by definition, never nods. So the Spirit-breathed text lacks the

contingency, the blank or slack passages, the dead water, that are to be found even in the Classic. To think otherwise, even of Classics, would be extremist. Anyone reading *Don Quixote* or *Macbeth* or the *Chanson de Roland* as the Bible has been read would be reckoned, Borges properly believes, quite mad. But this is precisely what has happened and is happening. Umberto Eco is right to observe that critical history is crowded with secular texts that are in fact treated as sacred for their culture ... *Finnegans Wake* is the big symptom and example of this. This particular acme of the (post)modernist text was set up precisely out of a desire to rival the Judaeo-Christian Scriptures in luring in the interpreter forever. Its wishes have been massively respected *per se* and *per exemplum.* (*In the Reading Gaol,* 389–90) [17]

By Cunningham's standard, Kermode appears something of an extremist, for not only does he wish to read '*Macbeth* ... as the Bible has been read,' but he also wishes to read the Bible as *Macbeth* has been read. This is the interpretative thrust of *The Literary Guide to the Bible,* which Kermode co-edited with Robert Alter. Together, they write in the 'Introduction' that 'the Bible, considered as a book, achieves its effects by means no different from those generally employed by written language ... Indeed literary analysis must come first, for unless we have a sound understanding of what the text is doing and saying, it will not be of much value in other respects' (2). There is sense in stressing the reader's preparedness this way, yet the thrust of what is said here and elsewhere is more than simply cautionary. In *Poetry, Narrative, History,* Kermode writes that it seems 'possible, even necessary, to read the New Testament stories not in order to study their historical references but to consider them as one might consider other instances of the art of fiction, and to do so in the conviction that this was the way to defend their religious value' (40–1). The phrase 'the art of fiction' recalls Henry James, and is telling with regard to the direction Kermode wishes to go in reading the Bible. There is a hankering to read it as a New Critic might read a nineteenth-century novel, which is to say in terms of its unity of narrative and style, unmindful of the fact that its composition, rooted in the realities of an oral tradition, was a very different from the conscious artistry of a James or Joyce. Or as Helen Gardner writes:

How can we compare, with any hope of arriving at any interpretative or literary judgement, enigmas and puzzles put in by a highly self-conscious literary artist, in a vast, expansive, encyclopaedic work such as *Ulysses,* whose author once said that they were put in 'to keep the professors busy for centuries,' with a writer putting together stories, brief sayings, parables, dialogues, as prelude to a continuous narrative of the Passion, matter which had lived and been shaped in the memories and speech of men as it passed by word of mouth, had been embodied in rites celebrated and hymns sung, which is set down with such reserve and concision, at times showing signs of being learnt oral material. It is not set down as a document, containing secret wisdom for a few, for adepts, or initiates, or to use Kermode's word, 'insiders,' but for all who have 'ears to hear.' The enigmas and riddles which Kermode finds in Mark lie in the nature of the material he is presenting and handling, not, as with Joyce, in the intention of the author. (*In Defence of the Imagination*, 123)

So, too, thinks George Steiner, who in reviewing *The Literary Guide to the Bible*, takes note of the way in which reading the Bible through the formalist lens of a modernist transforms it into something quite different than its original conditions of composition would warrant: 'Read or heard in light of the inheritance of Henry James or of Joyce, the brusque changes of intonation, of narrative point of view, of stylistic form in Genesis and in certain parts of Exodus or Matthew tell neither of multiple authorship nor of textual corruption but of the subtle literary skills and complex intentions of the ancient masters of storytelling and portraiture' ('The Good Books,' 95). Steiner's description, though it is meant as critique, is a fair description of the purposes of Kermode and Alter in *The Literary Guide to the Bible*, wherein literature is defined in terms of '[i]ts syntax, grammar, and vocabulary [which] involve a highly heterogeneous concord of codes, devices, and linguistic properties,' including 'genre, convention, technique, context of allusion, style, structure, thematic organization, point of view for the narratives, voice for the poetry, imagery and diction for both' (5). It is a notably formalist notion of literature, excluding all the other things (e.g., historical, philosophical, or religious interest) that also make writing memorable. In practice, it would tend to exclude from the realm of literature texts like Frederick Douglass's *Narrative*, Alice James's *Diary*, and William James's *Varieties of Religious Experience*. When applied to the Bible, it values those things which 'the purely literary reader' might notice (LGB, 400), even when it is admitted that many other readers' interests lie elsewhere. 'The concern here,' writes Kermode in his discussion of *Matthew*, 'is with the manner, not with the message as interpreted by the faithful; the Gospels are writings first of all, whatever use is subsequently made of them' (ibid.).

To argue that the Bible's books 'are narratives like any other narratives and that they are subject to the same constraints' is to take a stance likely to insult the feelings of many readers, for it demonstrates an insensitivity to that which they hold special and sacred (PNH, 70). In passing, Kermode quotes Herder's statement that 'whoever turns a gospel of Christ into a novel has wounded my heart,' but seems deaf to the remark, intent as he is on Hans W. Frei's purportedly more incisive point 'that the story *was* the meaning lay beyond' Herder's grasp (GS, 120). To his credit, Kermode dissociates himself from the Frei charge, calling it 'ingenious but questionable' (ibid.), but it is clear where his interests lie – in the Bible as literature. For too long, Kermode argues in *The Genesis of Secrecy*, Biblical scholars have treated the text as if it were transparent, a window onto a sacred world. It is time to reverse the priority, in order to examine the Bible not in terms of its reference but of its linguistic structure: 'the story of modern biblical criticism ... seems to confirm the view that it takes a powerful mind to attend to what is written at the expense of what it is written about' (GS, 119). Stating the argument this way makes it seem too much of an either/or matter, when it is not. Nevertheless, Kermode prefers to respond to the Bible as if it were an anthology of poems ('biblical poems need to be read as poems before they are disassembled or treated simply as clues to a theology' [LGB, 442]) and novellas. The Gospels themselves are read as if they were choice modernist narratives. Kermode says that these 'stories ... are well made. They ask the right sort of narrative questions, and provide satisfactory answers. What sort of Messiah is Jesus? How shall a visit that begins in a royal triumph end with the hero's death as a criminal? The possibilities are subtly realized' (AT, 198). The Biblical authors are said to be sensitive to nuance, experts at irony: 'These writers understand irony, as when the true king is given a mock coronation. The label on the Cross, "King of the Jews," is meant as a gibe, but it is the truth. All this is very deft' (ibid.).

It may be deft, but it is still worth wondering whether something crucial is not lost when we read religious texts as a subset of the secular literary canon. Steiner, in his review, puts the matter quite clearly:

The separation, made in the name of current rationalism and agnosticism, between a theological-religious experiencing of Biblical texts and a literary one is radically factitious. It cannot work. This is to say that the plain question of divine inspiration – of orders of imagining and composition signally different from almost anything we have known since – must be posed, must be faced squarely and unflinchingly, even if ... the answer is one of more or less polite dismissal. The author of Job – and there is a poet's voice and transcendent genius in almost every line – was not producing 'literature.' Nor were those who bore witness to the 'darkness upon the earth' the evening of Good Friday. A literary elucidation of such texts is legitimate and can be helpful, but only if it acknowledges, in however polemic a vein, its own principles of exclusion – only if it tells us that which it omits is the essential. ('The Good Books,' 97)

About this other Biblical narrative – speaking of the heights of joy as well as terror; of hope as well as despair – Kermode has rather little to say. It lacks the domestic irony and subtlety of the modernist narrative, and calls for more than an appreciative response. Kermode seems to know this, but also wants to keep the matter off to the side. He stresses the centrality of the Bible, but his reasons appear, somehow, not the right ones. In *The Literary Guide to the Bible*, he and Alter warn of the consequences – i.e., the political upheavals – that ensue when the Bible is carelessly read: 'It has been said that the best reason for the serious study of the Bible – for learning how to read it well – is written across the history of Western culture: see what happens when people misread it, read it badly, or read it on false assumptions' (2). They also warn of the consequences for the literary culture when the Bible is not read at all: the 'increasing neglect in our secularized times has opened a gulf between it and our general literature, a gap of ignorance which must in some measure falsify the latter' (LGB, 3). The Bible's importance is largely reduced to its role as a source book for Western literature. Granted, it is said to be 'of such quality' that those who have neglected it have done so 'to their immense cost' (ibid.), but this quality appears ill-defined, albeit literary.

Maybe this is, in fact, the extent of Kermode's interest in the Bible. Certainly, the aspects of it to which he attends – e.g., its 'complex language'; the handling of points of view; the problems of interpretation; the movement from an oral tradition to a written body of canonical texts; the motif of apocalypse – evince a decidedly secular mindset. The Bible is spoken as one text among others, attractive for the way in which certain literary questions find illustration within its borders – e.g., 'I have tried to use the gospels as prime examples of interpretation in narrative' (GS, xi). And always, Kermode reminds his reader that '[t]he opinions I express are those of the secular critic with nothing to say about the doctrine' (AP, 210). The word 'secular' is one of his favourite, though de Man, imputing a religious motive to his work, once turned it back upon Kermode, saying that matters are not 'settled by historical perspectives that see literature as a secularization of religious experience; the concept of secularity is itself a deeply religious concept' ('Blocking the Road,' 190). It seems true, especially in Kermode's case, wherein, as previously noted, humanity is viewed as 'still in the mourning period for God, whose absence is our unacknowledged subject' (AFK, 105). One might argue that Kermode's work represents something like a negative theology, but if so, it needs to be noted that, as the description suggests, such a practice entails a cost. It is not simply a paler version of theology. Rather, it is something that, even while holding on to that belief which it has a mind to let go, enfeebles it, as it exists both for oneself and for others. This is the point and force of Donald Davie's own, quite poignant response to Kermode's agnosticism, of which I can offer only a part:

> What is so insidious, or lethal, about his treatment of John [in *The Literary Guide*] is that it begins with several pages about the first 18 verses of the Gospel ... , pages that profoundly and delicately nourish awed devotion in the reader; and then this awe and trust are sedulously undermined, as Kermode goes on to tease out, still delicately, still patiently, how John *manipulates* his narrative. Manipulate, I fear, is the word. Kermode is much clearer than his collaborators about what he means by 'literature,' especially narrative literature. It means contrivance.
>
> For Kermode, John the evangelist is a very great, very gifted contriver – alone of the evangelists, a proto-novelist. As we turn the pages, this assimilation of John to somebody like Henry James is ever more marked ...
>
> The cumulative effect of all these expressions is obvious, and Kermode must have intended it: the figure of John the witness ... is lost to sight behind the figure of John the fabricator. To be blunt about it, Kermode writes as an unbeliever to convert us to his unbelief. The great learning and lucid eloquence, the suave and patient tact, are all harnessed to this end. This is what treating the Bible as literature can come down to. ('Reading and Believing,' 32–3)

It is a very strong statement, indictment even, and perhaps the wrong note on which to end the section. '[B]etween two worlds, and immobilized by his belief in disbelief' (AP, 32), Kermode comes across as a man who, like Stevens, almost finds his disbelief thrust upon him, it being the last thing he would consciously choose. He is unable to reconcile himself to disbelief, and while religious beliefs are found no longer tenable, he strikes out to find something that might be. Literature and its language are what he finds and, while some might scoff, these seem enough to get him through the night. I admit my own scepticism with regard to this elevation of literature to the position of a new theology. 'Poetry,' for Kermode as for Stevens, 'is the supreme fiction,' the one thing that, in a world bereft of religious hope, holds out the possibilities of consolation. Yet even Kermode finds the consolation somewhat lacking, and is forced to accent less this than the stoical integrity of the position. 'I suppose that one reason why Stevens has meant and means so much to me is because ... he ... had an apprehension of poverty as the human condition so general that particular cases ... simply become representatives of a poverty more universal, especially apparent to and felt by poets, and the more tragic because set against a world they know to be capable of freshness and plenitude' (AFK, 96). It is a frank if disheartening statement about what he takes our situation to be; and while one might feel tempted to counter with another view, more fronted towards the said plenitude, in the end, this is Kermode's view, spoken with the directness and honesty that are so characteristic of his work. If the view hurts – Davie: 'It is ten years since I heard him lecture on Mark – and found my faith shaken in consequence' ('Reading and Believing,' 32) – it is because his own sense of loss has been that much deeper; and we should do well to respect it and to figure it into whatever more consoling meanings we might manage to eke out.

The Theory Debates

'There is a war on,' wrote Kermode in 1983, referring to the critical debates, 'and he who ventures into no-man's-land brandishing cigarettes and singing carols must expect to be shot at' (AT, 7). It is an apt allegory for Kermode's own situation, interested in critical theory, but not so much so that he cannot make the argument for literature as such. Thus he has often found himself in no-man's-land, explaining the importance of theory to those who would resist it, and explaining the importance of literary value to those who would sacrifice it to other interests. The result is that he frequently ends up satisfying neither side and is shot at by both. From the right, Helen Gardner complains that the essence of his interest in indeterminism, mystery, secrecy, and the oracular 'is to want the *liberté pour rien* of the demoniac, and [to] prefer such total freedom to the constraints of rational and social intercourse with one's fellow men, through which we discover our true individuality, and grow in knowledge of ourselves, and of the world we find ourselves in' (*In Defence of the Imagination*, 131). From the left, Terry Eagleton speaks of him as a 'bourgeois liberal humanist' (AFK, 99). If he is what Gardner claims, he must not be what Eagleton claims, and vice versa. But things are not this simple, for this assumes that there is no problem in saying what he is in essence as opposed to what he is to others; and to Gardner, Kermode is a radical theorist, to Eagleton, a conservative humanist. And to me? Well, he is something of both. As David Sexton notes, 'Kermode is so evenhanded a critic that he resembles a one-man committee: himself his own interpretative community' ('Kermode as compère,' 19).

Of course, not everyone shoots at the person dispensing cigarettes in no-man's-land. There are those, this reader included, who value the efforts of one who believes that differences are better mediated than exacerbated. One can readily grant that persons and communities have interests that are, more or less, their own, and still hold to the conviction that we all benefit from communication and compromise. We live in communities within communities, or circles within circles, and it is to the advantage of everyone that these harmoniously co-exist. To think otherwise is to ignore how interdependent are our lives. In any event, Kermode's attractiveness as a critic has much to do with his tact, with the conviction that one's first duty to another's work is to take it seriously, to offer it the respect that one would wish for one's own. He is, as Sexton says, 'a famously hospitable critic' (19), not because he is accepting of all arguments but because he is, more or less, open to all arguments. He is, as Margaret Tudeau-Clayton observes, 'one who (not without personal cost) has stood for the tolerance of diversity within the academy of literary study' (AFK, x–xi), or, as Stephen Logan (reviewing *The Uses of Error*) observes, one who, at a time 'when the disputes between scholarly factions are chaotic,' finds 'the fence provides the best advantage-point. The wonder is not that Kermode should sit on it, but that he should do so with such poise' ('The don in Grub Street,' 29). By this, Logan does not mean to suggest that Kermode has no points of his own to make. Instead, he argues that Kermode, with his 'capacity for controlled misgiving,' makes his points best by indirection: 'By his readiness to give discriminate praise to the likes of Derrida and De Man, and by his scrupulous investigations of the theories they have engendered, Kermode demonstrates an evenly sceptical mistrust both of knock-down bluster and of sophisticated cajolery. Yet he rarely expresses opposition by open dissent. Rather, his views on the proper nature and function of literary criticism are implicit in his allegiance to a system of values which it would be crass to suppose him either unaware or anxious to conceal. Thus it is that this collection of essays on subjects as diverse as Biblical translation, the editing of Shakespeare, misinterpretation, and Tennyson's sense of sound constitutes an argument which is nowhere stated but everywhere implied' (29).

As Logan notes, Kermode prefers not to make his critical methodology explicit. Nor does he solicit acolytes. A believer in the virtue of modesty, he also appears to practise it. Nevertheless, there is a methodology; Kermode does value certain critical practices over others; and while he is not one to parade these, they are discernible. For starters, he is a great believer in what one might call (though he does not) a critical pragmatism. He is sceptical of theoretical systems when applied to the study of literature. For instance, he has long been an admirer of Northrop Frye's work, especially his *Anatomy of Criticism*, yet he has also made it clear that he finds the book too systematic, too prepared to neglect literature's here-and-now character in favour of a mythic timelessness. Thus he compares Frye unfavourably to Blackmur, a critic whose critical values are closer to Kermode's own: 'He is the polar opposite of Blackmur, who was essentially a very unsystematic critic and believed, dangerously but correctly, that criticism is mostly anarchic, though dependent on a difficult act of submission and then on the critic's having a mind with useful and interesting contents' (C, 12). The submission would be to literature, so heterogeneous as to seem almost irreducible to system. Kermode writes, '[c]riticism entails immediate encounter with particular texts, which is the sort of criticism I would like to do' (CS, 119). Yet criticism seldom means an encounter with *any* text, and there is good reason for theorizing the reasons why we attend to one text rather than another. In *Versions of Pygmalion*, Hillis Miller speaks of an obligation, felt by him if not by others, that he read everything that has been written: 'Each book, text, essay, scrap of written language, even those in languages I do not know, asks to be read. The call is directed to me personally and with equal force by each text' (18). Even if one were to acknowledge the obligation (cf. Emerson: 'Books are for the scholar's idle times' [The American Scholar']), a person would need to be a god to fulfil such an obligation, and barring this, a reader tends to make deliberate choices, as I am sure Miller does as well. The question is not whether a person can read all the world's texts, but whether this person takes note of the factors that lead to the reading of one text rather than another? Kermode speaks of no Adamic desire to read everything; he knows that a choice is involved, and is not chary (at least in interview) about saying what determines the choice: 'If literature is not a separate category, what the hell are we going to do in English departments? Pick up anything and read it? It really is a practical issue. There has to be a category of literature' (PNH, 91).

Whether there 'has to be a category of literature' or not is, at present, debatable. What is clear is that when Kermode speaks of criticism's submission to the text, he is speaking of his own sense of obligation to literature. This obligation amounts to something like a one-way street, with the critic speaking of the duty to find out what the text is saying in its own voice: 'A good part of the pleasure I derived from my profession had come from finding out what texts seemed to be saying as it were voluntarily, and in conveying this information to others; and I should have felt uneasy to join a party whose sole business it was to elicit what they were saying in spite of themselves' (AT, 5). The last part of the statement refers specifically to deconstruction, though it might also be understood to refer to those other critical practices (e.g., Marxism, New Historicism, cultural studies) that seek to foreground a text's 'political unconscious.' In *History and Value*, for instance, Kermode takes issue with Eagleton's contention that the text's 'self-knowledge is the construction of a self-oblivion' (99). 'In other words,' he retorts, 'nothing a work appears to be saying about its own ideological context is worthy of any notice except what may be necessary to its discounting. Criticism should concern itself less with what the work ostensibly presents than with the absences that make it incomplete – with what resides in an "unconsciousness" of which the work itself cannot be aware' (HV, 100). It is a testy response, having to do, I suspect, with Kermode's objection to the tenor of the ambition: here, the exploration of a text's hidden dimension is not provoked – as it is in, say, Kermode's *Genesis of Secrecy* – by the desire to celebrate its mystery and sacredness, but by the desire to expose its complicity with power structures deemed pernicious. Besides questioning this tenor, Kermode thinks it something like an ethical imperative that we increase the possibilities for novelists and poets to write and that, when they have done so, we pay attention. In his view, Eagleton, as critic, would usurp the literary artist's role, for, in a sense, Eagleton seeks to rewrite the narrative or poem, to put his own name to it. Thus does an ostensibly political project mask an aesthetic one. Kermode's criticism of Eagleton might be compared to Giles Gunn's criticism of Jameson when, in *The Political Unconscious*, the latter writes that contrary to '[t]he ideal of a purely immanent criticism,' it should be possible to practise an analysis that 'involves the hypothetical *reconstruction* of the materials – content, narrative paradigms, stylistic and linguistic practices – which had to have been given in advance in order for that particular text to be produced in its unique historical specificity' (57–8). Gunn replies: 'From this perspective, the ideological is not something added onto or inserted into the aesthetic. It should be conceived rather as something inscribed within the aesthetic in a way that makes aesthetic creation, and therefore literary production as a whole, an ideological act in and of itself. Unless I am mistaken, however, to reconceive their relationship this way also transforms the historical recovery of ideology itself into a fundamentally aesthetic act, since the historical reconstruction of the ideological is essentially an act of the imagination' (*Thinking across the American Grain*, 168). For Jameson and Eagleton, the aesthetic act is less deconstructed than displaced, with the critic muscling into that space previously occupied by the artist. For the critic unwilling to grant the artist special status, this might not be a problem. For Kermode, however, it does constitute a problem, for he is unprepared to think of criticism as on a par with art: 'As for criticism, it rarely brings tears to the eyes, and never stays sudden, is indeed never to be thought of as having a very intimate relation with "the the." Most of it is like the statue of the general in Stevens: perhaps honoured in its time, but rubbish in the end' (AFK, 95).[18]

That criticism and literature are distinguishable is a major tenet of Kermode's work. 'I disagree with Harold Bloom and Geoffrey Hartman,' he told Salusinszky, 'about the relative status of poetry and criticism' (CS, 104), meaning that he generally finds criticism ephemeral, while literature has 'values which can be realized in quite different historical circumstances from those of its origin' (HV, 100). This is not a claim that literature escapes the problem of social and historical contingency, only that it translates better than most other things, criticism included, into new circumstances.[19] The argument is not as self-evident as Kermode suggests. Historically, it was not that long ago when 'literature' meant only that something was written, as opposed to what it has, post-Romantically, come to mean, an aesthetically motivated writing hinting of larger truths. Kermode knows this but thinks that present efforts to dislodge literature from its position of primacy are premature. For him, literature expresses a truth that, if not universal, has about it a remarkable staying power. It also expresses this truth in a way that resists paraphrase. Literature requires from us, its readers, a singular sort of attention, demanding that we return to the text itself not only to verify what we remember having found there but also to find out how much we first missed, and then to be attentive to how later readings reshape earlier readings and call into question our own interpretation skills. This sense of literature, Kermode concedes, is itself rather recent ('a whole category called "literature," which we, after all, didn't have until quite recently'), but he also believes that 'it's always been around in essence' (PNH, 90). Readers have always 'attended to Homer with a special kind of attention, more attention and a different quality of attention than they gave to other people, and that is what, after all, we mean when we say that Shakespeare is literature and that Deloney, say, is marginally so, popular literature' (PNH, 91).

The attention that Kermode speaks of is, by and large, of a formalist nature, reflective of his own history and training. His generation 'inherited a way of thinking about the history of literature, especially of our own literature, which owed most to Eliot, though much also to the earlier Leavis; we had learned from Richards and Empson, and later from the American New Critics, to give the texts of poems a new kind of attention, and we had even thought quite a bit about theoretical defences of such procedures' (AFK, 90). It is an attention which, now, should be spoken of as conservative, and Kermode is often on the defensive. He complains that '[e]ven when what used, on the whole uncontentiously, to be thought of as literature is criticized, it is often not criticized as *literature*, and some criticism presupposes either that there is no such thing as literature or that there shouldn't be, or that, supposing there is, and that it has a right to exist, it is something the true nature of which we have come to understand that we do not understand' (AP, 24–5). An appeal of this nature can expect to persuade only those who do not need persuading. It presupposes a certain definition of literature – i.e., that it is exemplary of certain linguistic and formal properties – and then requires that the debate take place within the boundaries of this definition. It evades the fact that it is precisely literature's definition that is being contested. Thus if a feminist critic, say, should question the canonical status of William Carlos Williams's poetry for the reason that it appears regressive in its understanding of women and their concerns, one can say that the focus of investigation has moved away from the point of formal linguistic properties, but one can hardly say that the new discussion has no relevance to the adjudication of Williams's work, or to the way in which we define literature. Kermode does not argue otherwise, but his concessions appear reluctant. He does not wish to deny the relevance of a male poet's attitudes towards women, but he does, it seems, wish to make such discussions – i.e., political – something like a side issue. '[A]fter all,' he writes, 'we are continually dealing with other kinds of literature that reflect dead or distasteful ideologies and we do not feel bound to allow those dead ideologies to determine literary value' (HV, 90). But this is not true. These matters do determine literary value, and have always done so. The question is not whether they do so, but how do they do so? And for whom? But these are questions that Kermode mostly prefers to skirt.

For Kermode, literature is a received inheritance. Its value is taken as a given; and when this value is questioned, he can respond irritably. On such occasions, he tries not to persuade the reader of the importance – i.e., the relevance to his or her life – of a particular text so much as to assert literature's own ill-defined 'quality': 'Historically the concept of literature is inextricably involved with the presumption of quality in both text and reader. It is therefore not surprising that the dismissal of quality as irrelevant to the study of writing (or its exploitation for political purposes) should entail a denial of literature' (AP, 26). As used here, 'quality' – e.g., quality of the reader – smacks of self-election and points out the reason why many critics, rightly or not, prefer to speak of value as socially and historically situated, or contingent, rather than as a thing-in-itself. In *History and Value*, Kermode himself asks, 'How do we know that it is "our" kind of writing that has most "merit" and "aesthetic value"?' (96). The question is part of an honest effort to think about the contingencies intertwined in the determination of literary value, and is followed with the question, 'How dependent are these assumptions on the success of one class against another?' (ibid.). Nevertheless, the overall suggestion is that there is but a single genuine literature. It is not that Kermode would deny that different communities have different standards of merit and aesthetic value. Rather, it is that his emotional allegiance to canonical literature and its standards simply creates too much of an obstacle for the appreciation of the noncanonical. The consequence is that *History and Value*, while it seeks to go another way, ends up implying that there is one literature – in this instance, produced by the 'bourgeois intellect' – that has *most* merit, and that other writings are inferior, not only for the class of university graduates, but in general. It is in this mood that Kermode writes, 'in our role [vis-à-vis the Thirties' writers] as posterity we feel pretty secure in our valuations and are not grateful to be reminded of the virtues of insecurity' (ibid.).

If Kermode, in *History and Value*, appears praising of canonical literature, with its inbred class assumptions, it is not because his beginnings were privileged. The circumstances of Kermode's youth on the Isle of Man were, economically, very modest. His father earned, year to year, three pounds a week, and in a single year never earned, adding in moonlighting, over two hundred pounds (UE, 39–97). This period was followed by the War and five years in the Navy, the subject of his fine and moving memoir, *Not Entitled*. It is, in fact, one of Kermode's great assets as a critic that his experiences have been so atypical of the middle-class academic. The academy, today, is marked by an extraordinary amount of empathy for those outside its precinct, but it is an empathy that often feels abstract and inauthentic, especially when it runs parallel to the course of professional advancement. Kermode has (as noted) commented upon this; and his comments have registered more forcefully for the reason that he has experienced first-hand what many younger academics meet largely in theory. Kermode's work has always been notable for the qualities of its empathy and generosity, something that seems the product of his background, even as that might have pitched him in another direction. In his modesty, he is quick to point out what the experience held back, saying, when accused of bourgeois sympathies, 'I wasn't always a bourgeois liberal humanist, if I had been born one I might perhaps have got myself educated better and earlier, and even been taught to think in a respectably philosophical way' (AFK, 99).

Thus while Kermode's critical predilections favour canonical literature, it is not because he has not been forced to think about such issues as class and value. *History and Value* is itself an attempt, couched in terms that are often personal, to come to grips with the problem. Yet, ultimately, Kermode tends to discount those novels, poems, and plays that strike him as more attuned to politics than to aesthetics, and to discount their efficacy in the larger public realm. In the Michael Payne interview, for instance, he notes that while the demand for political relevance fluctuates with the times, the utility of such programs remains open to doubt: 'Spenser was engaged in politics after all, ... but I don't think anybody's ever suggested that his engagement made very much difference.[20] It may somewhat have reinforced the Elizabethan settlement. Swift was engaged in politics, and perhaps he's a counterexample, because it's probable that his writings did something to affect the issues, like in the case of Wood's halfpence and the *Drapier Letters*, for example. But when you think back into the great decade of political engagement for theatre, in Britain anyway, and you think of what went on at the Unity Theatre, or think of American plays like *Waiting for Lefty* and so on, what good did all that do? It hasn't affected American or British political history in any measurable way ...' (PNH, 87). One might argue that this is not exactly what is meant, today, by an attention to a text's politics, that such is more conceived as part of the fabric of a novel or poem, and need not address itself to explicit political disputes. For example, a poem such as Williams's 'The Young Housewife' makes no overt reference to any political matter, yet the poem has, vis-à-vis the housewife, a voyeuristic character and raises unsettling questions with regard to male poet and female object. These are questions that Williams can hardly be credited with provoking, even as they follow from a reading of his poem. Instead, the questions follow from the clash of present-day interests with a 1917 modernist poem. Kermode would probably agree, but his own critical values, emphasizing the critic's responsibility to what the text says in its own voice, tend to discourage such readings. Kermode emphasizes literature's here and now aspect, but as a critic, committed to divination, there is a strong impulse to respond to literature as the exemplum of permanent truths: 'One hears rather little about permanent truths in modern criticism; to Empson it was obvious that they existed and that it was dishonorable ... to "wince away" from them' (AP, 119).

There is nothing wrong with acknowledging permanent truths – in one form or another, after all, they must exist – and one of Kermode's critical strengths is his sensitivity to the way texts entice us to seek out these truths but then deceive us into mistaking one labyrinthian dead end after another for the path home: 'Thus do texts interpret, or deceive, their interpreters, who should know they do so, and make allowances for it' (GS, 13). One of the dangers of this position is that the critic can adopt a relation to texts that is conceivably too deferential. This can lead, as it does Kermode, to the view that if all texts are in some way immanent, it is enough simply to follow one's 'own nose.' Things of value are said to give off an aroma that the good critic will heed, even if others do not. Approvingly, Kermode quotes Empson's dictum that 'a critic ought to trust his own nose, like the hunting dog, and if he lets any kind of theory or principle distract him from that, he is not doing his work' (AP, 45). It is not untrue, for intuition is one of our most valuable critical tools. Still, if a critic is not careful, this reliance can easily begin to look more like a prejudice, which, even when spoken of as common sense, can do harm. As I have noted, Kermode tends to take literature's definition for granted, to esteem that '"our" kind of writing' has an almost inherent superiority to other kinds (HV, 96). Perhaps it is because he is aware of his own susceptibility this way that Kermode, in his theorizing about interpretation, is so attentive to the problem of error. In 'The Men on the Dump,' he, in effect, says as much. Speaking of an earlier moment in his career, he writes: 'I made mistakes, and I wrote things that are quite rightly thought biased or inaccurate, but I regret none of that, for ... the life of intelligent poetry and criticism is a life of error twinned with truth – like twins, they quarrel and are interdependent' (AFK, 99). It is an eloquent way to put the matter, and it is expressly true.

For Kermode, errors make further interpretation necessary, and are therefore an integral element of a larger pleasure. In *The Art of Telling*, he spoke of 'at least two kinds of pleasure' associated with reading. The first 'has its origin precisely in the gaps – gaps which may have various causes, including error, but which are inescapably present in all texts' (130). The second pleasure is, in a sense, consequent upon the first, for it represents the attempt to overcome those gaps or errors, so as to divine a truth. Or as Kermode writes, 'it consists in knowing what it is that "holds a book together"; it involves the divination of generic expectations and structures' (AT, 130). Meanwhile, there is yet another way, pointed out in *An Appetite for Poetry* (1989), in which error might be thought valuable. Referring to a textual error in Forster's *Passage to India* that went undetected for several decades, Kermode notes that as a rule we tend to be under-readers, too capable of letting an obvious error escape our attention. This is bad, but it also suggests something good, that 'if we miss such manifest errors, we may also miss less manifest subtleties' (AP, 158–9). There is good reason, then, to be suspicious of our pronouncements about 'the larger sense of' things, be these things novels or matters more weighty. The sense that 'minor puzzles reflect greater ones, and in particular one that is so great as to deserve to be called the only problem' (UE, 429), is evident throughout Kermode's work, though perhaps seldom so beautifully expressed as in his one sermon, 'The Uses of Error,' offered at King's College Chapel. Here, addressing the interpretative problems made manifest by Georges De La Tour's *Job Visited by His Wife*, Kermode brings all his fascinations with error together, observing both how error is a constitutive part of interpretation as well as an important guarantor of the text's – and by extension, the world's – mystery:

The history of interpretation, the skills by which we keep alive in our minds the light and the dark of past literature and past humanity, is to an incalculable extent a history of error. Or perhaps it would be better to say, of ambiguity, of antithetical senses. The history of biblical interpretation will provide many instances of fruitful misunderstanding. It arises because we want to have more of the story than was originally offered, or we want to see into the depths of that story. We have always been pretty sure that the literal sense is not enough, and when we try to go beyond it we may err, but sometimes splendidly. Job will serve the argument as a book which always was and always will be enigmatic, which will always attract interpretation. A mysteriousness pervaded the whole book ... The more deeply we consider that time and the world have made of Job's wife the more obvious it becomes that the mysteries of such stories, and perhaps of language itself, are familiar to us from our interpretations of our own lives. (UE, 431–2)

Kermode's interest in error relates to his ambivalent relation to contemporary critical theory. That is, his sense that error is intertwined with all of our interpretative efforts, combined with his longstanding scepticism regarding systematic thought, has placed him in a sometimes contentious relation to theory, even as his own work has been notably sensitive to, and informed by, current theoretical discussions. Hence, he starts with the sensible acknowledgment that 'in some form or other the dispute about the place of theory in literary criticism ... has always been with us' (AP, 6), and that criticism, no matter what its stripe, must first inform itself about what it would question. 'Those who reject the fashionable *in toto* rarely think it worth their time to find out what it is they are rejecting' (UE, 176). His disagreements, then, with theory have been, he thinks, particular disagreements, and not broadsides, though, in truth, he has executed a number of these, too many in fact. Among the latter are such statements like 'this great efflorescence of literary theory seems to entail an indifference to, and even a hostility toward, "literature"' (AP, 5), or, with regard to the postmodernist's relativizing of truth, 'What used to be called lying is now the only way to argue. Anything is true if I can say it persuasively' ('Freedom and Interpretation,' 56). Statements like these have been met with the rebuttal that his work is 'autocratic and old-fashioned' (Hermione Lee, 'Will's Power'), the splenetic canards of 'a grumpy old man [who] appears at the window and yells until he's hoarse, "Hey, you kids!!! Stop playing ball in the front of my house!" and then slams the window' (Michael Bérubé, 'Defending Literary Studies'). Such derogatory putdowns notwithstanding, Kermode has, in fact, tried to hold fast to the principle that theory is neither a good nor bad thing, such judgments being dependent on the instant case. When it comes to theory, however, the tone of misgiving is never too far away: 'My sense of the matter is simply that it would be quite wrong to deplore theory as such, though quite right to contest some of its claims. That is to say, any complaint must be leveled not against new critical practices; it would be as intemperate to deny their propriety as it would be to decline questions about their cost, which arises not so much from the theoretical practices themselves as from the hegemonic claims they are often thought to justify' (AP, 6).

Two theoretical movements that have most caught Kermode's attention and occasional ire are deconstruction and New Historicism. The two movements are themselves somewhat adversarial, with deconstruction being a text-based theory that often seems to slight history, viewing it as one trope among others, and with New Historicism refusing to grant sovereignty to those canonical texts that have such a secure place in the work of a Derrida, de Man, and Miller. Kermode has certainly been influenced by both theories: *The Genesis of Secrecy* is, in many ways, a post-structuralist reading of Mark's Gospel; and *History and Value* is a volume in which he, as Cunningham observes, 'nailed his historical colours in a finely principled way to the critical mast' (*In the Reading Gaol*, 52), just as his 1954 edition of *The Tempest* has, writes Colin MacCabe, 'a real claim to be the founding text of the critical school of "new historicism"' ('Wild and Whirling Words'). Nevertheless, Kermode has expressed his differences with both movements, sometimes in acrimonious terms. Respecting deconstruction, Kermode has expressed notable discomfort with what he speaks of as its 'ludic' element, and this despite the fact that his own theory of interpretation, with its notion of endlessness, has clearly borrowed from this same criticism. Yet, as noted earlier, Kermode has described deconstruction as 'the most frightening manifestation' among the newer criticisms, and which, 'when deployed with a fervour no less evangelical than ludic,' appears like 'a contravention of what I take to be the purpose of criticism – briefly, illumination' (AT, 5). Illumination is, in fact, the desideratum of Kermode's criticism, but it would be easy enough to forget this given, one, his Hume-like scepticism and, two, his deep interest in the problem of interpretative error. His criticism often plays on the edge, if it does not actually fall into, the abyss of indeterminability, as when in 'The Uses of Error' sermon he concludes: 'So I think that there is a peculiar truth in Job's wife when we cannot decide whether she is tender or cruel, blessing or cursing; and a peculiar truth also in a poem which, on the face of it, falsifies the gospel itself' (UE, 432).

Meanwhile, Kermode's misgivings about post-structuralist theory partly relate to its self-promotion, the implied claim that it offers an unprecedented critical approach. Addressing himself to Barthes's concept of *écriture* and the warning against premature closures, Kermode writes: 'We might once more ask whether Barthes, with rare extravagant (and for that matter, ideological) additions, is not saying something that in a way we know already' (AT, 76). He makes the same objection to New Historicism: 'It is surely from an ignorance extraordinary in historians that militant New Historicists can claim to have broken the mould of a universally stuffy, unexamined practice of history, till now protected by "institutional guardians" and anti-intellectual specialists ... For there were in those days [mid-century and later] very serious debates about history, and the philosophy and history of history, and the history of literature; and new ways of doing history, not at all stuffy or institutionally coercive or specialised in the wrong sense, were emerging for example at the Warburg Institute' (AFK, 91). That deconstruction and New Historicism provide 'little that might ruffle most conventional critics' is the first reason Kermode, repressing something here, gives for objecting to these methodologies (UE, 123). In fact, these two methodologies ruffled, and still ruffle, the feathers of an inordinate number of 'conventional critics.' Fortunately, Kermode has some better objections, including his sense that deconstruction is too much like 'a catastrophe theory,' especially as it assumes 'that the whole Western metaphysical tradition can be put into reverse' (AT, 7); that it transforms undecidability into another form of closure (AP, 33); that it evinces a somewhat hypocritical relation to canonical discussions, for even as it calls into question the values that have singled certain texts out from the morass of history, its practitioners are biased in the direction of these texts, apparently on the principle 'that only great works, which are great because they have already deconstructed themselves, are worth deconstructing' (AP, 207); and that it refuses to define itself. On this last point, Kermode seems to agree with John Ellis, whose book, *Against Deconstruction*, he reviewed in 'Talk About Doing':

> Why is nobody willing to say exactly what this word [Deconstruction] means? Because, says its users, 'a demand for clarity begs the question at issue.' Ellis disagrees, and offers this old-style definition: it is 'the illusion that the meaning of a word has its *origin* in the structure of reality itself and hence makes the *truth* about that structure seem directly *present* to the mind.' But the position was familiar long before Deconstruction came in

with its mystifying demands for demystification. What is now obscurely attacked is a view generally agreed to be naive and uninformed, especially by readers of Wittgenstein, Sapir, Whorf and others. And according to Ellis, Derrida has done little more than add to the existing consensus a kind of gratuitously revolutionary fervour – a 'rhetorical absolutism.' (UE, 121)

These are sound criticisms, though the reluctance to grant deconstruction its due – i.e., to acknowledge the wide-scale consequences of its critique – is too chary. This said, Kermode does perform a necessary role, which is to apply a brake to a theoretical movement at risk of taking itself too seriously, of not acknowledging how much of what it proposes has been said, in one way or another, before. It is not the most glamorous role to play, but it does seem a necessary one, and it does require someone like Kermode, who speaks not only from experience but also with authority. Like an academic Inspector 'Pagan' Morse, Kermode plays the curmudgeon's role perfectly, and while it often enough subjects him to the unwelcome charge of conservatism, he manages, somehow, to retain the respect of theorists and non-theorists alike. Even the scathing (as well as jejune) Bérubé attack quoted above comes prefaced with the remark: 'Frank Kermode, after all, is no right-wing thug. He is one of the century's most perspicacious, sensitive, prolific, and versatile critics writing in English; his breadth of mind and generosity of intellect are justly renowned.' Meanwhile, Kermode's objections to New Historicism have again first to do with the sense that its 'newness' is overplayed. For instance, reviewing *The New Historicism* volume, edited by H. Aram Veeser, Kermode says of Stephen Greenblatt's conception of 'cultural poetics' that it 'can, in fact, be thought of rather simply as a blend of the formalist and the historical, very interestingly applied but essentially less "new" than others tend to make it sound. As with Deconstruction, there is a certain amount of hype. You'd think, reading some of these pieces, that professional exponents of Renaissance literature had until yesterday still been swearing by Tillyard's *Elizabethan World Picture*' (UE, 125).

More important than this is Kermode's objection to seeing literature, once again, regarded as 'just one function of a cultural system, one discourse among others' (UE, 123). Included in this objection is a resistance to the New Historicist's efforts to blur the 'distinctions between text and context, so that the records intended to illustrate or provide the context become texts of equivalent status to the "literary" works which were the ostensible motive of the enquiry' (ibid.). For Kermode there is a priority involved. For the New Historicist, disenchanted with literary criticism as a form 'of secular theodicy' (Greenblatt, *Learning to Curse*, 168), this priority (i.e., elevating the art work above its cultural matrix) itself needs to be questioned. Or as Greenblatt writes, 'there is a tendency in at least some new historicist writings (certainly in my own) for the focus to be partially displaced from the work of art that is their formal occasion onto the related practices that had been adduced ostensibly in order to illuminate that work. It is difficult to keep those practices in the background if the very concept of historical background has been called into question' (169). New Historicism, in this sense, seems to conceive the world as immanent. Nothing is too trivial to merit attention, for everything is interdependent and inseparable from the larger 'resonance' of meaning. To view something – e.g., literature – apart from its context is to falsify it, to see it as privileged and appropriating. This may be the case, but the argument, designed to make things more textual, risks becoming, as Stanley Fish points out, ahistorical. That is, by demanding that we refuse the appeal of those historical determinations and boundaries which, whether they are inherited or chosen, are a large part of who we are, New Historicism 'asks us to be ... unhistorical, detached at some crucial level from the very structures of society and politics to which the' theory itself 'pledges allegiance' ('Commentary,' 311). Or as Fish, in an essay applauded by Kermode, goes on say:

> Now in essence this picture of the radiating or widening out effects of institutional action is an accurate one; for since all activities are interrelated and none enables itself, what is done in one (temporarily demarcated) sphere will ultimately have ramifications for what goes on in others. The question is can one perform institutionally with an eye on that radiating effect? Can one grasp the political constructedness and relatedness of all things in order to do one thing in a different and more capacious way? Given that disciplinary performance depends on the in-place force of innumerable and enabling connections and affiliations (both of complicity and opposition), can I *focus* on those connections in such a way as to make my performance self-consciously larger than its institutional situation would seem to allow? ('Commentary,' 314)

The answer to these questions, says Fish, is 'no.' All the world's facts – past, present, and future – can be understood as intertwined and thereby meaningful to whatever our subject of study, but the world is larger than we, and situated as we are, we are forced into making certain choices with regard to which facts are most significant in the light of our needs, including the need to hypothesize the ways in which this same, larger world holds together. For Fish, these choices are at the heart of what constitutes a discipline, the nature of which is to be bound by a more or less stable set of questions about the world or some part of it. Such a set is not indifferent to what is happening around it, nor is it exempt from finitude. Most sets worthy of the name 'discipline,' how-ever, speak of past practices, codified as a tradition, which current prac-tices tend either to perpetuate or react to, depending on what sort of future their practitioners imagine the discipline as evolving towards. Lit-erature constitutes one of these disciplines, and what Kermode thinks intolerable about New Historicism is the latter's readiness to imagine a future without it. Contrasting New Historicism to the post-Leavis and -Eliotian tradition of literary study that formed him, Kermode com-ments, 'Of course there were many possible conjunctions, confronta-tions, contradictions that we didn't perceive or feel obliged to take into account, far too many by such standards of today. On the other hand it did not occur to us to put the whole idea of literature into question – to deny that there was anything that should be so distinguished, or to claim that the distinction was conferred upon it by acts of arbitrary and selfish power – and I think that was right' (AFK, 91).

There is, however, a difference between wishing to abolish literature and wishing to modernize its definition. Kermode accuses the New His-toricists of the former, yet there is reason to think that the ambition is more like the latter. In *Learning to Curse*, Greenblatt, for instance, notes, 'my own concern remains centrally with imaginative literature, and not only because other cultural structures resonate powerfully within it' (170). It is true that Greenblatt tends to blur the distinction between traditional conceptions of literature and non-literature, and it is true that his sense of New Historicism implies a certain immanence in things. But in his Biblical studies, Kermode himself has been prone to blur the distinction between texts traditionally distinguished as literary and non-literary (i.e., sacred), and to justify the conflation by appealing to their shared quality of immanence. In both instances, we find evi-dence of critics enlarging the boundaries of literature, with the hope of making it more responsive to our sense of the world. Yet if Greenblatt and Kermode have each made efforts towards reconfiguring our under-standing of what constitutes literary study, they have also each made efforts towards reining in the boundaries as well. We have seen this to be the case with Kermode's notion of that 'radiance' or 'momentary utmost' found in those 'poems that can stop the heart' (AFK, 93, 94). And, if I read Greenblatt correctly, his own sense of the aesthetic remains bounded by the notion of wonder, that focused attention which the art object obliges us to offer it, and which is defined, says Greenblatt, quoting Albert the Great, 'as a constriction and suspension of the heart caused by amazement at the sensible appearance of something so portentous, great, and unusual, that the heart suffers a systole' (*Learning to Curse*, 181). For Greenblatt, this wonder, prompted by the art work, prompts our own search for a larger resonance rather than vice-versa: 'I think the impact ... is likely to be greater if the initial appeal is wonder, a wonder that then leads to the desire for resonance, for it is easier to pass from wonder to resonance than from resonance to wonder' (ibid.).

I do not mean to suggest that there are no differences between Kermode and Greenblatt. There are differences, but they are not so contrary that agreements cannot also be negotiated, especially in light of Kermode's clear admiration for Greenblatt's work. The fact is, while Kermode has harsh things to say about deconstruction, New Historicism, Marxism, structuralism and feminist criticism as movements, he tends to be respectful of the learning of those critics most identified with these movements. It is movements themselves that Kermode seems not to care for, and to the degree that a particular critical theory begins to assume the characteristics of such, so does his scepticism grow. He simply distrusts schools, seeing them as too reflective of the herd instinct. To Salusinszky, he confessed, 'The only school I've belonged to – and that was very briefly – was when I was an undergraduate and, under the influence of ferocious young teachers, became a Leavisite. I mimicked the jargon, and so on, but then saw that's not a thing you ought to do' (CS, 111).[21] That one ought to steer clear of schools remains his belief. This helps to explain the preference of following his own nose; and it also helps to explain some of his harsher remarks regarding theory, including remarks about its 'vacuity and inaccessibility' (AT, 8); its 'large quantity of deformed prose' (UE, 119); its 'self-important semi-illiteracy' (UE, 125); and its being 'unduly fogged by neologism' (AT, 92). Thus, in the same paragraph, he can say about Derrida that he 'is full of surprises and hardly ever dull,' but that his followers are 'extremely dull' and 'tend to say the same thing about everything they choose to discuss' (AT, 5). Maybe, it is simply a matter of a British empiricism at work, but whatever the case, Kermode tends to look too scornfully at the unnamed (perhaps because unread) acolytes, even as his admiration for the profession's high priests appears genuine.

The contemporary critics who have attracted Kermode's attention include Empson, Frye, Barthes, Eagleton, Jameson, Williams, Culler, Foucault, Trilling, Derrida, and de Man. There are others who come in for particular attention, but these are the names that find themselves repeated. Empson and Frye are probably the two critics who have captured Kermode's greatest respect, even though the first is said to have disliked him, thinking him too much a neo-Christian (CS, 110), and the second is found, as mentioned, too systematic. Still, Kermode says 'that in terms of pure intellectual capacity and force, Empson was the best critic of the twentieth century, in English' (ibid.). He brought, along with Richards and Eliot, 'a new kind of attention' to poetry (AFK, 90), an attention schooled in the tradition of poetry, aware of theories yet not the servant of such, preferring ultimately to trust the critic's own judgment. When praising Empson, Kermode has especially in mind the work exemplified by *Seven Types of Ambiguity* (1930), wherein ambiguity is defined as 'any verbal nuance, however slight, which gives room for alternative reactions to the same piece of language' (1); and wherein it is claimed that 'all good poetry' is 'ambiguous' (xv). As it is so, it is incumbent upon the reader not to approach a poem with too many preconceptions; instead he or she 'must rely on each particular poem to show ... the way in which it is trying to be good' (7). Kermode also fully admires Empson's awareness of 'the dreadful sense of the contradictions involved in living and thinking about it,' that is, '[t]he radical contradiction ... between the hope of human happiness, for which, at least at certain moments we feel ourselves so wonderfully suited, and the power of the world as it inescapably is to frustrate or even ridicule that feeling' ('William Empson'). The sense of contradiction in Empson, thinks Kermode, is just as acute as that in the later deconstructionists, so it does not surprise him to find later theorists speaking of Empson as an ancestor. Yet the prior work does give him, he thinks, the right to ask whether deconstruction is offering anything terribly new. Presented with post-structuralist claims about the 'openness,' 'intransitivity,' and 'literarity' of texts, Kermode finds himself regretting 'the bad communications with Paris, for we, who have had Professor Empson and the New Criticism with us for forty years, hardly need to be told that texts can be polysemous' (AT, 65).

Like Empson, Northrop Frye is admired by Kermode for his brilliance and his prose. *The Anatomy of Criticism* is an 'extraordinary book,' 'wonderfully well written,' and for which 'one confidently predicts long life' (PE, 64). But unlike Empson, Frye is too much the servant of a theory, that is, his ambition to understand literature in the light of myth. This ambition takes literature out of its real home, times and space, and thus 'invalidates Frye' (C, 120). That is, '[i]f literature does the work that ritual and myth once did, the arrangement is providential, for myth and ritual can obviously no longer do it' (ibid.). For Kermode, literature's first (though clearly not its only) responsibility is to realities more present, and to the extent that Frye's theory obscures these, it appears misdirected: 'The difference between *illud tempus* and *hoc tempus* is simply willed away in Frye's critical system, but it is essential to the very forms of modern literature, and to our experience of it' (ibid.). Nevertheless, it was partly in response to the force of Frye's theory that, says Salusinszky, Kermode, in the 1960s, embraced Stevens's notion of fiction: 'Like myths, fictions impose human meaning on the world, and human structures on the dizzying openness of space and time. But unlike myth, fiction does not *deny* space and time, and is always willing to abandon its structures for new ones as life itself changes' (*Criticism in Society*, 101–2). This is noticeably the case in *The Sense of Ending*, wherein Kermode writes that '[i]f we forget that fictions are fictive we regress to myth (as when the Neo-Platonists forgot the fictiveness of Plato's fictions and Professor Frye forgets the fictiveness of *all* fictions)' (SE, 41). This notion of fiction had its own mythic dimension, though it went largely unrecognized at the time. In any event, Kermode, while admiring of Frye's work, has overall found it, as he found the latter's reading of *The Faerie Queene*, guilty of a 'fatal ... reduction' of literature's 'actual complexity' (SSD, 24).

Roland Barthes is another critic whose rival influence Kermode first experienced in the 1960s, a fact that apparently did not sit well with some of his fellow British critics. There were whispers that 'his relation to literary and to pedagogical fashion' was inappropriate, unpatriotic even; and that Kermode must assume 'personal and professional responsibility' for the critical leasing out of the 'scepter'd isle.'[22] Kermode could give back what he got ('it really takes an English reviewer to suggest that the whole movement of thought to which he [Roman Jakobson] has so seminally contributed is a load of newfangled nonsense' ['Structuralism Domesticated,' 17]), thus ensuring that he would never, by the standards of a powerful few, be thought a true cultural insider. (Kermode: 'Some of us Manx who have made our lives in England have had to settle for a permanent condition of mild alienation' [interview with Katie Donovan].) Kermode, meanwhile, found himself drawn to Barthes for the reason 'he writes so beautifully' (PNH, 81). And yet he thought that Barthes engaged in a straw-man argument, involving issues that Empson and the New Critics handled with less braggadocio and more nuance. Addressing himself to Barthes's suggestion, in *S/Z*, that pre-modern novels are themselves modern to the extent that they will frustrate the reader who assumes their meaning to be limited, Kermode writes: 'Barthes, under the influence of a domestic French quarrel, always talks as if establishment critics deny that position. Outside France this is, of course, untrue. In a sense, he is saying, in a new way, something we have long known about the plurality of good texts' (AT, 68). As for the straw-man accusation, it particularly applies to Barthes's discussion of the *lisible* and the *scriptible*, a distinction which imputes, in Kermode's words, an 'ambiguous innocence' to classical texts. The problem is that Barthes's *lisible* text, with its promise of transparent meanings, demands such an innocent reader that the theory itself becomes suspect: 'The *lisible*, it appears, assumes that its relation to the world is one of specularity, or of transparence; the text pretends to be absent – as if, to recall Coleridge's invaluable expression, it is, in the course of reading, defeated to a pure transparency. This is the basis of Barthes's distinction between *écrivance* (classic, transparent) and *écriture* (modern, announcing its difference, a text among texts). People who believe in the simple specularity and transparency of novels are indeed very naive' (AT, 74–5). Kermode, nevertheless, credits Barthes with instigating 'a renewal of attention to aspects of narrative which did not cease to exist because they were not attended to' (AT, 70), and believes that when later scholars make judgments about the era, they will value Barthes's achievement, especially his brilliant combination of 'descriptive technique and literary sensitivity' (PNH, 81).

It is not certain that Kermode should make the same prediction about the three Marxist critics – Terry Eagleton, Fredric Jameson, and Raymond Williams – to whom he, from time to time, refers. For one, there may be some tension, or maybe just prickliness, between him and Eagleton, that is if we can read resentment in Eagleton's labelling him 'a liberal bourgeois liberal humanist' and Kermode's recall of the fact (AFK, 99).[23] Beyond this, Kermode, with his working-class antecedents, harbours some class resentments against academic Marxists, tending to see their interest in workers as more exploitative and abstract than genuine. Oxford and Duke, it is implied, are not the best places to meet workers; and 'even with Williams, you don't have a feel that there's the same sort of desperate desire to get into and help shape a working-class culture that you get in the communist writers of the thirties' (PNH, 88).[24] Resentments aside, Kermode takes exception, as noted, to Eagleton and Jameson's special attention to the '*non dit*,' to 'the gaps of the texts rather than in the text itself' (HV, 99). He sees the two critics borrowing from psychoanalytical practice, seeking 'to read absences as well as presences, working on distortions and unwilling omissions and so making contact with a subtext which is vaguely analogous to the unconscious' (ibid.). For Kermode, the methodology undervalues what the text says in its own voice, and overvalues the allegorical narrative discovered in its gaps. Too often, it results in overdetermined readings, with the absent text dictating the reading of the present. In fact, thinks Kermode, in Marxist readings, the absent text, denials aside, begins to function like an Ur-narrative or master code. Or as he says with reference to Jameson: 'He quotes with approval some disparaging remarks of Deleuze and Guattari about Freudian interpretation – 'a system of allegorical interpretation in which the data of one narrative line are radically impoverished by their rewriting according to the paradigm of another narrative, which is taken as the former's master-code or Ur-narrative and proposed as the ultimate hidden or unconscious *meaning* of the first one.' ... Having understood this danger, Jameson is of course anxious to explain that he himself has not fallen into it – that his 'political unconscious' is not just such a 'master-code' or 'unconscious *meaning*' (HV, 102).

For Kermode, Jameson is an allegorist, a situation not offset by his appeal 'to the totality of the work, just as bourgeois critics do or did' (HV, 102). This said, it might be noted that Jameson himself would object to the notion, one, that a text's manifest meaning can be isolated from a latent meaning, and, two, that interpretation can avoid a rewriting, or allegorization, of the text, so that the more pressing matter is not whether this takes place, but how it takes place? From what perspective or theory is the text read? In the *Political Unconscious*, Jameson writes in response to those critics who accent the primacy of a text's manifest meaning: 'Unfortunately, no society has ever been quite so mystified in quite so many ways as our own, saturated as it is with messages and information, the very vehicles of mystification (language, as Tallyrand put it, having been given us in order to conceal our thoughts). If everything were transparent, then no ideology would be possible, and no domination either: evidently that is not our case' (61). Regarding the way that interpretation 'demands the forcible or imperceptible transformation of a given text into an allegory of its particular master code or "transcendental significer"' (58), Jameson writes: 'to see interpretation this way is to acquire the instruments by which we can force a given interpretative practice to stand and yield up its name, to blurt out its master code and thereby reveal its metaphysical and ideological underpinnings. It should not, in the present intellectual atmosphere, be necessary laboriously to argue the position that every form of practice, including the literary-critical kind, implies and presupposes a form of theory; that empiricism, the mirage of an utterly nontheoretical practice, is a contradiction in terms; that even the most formalizing kinds of literary or textual analysis carry a theoretical charge whose denial unmasks it as ideological' (58).

Jameson writes with a noticeable stridency, and there is reason for thinking a critic might do well to ignore the demand that one 'blurt out' the 'master code' informing the work. For one, the values which inform such are always part and parcel of the work to begin with, and the astute reader will discern what these are without the critic having to promulgate a critical doctrine, one which he or she will likely soon contradict. As Greenblatt, explaining why he has not been more explicit about his 'subject position,' writes: 'If I have not done so to the same extent [as other critics], it is ... because I believe they are pervasive: in the textual and visual traces I choose to analyze, in the stories I choose to tell, in the cultural conjunctions I attempt to make, in the syntax, adjectives, pronouns' (*Learning to Curse*, 167). It remains true that Kermode's empiricism tends to suggest that others have positions, whereas he looks at things straight on. It remains, in fact, part of the appeal of his work, even when we admit that disinterest is itself an interest. The point might be, there are interests and there are *interests*, and disinterest, comparatively speaking, still remains a useful concept. Kermode's empiricism is a point of view, one which, as Parrinder notes, tends to redefine criticism as interpretation; and one that also tends to be rather receptive to other points of view. Again, Parrinder writes: 'It is in *The Classic* that Kermode emerges as an ideologist of the modern institution of literary study, which opens its doors indiscriminately to Marxist, Freudian, Lacanian, New-Critical, structuralist, feminist, deconstructionist, and all other systems of interpretation. His attachment is not to any particular interpretative system but to the notions of the canon of "classic" (or plurally interpretable) texts and of the professional practice of interpretation' ('Secular Surrogates,' 113). This seems true, even when one grants that Kermode's liberalism becomes testy when critics confuse criticism with doctrine. Eagleton and Jameson do this, he thinks, and he finds it difficult to believe 'their notions of the relationship between base and superstructure have any special validity' (CS, 119), the whole matter appearing too much like a 'Marxist theology' (HV, 102).

Theology – or a discussion of its relation to criticism – might be considered a likely point at which Kermode would engage Jonathan Culler's work. Culler, like Empson before him, has made his anti-religious position abundantly clear, and, hoping to stir up a debate about the 'complicity' of criticism with theistic belief, has boldly questioned the practice: 'To urge us to take up a critique of religion is not to deny that Christianity in particular has been the inspiration for many great works of art but to ask us to reflect on the consequences in our own day of criticism's relation to religious discourse. The complicity of literary studies with religion today is a subject that has scarcely been broached but cries out for attention, not least because religion provides a legitimation for many reactionary or repressive forces in the United States and is arguably a greater danger today than ideological positions critics do spend their time attacking' (78). Though Kermode had much to say about *Framing the Sign*, the volume from which I quote, he preferred to ignore the invitation to debate Culler on this point, saying that while he gathered Culler was seeking to subvert what he regards 'as evil social or intellectual tendencies,' he 'couldn't understand what Culler was doing, really' (CS, 119). It is, in some ways, too bad, for it would have made for an interesting debate. Instead, Kermode chose to respond to Culler's work along more familiar lines: literature and its relation to theory, politics, pedagogy, and canon.

Kermode's responses to Culler's work are found principally in two sites: the prologues to *The Art of Telling* (1983) and *An Appetite for Poetry* (1989).[25] In both instances, Kermode describes Culler as one of the more important practising critics: in the 1983 collection he speaks of 'Culler's conversion to deconstruction' as 'quite an important moment in the history of the American [critical] movement' (AT, 5); and in the 1989 collection he speaks of Culler as 'that most persuasive spokesman of modern theory' (AP, 8). But in the six-year interval between the two volumes, Kermode's respect for Culler's work has clearly waned. In *The Art of Telling*, Kermode speaks of Culler with noticeable affection; he is the boy-genius who in the early 1970s would make his way down from Cambridge to attend Kermode's London-based discussion group on topics pertaining to the newer, more theoretical, criticism. Kermode also expresses his dismay when Frank Lentricchia accuses the Modern Language Association's leaders of conspiring to award the 1975 James

Russell Lowell Prize to Culler for *Structuralist Poetics*. But by 1989, things had apparently changed, perhaps even soured, for Kermode introduces *An Appetite for Poetry* with what is, in good part, an attack on Culler's *Framing the Sign*.

The attack is perhaps not personal, for the disagreements in their stances towards literature and theory are, in fact, substantial. Kermode thinks that Culler's work, like that of the Marxist critics, is too fronted towards concealed meanings, treating literary texts as a way station to more important destinations: the 'interest is in what is officially, or by institutional consent, concealed. The only reason why it continues to concern itself at all with what Culler still refers to as "literature" is that literary works can better than others be induced to tell us things that bear 'crucially' on theoretical questions' (AP, 10). The distinction between literature and non-literature is, Kermode finds, disregarded, even as Culler 'cannot bring himself to deny precedence to the great' literature (ibid.), and thus to reconfirm the canon. Culler would resist this description, for 'as a practical political strategy,' he thinks it imperative that there be, at once, both a 'transformation of the canon and resistance to canons' (*Framing the Sign*, 48). But Kermode thinks this ambition fraught with problems, not because he minds change, but because the notion of resistance, as used here, demonstrates Culler's failure to understand the way in which canons transform themselves. I addressed this point at length earlier, so I will not pursue it further now, other than to say that intrinsic to Kermode's objection both to Culler's conception of the canon and of theory is that they subvert one discipline, literature, in favour of another, politics, and help to promote 'sociopolitical standards' which, whatever their usefulness, seem not fully responsive to the complexity (the Empsonian ambiguity) of literature (AP, 21).

The dispute comes down partly to one of interests, perhaps complicated by a misunderstanding of the other critic's loyalties. Kermode is a vigorous defender of literature as a discipline. Culler is not, his interests being more directed towards criticism and interdisciplinary studies, wherein literature functions as a subset of a larger matrix. Yet Kermode's criticism of Culler tends to assume that the latter's interests are, first and foremost, those of literature. It is not an altogether unfair assumption, for Culler, a prominent member of the Modern Language Association, teaches out of a literature department and his writings have influenced, as they still do, what is taught in other such departments. So the disagreement is not only a matter of personal interests, but does, as the vigorousness of Kermode's argument attests, pertain to how literature is studied, both outside and inside the classroom. What Kermode particularly objects to is Culler's framing the dispute as being between those who think universities exist 'to reproduce "culture and the social order"' and those who think universities 'as "sites for the production of knowledge"' (AP, 11). Kermode's values, including a respect for canonical literature and its interpretation, are, in Culler's hand, identified with the 'humanist' education of the sort which E.D. Hirsch's *Cultural Literary* represents. Less argument than caricature, Culler's distinction fails to discriminate between, say, Robert Alter and William J. Bennett, and tars as reactionary all those who think literature sustainable as a discipline. Kermode resents the charge and the suggestion that an attention to canonical literature is perforce backward looking. Rather, he thinks such an attention goes hand-in-hand with a concern for modernity, and that when interpretations cease to be modern, they cease to matter. In the present moment, being modern entails an awareness of politics, but it does not require that literature subordinate itself to politics. Literature may not be an absolute category, but neither is politics. So Kermode thinks the attempt by Culler and others to make literature do politics' bidding smacks of self-righteousness: 'It is clear that Theory (I follow Culler in using the term to describe the whole many-sided critical movement) thinks remarkably well of itself, and remarkably ill of its literary-critical predecessors, unless their reputation is such that, like Empson, they might, if presented in suitably legitimated versions, serve as honorable ancestors, household gods, or propaganda totems' (AP, 12).

To turn to Michel Foucault and Lionel Trilling, these are not critics whose work Kermode actually takes up, but there are passing references to them, and they hover in the background of certain discussions. For instance, Kermode appears mindful that his argument on behalf of the tradition's continuity is challenged by Foucault's influential concept of epistemological fields, or epistemes, discontinuous orders held together as much by hidden as by manifest determinations. In *The Classic* (1983), Kermode writes that 'even if one argues, as I do, that there is clearly less epistemic discontinuity than Foucault's crisis-philosophy proposes, it seems plausible enough that earlier assumptions about continuity were too naïve' (140). Trilling, meanwhile, figures in the discussions about both the common reader and pedagogy. In the first instance, Kermode found inspiration in Trilling's effort to 'keep the road open' between academic and public discourse (AFK, 103), an effort made on the behalf of literature with the hope that it should not collapse into an overly precious scholarly object. It was an effort undertaken first in the classroom and then in the space of review essays. Whatever the forum, the sense was that the teacher-critic had a responsibility to a larger community than one's own kind. He or she also needed to realize that failures in communication might be double-sided. This explains, perhaps, Kermode's affection for Trilling's story about how when he introduced his students 'to the abyss of the Modern, [they] gazed into [it] politely, said "how interesting!" and passed by' (UE, 118). The moral is that academics often take themselves and their fears rather more seriously than those who pass through their classrooms, and if in Trilling's day, students appeared to front the abyss – i.e., modern literature's existential angst – and then to carry on, perhaps the present generation of students, introduced to an even deeper abyss, shall do likewise. Or as Kermode, in a discussion of de Man, writes: 'Others may do the same to de Man's abyss, and carry on thematizing and totalizing because it is their pleasure to do so, even if it is shamefully human to do so; and they have a long resistance to puritanical imperatives' (UE, 118).

'Puritanical,' 'melancholy,' 'dark,' 'severe,' 'bleak,' 'inhuman' – these are some of the adjectives Kermode applies to de Man's thought and temper. There is no hostile intention, for Kermode thinks highly of de Man, who, he states, 'may well be one of the players within the field [of criticism] who will continue to have a powerful influence' (PNH, 84). In *An Appetite for Poetry*, Kermode writes that '[n]obody could read de Man – even in the old sense of the word – without being aware that his was a very remarkable mind, essentially a dark mind as well as an abnormally acute one; what he writes is, in a perfectly recognizable sense of the word, literature' (33). It is unusual praise from one whose instincts tell him that criticism is parasitic, and who has referred to only a handful of critics as being worthy enough to be recognized as contributors to literature. Yet as Kermode's descriptions suggest, he sees in de Man the tortured soul of the genuine artist, Romantic cliché though this be. What Kermode dislikes about much academic criticism is its perfunctoriness, the sense of scholars going through the motions while seeking tenure, promotion, and material well-being. De Man's publishing history was something of an affront to this paradigm. During his life, he published but two books, *Blindness and Insight* and *Allegories of Reading*, both of which were made up of previously published essays. Reviewing *Critical Writings, 1953–1978*, a posthumous collection of de Man essays, Kermode writes that 'one of their merits is that they often demonstrate how much can be said in a review or a relatively brief essays: which explains why de Man was so slow to publish a book, and why all his books are collections of essays' (UE, 111).

Kermode has his own reasons for making the observation, for most of his books have also been collections of previously published essays, and even some of those that were not, such as *The Romantic Image* and *The Sense of Ending*, have, he tells us, been charged with being essay-like: 'Both of these books are properly to be thought of as essays (I remember Graham Hough grumbling that the first essay was followed, not as one might expect after a ten-year gap, by a real book, but by just another essay, and at the time I felt rueful about this, though my view now is that we could do with more essays and many fewer large books)' (AFK, 92). But Kermode's respect for de Man goes beyond this resemblance, relevant as it is. He particularly values the seriousness of the work, and even finds in de Man something like a kindred spirit, notably in his wrestle with problems pertaining to belief. Earlier, I applied one of Kermode's descriptions of de Man ('by his belief in disbelief') to Kermode himself, for it seemed revealing with respect to his secular interest in the Bible and to his interest in Stevens, especially the Stevens of the Supreme Fiction. The point is, much of Kermode's work appears that of a man, cognizant of belief, yet arrested by his scepticism from yielding to it. Disbelief, in this sense, requires an understanding of belief, and this makes the scepticism more poignant. This partly has to do with one's place in history. Kermode writes: 'A critic of de Man's age (exactly my own) must of course have dragged into his later life a burden of notions about intuitions of value that are now questioned or discredited' (AP, 30). And it partly has to do with temperament, something that Kermode both shares and does not share with de Man: 'he knew a lot about standards of cultural excellence, but maintained that such standards are "in the last analysis always based on some form of religious belief." For this suspect foundation he wished to substitute "a principle of disbelief." It is not difficult to see that such a principle can mean little to a subject lacking the experience of belief, and de Man's formation was such that he had indeed experienced belief in a form that led him to believe he needed to cultivate disbelief' (AP, 31).

This sense of de Man conforms with something that I have heard Hillis Miller say, more than once, about de Man, and that was that the latter had told him, in his cryptic fashion, that the question of religious belief was the most important of questions. What this meant is open to interpretation. Less so is that Kermode links the question of disbelief with that of belief, and this connects to his interest in de Man. Kermode's temperament is more ruddy than de Man's, but he is still capable of appreciating the element of self-torment locatable in the Belgian exile's work:

> This is certainly not the place to enter into the controversy about his wartime juvenilia; it is nevertheless worth pointing out that the mature de Man was in many respects inconceivable except as the product of an education not to be had outside continental Europe, and he is often applying the principle of disbelief to beliefs it might never have occurred to the rest of us to hold ... For example, when Heidegger says that the German language alone 'speaks Being' while all the others merely 'speak of Being,' a person of my formation is likely to feel, if not say, that on this occasion at least Heidegger is being silly. But to arrive at a position of disbelief in respect to such views was for de Man an arduous and fruitful task, involving a deconstruction of a powerful philosophical tradition that sponsored certain beliefs he came to regard as abhorrent, whether they were related to German political and cultural hegemony or to the false idea of aesthetic totality. Thus it was for him a matter of moment that *no* poetry, not even Hölderlin's, can be said to 'speak Being,' whereas to most people the claim that this is what poetry does would hardly seem worth arguing about ... But none of this means that the principle of disbelief is not a valuable principle, or that de Man's often melancholy and sometimes desperate application of it is irrelevant to our present crisis. (AP, 31–2)

As the passage testifies, part of Kermode feels the bond with de Man, while another part prefers to keep at a distance. The first, reading both the wartime journalism and the later 'evolving, exacting, rather melancholy writings,' appears sympathetic even when put off by the efforts of de Man's contemporary colleagues, 'decently animated by affection for a dead and admired friend' (UE, 113), to explain away, as intellectual errors, the young man's Nazi and anti-Semitic sympathies. Kermode feels that such responses 'often seem to lack any serious understanding, of how even people of high intelligence are sometimes induced to behave, especially when they may be under stress of a kind the exculpators have the good fortune to know nothing about' (ibid.). Kermode does not wish to deny the gravity of de Man's wartime sins, even as he, knowing temptation, does not wish to deny kinship. But perhaps the more genuine kinship is to be found in the caution which both men, in their academic writings, have expressed towards large-scale truths. For Kermode, this caution found itself embodied in clerical scepticism; for de Man, in the aporia. About the latter, Kermode writes: 'Aporia, unde-cidability: these now ubiquitous expressions are often covert ways of achieving critical closures which the favored line of argument ostensibly forbids and avoids. But they can also reflect, in the best practitioners, a degree of prudence and sanity. For the great question of value and history may ... be described as undecided, if not undecidable' (AP, 33). Or, as Empson once said, 'the point I am trying to make is that this final "judgment" is a thing which must be indefinitely postponed' (*Seven Types of Ambiguity*, xv).

Though Kermode, doubtlessly influenced by de Man, can speak of 'the progress of criticism ... as a progress of error,' and can also, in an effort to explain his own 'mode of protective irony,' speak of 'an obscure conviction that in some way potential error is more useful than palpable fact to the conversation of criticism' (AFK, 97), he is hesitant to elevate what is, for him, largely a matter of caution into a theory. Thus his scepticism regarding deconstruction, even when practised by such a formidable critic as de Man. Kermode (in a slightly mocking tone, more directed, it seems, at Christopher Norris, a de Man scholar, than at de Man) writes: 'even if one breathes the air of pure theory, it must sometimes seem strained to argue that it is always impossible to say what one means, even if the statement you wish to make is that it is always impossible to make such a statement' (UE, 114). This criticism goes to the heart of the matter. Kermode knows the value of caution, of scepticism even, but he also knows that things need to be said and done; and that if one chooses to inhabit the realm of the aporia for too long, others, with perhaps more sinister motives, will occupy the main playing field. This leads Kermode to say of de Man that the 'real problem is to discover in him anything, outside rhetoric, that can be stated unequivo-cally' (UE, 115).

About Derrida, de Man's colleague in deconstruction, Kermode has less to say, even as most of what he says is flattering. Kermode describes him as 'very much a thinker with whom one has somehow got to tune into,' someone whose impact will, in future times, be equated with 'that of Nietzsche,' so that '[t]here will be very great arguments about what he was really talking about' (PNH, 81). For Kermode, Derrida's main subject is the critique of totalities, particularly of 'the ontotheological and humanist myths' (AT, 110). Kermode is, again, sceptical about the critique's newness, but he praises Derrida for the little-noticed quality of caution in his thought (he is 'more cautious than might be expected of one who has acquired the reputation of the Great Anarch' [AP, 35]) and for his recent responsiveness to social considerations (PNH, 86). This said, Kermode cannot avoid being somewhat put out by the prose's 'ludic' dimension. He speaks of the prose as 'ranging eccentrically over great tracts of literature and philosophy' (AT, 5), with Derrida 'always picking up the last phrase he used and looking at it and sort of doing a little dance around it' (PNH, 81). It is 'a deeply serious performance' (ibid.), yet Kermode, with his commitment to clarity and the conversational style, cannot really warm up to it. The work strikes him as too enamoured with obscurity, too ready to investigate the recesses of things at the expense of attending to that which the author has worked so hard to put into an expressive form. In short, we have, in Derrida and Kermode, not only two kinds of interpretation, but also two styles of criticism. One is happy casting forth words as if from his own spinnerets, weaving a web over one facet of a thing, but then rushing off to embellish another facet, never quite ceasing; whereas the other uses words more parsimoniously, striving for exactitude but also mindful that errors have been, and will be, committed, leaving one with fewer words than may be needed to get the job done. It is not imperative that we choose between the two styles, for in truth they appear to complement one another. Kermode grants the value of both, but he is the exponent of the latter; and it is that for which we value him. It is a beautiful style, about which another great stylist, Denis Donoghue, has written: 'it addresses men and women who are deemed to share common sense, literacy, a certain span of public allusion, and willingness to be interested in ideas upon which the survival of our species does not necessarily depend' ('Critics at the Top,' 54). Survival may not depend on an interest in such ideas or in the values that Kermode's writings exemplify, but without these, it would appear a more impoverished world than even Stevens might contemplate.

Chapter Three

GEORGE STEINER

The Uncommon Reader

In his chapbook *The Uncommon Reader* (1978), George Steiner points to Jean Simeon Chardin's portrait *Le Philosophe lisant* (1734) to underscore his conception of the ideal reader. The portrait shows a richly dressed man, seated at a table, his attention immersed in a thick folio volume. The scene is a nocturnal, domestic one, wherein we see only that portion of the room in which the reader, his back to a large-stone fireplace, sits. This is enough to suggest the reader's material well-being, for the various pewter vessels on the mantel, plus those objects visible on the table – the inkwell, the hourglass, the other folio volumes, and the three large coins – combine to create a mood of comfortable privacy. And this, thinks Steiner, is not irrelevant: 'What matters is the emphatic elegance, the sartorial deliberation of the moment. The reader does not meet the book casually or in disarray. He is dressed for the occasion, a proceeding which directs our attention to the construct of values and sensibility which includes both "vestment" and "investment"' (UR, 2). We should not be wrong to read into the word "investment" all its monetary connotations – Steiner clearly wants us to – even as the main thought evokes the reader's self-discipline: 'The primary quality of the act, of the reader's self-investiture before the act of reading, is one of *cortesia*, a term rendered only imperfectly by "courtesy." Reading, here, is no haphazard, unpremeditated motion' (ibid.). For Steiner, serious, thoughtful reading requires not only curiosity and determination but also social privilege: 'Implicit in the format and atmosphere of the folio ... is the private library, the wall of book-lined shelves, library-steps, lecterns, which is the functional space of the inner lives of Montaigne, of Evelyn, of Montesquieu, of Thomas Jefferson. This space, in turn, entails distinct economic and social relations: as between domestics who dust and oil the books and the master who reads them, as between the sanctified privacy of the scholar and the more vulgar terrain on which the family and outside world conduct their noisy, philistine lives' (UR, 14–15).

The rhetoric is less elitist than cold-hearted, leaving many readers rightfully offended. Steiner professes little, if any, sympathy with the democratic sensibility – he describes his own as 'entirely stoical and pessimistic and perhaps anti-democratic' (RI, 170) – and likes to dismiss the academy's egalitarian efforts as hypocritical 'cant,' useful in helping liberals feel good about themselves, but otherwise useless. 'There is,' he says, 'no democracy to excellence' (RGS, 284). Rather, excellence speaks of privileged schooling, hard work, and the gift of intelligence, the last of which is not necessarily distributed evenly among all races, but likely reflects 'sociological, climatic, [and] nutritional (i.e., the differing levels of protein consumption)' factors (E, 192). Steiner writes, 'I have never been able to disguise my faith in Spinoza's equation of excellence and difficulty. I am convinced that nearly everything worth close investment in philosophy, poetics, the arts, demands stringent schooling and, often, a body of knowledge such as was imparted in the education of the privileged and the gifted prior to the present' (RGS, 284). As a result, the uncommon reader is, more than likely, a well-ensconced member of a conservative, bourgeois order: 'A man sitting alone in his personal library reading is at once the product and begetter of a particular social and moral order. It is a *bourgeois* order founded on certain hierarchies of literacy, of purchasing power, leisure, and of caste' (OD, 189). There can be, he says, no disguising the fact that this readership is predicated on power relations that free the individual from those forms of work and existence thought least desirable: 'the classic act of reading ... is the focus of a number of implicit power relations between the educated and the menial, between the leisured and the exhausted, between space and crowding, between silence and noise, between the sexes and the generations (it is only very gradually that women come to read in the same way and context as their husbands, brothers, and fathers)' (ibid.).

When Steiner speaks of reading this way, it almost always entails an elegiac tone, for he is convinced that social conditions and values have changed in such a way that serious, disciplined reading is endangered. The 'power relations and value-assumptions have been drastically eroded. There are few libraries now in private apartments and fewer servants to dust them or oil the bookspines. Intensities of light and noise levels of unprecedented volume crowd in on personal space, particularly in the urban home. Far more often than not, the act of reading takes place against, in direct competition with another medium – television, radio, the record player' (OD, 189). Reading has, in effect, been pressed out of the private, domestic space, and into university libraries and offices, where it has become more the activity of the specialized academic than that of the layperson: 'We are almost back at the stage before Montaigne's famous circular reading room in the quiet tower. We read "seriously" as did the clerics, in special professional places, where books are professional tools and silence is institutional' (OD, 190). This may be so, though as a reader and writer, Steiner has done everything in his power to resist the professional pressure to specialize. He is, at heart, a polymath, wishing to hold on to the dream that one person can read and absorb all the books worth caring about. Thus, in *The Uncommon Reader*, he writes: 'He is no true reader, no *philosophe lisant*, who has not experienced the reproachful fascination of the great shelves of unread books, of the libraries at night of which Borges is the fabulist. He is no reader who has not heard, in his inward ear, the call of the hundreds of thousands, of the millions of volumes which stand in the stacks of the British Library or of Widener asking to be read' (4). The impressive thing about Steiner is the degree to which he has made the polymathic ambition, so genuinely quixotic, *appear* plausible. Not that he has actually realized his ambition, for the most frequently heard criticisms of Steiner's work usually come from specialists questioning his accuracy. Still, given the reach of the ambition, one can well take note, as Edward Said has, of what 'a brilliant reproach' he has been to these same critics: 'For Steiner is ... an unashamed amateur who works in the conviction that "serious literary and philosophic criticism comes from a 'debt of love,' that we write about books or about music or about art because 'some primary instinct of communion' would have us share with and communicate to others an overwhelming enrichment." Steiner is that rare thing, a critic propelled by diverse enthusiasms, a man able to understand the implications of trends in different fields, an autodidact for whom no subject is too arcane' ('Himself Observed,' 244).

Steiner is a generalist, but a generalist with a vengeance. His curiosity seems to go everywhere, and where it leads, his pen soon follows. Yet while he writes for the common reader, he wants, on all occasions, to be taken seriously by the specialist as well. Or as he writes in the 'Preface' to *On Difficulty* (1978), 'It is my hope that these discussions will interest the general reader as well as the specialist who, necessarily, prefers to work within a technical domain' (xi). About the latter individual, however, he professes more than a degree of ambivalence. For one, he abhors the increasing reliance upon technical terms, believing that the tendency makes whatever community we still retain more fragile. Working with a much smaller vocabulary, 'the sixteenth and seventeenth centuries realized,' he argues, 'a unique coherence of inheritance and innovation,' something that we ourselves have, by and large, given up the hope of re-obtaining. Our English vocabulary now approaches half a million words, but it falls 'increasingly short of the needs of a splintered, technological society. Where it is not mere commonplace, our usage grows more and more specialized. The mass jargon of the modern city is stranger to the names of stones and flowers, as it is stranger to the making of its bread. We communicate; but being second-hand and abstract, the modes of our communication do not achieve community' (LS, 205). And if both language and community are the victims of specialization, so too is wisdom: 'In our present culture we have increasing numbers of intense specialists as against the diminishing numbers of generalists. This is a large and complicated subject, involving the displacement by technicity or *techné* of *sophia* or wisdom' (RI, 185). For the fox, as opposed to the hedgehog, this means trouble: 'In the process, the fox smelling the way around with joy, not closing his bristles into a single ball of monomaniacal specialization, comes to seem terribly vulnerable' (ibid.).

An especially adroit fox, Steiner took pride in the fact that his University of Geneva chair (from which he has since retired) spoke of a large purview: 'The title of my Geneva chair, the oldest in the comparative rubric, is that of *littérature générale*. This tag honors me. Would that it was called, even more exactly, *de lecture* – a chair of reading, for those learning how to read and to read with others. It may be that cows have fields. The geography of consciousness should be that of unfenced *errance*, Montaigne's comely word' (RGS, 278). Steiner has a proclivity for venturing across traditional scholarly borders, even as he knows that gatekeepers will repeatedly challenge his visa, and that the further one ventures afield, the easier it is to get lost. Yet the venture seems worth the risk. It may be, says Steiner, that '[t]o ask larger questions is to risk getting things wrong,' but '[n]ot to ask them at all is to constrain the life of the understanding to fragments of reciprocal irony or isolation' (OD, xi). This is well put, and it explains, in part (personality explaining even more), the contempt Steiner often exhibits towards specialists: 'Specialization has reached moronic vehemence. Learned lives are expended on reiterative minutiae. Academic rewards go to the narrow scholiast, to the blinkered. Men and women in the learned professions proclaim themselves to be experts on one author, in one brief historical period, in one aesthetic medium' (RGS, 278). At the same time, Steiner has been at pains to distinguish the scholar whom he admires from the specialist whom he disdains, the distinction residing in the sense that true scholarship is a much rarer, and more sacred, thing than the more general profferings of specialized knowledge. Gershom Scholem, says Steiner, taught him the difference: 'There [in Scholem's presence] I knew the rarest of combinations: minute textual, philological scholarship, based on the idea that God is in the details – which I admire helplessly, not being able to do it well myself – with the huge scope. I am surrounded by these rancorous dwarfs who think that to be a specialist is in itself the way to God. The devil it is!' ('The Art of Criticism, II,' 92). Scholem's example led him to understand the truth of Housman's remark that "True scholarship is much rarer than poetic genius' (ibid.). Steiner's distinction between true scholars and their imagined imitators would prove more convincing were it not so obviously the reflection of a chary heart; but generosity towards those perceived as underlings, whether social or academic, is not his strength; quite the contrary. There might be some compensating justice in the fact that Steiner does not – rhetorically at least – view himself as a true scholar, thinking that his scholarship could have been better had he been of a more patient temperament: 'I have, on occasion, been careless over detail, over technical discriminations. Impatience, a disinclination to submit work in progress to expert scrutiny, the pressure of deadlines and public platforms – too numerous, too diverse – have marred texts which could have been, formally at least, unblemished' (*Errata*, 172). It is the failing that gives birth to his memoir's title, *Errata* (1997), for the sense of failing is made more heartfelt by the memory of his deceased father, whose greatest ambition for his son was that he become both a teacher and scholar: 'On this last point, I have failed him' (12).

In truth, Steiner does not wish to have it thought that his work has no interest to the specialist. When venturing into realms already well explored, he knows the importance of admitting the limits of his knowledge (e.g., 'I understand far less of Heidegger than Graham Ward intimates' [RGS, 278]; 'It would require more knowledge and aesthetic acumen than I possess to discriminate with precision between these late still-lifes by Chardin and a number of similar compositions by Cézanne'

['The Heart of the Matter,' 150]). All the same, he must work very hard to get as reasonably on top of as many fields as he does (e.g., Biblical, Classical, and Holocaust studies, linguistics, modern literature, philosophy of language, and theories of translation). And what Said says about *After Babel* (1975) might, with justice, be said of most of his writings: 'The rare thing about what Steiner does ... is that he puts himself at the inner core of a discourse, discipline, language, author and *then* communicates outward to the uninitiated, without losing either the intimacy or the urgent clarity of each realm. You could call it ventriloquism or, with Steiner's critics, charlatanism, but it is an impressive and on the whole enviable gift' ('Himself Observed,' 245). Actually, with *After Babel*, perhaps Steiner's most important book, the author made a concerted effort to make a contribution to the theory of translation. He came away from it with the sense that he had, only then to have it suffer notable neglect among experts. In the 'Preface' to the revised edition, he admits his hurt, saying that the book's claims were not so much contested or debated among 'the mandarin trade,' as they were afforded a '"passage under silence"': 'Wholly representative of this strategy is the footnote in a recent (highly intelligent) monograph on philosophy and translation: *After Babel* is designated as self-evidently the most important text in the entire domain of translation studies and of the philosophic issues they entail. After which no further mention or citation occurs' (AB, xi). Since its appearance, many of its arguments have, he says, 'been drawn upon and pilfered, often without acknowledgement' (xi).

Steiner is probably right. As a critic, he is known for the suggestiveness of his work – for putting forward theses that if pursued would require several lifetimes of work. It should not surprise, then, if more committed linguists (and *Sprachphilosophen* and *Kulturkritiken*) might think it warrantable to flesh out Steiner's ideas without properly acknowledging their point of origin. In a sense, Steiner encourages such a response due to his penchant for asking questions that he knows he has not the time to answer. An interview with *Maclean's* ends, not atypically, with a thesis left hanging in the form of a question: 'Could it be that the reason Europe continues to produce formidably, and it does, is attached to the tragedy of its history? I'm asking questions here; the interview would be very unfair if it turned these into answers. Answers, we don't have. I'm just asking' ('George Steiner Thinks,' 15). 'To end on a question, to make of questions a responsion to questions,' may, as Steiner says, 'be a Jewish vice' (RGS, 285), but it also leaves the reader free to pursue matters on his or her own. If this person goes on to enclose the question in the house of a larger theory, it might be best to welcome this not only as the completion of a prior problem but also as an opening to further inquiry or questions. This is what Steiner mostly does – that is, he sees every answer as the commencement of a new question, in the nature of a never ending process. '"Coming to rest,"' says Steiner in *Antigones* (1984), 'is always provisional' (201); and it is exactly this sense of things that Ronald Sharp takes to be a central feature of the work: 'It would be difficult to exaggerate the frequency with which Steiner thematizes questioning, both in his fiction and his essays, and it would be equally difficult to exaggerate the centrality that questions – carefully formulated but often unanswered ones – occupy in his work as a whole' (221).

This is quite true, but it is also true that Steiner's provisional rhetoric gives cover to an aggressive position-taking. Robert Boyers incisively writes that '[f]or all of his obviously genuine desire to get things right by consulting every conceivably relevant source and alternative opinion, he moves with a relentless determination toward the fullness of his argument. He has a marked fondness for conclusive insights that permit him to use such terms as "indisputable," "pre-eminent," and "decisive"' ('Steiner as Cultural Critic,' 25). In this mode, Steiner often replaces argumentation with assertion, something that might persuade when the audience is a familiar one, sharing his biases, as the audiences of *The New Yorker* and the *Times Literary Supplement* – the two journals to which he has most frequently contributed – presumably do. Yet when the audience is less simpatico, the want of full-fledged argumentation can prove a liability. This happens, for me, whenever Steiner dons his Comte de Buffon hat in order to belittle intellectual life in the United States. In his notorious essay 'The Archives of Eden,' Steiner, claiming that America is a '"museum-culture"' that 'will not produce first rate [intellectual] contributions,' stresses both the inferior cultural antecedents of its population and the falseness of its egalitarian principles. In the first instance, after allowing for the contributions of Puritans and Jews, he writes, 'But the great mass of emigrants were not pioneers; they were fugitives, they were the hounded and defeated of Russian and of European history. If there is any common denominator to their manifold flight, it is precisely this: the determination to opt out of history in its classical and European vein, to abdicate from the historicity of justice, of suffering, of material and psychological deprivation' (AE, 72). In the second instance, he writes that in this land whose 'ethnic-demographic elements' constitute a sort of '"Darwinian negative,"' the cultural 'pyramid is, as it were, inverted. It would make excellence fully accessible to the vulgate. This desideratum is inherently antinomian. It labours to correct the oversight or snobbery of God, the failure of nature to disseminate generally and equitably among men the potential for response to the disinterested, the abstract, the transcendent' (AE, 81). These remarks might play well enough in the British (e.g., in the relentlessly anti-American 'NB' section of *TLS*) and European journals, but without more substantive argument than what even Steiner admits amounts to personal conviction, their force on this side of the ocean is bound to seem slight.[1]

'The Archives of Eden' was written for a 1980 conference at Skidmore College; and the audience, mostly American, did receive it badly. Henry Patcher called its thinking 'shoddy' and 'dishonest' ('In Response to George Steiner,' 96, 97); John Lukacs called it 'a *haute Weimar* complaint' (Boyers, 'Discussion,' 117); and Susan Sontag bemoaned the fact that 'Steiner had [not] made his argument better,' for there are things in it with which she would have been more inclined to agree had not the job been done 'intemperately and with a good deal of inaccuracy' (Boyers, 'Discussion,' 118). It was not that Steiner was incapable of pleasing his audience. Steiner's brilliance is generally accepted, even among his critics. Nor was it that the essay worked too much on the level of assertion. Rather, what most annoyed his audience was the essay's ruthlessness. That Steiner, the recipient of so·many instances of American beneficence,[2] should appear so dismissive of all things American, is, no doubt, connected with his conception of himself 'as a Platonic anarchist' (*Errata*, 135), whose sole allegiance is to the realm of the Ideal. But it is difficult not to read the essay as a remarkable instance of ingratitude, and to wonder, as David Bromwich does, whether some of Steiner's more outrageous statements are meant to be taken as perverse jokes – or, more likely, the unrepressed sentiment of a misanthrope. Thus we are told that 'Ninety-nine percent of humanity conducts lives either of severe deprivations – physical, emotional, cerebral – or contributes nothing to the sum of insight, of beauty, of moral trial in our civil condition' (AE, 64). And: 'We are, on the whole, a cowardly, murderous bundle of appetites endowed with seemingly limitless instincts of destruction and self-destruction' (ibid.). Thinking so little of humans in general, Steiner can argue not only that '[t]he existence of a Plato, of a Karl Friedrich Gauss, of a Mozart may go a surprisingly long way towards redeeming that of man' (BC, 87), but also that if we are 'absolutely honest,' we will view 'the destruction of Galois at twenty-one, or the disap-

pearance of an important score, to be losses paradoxically but none the
less decidedly out of proportion with common deaths, even on a large
scale' (BC, 88). The uplift of the conclusion is too attached to a ghastly,
sardonic premise.

As with Swift, the hurtfulness and bitterness are seldom removed
from the desire to provoke. Steiner may think little of humanity, but he
is determined to prod it into something better than it is. Americans, he
says, 'would democratize eternity' if they could (RP, 33), but it is precisely by the standards of eternity, rather than America, that Steiner proposes – even insists – that we live. So he turns to provocation, which by
its nature bespeaks something excessive. Otherwise, it should go unnoticed. Steiner, meantime, is a master of the sthenian challenge. No
merely judicious individual would propose, for instance, that '[e]ven
the Gulag ... is less of a peril to the life of the spirit than is the detergent
tide of "Americanism"' (MH, 68). He makes the remark in a discussion
of Georg Lukács, and so is spurred on by the Marxist critic's own views.
Nevertheless, Steiner has made it a habit of provoking Western intellectuals by his claim that the totalitarian state, with its paternalism and censorship, is a more invigorating climate for the intellectual than the
democratic state, with its consumer values. '[I]n the world of the Gulag,'
Steiner writes, '[a]rtists, thinkers, writers receive the unwavering tribute
of political scrutiny and repression. The KGB and the serious writer are
in total accord when both know, when both *act on the knowledge* that a
sonnet (Pasternak simply citing the first line of a Shakespeare sonnet in
the venomous presence of Zhdanov), a novel, a scene from a play can be
the power-house of human affairs, that there is nothing more charged
with the detonators of dreams and action than the word, particularly the
word known by heart' (AE, 88). Steiner's point is that in the former
Soviet empire, the work of the intellectual garnered attention; and that
as perverse as it might seem, this is preferable to the large-scale silence
that meets artistry in the West: 'What text, what painting, what symphony could shake the edifice of American politics? What act of abstract
thought really matters at all? Who *cares*?' (AE, 89) In totalitarian societies, the artist can be sure that someone – i.e., Big Brother – does care:
'To imprison a man because he quotes *Richard III* during the 1937
purges, to arrest him in Prague today [1980] because he is giving a seminar on Kant, is to gauge accurately the status of great literature and philosophy. It is to honour perversely, but to honour nevertheless, the
obsession that is truth' (ibid.).

The claim has not gone unnoticed, even in our inattentive culture.

Cynthia Ozick tries to build a friendly frame about it, saying that '[o]f course Steiner doesn't mean us to think that tyranny is "good for" culture; *he* is being somewhat Aesopian too' ('George Steiner's Either/Or' 91). But other critics, like Ihab Hassan, have been more anxious to point out that what the totalitarian state takes seriously are not 'art and ideas,' but rather *'dissent in any form*, including jokes, whispers, dreams' ('The Whole Mystery,' 321). More angry than anxious, Henry Patcher cites the argument as an example of *'ignoratio elenchi*,' and adds that '[t]o decide ... that the artist has a choice between two alternatives: either to live comfortably in an open society, at the sacrifice of his art, or to live in a society of "creative hermeticism and censorship" – is a misuse of the excluded middle when there is indeed a third choice' ('In Response to George Steiner,' 96–7). I agree with Hassan and Patcher. For three years, I lived and taught in the Soviet empire, first in Lublin and later in Warsaw; and while sympathetic to the Greshaw's Law element in Steiner's thesis – i.e., all the tabloid and Hollywood dreck first makes suspect and then displaces work of a more serious calibre – I also recall how difficult it is to do good work when all the traditional sources of intellectual inspiration (i.e., uncensored and readily available journals, books, archives, conferences, recordings, etc.) are no longer at hand. Yes, there is some evidence that, in Steiner's words, '[w]e are an animal which when cornered becomes eloquent' (RI, 180). Vaclav Havel, Adam Michnik, Zbigniew Herbert, Milan Kundera, Andrei Sakharov, Krzysztof Kieslowski, Nelson Mandela, Zhang Yimou, and Aung San Suu Kyi are all illustrations, past and present, of this phenomenon. Nevertheless, the overall effect of oppression is that it makes people cowardly and cynical; and this is less a spur to, than a dismantling of, intellectual life. When borders make conversations with other artists and scholars difficult, if not impossible, and when governments, through their pervasive bureaucratizing of experience, keep a strict watch over what is said and done, intellectual life suffers much more than it gains. For Steiner's claims not to seem 'gratuitously provocative' (Boyers, 'Steiner as Cultural Critic,' 15), he would need to develop the argument and illustrate it not only with those examples whereby singular, albeit courageous, men and women have stood up to a tyrannical system but also with examples whereby entire disciplines have been seen to prosper. He would need to explain where we are to find the Soviet empire's major contributions (for they seem difficult to locate) in architecture, diplomacy, economics, jurisprudence, medicine, technology, transportation, and urban planning. These too are intellectual disciplines and not insignificant aspects of culture. If Steiner really thinks that oppression paradoxically encourages invention (thus his frequent citation of Borges's remark 'that censorship is the mother of metaphor' ['Language under Surveillance,' 36]), he should take into account the larger ambit of this intellectual culture for the reason that literature – the discipline most illustrative of his remarks – is always more than literature, reflective as it is of a whole host of other values, values which, depending on their states of sophistication, will either enhance or undermine the labours of the writer. Such was implied when Steiner, in the eighties, claimed that the literature 'coming from Eastern Germany ... is so much superior to what is being produced in West Germany that it is almost embarrassing' (RI, 180), but it left the reader with the problem of saying exactly how the West was so culturally inferior to the East, for all the details were smothered in innuendo.[3]

The matter has bearing on Steiner's conception of the common – or uncommon – reader. As he views things, the West has, over the course of decades, experienced an extraordinary erosion in traditional values, including literacy. '[T]hrough world wars and inflation, the transfer of material energies to various modes of populism and "mass culture,"' the West has come to a point wherein 'the shared habits of biblical-classical reference, of articulate formality, of "order and degree" both emblematic and expressly rhetorical on which the intellectual-social-political architecture of the Renaissance, the Enlightenment and the nineteenth century were built, is now largely in ruins' (OD, 8). In addition to the mutation in cultural values, the West has experienced all sorts of economic and material deformations that make the everyday life of the would-be serious reader more and more taxing. No longer does one witness 'the personal acquisition of libraries in the old manner,' for '[t]he pace of being, the surrounding noise-levels, the competitive stimulus of alternative media of information and entertainment (a plurality notably lacking in the Soviet Union), militate against the compacted privacy, the investment of silence, required by serious reading' (OD, 10). Yet if the West had become inhospitable to serious readers, there remained, wrote Steiner in *The Uncommon Reader,* a place where the situation was not so irredeemable: 'There is a society or social order in which many of the values and habits or sensibility implicit in Chardin's canvas are still operative; in which the classics are read with passionate attention; in which there are few mass media to compete with the primacy of literature; in which secondary education and the blackmail of censorship induce constant memorization and the transmission of texts from remembrance to remembrance. There is a society which is bookish in the root-sense, which argues its destiny by perpetual reference to canonic texts, and whose sense of historical record is at once so compulsive and so vulnerable that it employs a veritable industry of exegetic falsification. I am, of course, alluding to the Soviet Union' (19).

It is, at once, a view both realistic and romantic. It is realistic in the sense that Steiner acknowledges the crimes of censorship and falsification, and in the sense that it is – or, better yet, was – true that absent other forms of entertainment (i.e., television and radio stations with more than two or three channels and decent production values, a bevy of films, and other forms of popular culture), a university graduate does tend to read quite a bit. I know that I did when I lived in Poland. Even so, Steiner's claim appears that of someone who has never stood in a butcher's line for half an hour, then in another long line at the baker's, and finally, on the way home, in a line at the post office to pay telephone and electricity bills. The point is that life in the Soviet empire was quite arduous, even for the university man or woman; and it was not unlikely that once a person sat down to read, word would come that a new shipment of choice, or necessary, items had arrived at the neighbourhood store and that one must hasten there forthwith. Also, if comparisons are going to be made between the conditions of the serious reader in the West and East, it should be noted that the percentage of the population in the East that had the opportunity to participate in the common reader tradition was minuscule. The economies of the East were (until recently) predicated on the nineteenth-century model of heavy industry and labour-intensive farming. In the Eastern Bloc more than 30 per cent of the labour force worked in agriculture, compared to 6 per cent in the West.[4] Similar disparities were found in manufacturing, with the Eastern states employing a far greater percentage of people in jobs that have been made redundant in the West, due to better technology and stricter work rules. These are, in fact, important contingencies when discussing the common reader tradition, for if the point is that the conditions for this tradition were greater in the Soviet empire than in the West, then it must first be conceded that the percentage of the population that combined both a university education and the necessary leisure-time to read was but a fraction of what it was, and remains, in the West. As someone who began his career writing for *The Economist*, Steiner should be much more sensitive to these disparities.

Compared to the East, the West – or, more specifically, the United States – does not encourage a strong demarcation between intellectuals and all others. In the United States, we seldom employ the term 'intellectual' as a noun, the way it is often employed in Europe, and especially in Central Europe. There is a propensity to feel, as John Lukacs puts it in response to Steiner's essay, that 'This notion of *intellectual* as a noun is a very poisonous thing' (Boyers, 'Discussion,' 116). Steiner views things differently. For one, if there be American intellectuals, he is unimpressed by them. 'Even people at the top of the educational and social pyramid fall, on average, well below the standard of cultural recognition taken to be essential in Japan and Western Europe' (LRS, 106). This follows suit with his view that 'humane mediocrity' constitutes an American cultural ideal (WOW, 98). Contra this ideal, he offers the ideal of the gifted few: 'It is not difficult to formulate an apologia for civilization based firmly and without cant on the model of history as privilege, a hierarchic order. One can say simply that the accomplishments of art, of speculative imagining, of mathematical and empirical sciences have been, are, will be, to an overwhelming extent, the creation of the gifted few' (BC, 87). The 'gifted few' excludes most common readers, for the latter are not required to possess the creative talent displayed by the former. They are, though, required to recognize it when they see it; and they are also required to help keep it alive, most notably via the means of conversation and critical commentary: 'To be realized critically the work of literature must find its complete reader; but that reader ... can only quicken and verify his response if a comparable effort at insight is occurring somewhere around him' (LS, 223).

The true reader is answerable to the text. The text – i.e., the classic text – is that which endures almost outside of time: 'The reader's life is measured in hours, that of the book in millennia. This is the triumphant scandal first proclaimed by Pindar: "when the city I celebrate shall have perished, when the men to whom I sing shall have vanished into oblivion, my words shall endure"' (LS, 3). Steiner is aware of how worn this equation has begun to seem. Nevertheless, the book as a means – one of the most certain – of transcendence has been a constant motif in Steiner: 'Marble crumbles, bronze decays, but written words – seemingly the most fragile of media – survive. They survive their begetters – Flaubert cried out against the paradox whereby he lay dying like a dog whereas that "whore" Emma Bovary, his creature, sprung of lifeless letters scratched on a piece of paper, continued alive. So far, only books have circumvented death and have fulfilled what Paul Eluard defined as the artist's central compulsion: *le dure désir de durer*' (UR, 3). Books are what we are left by past generations; they are our greatest legacy. Steiner asks that readers adopt an almost worshipful, even kabalistic, stance towards them. The reader who passes over a printer's error in a book is 'no mere philistine' but 'a perjurer of spirit and sense' (UR, 8). For Steiner, books retain their spiritual aura, and while the times are secular, there still attaches a fragrance of grace to those who treat books as sacred: 'It may well be that in a secular culture the best way to define a condition of grace is to say that it is one in which one leaves uncorrected neither literal nor substantive *errata* in the texts one reads and hands on to those who come after us' (ibid.). In this spirit, Steiner speaks of the reader's inherent obligation to the text, of our being answerable to it: 'to read well is to be read by that which we read. It is to be answerable to it. The obsolete world "responsion," signifying, as it still does at Oxford, the process of examination and reply, may be used to short-hand the several and complex stages of active reading inherent in the quill' (UR, 7).

Steiner knows that this formulation will seem regressive to many readers. That the book has a life beyond its material conditions of production, that men and women can participate in this life by making themselves answerable to the text – these are anathemas to a majority of sophisticated readers. Such ideas speak of vestigial religious longings when religion has long been dismissed and pigeonholed as fundamentalist myth-making. But even the most worldly critic – if responsive to the ache of human longing – might concede Steiner's courage in seeking to keep alive the premise that human life has inbred meaning. Again, he is more than aware of how easy it is to judge men and women as aggressive, wasteful, inconsequential beings, the sort the planet needs no more of and would be better off with far fewer of. In fact, as suggested, the criticism can be lodged against Steiner that he is too insensitive to the overall human population's inherent worth. In 'The Long Life of Metaphor,' one of his most embittered essays, he speaks of a significant majority of 'this polluted and suicidal planet['s]' people as having regressed to a state of 'bestiality,' employing a '"post-human"' language. Looking around him, he sees more and more 'creatures' who are 'less than human. They are loud with emptiness, a volume made the more evident and barbaric by electronic media. Where the language is still humane, in the root sense of the word, it is being spoken by survivors, remembrancers and ghosts' (55).

Still, Steiner holds to the hope that, contrary evidence notwithstanding, a human being can count for something in the larger scheme of things. It may be a slim hope, but everything seems dependent upon it. Thus in an act of extraordinary wilfulness, he wholeheartedly attaches himself to the notion of the uncommon reader, to the Arnoldian-like ambition which would make itself conversant with all that past and present generations, in their best and most inspired creative acts, have given us. It is a quixotic ambition, for it means making oneself intimate, if not expert, with not one discipline but many; and it means doing so in a second, third, and fourth tongue. Yet if anyone is equal to the task, it is Steiner, whose zeal here acts as a provocation to the rest of us who possess neither his talent nor fortitude. It is the zeal of the most uncommon reader, the person who assumes it an obligation to engage the text – the classic text – as it were '*by heart,*' believing it the best repository for all that we may know of '*auctoritas*' (UR, 16). This person not only corrects textual errors and interacts with the text via marginalia, but also shares his or her findings with other readers. Nor are all these readers committed to the same discipline, for while the uncommon reader respects disciplinary knowledge, he or she does not feel at a loss outside its boundaries. This is why Steiner has compared his work to that of 'a mail carrier,' an analogy that he extends by quoting Pushkin's remark, 'Please, never despise the translator. He's the mailman of human civilization.' Making the connection explicit, Steiner says, 'I think of myself at best as a translator, not just between different languages but between different disciplines and interests' ('George Steiner Thinks,' 14). Disciplines are respected, even as the uncommon reader aspires, albeit humbly, to an understanding that transcends the discoveries of any one discipline.

Knowledge has always been about use-value; but for some, Steiner included, it has also been about use-value in the largest of senses, wherein the desire has been not only to acknowledge that we live, but also to ask the question of how we should live and why. This is knowledge as metaphysics, and it partly explains Steiner's disgruntlement with things American, for he sees our lives as dedicated to the principles of pragmatism: '[t]here are ... regards in which the tenor of American feeling is closer to the bias for magic, for pragmatic *bricolage*, current in non-western traditions than it is to the world of Plato and of Kant' (AE, 62). It is true enough, and it helps explain why Steiner, with his commitments, places so much value on 1) the concept of a school of reading; and 2) his own critical labours in the pages of such weeklies as the *Times Literary Supplement, The New Yorker,* and *The Observer.* In the first instance, Steiner has repeatedly spoken of the ideal classroom as a place less where one disciplinary discourse or another reigns than as a place where reading itself reigns: 'I carry with me a vision of "schools of creative reading" ("schools" is far too pretentious a word; a quiet room and table will do)' (UR, 21). Reading entails a sensitivity to ideas, history, language, form, and nuance, concerns that together constitute what we mean by literature in its broadest sense. Texts might include Descartes's *Discourse on Method*, Rousseau's *The Confessions*, Goethe's *Elective Affinities*, Coleridge and Wordsworth's *Lyrical Ballads*, Darwin's *On the Origin of Species*, and Proust's *Remembrance of Things Past*, the selection process being dictated less by narrowly conceived belletristic interests than by the power of these texts to provoke thought and feeling.[5] As literature, these texts will always raise questions of execution or expression, something Steiner is quick to stress. Students should be taught 'metrics and rules of scansion,' ... 'not out of pedantry,' but because in 'all poetry, and in a fair proportion of prose, metre is the controlling music of thought and feeling' (UR, 22). More broadly, Steiner writes: 'My students and I do our very best to learn to read together. We seek to bring to bear on the manifold and historically metamorphic lives of the text the "speculative instruments" (Coleridge) of linguistics, of philology, of hermeneutics. The result is, when luck and concentration hold, an *explication de texte*, always provisional, always and explicitly "at the service of" the poetic-creative act' ('Literary Theory,' 445). Throughout, Steiner stresses the centrality of the text, of how we bend more towards it than it towards us, and of how we interpret the text best when we live and read in the midst of a community of readers.

Given his goals, Steiner inevitably refers more often to texts from the humanities than from the sciences. But he values scientific work, and his writings include many references to it. He also thinks that any serious work must demonstrate an acquaintance with past and present states of scientific knowledge. In *Bluebeard's Castle* (1971), for instance, Steiner argues that it would be a mistake 'to speak of the Renaissance without knowledge of its cosmology, of the mathematical dreams which underwrote its theories of art and music' (133). The more the scholar knows about mathematics and the sciences, the more valuable will appear the study. And yet, Steiner makes a crucial distinction between the interests that operate in the humanities and the sciences. He believes science is too involved in technology's matrix, and that its ends tend towards immediate use-value and less towards ultimate meaning. In *Language and Silence* (1972), he writes: 'But though they are of inexhaustible fascination and frequent beauty, the natural and mathematical sciences are only rarely of ultimate interest. I mean that they have added little to our knowledge or governance of human possibility, that there is demonstrably more of insight into the matter of man in Homer, Shakespeare, or Dostoevsky than in the entirety of neurology or statistics' (6). Most scientists would likely disagree with this, though they might agree that science's conclusions, so far as they speak to humankind's purpose, are nested in a language that laypeople generally find unapproachable. But Steiner also makes the point, acceptable I suspect to both camps, that science tends to be more forward-looking than, say, literature; that science's most encompassing achievements are its latest, whereas it should be hard to make the point, for instance, that the fiction of Penelope Fitzgerald or Anita Desai, while exquisite, represents an advance over that of Virginia Woolf or Jane Austen. They are different writers, and judgments about the merits of their achievements can be put forth, but these achievements will mostly have less to do with their temporal relation to one another than those in the sciences. 'It is of the nature of the study of philosophy and of the arts – distinct, in this regard, from that of the sciences – that time and age do tend to bring them a better-informed, a more balanced, view of their object. But neither the questions one poses nor the answers one puts forward are necessarily progressive' (A, 297). Of course, there might, even in literature, be some questions that can be spoken of as progressive, but in the main, thinks Steiner, philosophy and literature address perennial concerns: 'it is, I believe, poetry, art and music which relate us most directly to that in being which is not ours. Science is no less animate in its making of models and images. But these are not, finally, disinterested. They aim at mastery, at ownership. It is counter-creation and counter-love, as these are embodied in the aesthetic and in our reception of formed meaning, which puts us in sane touch with that which transcends, with matters "undreamt of" in our materiality' (RP, 226–7).

Steiner thinks that scientists and other specialists bypass those questions of meaning that are most dear to us, fearful perhaps of their banality. The questions, nevertheless, remain important, and if the specialist refuses to consider them, perhaps the committed generalist can. This partly explains the attractiveness, for Steiner, of reviewing, for it offers a space where interdisciplinary, non-specialist interests can be raised. Steiner has his reservations about reviewing, especially to the degree that it appears quotidian and journalistic. But it remains not only a space where larger issues can be addressed but also one where literature can be talked about and, in effect, kept extant. There are, naturally, other forums – e.g., the scholarly monograph – where literature is examined, but few offer the feel and vibrancy of the review essay, with its suggestion of a topic that is alive and important now. The good reviewer awakens interests, makes a hitherto unknown text appear a necessary addition to the reader's intellectual biography. Sometimes the reality does not match the appearance, and the reader must proceed elsewhere. But what remains important is that the reviewer, addressing other general readers, generates interest, and moves people in the direction of bookstalls and libraries. Here, the reviewer performs a function that often goes under-appreciated, and yet is vital to literature's survival. It is what leads Steiner, quoting a phrase from Charles Péguy, to write, "'what a terrifying responsibility," but also what a measureless privilege; to know that the survival of even the greatest literature depends on *une lecture bien faite, une lecture honnête.* And to know that this act of reading cannot be left in the sole custody of mandarin specialists' (UR, 21).

As a reviewer, Steiner has done his job well. In journals such as the *Times Literary Supplement, Encounter, The New Yorker, The Observer,* and *Salmagundi,* among others, Steiner has contributed, over the years, a steady stream of book reviews, essays, and opinion pieces, most of which remain uncollected, even as this constitutes the bulk of his work. He estimates that he contributed close to two hundred pieces to *The New Yorker* alone (RGS, 280). Clearly, he thinks this work important, even as he believes that 'it is not easy for an honest man to be a literary critic,' there being 'so many more urgent things to' do (LS, 325). In fact, he has repeatedly, if contradictorily, lodged complaints against reviewing, which, he says, is predicated on 'the implausible theory that something worth reading is published each morning in the year' (ibid.). In *Real Presences* (1989), he writes: 'Each day, via journalism, via the journalistic-academic, the inherent value, the productive powers, the savings embodied in a creative currency, this is to say in the vitality of the aesthetic, are devalued. The paper Leviathan of secondary talk not only swallows the prophetic ... ; it spews it out diminished and fragmented. In the absence of the guarantor, a counterfeit mode of exchange, that of the review speaking to the review, of the critical article addressing the critical article, circulates endlessly. It is not, as Ecclesiastes would have it, that of "making many books there is no end." It is that "of making books on books and books on those books there is no end"' (48). Why does Steiner castigate the practice of reviewing? Reasons are available, but they do not make this criticism seem any less contradictory, for Steiner has long been one of our most accomplished reviewers. As Mark Krupnick, who believes Steiner 'the best generalist reviewer of books since Edmund Wilson' ('Steiner's Literary Journalism,' 43), notes, Steiner has 'the restless curiosity of the born journalist,' so 'deeply curious [is he] about everything and willing to look at things from which others fastidiously recoil' (44). Krupnick grants that Steiner's 'moral seriousness and purposefulness ... are anything but journalistic' (ibid.), but he also argues, rightly I think, 'that Steiner is at his best in his reviews and occasional essays rather than in his full-length studies' (46). The reason for this, says Krupnick, has to do with the diversity of the shorter pieces. Another reason, offered by Jay Parini, has to do with the suggestiveness of Steiner's work, a quality more effective in an essay than a book ('The Question of George Steiner,' 499). It might also be noted how essayistic are Steiner's books, where he often repeats, rather than develops, his themes. This is especially true of his last book, *Grammars of Creation* (2001), which while developing his interest in the distinction between artistic creation and scientific invention, mostly revisits old themes. In general, then, the books, to borrow one of Steiner's metaphors, progress less linearly than spirally. Consequently, many readers find Steiner's review essays and other shorter pieces more satisfying, for their brevity makes their insights more emphatic. Also, given the fact, noted by Said, that Steiner's 'terms of reference come from his experience – which is trilingual, eccentric and highly urbane – not from something as stable as doctrine or authority' ('Himself Observed,' 244), the review format, more accommodating here than the book, must appear to him (though I find no testimony to this effect) particularly congenial. It allows him to play the role of *kulturkritik*, a role requiring a quick and passionate response to those ever-occurring events judged relevant to culture's progress. Boyers speaks of Steiner's frank commitment 'to intuition and vehement speculation' ('Steiner as Cultural Critic,' 18), and goes further to say that there is hardly anything more distasteful to him 'than the posture of the drawing-room critic holding himself aloof from the changes taking place just outside his window. Steiner's engagement with his culture is aggressive. The very speed of his sentences as they follow hard on one another, the voracity with which he grabs now at one item, then another: these represent to us not only Steiner's singularity but also his indomitable curiosity, the visceral satisfaction he takes in immersion without submission' (19–20).

Thus it is that some of Steiner's best work has appeared in not only the *Times Literary Supplement,* that 'mailbox of the British intelligentsia' (GSR, 203), but also *The New Yorker,* a magazine that, Krupnick observes, 'has never been noted for an intellectual tone' ('Steiner's Literary Journalism,' 47). The observation, as applied to the more recent Newhouse era, rings true, and it helps explain the magazine's letting go, during Tina Brown's editorship, of Steiner (a hurt about which he has remained steadfastly silent). But in years prior, especially under the editorship of William Shawn, the observation would not seem to apply. In fact, Steiner's predecessor as chief reviewer was Edmund Wilson. Still, as Krupnick observes, there has always been a discrepancy of sorts between *The New Yorker*'s flagrant appeal to bourgeois materialism and its intellectual ambitions: 'Steiner's *New Yorker* reviews are typically printed in narrow columns often bordered on both sides by advertisements for expensive gifts, real estate, and other goods of upscale consumer culture. It is not a culture for which Steiner has a high regard. Yet that culture includes a sensitive, well-educated minority that has the highest regard for him. That nonspecialist American readership is probably larger than Steiner's readership in England, France, Germany, and Switzerland combined' (47). Krupnick is right about the well-educated minority. At the same time, without being censorious, it is possible to wonder whether Steiner's relation to the magazine's bourgeois readers has been as contradictory as Krupnick suggests. In some ways, the relation was a good fit, most notably in the context of Steiner's belief that the uncommon reader should be a man of property. It is not often that one finds a critic mourning the lost privileges that underwrote J.P. Morgan's Library. Steiner not only does so, but even identifies with those most disadvantaged by subsequent egalitarian measures: 'The entire economy, the architecture of privilege, in which the classic act of reading took place, has become remote (we visit the Morgan Library in New York or one of the great English country houses to view, albeit on a magnified scale, what was once the effective cadre of high bookishness)' (UR, 15). While it makes perfect sense to investigate the relation between reading as avocation and social privilege, it is dismaying to see how often Steiner sides with the forces of material well-being (besides, does he really believe that Morgan looked upon his rare books and manuscripts with anything other than a proprietary eye?), and how he weighs down the uncommon reader's freedom to travel with leather-bound volumes: 'To read classically means to own the means of that reading' ('The End of Bookishness,' 754). How bourgeois!

After the Fall

Maybe it is because Steiner writes on so many subjects that critics have felt it necessary to collapse the work down to one or another theme.

Whatever the reason, it does seem that critics of Steiner's work have a penchant for discovering a unifying thread. Ruth Padel believes that '[t]ragedy is the basis of Steiner's work' (RGS, 99); Ronald Sharp argues that 'we need to understand just how deeply [the] notion of translation informs his vision' (RGS, 207); for Edith Wyschogrod, the work is 'a Holocaust hermeneutics of language and culture' (RGS, 151); and for Ihab Hassan, '[e]verything in Steiner reverts to language, ineluctable Babel' ('The Whole Mystery,' 323). This even prompts Steiner, in reply, to say, '[a]s several contributors [to *Reading George Steiner*] emphasize, language has been its [his work's] pivot' (RGS, 281). Each of these critics is right. In fact, so long as there is no claim that one has hit on the *only* unifying thread, it would be difficult to make a mistake, so wide-ranging are Steiner's interests. In this section, I wish to address a theme that has not been, to my knowledge, fully addressed: that of elegy. I particularly wish to address this theme as it touches on a host of subthemes, including those of crisis, decline, epilogue, fallenness, homecoming, kaddish, loss, mourning, post-culture, remembrance, ruin, and silence. Together they constitute what must be considered major threads in Steiner's thought, and this, again, has to do with the elegiac sense that we live in a 'post-culture,' after the fall. As Steiner himself puts it, 'We come *after*' (LS, 4).

From the first, as in *Tolstoy or Dostoevsky*, where Steiner thinks it imperative to employ what he calls the 'old criticism,' to the more recent work, so attentive to the Holocaust as constituting another profound instance of men and women turning away from God ('the holocaust may be said to mark a second Fall' [BC, 46]), there has been a strong elegiac mood. The underlying suggestion is that things were better in the past. Even in *Bluebeard's Castle*, which Steiner, meta-critically, begins by noting how readily we construct images, or fictions, of the past that then loom larger over the present, the past still comes to stand as preferable to 'the dominant phenomenon of twentieth-century barbarism' (29). The 'main features' of the mythic 'garden in England and western Europe between ca. 1820s and 1915' are claimed to be 'unmistakable' (BC, 5). They include '[a] high and gaining literacy. The rule of law. A doubtless imperfect yet actively spreading use of representative forms of government. Privacy at home and an ever-increasing measure of safety in the streets' (ibid.). This leads Steiner into a series of generic reminiscences, creating in effect a virtual reality:

Depending on our interests, we carry with us different bits and pieces of this complex whole. The parents 'know' of a bygone age in which manners were strict and children domesticated. The sociologist 'knows' of an urban culture largely immune to anarchic challenge and sudden gusts of violence. The religious man and the moralist 'know' of a lost epoch of agreed values. Each of us can summon up appropriate vignettes: of the well-ordered household, with its privacies and domestics; of the Sunday parks, leisured and safe; of Latin in the schoolroom and apostolic finesse in the college quad; of real bookstores and literate parliamentary debate. Bookmen 'know,' in a special, symbolically structured sense of the word, of a time in which serious literary and scholarly production, marketed at low cost, found a wide or critically responsive echo. There are still a good many alive today for whom that famous cloudless summer of 1914 extends backward, a long way, into a world more civil, more confident, more humanely articulate than any we have known since. It is against their remembrance of that great summer, and our own symbolic knowledge of it, that we test the present cold. (BC, 5–6)

It is Steiner's argument that we can trace the roots of twentieth-century barbarism back to nineteenth-century *ennui*. But this '"summer of 1815–1915"' retains enough Scythian colour to make us rue its passing. And this occurs despite our realization that 'the intellectual wealth and stability of middle- and upper-middle-class life during the long liberal summer depended, directly, on economic and, ultimately military, dominion over vast portions of what is now known as the underdeveloped third world' (BC, 7). It is a distinctly privileged viewpoint. It is not likely, for instance, that an African-American would wax so eloquently about this long lost summer. It was not a pastoral for everyone, and there must be fair a number of others (e.g., ethnic minorities, liberated women, gays and lesbians, secularists, technologists, unionized labourers) who find the subsequent centuries preferable to the nineteenth. As Edith Wyschogrod points out, 'Steiner's description of it [this lost summer] reads like a bill of lading enumerating English and German Enlightenment values ... But this myth of present comfort and future promise concealed a substructure of poverty, class distinction, and the exploitation of underdeveloped countries' (RGS, 157).

Is Steiner's panegyric to the past, then, an illiberal, regressive gesture that needs to be checked? Yes, in part. But it is also more than this and bears investigation. Thus while Steiner's mappings of epochal change, focused upon evidence of loss and decline, reflect a critic more comfortable with past cultural achievements, the effort to discern history's large-scale transmutations remains worthwhile. Steiner's touch may not be as systematic or alluring as Michel Foucault's, whose chartings of epistemic changes in the human sciences have proven so influential. Yet they bespeak not only a like ambition but also an abiding belief that what it means to be human is crucially intertwined with these changes. Steiner's greatest fear is that after the manifest barbarisms of the recent 'black century' ('To Speak of God,' 7), symbolized by Auschwitz, we may have reached a point when it is no longer possible to speak of human beings as continuous (in a linguistic and ethical sense) with those who came before. In 'The Long Life of Metaphor: An Approach to "the Shoah,"' he writes: 'It may be that the Auschwitz-universe, for it was that, precisely marks that realm of potential – now realized – human bestiality, or, rather, abandonment of the human and regression to bestiality, which both precedes language, as it does in the animal, and comes after language as it does in death. Auschwitz would signify on a collective, historical scale the *death of man* as a rational, "forward-dreaming" speech-organism (the *zoon phonanta* of Greek philosophy)' (55). Whether future generations will view this as dismally hyperbolic or not is difficult to say, though in our own time the bloodletting in both Rwanda and Bosnia has bestowed a timeliness upon Steiner's suggestion. What was especially troubling in the instance of Rwanda, beyond the genocidal rampage's taking place at all, was that the world stood by and did so little to stop it. In short, it would be easier to accuse Steiner of doomsaying if there were not so many supporting instances upon which to draw, particularly in the 'black century' of two world wars, King Leopold II's Belgian Congo, the Ukrainian famine, the Gulag, the Rape of Nanjing, Dresden and Hamburg, Hiroshima and Nagasaki, the arms race, the Korean and Vietnam wars, Amin's Uganda, Pol Pot's Cambodia, Somalia, the AIDS epidemic, and other tragedies that leave us numbed by their madness.

It is because Steiner is so mindful of history's tragic side, of its '"apocalyptic mood"' ('Acids of Tiredness,' 4), that his vocabulary is saturated with words like 'breakdown,' 'collapse,' 'crisis,' 'decay,' 'decline,' 'end,' 'epilogue,' 'fall,' 'failure,' 'last,' 'loss,' and 'post-.' He has a clear Spenglerian side, bolstered by an inclination to imagine that the human species, its bad choices aside, might almost be programmed for extinction: 'No one is competent to rule on whether such mechanisms lodge within the very fabric of our biological and psychological identity (other and, apparently, even more adaptive species have become extinct). It is my own hunch ... that the particular intensity of current uneasiness ... tells of an epilogue to a religious-metaphysical order of imagining and social practice. Ours is, very precisely, a period of transition, in which the constraints and promises of authentic religious faith are less and less respectably available, while the decay, the wastage, of the religious millennia is still lying about in our psyche, in our language, in a good many of our institutions. Exhausted and moribund muscular tissue secretes acids of tiredness into the bloodstream' ('Acids of Tiredness,' 4). Steiner thinks that such human self-destructiveness has a long history, that it is almost one with history. And yet he also thinks that if we reach back far enough we can view something different, that moment at time's dawning when Homer and his fellow Greeks first found they could speak Being. In *Antigones*, Steiner writes: 'from the perspective of western sensibility after Rome, the Greek language and Greek literature *are* primary (as from a theological-liturgical point of view is Hebrew). We know ... that the speech and expressive conventions of Heraclitus, Archilochus, or Pindar are late products of processes of development and selection which we cannot trace. But to *us* they convey the authority of morning. It is by their light that we set out. It is they who first set down the similes, the metaphors, the lineaments of accord and of negation, by which we organize our inward lives' (133).

Steiner knows that even Greek literature postdates origin, that 'we have no access to the origins either of speech or of that disinterested and selective mode of speech we call "literature"' (A, 133). At the same time, he believes that *for us* the Greeks give every *appearance* of writing not only at the dawn of history but also in an epiphanic mode no longer available except as we travel back through them. The belief reflects the importance of Heidegger, whose analyses 'are the most radical and the most in tune with the problem of the inaugural (the *instauratio magna* in western consciousness). Heidegger's ontology is, in essence, a theory of beginnings. He ascribes to the Greek spirit and to the Greek language in their pre-Socratic phase a specific, unique proximity to the 'presentness and truth of Being.' Anaximander, Heraclitus, and Parmenides experienced, were in some measure able to articulate, a primordial equation between the "being of Being" – the hidden but also radiant principle of all existence – and the capacity of speech ... to be meaningful' (A, 131). Did such a moment happen? Only rhetorically. But this may be enough, for Steiner is enchanted by the notion that poets, in an originative time, spoke in a language as fresh as the morning light, creating figures of speech never before heard, and thereby enhancing the pleasure. 'That a brave man should be like a lion or dawn wear a mantle of the colour of flame were not,' for these most ancient of Greeks, 'stale ornaments of speech but provisional, idiosyncratic mappings of reality. No Western idiom after the Psalms and Homer has found the world so new' (AB, 195). But the newness did not last long, for by the time of Aristotle the Greek language had already lost its innocence and become workman-like, more a utensil for communication than for poetry. Or as Steiner, referring back to Heidegger, writes: 'The Aristotelian view of language was functional and pragmatic. These philosophic developments mark the irreparable fall of the western spirit from the numinous grace and immediacy of the word. We have never "spoken Being" again as did Parmenides in his identification of oneness with existence, as did Heraclitus when he saw the world as "harvested, ingathered by lightning"' (A, 132).

For Heidegger, this fall into *différance*, into language, was inescapable. 'The "fallenness" of *Dasein* is not a lapse from some golden age of economic parity and social justice'; rather, it 'is the inevitable quality that characterizes an individual's involvement with others and with the phenomenal world' (H, 98). It is in the nature of existence that it be incomplete, that we be made to search out that which should make it complete – Being. As such, the Greeks' fall into language might be likened to Adam's fortunate fall, as necessary and thereby unregrettable: 'The "positivity of fallenness" in Heidegger's analysis is an exact counterpart to the celebrated *felix culpa* paradox, to the doctrine which sees in Adam's "happy fall" the necessary precondition for Christ's ministry and man's ultimate resurrection. Via the inauthenticity of its being-in-the-world, *Dasein* is compelled to search out the authentic' (H, 99). It is compelled to seek its true home. Or as Steiner, quoting Heidegger, writes: '"The wandering, ... the peregrinations toward that which is worthy of being questioned, is not adventure but homecoming." Man in his dignity, comes home to the unanswerable. And that, of course, which is most *fragwürdig* is "Being"' (H, 57). 'Being' is that which Is, what remains present even as all other things move out of the past and towards the future, and what constitutes our most authentic Home. It is not a substance but a presencing, not a material thing but a spiritual. It is also something that inevitably finds itself enwrapped in, and obscured by, language. This is evident in the attempt, by first Heidegger and then Steiner, to gets its name right:

The Greek called 'being' *ousia* or, more fully, *parousia*. Our dictionaries translate this word as 'substance.' Wrongly, says Heidegger. The veritable translation would be a set or cluster of significations comprising 'homestead, at-homeness, a standing in and by itself, a self-enclosedness, an integral presentness or thereness.' German *Anwesen* corresponds accurately to the range and force of meaning. *Parousia* tells us that 'something is present to us. It stands firmly by itself and thus manifests and declares itself. It is. For the Greeks, "being" basically meant this standing presence.' Post-Socratic Greek thought, whether in Platonic idealism or Aristotelian substantiality, never returned to this pure and primal 'ground of being,' to this illumination of and through the presentness of the existing. But it is to just this ground that we must strive to come home ('homecoming' is, as we shall see, both the process and the goal of authentic being). (H, 46–7)

Is homecoming possible? Not if we have forgotten Being, something that the present moment – with its bias towards capital, technology, and nationhood – would appear to have forgotten. Yet there remain ways, even in a culture characterized by indifference, to put ourselves in a more satisfying relation to Being. For Steiner, homecoming remains most possible through the agencies of art, literature, and music. This belief helps to explain his fascination with the multitudiousness ways in which Sophocles' *Antigone* has been remembered and resurrected down through the centuries, even as Steiner acknowledges that literature's temporality generally undermines long-term meanings. In *Antigones*, he writes that '[i]t may be the late and necessary condition of "fiction"' that while it 'is recounted or performed now,' it '"actually took place" in the past,' and cannot thereby be said, if our terms are exact, to be 'ephiphanically present "here and now,"' the way that Christ, for instance, is said to be so in Eucharist. But to the extent that a text entails archetypal, mythic qualities, it affords a sense of homecoming. In those narratives that are truly mythic 'our consciousness finds its ever-renewed homecoming to the opaque comforts and terrors of its origins, a homecoming made compelling and endurable by the formality, by the narrative coherence, by the lyric and plastic comeliness with which the Greek spirit invested the uncanny and the daemonic' (125). This is why Steiner, in *Antigones*, offers such an extensive report on the ways the Sophocles drama has been picked up and revoiced throughout time. Each additional returning to the play offers further proof of its archetypal nature, proof that truth can be more than local. Thus what first appeared a problem – i.e., literature's temporality – is outweighed by another consideration, the ability of the narrative to express a pattern instinctively familiar to all. Such art 'can exercise its lasting spell, can survive and indeed foster repetition and variation over the ages, *only* if it conserves and makes palpable its links with those archaic, fundamental instinctive patterns ("archetypes") from which human consciousness grew and which continue alive in folklore and in ritual. We revert to "the archetypal analogies," to the primal constellations of gesture and image in art, because the conscious mind, however emancipated and secularized, is both repelled by and drawn towards its earlier stages of existence. Confronting these, it "remembers," it "knows that it has been here before." It is precisely this *déjà vu* within formal and executive originality which makes of our experience of great art and poetry a homecoming to new remembrance' (A, 126–7).

Literature and art are capable of shredding their historical dross, especially as they rise to the level of myth, but they never do this as well, thinks Steiner, as does music. This is why music figures so prominently in his thinking. 'I believe,' he writes in *Real Presences*, 'the matter of music to be central to that of the meaning of man, of man's access to or abstention from metaphysical experience' (6). The reason has to do with the sense of music's immediacy, with its untranslatability. It is what it is. 'In music, being and meaning are inextricable. They deny paraphrase. But they *are*, and our experience of this "essentiality" is as certain as any in human awareness' (H, 44). Literature is always being translated, either into another language or aesthetic form. It is why literature follows music in our esteem when the question pertains to Being. And it is also why literature and the other arts are deemed the more attractive as they approach the condition of music: 'Great poetry is, very exactly, that in which this homeward soughing of the musical tide is made to enrich, to deepen, the life of the word. A true poem, a live prose, a philosophic movement wholly consonant to its syntax, is one in which Odysseus sets observant words to the Sirens' song' (RP, 198). It seems right to speak of music and homecoming in the same breath for the reason that 'music puts our being as men and women in touch with that which transcends the sayable, which outstrips the analysable' (RP, 218). It is a debatable matter, but Steiner chooses to think of music (i.e., classical music) as something 'uncircumscribed by the world as the latter is an object of scientific determination and practical harnessing' (ibid.). That music depends on its material conditions does not deter Steiner from viewing it as the truest avenue to Being and, in a secular world, the nearest thing to religion itself: 'The meanings of the meaning of music transcend. It has long been, it continues to be, the unwritten theology of those who lack or reject any formal creed. Or to put it reciprocally, for many human beings, religion has been the music which they believe in' (ibid.).

For Steiner, art, be it in the form of myth or music, affords us an intuition of Being; but even as he believes this, he also appears to believe with Heidegger that the history of Western civilization has been the history of the forgetting of Being. For Heidegger, the moment of crisis came, as noted, sometime between the pre-Socratics and Aristotle. After that, it was understood that fallenness was essential to our condition, and that we should overcome the situation only when our sense of incompletion, of a presence knowable solely via its absence, compelled us to seek out the source of our being. It is a manner of thinking that Steiner, not surprisingly, finds attractive. He, too, believes that our state must be understood as something like a fall from Being, and from Grace. History is construed as the consequence not only of an originating crisis of meaning – be it Adam's fall, the Tower of Babel's collapse or the ancient Greeks' turning to Substance as the measure of their philosophy and linguistics – but also of a series of significant, subsequent crises. These include, most notably, the severing of the human from God in the seventeenth century following upon the advances of science; the severing of the word from world in the late nineteenth and the early twentieth century as a consequence of the modernists' quest for an exotic, private language, unsullied by the history of long usage; and the severing of humans from hope as a consequence of Auschwitz. It is this history of crisis that I now wish to examine.

To begin, we might note Steiner's conviction that narratives of crisis, or fallenness, are discoverable in all cultures, so even while the narratives are different, no culture is without its myth of an ancient Fall. 'The myth of the Fall runs stronger than any particular religion. There is hardly a civilization, perhaps hardly an individual consciousness, that does not carry inwardly an answer to intimations of a sense of distant catastrophe. Somewhere a wrong turn was taken in that "dark and sacred wood," after which man has had to labour, socially, psychologically, against the natural grain of being' (BC, 4). The feeling that existence was once fresher, more original, and thus truer, holds Steiner in its thrall. The sciences may look towards the future, but there is perhaps more to learn by looking back to our beginnings: 'Inevitably, the humanist looks back. The essential repertoire of his consciousness, the props of his daily life as a scholar or critic are from the past' (BC, 134). Who we are depends as much upon where we have come from as upon our notions of telos. Like a stream out of the past, language carries with it not only our basic semiotics but also our cultural idioms and memories. 'Because it carries the past within it, language, unlike mathematics, draws backward. This is the meaning of Eurydice. Because the realness of his inward world lies at his back, the man of words, the singer, will turn back, to the place of necessary beloved shadows. For the scientist time and light lie before' (BC, 135). The distinction might not have made sense to the person living before the seventeenth century, for only then did science begin to assert an alternative vision. It was, however, a vision that exacted a painful price, for it was in the nature of science to force attention outward, away from the privacy of inner verbalization and towards the newly esteemed fact, measurable in the abstract language of mathematics. At this point,

> significant areas of truth, reality and action recede from the sphere of verbal statement. It is, on the whole, true to say that until the seventeenth century the predominant bias and content of the natural sciences were descriptive. Mathematics had its long, brilliant history of symbolic notation; but even mathematics was a shorthand for verbal propositions applicable to, and meaningful within, the framework of linguistic description. Mathematical thought, with certain notable exceptions, was anchored to the material conditions of experience. These, in turn, were ordered and ruled by language. During the seventeenth century, this ceased to be the general case, and there began a revolution that has transformed forever man's relationship to reality and radically altered the shapes of thought. (LS, 14)

Steiner's regret follows on the conviction that the seventeenth century was both 'the classic age of soliloquy' (OD, 92) and the last moment when the relevance of classical and religious myth-making could be assumed (DT, 320). In the first instance, Steiner argues that middle- and upper-class life was distinguished by its verbal inwardness, a mode perpetuated by private reading, introspection, and prayer. The period's propitiousness followed both from its prosperity, making domestic values and private space more readily available, and from the Protestant revolution, with its stress on the individual's unmediated relation to God: 'The energies of domesticity (the turn towards and into the private room), the emphasis on individuation, the notion of psychic resources as being a capital worth amassing and investing prudentially, mark the movements of religious reform and the concurrent emergence of the modern middle classes during the sixteenth and, especially, during the seventeenth centuries. The seventeenth century can be documented as having been the classic period of inward religious address. We cannot dissociate virtuoso performances of sustained inward concentration such as the meditations of Pascal, the analytic introspections of Descartes or the monologues of ecstasy in St. John of the Cross, from a much wider executive form and practice' (OD, 81–2). Steiner here is less attentive to class (though this remains crucial) than to religious discourse, with its stress on meditation and silent supplication. 'Much of religious sentiment and performance is verbally internalized in the guise of prayer, invocation, supplication, self-admonition or penitential scrutiny. It is only when an individual addresses himself to the deity that one can speak of a "monologue with." This paradoxical rhetorical mode postulates a presence whose very silence does not negate the communicative act, but somehow confirms it, making of the monologue a dialectic structure' (OD, 56). Steiner has in mind a particular form of religious discourse (Protestant, mostly) at a particular historical moment: the Renaissance through the seventeenth century. As he notes, '[u]nvoiced invocation to the deity is, presumably, a primal and universal element in all religious experience. But in the history of religions, as in that of language itself, there have been variations of stress as between externalized collective utterance and the inaudible colloquy of the individual and the numinous presence' (OD, 81). And what he most wishes to stress is how important this latter mode – i.e., 'the inaudible colloquy' – was at this time to both the European and North American definitions of humanness. Steiner, I think rightly, claims that much has changed since, that we are less apt to define our humanity so wholeheartedly in terms of inwardness. Whether this change constitutes a 'decline' or not may be a more contentious matter. For Steiner, certainly, the discussion is framed in terms of lapse, loss, and reduction. He speaks of the 'almost programmatic "thinning out" of the interior medium' that has since transpired (OD, 58), and notes that even our religious discourse has seen a 'sharply diminished' reliance on inner verbalization (OD, 57). Looking back, he says, it appears that '[w]e have lost a considerable measure of control over the fertile ground of silence,' to the point that we expend 'more of our "speech-selves,"' and 'have less in reserve' (OD, 94). In short, we can 'almost define the decline of a classic value-structure, as felt in the Renaissance and seventeenth century, and active still among the literate until the great crises of world war and social revolution, as being a shift from an internalized to a voiced convention of personality and utterance' (ibid.).

This shift from a religious world-view, accentuating the privacy of the soul, to a scientific view, accentuating the materiality of experience, had consequences for literature. For one, as noted, the seventeenth century was probably the last to feel confidently that the classical and Judaeo-Christian descriptions were sufficiently explanatory. Milton, says Steiner, was the last major poet to feel this way, and '[h]is refusal in *Paradise Lost* to choose between the Ptolemaic and the Copernican accounts of celestial motion is a gesture both serene and sorrowful; serene, because it regards the proposals of natural science as less urgent or assured than those of poetic tradition; sorrowful, because it marks the historical moment in which the forms of the cosmos recede from the authority of humanistic judgement' (DT, 320). For Steiner, science's advance has been marred by its ambition to dominate, by its repudiation of our metaphysical and religious heritage and by its imposition of a material logic and axiology on a still deliberating humanity. The result of science's intervention was, says Steiner, that '[a]fter Milton the mythology of animate creation and the nearly tangible awareness of a continuity between the human and the divine order – that sense of a relationship between the rim of private experience and the hub of the great wheel of being – lose their hold over intellectual life' (ibid.). After Milton, 'the stars burn out of reach' (ibid.).

Before this occurrence, however, we do find positive correlations between the turn inward and literary production, correlations that do not all disappear with science's advances. For one, the English language was, in the Renaissance, more or less capable of saying all there was to say. By this, Steiner means that not only were the humanistic disciplines expressible in it, but so were those – e.g., mathematics, chemistry, physics – now conceded to have inhabit their own discourses. If '[a]fter 1640, the achievements of Bacon, Descartes, and Newton made the old order unrecapturable,' before that time, English 'realized a unique coherence of inheritance and innovation' (LS, 202, 203). The language, when used by a master, was capable of reconciling our inner and outer worlds. For proof, says Steiner, we need look no further than Shakespeare, whose writings demonstrate not only a remarkable quality of inwardness and 'at-homeness' but also what, in retrospect, seems like an Adamic relation to the English language:

Shakespeare's stance in language is a calm tenancy, an at-homeness in a sphere of expressive, executive means whose roots, traditional strengths, tonalities, as yet unexploited riches, he recognized as a man's hand will recognize the struts and cornices, the worn places and the new in his father's house. Where he widens and grafts, achieving reaches and interactions of language unmatched before him, Shakespeare works from within. The process is one of generation from a centre at once conventional (popular, historically based, current) and susceptible of augmented life. Hence the normative poise, the enfolding coherence which mark a Shakespearean text even at the limits of pathos or compactness. Violent, idiosyncratic as it may be, the statement is made from inside the transcendent generality of common speech. A classic literacy is defined by this 'housedness' in language, by the assumption that, used with requisite penetration and suppleness, available words and grammar will do the job. There is nothing in the Garden or, indeed, in himself, that Adam cannot name. (AB, 185)

This at-homeness in language would, argues Steiner, be put in question by the scientific revolution, but not before such genres as the diary, letter, and novel – forms particularly identified with subjectivity – would blossom. Steiner is particularly attentive to the role women played in what he calls the '"golden age" of letter-writing from the rise of feminine literacy during the latter sixteenth century to a period roughly preceding the First World War' (OD, 73). Their production was not only connected to the age's cultivation of inwardness, but also to the fact that 'the available resources of [public] verbalization were essentially in paternal-masculine hands' (OD, 71) and that the letter offered itself as an avenue in which women's efforts at expression remained unblocked: '[t]o a marked degree, the personal letter represented the most ready and acceptable guise in which women could act politically, socially, psychologically on society at large' (OD, 73). As a result, 'in the totality of epistolary production and exchange, the feminine component was major' (ibid.). The same conclusions apply to the genre of the diary, which, like the letter, has suffered a diminishment in modern times: 'The tempo of the middle-class day, the new licenses and positive valuation given to every kind of intimate "publication" and self-expression, the decay of hand-writing – a phenomenon whose socio-psychological implications have been little explored – the complex but radical changes in the whole theory and *praxis* of privacy – all these point to the gradual erosion of the diary's medium' (OD, 88).

People still write diaries and an occasional letter (excluding e-mail messages), as they still write novels, but the day when these activities seemed invested with presentness is, Steiner believes, no longer. It may seem odd that Steiner, a staunch advocate of traditional literary values, finds the novel a 'no longer very interesting medium' (LS, 83), but it has to do with his sense that the genre's historical moment is past. In *Extra-territorial* (1971), he writes, '[i]f so much non-fiction is better written than current novels, if it is far more adult and crowded with felt life, the reason is that the major period of the novel has come before' (E, 166). It is a disputatious claim, especially when the genre now boasts such recent talents as John Banville, John Barth, J.M. Coetzee, Don DeLillo, Anita Desai, Penelope Fitzgerald, William Gaddis, Kazuo Ishiguro, Ian McEwan, Toni Morrison, V.S. Naipaul, Thomas Pynchon, Salman Rushdie, and Graham Swift. It seems a theory disregarding of facts. Nevertheless, if one is prepared to grant the contention that the novel's roots and strength are locatable in those same felt privacies that gave rise to the letter and the diary, one might take the view that the novel either needs to redefine its relation to subjectivity (something the postmodern novel has done) or content itself with a more peripheral place in our cultural consciousness (as has been the case with many a first-rate talent). In *On Difficulty*, Steiner explicitly links letters and novels, speaking of them as the secular counterpart and eventual product of the seventeenth century's fixation with inwardness: 'With the very gradual decline of formal religiosity in common life or, more exactly, with the partial metamorphoses of this religiosity into more generally "humanistic" and worldly configurations of feeling, came a shift in the focus of self-address. Throughout the later seventeenth century we find a deepening fascination with the complexities of the ego, complexities not to be disciplined or even negated in the interest of immediacies of religious encounter, but on the contrary to be mapped and cultivated for their own sake. The prose novel, whose beginnings are so characteristically those of the fantasy-journey or of the epistolary dialogue, is the product of this fascination' (OD, 84). But neither the letter nor the novel has, thinks Steiner, remained viable, for their privacies represent a system of values not our own: 'The silences, the quasi-ritual privacies which accompanied the constant and voluminous production of epistolary acts in former times are no longer a current of personal usage.' In the bargain, '[a]n entire register of narrative, introspective, confessional, commemorative notation and articulation, of which the epistolary novel which extends from the late Renaissance through *Pamela* and *La Nouvelle Héloïse* the whole way to Dostoevsky's *Poor Folk* is the outward manifestation, has lapsed from normal awareness' (OD, 74).

Steiner's work has been criticized for various reasons, but one of the more reiterated complaints is that the author would recover that which is no longer recoverable: a closed-off, mythologized past, at home in large-scale meaning. Harold Fromm, a friendly critic, speaks of Steiner's *Real Presences*, for instance, as a 'somewhat desperate attempt to part the Red Sea of postmodernism and conduct the faithful to a new Promised Land of postdeconstructive meaningfulness' (review, *Georgia Review*, 398). He is not wrong. Nor is he wrong in his view (the hyperbole notwithstanding) that 'Western society, particularly the Anglo-American variety, appears to have lost all the traditional generators of cultural value – apart from moneymaking – that give meaning to life' (398–9). Paradoxically, perhaps, this is precisely why Steiner's work remains worthy of attention, for while its tenor strikes many readers as too crepuscular and mournful, as well as insensitive to life outside the bourgeois pale, he remains one of the few critics asking the sort of questions that goes to the heart of our existence. He also knows that the asking of questions entails a responsibility, that one should not ask a question unless one is prepared to live with the answer. Today, those who do front such questions often appear deaf regarding the answers – the negations. The latter get treated as abstractions, pieces in a game. The contradiction between discrediting notions like self-presence, economic security, justice, truth, literary distinction, and so forth, yet wanting these things for oneself, is seldom acknowledged. Professionalism does not require it, does not require that one live out the consequences of one's more radical critiques. Thus Fromm writes of the rootlessness of the 'academia that has largely sold itself as a commodity agent of the Information Society in return for professional success' (399), and Hassan, also in an essay on Steiner, writes that '[i]t is *our* riddle in the West, which Camus adduces when he wryly remarks that Europe believes in nothing and claims to know everything' ('The Whole Mystery,' 332). Steiner's work, meanwhile, remains pertinent for the reason that, in Hassan's words, 'we can no longer ignore the consequences of our beliefs or disbeliefs in a world so perilously fraught with our nihilism' (ibid.). Steiner's answers might not always seem right, but at least his work bears in mind that ideas have consequences, and that radical ideas – like the attack on human subjectivity – sometimes have radical consequences. It is because he has so evidently imagined life bereft of identity and its privacies, of human ballast, that he fights so hard to hold on to the forms and guarantees of this identity. And while he can be a Luddite, railing against the television and stereo, the level of human-made noise has, in fact, dramatically increased in his lifetime, and Steiner is right to wonder what are the consequences for subjectivity.

While Steiner is, on the whole, attentive to consequences, his dismissive tone regarding ordinary human beings appears otherwise. In 'The Archives of Eden,' he writes, not atypically, that the 'genuine teacher, editor, critic, art historian, musical performer or musicologist, is' that person who 'knows ninety-nine percent of humanity in the developed west may aspire to only one vestige of immortality: an entry in the telephone book,' and also knows 'that there is one per cent, perhaps less, whose written word alters history, whose paintings change the light and landscape, whose music takes immortal root in the ear of the mind, whose ability to put in the speech of mathematics coherent worlds wholly outside sensual reach, make up the dignity of the species' (87). Here, the 'dignity of the species' is too parsimoniously conceived. One need not deny that immortality, secularly conceived, makes minions of us all, to feel, at the same time, that men and women, each day going about their ordinary lives, offer all sorts of evidence that dignified behaviour is a more egalitarian thing than Steiner imagines. The tutor instructing children in the elements of mathematics, the nurse attending accident victims, the pilot guiding an airliner back to earth are common enough realities, yet each is expressive of an ethicity that would seem miraculous were it not so commonplace. The fact that they are commonplace should not blind us to the wealth of dignity they embody, or encourage us to remark insensitively, as Steiner does, that our obligation to the literary text, mathematical proof, or painting 'overrides the claims of social justice' and requires us to abide 'the hideous fact that hundreds of thousands could be fed on the price a museum pays for one Raphael or Picasso' (ibid.). Steiner may believe the desire to reconcile the concepts of aesthetics and justice an instance of 'puerile hypocrisy' (ibid.), but unless there be some relation between these concepts, the consequences are bound to be ill-fated. Meanwhile, Steiner's readiness to circumscribe the realm of human worth and dignity to an area no larger than the world's pre-eminent libraries and museums encourages him contumaciously to suggest that 'in some crazy way, the possibility that the neutron bomb (destroyer of nameless peoples, preserver of libraries, museums, archives, book-stores) may be the final weapon of the intellect' (AE, 88).

So far, neither our cities nor their cultural institutions have suffered the benefits of the neutron bomb, and so remain noisy and full of life. For better or worse, the seventeenth-century person of property's privacies have eroded, and in our cities even the wealthy live lives inordinately less quiet and private. Steiner attributes this not only to the increasing population but also to its democratization. The latter has entailed something like a shifting dominant, as cultures began to find their voice not in their elites but in their mid-level shopkeepers, manufacturers, and professionals. Telling evidence for this can be found, he says, in the transformation of the theatre-going populace between the seventeenth and nineteenth centuries:

> there are a number of things that can be said of the nineteenth-century public. Having become more democratic, it had deteriorated in literacy. The audience of Racine were, in the main, a closed society to which the lower orders of social and economic life had little entry. Throughout the eighteenth century, the centre of social gravity shifted toward the middle classes. The French Revolution, essentially a triumph of the militant *bourgeoisie*, accelerated the shift. In his *Essay on the Drama*, Sir Walter Scott shows how the liberalization of the audience led to a lowering of dramatic standards. The theatrical managers and their playwrights were no longer catering to a literate aristocracy or *élite* drawn from the magistracy and high finance; they were trying to attract the *bourgeois* family with its lack of literary background and its taste for pathos and happy endings. (DT, 115)

So much for the nineteenth-century garden. And if a reader should ask what about Elizabethan audiences, well known to have included society's more diverse elements, Steiner has an answer, of sorts. He says that while it may be true that the audience for, say, a Shakespeare play was representative of the culture at large, it also constituted something like a homogeneous community, sharing 'certain orders of value and habits of belief which made it possible for the dramatist to rely on a common body of imaginative response' (DT, 114). This meant, apparently, that while the lord and 'his lackey' might have found different pleasures in Hamlet, 'neither needed footnotes or a special gloss to prepare him for the possibility of ghostly action and for the implicit reference of human conduct to a scale of values reaching from the angelic down to brute matter' (DT, 114–15). As explanation, it does not truly tell us why Steiner thinks the paradigm of decline so operative here, or why we should think of Racine's, rather than Shakespeare's, audience as the standard from which we have fallen. Nor does the explanation help substantiate Steiner's suggestion that the failure of later dramas was possibly as much one of audience as of invention. 'Did the dramatic poets of the nineteenth century fail to produce good plays because there were available to them neither the necessary theatres nor the requisite audience?' (DT, 121). Steiner seems to think so, believing that when the 'new "historical" man ... came to the theatre with a newspaper in his pocket' (DT, 117), things were doomed. We live in a fallen time, victims of our failures (e.g., to control our numbers) and successes (e.g., in democratization). Even God, merciful no longer, lost interest in us at about this time: 'I would suppose that He turned away during the seventeenth century, a time which has been a constant dividing line in our argument' (DT, 354). No longer capable of recognizing 'His image in the mirror creation, ' God simply lost interest (DT, 353). We were, then, left alone among ourselves, creating narratives – first novels, now films – that the masses can understand, though they make evident how low we have sunk. 'The myths which have prevailed since Descartes and Newton are myths of reason,' and these, compared to prior religious myths, are 'less responsive to the claim of art,' the implied first claim (DT, 321).

The myth of reason offers us neither the epic nor the tragedy, but the novel, a form identified with the masses and middlebrow aspirations. Long ago, '[i]n the age of Dante, the mind moved in the world as in a drama of Christ's being,' so '[t]hat being and the miracle of its incarnation gave to reality its design and purpose' (DT, 331). That 'mythology' has expired, and now '[t]he saints no longer set their fiery feet on the high places' (ibid.). And so, with the expiration of one mythology there arose another, an event which, in its turn, precipitated 'the decline of serious drama' and 'the rise of the novel' (DT, 118). By the nineteenth century, 'the classic age of low-cost mass printing, of serialization, and the public reading room' (ibid.), the novelist, and other littérateurs working in a realistic vein, gained ascendancy. 'The novelist, the popularizer of humane and scientific knowledge, the satirist, or the historian now had far readier access to the public than the playwright. To see mirrors held up to nature by expert hands, the literate public had no particular need of theatrical performance. A man could stay by his fire with the latest part-issue of a novel, with the newest number of the *Edinburgh Review* or the *Revue des deux mondes*. The spectator had become reader' (ibid.). *Regnat populus* was the motto, and this spirit, intertwined with political and economic changes, led increasingly to a literary culture predicated upon marketplace values, wherein journalism, not poetry, carried weight. As Steiner, in *On Difficulty*, comments: 'the rapid proliferation of journalistic and popular media of communication – the press, the *feuilleton*, the cheap book – while beneficial to prose fiction, accentuated the minority status of the poem. With this industrialization of language and of the means of dissemination of language came the semi-literacies characteristic of a technocratic and mass-consumer society. To certain poets ... the ancient trope of inadequate discourse, the conceit whereby words fall short of the unique immediacies of individual experience, became a more general issue. Now it was language as a whole that was being cheapened, brutalized, emptied of numinous and exact force, by mass usage' (42).

Through its mass dissemination, writing became commonplace, at times tawdry; and this led, in the late nineteenth and early twentieth century, to yet another stage in the fall from Being: the severance of word from world. Steiner particularly addresses this motif, or crisis, in *After Babel* and *Real Presences*. He argues that for the modern writer – Mallarmé, Rimbaud, Joyce, Stein – language had lost, through overuse, its freshness and ability to surprise. The situation has not changed: '[o]ur words seem tired and shopworn, ... no longer charged with their original innocence or with the power of revelation' (DT, 314). This is because they not only echo back to us in everything we hear or read, but also because of our historical belatedness, of the fact that we come after Dante, Shakespeare, Milton, and Johnson. We appreciate the instruction and wisdom of our literary forbears, but we are simultaneously humbled and burdened by their achievement. In *After Babel*, Steiner writes: 'Language bends under the sheer weight of the literature which it has produced. Where is the Italian poet to go after Dante, what untapped sources of life remain in English blank verse after Shakespeare? In 1902, Edmund Gosse will say of the Shakespearean tradition: "It haunts us, it oppresses us, it destroys us"' (186). Gosse's timing is pertinent; it confirms Steiner's sense that in the period stretching roughly from 1870 to 1930, the West underwent an epochal change in its relation to language. Before this period, we assumed that the relation between word and world was covenant-like, two realms bound together beneath truth's umbrella. Shakespeare, Montaigne, and Hume were 'thoroughly at home in the house of language' (RP, 92). They presumed 'that being is, to a workable degree, "sayable"' (RP, 90), and that even a sceptic's relation to language was, ipso facto, one of trust. That is, 'until the crisis of the meaning of meaning which began in the late nineteenth century, even the most subversive of anti-rhetorics, remained committed to language' (RP, 92).

This all changed, however, with Mallarmé, Rimbaud, Joyce, Stein, and Wittgenstein: With them Western literature and speech-consciousness enter a new phase. The poet no longer has or can confidently hope for tenure in a generalized authority of speech. The languages waiting for him as an individual born into history, into society, into the expressive conventions of his

particular culture and milieu, are no longer a natural skin. Established language is the enemy. The poet finds it sordid with lies. Daily currency has
made it stale. The ancient metaphors are inert and the numinous energies
bone-dry. It is the writer's compelling task, as Mallarmé said of Poe, 'to
purify the language of the tribe.' He will seek to resuscitate the magic of
the word by dislocating traditional bonds of grammar and of ordered space
... He will endeavour to rescind or at least weaken the classic continuities of
reason and syntax, of conscious directions and verbal forms ... (AB, 186)

Dismayed by language's increasing conventionality, the moderns tried
to create something resembling a private language, so elliptical and esoteric that only the cognoscenti might catch its meanings. In one sense, it
constituted an Herculean effort to make language once again fresh,
even Adamic. This was the impulse behind, say, Stein's *Tender Buttons*
(1914) or Williams's *Spring and All* (1923). Williams himself justified
'incomprehensibility' as the most viable way to contend with 'layers of
demoded words' left 'empty ... through laziness or changes in the form
of existence' (188). In this vein, Williams celebrated the difficulty of
Marianne Moore's poetry, for it 'is witness to at what cost (she cleaves
herself away) as it is also to the distance which the most are from a comprehension of the purpose of the composition' (ibid.). Here, the modernist movement might paradoxically be conceived less as a falling away
from Being than as an attempt to rediscover it. Stein, for instance,
seemed to be seeking something like this – i.e., the reality extant
beneath the word – in *Tender Buttons*. Or as she said, when explaining
what occurred during the course of the text's composition, 'I began to
discover the name of things, that is not to discover the names but discover the things the things to see the things to look at and in doing so I
had of course to name them not to give them new names but to see that
I could find out how to know that they were there by their names or by
replacing their names' (235). Stein wanted, in effect, to recover the
sense of a thing's beingness, something far more elusive than conventional language could articulate. Like Steiner, Stein believed that in
Shakespeare's time English was in its springtime. The Bard said Being,
but the modern must find other, more experimental, ways to say the
same thing, so exhausted was the language:

Shakespeare in the forest of Arden had created a forest without mentioning the things that make a forest. You feel it all but he does not name its
names.

Now that was a thing that I too felt in me the need of making it be a thing that could be named without using its name. After all one had known its name anything's name for so long, and so the name was not new but the thing being alive was always new. (236–7)

Neither Stein nor Williams accomplished what they set out to do: to recover Being. They offer us less originality than a technique of originality, where certain stylistic features – e.g., parataxis, conflation of subject and object, syntactical and lexical disruptions, verbal playfulness, stream of consciousness, and, not least, aggressive polemics – stand in the place of originality. A naive reader takes the modernists at their word; others approach their claims with a modicum of scepticism. Steiner knows this. This is why he is ambivalent about the project. On the one hand, he applauds the artists' battle against the corporate takeover of language, with its ambition to employ it as a technocratic tool for the communication of information. On the other, he knows that private languages undermine the communal discourse and make all those matters that depend upon the commonality of linguistic reference more tenuous.

Let us first, however, look at this revolution – '*It is this break of the covenant between word and world which constitutes one of the very few genuine revolutions of spirit in Western history and which defines modernity itself*' (RP, 93) – from a sympathetic angle. The fundamental difficulty faced by this epoch's writers has to do with the fact that '[t]he discourse which knits social institutions, that of legal codes, of political debate, of philosophic argument and literary construct, the leviathan rhetoric of the public media – all are rotten with lifeless clichés, with meaningless jargon, with intentional or unconscious falsehood' (RP, 110–11). The situation leaves the writer with more or less three choices of action. The writer can accept things as they are and work in what is essentially a technocratic idiom; she can set out to offer something by way of substitution, for instance a private language intended for other artists and their followers; or he can refrain as much as possible from language altogether, and cultivate the virtues of silence. Each of these positions has something attractive and unattractive about it. In the first instance, though the language is co-opted by the technocracy, it still predicates a correspondence between word and world, in place since 'the beginnings of recorded history and propositional utterance (in the pre-Socratics) to the later nineteenth century' (RP, 93). In the second instance, though the modernists' cultivation of a private language smacks of self-exclusion, their sensitivity to language's moribund state and their readiness to investigate alternatives deserve respect, if not uncritical emulation. Finally, in the third instance, though silence, 'so far as language goes,' 'is, palpably, a dead end' (AB, 194), it is, perhaps, the mode of response least unfaithful to being. In promotion of this view, Steiner quotes Wittgenstein's memorable description of the *Tractatus* as consisting 'of two parts: the one presented here plus all that I have *not* written. And it is precisely this second part which is the important one' (AB, 192). Silence speaks of what it cannot say yet must respect, speaks of what, while mute, determines the rules of the sayable.

What intrigues Steiner about the modernist agenda is the way it can be imagined less as a falling away from Being than as an emulation of such. It can be conceived both ways. In the more familiar sense, the poetry of Mallarmé, for instance, represents the word's retreat into itself, away from the world. It represents a poetics of absence, a direct challenge to the Logos-order grounding Western thought. Steiner writes that a '*Logos*-order entails ... a central supposition of "real presence." Mallarmé's repudiation of the covenant of reference, and his insistence that non-reference constitutes the true genius and purity of language, entail a central supposition of "real absence"' (RP, 96). Understood this way, Mallarmé's gesture, like Stein's in *Tender Buttons* and Joyce's in *Finnegans Wake* (1939), positions us at something like 'the breakpoint with the *Logos*-order as Western thought and feeling had known it since, at least, the tautology spoken from the Burning Bush' (ibid.). It represents an extraordinary falling away. And yet, as my prior references to Stein and Williams were meant to suggest, it is possible to imagine this same gesture less as a denial of Being than as an attempt to speak it directly. Steiner himself makes this point when he connects modernist poetics to Heidegger's notion of '*Die Sprache spricht*,' a notion he describes as a 'direct reprise of Mallarmé' (RP, 97). He further underscores the point when he draws a parallel between the self-reflexivity of modernist poetics and music: 'Music is made of conventionally organized sounds. It signifies only itself. And it is proportionately to the degree that it approaches the condition of music and the self-contained autonomy of the musical code that, for Mallarmé and modernism, language comes home to its numinous freedom, to its disinvestment from the inchoate, derelict fabric of the world' (RP, 98). A modernist poetics does not attempt to re-present Being so much as enact it, or be it. It participates in the world's immanence, rather than positing it as lying elsewhere, a distant object. Imagined this way, the modernist poem (like the painting, sculpture, or musical composition) does not depend upon something external for its existence, but is self-referential, autotelic (Eliot: 'I have assumed as axiomatic that a creation, a work of art, is autotelic' ['The Function of Criticism,' in *Selected Prose*, 73–4]). This is what Stein meant when she compared her texts to the oil painting that, in defiance of tradition, exists for itself, expressive of being: 'I think the annoyance comes from the fact that the oil painting exists by reason of these things the oil painting represents in the oil painting, and profoundly it should not do so, so thinks the oil painting, so sometimes thinks the painter of the oil painting, so instinctively feels the person looking at the oil painting. Really in everybody's heart there is a feeling of annoyance at the inevitable existence of an oil painting in relation to what it has painted people, objects and landscapes. And indeed and of course as I have already made you realize that is not what an oil painting is. An oil painting is an oil painting ...' (*Lectures in America*, 84). And it is presumably what Eliot had in mind when, in 'The Music of Poetry,' he wrote: 'I know that a poem, or a passage of a poem, may tend to realize itself first as a particular rhythm before it reaches its expression in words, and that this rhythm may bring to birth the idea and the image; and I do not believe that this is an experience peculiar to myself. The use of recurrent themes is as natural to poetry as to music. There are possibilities for verse which bear some analogy to the development of a theme by different groups of instruments; they are possibilities of transitions in a poem comparable to the different movements of a symphony or a quartet; there are possibilities of contrapuntal arrangement of subject-matter. It is in the concert room, rather than in the opera house, that the germ of a poem may be quickened' (*Selected Prose*, 114).

Something else puts the new poetics' potential attractiveness in question, however. This is the collapsing of the subject-object distinction, a situation that Steiner illustrates with reference to Rimbaud's formula '*Je est un autre.*' It is a deliberately provocative gesture, undermining the Logos' implicit theological dimension, especially as this links Godhead with creation: '"*Je est un autre*" is an uncompromising negation of the supreme tautology, of the grammatical act of grammatical self-definition in God's "I am who I am"' (RP, 99).[6] Rimbaud's conversion of the 'I' into all the other 'I's not at one with it – i.e., all the 'others' – is not a moderating gesture, intent on acknowledging the 'I's identity as inseparable from other people and things. Rather, it seeks to undermine the authenticity of all 'I's, to suggest that they are less akin to one another than parodistic, or multitudinous and unreal: 'Rimbaud's decomposition introduces into the broken vessel of the ego not only the "other," the counter-persona of Gnostic and Manichean dualism, but a limitless plurality. Where Mallarmé alters the epistemology of "real presence" (theologically grounded) into one of "real absence," Rimbaud posits at the now vacant heart of consciousness the splintered images of other and momentary "selves." And he does so in ways and in contexts which render almost inescapable the intuition that these other selves are not some neutral or parallel alterity, but parodistic, nihilistic anti-matter, radically subversive of order and creation' (ibid.). Here, the self is less strengthened or corrected by its others than it disappears into them. These others, meanwhile, appear weightless and indistinctive, bereft of the individuality that more traditional descriptions afford the human. That the traditional description of the sovereign self needs reimagining is not questioned. Steiner does question the suggestion that the self is little more than a simulacrum, and that we should refrain from speaking of its authenticity or its genius for creation. What is particularly disheartening, thinks Steiner, about the new paradigm is the way in which it allows everything, people included, to float free in a relativistic space lacking the kinds of coordinates that have traditionally been used to define and judge human behaviour. In this hall of mirrors, it is difficult enough to fix the parameters of human behaviour in the most ordinary sense, not to speak of what it means to be an artist – the most exalted manner, thinks Steiner, of being human: 'Where the "I" is not "I" but a Magellanic cloud of momentary energies always in the process of fission, there can be no authorship in any single, stable sense. The maker's – the poet's, the painter's, the composer's – will and intentionality in regard to his work can have no fixed *locus*' (RP, 100). When this happens – i.e., when answerability and responsibility lose their character of urgency and specific summons – then the aesthetic can no longer be said to exist in a privileged relation to the ethical (RP, 101). For Steiner, this eventuality is imaginable only as a major loss, a falling away from an equation – that of the Logos – superior (in respect to our needs) to that which he calls, alternately, the 'after-Word' and 'the epilogue.' The whole question of the meaning of meaning – the polestar for history's finest minds, and one that will not go away – can appear only vaporous once we renounce the possibility of the sacred, and make *différance* an ultimate-in-itself. In *Real Presences*, he writes: 'The break with the postulate of the sacred is the break with any stable, potentially ascertainable meaning of meaning. Where the theologically and metaphysically posited principle of a continuous individuality, of a cognitively coherent and ethically responsible ego is dissolved ..., there can be neither Kant's "subjective universality," nor that belief in shared truth-seeking which, from Plato to the present, from the *Phaedrus* to now, had underwritten the ideals of modernism, of humanism and of communication. It is this very impossibility that defines modernism' (132–3).

This break with the sacred – and thus with the meaning of meaning – cannot be thought inseparable from the modern era's most barbaric events, from our most dramatic fall. The 'material and moral desolation of the First World War and its aftermath seem to mark a watershed' (OD, 91), Steiner has argued, meaning that this episode's violence opened the doors to a greater violence, itself exacerbated by the retreat of word from world. In *Language and Silence*, Steiner writes that '[w]hen the soldiers marched off to the 1914 war, so did the words. The surviving soldiers came back, four years later, harrowed and beaten. In a real sense, the words did not' (98). The statement has a rhetorical flourish about it that makes us cautious regarding its claim. Nevertheless, an event like Verdun or Auschwitz – the age's representative crimes against the human – does not occur in those climates hospitable to language and a reverence for the sacred. Nor can these things be thought irrelevant to our valuation of the human. When the human is thought one coin like any other, subject to capital-like fluctuations in value, it is difficult to fend off those powers that have no use for this or that group. Granted, the world has always been a more or less fallen place, even when it pretended to live under a sacred dispensation, and the definition of the human has forever been contingent upon a host of localized values. At the same time, when our lot is that of the alien or, worse, that of 'unaccommodated man,' we know it is best to look to, and to place our trust in, those communities that predicate their existences on the most generous understanding of the human, rather than those that are parsimonious and even cruel in their determinations. Modern Europe has offered illustration of both extremes, but in attempting to understand the Holocaust, Steiner's attention bends towards the latter.

Why should Europeans have turned, in the twentieth century, so murderous towards one another and particularly towards those ethnic minorities least able to defend themselves? This question is always near the surface of Steiner's work, and is itself enwrapped in the theme of decline and fall. For Steiner, the Holocaust is not a German atrocity only. The West at large also shares its responsibility. 'I cannot accept the facile comfort that this catastrophe was a purely German phenomenon or some calamitous mishap rooted in the persona of one or another totalitarian ruler. Ten years after the Gestapo quit Paris, the countrymen of Voltaire were torturing Algerians and each other in some of the same police cellars. The house of classic humanism, the dream of reason which animated Western society, have largely broken down' (LS, ix). The breakdown has its roots in the decline of 'religious feeling' or, more properly, in 'the ambiguous afterlife of religious feeling in Western culture' and in 'the malignant energies released by the decay of natural religious forms' (BC, 53). In modern times, religion has, thinks Steiner, become a parody of itself. Even the Nazis give evidence of this, for they were fond of appropriating Christian and Jewish practices (TGD, 45; LS, 153). In *Bluebeard's Castle*, Steiner writes: 'In our current barbarism an extinct theology is at work, a body of transcendent reference whose slow, incomplete death has produced surrogate, parodistic forms. The epilogue to belief, the passage of religious belief into hollow convention, seems to me a more dangerous process than the *philosophes* anticipated. The structures of decay are toxic. Needing Hell, we have learned how to build and run it on earth' (BC, 55). It is not certain that we need Hell. But humanity has been adept at building its simulacrum, a situation that might be thought as benefiting from either a forgetting or a perverting of the Commandments and Beatitudes. Modern infernos – Southern slavery, industrial slave mills, the Gulag, the Holocaust, among others – generally follow from a combination of the two, the result being that recent history has witnessed too many large-scale attempts to reduce various segments of the population to the state of the nonhuman.

If Auschwitz can, as Steiner states, be likened to a second Fall, it is an event that has its precursors and its successors. In *Bluebeard's Castle*, Steiner draws a link between nineteenth-century's industrial mills and the death camps: 'Thus there *are* links ... between mass manufacture, as it evolves in the late eighteenth and nineteenth centuries, and a movement towards dehumanization. Watching exhausted, brutalized factory workers pour into the street, Engels saw a reservoir of subhuman impulses was filling. There is, doubtless, a sense in which the concentration camp reproduces the life-forms of the factory, in which the "final solution" is the application to human beings of warehouse and assembly-line techniques' (50). What joins the mills with the death camps and then, later, with the South African gold mines and the Cambodian genocide, is the refusal to acknowledge the humanity of those persons whose difference from ourselves appears somehow marked, most commonly by way of class, ethnicity, or religion. This refusal is not the mill, camp, or mine overseer's alone, for we are speaking of crimes that occurred (and still occur) in the world's broad daylight, where all those who profess a concern for humankind might, pushing indifference aside, see them. Indifference on our part seems more the rule than the exception, however, and when met with the pain of long-suffering others, we too often find ourselves, like Lear, forced to admit that we 'have ta'en / Too little care of this!' And thus our indifference contributes to that climate most conducive to the overseer's crime, and makes us complicitous. It is Original Sin all over again, except that now the challenge is made even more complicated by events like the world's explosive population growth, which leaves each and everyone of us, says Steiner, wishing almost to lash out, to '"get air," to break the live prison-walls of an intolerably thronged condition' (BC, 52).

Steiner clearly values whatever privacy bourgeois well-being affords. He speaks often of the importance of being unhoused, but it is difficult to imagine this well-mannered scholar as ever being truly comfortable without various domestic amenities. This is why Steiner's statement that we are psychically overwhelmed by increasing numbers seems so personal, even as the author's testimony means to warn us of the situation's dangers. 'We conduct a good part of our lives amid the menacing jostle of the crowd. Enormous pressures of competing numbers build up against our needs of space, of privacy. The result is a contradictory impulse toward "clearance." On the one hand, the palpable mass of uniform life, the insect immensity of the city or beach crowd, devalues any sense of individual worth. It wholly deflates the mystery of the irreplaceable presence. On the other hand, and because our own identity is threatened by the smothering mass of the anonymous, we suffer destructive spasms, a blind need to lunge out and make room' (BC, 51). The two 'hands' seem of a piece. They speak of the difficulty – made harder in recent times – to imagine a personal, individual 'presence' in each of the six billion people with whom we share the planet. And assuming that we can do this – a big assumption – the difficulty is further compounded when we say that we have an obligation to treat each of these persons, and to see that they are treated, as we ourselves should wish, even demand, to be treated. We know the impossibility of the obligation, even as we are not yet prepared to turn our backs on the ideal that grounds it. Or at least many, if not most, of us (Steiner included) are not prepared to do so, for despite the categorical nature of the situation, there have always been those, nations as well as individuals, who have, in fact, turned their back on the ideal and its obligation. Certainly, Germany in the 1930s and 1940s was one nation that did turn its back,

and among the more deadly consequences of this denial was the genocidal lashing out against Jews, Gypsies, homosexuals, and various others.

I have spoken of the Holocaust as a major act of forgetting, of a turning away from an ideal that has long been, and continues to be, at the
heart of our civilization. As such, I tend to see the Holocaust – despite
the enormity of it crime – as not the first nor the last act of human
betrayal. The temptations that lead us to murder are always with us, and
civilized nations and their citizens are never immune to this temptation,
though they might like to think themselves above it. I like the statement
made by Connor Cruise O'Brien in a round-table discussion on 'The
Responsibility of Intellectuals' that included Steiner among its speakers,
and was moderated by the editor of *Salmagundi*, Robert Boyers. O'Brien
said at that time: 'Now there may be children of the Enlightenment in
this room (I am a kind of step-child of the Enlightenment myself), who
say, "sin, what's that?" I don't quite know what sin is, but I do know a little about what greed is, what ambition is, what rapacity is, what cruelty
is, and I have never been convinced that intellectuals are more immune
to these infections than other people. So, limitations of sin and fallibility
are there, and we can't ignore them when we set about defining what we
do and what we're good for' (RI, 168). I refer to this statement because
Steiner's discussion of the Holocaust – or to use the name he thinks
more appropriate: the Shoah[7] – has repeatedly circled back to his shock
that large-scale evil and civilization (or its forms) could co-exist in the
same place: 'We know now that a man can read Goethe or Rilke in the
evening, that he can play Bach and Schubert, and go to his day's work at
Auschwitz in the morning' (LS, ix).[8] I also refer to it because Steiner
thinks the phenomenon casts into doubt the Enlightenment's implied
promise – i.e., the conviction that the study of art, literature, and music
shall, in the end, make us better, more ethical, persons. He writes, '*Had
the Enlightenment and the nineteenth century understood that there
could be no presumption of a carry-over from civilization to civility,
from humanism to the humane, the springs of hope would have been
staunched and much of the immense liberation of the mind and of society achieved over four generations been rendered impossible' (BC, 79).

Like O'Brien, I confess scepticism about Steiner's supposed paradox.
There is no paradox, as far as I can see. Listening to Bach or reading
Goethe and Shakespeare does not make a person more ethical unless
he or she is truly responsive to that which makes itself felt as ethical. Say-
ing what this is will always be difficult, though perhaps not impossible.
The person who responds to Lear's newfound empathy, on the storm-

blasted heath, for 'what wretches feel' is responding to a dimension in the play that is inextricably ethical, and must be thought better for having done so, even as this response does not constitute an end of the matter. More proof is needed. I suppose this is a variation of what most readers would say when confronted with the attempt to sever the relation between classic texts and ethics. Steiner is dismissive of such a response (even as the body of his work depends on it), claiming that '[t]o say that he [the camp guard] has read them without understanding or that his ear is gross, is cant' (LS, ix). It is not cant, and if Steiner truly thinks so, he should make a greater effort to reconcile all the elements in his work which posit otherwise. But this is not the argument I wish to pursue, for there is something else in the Steiner claim that provokes me more, and this is the desire to see the cultured bourgeois as ethically superior to the charwoman and dock worker. Granted, Steiner allows that our reading may leave us more sympathetic to the injustice in the book than down the street, but he does so with regret, preferring the notion that we might so improve ourselves through our engagement with art that we should place ourselves above temptation, including the temptation of large-scale murder. As said above, I think that temptation never disappears, and that while we can, through habitual moral action, make ourselves (again either as communities or persons) strong against temptation, we can never put ourselves completely out of its path, no matter what our stations in life. (Undoubtedly, the nature of the temptation changes, as our social position changes [e.g., the millionaire feels little temptation to rob the liquor store; the office clerk feels little temptation to bribe high government officials], but temptation itself seems ever present.) This may sound like an old saw (which is fine, it is). But it needs restating because Steiner, smitten with the Enlightenment dream that education makes us not only bright but also virtuous, professes shock and dismay when it turns out – in a big way – not to be true. This then leads him to all sorts of fulminations about God having made this world a 'hellish' place (TT, 396), where it is no longer possible to pray to God (LLM, 143), fulminations that are more intemperate than wise.[9]

As a Jew, Steiner has reason for thinking the Shoah evidence of the ultimate fall from Grace. For one, it largely ended the extraordinary history of Jewish intellectual culture in Central Europe. This history was richest, thinks Steiner, in the pre-Holocaust generations, in the 'golden period, from 1870 to 1914, then again in the 1920's' (LS, 147). Readers of Steiner know this is where his heart is, with a culture that should have been his own had not the Nazis snuffed it out. 'I happen to be, first and foremost, "A Kind of Survivor." ... I come from the singularly productive world of emancipated Central European Judaism,' a world that, as he says, has left a remarkable legacy in the form of its investigations in economics, linguistics, literature, physics, psychology, sociology, and theology (GSR, 13). He takes no credit for this wealth, but he does feel it as his patrimony:

> The reflexes of consciousness, the styles of articulacy which had generated messianic Marxism, Freudian psychoanalysis, the philosophies of discourse of Wittgenstein, the art of Mahler and of Kafka, were almost immediate to my childhood and upbringing. The polyglot habits in this background, the peregrine ironies and premonitions, the scarcely examined investment of familial energies and pride in the intellect and the arts, make up what I am. Without pretence to comparison, I can say that books such as *Language and Silence* (1979), *In Bluebeard's Castle, Extraterritorial* (1975), *After Babel* (1975) or *On Difficulty* (1978) ... take their substance, and much of their 'voice,' from the legacy of Ernst Bloch, of Adorno, of Walter Benjamin and from the inheritance of Jewish poetic-philosophic investigations of the word as it is evident in Roman Jakobson, in Karl Krauss, in Fritz Mauthner and Noam Chomsky. The mapping of my identity, the inward orientations, remain those circumscribed by Leningrad, Odessa, Prague and Vienna on the one side, and by Frankfurt, Milan and Paris on the other. (ibid.)

A remnant of this culture found refuge in the United States and England, and in the personages of such luminaries as Adorno, Arendt, Bartók, Bloch, Einstein, Freud, Gödel, Jakobson, Marcuse, and Schoenberg, carried on, while they might, a proud tradition. Steiner's family was part of this migration, arriving in New York in 1940.[10] But the Shoah had put an emphatic and tragic end to the fruitful, symbiotic relationship which was the Jewish/Central European dyad. And the finality of this, in the context of the Shoah and the loss of so many millions, fostered, in Steiner, the sense that the Jew had no home more secure than the peripatetic text, as well as how singular these events were. He is led to wonder whether or not the Shoah might be construed as evidence of 'what modern physics calls a "singularity," a phenomenon and event outside the rules or patterns of the general system of reality' (LLM, 56). He professes to find the question 'deeply unsettling, even repellant,' but thinks 'it must be considered' (ibid.).[11] He offers no direct answer, but his claim that following the Shoah 'we no longer have cause or need to speak to or about God whose overwhelming attribute became that of absence, of nothingness,' is answer enough (ibid.). In the Shoah, Steiner, drawing from Paul Celan's 'Psalm,' suggests that 'the Jewish people ... can be seen, understood, to have died *for* God, to have taken upon itself the inconceivable guilt of God's indifference, or absence, or impotence' (LLM, 61). If so, this leaves those who have survived with but two avenues of discourse: the *kaddish* or silence.

Steiner's own work, even as it extols the second avenue, is an exemplification of the first. He is a remembrancer. 'Is there,' asks Steiner in 'Through That Glass Darkly,' 'for a Jew, any duty greater than that of bestowing loving burial on his parents, of saying *kaddish* for them aloud and under his remembering breath?' (36). He thinks not, and has explicitly linked his own work with this tradition, saying, for instance in the 'Introduction' to his anthology, 'Several of the texts in this *Reader* constitute an act of remembrance (a *kaddish*) ... These texts endeavour to wrest from forgetting one of the very great periods in the history of human thought, of language and of dreams, and to recall the crimes committed upon millions. It is, I believe, the task and dignity of those who, by miracle or chance dispensation, have survived to make of themselves remembrancers against time' (GSR, 13). For Steiner, the concept of remembrance, though it has come to be identified with that of the Jewish remembrancer in the epilogue, actually has its roots in Heidegger and the forgetting of Being. In *Martin Heidegger* (1978), Steiner writes: 'How was being forgotten; what has come of this forgetting; where and through what means can man regain remembrance?' (H, 39) In his later work, Steiner transmutes the concept to give it a specific resonance in relation to the Shoah. It is, as such, what leads him to title an essay on Benjamin 'The Remembrancer' and to praise this writer – who '[n]o less than Freud or Arnold Schoenberg or Wittgenstein, ... belongs to the radiant, doomed chronicle of twentieth-century European Judaism' (37) – for his work this way: 'Principally, Benjamin is a remembrancer. No modern sensibility has ached more vividly towards the scandal of the unjustly forgotten ... None has striven harder to recuperate the stricken past in order to embody it in the justifying motions of the future (the messianic)' (38). Benjamin died in flight from the Gestapo, and so while his work might offer itself as a model for the contemporary remembrancer, it has also become part of that now vanished culture which Steiner would keep present in our memories. Remembering is the Survivor's obligation. The guilt of the survivor has something to do with this, and Steiner acknowledges as much: 'Of the Jewish boys and girls in my school class and circle, two have survived (of whom I am one). The unmerited scandal of this survival, the pathological bent toward some immediate sharing of their hideous fate (how would I have behaved, how abject would my fears have been?) is with me always. It is inherent in my sense of lamed self and of my assignment. Which is that of "remembrancer" ..., of one who learns by heart in order to hand on what would otherwise be ash' (RGS, 276). The guilt of the survivor does not take us very far as explanation though, for the obligation is more deeply rooted than this, more mindful of the irreplaceableness of what has been lost, and, if this is so, then of its sacredness. Steiner thinks that with the Shoah, we lost whatever significant claims we had to humanity and truthfulness. In the first instance, he thinks that the Shoah has brought out, and kept out, the bestial element in us, to the point that we might as well be said to be living in a 'post-human' age (LLM, 55). In the second instance, he thinks that the Shoah has forever distanced us from truth, and while he is not so unswerving about this that he cannot appreciate, and urge forward, the work of those 'historians of the Shoah' who, through the 'simple virtue of their publication of the documentary records of the death-camps, of the massacres at large, of Jewish resistance,' 'have performed an absolutely essential act of truthful remembrance, or resurrection' (LLM, 58), he himself has come to think that 'it may be that after the Shoah, those metaphors, those projections and sublimations which made it possible for human words and human syntax to speak about God are no longer available to us' (LLM, 56).

For Steiner, the 'haunted music' of the Shoah 'is that of the embers which continue to crackle in the cooling ash of a dead fire. Eloquence after Auschwitz would be a kind of obscenity' (LLM, 56). Silence is better. It is, perhaps, the most respectful and fitful response to a loss whose magnitude so overwhelms description, and thereby makes all attempts to articulate its scope and meaning inadequate. The question is 'whether language itself can justly communicate, express, give rational or metaphoric constructs to the realities of modern torture and extermination' and whether we ought not 'to acquiesce in Adorno's famous dictum: "No poetry after Auschwitz"' (GSR, 14). Inevitably, there is a rhetorical, albeit eloquent, side to Steiner's posing of the problem. He urges silence, but at length. He says that 'to try to speak or write intelligibly, interpretatively, about Auschwitz is to misconceive totally the nature of that event and to misconstrue totally the necessary constraints of humanity within language' (LLM, 56), but then attempts to do just this, to make sense (negative) of the Shoah. Thus, Steiner speaks of the Shoah as reflective of an urge for clearance ('Elias Canetti has made the intriguing suggestion that the ease of the holocaust relates to the collapse of currency in the 1920s' [BC, 51]); or speaks of it as 'the logical culmination of the millennial Christian vision and teaching of the Jew as killer of God' (LS, 162), an interpretation that becomes more pronounced in Steiner's later writings. It is understandable, even unavoidable, that there be an attempt to work out the whys of the Shoah. Not to do so would be the true statement about our inhumanity. Yet Steiner is not wrong to urge silence, even when the exhortation must appear contradictory. As he says in *After Babel*, 'true understanding,' of a metaphysical sort at least, 'is possible only when there is silence' (301), truth being something that too easily gets lost in the babble of competing speech acts. And because the Shoah has such a gravity about it that questions here assume the nature of a metaphysical investigation, silence (no matter how often we breach it) does seem the appropriate response. Thus, in the spirit of an Ionesco, who thought that '[t]here are no words for the deepest experience,'[12] Steiner thinks that regarding the Shoah, '[t]he best *now*, after so much has been set forth is, perhaps, to be silent' (LS, 163).

The Shoah confirms all Steiner's suspicions about the decline and fall of Western culture. In the West, the cultural dominant in the twentieth century and after has been 'barbarism'; and there can be no serious discussions of this culture 'which do not have at their pivot a consideration of the modes of terror that brought on the death, through war, starvation, and deliberate massacre, of some seventy million human beings in Europe and Russia, between the start of the first World War and the end of the second' (BC, 29). Certainly, such modes have been pivotal to Steiner's own discussion, and have led to the conviction that 'we are now in a *post-culture*' (BC, 56), wherein history can no longer be conceived as ascendant or linear. Instead, history moves more like 'a spiral,' with every advance also entailing a return to an earlier stage: 'We know now, as Adam Smith and Macaulay did not, that material progress is implicated in a dialectic of concomitant damage, that it destroys irreparable equilibria between society and nature' (BC, 69). It is, in fact, more like a spiralling downward, so strong are the intimations of apocalypse: 'We can subscribe today, all too readily, to de Maistre's view that the barbarism of modern politics, the regress of educated, technologically inventive man into slaughter enact a necessary working out of the eschatology of the Fall' (BC, 79–80). For Steiner, things fall apart, loosening not only the centre but also the hierarchies that have hitherto defined the culture:

The loss of a geographic-sociological centrality, the abandonment or extreme qualification of the axiom of historical progress, our sense of the failure or severe inadequacies of knowledge and humanism in regard to social action – all these signify the end of an agreed hierarchic value-structure. Those binary cuts which organized social perception and which represented the domination of the cultural over the natural code are now blurred or rejected outright. Cuts between Western culture and the rest, between the learned and the untutored, between the upper and the lower strata of society, between the authority of age and the dependence of youth, between the sexes. These cuts were not only diacritical – defining the identity of the two units in relation to themselves and to each other – they were expressly horizontal. The line of division separated the higher from the lower, the greater from the lesser: civilization from retarded primitivism, learning from ignorance, social privilege from subservience, seniority from immaturity, men from women. And each time, 'from' stood also for 'above.' It is the collapse, more or less complete, more or less conscious, of these hierarchized, definitional value-gradients (and can there be value without hierarchy?) which is now the major fact of our intellectual and social circumstance. (BC, 81–2)

The passage comes from *In Bluebeard's Castle*, a book which, I think, has worn badly, though I find others speaking of its prescience. I myself am taken aback by how reactionary such a passage now seems (and probably seemed even when written [ca. 1971]). My response also perhaps explains why I find the argument of decline, finally, unconvincing, for it depends too much upon a halcyon past, which when given articulation seems not so halcyon (e.g., the hierarchy that has men standing 'above' women). I do not preclude the possibility that societies are capable of decay. But I would like the evidence to seem less rhetorical. This may be the wrong thing to ask of Steiner, for he is among our pre-eminent stylists, and not likely to confuse sociology with elegy. Steiner's own relation to history and culture has given him good reason for somber reflection and lamentation, and has doubtlessly made the motif of the fall all that much more compelling. For Steiner, the fall motif does take on a life of its own, building up to the point that apocalypse is inevitable. Yet this apocalypse represents not the complete conclusion of history so much as its entropic perpetuation. The culminating event here is the Shoah. It signals the end of civilization as it had been hitherto known, as well as '"the exit of God"' (LLM, 56). We now live in the epilogue, characterized by a failure to live mindful of the future. Earlier, I quoted Steiner's view that Auschwitz signalled 'the death of man as a rational, "forward-dreaming" speech-organism' (LLM, 55). To this, we can add his conviction that we, in the present, are in the singular historical position of having nothing to look forward to: 'it is ... a very new situation when there is no place which enlists the imagination' (RI, 175). It is as if the future has been removed from our thinking, our hopes, and there is nothing to do but find cover from the omnipresent dangers: 'The "modern world" is, in fundamental respects, a fairly hellish place. We inhabit the century of Himmler and Pol Pot. The nuclear arsenal has long since spiralled into homicidal lunacy. We are laying waste what is left of the natural resources and the vestiges of the Edenic on our planet. In many of its fundamental motions of spirit and of policy, the era of the superpower and the terrorist is one not of progress ... but of barbarism' (LRS, 109). If today we experience 'an "apocalyptic mood" or, more accurately, a Western intimation of decline, of negative entropy in the dynamics of individual and collective hope, the reasons,' we are told, are near 'to hand' ('Acids of Tiredness,' 4). Meanwhile, Steiner could not let the Millennium come and go without wresting from it all its subliminal and not so subliminal threats of ending. Written as his own '*in memoriam* for lost futures' (12), *Grammars of Creation* is a dirge for the 'twilight' of civilization (1): '[T]here is ... in the climate of spirit at the end of the twentieth century, a core-tiredness. The inward chronometry, the contracts with time which so largely determine our consciousness, point to late afternoon in ways that are ontological – this is to say, of the essence, of the fabric of being. We are ... latecomers. The dishes are being cleared. "Time, ladies and gents, time." ... [T]he shadows lengthen. We seem to bend earthward and towards night as do plants' (2).

A Religion of Abstraction

If Steiner's religious thinking were reduced to a sentence, it might well be Jesus's command, 'Be perfect as your heavenly Father is perfect' (Matt. 5: 48). This commandment is, as Geza Vermes argues, solidly based in 'Jewish teaching on the imitability of God's loving-kindness and the duty to follow him' (*The Religion of Jesus*, 204), and, as such, is one more testimony to the merit of viewing Jesus as part of the Jewish tradition. In 1935, Thomas Walter Manson wrote, 'We are so accustomed ... to mak[ing] Jesus the object of religion that we become apt to forget that in our earliest records he is portrayed not as the object of religion, but as a religious man' (quoted in Vermes, *The Religion of Jesus*, 184).

Steiner himself sees Jesus this way, as a religious man, specifically a Jew, compelled by an extraordinary idealism that should be intolerable to most. In his novel *The Portage to San Cristóbal of A.H.* (1981), Steiner has Hitler say of Jesus, 'Demand of human beings more than they can give, demand that they give up their stained, selfish humanity in the name of a higher ideal, and you will make of them cripples, hypocrites, mendicants for salvation. The Nazarene said that his kingdom, his purities were not of this world ... Ask of man more than he is, hold before his tired eyes an image of altruism, of compassion, of self-denial which only the saint or the madman can touch, and you stretch him on the rack. Till his soul bursts. What can be crueler than the Jew's addiction to the ideal?' (165). Hitler, the character, says nothing that Steiner himself has not said elsewhere, albeit in less belligerent circumstances. Steiner identifies Jesus with the summons to perfection, a way of life that sets itself in aggressive contradistinction to the lives of ordinary men and women. The desire is to escape reality's dross and to move towards the Ideal. In *Bluebeard's Castle*, Steiner writes:

> The Books of the Prophets and the Sermon on the Mount and parables of Jesus which are so closely related to the prophetic idiom, constitute an unequaled act of moral demand. Because the words are so familiar, yet too great for ready use, we tend to forget or merely conventionalize the extremity of their call. Only he who loses his life, in the fullest sense of sacrificial self-denial, shall find life. The kingdom is for the naked, for those who have willingly stripped themselves of every belonging, of every sheltering egoism. There is no salvation in the middle places. For the true disciple of the prophets and of Jesus, the utmost ethical commitment is like common breath. To become a man, man must make himself new, and in so doing stifle the elemental desires, weaknesses, and claims of the ego. Only he who can say with Pascal, 'le moi est haissable,' has ever begun to obey the Gospels' altruistic imperative. (42) [13]

Steiner views the summons to perfection not only as articulative of 'the religious element' (TD, 329), but also as particularly identifiable with Judaism. In the first instance, it might be noted that as a mostly non-practising Jew, Steiner's references to religion have generally been non-parochial. In his first book, *Tolstoy or Dostoevsky*, he urges his reader to understand his references to religion 'in its most spacious connotations' (ibid.). This conception of religion as an expression of larger, abstract purposes has held good throughout his career. Yet, as his work has increasingly discussed the Shoah, it has also increasingly made reference to his own Jewishness. This has not really altered his sense of the religious impulse as broad-based, though it has resulted in an increasing identification of Judaism not only with the murdered victims of German hatred and the world's indifference but also with the challenge of Abstraction. Moses was the first, Jesus was the second, and Marx was the third of three Jews, each of whom demanded that the world reform itself, that it put aside its suspect practices and gods and attend to the call of the Ideal: 'Three times, Judaism has confronted Western man with the merciless claims and exactions of the ideal. Three times – in its invention of monotheism, in the message of the radical Jesus, in Marxism and messianic-socialism – Israel has asked of ordinary men and women more than human nature wishes to give; more, it may be, than it is organically and psychically able to give. Nothing is more cruel than the blackmail of perfection' (LLM, 59).

Steiner finds several reasons for identifying Judaism with Abstraction. First, there is the reason of its God, this Presence who, after Mount Sinai, has been most notable for His Absence, an absence which has constituted the central fact of Judaic history, though perhaps never so painfully noticed as during the Shoah. 'In post-Shoah Judaism the question of the language of prayer – how can it be anything but cynical, accusatory or despairing? – is radically posed' (LLM, 143). How can one pray to a God who has abandoned one? This is the question that every post-Shoah Jew must struggle with, though the question is not, in Jewish history, without antecedent, for it was heard earlier on Golgotha: 'Eli, la'ma sabach-tha'ni?' (Matt. 27: 46). Belief makes extraordinary demands, as it always has, for how does one orient one's life towards that which appears seldom more palpable than the most ancient testimony and the most suspect intuition: 'The demands made of the mind are, like God's name, unspeakable. Brain and conscience are commanded to vest belief, obedience, love in an abstraction purer, more inaccessible to ordinary sense than is the highest of mathematics' (BC, 37). By contrast, the Christian's core of beliefs seems absolutely physical. Steiner remarks on this, noting how difficult it must have been for the ancient Israelites to hold to what, at the time, would have seemed a fantastic notion (i.e., one God). He says that Christianity, in effect, found a way to make the demands on the imagination less arduous by offering a blend of monotheism and polytheism, a blend of abstraction and household saints: 'it allowed scope for the pluralistic, pictorial needs of the psyche. Be it in their Trinitarian aspects, in their proliferation of saintly and angelic persons, or in their vividly material realization of God the Father, of Christ, of Mary, the Christian churches have, with very rare exception, been a hybrid of monotheistic ideals and polytheistic practices' (BC, 39). The more stringent monotheistic ideal predates Christianity, and it still seems unmindful of human needs, originating as it does from this 'jealous God,' who visits 'the iniquity of the fathers upon the children to the third and fourth generation' (Exod. 20: 5). This may be one more reason why the God of Moses must have received from the early Israelites only a lukewarm welcome: 'What we must recapture to mind, as nakedly as we can, is the singularity, the brainhammering strangeness, of the monotheistic idea. Historians of religion tell us that the emergence of the concept of the Mosaic God is a unique fact in human experience, that a genuinely comparable notion sprang up at no other place. The abruptness of the Mosaic revelation, the finality of the creed at Sinai, tore up the human psyche by its most ancient roots. The break has never really knit' (BC, 37).

Another reason for identifying Judaism with Abstraction connects with the Mosaic God's commandment against 'graven image[s].' In *The Critique of Judgement*, Kant wrote that there was perhaps 'no more sublime passage in the Jewish Law' than this (I, 127), his reason being that it forced the Jewish people away from the commonplace idols of more primitive communities, and instead forced them to stretch their imaginations and to reach out in the direction of the sublime: 'The fear that, if we divest this representation of everything that can commend it to the senses, it will thereupon be attended only with a cold and lifeless approbation and not with any moving force or emotion, is wholly unwarranted. The very reverse is the truth. For when nothing any longer meets the eye of sense, and the unmistakable and ineffaceable idea of morality is left in possession of the field, there would be need rather of tempering the ardour of an unbounded imagination to prevent it rising to enthusiasm, than of seeking to lend these ideas the aid of images and childish devices for fear of their being wanting in potency' (I, 127–8). Steiner agrees. 'To all but a very few the Mosaic God has been from the outset, even when passionately invoked, an immeasurable Absence, or a metaphor modulating downward to the natural sphere of poetic, imagistic approximation. But the exaction stays in force – immense, relentless. It hammers at human consciousness, demanding that it transcend itself, that it reach out into a light of understanding so pure that it is itself blinding' (BC, 38).[14] Images may be inescapable, but we can resist, thinks Steiner, the temptation to caress and worship them, and to think that they are all there is and that there is no copula between the realm of images and meaning itself. It is why he is so hostile to post-structuralism and its celebration of a linguistic indeterminacy, for he fears that it leaves us mired in language's detritus, with our backs turned away from the source of our being. In a discussion comparing Derrida and Levinas, Steiner writes: 'When Derrida postulates that semantic markers can be ascribed decidable and eventually stabilized sense only if "the sign is taken to look to God," he is in total accord with Levinas. But for deconstruction, of course, such an assumption is an absurd atavism and a ludicrous quest for beginnings, for an *auctoritas* that never was. For Levinas, no less self-evidently, a theory and practice of sense is underwritten by that very turn towards the "face of God"' ('Levinas,' 244–5).[15]

For Steiner, theology entails a grammar, a closed system: 'Grammatical postulates and demonstrations of God's existence ... can have validity only inside closed speech systems' (RP, 57). The system either finds its validation in the Deity, or it does not find it at all. But the sense is that all things, when understood in the light, or invisible centre, which is God, acquire meaning, a meaning more measurable than that locatable in an indeterminate system driven by forces that are as rapacious as they are blind. This, says Steiner, helps to explain the necessity of taboos, not only the Judaic taboo against graven images but also more general religious restrictions against blasphemy, or any other action that would invert the relation of the divine to the mundane through making God's name one name among others. The 'depth of the Judaic prohibition on the enunciation of the name or, more strictly speaking, of the Name of the Name, of God' relates to the fact that once this name is spoken, it 'passes into the contingent limitlessness of linguistic play, be it rhetorical, metaphoric or deconstructive,' where it finds 'no demonstrable lodging' (ibid.). But this restriction exacts a price, for it makes the Jewish God all that much more abstract and inaccessible, a God almost more wisely addressed, or acknowledged, through silence. Certainly, Steiner encourages the view that silence is the most fitting response to Divinity. He even imagines prayer as passing through into silence, as the supplicant is forced to adopt the language of his Interlocutor, 'the silence of live meaning' (BC, 106). Language severs us 'from the ... from the silences that inhabit the greater part of being' (LS, x). Silence, on the other hand, gives us 'access' to 'the categories of felt being' (RP, 103). It need not be a dead-end, and may be an avenue towards the Light (LS, 21); and for those who are most attentive to the world's unspoken articulacy, silence can be a form of active answering (RP, 7).

Yet to make silence the primary avenue by which God may be known furthers, again, the sense of His abstractness. Nor does it escape the charge of being rhetorical, for a polemics on behalf of silence remains a gesture lodged in language. Even when silence's gestures appear most pure, they still constitute a kind of language. This does not mean that we cannot imagine a realm outside the bounds of human linguistics. We can, and we do well to if we wish to avoid both an intellectual and spiritual impoverishment. For Steiner, the prohibition against graven images was a reminder of the need to seek out meaning even in the midst of a sea of images. In his essay 'Graven Images,' he celebrates a host of Jewish art historians – Adolph Goldschmidt, Fritz Saxl, Erwin Panofsky, Meyer Schapiro, Max Friedländer, E.H. Gombrich, and Aby Warburg – precisely for their ability to search out the meanings of meaning, which even if it did not offer itself plainly, evidenced itself in shadow, in the symbolic iconography of a Flemish canvas that if one, such as Panofsky, knew how to read it, could make the world seem luminescent with meaning. That these men were able to read as well as they did Steiner partly attributes to the Hebraic prohibition against graven images, a prohibition which helped teach them, as Kant would have it, the power of the imagination:

> The question leaps to mind: Why this dominance of a veritable galaxy of Jewish talent in art history and art interpretation? A possible answer ... lies to hand. Prohibited throughout its earlier religious and ritual history from the making and contemplation of graven images, emancipated Judaism turned to the study of Western art with a peculiar thirst but also with a vehement, if perhaps subconscious, bias. The art to which it turned had to be 'meaningful' – it had to be subject to intelligible readings and, ultimately, to rational analysis, as were the canonic texts in the Judaic tradition. There was in Warburg's obsession and in the great library that he gathered and handed on more than a touch of the Talmudic. But so there is, he would point out, in the assemblage of occult symbols, in the unwavering posture of intellectual and moral inquiry that Dürer delineated in his representation of human sorrow. (98)

Steiner's allusion to the Talmud also calls forth another reason for identifying Judaism with Abstraction, and this has to do with its being such a remarkably text-based religion. Of course, the Talmud calls up an image of a text that has taken on a life of its own, and Steiner admits the fact: 'Dialogue with the ultimately, but only ultimately, unfathomable text is the breath of Jewish history and being. It has proved to be the instrument of improbable survival. At the same time, the Talmudic genius and method have, very possibly, generated within Judaic sensibility certain philological-legalistic sterilities and circularities. The dance turns never-endingly on itself' (RP, 41). This image of the Talmud as emblematically textual has not gone unnoticed by commentators sympathetic to the post-structuralist point of view. Susan Handelman, in *The Slayers of Moses: The Emergence of Rabbinic Interpretation in Modern Literary Theory*, is most identified with the theory that finds a strong rabbinical element in post-structuralism's celebration of textuality, for her thinking here is both the most developed and presumptive. But other critics, including Kermode and Hartman, have also promoted the thesis that Talmudic commentary's strength lies in its offering a way of reading that accents 'revision, rather than more violent ways of denial, or trying to start *de novo*' (Hartman in Salusinszky, *Criticism in Society*, 87). Steiner would not dispute the point, but at the same time, it has been his contention that this method is different from deconstructive readings in that it assumes a theological order. In '"The Critic"/"Reader,"' he writes: 'the rabbinical exegete or Calvin on the Gospels can proceed without apology or rationalizing metaphor, "as if" the real presence were unambiguously operative in his text. He can, in short, make explicit the assumption, implicit in all true reading, that the warranty of meaning, that which finally underwrites the capacity of language to have sense and force beyond sense, is of a theological order' (GSR, 90). Steiner does not distinguish between Jewish and Christian commentary, conceiving more similarity than difference in the methodologies. Ten years later, in *Real Presences*, however, his shading acquires a different hue.

In *Real Presences* and other more recent work, Steiner demonstrates greater readiness to make strong distinctions between Jewish and Christian practices, including the difference in commentary styles. He still views Talmudic practice as predicating a theological order, but he also borrows something from post-structuralism in general and Handelman in particular, most notably the latter's view that 'Paul and the Church Fathers after him replaced the prolonged Rabbinic meditation on and meditation of the Text with the pure unmediated presence of Jesus, who resolves all oppositions, stabilizes meaning, provides ultimate identity, and collapses differentiation.'[16] For instance, compare this statement to the following in *Real Presences*: 'Note the radical difference between Catholic and Judaic textuality. There is no temporal singularity, no enigma of historicity ("why in this one place, why at that one time?") in

the Judaic sense of the Creation and of the Mosaic reception and transmission of the Law. There is a strict, utterly mysterious temporality in
the coming and ministry of Christ. Being so naturally, if inexplicably,
immersed in actual time, the meanings of that coming, the normative
consequences of the sayings of Christ and of the writings of the Apos-
tles, must, as it were, be stabilized in eternity. The Torah is indetermi-
nately synchronic with all individual and communal life. The Gospels,
Epistles and Acts are not' (RP, 44).[17] The antithesis, while not unhelp-
ful, seems too pat. We know of Christ, as we know of Moses, through narratives handed down, sometimes lost and then later found, redacted,
translated, and filtered through commentary, conflict, and ritual. We
make a mistake if we think that all the Christian needs to do is go back
to the source, the Gospel narratives, themselves a form of commentary,
or textuality, written decades after Jesus' death and often at odds with
one another as to even the basis facts. As Valentine Cunningham says in
response to Handelman, 'What, I wonder, would Lancelot Andrewes
have made of being dismissed as one not meditating on the text in prolonged ways or of accepting the a-textually "unmediated presence of
Jesus"!' (*In the Reading Gaol*, 399). Textuality is textuality, whether it be
Jewish or Christian, though we perhaps force the matter when we compare what amount to Jewish texts of law to Christian texts of revelation.
As Vermes writes: 'If Judaism is described exclusively on the basis of such
legal or near-legal documents as the Mishnah, the Talmud or the *Shul-
han Arukh*, it will appear more legalistic and casuistic than spiritual; but
so would Christianity if seen one-sidedly mirrored in the codes of canon
law, penitential books or manuals of moral theology of the various
churches' (*The Religion of Jesus*, 195). These texts announce their secondariness, their textuality, in a way that neither *Genesis* nor *Mark* does.
And yet we would be naive to think the latter narratives transparencies.
They are not. Steiner knows this; but it does not stop him from wishing
to make a distinction that places Christianity on the side of time-stop-
ping revelation and Judaism on the side of textuality (and, by extension,
on the side of Abstraction). As he writes in 'Our Homeland, the Text,'
'whether they are seen as positive or negative, the "textual" fabric, the
interpretative practices in Judaism are ontologically and historically at
the heart of Jewish identity' (7), of an identity that 'scorn[s] the natural
sphere' in favour of 'its extreme commitment to abstraction, to word
and text' (6).[18]

Crucial to Steiner's identification of Judaism with textuality is the
downplaying, even rejection, of a Messiah. That is, while Steiner is

keenly aware of the messianic elements in such historical movements as Christianity, Marxism, Zionism, and even Judaism proper, he thinks the concept of a Messiah bogus, whether understood in the frame of Jewish longing or Christian remembrance and promise. In the instance of Judaism, he believes that its messianic tenets have always been ambivalent, and that, in the post-Shoah period, they must be simply set aside, as something now widely recognized as unrealizable: 'The Old Testament and the Talmud, rabbinic teachings and Jewish historicism are unquestionably brimful of the messianic promise and of the awaiting of the Messiah in moods both anguished and exultant. But does the Jew, in psychological and historical fact truly believe in the coming? More searchingly: does he truly thirst for it? Or is it, was it perhaps from the very first, what logicians or grammatologists might designate as a "counter-factual optative," a category of meaning never to be realized?' (TGD, 37). It is not that radical an opinion, actually, even among more committed Jewish thinkers. Gershom Scholem, for instance, thinks that while the personal Messiah 'is undoubtedly connected with the historical origins of the messianic hope,' '[i]t has become immaterial for wide circles of Jews, even for some who harbor strong religious feelings' (*On Jews and Judaism in Crisis*, 287–8). Even as Scholem thinks of himself as a messianist, he sees the Messiah surviving mainly as a symbol, 'as a summation of everything implied by the messianic ideal' (288). This is the way things should be thinks Steiner, believing the ideal too anti-historical, too much a threat to the delivery of tomorrow's 'morning paper': 'Given the choice, the Jew prefers tomorrow's news, however grim, to the arrival of the Messiah. We are a people unquenchably avid of history, of knowledge in motion. We are the children of Eve whose primal curiosity has modulated into that of the philosophic and natural sciences. In denying the messianic status of Jesus, in subverting early Christian beliefs in the proximity of the eschatological, the Jew gave expression to the genius of restlessness central to his psyche. We were, we remain nomads across time' (TGD, 37–8).

Scholem once wrote that '[a]ny discussion of the problems relating to Messianism is a delicate matter, for it is here that the essential conflict between Judaism and Christianity has developed and continues to exist' (*The Messianic Idea in Judaism*, 1). The statement reflects both his temperance and wisdom. On the matter of messianism, however, Steiner steers a different course. In 'Through That Glass Darkly' (1992), the oppositions he celebrates mostly entail a far from delicate dismissal of Christian messianism. Again, his point is that Christianity would have stopped time – though it is not clear how – had it not been for the refusal of the Jews to recognize Jesus as the Messiah: 'The Jewish rebuke to Christ prevents the coming of the messianic realm. It pries and forces open the ravenous jaws of history' (TGD, 41). This forgets that Christians imagine their existences as situated between a First and Second Coming (or Parousia), and thereby see themselves historically. History and Logos co-exist, even as the former is imagined as living in and moving towards the latter. It is true, as Scholem writes, that what for Judaism 'stood unconditionally at the end of history as its most distant aim was for' Christianity 'the true centre of the historical process' (*The Messianic Idea in Judaism*, 1); and that this has had consequences in how the two theologies conceive this Ideal. Notably, says Scholem, Jews have long 'maintained a concept of redemption as an event that takes places publicly, on the stage of history and within the community,' whereas Christians have tended to imagine 'redemption as an event in the spiritual and unseen realm, an event which is reflected in the soul, in the private world of each individual, and which effects an inner transformation which need not correspond to anything outside' (ibid.). Also, says Scholem, the experience of the messianic has for Jews long been associated with the state of exile; and whereas Christians know Christ as a historical person, the Jewish image of the Messiah is necessarily abstract and entails no longing backward but only a looking forward: 'Thus in Judaism the Messianic idea has compelled a *life lived in deferment*, in which nothing can be done definitively, nothing can be irrevocably accomplished. One may say, perhaps, the Messianic idea is the real anti-existentialist idea' (*The Messianic Idea in Judaism*, 35). Clearly, then, there are differences, but to push these differences, as Steiner does, to the point where Christianity's embrace of Logos is seen as all-in-all, and Judaism's embrace of History is also seen as all-in-all, is to distort matters too much. Here, Judaism seems less anti-existential than quintessentially existential. 'In what measure, at what level of consciousness was the Jewish refusal of Jesus, at the time and thereafter, a symptom of radical psychic commitment to historical freedom, to the creative *daimon* of existential destiny on a changing earth?' (TGD, 38). We are expected to answer that the refusal of Jesus's messianic claim was a conscious, profound, and sound affirmation of history over telos, even over Judaism's own form of messianism. Or as Steiner himself says: 'We Jews have said "No" to the claims made for and, in certain opaque moments by, the man Jesus. He remains for us a spurious messiah. The true one has not come in his stead. Today, who but a fundamentalist handful awaits his coming in any but a formulaic, allegoric sense, a sense bitterly irrelevant to the continuing desolation of the human situation?' (TGD, 49).

For Steiner, this rejection of Jesus the Messiah is not a rejection of Jesus the man, or his teachings. About the latter, Steiner's views parallel Vermes', that the Sermon on the Mount and other such teachings are continuous with Judaic practices of the time, particularly 'the charismatic Judaism of wonder-working holy men such as the first-century BC Honi and Jesus' younger contemporary, Hanina ben Dosa, modelled on the biblical prophets such as Elijah and Elisha' (Vermes, *The Religion of Jesus*, 4). These teachings can be found to 'correspond very nearly point for point with cardinal tenets of the Torah and with the ethics, unsurpassed, of the Prophets, most especially Isaiah. Where there are departures from the canonic norm, in respect, for example, of the need to keep company with the publicans and the sinful, or in regard to the primacy of healing and salvational acts over the sanctity of the Sabbath, such dissents do not go signally beyond queries and challenges to Pharisiac observance as we find them among other Jewish "liberals" or apocalyptics at the time' (ibid.). Jesus was a paragon of virtue, the mouthpiece of 'a purified, humanly resourceful and compassionate Judaism' (TGD, 34), who summoned men and women to live not by their appetites but by an ideal of self-sacrifice and love for one another. That the message got distorted, thinks Steiner, is less the fault of Jesus than of Paul, John, and those who came after. He should probably agree with Vermes, when the latter writes: 'Today as in past centuries, the believing Christian's main New Testament source of faith lies, not so much in Mark, Matthew and Luke and their still sufficiently earthly Jesus, as in the centuries of speculation by the church on the theological Gospel of John with its eternal Word become flesh, and perhaps, even more on the letters of Paul with their drama of death, atonement, and resurrection. The Christ of Paul and John, on the way toward deification, overshadows and obscures the man of Galilee' (*The Religion of Jesus*, 210). Certainly, Paul comes across as the villain in Steiner's accounts, the one most responsible for the early Christian sect's separation from the larger Jewish community. In Paul, Steiner detects an element of Jewish self-hatred, a flaw that found its tragic denouement in the Shoah, as hatred originally directed inward found itself, after the divorce of communities, directed outward: 'The beginning of the macabre history of Jewish self-hatred are inextricably inwoven with those of Christianity ... [T]he thought presses on one that Christianity is at fundamental points a product and externalization of just this Jewish self-hatred' (TGD, 40). Reductive as this appears, Steiner nevertheless thinks the Shoah has its roots in those passages (he names *Romans* 9–11, *Ephesians* 2, and 1 *Thessalonians*) wherein Paul appears to blame the Jews for Christ's crucifixion. In 'Through That Glass Darkly,' he writes: '1 Thessalonians, 2, 15, proclaims the Jew to be a deicide, a slayer of his own Prophets and, therefore, one "contrary" or "enemy to all men." Vatican II sought to attenuate or even cancel this sentence of death in the troubled light of modern squeamishness and the Holocaust. In view of the "final solution" which this Pauline verdict determines. But the text is not accident: it lay, it continues to lie, at the historical and symbolic roots of Christendom' (49–50).[19] Steiner's vehement rejection of Paul contrasts with Vermes's more equitably managed judgment: 'To be fair, it has to be said that Paul, despite the many harsh polemical comments against Judaism, shies off in the end from damning his people for ever. His inventive poetic mind imagines that the rejection of Christ is a dreadful but only temporary lapse. The apostle of the Gentiles by attempting to graft the whole converted non-Jewish world on to the Jewish stock, thus making them the heirs of all the divine promises granted to Abraham and his posterity, secretly hoped that the elevation of the Gentiles would excite the jealousy of the Jews, and bring them to *teshuvah* and submission to Christ so that 'all Israel' might be saved' (212–13).

In short, Steiner blames the split between the Christian and Jewish communities on 1) self-hatred among the early Jewish-Christians for their own antecedents; 2) Paul's placement of blame upon the Jews for Jesus's crucifixion; 3) the Jews' refusal to acknowledge Jesus as the Messiah; and 4) Christianity's later inclination towards political power. About this last point, I have as yet said nothing. But it is an important issue for Steiner, and explains not only his dislike for the Church, but also his discomfort with the state of Israel, especially as it presents itself as both a religious and political entity. In the first instance, Steiner says that '[i]t is altogether possible that Judaism would have lost its identity, would have diffused itself in Christianity, if the latter had been true to its Judaic catholicity. Instead, Christendom became, itself, a political-territorial structure, prepared, on all practical counts, to serve, to hallow, the genesis and militancy of secular states' (OHT, 21). The suggestion that Judaism would have been absorbed into Christianity had the latter remained outside the political matrix is suspect. But whether or not this might have happened, Steiner's main point is that no corporate entity like a Church can do justice to the anarchic energy of a Jesus, to the intolerable demands that his teachings make upon us. 'Can,' he quotes Dostoevsky, 'any established church house the Galilean trouble-maker?' (SR, 59). He thinks not, not this prophet who, in the spirit of Amos (7: 14), demanded of his disciples that they go out into the world taking 'nothing for their journey except a staff; no bread, no bag, no money in their belts; but to wear sandals and not put on two tunics' (Mark 6: 8–9). To seek the homeland that is God requires that we not put down roots, that we remain restless searchers. To do otherwise is to convert the unearthly imperative into something much more tame – forms and rituals, empty of meaning and force: 'For the majority of "practicing" Christians – and what does "practicing" entail in this con-cept? – the Crucifixion remains an unexamined inheritance, a symbolic marker of familiar but vestigial recognitions. This marker is reversed and invoked in conventional idiom and gestures. Its concrete status, the enormity of suffering and injustice it incarnates, would appear to have faded from felt immediacy. How many educated men or women now hear Pascal's cry that humanity must not sleep because Christ hangs on his Cross till the end of the world? A "rationalized" Christianity hovers between an untenable literalism and symbolic insubstantiality, in the indistinct spaces of fitful imagining which we call myth' (SR, 62–3).

For his implacable formulation, Steiner makes no apologies. Instead, when pressed to adopt a more accommodating posture, he becomes more goading, telling us, for instance, that '[t]he death of Socrates out-weighs the survival of Athens' (GSR, 196). Or that the nation of Israel has become a 'death trap': 'The messianic vision was, precisely, that which strove to overcome the homicidal tribalism that inhabits man. Having to be peregrine on this earth, the Jew developed that inward restlessness, those antennae for danger to which he owes his survival. For the Jew, the nation-state is not a fulfillment but a death trap' ('A Jew's Grief,' 20). This last analysis has not won Steiner very many friends, certainly not among Jewish intellectuals. Morris Dickstein speaks of *The Portage to San Cristóbal of A.H.*, and its theories about Israel in its relation to nationalism and the Shoah, 'as a sideshow distraction from the serious business of thinking through the unspeakable horrors of the Nazi era' ('Alive and 90,' 21); and Lionel Abel writes that 'no Jew, religious or secular, can follow George Steiner, nor can Steiner follow himself. He still has to decide how it is possible to secularize the Torah and yet regard it as true, or how to make sacred the untrue text. With-out bringing off one or the other of these impossible feats, there cannot be Homeland for him' ('So Who is to Have the Last Word,' 371). Steiner is obsessed with the question of homeland, but he thinks, unlike

Abel and even unlike Scholem and Levinas, whose thinking he clearly respects, that the Jew's true homeland is not to be found in a piece of property alongside the Mediterranean, no matter how imbued with Jewish history. It is to be found in the text: 'In post-exilic Judaism, but perhaps earlier, active reading, answerability to the text on both the meditative-interpretative and the behavioural levels, is the central motion of personal and national homecoming. The Torah is met at the place of summons and in the time of calling (which is night and day). The dwelling assigned, ascribed to Israel is the House of the Book. Heine's phrase is exactly right: *das aufgeschriebene Vaterland.* The "land of the fathers," the patrimonie, is the script' (OHT, 5).

Abel has reason to worry that Steiner's allegiance to the text extends beyond Jewish sacred texts, and that these latter texts do not receive an attention distinctive enough to make clear their specialness. Steiner has long postulated a connection between literary texts and the spiritual, and his interest has, in this time, been more with secular than sacred texts. Still, in 'Our Homeland, the Text,' Steiner makes a concerted attempt to deal with the issues of text and textuality as they pertain to Jewish experience and longings – specifically the longing connected to the *aliyah.* He begins by drawing a connection between Judaism and the text as they both bespeak the condition of exile. It is easy, given the long history of the Diaspora, to understand the first connection; the second, however, needs spelling out. Steiner starts off by proposing the possibility that the Torah itself 'is a place of privileged banishment from the tautological immediacy of Adamic speech, of God's direct, unwritten address to man' (OHT, 5). Something's being written already confers on it the status of exile, with the text departing from the author like a child from a parent. God's Word, meanwhile, has an immediacy or originality about it that escapes transcription and confers a secondariness even upon sacred writings. Among the Hebrews, no less than the Greeks, says Steiner, there is 'a distrust of the written word, a critical regret at the passing of orality' (OHT, 8). For them, 'the written is always a shadow after the fact, a post-script' (ibid.). Nor does Steiner stop at writing. He also attributes a quality of belatedness and exile to reading, particularly in relation to praxis: 'Reading, textual exegesis, are an exile from action, from the existential innocence of *praxis,* even when the text is aiming at practical and political consequence. The reader is one who (day and night) is absent from action' (OHT, 5). Writing and reading, then, are noticeably textual, locatable in their own diaspora. This diaspora is not so unlike the Jewish people's own

Diaspora, for their situation has historically also been one of textuality:
'The "textuality" of the Jewish condition, from the destruction of the
Temple to the foundation of the modern state of Israel, can be seen, has
been seen by Zionism, as one of tragic impotence. The text was the
instrument of exilic survival; that survival came within a breath of anni-
hilation. To endure at all, the "people of the Book" had, once again, to
be a nation' (ibid.).

Steiner, however, rejects the Zionist conclusion. He acknowledges
that Jews are divided by their 'an unhoused at-homeness in the text'
(specifically the Hebraic text) and 'the territorial mystery of the native
ground' (OHT, 5), but he sees no reason for thinking that Israel as
homeland is preferable to the Book. This conviction has only been
strengthened by the events of the previous decades, events which have
demonstrated that an Israel conceived along the lines of nineteenth-
century nationalism will invariably fall into all the associated traps – the
inequities, the militarism, the bureaucratic subterfuge, and liming of
brutalities. Looking back to Theodor Herzel's *Judenstaat*, a founding
document of Zionism, Steiner is struck by how much 'the language and
the vision are proudly mimetic of Bismarckian nationalism' (OHT, 22),
and what an ominous foreshadowing this was of present-day Israel:
'Israel is a nation-state to the utmost degree. It lives armed to the teeth.
It has been compelled to make other men homeless, servile, disinherited, in order to survive from day to day (it was, during the millennia,
the dignity of the Jew that he was too weak to make any other human
being unhoused, as wretched as himself). The virtues of Israel are those
of beleaguered Sparta. Its propaganda, its rhetoric of self-deception, are
as desperate as any contrived in the history of nationalism. Under external and internal stress, loyalty has been atrophied to patriotism, and
patriotism made chauvinism' (ibid.).

The homecoming has been a disappointment, at least to the extent
that Zionism provoked a messianic promise which it has, so far, failed to
keep. The future may change this, though it seems unlikely. This does
not make any more agreeable, to most Israelis, Steiner's notion that they
should prefer the abandon of the nomadic life to the comforts and pleasures of material at-homeness. But he believes Jews remarkably different
from other people, even to the point of promoting a racialism that,
among contemporary intellectuals, is now rarely heard: 'if one is a Jew,
one has quite extraordinary experience, perhaps illusory, perhaps not,
of going down a street in a distant land, even where one does not know
the language, and the other Jew in the street is one one recognizes by

the way he walks. I know this to be true of my own experience' (TT, 393).[20] Whether or not this is the case, Steiner thinks that the Jew's religion and proud heritage must make him or her a partisan of transcendence, in a way foreign to the majority of non-Jews. He cites Hegel's description of Abraham as seeking an 'almost autistic intimacy with God,' and as one 'radically uninterested in or even hostile to other men, to those outside the covenant of his search' (OHT, 6). The search is the most important thing, and others are not expected to take a like interest in it. From the Jew's perspective, thinks Steiner, they do not: 'More than any other people, Jews claim, indeed they seem to achieve, nearness to the concept of God. They do so at the suicidal cost of mundane renunciation, of self ostracism from the earth and its family of nations' (ibid.). Steiner seems to be speaking for Hegel here, though it is not clear. He does concur with Hegel's description, but not his conclusion. The reason is that while Hegel found the Jews an exceptional people, he also thought them the victims of 'an awesome pathology, a tragic, arrested stage in the advance of human consciousness towards a liberated homecoming' (OHT, 7). Steiner thinks otherwise, believing this same movement away from the world and towards transcendence a sign 'of the Jewish genius and of its survival' (ibid.), forgetting, for the moment, his touting of history as crucial to Jewish identity. In any event, he may be right, but the cost has been great.

There remains the question that if the Jew is not to think of Israel as his or her homeland because its model is conventional nationhood, why should this person think better of the text, which, as we have seen, is also equated with exile? Steiner has an answer, though it seems to entail an evasion. I say this because Steiner, as we have seen, has long railed against the essential parasitism of commentary, imagining such activity as occluding that which should be held primary. And yet, when it comes to Jewish commentary upon the Torah, he takes a somewhat different stance, approving what he formerly scorned (and sometimes still does). The point is, in 'Our Homeland, the Text,' he demonstrates a readiness, influenced perhaps by Handelman and other post-structuralists, to view commentary not as a killing of the thing one loves, but as a means of keeping it alive in people's hearts. 'The text is home; each commentary a return. When he reads, when, by virtue of commentary, he makes of his reading a dialogue and life-giving echo, the Jew is, to purloin Heidegger's image, "the shepherd of being." The seeming nomad in truth carries the world within him, as does language itself' (7). Without commentary, texts – original and incarnated – would be forgotten and, in effect, die. The sacred would wither away into anthropology. Yet so long as the holy books 'are read and surrounded by a constancy of secondary, satellite texts,' their authority cannot be abrogated, and we can say of the secondary texts that they 'rescue the canon from the ebbing motion of the past tense, from that which would draw live meaning into inert and merely liturgical monumentality' (ibid.).[21]

Everything that Steiner says in 'Our Homeland, the Text' suggests a privileging of sacred writ over all else, though with Steiner one never quite knows whether it is he or the rhetoric that is speaking. This is not to accuse him of dishonesty. It is, rather, to acknowledge the brilliance of his writing and to wonder whether this brilliance does not, at times, reverse the order of author and pen. Dickstein puts this matter more harshly than I would, but because I think he is on to something, I will quote him: 'Mr. Steiner's writings often have this hollow feeling to them, as if his language were running away from him, and as though this gifted rhetorician were treating the blood and bone of history as a literary text, a conceptual challenge, an occasion for ingenious exercises in interpretation' ('Alive and 90,' 13, 21). This comes from the review of Steiner's controversial novel, and the statement's harshness is undoubtedly connected to that fact. But there is a strong element of truth in it, and in 'Our Homeland, the Text,' the rhetorical performance is of such an extraordinary calibre that even Steiner, near its conclusion, must pull back and confess that 'this, of course, is only a part of the truth' (22), that while it makes wonderful poetic sense to identify Jews as the people of the Book, thirsting for transcendence, it must be acknowledged that '[t]he overwhelming majority of Jews ... seek neither to be prophets nor clerics deranged by some autistic, otherworldly addiction to speculative abstractions and the elixir of truth' (22–3). Then, in a statement that seemingly has forgotten from whence the matter originated, he writes: 'What mandarin fantasy, what ivory-tower nonsense, is it to suppose that alone among men, and after the unspeakable horrors of destruction lavished among him, the Jew should not have a land of his own, a shelter in the night?' (23). This is to grant the opposing view its legitimacy, not to acquiesce to it. And in the remainder of the essay, Steiner returns to his theme, albeit in a more modulated, even chastened – '*Personally*, I have no right to this answer' (ibid.) – tone.

Steiner's preference of the homeland of the text over that of the state employs rhetorical strategies – i.e., the drawing of a line of inheritance that connects Jewish sacred texts back to the Word of God – that could just as well be used to justify the excellence of the state; and that have, in fact, been so used, as for instance by Levinas, when he argues that the state of Israel achieves its 'true sovereignty' through its institutionalizing the justice of God, the justice that makes it possible 'for a man to see the face of an other' (*The Levinas Reader*, 260, 261):

> Like an empire on which the sun never sets, a religious history extends the size of its modest territory, even to the point where it absorbs a breath-taking past. But, contrary to national histories, this past, like an ancient civilization, places itself above nations, like a fixed star. And yet we are the living ladder that reaches up to the sky. Doesn't Israel's particular past consist in something both eternal and ours? This peculiar right, revealed by an undeniable Jewish experience, to call our own a doctrine that is none the less offered to everyone, marks the true sovereignty of Israel. It is not its political genius nor its artistic genius nor even its scientific genius (despite all they promise) that forms the basis of its majority, but its religious genius! The Jewish people therefore achieves a State whose prestige none the less stems from the religion which modern political life supplants. (260)

For Levinas, there is the homeland of Israel, for Steiner, that of the text, sacred and secular (political, artistic, scientific). Both scholars employ an argument that begs the question, and begs it in a similar way, so it is perhaps wrong for Steiner to promote the text over the state by claiming that the text is articulative of something – i.e., divinity – that a state can never be. Which text? Which state? Not Israel, thinks Steiner, but maybe its texts. That is, while he argues that all texts have a quality of the secondary, of the exilic, about them, some texts – most notably, sacred texts – exhibit a greater sense of recognition, of a recall of a mystery which, in our postlapsarian condition, escapes too rapidly into the crevices of the quotidian. Before the Fall, things were otherwise. Then, '[t]hings were as Adam named them and said them to be. Word and world were one' (OHT, 8). But '[a]fter the Fall,' says Steiner, 'memories and dreams, which are so often messianic recollections of futurity, become the store-house of experience and of hope. Hence the need to re-read, to re-call (revocation) those texts in which the mystery of a beginning, in which the vestiges of a lost self-evidence – God's "I am that I am" – are current' (ibid.). For someone whose Jewishness has been described as 'secular' (RGS, 267), this predicates much of the argument upon what almost amounts to a literal reading of the Bible. Steiner knows this, and undoubtedly does not wish to proceed too far this way, but he is almost obliged to, given the emphasis placed on the textuality of Jewish experience. By claiming that Judaism 'holds Christianity, and, indeed, mankind ..., hostage' and that its rejection of Christ 'has condemned man to the treadmill of history' (TGD, 41), Steiner is in danger of making too much of Jewish textuality, to the point that his blueprint threatens a permanent exile to the people of the Book. He is proud of this textuality, proud that '[i]n Judaism, the letter is the life of the spirit' (OHT, 17), and proud that 'the God to whom the Jew would stand so near is, by virtue of implacable abstraction, of the unfathomable elevation attributed to Him, furtherest from man' (OHT, 6). But unless there be some reversal of direction, away from an argument that has so much post-structuralist colouring about it, there can be no real talk of homecoming. Textuality will have won out.

In his later work, Steiner moves in seemingly contradictory directions. He likes opposing Jewish textuality to Christian a-textuality, and suggesting that this shows the greater fortitude and wisdom of the Jewish people. But by composing a binary grounded in an antithesis, something is also lost, not only as far as Christianity (now opposed to History) is concerned, but also as far as Judaism is concerned. That is, by placing Christianity on the side of Logos, and Judaism on the side of History, Steiner threatens to cut off Jewish experience from all that makes it first meaningfulness: the claim to be God's chosen people. Steiner is ambivalent about this claim, and has angered many Jews by the linkage made, in *The Portage to San Cristóbal of A.H.*, between it and the claim of Nazism. (Hitler: 'My racism was a parody of yours, a hungry imitation. What is a thousand-year *Reich* compared with the eternity of Zion? Perhaps I was the false Messiah sent before. Judge me and you must judge yourselves. *Übermenschen*, chosen ones!' [164].) Without this claim, and without some credence in it, the propensity to see both Jewish *and* Christian Scripture as sacred would quickly lose its valence. Steiner is unready to give up this much. But his ambivalence makes his appeal to *Genesis* and the Fall seem forced, and makes his argument that between God and the Jews 'the concepts of contract and of covenant are not metaphoric' (OHT, 8) seem rhetorical. Nevertheless, Steiner chooses not to abandon the Jew to a textuality that is all post-script, and he or she is said to act out a 'pre-script,' 'to inhabit the literal text of his [or her] foreseen being' (OHT, 12): 'No other community in the evolution and social history of man has, from its outset, read, re-read without cease, learnt by heart or by rote, and expounded without end the texts which spell out its whole destiny. These texts, moreover, are felt to be of transcendent authorship and authority, infallible in their *pre*-diction, as oracles in the pagan world, notoriously, are not. The script, therefore, is a contract with the inevitable. God has, in the dual sense of utterance and of binding affirmation, "given His word." His *Logos* and His bond to Israel. It cannot be broken or refuted' (ibid.).

It is because Jews conceive of their relation to God as contractual, says Steiner, that they have cultivated a clerical mode, attentive to the preservation and dissemination of the contract as well as the obligations enjoined by it: 'The mystery and the practises of clerisy are fundamental to Judaism. No other tradition or culture has ascribed a comparable aura to the conservation and transcription of texts. In no other has there been an equivalent mystique of the philological' (OHT, 17). All this has importance to Judaism's doctrinal demands and more general axiology. Steiner is more interested in the latter, in the consequences ensuing from the Jewish people's subservience to the Book. For him, there is, as noted, something exilic about books. They also encourage our own separation from the activity and commotion about us. Reading a book, we step out of the 'real' world, and into an extraterritorial space. This departure, or chosen exile, often increases our detachment regarding the world as found. We become more disinterested. It is this relation between bookishness and detachment, or disinterest, that helps to explain, says Steiner, the Jewish character, especially as it has been shaped by its long, historical relation to the Book: 'It is because he lives, enacts privately and historically, a written writ, a promissory note served on him when God sought out Abraham and Moses, it is because the "Book of Life" is, in Judaism, literally textual, that the Jew dwells apart' (OHT, 12). Jewish bookishness, however, does not stop with the Bible; it carries over into a more general respect for books, and this respect, in turn, has dialectically molded and distinguished the Jewish character. Thus Steiner speaks of 'the sometimes hallucinatory techniques and disciplines of attention to the text, the mystique of fidelity to the written word, the reverence bestowed on its expositors and transmitters, concentrated within Judaic sensibility unique strengths and purities of disinterested purpose' (OHT, 17).

For Steiner, it is this latter phase – where would-be clerics, raised in the tradition of the Book, begin to take an interest in secular texts – that has always most interested him. It is a phase that only begins to acquire bulk in the late nineteenth and early twentieth centuries, after the processes of assimilation (itself related to the factors of urbanization and the growth of the middle class) made it possible for Jews to participate in the larger intellectual life of Europe and North America. Earlier, I mentioned Steiner's conviction that Jewish intellectual life experienced something like a golden age during this period. If it were so, it is because Jewish clerical traditions easily adapted themselves to the disciplines of humanistic scholarship, mathematics, and science. The accomplishments were not, at first, as significant in the arts because the Hebraic restrictions regarding mimesis discouraged them ('Graven Images'). This has changed in the ensuing generations, as witnessed by the extraordinary achievements of Kafka, Proust, Chagall, Celan, Schoenberg, Mandelstam, Gershwin, Rothko, Bellow, Roth, and others. In any event, this history of bookishness, first religious and then less so, must be credited with placing a disproportionate number of Jewish intellectuals at the forefront of modern culture: 'The "bookish" genius of Marx and of Freud, of Wittgenstein and of Lévi-Strauss, is a secular deployment of the long schooling in abstract, speculative commentary and clerkship in the exegetic legacy (while being at the same time a psychological-sociological revolt against it). The Jewish presence, often overwhelming, in modern mathematics, physics, economic and social theory, is direct heir to that abstinence from the approximate, from the mundane, which constitutes the ethos of the cleric' (OHT, 17). Steiner can be chauvinistic about this achievement. As noted earlier, it is a little disconcerting to find that there is little in U.S. culture that merits attention once the contributions of the Puritans and the Jews have been accounted for. Or, as Steiner says in regard to post-war American culture: 'Think away the arrival of the Jewish *intelligentsia*, think away the genius of Leningrad-Prague-Budapest-Vienna and Frankfurt in American culture of the past decades, and what have you left? For the very concept of an *intelligentsia*, of an élite minority infected with the leprosy of abstract thought, is radically alien to the essential American circumstance' (AE, 73–4). This kind of thinking, so captive to ethnic and cultural stereotypes and the partisanship that goes with them, has a tragic enough history already, and it is a little dispiriting to see Steiner participating in it.

In any event, this clerical tradition, that first engaged sacred and later secular texts, carried with it not only an expertise in hermeneutics, but also the faith – or maybe just the hope – that the text *sui generis* remains somehow valuable and sacred. It is a faith that initially cannot imagine the text existing other than as a conduit of first meanings. Later, when it can imagine this, it must change its relation to texts, either by dramatically narrowing down the range of texts thought worthy of serious investigation or by changing its strategy vis-à-vis texts. This might mean moving away from a hermeneutics that engages texts ontologically and towards one that engages them otherwise, for instance, ethnographically, historically, psychologically, sociologically, and so forth. The fact is, current criticism has thought it best to pursue the second avenue, to alter its strategy vis-à-vis texts. Steiner, however, still thinks it worthwhile, even important, to pursue the first avenue. He knows that this means ignoring the majority of texts, though it is not clear that he has fully weighed the consequences of this exclusion. Those critics who have chosen otherwise would no doubt find his selectivity this way neglectful and elitist. He, in turn, would fault them for prematurely withdrawing from the most important of investigations: the pursuit of the meanings of meaning. Steiner knows that for secular texts one cannot make the claim – made for sacred texts – that they issue from the very first source of meaning. But if they are not this – i.e., God-spoken – they may still be understood as participating in the sacred, to the extent, or in the sense, that this is identified with Order in its most transcendent, and thereby Divine, manifestation. If God has spoken Himself in the world, either through the prophets or the world itself, then we must assume that the voice is distinctive enough that those who seek it out, who are receptive, and honest with themselves and others, can hear it, if not all the time, at least some of the time, and that what they hear concurs, more or less, with what others of like attentiveness also hear. It is the assumption that underwrites religious life in general; and while artists ostensibly pursue other purposes, they have long been identified with a similar attentiveness or hearing, though this history seems to be coming to a close. It *has* closed for many, if not the majority, of artists working in the West. This latter fact helps to explain Steiner's own disenchantment with contemporary Western art – 'God, look at our literature in free Britain. Mountains of trivia and pretentiousness!' (RI, 180) – especially when compared to its Eastern European and Russian counterparts. In fact, Steiner is specifically attentive to that art which presumes an unheard music, a divine presence capable of underwriting the world's dailiness. Here, '[w]hat is implicit is the notion of and expression of "real presence"' (GSR, 85). This leads the critic, or reader, to proceed '*as if* the text was the housing of forces and meanings, of meanings of meaning, whose lodging within the executive verbal form was one of "incarnation." He reads *as if* – a conditionality which defines the "provisional" temper of his pursuit – the singular presence of the life meaning in the text and work of art was "a real presence" irreducible to analytic summations and resistant to judgement in the sense in which the critic can and must judge' (GSR, 85).

Steiner's most eloquent statement this way is found in *Real Presences*, a book that must be thought of as near, if not *the*, pinnacle of his work, so beautifully does he articulate the argument that inscribes not simply art but all meaning in an Absolute. The book's success partly follows from the fact that, unlike some of the earlier books, Steiner achieves a less acrid, more conciliatory, tone.[22] There is enough acridity for those who want it – e.g., '[t]he entire notion of research in modern letters is vitiated by the evidently false postulate that tens of thousands of young men and women will have anything new and just to say about Shakespeare or Keats or Flaubert' (35) – and by ordinary standards, there should seem a lot. But, on the whole, the book is a more measured and thoughtful effort than his previous work in cultural criticism, *In Bluebeard's Castle*. Included among its strengths are not only the lucidity of the analysis but also the willingness to front the embarrassment that holds forth in the academy with regard to questions about ultimate meaning, especially about the Deity. He is perfectly cognizant that ours is a time 'in which embarrassment terrorizes even the confident' and that the prevailing criticisms prefer to '"play it cool"' (RP, 178), avoiding those risks that might easily be confused with intellectual naiveté.[23] Steiner is not immune to these embarrassments, yet he thinks the question of meaning – i.e., of what we take, or do not take, to be the foundation of what we say and do – is of such extraordinary importance that it is worthwhile to put fears momentarily aside. Thus in *Real Presences*, Steiner proposes what only a neophyte or a *provocateur* would dare to suggest – that is, 'that any coherent understanding of what language is and how language performs, that any coherent account of the capacity of human speech to communicate meaning and feeling is, in the final analysis, underwritten by the assumption of God's presence' (RP, 3).

It is a daring thesis, and Steiner does not imagine it attracting many sympathetic readers among academicians. Towards the end, he says as much and offers a reason: 'I know that this formulation will be unacceptable not only to those who will read a book such as this, but also to the prevailing climate of thought and of feeling in our culture. It is just this unacceptability which characterizes what I have called a time of "epilogue," an immanence within the logic of the "afterword"' (RP, 228). By this, he means that in the present, after the lessons of Mallarmé, Stein, Joyce, and Derrida, our current paradigm of meaning is less transcendent than self-reflexive, of words calling forth other words calling forth other words, in an unending round robin of textuality. And it is not only words which are imagined as operating this way. Events, too, including the events of our lives, are mired in a history that moves nowhere except further into the recesses, or black holes, of contingency. There are stoics among us who are not threatened by such a paradigm, and who tend to pooh-pooh the expressed misgivings of those who are. There are others who, while less stoical, view matters as out of their hands, and who resign themselves to whatever scenario appears most aggressive and powerful. Forcefulness gets identified with things as they are, or as they are entropically predetermined to be. Steiner is cognizant of this, and knows that the scenario he offers may, to the present generation and its heirs, appear passé, or nostalgic, something better sloughed off like an old skin. If this happens, as it already is happening, then, believes Steiner, the whole nature of our thinking about aesthetics will change dramatically: 'It may well be that the forgetting of the question of God will be the nub of cultures now nascent. It may be that the verticalities of reference to "higher things," to the impalpable and mythical which are still incised in our grammars, which are still the ontological guarantors of the arcs of metaphor, will drain from speech ... Should these mutations of consciousness and expression come into force, the forms of aesthetic making as we have known them will no longer be productive' (RP, 230). It is almost a truism, something that those on both sides of the debate can agree on: our definition of aesthetics is crucially intertwined with the way we understand the meanings of meaning. Things get contestable only when we try to fill in the equation.

In the present climate, Steiner's conviction that all things, aesthetics included, lean either towards or away from an Absolute, the determinant of their worth, is almost quarrelsome. No matter, he thinks, for while it may be possible to imagine the universe as something like an unending, directionless flux, the fact that this scenario offers so little in the way of human consolation, so little to offset the blunt fact of death – not only our own but that of those nearest to us – almost forces us to imagine things otherwise. Steiner's devoutness is never less than tentative, yet he still thinks a Pascalian wager almost required. In *Real Presences* he writes that a 'wager on the meaning of meanings, on the potential insight and response when one human voice addresses another, when we come face to face with the text and the work of art or music, which is to say when we encounter the *other* in its condition of freedom, is a wager on transcendence' (4). The wager is that these interactions not only mean something (for contingency theory says nothing less), but that they are reflections of a larger meaning, underwriting and reinforcing them to the degree that they are truthful. The wager, then, predicates not only meaning but meaningfulness. Steiner writes: 'This wager – it is that of Descartes, of Kant and of every poet, artist, composer of whom we have explicit record – predicates the presence of a realness, of a "substantion" (the theological reach of this word is obvious) within language and form. It supposes a passage, beyond the fictive or the purely pragmatic, from meaning to meaningfulness. The conjecture is that "God" *is*, not because our grammar is outworn; but that grammar lives and generates because there is the wager on God' (RP, 4).

The reference to grammar has a Wittgensteinian ring to it, especially the Wittgenstein of the *Tractatus*, wherein the philosopher postulates an invisible form, or grammar, that conjoins representations and their objects: 'It is clear that however different from the real one an imagined world may be, it must have something – a form – in common with the real world' (35). Steiner believes this, believes that what we say and do – even our scepticisms and stoicisms – postulates a 'tenor of *trust*' (RP, 89) whereby we take for granted all sorts of benevolent facts about the world, including that of its logicalness and our ability to imitate this. Also included is our belief, affirmed each time we write or speak a sentence, that words, singular or networked, can refer (even with startling accuracy and beauty) to things beyond themselves, and thereby make sense to others. 'There would be no history as we know it, no religion, metaphysics, politics or aesthetics as we have lived them, without an initial act of trust, of confiding, more fundamental, more axiomatic by far than any "social contract" or covenant with the postulate of the divine. This instauration of trust, this entrance of man into the city of man, is that between word and world' (ibid.). To say otherwise only throws us into the paradox of the Cretan calling all Cretans liars, whereby we would have to imagine that while all claims to speak the truth of things are essentially specious, this one claim must be thought otherwise. It makes for a spissatus-like truth. It seems wiser, then, to grant (like Augustine, who believed, 'Not everything we make up is a lie') the 'Hebraic-Hellenic copula,' so syntactically crucial to the history of our thought and language, a continuing centrality (RP, 119). Here, Steiner argues that every time we join subject to predicate with the purpose of putting sense in a form recognizable to others, we also do something else: we affirm our belief in an equation that transcends the strict grammars of language and nature; we affirm our belief that the world holds together. Steiner quotes Derrida to the effect that '[t]he age of the sign is essentially theological' (ibid.), but whereas Derrida launches a revolt against this knowledge, Steiner wants to build on it: 'The archetypal paradigm of all affirmations of sense and of significant plenitude – the fullness of meaning – is a *Logos*-model' (ibid.). Things originate with the Logos. We do not call upon it so much as it calls upon us; it summons us. 'That which comes *to call on us* – that idiom ... connotes both spontaneous visitation and summons – will very often do so unbidden. Even where there is a readiness, as in the concert hall, in the museum, in the moment of chosen reading, the true entrance into us will not occur by an act of will' (RP, 179).

For Steiner, sacred and secular texts of the highest sort overlap. Distinguishing them both is the quality of summons, though one assumes it will be greater in Isaiah than in Henry James. In one sense, Steiner agrees with this; it is this agreement, as we saw in the Kermode chapter, that leads him to recoil from the whole premise of *The Literary Guide to the Bible*, with its implicit embarrassment regarding the claims that sacred texts, including the Hebrew and Christian Bibles, make: 'The separation, made in the name of current rationalism and agnosticism, between a theological-religious experiencing of Biblical texts and a literary one is radically factitious. It cannot work' ('The Good Books,' 97). In a second sense, however, he finds the distinction difficult to make, for it is precisely this imputation of summons that he believes characterizes art work at its most profound. 'The relations between the sacred and the legally or ethically prescriptive ("the worded") on the one hand, and the poetic or fictive on the other, have always been vexed. What matters is that literary invention should be regarded, be it with welcome or with mistrust ..., as one of the foundational triad. In the poem, in the prayer, in the law, the reach of words is made very nearly equivalent to the humanity of man' (RP, 189). Here, Steiner seeks to offer a definition of civilization, but even from this, it is clear that he imagines an unusual intimacy between the sacred and aesthetic. They both summon us to an experience thought to originate outside of not only ourselves but of our world. Or as Steiner, making more explicit the relation between the aesthetic and the theological, writes: 'The ascription of beauty to truth and to meaning is either a rhetorical flourish, or it is a piece of theology. It is a theology, explicit or suppressed, masked or avowed, substantive or imaged, which underwrites the presumption of creativity, of signification in our encounters with text, music, art. The meaning of meaning is a transcendent postulate. To read the poem responsibly ("respondingly"), to be answerable to form, is to wager on a reinsurance of sense' (RP, 216). The suggestion is that while not all texts reputed to be sacred

are so (i.e., command our full-fledged respect), not all aesthetic texts –
which make no overt claims of inspiration – need to be thought as existing outside the realm of the sacred. In the first instance, Steiner grants
that 'much in the Old Testament burns with tribal folly' and brutality
(SR, 69), while, in the second instance, he argues that art, when it
appears (in Joyce's words) 'grave and constant,' may well be thought of
as sacred, or at least religious:

> I am arguing that the 'gravity' and the 'constancy' are, finally, religious. As
> is the category of meaningfulness. They are religious in two main senses.
> The first is obvious. The *Oresteia, King Lear,* Dostoevsky's *The Devils* no less
> than the art of Giotto or the Passions of Bach, inquire into, dramatize, the
> relations of man and woman to the existence of the gods or of God. It is
> the Hebraic intuition that God is capable of all speech-acts except that of
> monologue which has generated our arts of reply, of questioning, and
> counter-creation. After the Book of Job and Euripides' *Bacchae*, there *had*
> to be, if man was to bear his being, the means of dialogue with God which
> are spelt out in our poetics, music, art.
>
>   The gravity and constancy at the heart of major forms and of our under-
> standing of them are religious in a second, more diffuse sense. They enact
> ... a root-impulse of the human spirit to explore the possibilities of mean-
> ing and of truth that lie outside empirical seizure or proof. (RP, 225)

Crucial to Steiner's grasp of the religious element in our texts, be they
sacred, judicial, or aesthetic, is the suggestion of dialogue. They begin in
response to a summons, to something larger than ourselves requiring us
to bend towards it, to give answer. The summons may, as in Scripture,
have the force of God's impress, or it may, as in the art of a Schoenberg,
Rothko, or Kieslowski, have a lesser force, more akin to intuition than
revelation. Yet, whether it be one or the other, a response appears called
for. This response may take the form of a respectful silence, the sought
advocated by Wittgenstein and often spoken of approvingly by Steiner:
'For the *Tractatus*, the truly "human" being, the man or woman most
open to the solicitations of the ethical and the spiritual, is he who keeps
silent before the essential' (RP, 103). Or the response may take the form
of the poet's or musician's most expressive articulation of what it means
to be human, what it means to be unhoused, to dwell apart from, and
largely ignorant of, the source of our being: 'Serious painting, music, literature or sculpture make palpable to us, as do no other means of communication, the unassuaged, unhoused instability and estrangement of

our condition' (RP, 139). In the latter instance, the artist's work can also function as a summon to others capable of responding to that which in the art transcends its own boundaries and somehow gives voice to the source of its inspiration. Thus it is that '[t]he encounter with the aesthetic is, together with certain modes of religious and of metaphysical experience, the most "ingressive," transformative summons available to human experiencing ... [T]he shorthand image is that of an Annunciation, of "a terrible beauty" or gravity breaking into the small house of our cautionary being' (RP, 143). At this level, art is both a response and an enticement to a response, implying a dialogic equation that makes our relation with the Creator more than simply a passive experience. William James, in *The Varieties of Religious Experience*, once wrote:

> The religious phenomenon, studied as an inner fact, and apart from ecclesiastical or theological complications, has shown itself to consist everywhere, and at all its stages, in the consciousness which individuals have of an intercourse between themselves and higher powers with which they feel themselves to be related. This intercourse is realized at the time as being both active and mutual. If it be not effective; if it be not a give and take relation; if nothing is really transacted while it lasts; if the world is in no whit different for its having taken place; then prayer, taken in this wide meaning of a sense that something is transacting, is of course a feeling of what is illusory, and religion must on the whole be classed, not simply as containing elements of delusion, – these undoubtedly everywhere exist, – but as being rooted in delusion altogether, just as materialists and atheists have always said it was. (465)

Steiner, I think, would agree. We pray and we make art because we anticipate a response. We imagine an Other, a Deity, whose investment in us is not unlike our return investment. We assume that the world's final shape is not predetermined and that we can make a difference. If this be not the case, then the purposes of religion and art (as conceived here) must appear terribly empty. But we – or many of us – proceed as if this is the case. We see this in the rabbi's unending dialogue with the sacred texts; and we see this in the artist's assumption of authorship, a model taking the Creator as its inspiration. 'I take the aesthetic act,' says Steiner, 'the conceiving and bringing into being of that which, very precisely, could not have been conceived or brought into being, to be an *imitatio*, a replication on its own scale, of the inaccessible first *fiat*' (RP, 201). The reasons for this imitation can be complicated. The motivation can be one of emulation, or it can be one of rivalry, of an attempt to provoke God, to make God step out from behind the plane of invisibility. In either case, the gesture postulates that we are not mere passive adjuncts to reality but that we can author our own responses: 'A *Logos*-aesthetic and hermeneutic is one of reference to authorship, to the potential of 'authority' contained within that word and concept. All *mimesis*, thematic variation, quotation, ascription of intended sense, derives from a postulate of creative presence' (RP, 101). Inherent in this postulate is the sense that our authored responses to the world, our answering to the Deity, entail the demands of responsibility, of answerability. Question and answer bespeak the same equation. 'There can be,' writes Steiner in *Heidegger*, 'no life-giving precision, no responsibility when question and answer do not relate, where they do not spring from a common ontological center' (31). The artist engages in a dialogue with the universe, and with the Author of this universe. And yet, whatever confidence the artist places in this dialogue, he or she cannot escape the fact that we dwell apart from the home of being and are unhoused: 'It is poetics, in the full sense, which informs us of the visitor's visa in place and in time which defines our status as transients in a house of being whose foundations, whose future history, whose rationale – if any – lie wholly outside our will and comprehension. It is the capacity of the arts, in a definition which must, I believe, be allowed to include the living forms of the speculative (what tenable vision of poetics will exclude Plato, Pascal, Nietzsche?), to make us, if not at home, at least alertly, answerably peregrine in the unhousedness of our human circumstance. Without the arts, form would remain unmet and strangeness without speech in the silence of the stone' (RP, 140).

For Steiner, men and women are unhoused, but often do not know it. The artist knows it, and this puts him or her in alliance with the rabbi or priest. They each seek to find the way home, be it through sacred texts, moral action, or aesthetic form. For the artist, it is mostly via the last of these that he or she works, attempting to seduce us into a recognition of what has been lost but might be recovered. The work will mean nothing for us, however, if we ourselves 'do not redefine, if we do not re-experience, the life of meaning in the text, in music, in art' (RP, 49–50). This life has nothing to do with newness or originality as more generally conceived; rather, it has to do with something like a return to first being. 'Originality' in art, says Steiner, 'is antithetical to novelty. The etymology of the word alerts us. It tells of "inception" and of "instauration," of a return, in substance and in form, to beginnings. In exact relation to their originality, to their spiritual-formal force of innovation, aesthetic inventions are "archaic." They carry in them the pulse of the distant source' (RP, 27). This is why art, at its most powerful, must be conceived as a form of anagnorisis, of recognition in its fullest and most transcendent sense: 'We must come to recognize, and the stress is on *re*-cognition, a meaningful which is that of a freedom of giving and of reception beyond the constraints of immanence' (RP, 49). This is the way towards homecoming, the way toward what Steiner, in 'Our Homeland, the Text,' refers to as the '"Israel" of truth-seeking' (19). This is not a physical place, not a state alongside the Mediterranean, but that *trópos* which signifies the place wherein all contradictions vanish, and the universal reigns. Of course, religions can and have pointed the way. Steiner credits Judaism for its invention of monotheism and the primacy its bestows upon the Book; and he probably would agree with Vermes when he credits Christianity, or better yet Jesus, for 'the underlying universalism' of his 'doctrine of *imitatio Dei*, a God whose providence includes all, and his primary concern for the individual, thus permitting an easier dispensation from the mostly communal and social aspects of the Law of Moses' (213).[24] But Steiner's religiosity feels ultimately uncomfortable when housed in doctrine. He cannot quite accept a Judaism that, in its orthodox manifestation, 'continues in its often jejune formalism, in its feverish atrophy in ritualistic minutiae,' that, in its Zionist manifestation, encourages the state of Israel's 'savagery and corruption,' and that, in its liberal manifestation, seems spiritually and metaphysically inert (TGD, 48). Nor can he accept a Christianity which, since the Shoah, is 'sick at heart' and 'lamed, possibly terminally, by the paradox of revelation and of doctrine which generated not only the Shoah but the millenia of anti-Jewish violence, humiliation and quarantine which are its obvious background' (TGD, 47). In the end, for Steiner, there can be 'no synagogue, no *ecclesia*, no *polis*, no nation, no ethnic community which is *not* worth *leaving*' (TT, 397). It is a melancholy conclusion, predicated on his belief that a nation, in time, will always act in an unacceptable manner, and that '[a] synagogue will one day excommunicate Spinoza, it must' (ibid.). It is better, he thinks, to place one's trust directly in the Absolute, and to distrust all those instances wherein two or more are gathered in the name of some cause, or Lord: 'Personally, I believe that anarchy is one of the ideals and hopes and utopias of anyone who wants to do serious thinking and work. It is when you find yourself agreeing with another person you should begin to suspect that you are talking nonsense. I repeat: there is no community of love, no family,

no interest, caste, profession, or social class not worth resigning from'
(TT, 397–8).

There is something too hubristic about Steiner's stance, about the suggestion that one's salvation is an individual matter, unrelated to the good
works and faithfulness of others. William James once noted that '[o]ur
faith is faith in someone else's faith, and in the greatest matters this is
most the case.' It is difficult to believe in anything, not to mention something invisible, without some form of concurrence. As is his wont,
Steiner prefers to go it alone, to conceive of the Deity as an abstraction
characterized as much by Its absence as by Its presence. This sense of
absence is heightened by the Shoah, when so many Jews experienced
'the dark of God's absence' (LS, 167). And while this emotion is, certainly, not to be discounted, there also seems something personal about
Steiner's stress on God's absence. Or maybe I am misreading him here;
and his stress on God's absence has more to do with the fact that there is
something almost archaic about the Hebrew Bible's God, making it easier to imagine Him in the past tense. Even before the Shoah, this God,
says Steiner, seemed notably absent. In *Bluebeard's Castle*, he writes, 'To all
but a very few the Mosaic God has been from the outset, even when passionately invoked, an immeasurable Absence, or a metaphor modulating
downward to the natural sphere of poetic, imagistic approximation'
(38). This is the way Steiner imagines Him: an unfathomable First Cause
and Principle of Perfection, almost more tellingly revealed in the work
of the greatest artists than of those more ostensibly religious. 'Above all,'
he writes in 'Language under Surveillance,' 'it is in art and literature
that the Messianic challenge, the potential of human ripening and deliverance, is enacted and transmitted across time' (36). Resistant to the
matrix of power, and working in isolation, the artist feels, as few others
do, 'responsible toward the claims and provocations of the ideal' (ibid.).
The demand on the artist is to acknowledge the Ideal, that place which
counts as home. In *Antigones*, Steiner speaks of the 'co-ordinates of
Idealism' as 'exile and attempted homecoming' (14). Until one completes the journey of becoming (which, by definition, never ends), a person exists as an exile from being. Mindful of this, the artist, more than
others, holds to the path. But as described by Steiner, it is a rather solitary adventure, not suitable for those of a social or non-intellectual temper. Thus, he praises Benjamin for withdrawing from life (R, 38) and
Lukács for making a homeland of the mind (MH, 67). And when Steiner
considers his own demise, he thinks that '[a] man need not be buried in
Israel. Highgate or Golders Green or the wind will do' (LS, 154).

In the interim, Steiner is increasingly drawn to music, thinking it an embodiment of the Ideal. 'Personally,' he writes in the 'Introduction' to his *Reader*, 'I find myself *needing* music more and more. The number of books one feels one *must* read diminishes; it is re-reading that matters. Music, on the contrary, grows indispensable, as if it had become the elect companion of identity, the homecoming to that inside oneself which time has in its keeping' (GSR, 18). It is a thought that he has expressed throughout his writings, though in the fullness of the claim, it also harks back to his statement, in *Bluebeard's Castle*, that music increasingly served him and those he knew as a substitute for a religion no longer thought tenable: 'one does know of a good many individual and familial existences in which the performance or enjoyment of music has functions as subtly indispensable, as exalting and consoling, as religious practices might have, or might have had formerly. It is this indispensability which strikes one, the feeling (which I share) that there is music one cannot do without for long, that certain pieces of music rather than, say, books, are the talisman of order and of trust inside oneself. In the absence or recession of religious belief, close-linked as it was to the classic primacy of language, music seems to gather, to harvest us to ourselves' (122).

The stance mistakenly conflates two things – religion and music – which, whatever their affinities, need, more importantly, to be understood as separate. If the consolations that music offers do not seem pale in comparison to those offered by this or that religion, then the religion must be weakly imagined. To return to James's suggestion, if the practice of religion changes nothing in the world, if everything is as it was found, and if there be no felt experience of real conversation between one-self, or -selves, and the Deity, then yes, music can be compared to religion, for the consolation that each offers, in this instance, is of a largely psychological, or therapeutic, nature; it is a consolation enwrapped in the individual's own estimation of self, and its 'harvest' may well be understood reflexively, as a homecoming 'to ourselves.' Steiner would, no doubt, resent this representation of his thinking, but his extolling of music to the point that it becomes something akin to an object of worship forces us to ask, if not to Whom, then to What are we answerable, and in exactly what way? In *Real Presences*, he writes that 'music puts our being as men and women in touch with that which transcends the sayable, which outstrips the analysable. Music is plainly uncircumscribed by the world as the latter is an object of scientific determination and practical harnessing. The meanings of the meaning of music transcend. It has long been, it continues to be, the unwritten theology of those who lack or reject any formal creed. Or to put it reciprocally: for many human beings, religion has been the music which they believe in' (218). It is an extraordinary rhetorical flight, but once it is over, what are we left with? Are we to worship music? mathematics? or the Abstraction that they imply? Steiner comes close to suggesting that we are to do just this. This view is implicit, for instance, in the praise bestowed upon the 'Jewish abstractionists,' by whom Steiner means Lukács, Bloch, Benjamin, Adorno, Marcuse, Wittgenstein, and others. In an essay on Lukács, he writes: 'Unhoused, peregrine, domestic in ostracism, he is one of that tragic constellation – Ernst Bloch, Walter Benjamin, Adorno, Herbert Marcuse – of Jewish abstractionists, possessed by a messianic rage for logic, for systematic order in the social condition of man. Lukács's Marxism is, in essence, a refusal of the world's incoherence, of the murderous stupidities whereby men and women misconduct their lives. Like the other Jewish self-exiles whose radicalism out of Central Europe has so incisively marked the century, Lukács is an heir in immanence to the transcendent absolute of Spinoza' (MH, 67). And it is implicit in his monkish, but not monkish, fantasy about a temperate clime, distant from the 'hellish' world, where one can indulge in the pursuit of abstraction for its own sake:

> It is perfectly conceivable that there is a small strip on the world's map (this was Herodotus's view, also Thucydides,' also Plato's) where the climate is more or less bearable, temperate, where there is enough protein to eat, where there are *slaves* – that is, subject peoples who allow you to get on with the business of thinking, which means that you can spend your day doing something fantastic, like examining the geometry of conic sections (which is what Archimedes dies for), that you can do this quite insane and obsessive thing – to give your life to abstraction, to a speculation, to pure mathematics. Perhaps there is one part of the earth that produces complex theorems, algebraic theorems, of a very involved and difficult and totally useless nature, that produces not religious faith but that immense luxury we call metaphysical speculative systems. (TT, 396)

This happy 'strip' where abstraction is indulged appears more a temptation than an answer. Throughout his career, Steiner has reminded us of abstraction's cost, of how the cry that originates in a novel is often experienced as more moving than that which originates in the next street, not to mention among the world's poor. And in the passage just quoted, Steiner ends by saying that '[c]limatically, foodwise, survival-wise, this is not open to everyone' (TT, 396). Yet the temptation has always been an especially seductive one for Steiner, and it colours what he has to say about 'real presences' underwriting the text. He makes reference to God often enough, but it is a God lacking in warmth and other, decidedly anthropomorphic, characteristics that we like to attribute to 'Him': caring, mercy, justice, and so forth. Instead, Steiner's God easily slips into the dress of abstraction, identified in terms – e.g., Being, Logos, Presence – more likely to warm the hearts of philosophers than ordinary men and women seeking something, or rather Someone, to place their trust in. Steiner's critics have noted this. Robert P. Carroll, referring to *Real Presences* (where 'the question of God [is addressed] more fully than in anything else' Steiner has written), says that its God is likeable to '"transcendence," that is, the undefined, unknown God, rather than the overdetermined, overdefined God of traditional Jewish religion and Christian ecclesiastical creeds' (RGS, 266). And Harold Fromm, taking a harsher view, says that 'his God is not really God, his transcendence has no literal characteristics he can clearly name apart from his own feelings, his religion has no tenets or contents' (review, *Georgian Review*, 402). Somewhat along this line, Wendy Steiner writes that '[i]f truth be told, ... Steiner seems closest to Protestant fundamen-talism. Down with the priestly caste of expositors who stand between the populace and art: only direct communion with aesthetic presence will do' ('Silence,' 11). Finally, Graham Ward notes that Steiner's 'ontology of reading is described in distinctly Catholic (Heidegger's theological background) terms: "transubstantial," "real presence," "sacramental," "incarnation," "icon," and "revelation"'; but that much is also unre-solved for the reason that 'he is attempting to interlace a sociology and an ontology of literature' (RGS, 192). In short, says Ward, Steiner 'wants a synthesis of the ontic and the ontological, and it is all too easy to cre-ate the synthesis by being "eloquent of God"' (ibid.).

Steiner invokes the terms of theology, but in the end he is really drawn to other things – to literature, music, philosophy, rhetoric, and the Shoah. But his work is also about longing, and this is what most truly justifies our thinking of him as a religious thinker. That is, what I find especially attractive about Steiner's work here is just how emotionally involved he is in wanting the world to make sense, to hold together. It is true that this is not necessarily a religious project, but the asking of such questions is at the heart of theology, especially a theology (Steiner's Judaism) that thinks the asking of questions one of the most valuable things we can do. Steiner has, meanwhile, suggested that Judaism is itself a-theological, that its textuality makes its ill at ease with the construction of answers that are inherently a-historical. In 'The Long Life of Metaphor,' he writes that 'the very notion of "theology," in the post-Pauline, post-Johannine, and post-Augustinian sense, has no real counterpart in Jewish religious feeling. The most authentic and lasting strength in Jewish sensibility is not a reflection or metaphysical discourse on the nature and attributes of God, but a "living in His presence"' (55). Again, for Steiner, Judaism's relation to God is thought more dialogic, and Christianity's more duty bound. It is a difficult antithesis to maintain, dismissing (among other things) the importance of the Torah for the observant Jew and the importance of prayer for the observant Christian. It is better to admit the importance of questioning to both religions, something that Steiner, in effect, does when, in 'Anglican Inadequacies,' he approvingly quotes the Protestant theologian Donald MacKinnon: 'If Christianity survives it will be in part at least because the lonely figure, dying in agony upon the cross, crying out in dereliction to the Father, whom he believes to have forsaken him, remains ceaselessly interrogating men and women, outside as much as within the Christian churches, concerning his significance and that of his supreme hour. "What think you of this man?"' (1238). In truth, Steiner has, as Robert Carroll points out, always combined a 'knowledge of things Jewish with a sensitivity to things Christian' (RGS, 269), and it is this, rather than what Ward describes as an inexplicable 'Christocentric' imagery, that best explains the beautiful closing passage in *Real Presences*: 'But ours is the long day's journey of the Saturday. Between suffering, aloneness, unutterable waste on the one hand and the dream of liberation, of rebirth on the other. In the face of the torture of a child, of the death of love which is Friday, even the greatest art and poetry are almost helpless. In the Utopia of the Sunday, the aesthetic will, presumably, no longer have logic or necessity. The apprehensions and figurations in the play of metaphysical imagining, in the poem and the music, which tell of pain and hope, of the flesh which is said to taste of ash and of the spirit which is said to have the savour of fire, are always Sabbatarian. They have risen out of an immensity of waiting which is that of man. Without them, how could we be patient?' (232).

True, Steiner employs an Easter allegory, but he also intersects it with the Jewish Sabbath, and it is the Sabbath – the Saturday characterized by waiting for the 'Utopia of Sunday' (the release day from history's bondage), as well as the art and music composed in this period – that is the reality in place: 'ours is the long day's journey of the Saturday.' The image might be critiqued for the way it sets Judaism and Christianity in opposition, but it also quite beautifully yokes them together. In doing so, it also calls forth all Steiner's own longings and doubts, which need not be thought of as a-theological, and are not thought of so here.

The Theory Debates

Steiner subtitled his first book, *Tolstoy or Dostoevsky*, 'An Essay in the Old Criticism.' The subtitle signalled his displeasure with New Criticism, and offered as an alternative a criticism more willing to range beyond the strict confines of a text's boundaries. The New Criticism, he thought, was particularly inapplicable to such novelists as Tolstoy and Dostoevsky, whose 'religious, moral and philosophic preoccupations' could only be slighted by a methodology that restricted its attention to image patterns and themes. Steiner wrote that New Criticism's 'concentration on the single image or cluster of language, its bias against extrinsic and biographical evidence, its preference for the poetic over the prosaic forms, are out of tune with the governing qualities of Tolstoyan and Dostoevskyan fiction. Hence the need for an "old criticism" equipped with the wide-ranging civilization of an Arnold, a Sainte-Beuve, and a Bradley' (TD, 58). It was a characteristic gesture, given Steiner's penchant for going his own way. On the one hand, he demonstrated a keen sense of New Criticism's weaknesses; on the other, he demonstrated a chariness respecting the criticism's contribution to literary studies. What was so provocative about the New Criticism was its demand that the reader attend as much to the particulars of a text as to its circumference. It assumed that if an author worked hard on getting the details right, then the reader should reciprocate the effort by giving attention to what had been done. In this sense, it was a criticism remarkably generous towards authors, for it paid them the compliment of taking their work so seriously that the reader was willing to renounce his or her own preoccupations. Now, forty-plus years later, we are well schooled in the failings of New Criticism, and we know, for instance, that readers' values are not insignificant to interpretation and that we make a mistake to divorce texts from contexts. Yet knowing this should not make us think that we have no other choice but to dismiss New Criticism, for its insights are not all suspect and much of the work remains remarkably valuable, even a tonic to our own criticism, which has become almost indifferent to the values that distinguish literature, as aesthetically conceived, from other disciplines. Nor do I find that Steiner's rejection of New Criticism makes *Tolstoy or Dostoevsky* a necessarily better book than it might have been had he borrowed some of the criticism's precepts. The book is too impressionistic, too much an articulation of Steiner's own sense of the tragic. To this reader, Caryl Emerson's criticisms of *Tolstoy or Dostoevsky* ring true, as when she writes that 'aspects of Tolstoyan aesthetics that do not fit the Homeric model (Tolstoy's rejection of heroism, for example) Steiner does not hide, but he also does not elaborate. Well he might not, because to a very large extent Tolstoy's militant antiheroicism is what makes the Tolstoyan novel what it is' (RGS, 92). And when she writes, more broadly, that '[w]hat is missing ... from this earnest postscript in redemptive reading is any serious attempt on Steiner's part to respect or, better, to understand from within, Tolstoy's own world view' (RGS, 89). In *Tolstoy or Dostoevsky*, Steiner's love for truth in general too often rides roughshod over truth in the particular, an affective imbalance that might have been cured by a dose of the New Critical medicine.

I begin this last section with reference to Steiner's early rejection of New Critical practices because it strikes me as a precursor to his more recent rejections of contemporary theory. His dismissal of New Criticism and of theory seem of a piece. For instance, the characterization of New Criticism as marred by academicism, 'jargon,' and 'shimmering technical obscurities' (LS, 324, 224) anticipates the characterization of contemporary theory as marred by 'narrow' academicism, 'repulsive jargon,' and 'contrived obscurantism and specious pretensions to technicality' (RGS, 278; RP, 116).[25] In each instance, Steiner allows overreaching generalizations and invective to get the better of him, and this, in turn, allows a critic such as Said, in 'Himself Observed,' to dismiss his 'Marxist and deconstructionist criticism' as evidencing an 'embarrassing ... ignorance of recent work in those fields' (244). Said's comments evince their own characteristic harshness. But it is true that while Steiner has an enviable knack for discerning a thing's essence, he is not one to get bogged down in points of fact or in theoretical shadings. From Steiner, a reader learns only as much about Marxism or deconstruction as a shorthand discussion will allow. This sort of discussion is not necessarily without value. But if a reader expects Steiner to substantiate his more caustic charges against theoretically minded critics, he or she will be disappointed. True, Steiner refers occasionally to those critics (e.g., Blackmur, Richards, Derrida, de Man, Barthes, Lacan) most identified with this school or that, but these references, as must be the case, always balance praise with critique. However, the less well-known critic receives little, if any, mention. For Steiner, this person is mostly a caricature, a ghost in the machine, reducible to the generic nomination of 'structuralist,' 'post-structuralist,' or some third or fourth type. We see this, for example, when he (rather like Kermode in this respect) haughtily dismisses the bulk of academic work as 'trivial' and moribund: 'The mushrooming of semantic-critical jargon, the disputations between structuralists, post-structuralists, meta-structuralist and deconstructionists, the attention accorded both in the academy and the media to theoreticians and publicists of the aesthetic – all these carry within their bustling pretence the germs of more or less rapid decay' (RP, 48). For Steiner, criticism, like literature, is a game which only three or four can play. The critic's function, we are told in *Tolstoy or Dostoevsky*, 'is to distinguish not between the good and the bad, but between the good and the best' (4). Steiner's view, in the interim, has not changed a jot.

Steiner makes his most all-embracing criticism of contemporary theory first in his brief 1983 contribution to the *New Literary History*-sponsored symposium, 'Literary Theory in the University,' and then in *Real Presences*. The gist of his criticism is that the term 'theory' has been misappropriated from the sciences, wherein, since the seventeenth century, it has had a specific meaning: the proposing of a hypothesis verifiable by subsequent material experimentation. 'It is only in the latter half of the sixteenth century that "theory" and the "theoretical" take on their modern guise. And it is not before the 1640s, it would seem, that a "theorist" is one who devises and entertains speculative hypotheses' (RP, 69). The definition still holds good for Steiner, and he resents what he views as a mistranslation, whereby humanists, wishing to obtain respect for their work, have stolen a term, only to devalue it. In *Real Presences*, he writes, 'the extension of this imperial model to the interpretation and judgement of literature, music and the arts, is factitious. Here the concept of theory and the theoretical, in any responsible sense, is either a self-flattering delusion or a misappropriation from the domain of the sciences. It represents a basic confusion, an "error of categories" as it is called in classical logic and metaphysics. To invoke and put forward a "theory of criticism," a "theoretical poetics and hermeneutic" in reference to the signifying forms of the textual and aesthetic, in anything but the most scrupulously avowed metaphorical or mimetic sense, is to "translate," to "be translated" in the suspect, profoundly comical mode in which Bottom is "translated" in *A Midsummer Night's Dream*' (72).[26]

For Steiner, the sciences and the humanities are not only separate disciplines, but they also invoke separate, and virtually antithetical, methodologies. The scientist looks to the future, the humanist to the past. The scientist seeks to surpass, or vitiate, the achievements of the past; the humanist returns to past achievements, knowing that while they – as in the instance of Shakespeare – can be imitated or, more perversely, decried, they cannot be said, in any logical sense, to be subject to improvement. They are what they are; and the history of literature is not a fit field for the technologist. In *Bluebeard's Castle*, Steiner first offers a sentiment that he often comes back to, that 'even if a Rembrandt or a Mozart may, in future, be equaled (itself a gross, indistinct notion), they cannot be surpassed. There is a profound logic of sequent energy in the arts, but not an additive progress in the sense of the sciences. No errors are corrected or theorems disproved. Because it carries the past within it, language, unlike mathematics, draws backward. This is the meaning of Eurydice. Because the realness of his inward world lies at his back, the man of words, the singer, will turn back, to the place of necessary beloved shadows. For the scientist time and light lie before' (134–5). It seems true. Methodologically, scientists and humanists work differently.

Still, we might ask whether or not the humanist can adopt a term – even one that goes to the heart of what makes science science – and convert it to his or her discipline's own purposes. This has certainly happened, so that while some critics may use the term 'theory' as a scientist might, most do not. Instead, most critics interested in 'theory' use the term to highlight anti-foundational notions of interpretation. Sceptical of objective determinations, these critics wish to announce from what angle, or theory, their own judgments begin. Theory here speaks not of hypothesis and testing, but of pre-conceived principles used to guide the critic in the reading of texts. As such, the term's meaning has been clearly altered, a situation that we can either accept or reject. If we accept it, it is incumbent upon us to clarify our new meanings. If we reject it, our explanatory obligations are significantly reduced. Yet the rejectionist should be mindful of what new claims are being made, as opposed to rejecting such out of hand. Steiner's own record this way tends to be mixed. He is not unmindful of what contemporary theorists are up to, but he does not convince one that he has truly spent time with that which he is so ready to castigate, or that his dismissal of theory for reasons of nomenclature is as sinking a blow as he imagines:

> However abstract, the explicative and the judgemental discourse about the text, the statue, the symphony, do not empower us to invoke the concepts of 'theory,' of the 'theoretical,' as these are used, fundamentally, in the

exact and the applied sciences (music being, evidently, the complex and intermediary case). Those who proclaim and apply to poetic works a 'theory of criticism,' a 'theoretical hermeneutic' are, today, the masters of the academy and the exemplars in the high gossip of arts and letters. Indeed, they have clarioned 'the triumph of the theoretical.' They are, in truth, either deceiving themselves or purloining from the immense prestige and confidence of science and technology an instrument ontologically inapplicable to their own material. They would enclose water in a sieve. (RP, 75)[27]

Steiner proposes that rather than using the term 'theory,' critics employ the term 'narrative': 'Where it is not arrogant pretense or mere impatience, what passes, quite falsely, for "theory" in the humanities is, in fact, narrative, a storytelling of ideas' (RGS, 280). Such a term would make clear the degree to which the critics' presuppositions are, in fact, constructed. Of course, most critics would not think it a failing to acknowledge the constructedness of their work, even as they aspire, like scientists, to get at the truth of things. But in the present instance, given the source of the suggestion, one might anticipate some rankling. The reason is that while Steiner is a humanist critic, his presuppositions are in keeping with those of the Popperian celebration of theory wedded to fact – of a science propelled by imaginative genius but always needing to verify its claim in the realm of the concrete. He speaks of the pressure the 'Cartesian-Kantian paradigm' has been under, as the notion of 'indeterminacy' 'has put in doubt the deterministic classical conditions of proof, of experimental verification' (RP, 70). But mostly, Steiner views indeterminacy as a problem affecting only a small portion of scientific work, for example, 'atomic and sub-atomic interactions' (ibid.). Meanwhile, '[p]hysics, molecular biology, astrophysics proceed as if the Cartesian-Kantian contract between theory and trial (the "falsifiability criterion" of Karl Popper) continued to be valid and universal' (RP, 71). In this contract, theory and fact reside in the camp of science, and myth and narrative in the camp of the humanities. Yet, to consign things this way is not only to divvy knowledge into workable subdivisions, it is also to prioritize it in a way detrimental to non-scientists. Steiner surely knows this, but his own sense of the factual, and its palpability, is great enough that he is willing to grant science its more cherished notions about its priority and sovereignty: 'The history of modern science and technology demonstrates blindingly (consider our colonized planet) that mensuration, the *tempora spatiis mensura mundae* of Bacon, of Descartes and the aeroplane designer, works. Theory applies' (RP, 72).

I do not wish to disparage science, or to question its unique attentiveness to the realm of fact. Science's achievements have been so often
astonishing that to refuse this acknowledgment can only invite charges
of obstinacy. This said, there remains good reason for not wishing to
beat down the accomplishments of contemporary theory with the stick
of science. There also remains good reason for not wishing to see critics
too fully emulate classical science, with its confident assumptions about
objectivity and truth value. Truth, when housed in human institutions
and experience, is a much more refractory thing than when housed in
stones and stars. Steiner knows this, proof of which is in the credence
that he gives to the concepts of mystery and incarnated being. Nevertheless, there is much in Steiner's theory of criticism that does borrow from
the methodology of science. This is most apparent in the 1979 essay
'"Critic"/ "Reader,"' his most vigorous attempt to provide an alternative
to the newer critical practices. A masterful essay, '"Critic"/ "Reader"'
evinces a rather careful and discriminating attention to the details of
argument that one would like to see more of from Steiner. The prose
stays close to the ground for long stretches at a time and only begins to
take flight, at the end of each section, once the author is convinced that
he has made his case. In a sense, Steiner's strength – a rich, rhetorical,
self-conscious prose – is also, at times, his weakness, for the critic, knowing that he can charm and persuade (or, in his least attractive mood,
browbeat) an audience, sometimes appears less responsible to eviden-
tiary details and the logic of cause and effect. In '"Critic"/ "Reader,"'
things are generally otherwise; and Steiner makes a concerted effort to
justify a criticism that, one, has a strong sense of truth value and, two,
equates art of the highest achievement with incarnation. In the first
instance, Steiner forcefully argues the importance of clarity, disinterest,
epistemology, perspective, and 'ordering sight.' These are classical values, the sort identified with Foucault's own classical episteme, wherein
sight is afforded 'an almost exclusive privilege, being the sense by which
we perceive extent and establish proof, and, in consequence, the means
to an analysis *partes extra partes* acceptable to everyone' (133). They are,
as such, values that have come under serious scrutiny, and while it is
doubtful that they can ever manifest the authority that they once did,
they remain attractive. As for instance, when Steiner writes: 'To "criticize" means to perceive at a distance, at the order of remove most
appropriate to clarity, to *placement* (F.R. Leavis's term), to communicate
intelligibility. The motion of criticism is one of "stepping back from" in
exactly the same sense in which one steps back from a painting on a wall

in order to perceive it better' (GSR, 68). Perspective here represents more the matter of getting the art object into proper focus than the relativization of judgment. Steiner speaks of the need for the critic to be aware of one's position vis-à-vis the object, but this need is subject to another need: to see one's criticism as part of an epistemological understanding. The critic, says Steiner, 'details his recessional steps so as to make the resultant distance, the elucidative measure, the prescriptive perspective – distance entails "angle" of vision – explicit, responsible, and, therefore, open to argument. It is this activation of distance between critic and object (the "text" from which he is stepping back ...) that makes all serious criticism epistemological' (ibid.).

For Steiner, criticism entails elements both of apprehension and intentionality. In the first instance, he writes that the critic is 'an activist of apprehension'; in the second, he quotes Husserl to the effect that '"to perceive" at all is "to intend"' (GSR, 69). From this, it follows that '*criticism is ordering sight,*' by which Steiner means that '[t]he act of critical viewing takes place in, it delimits and externalizes for argument, an intentional distance from the object' (ibid.). It aims not only to see but also to judge things clearly, for the two activities are closely allied: 'when we say "ordering sight," when we say "placement," when we say *critique,* we say "judgement"' (GSR, 70). The judgment is intentional, directed towards '"this painting," "that piece of music, 'this text'"' (ibid.). It also entails a ranking of these objects, so that it becomes possible to say that *this* painting is better than *that* painting. It is understood that such ranking is 'preferential and discriminatory' (GSR, 73), though Steiner's imperiousness makes this caveat seem grudging. Thus when speaking of the critic's syllabus, Steiner explains that its rationale is that 'of purgation' wherein 'vital space is cleansed and converted for the "enduring," for the "authentic," for the "classical"' (GSR, 74). Presumably, the 'august broker' knows the 'authentic' when he or she sees it (GSR, 73), but for many, the debate extends beyond the reach of the strictly aesthetic and becomes a debate over other matters – e.g., class, gender, ethnicity – as well. But it is precisely these things that are occluded in Steiner's scheme of criticism. Steiner writes that '[r]ecent emphasis by Marxist, sociologist, or semiotic critics on the economic structures of all "textuality" – texts are manufactured, they compete for attention in the market, they are objects of merchandising and accumulation – only dramatize an obvious constant' (GSR, 76). To say so – to reduce all such factors to a unity, a constant – is, in effect, to deny their importance. It reminds us that, here as elsewhere, we need to be as attentive to what the criticism hides as to what it makes visible. Steiner's criticism would hide, or downplay, the values that the critic brings to the scene. These values can be many, and they might even affront the 'taste' of the critic fronted towards the object-in-itself, for the reason that they speak of interests that are deemed, almost categorically, to be extra-aesthetic. In '"Critic"/"Reader,"' Steiner does think of the critic's task as something like this, as fronted towards the object-in-itself, where anything that distracts from the penetrative, telescopic vision of the thing is an impertinence. The critic, he says, 'argues distance in order to penetrate. He widens or narrows the aperture of vision so as to obtain a lucid grasp' (GSR, 69). One might think that Steiner's own history of conflating aesthetic judgment with philosophical and religious interests would make him more receptive to those critics who foreground their own interests; but instead, he argues the view that the 'correct' determination of the aesthetic object transcends this or that bias. 'The point I am putting forward is not the suspect commonplace whereby there are supposed to be no value free, no rigorously neutral perceptions – "suspect" because it is, at least, arguable that one's perception of the correct solution of an equation is not, except in some quasi-mystical sense, a value judgement' (ibid.).

Crucial to Steiner's understanding of the critic, in '"Critic"/ "Reader,"' is the conviction that he or she comes *after*. The art object has priority; it is there, present, before the critic arrives. The critic is not a maker, but a witness; whatever he or she says about the object will perforce seem derivative: 'All criticism is posterior, and this sequent status is not only temporal but existential. The work of art, the text, the musical composition exists not only prior to the ordering sight of the critic; it can exist without it' (GSR, 80). The view is attractively commonsensical, but it plays down the fact that the aesthetic object is not the first link in a chain, and that we might even find, among the things to which it responds, an earlier critic's text. How many poems have been written mindful of Aristotle's *Poetics*, Wordsworth's 'Preface to the *Lyrical Ballads*,' Pound's 'A Few Don'ts for an Imagist,' or Charles Bernstein's critical writings on behalf of language poetry? Quite a few, I imagine. Are these not, then, examples of artists responding to the work not only of prior artists but also of prior critics? Steiner thinks not; rather, he sees such critical statements more in relation to what came before than what came after: 'The Sophoclean versions of Oedipus are prior to the *Poetics*; the *Lyrical Ballads* come before the brilliancies of Coleridge's "practical criticism" in which so much of the modern technique of vision is rooted; Marvell's poems long antedate T.S. Eliot's insights' (ibid.). It is a selective history, but the point is obvious: for Steiner, the critic's stature is subordinate to that of the artist: 'This existential posteriority, this dependence of the perceptual and normative act on the prior and autonomous nature of the object, signifies that all criticism is, ontologically, *parasitic.* The Platonic paradigm makes graphic the degree of derivation. The carpenter imitates the Idea of the table. The painter mimes this mimesis whose literal form he can neither execute nor judge properly. The critic of the painting expatiates at fourth hand on the mimicry of a shadow. But even in any less caustic model of the orders of executive action and perception, the dependent, ancillary, occasional – because "occasioned from outside" – nature of all critical vision and utterance is manifest. *The critic is not the maker'* (GSR, 81).

It is difficult to know how to respond to this declaration, for while it would be easy to think of exceptions to Steiner's claim (e.g., Whitman's response to Emerson; Eliot's response to Symons; Mark Tansey's response to post-structuralism), the claim is offered in such an aggressive, polemical manner that it forbids contestation. Certainly, there is plenty of current criticism that examines the way in which the strong reader plays a performative role much like that of the artist. Derrida, for example, writes that 'when I read a sentence from a given text in a seminar (a statement of Socrates, a fragment of *Das Kapital* or *Finnegans Wake,* a paragraph of *The Conflict of Faculties*) I do not merely fulfill an already existing contract; I am also writing, or preparing for signature, a new contract with the institution, between the institution and the dominant forces of society.'[28] Writing here provokes reading, and reading writing. So much does Steiner himself acknowledge, for it his own contention that a novelist creates first by reading those who came before, to the point that an act of reading becomes the impetus for an act of writing. James reads *Middlemarch,* and then he writes *The Portrait of a Lady.* Is the James novel art or criticism? In *Real Presences,* Steiner contends that it is both, and that the artist's work is, in fact, the truest form of criticism. He also argues, taking his lead from Borges, that in a relation such as that between the Eliot and James novels, we can speak of a certain reversal in chronology, wherein we begin to understand the prior novel through the offices of the latter: 'We learn to read *Middlemarch* in the probing light of James's treatment; we then return to *The Portrait of a Lady* and come to recognize the transformative inflections of its source' (RP, 14). Here, Steiner says nothing that a deconstructionist critic would challenge. What this critic would challenge, however, is the claim that there is a categorical distinction between Derrida's rewriting of *Finnegans Wake* and James's rewriting of *Middlemarch*. About the latter, Steiner writes, '[t]hese inflections are not parasitical as in the case of purely critical, pedagogical commentary and verdict' (ibid.). The word 'purely' begs the question in favour of the distinction, but it cannot hide the fact that Steiner wants to erect a wall where a friendly border crossing would do. Naturally, it is one thing to argue that the ordinary teacher-critic is not a 'maker' and another thing to argue that Derrida is not. Even Steiner is prepared to admit, for instance, that '[t]he relevant sections in Coleridge's *Biographia Literaria* are "literature" in a sense not drastically removed from that which we attach to the poetry they analyse and judge' (GSR, 82). He also admits that we would not wish to throw away Vasari's writings even though many of the paintings and statues that he wrote about have not survived; and, finally, he admits that few would rather read the minor poets who make it into *The Lives of the English Poets* than what Johnson has to say about them. But for Steiner, these are rare instances, the consequence of 'accidental' and 'involuntary' circumstances 'outside the critic's purpose and control' (GSR, 83). They may be such, but they do undermine the notion that criticism is a necessarily inferior thing to painting or poetry. Nor is the argument helped by Steiner's allusion to Roland Barthes, accompanied by the suggestion that the French critic's attention to minor aesthetic artifacts – 'an inferior Balzac novella, the rhapsodies of Lautréamont, a *kitsch* film' (ibid.) – is motivated by a jealousy: 'Subconsciously, perhaps, it [the criticism] seeks compensation, even vengeance for its own parasitism on the object which is, eternally, its precedent and cause of being' (ibid.). That criticism, like art, might mix elements that are connoted as secondary (e.g., its aboutness) with those connoted as primary (e.g., freshness and vitality of language) is an all but suppressed understanding, even as Steiner, himself a critic, has an interest in seeing the work that critics do receives its fair share of recognition.

That critics are as interested in creating as in honouring is, in fact, the underside of Steiner's contention that '[i]mplicit in all criticism ... is the instinct for autonomy' (GSR, 81). He argues that the critic is always pulling away from the aesthetic object, no matter what the initial intention. There is, thinks Steiner, a competitive, even agonistic, relation between critic and artist. This leads him to say that 'the absolutely central fact' of criticism is that it is '"adversative to" its object,' and to add that 'criticism stands not only "outside" and "after" its cause: it stands "against" it' (GSR, 81). The critic not only makes something over but also makes something new. He or she offers, says Steiner, 'a *counter-statement* to' the object (ibid.), seeking to borrow its creative energy. The scenario evokes less an image of Platonic simulacra than of post-structuralism's *différance*, as one thing becomes generative of a second, and that of a third, and so forth. It is not a comparison that Steiner might welcome, for like Plato, he believes that origin is essential. Or if he should welcome the comparison, it is because he is, ironically, not a fan of critics, and views this counter-statement on par with the post-structuralist's obscuring the hierarchical distinction between artist and critic. Here, Steiner views the critic's relation to the aesthetic object as less honouring than appropriating, even ingesting: 'The act of criticism has "ingested" its object, and now stands autonomous' (ibid.). The situation has always been latent in criticism, even as instances in recent times appear to loom large. It is what leads Steiner to conceive of the critic less as 'a failed artist' than as a 'rival,' even a 'counterstater' (GSR, 82).

For Steiner, the problem with critics is that they let their distance from the aesthetic object undermine their primary responsibility. At first they go tethered, but soon they begin to imagine that they can propel themselves in new directions, away from the source of inspiration. At this point, they relinquish their obligation to the text, forgetting that it is in the text that being is most fully housed and present. When this happens, they fail not only in their capacity as critics, but also in their capacity as readers, the more esteemed activity. That is, criticism for Steiner is a weak form of reading; it is a putting distance between oneself and the text when distance is least wanted. In contrast, reading speaks of the effort to defeat distance, to bring oneself into as co-present a relation to the text as possible. Criticism speaks of the desire to master the text, reading the desire to be servant to it (GSR, 95). The critic's relation to the text is wilful, egotistical; the reader's relation is neither. Rather, the reader seeks to let the text speak through him or her, to be its transmitter rather than its transmuter. This explains why memorization is so valued by Steiner, for its relation to the text is the least adversarial and the most faithful, even loving: 'At its most primary and most radical level, the thorough act of reading, the full apprehension of the *présences transcendantes* in language and music, entails memorization. The act of learning *by heart* – an idiom of notable precision – is no technical auxiliary or carry-over from liturgical and pedagogical practice. It is of the essence of the reader's attempt to abolish or sublate that very distance which the critic stakes out. To memorize is, simultaneously, to enter into the text and to be entered into by the text' (GSR, 88). A reader values apprehension over comprehension, guardianship over salesmanship. The relation to the text is not loud and public, but quiet and private, bespeaking the most profound respect and admiration:

> The reader is *servant* to the text. The genuine reader, textual editor, scribe are called to a clerisy of service. The text finds out its condign reader. Often he would resist its peremptory ingress, even as the prophet seeks to shut his teeth against the imperatives of his calling (Jonah was a 'reader'). The reader's acceptance of the canon comports a trusteeship, mute and private except in those practices of collaborative reiteration, commitment to memory, and heuristic commentary mentioned above. But whether singular or participatory, unspoken or communicated, the reader is 'in service' to the text. Roy Campbell recounts how the back of his spirit and the back of his body were bent when the text of St John of the Cross 'leapt upon him' from fortunate ambush. He became, as every true reader must become, a shepherd to the being of the text, a doorkeeper at the always opened gates to meaning. (GSR, 95)

Steiner's hierarchy depends on there being something very special, even sacred, about aesthetic texts. If otherwise, it would make little sense to postulate a relation of obligation wherein the lines of force run so much in one direction, back to the originating object. But Steiner (like both Donoghue and Kermode) does imagine aesthetic texts as unique and perhaps sacred, even as he grants that the proximate relation between the aesthetic and the religious is historically contingent. Steiner's view here does not require that one think that all other articulations of experience (e.g., business, politics, science) are entirely indifferent to, or inexpressive of, the meanings of meaning; it does, however, require that one think that the artist, like the religious, makes a concerted effort to hear an unheard music. The view has, of late, come under considerable attack, yet it has a long and estimable tradition and should not be dismissed out of hand. It is the same imagining that Shakespeare, via Lorenzo, gives voice to in *The Merchant of Venice*, when Jessica is urged to make herself present to a celestial music ('There's not the smallest orb which thou behold'st / But in his motion like an angel sings, / Still quiring to the young-ey'd cherubins; / Such harmony is in immortal souls, / But whilst this muddy vesture of decay / Doth grossly close it in, we cannot hear it'). And it is same imagining that urges us to view the world as something larger than human history, linguistics, and politics, and thus commanding our attention and respect. It is, then, because the artist has historically had an ear cocked to hear the world's 'sweet music' that Steiner thinks of art as a superior form of understanding, attentive to transcendence. The reader, meanwhile, is not the artist, but seeks to learn from the artist, and is likewise motivated by, and desirous of, 'a contract with the transcendent' (GSR, 95). 'In the final analysis,' writes Steiner, 'the reader has subscribed to a contract of implicit presence. He must "enact as if" the letter is the vessel, however opaque, however fragmented, of the spirit. He must venture a Pascalian wager on the iconic potential of the work' (ibid.).

This wager is, at bottom, theological in nature. It is a statement of belief that the world is not an adrift, rudderless vessel, with no rules, no order and no Captain, but rather its opposite. We have embarked from one place and head towards another, all the while watched over by a Presence whose nature baffles us even as we seek to live out Its will. Here, Steiner's theological presuppositions have, as noted, an almost non-denominal, universalist character. This is evident when he, furthering the distinction between the critic and reader, writes that '[t]he contract with transcendence cannot be empirically validated. Its guarantor is theological, if this word is allowed its widest compass. As is "theological" the warranty which underwrites the validity of metaphor and analogy ... This is the obvious weakness of the reader's theoretical position. The critic owes no hostage to mystery. The reader does' (GSR, 96).

In an earlier era, such an articulation might have earned Steiner a reprimand for his areligiosity. In the present, however, it earns him a reputation as a conservative, theologically minded critic wishing to anchor axiological determinations in a realm saturated with mystery. The view presumes Steiner's identification is less with the critic than with the reader, which is correct. Whether it is correct in other respects, particularly in its suggestion that Steiner's position is irredeemably rearguard, is less certain. What is certain, as Steiner himself knows, is that most of his colleagues, especially those of a later generation, will disagree with him; and that his refusal, in this context, to give greater importance to more material considerations like economics, history, and politics will earn him the further reputation of being resistant to theory. He *is* resistant to theory (as this activity has been defined in literary studies), and his alternative – that we should set up houses of reading – will strike most academic readers as a wilful aberrancy, which it is, of course. But it carries with it genuine conviction, as is made clear in his conclusion to the '"Critic"/"Reader"':

> What we need ... are not 'programmes in the humanities,' 'schools of creative writing,' 'programmes in creative criticism' (*mirabile dictu*, these exist). What we need are places, i.e. a table with some chairs around it, in which we can learn again how to read, how to read together. One aims at such a desideratum at the most literary levels. Elementary lexical and grammatical analyses, the parsing of sentences, the scansion of verse (prosody being the inseparable pulse and music of meaning), the ability to make out even the most rudimentary lineaments of those innervations and figures of rhetoric which, from Pindar to Joyce, have been the carriers of felt life – all these are now esoteric or lost skills. We need 'houses of and for reading' in which there is enough silence for the sinews of memory to awake. If language, under the pressure of wonder (the 'surplus value') of multiple meaning, if the music of thought are to endure, it is not more 'critics' we require but more and better 'readers.' (GSR, 97)

Herein lies the crux of Steiner's conflict with most contemporary theorists. He believes, as they generally do not, that the aesthetic can be grounded in wonder and mystery; and that, short of this, our best approach to the arts is to investigate their inner workings, not with the aim of domination, but with that of enhancing our acquaintance with, and our respect for, the painting, poem, or sonata. Granted, we cannot simply group together contemporary schools of criticism as if they were one; and while I think this general distinction sound, I would like to particularize the discussion more, beginning with Steiner's relation to deconstruction, the critical movement that has most captured his attention and the one that bears the closest affinity to his own work, despite his own refusal to play it cool and to consign a larger, more metaphysical hope to the dustbin of history. Yet, as critics such as Edith Wyschogrod and Graham Ward have argued (RGS, 164, 198), Steiner's relation to deconstruction is more marked by ambivalences than by outright rejection. For starters, there is, as earlier noted, the clear connection between his understanding of Judaism and deconstruction. In *Real Presences*, and later *Grammars of Creation*, this connection is made explicit: 'Out of Judaism grown impatient at the everlasting delay of the messianic came strange fruit. Today, this impatience has taken on extreme, nihilistic urgency. It questions the very concepts of meaning and of form. It queries the possibility of any significant relation between word and world. It exalts the myths of theory above the facts of creation' (86–7). And this has followed directly on the statement that 'theory in the humanities' can be defined 'as impatience systematized' (RP, 86). Steiner, we know, is not adverse to textuality itself. Much of his work, particularly lately, has extolled the condition of textuality, and his refusal to embrace any one religion, state or theory is in line with this. Meanwhile, Steiner has always stressed that reading is a 'potentially unending' exercise (AB, 8) and that any coming to rest must be considered, at best, 'provisional' (AB, 201). He has also stressed that the genius of language is to be located in it aporias, in its '[a]mbiguity, polysemy' and 'violation[s] of grammatical and logical sequence' (AB, 246). In *After Babel*, he writes that the '[u]ncertainty of meaning is incipient poetry' (246), a definition that parallels de Man's own belief that he 'would not hesitate to equate the rhetorical, figural potentiality of language with literature itself' (*Allegories*, 10). Finally, Steiner has long made favourable (if not unambivalent) comparisons between Jews, gays, and blacks and the modern notion of language as indeterminate and game-like, the suggestion being that such persons have had, historically, an important role in deconstructing society's pieties. In *On Difficulty*, for instance, he writes that '[s]o far as much of the best, of the most original in modern art and literature is autistic, i.e. unable or unwilling to look to a reality or "normality" outside its own chosen rules, so far as much of the modern genius can be understood from the point of view of a sufficiently comprehensive, sophisticated theory of games, there is in it a radical homosexuality' (117). And what was true earlier in the century with regard to gays also started to be true, later in the century, with regard to 'other "offending/offensive exiles" such as those of the Jew and of the Negro' (OD, 118).

Still, even as Steiner's work bears numerous affinities with deconstruction, he feels uncomfortable with the theory's unrelenting efforts in the direction of *différance*. In *Real Presences*, he writes 'that the notion of language as a purely interrelational play of differences, and the notion of man's life in speech as one of diverse language-games with no imperative of reference except for the pragmatic, are radically inadequate' (85). His reservations are much like those he has about psychoanalysis, which he criticizes for its refusal to imagine anything like a boundary condition to its investigations: 'The logic, the motor principle of free association, on which the theory and practice of psychoanalysis depend, are those of an infinite series. Each unit in the associative chain does not only connect horizontally and in linear sequence with the next;

it can itself become the starting point for an unbounded set of new linked connotations, associations and recall' (RP, 45). The problem is not that the world cannot be spoken of in terms of its unendingness, its infinite regresses. It can, and Steiner admits that when our view is geared this way, deconstruction makes perfect sense: '*On its own terms and planes of argument*, terms by no means trivial if only in respect of their bracing acceptance of ephemerality and self-dissolution, the challenge of deconstruction does seem to me irrefutable' (RP, 132). It is, however, when we try to imagine what the world is like in itself, in its essence, not as something in infinite motion, but as something that contains this motion even as it retains its integrity, that deconstruction fails us. That is, in Heraclitean fashion, it is when we seek to say something about the river as opposed to its current that deconstruction comes up short, for its attentions are all directed toward the current. Its attentions are directed to only half the story, and Steiner longs to know the other half as well. About death, about God, deconstruction has next to nothing to say. De Man's defining death as 'a displaced name for a linguistic predicament' speaks, thinks Steiner, of a shallowness, of a refusal to imagine the radical otherness extant outside the realm of our material linguisticity.[29] And yet each of our lives is lived in the shadow of death, a situation that not only accentuates our guest-like character, but also demands from us the framing of a response, be it philosophical, aesthetic, or religious: 'It is the facticity of death, a facticity wholly resistant to reason, to metaphor, to revelatory representation, which makes us "guest-workers," *frontaliers*, in the boarding-houses of life. Where it engages, uncompromisingly, the issues of our condition, poetics seeks to elucidate the incommunicado of our meetings with death (in their terminal structure, narrations are rehearsals for death). However inspired, no poem, no painting, no musical piece – though music comes closest – can make us at home with death, let alone "weep it from its purpose"' (RP, 140–1).

Deconstruction does, in fact, offer a response. But this response is so lacking in consolation that unless one has been weaned on the verities of existentialism, its truth value will be difficult to reconcile with one's hopes. That is, it will be difficult to reconcile with those hopes that have a messianic or religious tenor about them, for these are exactly what deconstruction discourages. Urged to play it cool, and not to be taken in by the metaphors of presence, we have pitched ourselves into a situation where 'you are taken for a damn fool if you invest in such hope' (RI, 171).[30] Caution has become the rule. Or at least ostensibly it has, for there is evidence that even as it rejects the dogmatisms of the past, deconstruction creates its own dogmatism: 'The negations of post-structuralism and of certain varieties of deconstruction are precisely as dogmatic, as political as were the positivist equations of archival historicism. The "emptiness of meaning" postulate is no less *a priori*, no less a case of despotic reductionism than were, say, the axioms of economic and psycho-sociological causality in regard to the generation of meaning in literature and the arts in turn-of-the-century pragmatism and scientism' (RP, 175). Deconstruction's practitioners, not surprisingly, do not see the matter this way. For one, they argue that deconstruction is not a methodology, finding its force outside the text, but is something that happens within texts themselves. Hence, there is de Man's statement that '"the text deconstructs itself, is self-deconstructive" rather than being deconstructed by a philosophical intervention from the outside of the text' (*Resistance to Theory*, 118). And there are also Derrida's statements that 'language bears within itself the necessity of its own critique' (*Writing and Difference*, 284) and that deconstruction is not 'another science, a new discipline charged with a new content or new domain' but a process (*Positions*, 36). For another, deconstructionists argue less the emptiness of meaning than that meaning is never present in, or to, itself, but always finds aspects of its determination outside of itself. Or as Derrida puts it: 'In the extent to which what is called "meaning" (to be "expressed") is already, and thoroughly, constituted by a tissue of differences, in the extent to which there is already a *text*, a network of referrals to *other* texts, a textual transformation in which each allegedly "simple term" is marked by the trace of another term, the presumed interiority of meaning is already worked upon by its own exteriority. It is always already carried outside of itself. It already differs (from itself) before any act of expression' (*Positions*, 33).

Steiner knows this, yet remains generally opposed to deconstructive practices. For one, he believes that he has good reason, statements of post-structuralists notwithstanding, to think that deconstruction is, in fact, a methodology, a particular practice of reading that one such as Derrida, de Man, or Miller consciously employs. To suggest, as deconstructionists do, that texts deconstruct themselves and that deconstruction is, therefore, something like a neutral, non-intervening practice, strikes Steiner as self-deception. Granted, when pressed, such critics back off from the stance of neutrality (Derrida: 'Deconstruction, I have insisted, is not neutral. It intervenes' [*Positions*, 93]). Yet the overall tenor of their work is to shift responsibility away from subjects in the direction of a system of differences. Or as Derrida puts it, 'the subject, and first of all the conscious and speaking subject, depends upon the system of differences and the movement of *différance*' (*Positions*, 29). One does not have to possess a naive faith in individual autonomy, thinks Steiner, to see this description as, one, itself interventionist and inscribed in the same Logos discourse that it critiques and, two, fraught with all sorts of serious consequences as it becomes commonplace to locate 'movement,' if not responsibility, in a system of differences. Steiner writes: 'The deconstruction of the "I" and of authorship separates the aesthetic from the ethical. Where is responsibility, where is responsibility to be located?"' (RP, 101). Steiner here disagrees less with Derrida's description than with his emphases. He wants to hold on to the sense of a strong subject, but deconstructionists undermine this hope. They might, says Steiner, be thought of as making more systematic a situation that was already evident in the work of nineteenth-century writers such as Rimbaud and Mallarmé, especially when the consequences of the formula '*Je est une autre*' are allowed to ripen and disseminate, to the point that the self begins to appear more and more parodistic. When this happens, and when, parallel to this, the structures of existence begin to be increasingly referred to in terms of game theory, then the large-scale assumption that life is purposive begins to be lost. If this is now happening, the fault is, certainly, not post-structuralists' alone. Still, to the extent that they accentuate absence over presence, the epilogue over the Logos, they bear some responsibility. Or as Steiner says in *Real Presences*, when concluding his discussion of deconstruction: 'There is a distinct possibility that these questions [i.e., of metaphysics and of theology] no longer admit of an adult, let alone consoling, answer. They may be mere flourishes of nostalgia and pathos. The cruelest of paradoxes in deconstruction is this: there was no "place to start," but there is, in regard to our innocent, factitious, opportunistic habitation in meaning, a place at which to end. What seems clear is that the challenge cannot be evaded. The reader (the misreader) at our shoulder can be either a Roland Barthes or a Karl Barth. For the current masters of emptiness, the stakes are indeed those of a game. That is where we differ' (134).

Steiner's interest in deconstruction connects with the fact that despite its evident success in North America, its antecedents are locatable in the European philosophical tradition, in the work of Hegel, Nietzsche, Wittgenstein, Husserl, Sartre and, most especially, Heidegger. In fact, Steiner argues that deconstruction is first and foremost a venture in phi-

losophy and has little to tell us about literature: 'The classics of deconstruction ... are 'misreadings' not of literature but of philosophy; they
address themselves to philosophical linguistics and the theory of language. The masks they seek to strip off are those worn by Plato, by
Hegel, by Rousseau, by Nietzsche or Saussure. Deconstruction has nothing to tell us of Aeschylus or Dante, of Shakespeare or Tolstoy' (RP,
128). There is some truth in this, for it is difficult to deconstruct a text
whose purposes are, from the very start, rhetorical, as any play by
Shakespeare or novel by James undoubtedly is.[31] It should take a great
deal of presumption, for instance, to say what meanings Shakespeare
did, and did not, intend in Richard II's soliloquy in Pomfret Castle ('My
thoughts are minutes, and with sighs they jar / Their watches on unto
mine eyes, the outward watch / Whereto my finger, like a dial's point, /
Is pointing still in cleansing them from tears'). It is true, as Hegel says in
the *Phenomenology of Spirit*, that '[w]e learn by experience that we meant
something other than we meant to mean, and this correction of our
meaning compels our knowing to go back to the proposition, and
understand it in some other way' (39); yet to push this further and to
suggest, as deconstruction does, that we can read the past linguistic
intentions of others as well as (if not better than) we read our own is to
claim too much; and it raises the question of whether or not deconstruction does not assume an innocent relation to texts, for the contention
that one can deconstruct a text predicates, denials aside, that the text's
meaning is already constructed, or determined. We know (or think we
know) that it is not, and so there is reason for thinking those readings
that purport to be deconstructive as no different from other, less self-
promoting, readings. Like other readings, a Derridian or a de Manian
reading is less a deconstruction than a construction, even as its attendant interests are different. This is to say nothing that a post-structuralist critic does not already know, but it does give further credence to
Steiner's remark, echoing both Donoghue and Kermode, that '[i]n
regard to poetry and prose in the Anglo-American tradition, nothing in
post-structuralist and deconstructive reading surpasses the playful, but
linguistically and historically informed exercises of William Empson,
most especially in his *Structure of Complex Words*, or the philological but
politically-lit penetration of Kenneth Burke's studies in rhetoric, motive
and grammatology' (RP, 128).

I began the last paragraph by saying that Steiner shares similar intellectual antecedents with the deconstructionists. These antecedents are
principally in Continental literature and philosophy. Steiner observes

the importance of these antecedents for the deconstructionists, saying for instance that the philosophy represents the '[d]eveloping' and 'radicalizing' of 'a Nietzschean intuition' (RP, 119); and that 'Derrida's famous neologism, la *différance*,' is '[i]tself an echo to Hegel's *Aufhebung*' (RP, 122). He also observes that '[t]here is little in Deconstruction or in Foucault's "abolition of man," with its background in Dada and Artaud, which is not voiced in Heidegger's *a*-humanism' (H, xxiv); and that 'it is beginning to look as if this seminal period of French argument, from the late nineteen-forties to the early eighties, were itself an epilogue to German and Central European philosophy, psychology, language theory, and political sociology. Sartre came after Heidegger, as Lacan came after Freud, and Foucault and Derrida after Nietzsche. It is as if the German occupation of France had left deep scars that turned into furrows' ('Power Play,' 105). Steiner is, as noted, interested in notions of epilogue, but his strongest affections here are for the writers of the prologue, not only for Nietzsche, Freud, and Heidegger, but also for Adorno, Arendt, Benjamin, Bloch, Canetti, Hegel, Jakobson, Kafka, Kraus, Levinas, Lukács, Marcuse, Marx, Scholem, and Wittgenstein. As he has several times said, he likes to think of his intellectual roots as having sprung from the libraries and parlours of such European cities as Vienna, Prague, Leningrad, Berlin, Frankfurt, Paris, and Cracow. The emphasis has always been on the Central European tradition, especially in its Jewish variant, but also as this variant intersects with the Enlightenment. In a helpful essay, 'Heidegger in Steiner,' Graham Ward notes the influence of this latter project, as it found itself manifested in the writers of the Weimar Republic and later in the Frankfurt School, upon Steiner's thinking. He notes, partly in defence of Steiner's own pronounced cultural elitism, that the 'liberal dream – of humanism, rationalism, literacy, and the political commitment to what Leibniz termed "un instinct général de societé" – has always been dizzy with nostalgia, because it balanced on the shoulders of tradition. It looked back, in its appeal to *auctoritas*, and affirmed as necessary the interrelationship of social élitism, philosophical universalism, and the cultured (*gebildet*) consciousness' (RGS, 181). Steiner, thinks Ward, first came into his own, 'in the late 1950s and early 60s, dreaming the liberal dream' and extolling 'a "humane literacy"' even as what he mostly heard all around him was 'a "sub-human jargon"' (RGS, 182). When his career is looked at this way, says Ward, '[t]he tensions in his work [between dream and reality] become understandable' (ibid.). I think that Ward is right, and that Steiner's work appears most impressive when it is understood as an outgrowth of the German and Central European tradition rather than when it is placed in relation to French theory and its American off-shoots. This prior tradition is, naturally, the frame in which Steiner himself prefers to see his work.

In this tradition, it is probably Karl Marx who, for Steiner, most assuredly brings together messianic and Enlightenment values. These values are most important to Steiner, and while Marx might not be a thinker whom he would otherwise esteem, the combination of interests, or ambitions, makes him a central reference point in Steiner's discussions. True, Marx is hardly a willing subject in the tradition of Judaic messianism, but Steiner has his own thoughts about this and, as we have seen, chooses to think of him, alongside Moses and Jesus, as one of Judaism's three most important proselytizers for the realm of the ideal and the demands that it makes upon us. Making explicit the comparison with 'Jesus the Jew,' Steiner writes that '[t]his summons [in Jesus's Sermon on the Mount] to abnegation – to the abolition of the ego and of private property and privilege – this annunciation of the inevitable sacrificially-prepared coming of the kingdom of justice on earth, constitutes the core of that utterly Judaic secular messianism which we call Marxism. When Marx asks that man "exchange love for love, and justice for justice," he is speaking the exact language of Isaiah, of Amos, of the anarchist from Nazareth and Galilee' (LLM, 59). Steiner's understanding of the messianic here, as elsewhere, has a strong secular ring to it. This messianism awaits no Jewish Messiah coming down from the clouds. Rather, it is the substitute for such longing; it is the ambition to get on with the work, to transform the earth, with or without a Messiah, into a heavenly kingdom. In this sense, 'Marxism,' thinks Steiner, 'is Judaism grown impatient. The Messiah has been too long in coming or, more precisely, in not-coming. The kingdom of justice must be established by man himself, on this earth, here and now' (TGD, 44). Steiner is clearly not the critic to look to for detailed analysis of Marx's social and economic theories. Despite the numerous references to Marx, there is seldom, if ever, references to matters like exchange value, surplus-value, workers' struggle, and so forth. The closest Steiner comes to a discussion of social theory is in his reference to Marx's internationalism, though even this is intertwined with mention of his messianism: 'This is where Marx is most profoundly a Jew – while at the same time arguing the dissolution of Jewish identity. He believed that class and economic status knew no frontiers, that misery had a common citizenship. He postulated that the revolutionary process would abolish national distinctions and antagonisms as industrial technology had all but eroded regional autonomy. The entire socialist utopia and dialectic of history is based on an international premise' (LS, 153). From Steiner, then, we can anticipate little that might offer itself as solace to the ordinary man or woman in the street, the eight-dollar-an-hour labourer, for his interest in Marxism has always been as it evokes justice in its most abstract, universal sense, not as it finds itself negotiated on the shop floor. As he writes in an essay on the French Marxist, Louis Althusser: 'Marxism is ... a messianic dream of immanent justice. Its source is twofold: the Judaic prophetic vision of human redemption, and the millennial promise of the French Revolution and European Romanticism. Marx's peers are not the exact scientists but the panoptic dreamers of historical progress and fulfillment, such as Hugo, Michelet, and Wagner' ('Stranglehold,' 118).

It is, perhaps, because Steiner's interest in Marxism is so intertwined with the promises of messianism and the universal that he comes across, at times, as indifferent to the cruelties perpetuated in its name. I have touched on this subject previously, and will not pursue it here at any length; but it does seem likely that this has something to do with Steiner's penchant for saying how much better it was under the Soviet system for people of a bookish temperament. That is, it seems that only a penchant for abstraction, wherein words like 'inhumanity' do not seek reification and can be tucked away in subordinate clauses, permits him to write a sentence like the following: 'For all its obscurantism and *inhumanity*, the Marxist conception of literature is neither academic, in the manner of some of the "New Criticism" practices in America, nor provincial, as is so much of current English criticism' (LS, 323–4; italics added). And only a real lack of experience in living under 'the political régimes' spoken of in the following should make their interest in literature at all enticing: 'Marxist-Leninism and the political régimes enacted in its name takes literature *seriously*, indeed desperately so' (LS, 323). The point is, there are times when, for Steiner, Marxist-Leninism's threat to basic human liberties and decencies appear hardly more punitive than the house-arrest visited upon Georg Lukács – Lukács to Steiner: 'You want to know how one gets work done? It's easy. House-arrest, Steiner, house-arrest!' (MH, 67) – a story told in the spirit that sees bookishness and totalitarianism as brothers-in-arms. And so, rather than responding to the very real historical consequences of Marxist-Leninist practice, Steiner blindly glosses this as the facilitator of exemplary artistry. 'Communism,' he writes, 'has been a central force in much of the finest of modern literature,' and '*even where it has gone venomous*, is a mythology of the human future, a vision of human possibility rich in moral demand' (LS, 356; italics added).

That Steiner does not see the madness of this position is not unconnected with his identification of Communism with Judaism. It may be, as Steiner writes in the Althusser essay, that '[i]n their doctrinal absolutism, their organization, and their altruistic ideals, Catholicism and utopian Marxism are akin' ('Stranglehold,' 118), but mostly Steiner's work suggests that, in the words of *Proofs*' professore, '[t]here can be no Communist, no real socialist who is not, at bottom, a Jew' (35). The reason, again, has to do with Communism's messianic aspect, though this, as suggested, places Communism in a rather small container, one in which it, as history has shown, has refused to remain lodged. Yet it is this container, or thesis, that has the greatest appeal to Steiner; and it helps to explain his interest in Marxist critics such as Lukács, Benjamin, Bloch, Adorno, and Marcuse, authors whom he refers to as 'Jewish abstractionists,' for the reason that they each seem motivated by a particularly abstract and universal sense of justice, a sense which seems religious whether it is called this or not (MH, 67). Here, Lukács, despite his own protestations, is described as 'a Jew to the tip of his fingers' (ibid.), and is praised, with Benjamin, for a 'style of vision' wherein 'literary judgment' entails 'a critique of society, a utopian or empirical comparison of fact and possibility in human action' (LS, viii). Living 'in the book-crammed study, ... high over the river in Budapest,' he is said to be 'a lone and splendid tower amidst the gray landscape of eastern Europe and Communist intellectual life' (LS, 350, 311). For Lukács, as for the Frankfurt School in general, there was 'the problem of how abstract thought, the life of the intellect,' could 'be knit to historical reality, to the exactions and dignity of concrete existence' (MH, 67). Brought up in wealth, wherein it was assumed 'that the values to be realized by man and society are those of the spirit, of the thinking intellect' (ibid.), Lukács, convinced that America was a greater threat than the Gulag, laboured, '[c]onsciously or not,' 'to make the world not only "safe for," but actively answerable to Goethe, Pushkin, Balzac or Thomas Mann' (ibid.). He laboured, like Marx himself (LS, 153), on behalf of the 'ideal of "man's becoming man"' (MH, 67). That this meant aligning himself with the forces of Stalin led to no apologies, not even in later life, for he was, says Steiner, a 'hard-liner,' who believed that '[t]here are situations – perhaps all genuine political and revolutionary situations are such – in which one must act rightly (*richtig*), even "justly," yet "unethically" (*unethisch*)' (ibid.). Steiner says that we should be naive to 'habour the belief that any man of obvious intellectual stature and moral awareness who has committed his strengths to Communism must, in the face of the Gulag and of Soviet realities, end his days in more or less avowed disenchantment and remorse' (ibid.). The unstated assumption is that genius does what it will, notwithstanding the consequences for others. That Steiner, so fearful regarding vulgar people and their kitsch, has not thought through the ethical implications of his embrace of genius, is, I think, self-evident. And unfortunate. It does, however, help to explain his interest in the Frankfurt School, for the school was also known for its fear of kitsch, especially when it emanated from the United States. Or as Steiner writes: 'Of course what they [Horkheimer, Adorno and the Frankfurt School in general] feared here [in America] most was not, in any simple sense, democratic institutions: it was kitsch. It was mass vulgarisation' (RI, 178).

Other Frankfurt School critics who attract Steiner's attention include Adorno and Benjamin. Again, the reason has much to do with their identity as Central European Jews. Steiner speaks of Adorno as a survivor, whose work carries within it the 'common note of desolation' that marks the work of other survivors – Arendt, Bloch, Kahler, Lévi-Strauss – and that makes it appear 'contemporary' (LS, 149). Steiner values the work's 'context of reference' and its 'understanding of the philosophic, political, aesthetic roots of the inhuman; of the paradox that modern barbarism sprang, in some intimate, perhaps necessary way, from the very core and locale of humanistic civilization' (ibid.). Steiner further values Adorno's work for raising the question of whether after Auschwitz there can be any poetry? It is a question that Steiner comes back to again and again, as in 'The Long Life of Metaphor,' where he defends Adorno's statement against those who have wondered about its logic, and where he even expands its terms with the statement that eloquence itself (with all its presumptions about the goodness of God's creation) constitutes a sort of obscenity after the Shoah: 'this is the meaning of T.W. Adorno's so often misunderstood call for "no poetry after Auschwitz"' (56).[32] I am not sure that Steiner's addition clarifies things, except perhaps in the heart, where these sorts of matters tend to register most fully. Steiner speaks of Benjamin as one of the twentieth century's 'two master-readers' (the other is Heidegger [GSR, 21]), and one who must be understood first and foremost within the constellation of European Jewish intellectuals. There can be, says Steiner agreeing with Scholem, 'no worthwhile reading whatever, that is not scrupulously

respondent to his Judaism'; and '[t]hose intellectually or psychologically unprepared to face this fact, and the modes of interpretation it
entails, have no true business with him' (R, 37). Steiner takes notes of
Benjamin's '"Moscow-Jerusalem" dream' (FF, 136), the messianism that
sought, much to his friend Scholem's horror, to make Marxism the
focus of its hope: 'The messianic did not signify Zionism. It implied the
recovery of the voices of the humbled and the defeated, plowed under
by the history and historians. It would restore the lost Adamic tongue
that secretly underlay all human languages, and whose generative presence made both possible and impossible the act of translation. For Benjamin, the coming of the Messiah would reveal itself via a transparency
to truth, to social justice, to loving rationality extending beyond Judaism
and the rebirth of Israel (miraculous as he sensed that to be)' (FF, 134).

Steiner does not exactly choose sides in the Scholem-Benjamin
debate over what form messianism might be expected to take. He is too
admiring of both men to do this. Yet, as we have seen, Steiner's own
sense of messianism is much more analogous to that of Benjamin, with
its implication of an ideal social justice, and he goes easy on Benjamin
when he fails to see the horrific dimension of the Marxist-Leninist equation: 'He did not choose to perceive the tragic dimensions of that
degeneration from messianic ideals, from the utopian but incessant call
for social justice as it is already eloquent in the Prophets' (FF, 135). In
addition to an interest in Benjamin's messianism, Steiner is interested in
Benjamin's thinking about remembrance, aura, and translation. I earlier addressed the matter of remembrance, and so will say nothing here.
As for Benjamin's concept of aura, its importance for Steiner, like that
of translation, relates to an 'undeclared theology,' to the writer's willingness to draw 'on the back-credit of theology, on the ultimately theological re-insurance of the very concept of meaningful, without offering in
return the collateral of an avowed faith' (GSR, 21). But even as Steiner
critiques Benjamin's hesitancy, he identifies with it, for his own work
borrows heavily from this same bank with not that much more show of
collateral. In any event, Steiner thinks that Benjamin's concept of aura,
like Joyce's of epiphany, speaks of 'the freedom and mystery of being'
whose source is 'deeper than language, and must, if' it is to retain its
truth-claim, 'remain undeclared' (RP, 112). Any attempt to say in words
what is experienced intuitively, or in music, must, by the nature of
things, fail, as must any attempt to translate from one language into
another. Steiner's interest in this failure – which again must be understood in the light of something that is deeper than language – takes

inspiration from Benjamin's own insights about translation, particularly as offered in 'The Task of the Translator': 'Benjamin founds his metaphysic of translation on the concept of "universal language." Translation is both possible and impossible – a dialectical antinomy characteristic of esoteric argument. This antimony arises from the fact that all known tongues are fragments, whose roots, in a sense which is both algebraic and etymological, can only be found in and validated by "die reine Sprache." This "pure language" ... is like a hidden spring seeking to force its way through the silted channels of our differing tongues. At the "messianic end of their history" (again a Kabbalistic or Hasidic formulation), all separate languages will return to their source of common life. In the interim, translation has a task of profound philosophic, ethical, and magical import' (AB, 66–7).

What gives Benjamin's work on translation its special importance, thinks Steiner, is his refusal to think of it as strictly a matter of linguistics or philosophy. For Benjamin, translation is, in the most fundamental sense, a theological problem (AB, 290). It is about the search to recover a lost meaning, to recover that something – that 'more final realm of language' (AB, 257) – which hides in the interstices of original and translated texts. 'The true interlinear is the final, unrealizable goal of the hermeneutic act' (AB, 324). And when 'rigorously conceived, it embodies that totality of understanding and reproduction, that utter transparency between languages which is empirically unattainable and whose attainment would signal a return to the Adamic unison of human speech' (ibid.). It was, observes Steiner, a sign of Benjamin's genius to understand this, and to be able to write that 'literalness and freedom must without strain unite in the translation in the form of the interlinear version ... The interlinear version of the Scriptures is the best archetype or ideal of all translation' (ibid.).

Graham Ward has argued that Steiner's early interest in the Frankfurt School, an interest tied to his wanting to orient his literary interests in a larger social-historical matrix, came at a time when the school itself was beginning to shift direction, to put behind it a critique that had strong post-Kantian elements and that was short on actual political commitment. A sceptic with regard to intellectuals' professions of political commitment,[33] Steiner was drawn to the school in its earlier manifestation:

> Steiner adopts the 'process of dialectical analysis' (*LS*, 342) he admires so much in the work of 'para-Marxist' critics. This is a process that analyses a text in its dialectical relationship to its sociohistorical context, a process in

which the text is examined in terms of how it reflects, creates, and acts as a critique upon that context. It is a process that, as Adorno wrote, 'cannot, therefore, permit any insistence on logical neatness.' But Steiner also proceeds to trace logical development and to argue toward an idealistic synthesis or a messianic revolution. Thus in his writing there emerges a complex weave of trenchant social critique and Romantic idealism. But unlike the writers of the Frankfurt School, Steiner's employment of 'dialectical analysis' is not concomitant with a political and philosophical program. He employs the technique in order to breathe a new life into 'old criticism' and its belief in civilizing values; but these are values that 'para-Marxist' dialectics are calling into question. (RGS, 182)

Ward supports his argument with reference to Steiner's early work, particularly *Tolstoy or Dostoevsky* and *The Death of Tragedy* (1980). But he also notes that sometime 'in the mid-1960s,' 'something changes in the tone of Steiner's work': 'Steiner becomes preoccupied with the relationship of eloquence to silence' (GSR, 184). Though Ward mentions Wittgenstein, this change in tone is most directly linked with Heidegger (ibid.). Ward offers a masterful discussion of Steiner's relation to Heidegger; and while I cannot explore the subject with the same detailed attention, I would, before concluding, wish briefly to speak of not only Heidgger's but also Wittgenstein's influence on Steiner. I shall begin with Wittgenstein.

Wittgenstein influences Steiner in several areas, including grammar, language games, translation, silence, and the numinous. The *Tractatus Logico-Philosophicus* and the *Philosophical Investigations* are key texts, though Steiner's instinct for the sublime sends him back more to the former than the latter. But it is in the latter wherein Wittgenstein develops his theory of a linguistics that builds up its rules as it goes along; and this conception is important with regard to Steiner's thinking on the epilogue and translation. It is in the *Investigations*, for instance, that Wittgenstein writes, 'We are under the illusion that what is peculiar, profound, essential, in our investigation, resides in its trying to grasp the incomparable essence of language' (44), and then follows this with the suggestion that rather than searching out a '*super*-order' via the means of '*super*-concepts,' we might begin our investigations more modestly, with the experience and vocabulary most near to hand: 'if the words "language," "experience," "world," have a use, it must be as humble a one as that of the words "table," "lamp," "door"' (ibid.). It is also in the *Investigations* that Wittgenstein likens this pragmatic linguistics to the way people begin to make up rules once they start throwing a ball around:

> Doesn't the analogy between language and games throw light here? We can easily imagine people amusing themselves in a field by playing with a ball so as to start various existing games, but playing many without finishing them and in between throwing the ball aimlessly into the air, chasing one another with the ball and bombarding one another for a joke and so on. And now someone says: The whole time they are playing a ball-game and following definite rules at every throw.
>
> And is there not also the case where we play and – make up the rules as we go along? And there is even one where we alter them – as we go along. (39)

This discussion colours Steiner's own on the epilogue, an epoch characterized by an increasing readiness among writers to repress language's referential function and to celebrate its more self-reflexive, or 'letteral,' dimension. Inspired by Mallarmé, Stein, and Joyce, these (postmodern) writers accent their work's playfulness, its qualities of *jouissance, différance*, and textuality. For many, writing constitutes play in its most positive and energetic sense, but for Steiner, this play, while not unattractive, especially as it questions more staid pieties, also has a dark side – that which is *just* play, unmoored from purposiveness. In *Real Presences*, Steiner expresses this anxiety and wonders, when faced with the postulate that the human is not a 'speech animal' but a 'playing animal,' why any writer bothers 'to write and readers to misread?' (131). He considers Barthes's 'concept of jouissance, of the lightly orgasmic effects produced by the eroticization of the discursive process and of its reception' and Derrida's 'more covert resort to language-games' (ibid.). But in the end, Steiner finds both of these concepts – as answers to why write? why read? – unpersuasive. They do not console; they do not even pretend to; and unless one is prepared to think of life as one large game, we will, thinks Steiner, need to look elsewhere for answers.

Steiner does have his own uses for the Wittgensteinian concept of game, however. First, it strikes him as important for what it – or its variant – suggests about the nature of translation. In *After Babel*, Steiner quotes Wittgenstein comparing translation to a mathematical problem – i.e., to the type of problem that admits of a solution even though it, in Wittgenstein's words, presupposes no 'systematic method of solving it' (290). It is, thinks Steiner, a crucial concept; and he stresses the point to the reader: 'It is of extreme importance to grasp the distinction which Wittgenstein puts forward, to understand how "solution" can coexist with the absence of any systematic method of solution' (ibid.). The concept has particular relevance to translation, and 'the descriptions and judgements we can make of it,' so much so that Steiner predicates his subsequent discussion in *After Babel* on its principle: 'The rest of this book is an attempt to show this as clearly as possible, and to suggest the reasons why' (ibid.). In addition to the help that the *Investigations* offers Steiner in conceiving the problem of translation, it helps him to understand how ultimately private some of our most cherished beliefs must remain. In *After Babel* (167–77), Steiner offers a lengthy discussion of Wittgenstein's concept of private language (found in sections 203–315 of the *Investigations*); and while, like most commentators (Kripke included),[34] he finds Wittgenstein's discussion muddled, he takes away from it not only the idea that language is public, or translatable, but also that it affords all sorts of private recesses: 'Active inside the "public" vocabulary and conventions of grammar are pressures of vital association, of latent or realized content. Much of this content is irreducibly individual and, in the common sense of the term, private' (AB, 181). This concept of private language, with that of language games, helps Steiner understand how it is that concepts that are capable of having the greatest importance for us, both as individuals and communities, can, once they leave their privileged space, so easily meet with deafness:

> Strictly considered, the 'holy' script is revealed to itself by its readers and exegete within the house of shared beliefs. Modern epistemology provides some access to this situation. The 'language-games' of the sacred may well be more widely sovereign, more poignant and unsettling, than any others played (i.e., spoken and written) by men. But they remain language-games whose only rules and validation must be internal. They cannot be demonstrated 'from outside'; they have no self-evident proof. I take this to be the import, profound and far-reaching, of Wittgenstein's note in the Philosophical Investigations (I, 373): 'Theology as grammar.' Any reading of the cock of St. Peter as inserted in an ontologically different context from that of the sacrifice to Asclepios, is, in Kiekegaardian terminology, a leap into the light. ('The Scandal of Revelation,' 68–9)

Steiner obviously refuses to let the concepts of game and privacy, applied to language, quench his longing for that sort of consolation which systems themselves, be they linguistic, mathematical, or even theological, forfend. He wants not a wall but a window, not the darkness of the labyrinth but the light of daybreak; and while the *Investigations* is valued, it is more often the case that Steiner turns to the *Tractatus*, the text that more clearly plays on the edge of the unknown and its radiant mystery. In *Language and Silence*, he writes of his preference: 'The *Philosophic Investigations* take a more optimistic view of the inherent capacities of language to describe the world and to articulate certain modes of conduct. But it is an open question whether the *Tractatus* is not the more powerful and consistent statement. It is certainly deeply felt. For the silence, which at every point surrounds the naked discourse, seems, by virtue of Wittgenstein's force of insight, less a wall than a window. With Wittgenstein, as with certain poets, we look out of language not into darkness but light. Anyone who reads the *Tractatus* will be sensible of its odd, mute radiance' (21).

What Steiner finds especially attractive about Wittgenstein's work in the *Tractatus* is the monk-like cultivation of silence as not simply a mode of speech but its most ambient mode. Like Pascal's silence of the heavens, Wittgenstein's silence is what envelops us, even on this most noisy of planets. And in the *Tractatus*, thinks Steiner, there is an almost tragic sense of the 'gap between what is apprehended and what can be said' (LS, 134). This is true not only in the famous pronouncement that 'whereof one cannot speak thereof one must be silent' (*Tractatus*, 27), but also in the aposiopetic direction of the work, with all its suggestion that the most important and determinative things are precisely those that do not get spoken of. This conviction is most expressively evoked in Wittgenstein's 1919 letter to Ludwig Ficker (mentioned earlier), wherein the philosopher tries to explain his purpose in the *Tractatus*: 'my work consists of two parts: the one presented here plus all that I have *not* written. And it is precisely this second part which is the most important to me' (AB, 192). The statement is not only crucial for what it says about Wittgenstein's work, but also for what it says about Steiner's, for even as Steiner is more prolix than Wittgenstein, his entire œuvre is, in part, an attempt to evoke, or tease out, the silence of being – the silence identifiable with the 'more,' as when Steiner writes, 'A sentence always means more' (RP, 82). About this realm, it is felt that 'words distort,' and that 'eloquent words distort absolutely' (LS, 134) – a statement fraught with contradiction, for few, if any, speak more eloquently about silence than Steiner. Still, whatever difficulties adhere to the discussion of that which transcends not only language but perhaps materiality itself, the conviction remains that Steiner's work is oriented in the same direction as Wittgenstein's: towards that Presence which wordlessly words our world: 'In the vision of the early Wittgenstein – and "vision" is the least inaccurate term – the existential realm "on the other side of language," the categories of felt being to which only silence (or music) give access, are neither fictitious nor trivial. On the contrary. They are, indeed, the most important, life-transforming categories conceivable to man (but how?). They define his humanity' (RP, 103).

In his 1991 'Introduction' to the reissued *Martin Heidegger*, Steiner writes that '[i]t is ... the conjunctions in depth between Wittgenstein and Heidegger, the two foremost philosophic-linguistic thinkers of the age, so seemingly antithetical, which offer the most fertile ground for coming investigation and comprehension' (H, xiv). In the 1984 *Antigones*, Steiner pointed to what might be thought as one of the most important of these conjunctions, and this was, again, the apophatic nature of both Wittgenstein's and Heidegger's work. Following a comparison between Shakespeare and 'the early Wittgenstein' – 'In Shakespeare, as in the early Wittgenstein, the limits of language coincide with those of that which is' (230–1) – Steiner segues into a discussion of Heidegger: 'Yet where it is convincing, the *felt* pressure on mortal saying by that which lies "outside" may well represent the ultimate in thought and in poetry ("of that of which one cannot speak one cannot be silent").[35] Heidegger, who observes this pressure on the texts of Sophocles, of Hölderlin, and, at moments, of Rilke, marks therein the vestigial presentness, the after-glow of Being itself, of the ontological nucleus which precedes language and from which language, in passages of supreme risk and extremity, derives its numinous validity, its power to mean so much more than can be said' (A, 231).

For some time, Steiner has been taken with the Heideggerian thesis that there is more to reality than we generally grant, and that this 'more' (or 'Being') is 'hidden' in the recesses of what is ('being'). In his monograph on Heidegger, Steiner gives the point much attention, and in passages such as the following, he almost appropriates the concept:

> There could be no experience of Being, such as we manifestly have, unless Being were hidden in beings, in the essents which comprise man and the world. It is precisely this negative character of Being, the fact that Being is not an entity in itself (the Kantian *Ding an sich*), which generates the powers of manifestation in beings. It is hidden Being that gives the rock its dense 'thereness,' that makes the heart pause when a kingfisher alights,

that makes our own existence inseparable from that of others. In each case, wonder and reflection tell us of an intensity of presentness, an integral unfolding or self-statement, *clearly in excess of sensory data and neutral registration*. The sum *is* so obviously greater, 'more there' than the parts. There *is* so much more in front of us than meets the eye or hand or analytic brain. To grasp it we must think dialectically, we must understand how the negative, the hidden, the 'not-there' can engender the manifest and positive. (H, 68)

We see this appropriation, or borrowing, also in his comparison of Heidegger's concept of Being to music: 'Halting as it is, this analogy [with music] may suggest a first approximation to Heidegger's concept of being. Here too there is brazen obviousness and impalpability, an enveloping nearness and infinite regress. Being, in the Heideggerian sense, has, like music, a history and a meaning, a dependence on man and dimensions transcending humanity. In music, intervals are charged with sense. This ... may help us to understand Heidegger's relation to being of an active "nothingness" ... We take the being of music for granted as we do that of the being of being. We forget to be astonished' (H, 44–5).

Steiner thinks Heidegger's neglect of music a 'drawback' (H, 131), but this does not undercut his conviction that, as Heidegger argued, Being has now largely been forgotten. We have become inured to the vitality of experience, and it shows in our language. It is overused and tired, weighted down with clichés. Or as Steiner quotes Heidegger: 'Many words, and precisely the essential ones, are in the same situation: the language in general is worn out and used up – an indispensable but masterless means of communication that may be used as one pleases, as indifferent as a means of public transport' (H, 45). Steiner, not surprisingly, seconds Heidegger's judgment, saying that 'this exhaustion is itself symptomatic of the fact that our relations to existence, which constitute the core and rationale of human speech, have receded into grammatical banality (the word "is" diminished to a mere copula) or into forgetting' (ibid.). And because we have forgotten Being, we find ourselves unhoused and lost, unsure about how to find our way home.

True, Heidegger's concept of Being is irritatingly nebulous, and Steiner admits as much: 'It may be that we cannot provide for the term "being" an adequate syntactic analysis or paraphrase (an unambiguous, exhaustive definition). But being lives essentially in and through language. If we had no comprehension of being, if the word were "only a word" – as Heidegger's critics may argue – there could be no meaning-ful propositions whatever, no grammar, no predications. We would remain speechless' (H, 50). But we do not remain speechless, says Steiner, and while it may be impossible to pin down the term's meaning, and while it may, at times, seem like 'mystical bullying,' Steiner argues (at least in the monograph) that 'much of Heidegger does "get through,"' despite the 'idioletic' nature of the discourse (H, 12, 9). What particularly gets through is the sense of Being's oneness with 'What Is.' It is not something outside of experience, but part and parcel with it, something that determines events even as it remains hidden. It is, says Steiner, something that exists before the subject, before logic – something that needs to be experienced, or listened to, rather than mas-tered. This helps to explain the importance of music and poetry, for they, more than any other human invention, are alive to the presence of Being, even as it remains knowable only through indirection: 'The work of art shows us that "truth happens in the guise of the primordial strug-gle between 'clearance' and 'concealment'"' (H, 135). Art allows Being to speak through it, for it presumes that Being pre-exists all else and must be welcomed. As such, Steiner thinks that Being has been misrep-resented by Platonic thought, with its accent on mimesis, and by scien-tific thought, with its accent on an 'imperialistic subjectivity' and domination (H, 70). It has also been misrepresented by theology, with its anthropomorphism. In fact, Heidegger's attempt to think Being is itself an attempt to conceive the problem of existence as apart from that of a Deity. 'Heidegger is determined to think outside theology. He insists that his fundamental ontology is extratheological, that it has nothing to tell us, either way, of the existence or attributes of God' (H, 155). Steiner himself is sceptical, and believes that Heidegger's notion of Being depends on theology's legacy. He does, however, grant that Heidegger's ambition to think beyond theology requires that we speak of the work as a 'post-theology': 'It is ... my own experience that Heideg-ger's paradigm and expression of Being, of the ontological cut between Being and beings, adapts at almost every point to the substitution of "God" for the term *Sein*. This *does not* prove that such substitution is latent in Heidegger's design. He would repudiate it. But it does mean ... that the philosophy, the sociology, the poetics and, at some opaque level, the politics of Heidegger embody and articulate an "after-" or "post-theology"' (H, 155–6).

In *Martin Heidegger*, Steiner maintains a distance between Heidegger's theories and his own; and he repeatedly weighs the pros and cons of this or that proposal. At the same time, he clearly values Heidegger's work, especially for what it has to say about Being, homecoming, and art. And also, I believe he values Heidegger's attempt to imagine a theology without God, a 'post-theology.' Steiner believes the attempt is probably doomed from the start, that Heidegger's notion of Being is likeable to a lapsed theology. But because his own theological commitments have long been more nostalgic than piquant, he appears to value the attempt, and places it in the context of earlier work done by Marx, Nietzsche, and Freud. Steiner's point is that there is something messianic about each thinker's work, even as they are said to live in a period 'following on the eclipse of God' (H, 156). It is because Steiner believes this that he ends the monograph on a note that appears to grant Heidegger his own messianic status, saying that due to the fact that 'Heidegger has been among us, the notion that the asking of questions is the supreme piety of the spirit, and the uncanny idea that abstract thought is man's preeminent excellence and burden have been affirmed' (H, 157).

Heidegger is a major influence upon Steiner, especially during the 1970s and 1980s. This is most noticeable in Steiner's interest in concepts like 'Being,' 'forgetting,' 'unhousedness,' and 'homecoming.' The monograph on Heidegger, first published in Frank Kermode's Modern Masters Series in 1978, is itself a testimony to this influence. And while Steiner addresses, in *Martin Heidegger*, all the questions pertaining to the philosopher's relation to Nazism, questions that have, since the 1987 publication of Victor Farias's *Heidegger et le nazisme*, received considerably more attention, his overall judgment of the philosopher remains favourable. This does not mean that Steiner does not have some stinging things to say regarding Heidegger's relation to National Socialism or his silence, even long after the war, about the Shoah. He does, calling him a 'very small man' in his personal life, whose 'complete silence on Hitlerism and the holocaust after 1945 is very nearly intolerable' (H, 124, 123). But there is also an attempt to place Heidegger's failings in the context of the larger history. For instance:

> My own reading of the evidence is this: Like millions of other German men and women, and a good many eminent minds outside Germany, Heidegger was caught up in the electric trance of the National Socialist promise. He saw in it the only hope for a country in the grip of economic and social disaster. The Nazism to which Heidegger adhered, moreover, was, as yet, masking its essential barbarism. It was Heidegger's error and vanity, so characteristic of the academic, to believe that he could influence Nazi

ideology, that he could bring his own doctrine of existential futurity to bear on the Hitlerite program, while at the same time preserving the prestige and partial autonomy of the scholarly establishment. He was fatuously mistaken. But if the photograph I have referred to is anything to go by, Heidegger was, already by November 1933, acutely uncomfortable among his Nazi colleagues. His official implication in the movement lasted only nine months and he quit – the point is worth reiterating – before Hitler's assumption of total power. Many eminent intellectuals did far worse. (H, 121)

The paragraph, like the monograph, is thoughtful and measured. Steiner neither exculpates Heidegger of the charge that both he and his work are implicative in the German crimes of the 1930s and 1940s, nor makes this implication the final statement about either. How could he, given the influence that they (the work especially) had begun to have on his own thinking? But between the time when the book was written, in the mid-1970s, and the time when Steiner wrote the introduction, 'Heidegger in 1991,' for the reissued edition, something had changed. What had changed, of course, was the heightened public attention to Heidegger's Nazi sympathies, an attention prompted by the Farias book and the subsequent revelations about de Man's own collaborationist writings in *Le Soir,* as well as by the noticeably more prosecutorial tone to intellectual work in general. In any event, the tone of Steiner's own 1991 introduction, compared to the monograph, is noticeably harsher and less forgiving of Heidegger's alliances and silences. And here, the concept of silence begins to acquire a new valence, for now rather than being identified with a Wittgensteinian silence – that which speaks of an other world – silence speaks of a refusal, a failure to acknowledge one's complicity in a crime. It conceivably calls into question the value of the prior work – 'Heidegger's silence after 1945 would [for anti-Heideggerians], in essence, deconstruct the claims of his philosophy to any serious insights into the human condition and into the relations between consciousness and action' (H, xxix) – and it also conceivably represents (in the light of what Steiner then thought was the philosopher's rejection of Celan's personal request for explanation) an act of 'self-ostracism ... from the city of man' (H, xxxiii).[36] Yet, whereas Steiner in the monograph took a somewhat kindly view towards Heidegger's attempt to think outside the frame of theology, in the 1991 introduction the suggestion is that this ambition relates to, one, his failure to recognize, or to articulate a theory of, evil; and two, 'his defeat, as a thinker, as a human person' (xxxv). Both failures are mentioned in the following passage: 'In the massive, reiterative body of Heidegger's writings, the signal absence is very precisely that of the concept of evil ... Far beyond Nietzsche, Heidegger thinks, feels in categories *outside* good and evil. Heidegger's precept and image whereby death is a 'shrine' in which Being is most nakedly, most epiphanically present, categorically sublates (the dialectical *Aufhebung*) the problem of good and evil as this problem attaches to metaphysics in traditional systems of thought. Had Heidegger sought the understanding of the evil of Nazism and of his role therein, had he striven to 'think Auschwitz' at anything near the requisite depth ..., the domain of the ethical would have been indispensable. It is, I venture, this domain which he had, in his renunciation of theology, excluded, and that exclusion crippled his humanity' (xxxiv).

The statement is quite interesting, and raises a legitimate concern about how seriously we can think through the question of good and evil outside the frame of a theology. But it is also a statement that says as much about Steiner, and the way that his thinking has changed, as it does about Heidegger. In the monograph, Steiner suggests that Heidegger's concept of Being carries with it the most arduous ethical demand. He speaks of our responsibility to Being and the Other, and of how this dialectical situation is preferable to the more traditional ethics exalting the Cartesian ego: 'Man is only a privileged listener and respondent to existence. The vital relation to otherness is not, as for Cartesian and positivist rationalism, one of "grasping" and pragmatic use. It is a relation of audition. We are trying "to listen to the voice of Being." It is, or ought to be, a relation of extreme responsibility, custodianship, answerability to and for. Of this answerability, the thinker and the poet, *der Denker und der Dichter*, are at once the carriers and the trustees. This is because it is in their oneness to language (to the *logos*), in their capacity to *be spoken* rather to speak ... that the truth, or can we say with Wordsworth and Hölderlin, 'the music of being,' most urgently calls for and summons up response' (H, 32).

In the interim, Steiner has grown more distrustful of an ethics that emphasizes the individual's obedience to something outside of him or her (be it Being or Nazism), and places markedly less emphasis on the individual's capacity to say yes or no. The revelations concerning the war-era activities of not only Heidegger and de Man, but also of Sartre, Lukács, Waldheim, and Mitterand, can only have heightened this anxiety. So have movements like deconstruction, with their calling into question the self's integrity. I have already quoted Steiner as saying, in *Real*

Presences, that '[t]he deconstruction of the "I" and of authorship separates the aesthetic from the ethical. Where is responsibility, where is
responsible response to be located?' (RP, 101); but it is worth repeating,
for the point has, lately, become more important to Steiner. It is part
and parcel with his contention, also made in *Real Presences*, that 'any thesis that would, either theoretically or practically, put literature and the
arts beyond good and evil is spurious' (142). This needs to be put in the
context of the fact that Steiner, as much as any deconstructionist, was
previously intrigued by the Heideggerian notion that we do not speak
language so much as it speaks us. But the problem with this notion, as
Steiner has come to see, is that so strongly does it suggest that human
beings (as spoken) are determined rather than determining that it
leaves us with little to say, by way of moral judgment, against those who
run with the tide even when the tide is patently evil. It comes close to
making a mockery of ethical discourse, at least as this implies an individual's power both to recognize and to refuse evil. Without some notion
otherwise, Steiner would find it difficult to claim, as he does, that
'[w]ords failed Heidegger and, at pivotal stage in his life and work, he
failed them' (H, xxi); and he would also find it difficult to claim that the
Shoah, terrible as it was, was something more than an historical nightmare, that it was an in-the-bone evil. What then has most notably
changed since Steiner first wrote the Heidegger monograph is his growing conviction that ethics grounds itself less in aesthetics than in theology. The link has long been part of his work's subtext, but the later work
brings it more to the fore, sparked no doubt by his further thinking
about the Shoah, as well as the ethical dilemmas posed by Heidegger, de
Man, Lukács, and Sartre, and their fall from grace.

   In the 1991 introduction, I would also call attention to Steiner's linkage of Heidegger, no longer revered, with deconstruction. Steiner has
always made a link between the work of deconstruction and Heidegger,
but the linkage usually elevated the German philosopher to a pinnacle-
like position, and belittled deconstructionists as epigones. In the monograph, for instance, Steiner begins one discussion by saying that 'the
language of the master [Heidegger] exercises a mesmeric force. It literally spellbinds, making the prose of other philosophers and even the
work of contemporary poets seem shallow' (H, 10). By way of example,
he names Sartre, Celan, Lacan, and Derrida, saying of the last two that,
'[c]urrently, the French school of psychoanalysis, under Jacques Lacan,
and the French school of semiotics, led by Jacques Derrida, are trying to
achieve in their own tongue Heidegger's etymological immersion'

(ibid.). Things are somewhat different in the 1991 introduction, however. Here, too, there is some discussion on the order of there is little in deconstruction that is not found in Heidegger (e.g., 'His punning ... has bred, to the point of parody, the poststructuralism and deconstruction of today' [H, xiii]). But there is also something new as well, and this is the more emphatic identification of deconstructionists and Heidegger together as preachers of a philosophy that is, perhaps, less a dance around the nihilistic abyss than an actual slide into that same abyss:

> The crux [of *Being and Time*], made more complex by the problem of Deconstruction and of such post-Heideggerians as De Man, is this: are there in Heidegger's incomplete ontological *summa* categories, advocacies of inhumanism, eradications of the human person, which, in some sense, prepare for the subsequent program of Nazism? Is Heidegger's play with and on Nothingness (a play intimately analogous with negative theology) a nihilism *in extremis* rather than, as it professes to be, an 'overcoming of nihilism'? Assuredly, *Sein und Zeit* and Heidegger's theory of language that speaks man rather than being spoken by him is utterly seminal in the modern anti-humanistic movement. There is little in Deconstruction or in Foucault's 'abolition of man,' with its background in Dada and Artaud, which is not voiced in Heidegger's *a*-humanism – where the *privativum* of the prefix does seem to me more accurate and just than would be that of *in*-humanism. (H, xxiv–v)

Steiner is distancing himself from a philosopher who, though never fully embraced, has had an immense influence on his work. There is not only a distancing from the philosopher but also from the work (cf., the way Steiner speaks here of 'Heidegger's theory of language that speaks man' with the way it is spoken both in the monograph and other early work), which means, in part, a distancing from his own earlier work. This change is one of the reasons why I have focused as much on Steiner's relation to earlier theorists as on his relation to those more contemporary. My feeling is that Steiner's relation to one such as Heidegger helps in fact to explain his own vexed relation to contemporary deconstruction.

Another reason for focusing the discussion this way is that Steiner's interactions with contemporary theorists do not reach far beyond the circle of deconstructionists, Marxists, and linguistics. As for what Steiner has to say about such critical discourses as feminism, gay studies, postcolonial studies, New Historicism, and cultural studies, I have purposely let this go. For one, he has rather little to say about such discourses; and, two, what he does say is couched in terms that are, on the whole, so unexamining and abusive that it would ill-benefit his own otherwise well-deserved stature as a critic to direct attention this way. Wendy Steiner's harsh rebuke of Steiner for his insensitivity to the concerns of women and minorities ('Steiner advocates a race-and-gender-restricted canon, the legislation of taste by "the few," an explanation of creativity that perpetuates female marginality, and a state of affairs that is undisguisedly self-promoting')[37] is, I am afraid, a good indication of where such a discussion should likely lead, and no doubt eventually will, pushed there by critics far less measured and thoughtful than Wendy Steiner. We are each provincial in one way or another, and sometimes the best thing we can do for one another is to take note of the fact, and then move on to other considerations. Steiner is less provincial than most, but even when one's province is that of the European man of letters, one cannot expect to be all things to all people, or expect that others must give way to one's greater learning and wisdom. Steiner knows this, but just barely. He has a weakness for the apodictic statement – e.g., 'It has, I believe, been given to only one literary text [*Antigone*] to express all the principal constants of conflict in the condition of man' (A, 231) – and for magniloquence. When Hassan notes that Steiner 'can seem too vehement, hortatory, [and] overbearing' ('The Whole Mystery,' 332), he is right; he is also right when he claims that there is 'no mind more *serious*, fecund, and comprehensive in criticism today' (333). In the end, I myself find that we have much to learn from him; and that if we think otherwise, we only make our own provincialism that much more apparent.

AFTERWORD

If in my 'Introduction,' I gave prominent attention to Geoffrey Hartman's argument, in *Minor Prophecies*, that the public critic, writing in a
'conversational style,' was passé, I would, in closing, like to bestow attention upon an opposing argument, articulated by Edward Said, that the
public critic, or intellectual, remains a perennial figure of importance.
Said makes this argument in *Representations of the Intellectual*, first offered
in the form of the Reith Lectures. It is an interesting performance, especially as it goes against the grain of current academic conviction, which
urges us to think of knowledge as local and contingent, a reflection of
our subject positions. We live, we are told, in a postmodern age, inhospitable to grand narratives. Our most realistic objectives are mini-
narratives, fictions that we ourselves forge. In *Representations of the
Intellectual*, however, Said refuses the demand that we think locally, or
postmodernly. Rather, he argues that '[r]eal intellectuals constitute a
clerisy, very rare creatures indeed, since what they uphold are eternal
standards of truth and justice that are precisely *not* of this world' (5).
Said is not unmindful that if this is the case, the ratio of academics
entering into the circle of 'real intellectuals' will be only slightly better
than that of the rich entering into the kingdom of heaven. Nevertheless,
he thinks that a preponderance of his colleagues have sloughed off
whatever spirit of free-ranging intellectual curiosity – Said's 'amateurism' – might have once motivated them, preferring the safety of professionalism, understood here not as competence but as role-playing: 'The
particular threat to the intellectual today ... [is] an attitude that I will
call professionalism. By professionalism I mean thinking of your work as
an intellectual as something you do for a living, between the hours of
nine and five with one eye on the clock, and another cocked at what is

considered to be proper, professional behavior – not rocking the boat, not straying outside the accepted paradigms or limits, making yourself marketable and above all presentable, hence uncontroversial and unpolitical and "objective"' (74).

Characteristic of this professionalism is specialization, which in literary study 'has meant an increasing technical formalism, and less and less of a historical sense of what real experience actually went into the making of a work of literature' (77). It has meant a movement away from literature and towards its theorization, a movement away from the emotional and intellectual energy that first sparked the creative act. 'Specialization means losing sight of the raw effort of constructing either art or knowledge; as a result you cannot view knowledge and art as choices and decisions, commitments and alignments, but only in terms of impersonal theories or methodologies' (ibid.). As an alternative to this technological spirit Said proposes 'amateurism, the desire to be moved not by profit or reward but by love for and unquenchable interest in the larger picture, in making connections across lines and barriers, in refusing to be tied down to a specialty, in caring for ideas and values despite the restrictions of a profession' (76). Specialists will continue to have their place, but if the tie is cut between their interests and the larger public's, mandarinism will triumph. It is imperative, then, for the intellectual to keep in touch not only with life outside the academy but also with a spirit of independence. Intellectuals are 'precisely those figures whose public performances can neither be predicted nor compelled into some slogan, orthodox line, or fixed dogma' (xii).

There are things to disagree with, or dislike, in the Said book, including its polemical stereotyping, its shortchanging of literature, and how it forces us to choose between the spirit of the professional and amateur.[1] Still, it is an impressive performance, especially as it garners verve from the force of Said's own iconoclasm. He is a passionate writer, and one always comes away impressed by the emotional investment given to a subject. For him, events exude meaning, requiring response. Yet not any response, for Said has little use for the conventional, 'this is what we think,' response. Rather, he insists that fears (e.g., of embarrassment) be put aside, so that the truth of things be properly searched out: 'Universality means taking a risk in order to go beyond the easy certainties provided us by our background, language, nationality, which so often shield us from the reality of others' (xiv). This is said with the understanding that no one person or group has a proprietary relation to truth and those inclined to think otherwise often wreck havoc. Nevertheless, as a desideratum, truth matters, and it is not often reached by committee. This is also the impression created by the criticism of Donoghue, Kermode, and Steiner. They are different critics, certainly, but what allies them is a readiness to go their own way, to refuse the comfort of collegiality when their instincts tell them that better answers are to be found elsewhere. They may not always be better answers, yet they often are, and they would not even be discussible were it not for the fact that there remain critics like them willing to suffer the professionals' snickers.

Donoghue, Kermode, and Steiner are neither academic nor conservative critics, but public critics, prepared to work in the large middle ground that has been vacated during the cultural wars. Their politics are essentially liberal, especially as the latter tradition has celebrated the importance of the individual and of dialogue, the back-and-forth negotiations that must take place if solutions are not to be viewed, by one constituency or another, as forced upon it. Their prose styles are in keeping with such a politics, and can be described as conversational. They are each expert at bringing the reader into the discussion, a situation bolstered by their inclination to think of answers as that which their work moves towards rather than that with which it starts. Naturally, they each have their various beliefs and convictions, but foremost among these is that an argument needs evidence, and as the totality of evidence always eludes our grasp, we generally live our lives in the middle of things, seeking answers, but mindful of alternative understandings. The alternative understandings are always before them, not only as the world becomes more cacophonous, but also as their beloved discipline, literary studies, moves away from itself, as younger scholars invert the relations between literature and philosophy, literature and politics, literature and history, literature and anthropology, and so forth. The critics continue to profess a commitment to literature as a discipline, which is not to say that they oppose interdisciplinarity or that their work remains fenced in by literature's boundaries. Yet they believe that just as there is something recognizable as history or politics, there is also something recognizable as literature; and they are not happy to see literature's study so entirely eclipsed by other interests. They were moulded in an earlier time, when literary values were more esteemed. But values have shifted, and the patient, honest, self-sacrificing attention to literature – both as it (literature) expresses individual and cultural longings and as it is composed of the most intricate poetic detail – no longer commands the respect that it once did. So they grow more stoical, struggling to hold on to meaning, to the conviction that things hold together, even as they are mindful that they might not, that the crowded, noisy city with its capitalist exchange values might be the truest comment on where humanity is headed. They hope not, and though somewhat exiled from the mindset of current critical discussions, they, like Philocetes, seem prepared to return to the fray, yet do not count on the call. So much has changed, and they, born shortly after the First World War and raised during the periods of the Depression and the Second World War, now find themselves being lectured to about history and other realities by Trilling's abyss-fronting students now grown older. That the younger academics' experience of poverty and war has mostly been mediated by television, and their fronting of nihilism's abyss has mostly been carried out in the spirit of a field trip, might be thought to undercut their theses, but not entirely, and Donoghue, Kermode, and Steiner have the good sense to acknowledge this. The world changes, and adjustments, not all for the worse, are necessary.

This said, it remains too early for elegies, not only for the individual critics but also for what they – as public critics attached to what Trilling spoke of as the 'Liberal Imagination' – represent. Said has, rightly, spoken of the university as offering the possibility of something like an 'utopian space,' where it still remains possible to investigate, discuss, and reflect on vital issues, prior to the making of determinations (ibid.). It would be most unfortunate should things become otherwise, should the university 'become a site where social and political issues are actually either imposed or resolved'; this, he says, 'would be to remove the university's function and turn it into an adjunct to whatever political party is in power' (*Culture and Imperialism*, xxvi). Donoghue, Kermode, and Steiner would agree, though where they should differ from Said is in the greater trust that they place in literature to keep this 'utopian space' alive. That is, if Said is thinks 'it is Panglossian to imagine that the careful reading of a few works of art considered humanistically, professionally, or aesthetically significant is anything but a private activity with only slender public consequences' (*Culture and Imperialism*, 318), they are more inclined to agree with Trilling, in *The Liberal Imagination*, recalling something said by Shelley: 'whenever it becomes a question of measuring the power of literature, Shelley's old comment recurs, and "it exceeds all imagination to conceive what would have been the moral condition of the world" if literature did not continue in existence with its appeal to limited groups, keeping the door open' (103). Listening to one's contemporaries, however, one begins to wonder whether the world might not have been better off without literature, especially if one thinks, as Regenia Gagnier says her students do, that 'aesthetics is a limiting category, a tool of hegemony, either dividing the people by hierarchies of taste or operating in practice as a subtle tool of control (as in aesthetic applications of Foucault's *Discipline and Punish*)' (264). Still, if forced to choose, few, if any, would will away our accumulated literary heritage. For the cynics, it simply provides too much evidence of people's reprobacy. Witness Anthony Julius who, while 'appalled' by the moral cowardliness locatable in Eliot's poems, still thinks 'the opportunities that they offer for the study of anti-Semitism ... probably outweigh the damage that they can do' (*T.S. Eliot*, 40). As he says, 'I censure; I do not wish to censor' (ibid.). For others, wishing neither to censor nor to censure, but to weigh and to judge, with the hope of being pleased, even enlightened, there remains the conviction that literature keeps the 'door open,' that it, like Said's university, but even more so, provides an utopian space. This space speaks less of final determinations than of things that exist as virtual, where the invitation is less to act than to perceive, and to make this perception the object of one's contemplation, not ruling out action, but not demonstrating any eagerness towards it either. Donoghue, paraphrasing Suzanne Langer, writes: 'a work of art is an object offered only or at least chiefly for perception: its mode is not real but virtual' (*Walter Pater*, 289–90). Does this mean that art has no utility? I do not think so, though it depends on how one uses the term. Wendy Steiner, in her intelligent defence of art, *The Scandal of Pleasure*, writes: 'This book is an argument for the subjectivity of aesthetic response, an attempt to explain what it means to invest art with value and derive pleasure from it. It tries to demonstrate the utility of a liberal aesthetics in which art is neither identical to reality nor isolated from it, but a virtual realm tied to the world by acts of interpretation. Experiencing the variety of meanings available in a work of art helps make us tolerant and mentally lithe. Art is a realm of thought experiments that quicken, sharpen, and sweeten our being in the world' (8).

Similarly, Donoghue, Kermode, and George Steiner think that criticism, at its best, seeks not an adversarial but an imitative relation to art: it tries to borrow its litheness, its liberality, its tolerance. Some might object that art does not always possess these qualities, or that they are just another bourgeois luxury. Our critics would respond that if something making the claim as art lacks these qualities then perhaps we should further scrutinize the claim; and, in the second instance, that what we are talking about here is less a luxury than a necessity, though this is not to deny the fact that any number of states – e.g., Stalin's Russia, Mao's China, Pot's Cambodia – have sought to do without such. The necessity applies to civil societies; or better yet, it is what defines them as such. In any event, a criticism that seeks to borrow from a liberal aesthetic should be one committed, in Kermode's words, to 'the old contract between critic and reader' with its 'assumption that although a writer was likely to be better informed on the particular subject, he and the reader were essentially the same kind of person, similarly educated and likely to be brought to agreement, or left in informed disagreement, by a familiar, sanctioned mode of discourse: "This is so, is it not?" It is an assumption of likemindedness, of literate community, of the possibility of consensus' ('Novels about Adultery,' 2). Kermode's use of the past tense is disheartening, with its acknowledgment that there are those, at present, who think the contract bogus, the consensus unobtainable. Before giving the latter their due, we might note that the contract continues to have its adherents, not only among an older generation of critics who (in this instance, Steiner) still recall Leavis's admonition: 'the critical judgment (the "placing") is put forward with an attendant query: "This is so, isn't it?" And what the critic hopes for is a qualified assent, a "Yes, but ..." which will compel him to re-examine or refine his own response and lead to fruitful dialogue' ('F.R. Leavis,' 38). But also among some of the younger critics, as for instance Wendy Steiner, Louis Menand, Andrew Delbanco, and Mark Edmundson, the latter of whom, much in the vein of Kermode and Steiner, writes: 'I hope my work has the dialogical tone commended, if not always practiced, by F.R. Leavis. To him a critical observation ought to take the form "This is so, isn't it?" and the speaker should expect a return that begins, "Yes, but," with the yes, naturally, flavored by varying measures of irony' (26). Two: the contract, like the aesthetic, assumes the importance of tolerance, not the tolerance of an everything is commensurable with everything else sort, but a tolerance for those views and beliefs that we do not share, though we can imagine how other, well-meaning people just might. As Christopher Ricks reminds us in T.S. *Eliot and Prejudice*, 'tolerance has come to mean *not disapproving*, whereas the indispensability of tolerance, its unique social and human triumph, consists in its disapproving yet permitting; there is no particular virtue in – or even a meaning to – permitting or tolerating that of which you in any case approve. Tolerance itself then is reduced to being a human device which has served its turn and been scrapped' (53–4).

And yet some critics argue that neither the conversational model of discussion nor the toleration of viewpoints that we disapprove of makes

sense. Thus John Beverley writes: 'It is not only Khomeini-style fundamentalisms (or, for that matter, the realpolitik of the Indian government) that may have problems with the aesthetic and ideological
strategies represented by a novel like *The Satanic Verses*. In something
that is so obviously connected via the education system to the state and
to the formation of elites, there is always the danger that even the most
iconoclastic or "progressive" literature is simply forging the new forms
of hegemony' (*Against Literature*, xiv). Beverley's is a regrettable stance,
whether in criticism or the classroom, for the latter locus is also, as Trilling stressed, covered by the said contract, though the relation here is no
longer one of critic to reader but of teacher to student. Still, the rules of
dialogue and tolerance remain in force, or at least they do under our
preferred dispensation.[2] Remember, for instance, not only the story that
Trilling, in 'On the Teaching of Modern Literature,' tells about his
abyss-loving students, but also about those few who did not take warmly
to the abyss, who did not understand, and did not really want anything
to do with it:

> When the term-essays come in, it is plain to me that almost none of the stu-
> dents have been taken aback by what they have read: they have wholly con-
> tained the attack. The chief exceptions are the few who simply do not
> comprehend, although they may be awed by, the categories of our dis-
> course. In their papers, like poor hunted creates [*sic*] in a Kafka story, they
> take refuge first in misunderstood large phrases, then in bad grammar,
> then in general incoherence. After my pedagogical exasperation has run
> its course, I find that I am sometimes moved to give them a queer respect,
> as if they had stood up and said what in fact they don't have the wit to stand
> up and say: 'Why do you harry us? Leave us alone. We are not Modern
> Man. We are the Old People. Ours is the Old Faith. We serve the Old Gods,
> the gods of the copybook maxims, the small, dark, somewhat powerful dei-
> ties of lawyers, doctors, engineers, accountants ...' (*Beyond Culture*, 23)

Trilling, naturally, does not agree with the response, but he respects
it; he finds it 'authentic' (*Beyond Culture*, 24). In short, Trilling offers us
an example of tolerance, of 'disapproving yet permitting'; and I was
reminded of it this week when my university's newspaper featured a similar provocation, this time by a student who, in an essay entitled 'What's
Liberal about this Education?,' complained that too many of his classes
– English classes most notably – were carried out in a spirit of indoctri-
nation. The essay was not especially felicitous; but it too had its authen-

ticity, as when the student wrote: 'It seems ... [the faculty] is set on debunking beliefs which most students already don't adhere to. Does anyone really believe that we have been sheltered all our lives and never taught anything but to love those great oppressive evils: God, family and America?' The essay itself, meanwhile, was less notable than the response it engendered from a faculty member who, treating the essay as a personal affront, set out to expose its hidden agenda: 'Though he presents himself as a defender of apolitical, objective standards, he cannot hide his advocacy of right-wing political correctness: in the name of "God, family, and America," he is prepared to silence those who don't agree with his ideology, and to reject traditions that don't fit his agenda.' And then, in an attempt to demonstrate his own evenhandedness, the English instructor offers the following mixed message: 'The works of Jefferson, Thoreau, Hemingway, Twain, Lawrence, and Joyce have also been assigned [in his own classroom], and I have never condemned any of these authors as white male heterosexual pigs.' As one concrete instance, the vignette offers testimony that the liberal dispensation underlying the criticism and pedagogy of Trilling is undergoing all sorts of stress. The tone has become more righteous, more hectoring, a fact which I suspect, in the case of the university in question, has contributed to the precipitous decline in the number of its English majors. The road has not been kept open. Or to quote Kermode, speaking to our responsibility to those undergraduate students who will never join the profession or even major in English but who might, with the proper encouragement, develop a serious love of reading: 'That is why, like Lionel Trilling, I regard it as essential to "keep the road open" – to maintain, somehow, a style of talking about literature (which we must presume to recognise) from destruction. I regard this as by far the most important single element in the task of university teachers of literature' (AFK, 103).

Yet if not the liberal imagination, then what? In *No Respect*, Andrew Ross urges that we substitute the *'liberatory imagination'*:

Unlike the liberal imagination, which exercises and defends autonomous rights and privileges already achieved and possessed, the liberatory imagination is *pragmatically* linked to the doctrine of 'positive liberty,' which entails the fresh creation of legal duties to ensure that individuals will have the means that they require in order to pursue liberty and equality. But it is also this liberatory imagination which sets the agenda of radical democracy beyond liberal pragmatism in a pursuit of claims, actions, rights, desires, pleasures, and thoughts that are often still considered too illegitimate to be recognized as political. Such claims, actions, and rights, etc., invariably do not arise out of liberalism's recognition of the *universal* rights of individuals. Instead, they spring from expressions of difference, from the differentiated needs and interests of individuals and groups who make up the full spectrum of democratic movements today. These differences do not necessarily converge, and they can rarely be posed in relation to rights that would concern or embrace all individuals. (177)

Ross seeks to offer a politics that takes into account our growing loss of commonality, and which puts aside the concept of a single set of rights in favour of an ever-expanding set. It is an utopian vision, as Ross appears to acknowledge when he speaks of 'a culture self-consciously devoted to liberatory or utopian moments grounded in the bodily present as opposed to the hard, guilt-ridden school of cultural maturity' associated with the liberal imagination (222). We are back in the realm of mini-narratives, of a postmodern culture where what counts as true for one person will count as something quite different for another. The scenario raises the question of whether we can put together legislative guarantees, originating from a putative centre, whose legitimacy, unlike that of other 'credentialist institutions and foundations,' is not 'compromised' (223). Claims are made, rights are demanded, but with little sense of entering into a relation of reciprocity. Without this acknowledgment, Ross's notion of an overreaching politics is likely to collapse into an array of warring factions, each committed to its notion of what constitutes 'a liberatory sphere,' wherein they can uninhibitedly pursue their dreams of pleasure: 'Their ethical sense of the personal as a liberatory sphere means that their responsibility to "objective" political causes will be experientially inflected by a deeply subjective psycho-history. Their relation to daily life will not be guilt-ridden by correctional codes of political behavior, especially in the cultural marketplace of consumer options and choices; it will be informed by the matrix of power, pleasure, and desire experienced by other consumers' (230).

'Consumers' aside, for whom exactly is this thought to be a viable alternative to the liberal imagination? And if, as Ross acknowledges, 'the wars of cultural taste are likely to be sharpened by new kinds of disrespect' (231), what is to prevent these wars from becoming truly conflagrative? Why this desire to throw gasoline on the fire? It seems so unmindful of history, of what happens when peoples choose both to embrace and extol their differences, while repressing all those things that make them much like their neighbours. Given the long history of colonialism, it makes some sense for Chinua Achebe to 'announce not just that we [Africans] are as good as the next man but that we are much better' (quoted in Raine, 'Conrad and Prejudice,' 18); and given the long history of female suppression, it makes similar sense for Nina Baym to wed feminism criticism with morality, even when it verges on misandry: 'Because ... moral significance has always been the main criterion for literary value, when feminist image study disclosed that revered repositories of transcendent moral values were denigrators of women, these great writers' breadth was rightly compromised, their transcendence rightly undermined. Men as well as women readers and scholars have been influenced by this unimpeachable demonstration of the moral limits of the literary great ... The point ... is not that the writing of this or that dead white male is politically incorrect in some extremely local sense but that it fails on precisely the grounds of moral spaciousness ...' ('The Agony of Feminism,' 109). We are used to making allowances for people to vent their legitimate anger. Yet this accomplished, do we really wish to institutionalize a politics that encourages us, as Ross's libertatory imagination does, to pit our differences against one another? It is only because Ross imagines that he and his friends unfailingly represent virtue that he can appear so cavalier about the dismantling of liberalism's safeguards. But it is a dangerous way to think.

Most people naturally try to maintain an allegiance both to a group (e.g., economic, ethnic, professional, religious, etc.) and the larger community; and in doing experience the tension of competing demands. Consider Henry Louis Gates's confession: 'The truth is that blacks – across the economic and ideological spectrum – often feel astonishingly vulnerable to charges of inauthenticity, of disloyalty to the race. I know that I do, despite my vigorous efforts to deconstruct that vocabulary of reproach' ('The Charmer,' 116). The confession comes in a *New Yorker* article on Louis Farrakhan, the Muslim minister whose anti-Semitic and other incendiary remarks have aroused fears in whites even as he remains a hero to many African-Americans. The article, in fact, represents an admirable attempt to mediate the differences between the country's white and black citizens, though the attempt has not always been welcome: 'a few of his [Farrakhan's] more impetuous followers had shared with me their fervent hope for my death' (ibid.). The threat is criminal, or so we think if we hold to the notion of tolerance, the belief that others should grant to us what we, in turn, are prepared to grant to them: respect for differences. Gates would likely agree, for his work is rooted in the liberal tradition. Others in the academy – a small, albeit vocal, minority – might not be so agreeable, thinking the principle something like a sell-out. It may be so, but the alternatives look so much worse. But to return to the distinction between the liberal and liberatory imagination: first, what is at issue is less that of commonality over difference, or difference over commonality, than their reconciliation. True, this usually runs parallel with the assumption that a society's nucleus has a gravitational pull that its more distant spheres do not have; and with the accompanying assumption that an inclining towards the centre is not a bad thing, especially if the centre has not done anything so grievous as to lose our larger respect. By contrast, in the liberatory imagination there is a genuine resistance to the centre, paralleled by a hesitancy to grant that there is anything reciprocal about the relation of one's sphere with the centre. Instead, the interest seems more unidirectional, marked as it is by the overarching desire to see one's sphere the object of respect. If there is reciprocation, it is of a mock order, the way the radical Left directs all its scorn rightward; and the radical Right directs all its scorn leftward. The result is that two extremes begin, their protests notwithstanding, to mirror each other. Or as Richard Levin, in his fine essay 'The Current Polarization of Literary Studies,' writes:

> Because of the dynamics of polarization, both sides are defined, by themselves and by their enemies, at the opposite extremes of the political spectrum – at the far Right and far Left. And each side treats anyone who is not at its extreme position as belonging to the opposite extreme, according to the basic principle of polarizing, that all those who are not with us are against us and so must be with *them*. Political rightists regard all those to their left as 'left-liberals,' which is often hypenated as a single word and conflated with 'radicals,' while the religious Right lumps them all together as 'secular-humanists.' And leftists regard all those to their right as 'liberal-humanists,' which they often conflate with 'reactionaries.' (There is an eerie resemblance between 'secular-humanism' and 'liberal-humanism': the former is a pseudoreligion invented by the far Right to serve as its demonic enemy, while the latter is a pseudoideology invented by the far Left for the same purpose.) For both extremes homogenize as well as demonize the enemy and try to erase any intermediate positions. They also try to erase any differences among those intermediate positions: Marxists called our two major parties 'tweedledum and tweedledee,' and George Wallace insisted that 'there's not a dime worth of difference between them.' (65)

This has had unsettling consequences for those in the middle, those who think that the liberal imagination is, like Churchill's description of democracy, 'the worse form of [g]overnment' until one examines the alternatives. By forcing people to choose sides, by putting everything, the most extraordinary intellectual and aesthetic achievements included, to a political litmus test, those of staunch (left or right) temperaments have made it more difficult to keep the road open. That 'literary situations' can be read as 'cultural situations,' that 'cultural situations' can be read 'as great elaborate fights about moral issues,' and that the connection 'between literature and politics' is 'a very immediate one' – all of this Trilling has argued (*Beyond Culture*, 12; *Liberal Imagination*, xi). Just as such has been argued by Donoghue, Kermode, and Steiner. In this sense we can see them not only as literary but also as cultural critics. To a point, however, for they resist that insistence which would require them to see literature as reducible to its determinations, and thus removed from the claims of the liberal imagination. And it is this resistance that has been such a crucial element of their longevity.

Since the 1950s, Donoghue, Kermode, and Steiner, in very public fora, have each been making, year after year, significant contributions to our understanding of literature. During this time, they have seen critical movements come and go. Yet they have held to their independence. Now, in a new century, they can, like Sondheim's Carlotta Campion, each boast, 'I'm Still Here.' In fact, this might be imagined as the feistier title for the present study. That they are here, that they continue to be read by a broad spectrum of readers – outward from the middle in directions both left and right – might surprise some, yet it should not. The point is, just as everyone, someday, passes through Leicester or Times Square, so do most intellectuals return, from time to time, to that middle space that we call the common reader tradition, and which Donoghue, Kermode, and Steiner have done so much to keep alive, even when its death knell has been repeatedly sounded. And still they come, not only to read what others have on offer, but also to make their own contributions, in the manner of Gates, Jamaica Kincaid, and Helen Vendler in *The New Yorker*; Timothy Garton Ash, James Fenton, and Alan Ryan in the *New York Review of Books*; Marilyn Butler, Wendy Steiner, and Elaine Showalter in the *London Review of Books*; Anne Barton, Valentine Cunningham, and John Sutherland in the *Times Literary Supplement*; and Stephen Carter and Cornell West in the *New York Times Book Review*. One is welcome to scramble the affiliations here somewhat, for most of these critics write for more than one publication. The same is true of Dono-

ghue, Kermode, and Steiner, whom I have, respectively, associated with
the *New York Review of Books*, the *London Review of Books*, and *The New
Yorker*, though they have each written for a wide range of publications.
Kermode, for instance, has often written for the *New York Review*, just as
Donoghue, in the mid-1980s, wrote a number of essays for the *London
Review*. Steiner often writes for the *Times Literary Supplement* and *The
Observer* (now that he has severed his ties with *The New Yorker*), and like
Donoghue and Kermode, he was a regular contributor, in the 1960s, to
Encounter. The key point is that Donoghue, Kermode, and Steiner have
done quite a lot to keep the tradition of public criticism alive. Not so
long ago – in the late 1970s, after the decline of *Encounter*, before the
birth of the *London Review*, and 'when some newspapers were in abeyance, and others had taken to cutting back on the space allowed for the
discussion of books' (Karl Miller, 'London Review of Books,' 3) – the
tradition was thought moribund, so much so that Miller, the *London
Review*'s first editor, opened that journal with what seemed more like an
elegy than an inaugural: 'Literary journalism in this country shares at
present in the country's contracted and suspended state – a state that
will not improve if we keep our appointment with the worsening world
of recession ... The prestige and velocity of the "critical comment," that
notable and often dubious feature of the Fifties, have failed. For reasons
that can't all be separated from the facts of national decline, criticism,
and the literature it serves, have suffered a loss of confidence' ('The
London Review of Books,' 2).

As one reader, Stephen Fender, wrote in response to the *Review*'s first
issue, 'Has a journal ever been launched with such a general wringing of
withered hands? The wicked godmother [Ian] Hamilton comes to poison the baby in its crib with bile drawn from the corpse of the *New York
Review*, John Sutherland returns hot-wing from the States with new evidence that London lives in New York's shadow, while you muse darkly
on whether the *London Review* can escape the laws of history long
enough to survive the collapse of Western civilisation scheduled for
next year' (Letter, 2). However, Fender also had the good sense to
notice something else: 'Fortunately, the vigour and seriousness of your
other contributors belie your pessimism and show that you can still pick
your authors' (2). The *London Review* – which Kermode was instrumental in starting and on whose small editorial board he has from the first
been a member – has, in fact, since its inception, been a remarkable
showcase for criticism of the highest order. Its regular contributors have
included (among those not already named) John Bayley, Mary Beard,

Peter Campbell, Donald Davie, Stephen Greenblatt, Martha C. Nussbaum, Adam Phillips, Christopher Ricks, Richard Rorty, Lorna Sage, Edward Said, John Searle, John Sutherland, Bernard Williams, and Michael Wood. They have also included Donoghue, Kermode, and Steiner; and if the question should be posed as to what contribution these critics make to present interests – so inflected by a concern for ethnicity and gender – I should stress the fact that they have been instrumental in keeping 'the road open.' Today, when someone like Stephen Carter, Henry Louis Gates, Cornell West, or Patricia J. Williams commands a newspaper's or review journal's space with the purpose of engaging a larger, less-partisan audience – thinking that whatever our differences might be, we cannot give up on the notion of commonality and the ideal that grounds it (West: 'Once you lose that moral high ground, all you have is a power struggle, and that has never been a persuasive means for the weaker to deal with the stronger' [quoted in Robbins, *Secular Vocations*, 247]) – I would argue that they are participating in that same common reader tradition that our three critics have done so much to keep vital. It was, of course, a woman, Virginia Woolf, who, in both *The Common Reader* (1925) and *The Second Common Reader* (1932), did so much to make us mindful of the tradition to start with. Others have preferred to speak of this tradition as that of the 'man of letters,' and thereby either, as in the instance of John Gross, seemingly to exclude women, or, in the instance of Patrick Parrinder, to remind us that such exclusions have historically been associated with the tradition.[3] They may well have been, yet as my preference for the 'common reader' appellative suggests, I prefer to imagine the tradition otherwise – i.e., as welcoming rather than excluding – and to think that unless we do so there should be no reason for us to wish to see the tradition continue. Meanwhile, as I have noted, all current evidence suggests that we do imagine it otherwise, and that there is every reason to hope that the tradition has before it a long future.

Before closing, I would like to make a few final comparisons regarding Donoghue, Kermode, and Steiner. That is, while I have designed my chapters to suggest parallels among them, I would like to restate, for purposes of emphasis, the reasons why it makes sense to group these critics together, even as they could never be said to form a critical school. In fact, one of things that joins them is a refusal to submit their criticism to a theoretical program, thinking that 'in solitary pursuit of true judgment' one will reach the sought-after destination before the rest (Donoghue, 'The Gay Science,' 84). Again, this is not because they are against theory. Rather, it is because they think that whatever contribution theory makes, its proclivity is, in Leavis's words, towards a 'blunting of edge, blurring of focus and muddled misdirection of attention: consequences of queering one discipline with the habits of another' (quoted in Steiner, 'F.R. Leavis,' 39). Better, they think, to 'isolate your object, establish your subject matter,' and then proceed (Donoghue, 'The Gay Science,' 82). Theories, or large-scale generalizations, will come, but they will not be so mindful of, or obsessed with, errors of consistency, that they lose sight of that – be it a poem, a novel, an œuvre – which provoked the observation. Or as Donoghue remarks, 'a defence of criticism might well remark the plentitude of the error it accommodates.' Theorists seem 'to say: get it right, or give it up. I would prefer to say: *etiam peccata*. In criticism many a *culpa* is *felix*' (ibid.).

I have been arguing the importance of criticism vis-à-vis theory, and the pre-eminence of Donoghue, Kermode, and Steiner among critics. They offer less new theories than new readings, it being felt that the conversational, or dialectical, engagement that the critic enters into not only with the artist but also with the reader is central to what they do. This makes their work different from theory, with its greater readiness to impose itself upon the text, as well as its blithe indifference to the common reader. It is what provokes Steiner to write: 'No less than the artist – indeed, more so – the critic is in need of a public. Without it the act of ideal reading, the attempt to re-create the work of art in the critical sensibility is doomed to becoming arbitrary impression or mere dictate. There must exist a body of readers seeking to achieve in vital concert a mature response to literature. Only then can the critic work with that measure of consent which makes disagreement creative' ('F.R. Leavis,' 38). Like Donoghue's 'errors,' disagreements here are felicitous to the degree that they promote further conversation, as well as further discoveries. We live in a world whose definition manages to exist outside our grasp, no matter how often we think that we have captured its essence, or ensnared it in our theories. Good criticism has the grace to recognize this, as does good theory. But the difference is that theory, seeking to pin things down, is more prone to confusing what it wants to see with what it does see. To a point, it respects the world, and its conversation with it; but then, thinking it has things figured out, it sets out to control the stage; whereupon, both conversation and fresh discoveries diminish. For those seeking the truth of things, it is easy to grow impatient with conversation; and while criticism may not be its only home, it is one of its clearest sanctuaries, especially as it is reliant upon a public discourse that shares some of literature's virtues. These include the condition of being virtual as well as the discipline entailed in form, itself a version of otherness.

I do not mean to suggest that Donoghue's, Kermode's, and Steiner's work is bereft of theoretical significance. Quite the opposite is the case; and it has been an ambition of this study to say what this is. Earlier, I quoted Stephen Logan to the effect that in Kermode's criticism one discerns 'an argument which is nowhere stated but everywhere implied' ('The don in Grub Street,' 29); and what is true of Kermode's work is also true of Donoghue's and Steiner's. That is, because these critics have written so much, and most often in the form of the review essay, many readers may find it difficult to say exactly what principles impel the work. Yet there are such principles, and I have sought to delineate some of them (e.g., the centrality of the imagination for Donoghue; of the canon for Kermode; of elegy for Steiner; and for all three the values of criticism in relation to the common reader tradition), as a way of demonstrating, contra Hartman, that each is more than simply a translator of ideas. I have sought to clarify some of their more important themes or concerns, with the hope of understanding how they hold together.

By this point, I have said a great deal about the critics' relation to the common reader, and its consequences for criticism, for the reader to realize the connectedness of their interest. I might, though, say something more about the interrelationship of the specific themes – the imagination, the canon, and elegy – that I chose, respectively, to discuss in relation to Donoghue, Kermode, and Steiner. The themes are rather specific to each critic. While one might find Donoghue saying that his favourite writers on canonicity are David Hume and Frank Kermode – 'Hume's values may be hard to recover, but Kermode's argument that certain works of art become canonical by being "patient of interpretation" has the great merit of acknowledging the work of readers as well as of writers' ('The Book of Genius,' 3) – one does not find him developing a theory of canonicity. Likewise, while both Kermode and Steiner think the imagination important – as for instance when the latter asks whether there is 'something that would make the imagination responsible and answerable to the reality principles of being human all around us?' (AC, 54) – one does not find either developing a theory of the imagination, the way that Donoghue has.[4] Yet if each can be identified with one of the themes more than the others, we can nevertheless say that the themes of the imagination, canon, and elegy have a certain kinship. In particular, they have in common an attachment to humanistic values, to the belief that men and women, as not entirely determined beings, have it within their power to develop forms of inwardness, of consciousness, wherein reside not only conscience but also a faculty for making judgments about the world, including art objects. The attachment is hardly exceptional, yet it has come under attack from many theorists,[5] something that no doubt explains the defensiveness of Kermode's remark, in *Not Entitled*, that without this same attachment he could scarcely write a memoir at all: 'I have difficulty with the idea that I, or for that matter you, can be understood as merely the site of conflicting discourses, merely the product of practices we have no control over and no direct knowledge of. Frankly, if I could not continue to assume, unphilosophically, that I have a self, I shouldn't be bothering with all this' (158).

This sense of a self, which must posit an other, in order to distinguish itself, is closely related to the imagination; for it could never posit another self like its own by staying strictly within its own confines. There must be a way outward; and the suggestion is that this way is via the imagination, something that works in coordination with states of inwardness, even as it reaches outward. Notions like self and consciousness are predicated upon our holding to the metaphor of inwardness and outwardness, with consciousness itself allied with the former, and imagination with the latter. But the two states are bound in a constant dialectic, as is evident, for instance, in that group of painters – Giotto, Bosch, Rembrandt, Turner, Cézanne, Braque – who, writes Steiner, 'have created visual totalities which are intensely personal yet so powerfully and richly translated into expressive form that they add to and alter the repertoire of sight, of significant visual recognition and location in western culture. They have done so by finding ways through which to externalise what was in each of them an internal space' ('The Thinking Eye,' 64).[6] Here, not only do consciousness and imagination intersect, but they also work in tandem to create distinctive aesthetic forms, forms which by virtue of their distinctiveness give birth to the notion of canon, the notion that some things are not only expressive of a unique creative act but also require a different form of recognition and attention. Yet, if it is true that the imagination and canon are related, we might nevertheless be hesitant to associate them with elegy. This is, in a sense, a proper response, for the imagination is as capable now, as ever, of creating what in time will be deemed memorable works. That they become this – i.e., memorable – implies a readiness on our part to think of art as something that resists the passage of time, and that in time – be it a moment of decades or even centuries – will either, through the reader's refusal to let go, be kept alive or, if there be no refusal, simply disappear. Here, we might recall Roland Barthes's own refusal to let go of something that meant just as much to him (i.e., the sole surviving photograph of his father and mother) as the art object means to the true critic:

> What is it that will be done away with, along with this photograph which yellows, fades, and will someday be thrown out, if not by me – too superstitious for that – at least when I die? Not only 'life' (this was alive, this posed live in front of the lens), but also, sometimes – how to put it? – love. In front of the only photograph in which I find my father and mother together, this couple who I know loved each other, I realize: it is love-as-treasure which is going to disappear forever; for once I am gone, no one will any longer be able to testify to this: nothing will remain but an indifferent Nature. This is laceration so intense, so intolerable that alone against his century, Michelet conceived of History as love's Protest: to perpetuate not only life but also what he called, in his vocabulary so outdated today, the Good, Justice, Unity, etc. (*Camera Lucida*, 94)

Whereas most are too ready to let the photograph or poem die, thinking of such as completely replaceable by new photographs and poems, ad infinitum, the true critic seeks to keep it somehow alive, by going back to it, talking about it, and making others – especially the young – pay attention to it. The critic does something else as well: he or she helps to foster the *belief* that everything is not reducible to everything else, that the individual art object, like the person, has a worth resistant to the spatial and temporal factoring so beloved by the materialist.[7] That there is something elegiac about this effort is, I think, clear; and that it attaches not only to matters of the imagination and canon, but also, as Barthes suggests, to love itself, is I hope likewise clear. If the reader does not believe this, he or she might at least grant that it is thought to be so by Donoghue, Kermode, and Steiner.

When, in the Steiner chapter, I used the term 'elegy,' it also meant something more encompassing, for the suggestion was that Steiner's work is imbued with an apocalyptic sense of history, the consequence of some extraordinary 'dis-grace': '*dis-grace*, fall from grace, interruption of some kind of relationship with God' (AC, 60). We live in the period, says he, of the epilogue, when in our worst, or most nightmarish, moments, we feel as if 'we have stumbled into history essentially to suf-

fer and we will continue so till the end, until we either massacre ourselves with a thermonuclear bomb, or our cities implode, as they now
may, or there is famine, or finally there is an AIDS which cannot be
checked' (ibid.). In moods like this, Steiner seems like a twentieth-
century Hieronymous Bosch, yet because his pessimism is not without
reason his view here, like his criticism in general, cannot be dismissed. It
is, however, not a view necessarily shared by either Donoghue or Kermode, who, while they grant the force of an End-directed narrative, take
more sanguine views. For instance, Donoghue thinks that no one time is
intrinsically better or worse than another, much like Robert Frost, who
believed that 'the time was neither wrong nor right' (quoted in *The Old
Moderns*, 3). In *The Old Moderns*, Donoghue admits that he once contemplated writing a book, to be entitled *Gasping on the Strand*, on the theme
of crisis, but after considering it for a while had to concede that there
was not enough in the matter: 'It seemed reasonable to suppose that
certain forms of literature were developed in response to mass society,
the Great War, the October Revolution, unemployment, inflation, the
internal combustion engine, and other exacerbations. But the book
didn't progress beyond its title; it was stopped by the consideration that
many gifted writers managed to ignore crisis and to continue writing as
if one day were much like another' (ix–x). And yet, one does find a
darker, if not quite apocalyptic, mood in Donoghue's later work, especially in *Being Modern Together* (1991), where the modern city threatens
to make aliens of us all. As for Kermode, though I bracket him with
Donoghue, it might be truer so say that his is a more mediating view.
That is, like Steiner, he takes the notion of crisis quite seriously – witness
The Sense of an Ending, wherein notions of crisis and end are said to be
constitutive to contemporary thought – yet, like Donoghue, he thinks
that such notions have always, albeit in less familiar forms, been with us:
'It seems doubtful that our crisis, our relation to the future and to the
past, is one of the important differences between us and our predecessors' (95).

The critics also seem to part company in the estimation of myth. For
Steiner, myth has a real importance, most noticeably in *Antigones*, where
he claims that 'because Greek myths encode certain primary biological
and social confrontations and self-perceptions in the history of man,
they endure as an animate legacy in collective remembrance and recognition. We come home to them as to our psychic roots ...' (300–1). It is a
suggestive thesis, the sort which Steiner has a knack for proposing, even
as what might count as proof appears elusive. It is what leads Oliver Tap-

lin, otherwise favourably disposed to Steiner, to remark that the critic 'lavishes too much tumid language on it' (13). It is also the sort of claim that most distinguishes Steiner from Kermode and Donoghue, who are so much more rooted in the Anglo-American tradition of practical criticism. There is a strong element of practical criticism in Steiner's work as well, most notably in the review essays; still, he is a Central European at heart, and this makes him more inclined to the sort of philosophical speculation that Kermode and Donoghue tend to shun. For instance, as noted, myth in Kermode's work receives, on the whole, a rather bad reception; in *The Sense of an Ending*, most famously, it is the bad brother to fictions; it represents what happens when fictions become indolent, thus regressive: 'We know that if we want to find out about ourselves, make sense, we must avoid the regress into myth which has deceived poet, historian, and critic' (43). Then, elsewhere, Kermode likes to identify myths with overreaching abstractions, as when, in his criticism of Northrop Frye, he writes by way of warning, 'when you hear talk of [mythic] archetypes, reach for your reality principle' (C, 121).[8] Donoghue also prefers the reality principle to myth, though he is prepared not only to countenance but also to embrace those myths that have a more local or historical colour, and strike him as suitable. The clearest instance of this occurs in his debate with those Irish social historians, or revisionists, who would substitute the categories of demographics, economics, and politics for the myth of Ireland embodied not only in the story of revolution but also in Yeats's poetry and plays. But Donoghue sees harm in the dismissal of the stories that a people employ to help explain themselves to themselves: 'A myth is a story told over and over again for the comfort of the community that receives it: its status apart from that community is of no account' (W, 170). To take their stories, or myths, away from the Irish would, thinks Donoghue, be an extraordinary mistake: 'Social history is an attempt to remove from Irish history the glamour of its sacrifices and martyrdoms. Revisionism is a project of slow history, or confounding the drama, thwarting the narrative. Unfortunately, Ireland without its story is merely a member of the EC, the begging bowl our symbol' (W, 172).

Sometimes, the relation between myth and religion finds itself blurred. They both rely upon narrative, and this can contribute to this blurring, as Donoghue appears to note when he, again writing about the Irish, says: 'In Ireland, Sunday Mass is the clearest form of customary knowledge. To the extent to which this knowledge has been eroded, the erosion has come about not mainly because of secularism at large but because, for many people, narrative has lost its power. All that remains of the mystery is the tale, and now, for those people, not even that' (W, 171). For Donoghue, the religious narrative of 'the life, death, and resurrection of Christ, the lives of the saints, the commemoration of Christ's life in the sacraments, as elucidated by the teachings of the Church through its doctrines and rituals' (ibid.) retains dominion, making it impossible to speak of it in terms of myth. He knows that the case is otherwise for many of his contemporaries, especially among academics. Nevertheless, he places his faith in this soteriology, thinking it true; and if this means that he must live his life against the grain, he seems prepared to do this. Yet while his religious belief clearly informs all his criticism, it seldom offers itself as an overt matter. Rather, like Auden who believed 'That love, or truth in any serious sense, / Like orthodoxy, is a reticence,' Donoghue prefers to judge literature as literature, all the while treating his religious belief as if it were, says Alfred Kazin, 'a precious personal possession, something apart, and not to be trafficked in this world of many issues' (45).

Something like a religious sense of the world also informs Steiner's and Kermode's criticism, but the blurring of religion and myth seems more apparent. For instance, Steiner, whose criticism has become, of late, much more invested in religious questions, especially after *Real Presences*, a book which Steiner has spoken of as representing his own 'coming around that immensely difficult corner, towards theology' (AC, 54), seemed, in his earlier criticism, to want to make myth stand in the place of religion, even to the point of suggesting, in *Antigones*, that Antigone is a precursor to Christ: 'What intention attaches to the repeated hints (in de Quincey, in Kierkegaard, they are more than hints) that Antigone is to be understood as a counterpart to Christ, as God's child and messenger before Revelation?' (19). Yet Steiner's later work is much more comfortable with theology than before, to the point that he even claims, when looking back over his writings, that it has been focused about 'almost a single point' – that is, 'the theological dimension, the question of the existence of God' (AC, 83). This may, or may not, be true, but it does seem to have become true, and if unlike Donoghue, Steiner eschews orthodoxy, he still has many valuable things to say about the relation of theology to art, to the point that he has become one of the most interesting critics on this matter. As for Kermode, he has said, 'I have no religious experience but I claim to be familiar with the experience of poetry' ('Theory and Truth,' 10). The bracketing of the two concerns is no accident, for while Kermode, as a lapsed Anglican, may have no religion per se, he has long treated poetry, and art in general, as akin to religion; or as he writes in *Not Entitled*: 'The incense reserved for my sacrifices, if any of my losses deserve that name, has been figurative; it has been poetry' (261). Kermode might consider this as his own fiction, but it really has become something like his own myth, that is, something he has accepted without obvious warrant. It is a view that Donoghue has always distanced himself from, whereas there was a time when Steiner might have said much the same thing. Now, however, Steiner seems to be moving away from culture as religion, and toward granting religion its own force. And maybe this, too, is the suggestion of the moving meditation on holiness that closes Kermode's memoir. I do not know for sure; but the passage does hint of a belief in, or longing for, something that transcends even the specialness of art:

> From poetry and music I derive the little I know about holiness. They continue to inform me. I am well aware that there are other kinds of holiness, kinds that I can hopelessly admire, that impel people into action, tending AIDS patients or children dying in poverty; also other kinds that call for silence, a sacrifice almost unimaginable to unholy talkers. Knowing of them I am persuaded of the reality of vocations, other people's vocations, and I know that holiness of this sort has nothing to do with bishops promulgating ... But I know also that these holinesses normally have little to do with the kind I have attributed to poetry and music. I can faintly sense a rare coming together of these disparate holinesses in certain Bach cantatas, especially the one known as the *Actus Tragicus*, which begins by assuring us that God's time is the best, and then urges us to set our houses in order, for we must die and not remain among the living. God is serenely invited to incline us to consider that our days are numbered. What seems to me an especially luminous junction of holinesses occurs in a performance of this cantata in which the soprano, Teresa Stich-Randall, seems to have known, as she sang, not only what the words and the music but what holiness meant. (*Not Entitled*, 261)

Like Donoghue and Steiner, Kermode may be first and foremost a critic of literature, yet as this passage testifies, he, like them, has almost a spiritual regard for music, be it for Bach's *Sacred Cantatas*, Dietrich Fischer-Dieskau's *lieder*-singing, or Beethoven's last *Quartets*. Donoghue, for instance, mindful of Barthes's contrary opinion, still finds in Fischer-Dieskau's singing a 'spirituality [that] seemed to claim not only an extraordinary degree of inwardness, but the transcendence of human limitation in every respect' (W, 90). And Steiner, recalling Lévi-Strauss's remark 'that the invention of melody is "the supreme mystery,"' goes on to say that there will always be something in this invention that escapes him, that comes to signify existence in its profoundest mood: 'but it's not just melody that I don't get. I don't get Bach being able to do the forty-eight preludes out of a four-note motif. I don't know how a Wagner holds in himself the arching construct from the opening chord of the *Ring* to the last. Or a Beethoven quartet' (AC, 89). That these three critics should all feel such reverence for music is not, I think, a coincidence, but reflective of the fact that as among our pre-eminent stylists they should rightly be in possession of an ear for rhythm, a feeling for harmony, and a longing to make their prose mimic some of music's sweeter sounds. More than any other reason, this is why I group them, for I can think of no three critics who so wonderfully remind the reader that, in the best instances, criticism can be a version of what, in more ordinary occasions, it simply studies: literature. Yet this said, we should also take note of the fact that as writers, or stylists, they have their differences, for they each display a particular strength: Kermode writes perhaps the most limpid prose in English; Donoghue the most graceful; and Steiner the most prophetic. So rather than mirroring, they seem more to complement one another, as if together they constituted the finest of classical trios. Meanwhile, they are still at work, still making lovely music, as if in testimony to the poet's belief that 'music at the close' is 'writ in remembrance more than things long past.'

NOTES

Introduction

1 The quotation appears in Michiko Kakutani's review (*New York Times* [12 March 1996], nat. ed., B 2) of Heywood's book, *Dedication to Hunger: The Anorexic Esthetic in Modern Culture.*

2 Critiquing Eagleton's *The Rape of Clarissa: Writing, Sexuality, and Class Struggle in Samuel Richardson,* Elaine Showalter argues that 'when theorists borrow the language of feminist criticism without a willingness to explore the masculinist bias of their own reading system, we get a phallic "feminist" criticism that competes with women instead of breaking out of patriarchal bounds' ('Critical Cross-Dressing; Male Feminists and the Woman of the Year,' 127).

3 In the first chapter of *Politics by Other Means: Higher Education and Group Thinking,* David Bromwich offers a full discussion of this theme, called 'stealing the discourse of the Other.'

4 The first Jewish member of the Columbia English Department, Trilling had to fight to hold on to his job, for the department made a concerted effort to dismiss him. Other Jewish intellectuals, at this time, had difficulty even getting in the door. Or as James Atlas, in 'The Changing World of New York Intellectuals,' writes: 'If Jews became freelance intellectuals, it wasn't necessarily by choice. The English departments of universities weren't open to them in the 30's and 40's' (71).

5 What I mean by Arnoldian play is explained in the text, but here I would like to explain Schiller's notion of play, one that has been the object of many recent allusions, as critics seek a middle ground between the New Historicists' determinisms and the Derrideans' uncorralled play of difference. Thus, Peter Brooks writes that 'Schiller's *On the Aesthetic Education of Man* (1795) ... remains in my view one of the most powerful and, for all its dated-

ness, most persuasive arguments for the centrality of the aesthetic in culture and the need to make it a core concept in education' ('Aesthetics and Ideology,' 159); and Donoghue writes, 'Schiller extended Kant's sense of art by appealing to the experience of play as an act of the mind superior to both the impulse to sense and the impulse to form, removing the deficiencies of each. A person is only and completely a person while at play. The source of play is excess of energy, beyond need. We have the basis of a theory of aesthetics if to Kant's third Critique and Schiller's *Letters on the Aesthetic Education of Man* we add Goethe's letter to Louise Seidler (February 1818) in which he describes that excess as the emotion of hope, anticipation, and astonishment. The condition of art, Goethe said, is probability, "but within the realm of probability the highest ideal must be supplied which does not otherwise appear"' (*The Old Moderns*, 85–6).

My point, then, in alluding to Schiller is to suggest the possibility of a space – here identified with that of the 'play impulse' – between the realms of the determinate and the indeterminate judgment. Or as Schiller writes: 'Reason demands, on transcendental grounds, that there shall be a partnership between the formal and the material impulse, that is to say a play impulse, because it is only the union of reality with form, of contingency with necessity, of passivity with freedom, that fullfils the conception of humanity' (*On the Aesthetic Education of Man*, 76).

6 Quoted in Dickstein, *Double Agent*, 79.
7 In the 'Preface' to *Literary Criticism*, Trilling writes: 'As it has been traditionally conceived, criticism is (among other things) a speculative discourse about the nature and function of literature. Its etymology reminds us that its practical end in view is the making of judgments, but from the first it is understood that it could not proceed to that end without specifying the grounds on which judgment is to be made, and this requires it to say what the thing is that it judges. The discourse that ensues has always been thought highly pleasurable. The pleasure is a natural one – criticism, as Eliot has said, "is as inevitable as breathing"' (ix).
8 See John Gross, *The Rise and Fall of the Man of Letters*, for a full-fledged history of this tradition, particularly in its nineteenth- and early twentieth-century variants.
9 In 'Intelligent Theory,' Kermode writes more fully in response to a position articulated by Stephen Logan, but thought to be expressive of that of many British critics:

Mr. Stephen Logan ... elegantly transforms Eliot's parenthetic observation that 'there is no method except to be very intelligent' into a pronouncement that intelligence is 'largely a matter of perceiving the disabling restrictions of method.' I doubt whether Eliot would have approved of this stronger version. He made the original remark in the context of a brief but admiring allusion to Aristotle's *Posterior Analytics*, a fragmentary yet still methodical work. Eliot offers it as an instance of 'intelligence ... swiftly operating the analysis of sensation to the point of principle and definition,' and is certainly saying that we should admire the intelligence of the operation rather than its method: but he is not saying what Mr. Logan says.

It would surely be unfortunate if it became the fashion to regard any sign of interest in literary theory and method as in itself a failure of intelligence; and it would be positively bizarre if those who held this view further asserted that merely by doing so – by the fact of their having perceived 'the disabling restrictions of method' – they had proved their own intelligence. Intelligence has enemies, and ought to defended (the enemy identified by Eliot in 'The Perfect Critic' is, by the way, emotion, not method), but that is not equivalent to calling whatever one chooses to defend by the name of intelligence. (8)

10 In a spirit analogous to that of Bradbury, David Bromwich writes: 'Until recently, we had in America a class of intellectual journalists who showed an unintimidated interest in the works of scholarship. That class has vanished – a fact so perplexing that, though the membership of the class was widely recognized twenty years ago, many scholars now want to deny that such persons *could* have existed. The decline of a public intellectual style meant the loss of a practical wisdom that could challenge academic pieties without an edge of philistinism' (*Politics by Other Means*, xiii).

11 Quoted in Wendy Steiner, *The Scandal of Pleasure*, 67; and in Rothstein, 'Musicologists Roll Over Beethoven,' 1.

12 In *The Function of Criticism*, Terry Eagleton also writes that for Leavis criticism was not 'a mere matter of "good sense," but must engage modes of analysis and forms of specialized experience denied to the "common reader"' (72).

13 Quoted in Kaplan and Rose, *The Canon and the Common Reader*, 55.

14 In his review of Gates and West's *The Future of the Race*, 'Blacks Like Them,' Gerald Early writes: 'The question, inescapably Victorian in its aspect, that the authors wish to answer – what is their duty to the lower or less fortunate class of blacks? – indicates the black bourgeoisie's inability to understand precisely what their success means to themselves or to blacks generally' (7).

Meanwhile, for a fine discussion of the successes that minority writers have had as public critics, see Robert S. Boyton's essay, 'The New Intellectuals.'

15 Compare what Kundera, from the writer's point of view, has to say about this relation: 'We should not denigrate literary criticism. Nothing is worse for a writer than to come up against its absence. I am speaking of literary criticism

as meditation, as analysis; literary criticism that involves several readings of the book it means to discuss (like great pieces of music we can listen to time and again, great novels too are made for repeated readings); literary criticism that, deaf to the implacable clock of topicality, will readily discuss works a year, thirty years, three hundred years old; literary criticism that tries to apprehend the originality of a work in order thus to inscribe it on historical memory. If such meditation did not accompany the history of the novel, we would know nothing today of Dostoyevsky, or Joyce, or Proust. For without it a work is surrendered to completely arbitrary judgments and swift oblivion' (*Testaments Betrayed*, 24).

16 Patrick Parrinder, in *Authors and Authority*, writes: 'Already the term "Anglo-American," applied to generalisations about the state of criticism and teaching in both Britain and America (and by extension, in the other English-speaking countries) is in most cases an empty formality. It is becoming misleading to assume that criticism and English literature have the same status in British culture as they have in the United States, to go no further. This is clearly visible in the criticism itself. Most good criticism published in America is addressed in the first place to an exclusively American reader, and much good British criticism is addressed to a British reader, with some strenuous exceptions ... Book publishing in Britain and America is increasingly unified, but this is not the case with book reviewing, and still less with the actual reading of contemporary fiction and poetry. Nor are the two cultures as closely interrelated as it might appear from the fact that, by and large, they acknowledge and study the same literary tradition. Great Britain is no longer the centre of English-speaking culture, and is in some (though not all) respects politically and culturally subordinate both to America and Europe. The United States has a national language and literary culture which it happened to acquire from one of the many European nationalities which make up the vast bulk of its population' (339–40).

17 Wellek, for instance, writes: 'Criticism aims at a theory of literature, at a formulation of criteria, and standards of description, classification, interpretation, and finally judgment. It is thus an international discipline, a branch of knowledge, a rational pursuit. If we want to arrive at a coherent theory of literature, we must do what all other disciplines do: isolate our object, establish our subject matter, distinguish the study of literature from other related pursuits' (quoted in Donoghue, 'The Gay Science,' 81).

18 In his 1991 essay 'The Man of Letters in a Closed Shop,' John Gross writes: 'The great names of critical theory are either Continental European or American. By comparison, Barthes, Foucault, de Man, Derrida, Genette, Jameson, Habermas, Hartman, Said, Fish: a Night of a Thousand Stars. On

the other hand, Terry Eagleton, Terence Hawkes, Catherine Belsey, Stephen Heath ... But it would be a mistake to measure the impact of theory in Britain purely in terms of the local practitioners. We are dealing with a phenomenon in which national boundaries count for comparatively little. Foreign theorists speak directly to British readers; they also confer authority on their British disciples' (15).

19 Compare Stephen Greenblatt and Giles Gunn's embrace of fashion as a significant force in literary studies. In the 'Introduction' to *Redrawing the Boundaries*, they say, with regard to the newer critical methodologies, 'It is easy to dismiss these transformations as "mere" changes in intellectual fashion, as if fashion were not – or at least should not be – important to literary intellectuals. But in fact continual refashioning is at the center of the profession of literary study' (5).

20 Another public critic of independent bent who should fit into this notion of articulating an exile's point of view is Edward Said, who in the 'Introduction' to *Culture and Imperialism* speaks quite specifically of the benefits to be had from having resided both inside and outside of this or that culture: 'The last point I want to make is that this book is an exile's book. For objective reasons that I have no control over, I grew up as an Arab with a Western education. Ever since I can remember, I have felt that I belonged to both worlds, without being completely *of* either one or the other. During my lifetime, however, the parts of the Arab world that I was most attached to either have been changed utterly by civil upheavals and war, or have simply ceased to exist. And for long periods of time I have been an outsider in the United States, particularly when it went to war against, and was deeply opposed to, the (far from perfect) cultures and societies of the Arab world. Yet when I say 'exile' I do not mean something sad or deprived. On the contrary belonging, as it were, to both sides of the imperial divide enables you to understand them more easily. Moreover New York ... is in so many ways the exilic city *par excellence*; it also contains within itself the Manichean structure of the colonial city described by Fanon. Perhaps all this has stimulated the kinds of interests and interpretations ventured here, but these circumstances certainly made it possible for me to feel as if I belonged to more than one history and more than one group' (xxvi–xxvii).

21 It may be a small matter, but I am struck by how important the father appears in the lives of Donoghue, Kermode, and Steiner. *Warrenpoint* is in large part a testimonial to the author's father; and in *Not Entitled*, the father also appears, if not as handsomely as in the Donoghue book, a strong presence, about whose opinion of him the author appears most anxious. Meanwhile, Steiner's memoir, *Errata*, is full of praises and statements of obligation

respecting the author's father. One instance: 'It may be that too much of my father's "library," of his "syllabus" of the supreme and caustic certitude that in the face of a Homer, of a Goethe, of a Beethoven or a Rembrandt, the second-rate is precisely that, conditions and confines me still' (174). Mothers, meanwhile, are a less dominant presence, even to the point that Donoghue says of his mother that '[i]t was taken for granted that whatever my mother did, she did badly' (24).

22 Quoted in Davie, 'The Clans,' 98.

23 Donoghue also experienced a difficult relation with Davie, one which he recounts at length in the seventh chapter of *Words Alone*. Davie – whom Donoghue describes as having been 'morally intimidating, with a touch of the commissar about him. He used the word "infidel" more freely and more deliberately than I supposed it had ever been used since the seventeenth century' (1138) – broke off their friendship following a Donoghue review: 'Donald Davie brought his friendship with me to an end because of one sentence in a long review I published of his second book on Pound: "The relation between Davie's mind and its contents has always been experimental." Davie interpreted it as saying: "Davie has never been able to think"' (226).

24 Compare Steiner's characterization of the English intellectual in his 1962 essay on Leavis: 'Being geographically compact, English intellectual life is sharply susceptible to the pressures of club and cabal; the artifice of renown can be swiftly conjured or revoked. In small waters sharks can be made to pass for momentary leviathans. It is also true that there is between the universities and the world of press, magazine, and radio an alliance of brisk vulgarisation. An unusual number of academics have a flair for showmanship; too often, ideas which are, in fact, intricate, provisional, and raw to the throat are thrown to the public as if they were bouquets. Watching some of the more brilliant performers at work, one would scarcely suppose that thought and scholarship are a rare, lonely, often self-consuming exercise of the soul when it is at full, painful stretch. Above all, there *is* in the English intellectual and artistic establishment a dangerous bias towards personal charm, towards understatement and amateur grace' ('F.R. Leavis,' 42).

25 In a similar vein, Donoghue, in his essay 'The Englishness of English Poetry,' wonders whether British poetry might have earlier put off some of its provincialism if, instead of having Yeats edit, in 1936, *The Oxford Book of Modern Verse*, the publisher had taken a chance with Pound or Eliot: 'It would be bold speculation to imagine, in 1936, that a contract for *The Oxford Book of Modern Verse* might have been offered to Pound or Eliot rather than to Yeats. But suppose it had been. A publisher willing to see Yeats play ducks-and-drakes with Pater's prose would have had to give any other editor a certain

latitude. It's at least conceivable that Eliot or Pound would have disclosed the possibility of being an English poet in a context of International Modernism (to use Hugh Kenner's phrase). It would then have appeared as an option for younger poets. I'm thinking of a poet in England, writing poems addressed not (or not necessarily) to readers of Palgrave or Quiller-Couch or even of Michael Roberts, but to readers of international literature' (49).

Compare Kermode and Donoghue's view with that of Hugh Kenner in *A Sinking Island: The Modern English Writers*. And, by contrast, with Dame Helen Gardner, borrowing from Graham Hough: 'There is truth in Graham Hough's feeling that the kind of literary campaign that Pound and Eliot waged for a truly "modern" poetry was something alien to the English literary tradition, which has not been given to movements and manifestos' (*In Defence of the Imagination*, 22).

26 Quoted in Alter, 'Outside the Academy,' 15.
27 About this same affair, Donald Davie wrote: 'Kermode's is the 20th-century sensibility; hers [Gardner's] is, charmingly but irrelevantly, stalled with, perhaps, Michael Drayton. In that once again, I dare say, the consensus is with her' ('Certainties,' 6).
28 Kermode writes: 'Literature, or the reading of literature, seems always to be concerned with the immanence of the intemporal in the temporal. There are of course many ways of talking about this, including the modern fashion for horizontal and vertical codes, melody and harmony. But the real point is surely that reading is, or mimes, a matter of life and death – the structuring of a life by a death or by a *Vorverständnis* that includes death before it comes' ('A Reply to Joseph Frank,' 588).
29 Quoted in White, 'Kermode and Theory,' 14.
30 In a persuasive critique of recent American value theory, especially Smith's, John Guillory writes: 'Liberal pluralism confronts the absolutist posturing of particular discourses of value with the philosophical bad news that no metaphysical grounds exist for such posturing. The alternative to the tendential absolutism of value judgments seems obviously to be that all values are "contingent," a condition for which the variability of price in the market provides the most readily available analogy. But the fact remains that the market is the historical *condition* and not merely the proper analogy for the extension of the value-concept to all acts of judgment. The failure to recognize this fact has had the effect of making the economic analogy in recent critiques of aesthetics merely empty, an analogy that fails to represent the real complexity of economic relations, an analogy that erases the history of economic discourse. In the absence of any sense of what has been at stake historically in the emergence of political economy, the cri-

tique of value has been conducted as the most arid exercise in philosophical debate, as the choice between the two positions of relativism and absolutism. Hence the relativist critique of the absolutist position congratulates itself for having exposed the groundlessness of "absolute" values, without raising its own discourse of commensuration to the level of historical self-reflection' (*Cultural Capital*, 324).

31 Guillory writes: 'To return ... to Barbara Herrnstein Smith's critique, we can recognize the historical irony of cultural relativism's celebration of the plurality of values; for what is really being celebrated is precisely the condition of the absolute commensurability of everything' (*Cultural Capital*, 323).

32 Quoted in Shattuck, *Candor and Perversion*, 27.

33 Quoted in Fish, *Professional Correctness*, 77.

34 Quoted in ibid., 78.

35 Quoted in ibid., 78.

36 Quoted in Brooks, 'Aesthetics and Ideology,' 161.

37 John Hollander has expressed the same sentiment: 'The *gauchisme* of many younger scholars reads like the deeply unpolitical cant of an exceedingly careerist generation. Many of the scholars wielding disproportionate power in the professionalized study and teaching of literature in the universities today have the same character as CEOs who look only for the quarterly bottom line, as lawyers who have been contriving to give that profession an even – did it seem possible? – worse name' (quoted in Robbins, *Secular Vocations*, 231).

38 Quoted in Edmundson, *Literature against Philosophy*, whose argument I am here recalling, 54.

Chapter 1: Denis Donoghue

1 Quoted in Donoghue, 'Kenneth Burke's Dangling Novel,' 84.

2 In the first issue of the *London Review of Books*, Karl Miller, its editor, wrote: 'The writers we publish, and the writers and publishers whose books we review, will generally be British. There have been some jokes to the effect that the same thing could be said of the *New York Review*, and these jokes can be taken to reflect certain realities of the English-speaking literary world. It is a world in which many books come out both in Britain and America, and, quite often, at about the same time, and in which British and American writers, and readers, are very much aware of one another. The *London Review* will therefore have to be very much aware of the *New York Review*. We may on occasion publish some of the same books, and we shan't always be straining

to make our coverage different or complementary. But it will not be hard to tell which journal is which' ('The London Review of Books,' 2).

3 Hannah Arendt's phrase 'enlarged mentality' might be thought useful here.

4 Donoghue takes his title here from Yeats's poem 'The Statues,' wherein the poet writes: 'We Irish, born into that ancient sect.' See *We Irish* (3).

5 Donoghue specifically mentions 'the French salon-keepers, the critics who rejected the first Impressionist paintings; Nietzsche, Tchaikovsky, Hugo Wolf, and Shaw in their denunciations of Brahms; Walton, who has dismissed Mahler; Ernest Newman, ridiculing Bartok's Violin Sonata' (AWM, 56).

6 In 'Slow Deconstruction,' David Bromwich also finds de Man's errors of scholarship telling: 'He was involved twice, to revealing effect, in controversies over his interpretations of philosophers – with Stanley Corngold on Nietzsche's conception of error, and with Raymond Geuss on Hegel's understanding of art. De Man had translated Nietzsche's remark that the world is a place where a mistake can happen and made it say instead that the world is a realm where "error reigns." He had taken Hegel's sentiment that art is for us a thing of the past, a description of one phase of civilization, and made it apply to all art at all times. In both disputes, he managed to concede every pertinent detail and yet to imply it could not possibly affect the truth he was getting at' (23).

Meanwhile, Donoghue can also be found pointing out lapses in scholarship among critics whom he clearly likes, as in his review of Harold Bloom's *The Western Canon* ('The Book of Genius'), wherein he repeatedly points out misquotations, and in his review of J. Hillis Miller's *Topographies* ('Textual Abuse'), wherein he begins by chastizing Miller for repeatedly misquoting a de Man passage, articulating a program for 'the linguistics of literariness,' in *Resistance to Theory*: 'This programme evidently means a great deal to J. Hillis Miller. He has quoted and misquoted the passage in several recent essays as if it were a manifesto he signed with de Man. By misquoting it, he takes possession of it. In "Paul de Man's Wartime Writings" (1988) he substituted "Deconstruction" for "the linguistics of literariness." In *Topographies* he quotes the entire passage from which the excerpt is taken, substitutes "sun" for "day" in an earlier sentence, and calls on the whole essay as if de Man's authority coincided with his own' (24).

7 In *Wallace Stevens*, Kermode also takes special note of these lines, calling the poem's fourth section, wherein they are located, 'Stevens's most ravishing explanation' (105).

8 In a much later discussion, the chapter 'On "Burnt Norton"' in *The Old Moderns*, Donoghue offers a very different view, in response to F.R. Leavis's dismissal of Eliot's late poetry:

Leavis allowed himself to be scandalized, in his commentary on 'Burnt
Norton,' by Eliot's insistence – at least it appeared to Leavis to amount to
an insistence – on 'the unreality, the unlivingness, of life in time.'

   Eliot is not insisting on anything of this kind: he couldn't have believed
it while in communion with a church founded on the redemption of time
by the Annunciation. (230)

9 In *Thieves of Fire*, Donoghue says of *Paradise Lost* 'that I would read the poem
   in a spirit comparable to that of Sri Ramakrishna who, when asked why an
   omnipotent God permits the operation of evil in the world, answered: "in
   order to thicken the plot"' (43).

10 Valentine Cunningham's *In the Reading Gaol* is, in fact, a book-length meditation on the difference of this one letter, nicely begun by taking notice of a
   slip of pen that, in Viriginia Woolf's diary, transmuted 'underworld' into
   'underword.' Or as Cunningham writes, 'For this text [Woolf's diary] is a
   curious, arresting, even puzzling amalgam of word-stuff and world-stuff. It is
   certainly neither all of the word nor all of the world. And it is the argument
   of this book that this amalgamation of word and world is the condition not
   just of Virginia Woolf's writing but of all writing' (10).

11 This artist will also have to contend with those artists and critics who argue
   that all is image or surface, and that depth is but imaginary. Mark C. Taylor,
   discussing the work of the painter David Salle, writes: 'To be obsessed with
   presentation is to be preoccupied with appearances, and to be preoccupied
   with appearances is to be consumed by what *is* rather than by what *ought to be*.
   In the world of consumer capitalism, what is, is image. Salle concludes that
   you can make a presentation without the *thing* presented but not without the
   image presented. From this point of view, *the real is the image and reality is imaginary*. The task of the artist in the age of electronic reproduction is to
   present presentation by displaying the omnipresence of images' (*Nots*, 179).

12 Compare *Walter Pater* (1995), 252; and The *Practice of Reading* (1998), 78.

13 A reader who would prefer not to be identified.

14 In *The Arts without Mystery*, Donoghue makes a tentative stab at a definition of
   art: 'I suppose most people, if asked what art is, would say something along
   these lines. A work of art is a work designed as such, even when a practical
   use is primarily intended, as in architecture; it is offered to our perception as
   a work at once expressive, formal, and unified; offered in the hope of arous-
   ing and gratifying our aesthetic sense, our sense of the beautiful in the manifestation of form. The relation between the work of art and the given world
   may be close or distant. It may be close, as in art which seeks to resemble,
   refer, allude, or denote; or it may be so distant that it shows more interest in
   the world as it might be or a world quite different from our own than in the

common world given to us in its appearances. Some forms or art, like painting, sculpture, or the novel, are comfortable with the possibility of resemblance: others, like music, are not. The pleasure offered by a work of art is
the pleasure of understanding an object for its own sake even though understanding can't be more than partial. A work of art is then admired for various
reasons; for durability, in the sense that it has survived, valued by generations
of people who in one degree or another have admired it; or it has shown
notable power to move a wide range of people, so that it is easy to believe
that it testifies to some permanent feature of human life' (100).

15 Quoted in Mark C. Taylor, *Nots*, 178.

16 Phillips here is discussing Trilling in the light of what might have tempted
him. He doesn't say that he succumbed, at least not entirely. That Donoghue
is liable to the same temptation is my implied sense.

17 In her perceptive 'Introduction' to *The Pure Good of Theory*, Pauline Fletcher
notes how the whole debate regarding the imagination changed over the
course of Donoghue's career, forcing him to defend strongly what he previously spoke of with reservations: 'At one time the imagination was under
attack because it placed man, rather than God, at the centre of the universe;
indeed, that was the basis of Donoghue's own attack on Stevens in *The Ordinary Universe*. But now the attack comes from structuralists, anthropologists,
Marxists, and Freudians, and it is directed not merely against God (long
since declared dead), but against the very concept of man as creator, author,
autonomous being. Donoghue is now [in *The Sovereign Ghost*] led to ask: "Is it
necessary to revise the standard account of the imagination under pressure
from those forces which would displace man from the creative centre of
experience and make him rather a function of certain governing systems or
codes?"' (PGT, 9–10).

18 In *Adam's Curse*, Donoghue writes: 'To survive as a religion, if [Emilc]
Durkheim is right, Christianity had to become a church. There has never
been a religion without a church. There have been magical practices and
cults, but these lack the social and communal identity that makes a religion.
"A Church," as Durkheim says, "is not a fraternity of priests; it is a moral community formed by all the believers in a single faith, laymen as well as priests"'
(30).

19 In *Nots*, Mark C. Taylor offers a much more favourable – albeit perverse –
judgment on Madonna's work: 'Madonna's Joycean masturbatorysexualpas-
sionate thing is the moment of passion, which, as Bataille insists, is the
instant when self-division is overcome and the presence of the self to itself
becomes *total*. In this moment, the passion of Christ is translated into the
passion of the "believer." While awaiting the coming of Christ, Madonna

comes on the altar. Like Bernini's *St. Theresa* coming all over the cover of Lacan's *Encore*, Madonna's mastubatorysexualpassionate thing is the moment of *jouissance*, which, in some cases, marks the climax of the female mystic's spiritual quest' (195–6).

20 Or patriarchal, though it is this, a notion that, biographically speaking, Donoghue offers us warrant for dwelling upon by his likening of his awe, while a child, for his father with that felt for the Deity: 'He [John Crowe Ransom] takes it for granted that the faithful think of God the Father in his imperious bearing; even if ... they deem awe or fear of Him to be the beginning of wisdom, and love of end the end. That's an entirely workable program, by the way. I started out in awe of my father, went on to revere him, and ended by loving him in a style that never presumed on intimacy' (*Adam's Curse*, 21).

21 Donoghue calls it '[o]ne of Christ's strangest sentences' (OU, 93).

22 In *Resistance to Theory*, de Man says something similar about the need to define literature and how its relation to the question of form seems the most expeditious avenue. As one might expect, de Man's own tone lacks Donoghue's confidence that we can 'say what form means': 'The main theoretical difficulty inherent in the teaching of literature is the delimitation of borderlines that circumscribe the literary field by setting it apart from other modes of discourse. Hence the nervousness which any tampering with canonical definition of a literary corpus is bound to provoke. In a manner that is more acute for theoreticians of literature than for theoreticians of the natural or the social world, it can be said that they do not quite know what it is they are talking about, not only in the metaphysical sense that the whatness, the ontology of literature is hard to fathom, but also in the more elusive sense that, whenever one is supposed to speak of literature, one speaks of anything under the sun (including, of course, oneself) except literature. The need for determination thus becomes all the stronger as a way to safeguard a discipline which constantly threatens to degenerate into gossip, trivia or self-obsession. The most traditional term to designate these borderlines is "form"; in literature, the concept of form is, before anything else, a definitional necessity. No literary metadiscourse would ever be conceivable in its absence. Before berating a critic or a theoretician for his formalism, one should realize that it is the necessary precondition to any theory. This does not mean, however, that the concept of form is itself susceptible of definition' (29–30).

23 *Aesthetics and Ideology* (1994), edited by George Levine, is an indication that the issue of form will not quietly go away. Levine writes, 'In effect, the book is a plea for a new kind of formalism, one that recognizes the ideological impli-

cations of the formal even as it values and deliberates over nuances of the text in ways that might, to vulgar eyes, seem like "mere formalism'" (23). Two of the book's essays especially stand out here: Derek Attridge's 'Literary Form and the Demands of Politics' and Peter Brooks's 'Aesthetics and Ideology – What Happened to Poetics?' In the first, Attridge writes: 'If the literary work exists as a unique act, then, that uniqueness is constituted by its form, understood as its singular performance of linguistic and cultural norms. But in this sense *form is always already meaning*; as an act of signification a literary work is meaning in motion, and there is no moment, not even a theoretical one, at which it is possible to isolate a purely formal property – at least not without turning the literary text into something else. The sounds or shapes of the text are *meaningful* sounds and shapes, and it is as such that they participate in the literary act. The effect of this mobilization of meaning by formal properties is that it can never close down on a represented world, can never become solely the reflection of or pointer to a set of existents outside language. The question of meaning and reference is kept alive as a question; referentiality is enacted – but not simply endorsed – in every literary act' (247).

And Brooks – addressing himself to not only the artist's but also the critic's obligation toward form – writes: 'The critic needs the self-imposition of the formalist *askesis* because this alone can assure the critic that the act of interpretation has been submitted to an otherness, that it is not simply an assimilation of the object of study. The realm of the aesthetic needs to be respected, by an imperative that is nearly ethical. It's not that the aesthetic is the realm of a secular scripture, that poetry has taken the place of a failed theodicy, that critics are celebrants at the hight altar of a cult of beauty isolated from history and politics. It is rather that personality must be tempered by the discipline of the impersonal that comes in the creation of form. "Form" in this sense is really an extension of language, which is itself impersonal in the same way. The human subject comes to being in language, as a system that preexists the individual locutor, that is transsubjective. To believe that we possess the language when we speak is an illusion. To understand that it possesses and defines us – that it is a formal system in which and through which we speak – is a necessary condition of subjectivity' (165).

24 The initial quotations here are drawn from Emmanuel Levinas, *The Levinas Reader*. The Socrates quotation was a favourite of Eliot's and is quoted in Donoghue's essay on Eliot, 'The Idea of a Christian Society' (228).

25 Again, Donoghue is quoting Langer.

26 De Man, of course, does not deny that language is metaphoric or symbolic. Even as he emphasizes the allegorical nature of language, he reminds us that

we have not left the realm of metaphor. For instance, in the chapter on 'Allegory' he writes: 'The paradigm for all texts consists of a figure (or a system of figures) and its deconstruction. But since this model cannot be closed off by a final reading, it engenders, in its turn, a supplementary figural superposition which narrates the unreadability of the prior narration. As distinguished from primary deconstructive narratives centered on figures and ultimately always on metaphor, we can call such narratives to the second (or the third) degrees *allegories*. Allegorical narratives tell the story of the failure to read whereas tropological narratives, such as the *Second Discourse*, tell the story of the failure to denominate. The difference is only a difference of degree and the allegory does not erase the figure. Allegories are always allegories of metaphor and, as such, they are always allegories of the impossibility of reading – a sentence in which the genitive "of" has itself to be "read" as a metaphor' (*Allegories of Reading*, 205).

Still, the tendency is to identify either the symbol or the metaphor with error – 'Metaphor is error because it believes or feigns to believe in its own referential meaning' (*Allegories of Reading*, 151) – as if the user of such could never tell the difference between, or avoid the conflation of, the word and the thing.

27   Here, I borrow again from Pauline Fletcher, who, in reference to the same passage from the Yeats book, writes that 'Donoghue ... has found a way to accept symbolism and the power of the transforming, Promethean imagination by assimilating these forces to his own epistemology. The moment marks a remarkable transformation in his critical stance. Symbol now guarantees "the presence of the supernatural in the natural"; symbols "mediate between the individual consciousness, which would otherwise be solipsist, and the given world, which would otherwise be alien"' (PGT, 8).

28   About Stevens's *Notes Toward a Supreme Fiction*, Donoghue writes that '[t]he basic motive ... is to offer man a substitute for God; to show him how he may transfer to himself the attributes and reverberations of the divine. This involves the replacement of certain fundamental terms in accordance with the idea that "God and the imagination are one." If they are one, the former may be replaced by the latter. So the idea of God is replaced by the idea of the imagination. Theology becomes Poetry, Metaphysics becomes Aesthetics. Faith is now addressed to the relation between the imagination and the structures of its own invention. The priest is replaced by the poet' (OU, 267).

29   Even as I say this, I still find room to agree with Alfred Kazin when he writes: 'As a modern critic of English and American writers – his special interest, his chosen country – Donoghue fascinates by the way he almost never brings his

religious beliefs to bear on the poetry and criticism ... he can analyze so shrewdly. The reason, I see from *Warrenpoint,* is that his Catholicism is a precious personal possession, something apart, and not to be trafficked in this world of many issues' ('Habits of Home,' 45).

30 It is indisputable that many criminal acts have been perpetuated in the name of God. In light of this, some would argue that we should impose a moratorium on the mention of God. I like however what Martin Buber, regarding this same suggestion, has to say, and will risk quoting him at length: 'Yes, it [God] is the most heavy-laden of all human words. None has become so soiled, so mutilated. Just for this reason I may not abandon it. Generations of men have laid the burden of their anxious lives upon this word ... it lies in the dust and bears their whole burden. The race of men with their religious factions have torn the word to pieces; they have killed for it and died for it, and it bears their fingermarks and their blood. Where might I find a word like it to describe the highest! If I took the purest, most sparkling concept from the inner treasure-chamber of the philosophers, I could only capture thereby an unbinding product of thought. I could not capture the presence of Him whom the generations of men have honoured and degraded with their awesome living and dying. I do indeed mean Him whom the hell-tormented and heaven-storming generations of men mean. Certainly, they draw caricatures and write "God" underneath; they murder one another and say "in God's name." But when all madness and delusion fall to dust, when they stand over against Him in the loneliest darkness and no longer say "He, He," but rather "Thou," shout "Thou," all of them the one word, and when they then add "God," is it not the real God whom they all implore, the one Living God, the God of the children of man? Is it not He who *hears* them? And just for this reason is not the word "God," the word of appeal, the word which has become a *name,* consecrated in all human tongues for all time? We must esteem those who interdict it because they rebel against the injustice and wrong which are so readily referred to "God" for authorisation. But we may not give it up. How understandable it is that some suggest that we should remain silent about the "last things" for a time in order that the misused words may be redeemed! But they are not to be redeemed *thus.* We cannot cleanse the word "God" and we cannot make it whole; but, defiled and mutilated as it is, we can raise it from the ground and set it over an hour of great care' (quoted in Murdoch, *Metaphysics as a Guide to Morals,* 420–1).

31 Donoghue is mindful of the insipidity of our religious discourse, and he urges a retreat from the reduction of religion to 'a matter of conscience, a value hard to distinguish from one's desires' (*Adam's Curse,* 39–40), but he also sees the advantages of keeping Church and State separate: 'Indeed, the

separation of Church and State, as in the United States, has at least this
advantage, that it enables the Church at once to be in the world and to stand
aside from its purposes. I agree with the late John Howard Yoder that the
Church should not engage in what he called "Constantinianism," the
assumption of responsibility for the moral structure of non-Christian society.
I agree, too, with Stanley Hauerwas and William Willimon when they call
upon Christians to live as "resident aliens" in modern America.' Resident
aliens pay their taxes, but they do not vote in state or general elections: they
live in society at a distance from its ideology. I note, too, that the experience
of having Church and State ostensibly at one, in my own country, has proved
a specious blessing ... There appears to be no alternative to the American
constitutional arrangement that keeps Church and State officially and for
most purposes separate. The Church is then in a better position to be vigi-
lant and to criticize the State and the World where such criticism is war-
ranted' (*Adam's Curse*, 47).

32 The allusion to Kermode is Donoghue's own ('The Idea of a Christian Society,' 229). It follows a discussion wherein Donoghue comments on the
darker consequence that may ensue from a life lived only mindful of an
abstract ideal: 'But there is always a risk, if your respect for a pattern laid up
in heaven compels the spirit in which you recognize what goes on in the
street, that you will get into the habit of thinking the events in the street
unimportant. If the pattern has priority, the immediate events are likely to
appear merely secondary' (ibid). I mention this because it is an argument
that Steiner himself has often made, as for example in his interview with
Ronald Sharp: 'We are trained our whole life long in abstraction, in the
fictive, and we develop a certain power – allegedly a power – to identify with
the fictive, to teach it, to deepen it ... Then we go into the street and there's
a scream and it has a strange unreality' (AC, 52).

33 Steiner's criticism of Eliot this way has grown stronger over the years. *In Bluebeard's Castle*, his 1970 'T.S. Eliot Memorial Lectures,' bears the subtitle *Some
Notes Towards the Redefinition of Culture*, 'intended in memoration of Eliot's
Notes of 1948' (BC, 3). At the time, Steiner said of the earlier volume: 'Not an
attractive book. One that is gray with the shock of recent barbarism, but a
barbarism whose actual sources and forms the argument leaves fastidiously
vague. Yet *Notes towards the Definition of Culture* remains of interest. They are,
so obviously, the product of a mind of exceptional acuteness' (BC, 3).

Meantime, in 1989, when more attention surrounded the question of
whether Eliot might be thought anti-Semitic, Steiner wrote in a letter (from
which I have already quoted) to the *London Review of Books*: '*Notes Towards a
Definition of Culture* continues to strike me as an often frigid, innerly confused
text. To approach the theme of any such redefinition within the immediate

wake of the Holocaust without addressing the event, without seeking to elucidate its possible roots within European civilization and Christendom, without examining the very notion of culture in the light (in the absolute dark)
of the new barbarism, remains frivolous or worse. For Eliot to do so when his
earlier sympathies with certain aspects of European reactionary sensibility
were fully known, and, by 1948, deeply embarrassing, remains a challenging,
saddening puzzle ... It is the central silence in Eliot on culture, on European
civility, on the future of poetry and thought, in respect of the Auschwitz
world. That silence utterly perplexes me and the comparison with Heidegger's – another man of eminent genius but of the most conservative and
"masked" political tenor – is perfectly admissible' (Letter ['Conrad and Eliot
and Prejudice'], 4).

34 Here, I think that maybe Derek Attridge finesses this matter better, when he
writes: 'The danger that I see in current modes of cultural and historical criticism, immensely valuable as they are, is that unless handled with extreme
subtlety and responsibility they can miss precisely what it is that literature as
literature has contributed, and has to contribute, to our political and ethical
thinking – and acting. This is not to deny the significant effect that literary
texts have had in thematizing historical issues, in forming and changing ideology, in popularizing worthy – or unworthy – causes, in providing education
and information. But it is to assert that the *literary,* in spite of, or rather
because of, the difficulties of categorization and definition it presents, is also
worth our continuing attention' ('Literary Form and the Demands of Politics,' 258).

The weakness of Attridge's view, however, is that it makes literary study
seem too much like a version of apologetics.

35 It was also reprinted in Lisa Jardine and Paul Smith's edited volume, *Men in
Feminism,* 146–52.

36 Witness Morris Dickstein's interesting statement regarding his own eventual
weariness with something that he began by applauding. I offer a small
excerpt:

No critic enters the academic arena [today] without a sanctioned battle
strategy – Marxist, feminist, poststructuralist – and an arsenal of currently
approved theorists. An immersion in the historical and institutional surround of literature has replaced a more direct engagement with writing
and writers. What we love about literature is not reflected in what we write
about.

As a result of these changes, the old New Critics whom I once set aside
as narrow formalists now look much better, as do older traditions of essays
and literary journalism that at least made writers and their world more,
not less, accessible to readers. Meanwhile, academic criticism has gone

into a free fall, more clever than ever, impeccably postmodern in its contempt for the living subject, proudly counterintuitive, yet also the laugh-
ingstock of scholars in other fields, despised by writers themselves and the
public at large. The old positivism and empiricism have been discarded,
but no accepted norms of argument and evidence have taken their place.
   Lately, there has been a reaction – a renewed interest in the aesthetic,
an embarrassment over jargon, a search for a more public intellectual style
– but this has not yet succeeded in pulling us out of the cul-de-sac in which
we are stranded, a dead end of arid abstraction, interpretive angst, and
misplaced political commitment. (Letter, *PMLA*, 1999).

37 In *Writing and Difference*, Derrida himself refuses the choice between the two
positions: 'For my part, although these two interpretations must acknowledge and accentuate their difference and define their irreducibility, I do not
believe that today there is any question of *choosing* – in the first place because
here we are in the region (let us say, provisionally, a region of historicity)
where the category of choice seems particularly trivial; and in the second,
because we must first try to conceive of the common ground, and the *différance* of this irreducible difference' (293).

38 Donoghue makes this same argument both in *The Arts without Mystery*, in the
'Commentary' to the third chapter (pages 60–6), and in *The Pure Good of Theory* interview. In the latter, he observes: 'What I resented at that stage [the
time of *Ferocious Alphabets*] in Derrida was that he was taking a perfectly valid
and very serious terminology, Schiller's terminology of play, and I thought
he was trivializing it. I'm thinking of *Glas* and Derrida's breaking up of words
and putting brackets around certain syllables and so on. I cannot believe that
that is what Schiller had in mind when he was talking about play. I think I
was resenting the kidnapping of the vocabulary of play. Derrida doesn't do
that always. For example, in "Structure, Sign and Play," it seems to me, he's
still using that term in a thoroughly Schillerean and valid way. The distinction he makes in that essay is very useful and one that could be developed.
The notion of play is important but questionable, in the sense that it could
go either way. It could become, in a Schillerean tradition, a serious activity
and a creative one; but equally you could tip it over into mere lexical fid-
dling. I felt that in *Glas* Derrida was doing that' (PGT, 95).

39 He attends to de Man's discussion of the poem in *Ferocious Alphabets* (174–5),
'The Limits of Language' (44), and 'The Strange Case of Paul de Man' (35).

40 In response to a question put by Harold Schweizer, Donoghue attempts to
explain further his difference with Miller over this question of ethics, saying
that for him ethics is more bound up with form than it is for Miller: 'I've
argued with Hillis Miller a little about *The Ethics of Reading*. I would use the

word "ethics" in a far more fundamental way. I respect the way in which Miller uses the word "ethics." He means the kind of ethical inclination or decision which is represented by writing a footnote to one's own work, that you qualify something you've just written. For him, ethics is a second thought brought to bear upon a first. My ethical emphasis – and this is where Levinas keeps coming into it – is primordial. It is not a footnote to the text. It is the text, in so far as it has achieved itself under ethical impulsion or ethical recognition. What I'm trying to do is to posit the ethical as the primordial and to see its trajectory culminating in an achieved form ...' (PGT, 93–4).

41 See Karen J. Winkler, 'Scholars Mark the Beginning of the Age of "Post-Theory."' The Fish quotation is also found here on page A 17.

Chapter 2: Frank Kermode

1 A reader who prefers to remain anonymous.

2 John Guillory writes: 'In no classroom is the "canon" itself the object of study. Where does it appear, then? It would be better to say that the canon is an *imaginary* totality of works. No one has access to the canon as a totality. This fact is true in the trivial sense that no one ever reads every canonical work; no one can, because the works invoked as canonical change continually according to many different occasions of judgment or contestation. What this means is that the canon is never other than an imaginary list; it never appears as a complete and uncontested list in any particular time and place, not even in the form of the omnibus anthology, which remains a selection from a larger list which does not itself appear anywhere in the anthology's table of contents' (*Cultural Capital*, 30).

3 In *Warrenpoint*, Donoghue says something quite similar with regard to sentences: 'But I don't think I understood that my reverence for the sentence as a form expressed not just my pleasure in the official relation between beginning, middle, and end, but my desire to see life as already intelligible. I'm sure I felt, at least vaguely, that even if life had many other qualities, it started by being intelligible. Sentences acted on that assumption and developed it further. The idea of a complex sentence, as in Henry James, showed the thrill of seeing risks taken and in the end the ship coming majestically into port' (139).

4 For instance, in 'Sacred Language and Open Text,' Betty Roitman – I think more sensibly – writes: 'The mobility and indeterminacy of midrash no doubt explain its attractiveness to present-day theoreticians who understand midrash in a way that feeds their faith in an infinite unfolding of textual signification. But this contemporary understanding of midrashic

428   Notes to pages 183–94

interpretation involves some considerable adaptation of the données of midrash. The opening of a text, to a western mind, presupposes an a priori renunciation of any "truth" of meaning. For many contemporary critics it is in the very gap between writing and its object, or between writing and its intent, that the plurality of meaning is said to establish itself, whereas in midrash the alignment of some of the same elements that go into the contemporary attitude produces a significantly different perspective. To describe midrash accurately it is important to acknowledge the force of the paradox represented by the classic midrashic position, which enacts at the level of interpretation a dialectic formulated on the ontological plane by Rabbi Akiva: "All is foreseen, but freedom of choice is given." All is determined, and yet all is open' (159–60).

5 Compare this to the non-parable passage in John 11: 41–2, where Jesus, standing before the tomb of Lazarus, speaks his thought out loud, in order that the crowd may perfectly understand his purpose: 'Father, I thank thee that thou hast heard me. I knew that thou hearest me always, but I have said this on account of the people standing by, that they may believe that thou didst send me.'

6 In *Hawthorne and History*, J. Hillis Miller says something similar about the opacity of the parables: 'According to the parables of Jesus, a chief way to get to the kingdom of heaven is to be a good reader of parables, or a good listener when they are presented orally, but most of us are among those who having eyes, see not, ears that neither hear nor understand. The parable is therefore both the means of getting to the kingdom of heaven and the blocking agent forbidding access. If you do not already understand the parable, the parable itself is not going to help you understand it' (72). Miller repeats the point in *Topographies* (187).

7 Cf. Steiner's belief that great works hold their value, whether there be present-day interpreters or not: 'Walter Benjamin said a book can wait a thousand years unread until the right reader happens to come along. Books are in no hurry. And act of creation is in no hurry: it reads us, it privileges us infinitely' (AC, 51).

8 Guillory further writes: 'The reason more women authors, for example, are not represented in older literatures is not primarily that their works were routinely excluded by invidious or prejudicial standards of evaluation, "excluded" as a consequence of their social identity as women. The historical reason is that, with few exceptions before the eighteenth century, women were excluded from *access to literacy*, or were proscribed from composition or publication in the genres considered to be serious rather than ephemeral. If current research has recovered a number of otherwise forgotten women

writers from the period before the eighteenth century, this fact is not directly related to canon formation as a process of selection or exclusion on the basis of social identity, but to the present institutional context of a valid and interesting *research program* whose subject is the history of women writers and writing. No other defense is required for studying these writers than the aims of the research program (and these could well be *political* aims). It is not necessary to claim canonical status for noncanonical works in order to justify their study, as the archive has always been the resource of historical scholarship' (*Cultural Capital*, 15–16).

9 Quoted in Baym, 'The Agony of Feminism,' 107.

10 About Gordon's *Eliot's New Life*, Kermode writes, 'But I'm bound to say that there is something disturbing about Gordon's handling of all this [Eliot's relation to Emily Hale]. Her religiose attitude to the facts, a sort of muckraking sublimity, affects her prose as well as her argument, and the whole pseudo-allegorical and hagiographical enterprise is vaguely disgusting, though I ought to add that it might seem just right to readers of different disposition' ('Feast of St. Thomas,' 4).

11 In *History and Value* (113–14), Kermode again refers to the Baker article, repeating the charge.

12 Gulliory writes: 'The movement to open the canon to noncanonical authors submits the syllabus to a kind of demographic oversight. Canonical and noncanonical authors are supposed to *stand for* particular social groups, dominant or subordinate. One can easily concede that there must be *some* relation between the representation of minorities in the canon, but what is that relation? The difficulty of describing this relation is in part a consequence of the fact that a particular social institution – the university – intervenes between these two sites of representation. Given the only partially successful social agenda of educational democratization in the last three decades, we may conclude that it is much easier to make the canon representative than the university. More to the point, those members of social minorities who enter the university do not "represent" the social groups to which they belong in the same way in which minority legislators can be said to represent their constituencies. The sense in which a social group is "represented" by an author or text is more tenuous still' (*Cultural Capital*, 7).

13 Favouring the inclusion of creative writing programs into the university, Kermode recalls his own positive experience while teaching at the University of Houston in the late 1990s: 'When I taught at the University of Houston in Texas, the students had been taught certain techniques of writing poetry. As a result they could relish the sense of difficulty overcome in Donne's poetry, how he follows an argument in a stanza form that opposes it at every turn. It

makes sense. If you studied music it would seem absurd not to learn the whole grammar of music' ('Interview with Katie Donovan').

14 It is in his concluding chapter ('Religious Criticism') to *The World, the Text, and the Critic* that Said groups Kermode with a number of other critics whom he identifies as part of a religious trend in criticism: 'When you see influential critics publishing major books with titles like *The Genesis of Secrecy, The Great Code, Kabbalah and Criticism, Violence and the Sacred, Deconstruction and Theology,* you know you are in the presence of a significant trend. The number of prevalent critical ideas whose essence is some version of theory liberated from the human and the circumstantial further attests to this trend' (291).

15 Frank Lentricchia, in *After the New Criticism,* writes: 'There is something misleading and even cruel in Kermode's citing anti-Semitism (a projection of death onto others) as his example of mythical thought and *King Lear* (which involves us in our own end) as the example of fictional thinking. For anti-Semitism can be held fictively, as well, as long as one encases the virulence in tonally, playful discourse – attaches an "as if " here, a "so to speak" there – and as long as one does not attempt to consummate one's fictions about Jews by murdering six million of them. It is the principle of self-consciousness and not anything in the structure of the fiction itself which is the true desideratum' (38). Meanwhile, in *T.S. Eliot, Anti-Semitism, and Literary Form,* Anthony Julius writes: 'Frank Kermode has argued that "[f]ictions can degenerate into myths whenever they are not consciously held to be fictive. In this sense anti-Semitism is a degenerate fiction, a myth; and *Lear* is a fiction." This is too categoric. Anti-Semitism does not consist solely of lies. It is also bulky with descriptions, which is why it cannot be defeated by counter-proofs and refutations alone. It is a way of imagining Jews, a pernicious, elaborate fiction, and not just a series of theorems about the Jewish people. Furthermore, Kermode's distinction depends either on imputing a reflexive consciousness to the work, which is fanciful, or on making the sincerity of the author determinative, which is futile. If it depends on the first, it imports the pathetic fallacy into literary criticism: if on the second, it imports a variety of the intentional fallacy especially difficult to defend' (96).

16 In her Charles Eliot Norton lectures, 1979–80, *In Defence of the Imagination,* Helen Gardner attacks Kermode on this matter, as well as many others: 'For sociological analysis we must, I suppose, call churches and universities institutions; but this is not how they feel, or should feel, to those who are within them. Both, if living organisms and not mere structures for analysis, are communities of persons professing a common faith, with a principle of unity that admits of wide possibilities of diversity, and both bear relations to the societies in which they exist' (132).

17 As in illustration of Cunningham's point, Kermode says of Joyce's other large novel: 'The fact is, I think, that when a book reaches the quasi-sacred status attained by *Ulysses* we assume that everything we can find out about it is valuable, including every possible parallel, whether intended or not; and whether we are baffled or not by this magical view of the world' (AP, 214). Meanwhile, in *The Genesis of Secrecy*, he observes that the Protestant hermeneutic tradition stands at risk 'for I do not see how, finally, it can distinguish between sacred and secular texts, those works of the worldly canon that also appear to possess inexhaustible hermeneutic potential' (40).

18 That theory is our new literature is, in large part, the thesis of Elizabeth W. Bruss's *Beautiful Theories*. See especially her chapter 'Theory of Literature Becomes Theory as Literature.'

19 In *Topographies*, Hillis Miller offers a very different claim, that it is theory that now moves most easily across borders: 'These days, in the fields of literary and cultural studies, theory "travels" everywhere' (317): 'Just why it should be literary theory that seems to be carried over so easily, that crosses borders with such facility, is not immediately clear. Nor is it quite clear what it means that literary theory originally developed in Europe and the United States should now be traveling everywhere in the world, often by way of its North American versions. Why is this happening? Is it because theory is conceptual and generalized, therefore applicable in any context and culture and time? Theory would, it might seem, in this differ from pedagogical techniques or specific readings of specific works. The latter are tied to particular sites and situations. Therefore they do not translate well or "travel" well, as they say of certain delicate wines that are best drunk where they are made. Literary theory, on the other hand, is like the vacuum-sealed box wines that travel anywhere and keep for a long time even after they are opened' (318).

20 In his chapter, 'Political and Ecclesiastical Allegory in *The Faerie Queene*,' in the co-authored collection *English Renaissance Literature* (1974), Kermode himself suggests just this, that the Spenser epic played a key political role in helping to legitimize the Elizabethan Settlement: 'The conclusion of the entire Book [I] is clearly apocalyptic, with the slaying of the dragon, the harrowing of Hell and the apocalyptic marriage of Redcrosse to Una – all these were regularly allegorized in commentaries on the Book of Revelation as the restoration of the true Church of England, and all became part of the business of praising the Elizabethan Settlement, which was obviously necessary, simply in order to try to restore political stability in the country. So you see, there is an immediate political end in all this use of the Book of Revelation' (6).

21 Kermode would later earn Leavis's ire, when with the termination of *Scrutiny*

in 1953, the former was asked by P.H. Newby, the director of the BBC Third Programme, to offer comment upon what the journal meant to English literary culture. Kermode seems to have meant well, praising both Leavis and his journal, but Leavis felt as if he was being patronized, and wrote an angry letter, to Newby, in response. See Ian MacKillop, *F.R. Leavis: A Life in Criticism*, 282–3.

22 A reader who prefers to remain anonymous.

23 In *Against the Grain*, however, Eagleton speaks of Kermode as 'the sole exception' to the contention that British literary critics fall down, both in 'substance or flair,' when compared to 'their American counterparts' (56).

24 Eagleton, naturally, views his allegiances somewhat differently. In *The Significance of Theory*, he writes: 'One of the reasons that I find it possible to work in Britain ... is that there is still a sense ... in which the working intellectual in Britain is not entirely cut off from the wider society. The intellectual in Britain is, in however partial and limited way, in a position of mediation with the society as a whole. My feeling is ... that if I worked in the United States, then I would be saying that my identity belongs almost wholly to a specific academic community or, as they would say in the States, to the profession, a word that almost never passes our lips. So this is, as it were, an existential matter as well as a theoretical one. It's a question of whether one feels, at least in principle, there are wider connections that can be made. Some of the work I do is connected with educational television and with the Open University and increasingly with school teachers, seeing if these rather highbrow ideas make some kind of sense in schools, I mean schools in our sense of the term. And that takes us back to the issue of the public sphere, with a different kind of definition of what intellectual work could be' (84).

25 Kermode's earliest response to Culler's work is in a 1966 review, 'Harvard Cheer,' of an anthology of writings from the *Harvard Advocate* edited by Culler.

Chapter 3: George Steiner

1 The difference an ocean makes does seem apparent in John Gray's appraisal of this same essay. Writing in *The Times Higher Education Supplement*, he states that 'Steiner's polemical exercise in the interpretation of American culture strikes me as worthwhile and on the whole plausible. If one thinks of writers of various sorts, how many of those who have been true innovators in the past century or so have been American? Indeed it is not easy to imagine the poetry of Rilke or Celan, the essays and aphorisms of Rozanov or Cioran, the short stories of Kafka, Borges or Ballard, the novels of Beckett, Dostoevsky,

Musil or Canetti, the "philosophical" works of Nietzsche, Shestov of Wittgenstein coming from within American civilization at all' (28).

Or, given Gray's examples, as coming much from within English civilization, either. Even Ballard is something of a foreigner, having been born in
China. In any event, the grouping of the writers for this purpose – the smug
dismissal of American culture – is an ill-considered gesture.

2 Steiner: 'My debt to the United States is enormous. It is not only saved our
lives in 1940, but it also gave me its education, its American citizenship and
the Rhodes Scholarship. My wife is a native New Yorker: my children are all
young academics in the United States. For twenty-seven years I've been a
critic on *The New Yorker*' ('The Art of Criticism, II,' 70).

3 In his 1964 essay 'Out of Central Europe,' Steiner offered a much grimmer
picture of East German culture: 'The reduction of East Germany to brutal
parochialism and servility leaves a dangerous gap. The D.D.R. stands, in
denial of human contact, between the vulnerable energies of independent intellectual life in eastern Europe and the efforts of the West to "get
through" on a basis of argument and response. Moreover, by virtue of history
and language, East Germany is intensely a part of Europe, and the diminu-
tion of any such part to barbarism is a threat to the vitality of the whole. In
cities where Goethe and Wagner composed, generations are coming of age
in a miasma of lies and controlled hatreds' (112).

4 In China, the percentage is as high as eighty, whereas it is '3 percent in the
United States, 4.8 percent in (West) Germany, 2.1 percent in Britain, 6.7 percent in France, 8 percent in Japan, 9.1 percent in Italy' (Kennedy, *Preparing
for the Twenty-First Century*, 170, 75).

5 'Steiner's troupe of poets and philosophers is conspicuously men-only,'
writes Roy Porter ('Original Bliss').

6 About this same 'self-definition,' Paul Ricoeur, in a chapter entitled 'Naming God,' interestingly writes: 'Thus the appellative "Yahweh" – he is – is
not a defining name but one that is a sign of the act of deliverance. Indeed,
the text [Exodus] continues in these terms: "God also said to Moses, 'Thus
you shall say to the Israelites, "Yahweh, the God of your ancestors, the God
of Abraham, the God of Isaac, and the God of Jacob, has sent me to you":
this is my name forever, and thus I am to be remembered throughout all
generations.'" Far, therefore, from the declaration "I am who I am" autho-
rizing a positive ontology capable of capping off the narrative and other
namings, instead it protects the secret of the "in-itself" of God, and this
secret, in turn, sends us back to the narrative naming through the names of
Abraham, Isaac, and Jacob, and by degrees to the other namings' (*Figuring
the Sacred*, 228).

7 In 'Totem or Taboo,' Steiner writes, 'I prefer never to use "holocaust" which is a beautiful Greek word meaning sacrifice, solemn and festive' (391).

8 In *Secular Vocations* Bruce Robbins offers an extended discussion of this figure he calls the 'cultured Kommandant' (128–31), particularly in terms of the way it exemplifies the mistaken belief that the public and the private (or the worlds of daytime and nighttime) are separable. About Steiner, he writes: 'He offered this figure as a challenge to the belief "that culture is a humanizing force," and thus that the work of scholars and humanists is socially meaningful. Contemplating his Kommandant, Steiner said he could no longer believe, with Matthew Arnold and F.R. Leavis, that the humanities humanize. And yet Steiner almost immediately backs down from his challenge (perhaps under pressure from the "engagement" of Sartre, the post-war voice who took the same challenge in the opposite direction), retreating to the Arnoldian humanist position, with its immense nostalgia for Europe's lost cultural splendors. The logic of his retreat is as clear as it is paradoxical. What he wants is culture in privacy – or, rather, culture *as* privacy. Since public life has proved a nightmare, let us withdraw into the patient, self-sacrificing, apolitical work of cultural transmission – even if (here is the paradox) the *capacity* of culture to remain apolitical, its *in*capacity to prevent or even resist the horrors of the war, is what has thrown what we mean by culture into question, and even if the contiguous but separate coexistence of high culture with the horror of the camps has been (for the cultured) the greatest horror of all. In short, the solution repeats the problem' (130–1).

9 Cf. Kermode: 'How did we ever come to suppose that we were equipped to make people good? To be realistic, we cannot do that, any more than we can fill the humps of the young with supplies of reading for later use' (AP, 57–8). And Harold Bloom: 'Reading deeply in the Canon will not make one a better person or a worse person, a more useful or more harmful citizen. The mind's dialogue with itself is not primarily a social reality. All that the Western Canon can bring one is the proper use of one's own solitude, that solitude whose final form is one's confrontation with one's own mortality' (*The Western Canon*, 30).

10 See 'The Art of Criticism II' (62–9) for Steiner's account of his family's own migration.

11 Steven Katz, in *The Holocaust in Historical Context*, sets out to do just this, to consider the 'phenomenological uniqueness' of the Holocaust.

12 Quoted in Steiner, *After Babel*, 193.

13 For a prior, yet analogous reading of Jesus in relation to this notion of perfection and the extraordinary demands it makes upon us, see Dietrich Bonhoeffer's moving 1937 book, *The Cost of Discipleship*. Especially relevant is the

chapter 'The Call to Discipleship,' wherein Bonhoeffer offers brilliant commentary upon the passage in Matthew wherein the rich man inquires of the 'Good Master, what good things shall I do, that I may have eternal life?' To which Jesus, in part, responds: 'If thou wilt be perfect, go and sell that thou hast, and give to the poor, and thou shalt have treasure in heaven: and come and follow me.'

14 As he acknowledges, Steiner here is borrowing an idea or two from Freud's *Moses and Monotheism.* For instance, Freud himself writes:

> Among the precepts of Mosaic religion is one that has more significance than is at first obvious. It is the prohibition against making an image of God, which means the compulsion to worship an invisible God. I surmise that in this point Moses surpassed the Aton religion in strictness. Perhaps he meant to be consistent; his God was to have neither a name nor a countenance. The prohibition was perhaps a fresh precaution against magic malpractices. If this prohibition was accepted, however, it was bound to exercise a profound influence. For it signified subordinating sense perception to an abstract idea; it was a triumph of spirituality over the senses; more precisely, an instinctual renunciation accompanied by its psychologically necessary consequences. (144)
>
> * * * *
>
> The religion that began with the prohibition against making an image of its God has developed in the course of centuries more and more into a religion of instinctual renunciation. Not that it demands sexual abstinence; it is content with a considerable restriction of sexual freedom. God, however, becomes completely withdrawn from sexuality and raised to an ideal of ethical perfection. Ethics, however, means restriction of instinctual gratification. The Prophets did not tire of maintaining that God demands nothing else from his people but a just and virtuous life – that is to say, abstention from the gratification of all impulses that, according to our present-day moral standards, are to be condemned as vicious. And even the exhortation to believe in God seems to recede in comparison with the seriousness of these ethical demands. (152)

15 In his own essay on Levinas, 'The Philosopher of Selfless Love,' Donoghue also notes the resemblances between Levinas and Derrida, as well as what sets them apart, a comparison that, like Steiner's, works to Levinas's advantage: 'Both philosophers emerged from the phenomenological tradition pioneered by Edmund Husserl and Martin Heidegger, and both came to question that tradition. Both believed that most philosophers pay too much attention to ontology (studying the nature of reality) and epistemology

(studying the nature of knowledge). Both men believe that the language philosophy uses, and even language as a whole, are deeply flawed and need to be reexamined. Levinas's response was to shift philosophy from epistemology and ontology toward ethics. Derrida, conversely, launched a head-on attack against philosophy itself' (37).

16 Quoted in Cunningham, *In the Reading Gaol,* 399.

17 In 'The Question of Voice,' Donoghue, borrowing from Handelman, also remarks on the difference between the two religious traditions, something that has become more noticeable with the work of Derrida:

> According to her [Handelman], Derrida is undermining Greco-Christian logocentrism and phonocentrism from the standpoint of a Hebraic sense of Scripture; Scripture as 'far more important than Nature.' Greek ontology separates language from being, and points the truth-seeker toward a silent ontology; but to the Hebrew, on the other hand, the central divine act is interpretation, not incarnation. Derrida, Handelman says, 'will undo Greco-Christian theology and move us back from ontology to grammatology, from Being to Text, from Logos to *Ecriture* – Scripture.' In Derrida, exile is a permanent condition, alleviated only by the freedom it makes possible: in that state, there is no return of speech to nature, nor is there a fulfillment of signs. But in describing Derrida's position as Hebraic, we have to allow for the second character of his writing, that its relation to the Torah is heretical. However, it is a well-established fact that in Judaism there are only wavering lines between the text and commentary; the commentary is received in the sense of the text, heresy is inseparable from orthodoxy. The most memorable parable of this incrimination of heresy and orthodoxy is a passage in Kafka:
>
> > Leopards break into the temple and drink the sacrificial chalices dry; this occurs repeatedly, again and again: finally it can be reckoned on beforehand and becomes part of the ceremony.
>
> What the parable means to say is that Rabbinic interpretation breaks open the Torah as a strategy of survival, not only against historical catastrophe but against what Handelman calls 'an overwhelming, authoritative Sacred Text that can never be overcome.' (44–5)

18 In 'Against Messiness,' Robert Alter takes strong exception to this aspect of Steiner's argument: 'There is no "extreme commitment to abstraction" in Jewish tradition. Quite the contrary, rabbinic culture is founded on the analysis of concrete details of quotidian life and does not even have a vocabulary of abstractions, which would enter the Hebrew language only after the

encounter with Aristotelianism through Arab mediation in the High Middle Ages' (23).

19 About such passages, Robert Alter sensibly writes: 'Because Steiner is impelled to express such notions of direct, linear causation rather histrionically, he makes a good many pronouncements that are not only terrible simplifications but are also offensive: "That night within night, into which Judas is dispatched ... is already that of the death-ovens." Similarly, even without the claim of historical concatenation, after quoting from the harrowing death-wish poem in Job 3: "The facts of Auschwitz and Rwanda are there." Since history is imagined as unfolding teleology, great writers can be represented as quite literally prophetic, and so we hear of "Amos's clairvoyance as to Zionism" and "Kafka's blueprint [!] of the concentration-camp world."' ('Against Messiness,' 23). The point is, says Alter, '[h]istory is surely too multifarious, too ambiguous and indeterminate in its shifting patterns of causation, to be adequately represented by such drastically linear schemes. And, as the American critic Michael André Bernstein has trenchantly argued in his *Foregone Conclusions*, we rob those who have lived before us of the variety of their life-experiences and their choices by locking them into the "inevitability" of what happened after them, reducing their flesh-and-blood existence to the ghostly foreshadow of later catastrophes' (24).

20 Cf. this to Donoghue's claim, in *Warrenpoint*, that as a child he 'could spot a Protestant at a hundred yards': 'In the North a Protestant walks with an air of possession and authority, regardless of his social class. He walks as if he owned the place, which indeed he does. A Catholic walks as if he were on sufferance. O'Neill is a Catholic name. How it settled upon Captain Terence [former Prime Minister of Northern Ireland] or his father or grandfather, I have no idea. But if I saw him walking along Royal Avenue in Belfast and didn't know him from Adam, I would know that he was a Protestant' (46–7).

21 In this vein, Steiner offers an argument that is, naturally, dear to Kermode's heart: 'When you speak of a canon you speak not just of texts but of texts plus commentary. Commentary, to put the matter at its lowest, is the medium in which texts survive – even texts in remote languages, texts from remote societies, in which a community or a civilization has invested its care' ('The Future of the English Literary Canon,' 19).

22 Latter books – *Errata* and *Grammars of Creation* – are even more successful in this one respect.

23 Speaking from the perspective of a Christian, Paul Ricoeur writes thoughtfully regarding this embarrassment: 'In such a society as our own, being ashamed of Jesus and his words take on the more subtle forms of abstention

and silence. I admit that the answer to the question of Christian witness in a liberal society is an extremely difficult one to formulate. Most of us, myself included, feel repugnance when confronted with the advertising-like quality much Christian witnessing has taken on in the media. Between the arrogance, the indiscretion, and the vulgarity of such testimony, on the one hand, and the flight into polite and prudent silence in the name of the private character of belief and respect for others, on the other, the most honest and courageous form of testimony, where it is needed and required by both the situation and our fellow human beings, is neither easy to discover nor to formulate. On both the individual and the communal planes, the question remains open what such honest and courageous testimony would look like in a liberal society' (*Figuring the Sacred*, 286–7).

24 In *Language and Silence*, Steiner points to another side of Judaism, that which advocates a boundless 'radical humanism.' Jesus is in this camp, and so is Marx: 'But if the poison [i.e., of sectarianism] is, in ancient part, Jewish, so perhaps is the antidote, the radical humanism which sees man on the road to becoming man. This is where Marx is most profoundly a Jew – while at the same time arguing the dissolution of Jewish identity. He believed that class and economic status knew no frontiers, that misery had a common citizenship. He postulated that the revolutionary process would abolish national distinctions and antagonisms as industrial technology had all but eroded regional autonomy. The entire socialist utopia and dialectic of history are based on an international premise' (153).

25 In this respect, Steiner is much like Kermode, whose objections to more recent criticisms (i.e., that it is badly written and cares little about literature as literature) are, in fact, a reprise of what he has been saying about academic criticism all along, as for instance when in the 1966 essay 'Marvell Transprosed,' Kermode attacked a proponent of the then in vogue history-of-ideas school for the reason that '[h]e cannot reconcile the big graduate words with poetry. If, as seems likely, the major graduate schools are going to bear a heavier responsibility for the perpetuation of a genuine literary public, they ought to be considering whether their better young men should be allowed to write in this way; if they continue to do so it may simply become impossible to defend the academic study of literature against all the people who want to condemn it' (82).

26 In *Topographies*, Hillis Miller also conflates theory with Bottom's being translated, though his purposes are more positive: 'In the new place a theory is made use of in ways the theory never intended or allowed for, though it also transforms the culture or discipline it enters. When theory crosses borders it is translated in the sense that Puck fits Bottom out with an ass's head in

Shakespeare's *A Midsummer Night's Dream*. When theory travels it is disfig-
ured, deformed, "translated"' (331–2).

27 On this point of theory, Steiner has a formidable ally in Rodolphe Gasché,
who in his book on Derrida, *Inventions of Difference*, writes: 'In the wake of
New Criticism, which rightly showed that literary criticism was not derivative
and was not simply a parasitic response to literature, but an autonomous discipline, it has become fashionable to conceive of literary criticism as *theory*.
Yet, what does theory mean in this context except the all too often naive and
sometimes even, given its uncontrolled and unwanted side effects, ridiculous
application of the *results* of philosophical debates to the literary field? It is on
this unproblematized and rarely justified application, as well as on the lack
of any questioning of the applicability of such philosophemes to the specific
levels of texts, that theory rests. It rests especially on a generally intuitive
understanding of conceptual systems, situated as it is in the (institutionally
motivated) absence of all rigorous formation in pilot sciences such as
anthropology, linguistics, psychoanalysis, and especially philosophy. In this,
theory is no different from the impressionistic approaches and loose conceptual instruments of traditional academic criticism, which seldom reflect its
own presuppositions' (23–4).

28 Quoted in J. Hillis Miller, *Versions of Pygmalion*, 84.

29 Quoted in Steiner, *Real Presences*, 148.

30 In his chapter 'Hope and the Structure of Philosophical Systems,' Paul
Ricoeur writes: 'What is hope? What does hope mean for biblical theology? If
we want to respect the specificity of the notion, we must say first that hope
does not primarily belong to philosophical discourse; the theologians of the
past were right when they called it a "theological virtue" – along with faith
and love. Under that title they preserved the dimension to which hope
belongs. It is this dimension that we have to recognize' (*Figuring the Sacred*,
204). And also: 'Hope is not a theme that comes after other themes, an idea
that closes the system, but an impulse that opens the system, that breaks the
closure of the system; it is a way of reopening what was unduly closed' (*Figuring the Sacred*, 211).

31 It is just this rhetorical nature of the poet's art that leads Socrates to com-
plain: 'The poet, when he sits on the tripod of the muses, is no longer in his
right mind. Like a fountain, he willingly lets whatever enters into him stream
forth. And since his art is only imitation, he is forced to create characters
which oppose each other and thus always to speak against himself (to contradict himself), and he does not know if the one thing or the other of that
which he has said is true' (*Laws* 719 c).

32 It was in such a context that Frank Kermode, in a review of Steiner's *Lan-*

guage and Silence, was provoked to speak of Steiner as a 'moral terrorist [who has] a certain readiness to abandon himself to the apocalyptic gesture ... and overstatement, into the preacher's loose immodest tone ... The root image of the terror underlying this intellectual terrorism is that of the concentration camps ... Whether one likes his leading ideas, his stage army of heroes (Kafka, Broch, Wittgenstein, Schoenberg), or his prose, one has to respect the motives of Steiner's terrorism, and the power of intellect with which he feeds it' (review of *Language and Silence*, 3).

The phrase 'moral terrorist' is Kant's, and is also used by Kermode in reference to Lawrence. See Kermode's *D.H. Lawrence*, 57; also see, on 153, footnote 13, for a further explanation of the phrase.

33 In 'The Responsibility of Intellectuals,' a symposium moderated by Robert Boyers, Steiner repeatedly addresses this issue of an intellectual's political responsibilities. He believes that academics are not, by and large, revolutionaries and that their first order of business is in the classroom, where they should avoid making pronouncements about how the world should be run: '[T]o be sitting in opulent safety in some rewarded university chair and make oneself a spokesman for terrorism in a far part of the earth is contemptible. It's sheer cant. For my part, I teach, or try to teach, and live by, the masters, the great texts, the philosophic traditions, the things handed on to us. And to do this while deriving every privilege – and what's much more important, every discipline of ecstasy, of inner joy – from one's position, and then to mouth egalitarian or radical or populist slogans, to attempt to run with the wolves of Philistinism as did so many in '68 and '69 is, I think, suicidal. So, I would interpret Rieff's remark as saying, "have the pride of being what you are"' (164–5).

34 See Saul A. Kripke, *Wittgenstein: On Rules and Private Language*.

35 This appears to be a misprint in the Steiner text; the second 'cannot' should read 'must,' if it is to agree with Wittgenstein's statement, 'und woven man nicht reden kann, darüber muss man schweigen' (*Tractatus*, 26).

36 In his 1995 review of Elzbieta Ettinger's book *Hannah Arendt / Martin Heidegger*, 'The New *Nouvelle Héloïse*,' Steiner writes: 'Ettinger implies, strongly, that Celan's inability to elicit from the master any responsible word as to the Holocaust helped bring on the poet's suicide. I implied just this on a public occasion in Paris some ten years ago. We are both mistaken. A letter from Celan to Franz Wurm, dated August 8, 1967 (only recently published), refers to the famous visit to Todtnauberg as having been eminently satisfactory and amicable. There is no shred of evidence that, as Ettinger would have it, Celan left Heidegger "crushed" and broken' (4).

37 'Silence' (11). In the same review essay, Wendy Steiner writes: 'And lest this

reference [by George Steiner] to black women of the Eighties appear a random example, we might look at Steiner's musing on the relation between gender and art. He considers the act of aesthetic creativity an imitation of God's *fiat.* "In stating this hypothesis, I am wholly conscious of its possible bias toward maleness. I fully sense its more than metaphoric inference both of a masculine primacy in the creation of great fictive forms ... and of a patriarchal, militant image or metaphor of God." Though women have written great novels, Steiner continues, is it not strange that they have produced almost no major drama? Could it be that the creativity involved in childbearing is so overwhelming that the begetting of fictive characters pales besides it? Of course, "the vengeful impatience of the feminist indictment of traditional aesthetic and philosophic theory" makes further inquiry on this point difficult, but Steiner is convinced of its centrality. In his utopia, the core curriculum is unencumbered with contemporary black women's writing, and the agonistic competition with God the Creator does not appeal to those big with child' (11).

Afterword

1 A fine counter argument to Said's book can be found in his Columbia colleague David Damrosch's *We Scholars.* Addressing himself to the figure of Lionel Trilling, whose ghost still haunts the Columbia English Department, Damrosch argues that the spirit of amateurism invoked by Trilling's career is simply no longer viable in present-day academia: 'What has changed is not the viability of Trilling's solution in cultural terms but the close fit that could still exist in his day between such a cultural perspective and a parallel scholarly method. In his writing as in his teaching, Trilling was a generalist, ranging easily and widely over modern culture. If his essays on Freud, on Marx, and on the liberal imagination are more focused than the timeless great conversations of the [Columbia] core courses, the difference is one of degree rather than one of kind. All his life, Trilling was a devoted member of the College faculty at Columbia, then still the heart of the university. His ideal reader was "the general reader," and even in his own time he was exceptional in maintaining a general outlook from within the academic base. The triumph of specialization during the past several decades has almost entirely eliminated such figures from the university ... The clock cannot be turned back sixty years, even if that were desirable; what is likely to be more constructive is to ask how, if at all, something resembling the ideal of general education can be restored in an age of specialization' (122).

2 Reviewing the influential collection of academic essays, edited by Patricia

Meyer Spacks, *Advocacy in the Classroom: Problems and Possibilities* (1996), Roger Shattuck notes that the ' constant appeal in these essays to academic freedom, treated as a special privilege for professors to speak their minds, neglects the accompanying principle of academic responsibility. Quite properly, ordinary citizens do not forget it. Since one is trained and carefully selected for one's scholarly knowledge of a field, a college teacher has a higher responsibility than the ordinary citizen to speak circumspectly and with documented evidence about the subject on which he or she offers courses. The professor is professionally on trust not to pop off in the classroom and in scholarly work, particularly on political subjects. One may do so in other settings such as conversation and journalism' (*Candor and Perversion*, 30).

3 In *Authors and Authority*, Parrinder writes: 'The very notion of the "man of letters," stemming from Carlyle's *On Heroes*, speaks of male domination: the "woman of letters" sounds as though she might be an inferior species. Carlyle was writing at a time when the profession of female authorship was coming to be widely acknowledged, and when a few advanced intellectuals were beginning to advocate equal rights for both sexes. The tradition of "men of letters," remained, however, a male preserve. John Gross in his history of *The Rise and Fall of the Man of Letters* (1969) unceremoniously debars the most distinguished modern female critic from the company he is celebrating. "The typical Virginia Woolf essay is a brilliant circular flight, which, as criticism, leads nowhere," he writes. This seems to imply that men of letters think in straight lines, like Woolf's own character Mr Ramsay in *To the Lighthouse*, whereas women, however gifted, flap around in circles' (326–7).

4 In his review of *The Uses of Error*, Patrick Parrinder observes, however, 'Had not Dame Helen [Gardner] pre-empted the phrase, he [Kermode] might have called it *In Defence of the Imagination*' ('Civil Service,' 45).

5 Terry Eagleton, for examples, writes: 'Liberal humanism is fond of imagining an inner space within the human subject where he or she is most significantly free. A sophisticated liberal humanist will not of course deny that human subjects are externally or even internally afflicted by all kinds of grievous determinants and constraints; it is just that what these forces seek to determine and constrain is some transcendental core of inner freedom. The bad news for the liberal humanist is that this "inner space" is actually where we are least free' (*The Significance of Theory*, 36).

6 The passage continues: 'All men spatialise internally and perform the act of perception through a conventional adjustment of external stimuli and internal constructs. The internal spatialisation in a sensibility such as Bosch's or Cézanne's is so detailed, so finely structured, that it translates the outside world wholly into its own values and focus. It is not a new window on to the

"outside world" that the revolutionary painter opens for us; it is a window into his own consciousness, a consciousness so coherent and expressive that we come to recognise in it alternative ways of seeing and feeling, that we borrow from it, that we learn to experience aspects of our own conventional reality in the new ordering given them by the artist' ('The Thinking Eye,' 64).

7 Or as Barthes, again in *Camera Lucida*, writes: 'What characterizes the so-called advanced societies is that they today consume images and no longer, like those of the past, beliefs; they are therefore more liberal, less fanatical, but also more "false" (less "authentic") – something we translate, in ordinary consciousness, by the avowal of an impression of nauseated boredom, as if the universalized image were producing a world that is without difference (indifferent), from which can rise, here and there, only the cry of anar-chisms, marginalisms, and individualisms: let us abolish the images, let us save immediate Desire (desire without mediation)' (119).

8 In 'Apocalypse Now and Then,' Kermode is also quite disparaging of myth, writing: 'Belief in myths can be devastating, even if it is associated with great political causes: we hardly need Palestine and Ireland to remind us of that. Perhaps the value of knowing about such people as Brothers and their absurd delusions is simply that they exhibit, in a form that proved harmless, the motives which, endowed with political power, can bring tyranny and destruction on a scale undreamed of by calm intellectuals who know a myth from a fiction and a fiction from a fact' (11).

BIBLIOGRAPHY

Abel, Lionel. 'So Who Is to Have the Last Word? (On Some of the Positions Taken by George Steiner).' *Partisan Review* 53, no. 3 (1987): 358–71.

Abrams, M.H. *Natural Supernatural; Tradition and Revolution in Romantic Literature*. New York: Norton, 1971.

Abrams, Robert. 'Public Faces.' Rev. of *The Portage to San Cristóbal of A.H.*, by George Steiner. *New York Review of Books* (12 August 1982): 11–12.

– 'Interfering with Literature.' Rev. of *The Ordinary Universe*, by Denis Donoghue. *New York Review of Books* (10 April 1969): 33–5.

Adorno, Theodor. *Aesthetic Theory*. Trans. C. Lenhardt. New York: Routledge and Kegan Paul, 1986.

Alter, Robert. 'Against Messiness.' Rev. of *No Passion Spent* and *The Deeps of the Sea and Other Fiction*, by George Steiner. *Times Literary Supplement* (12 January 1996): 23–4.

– *Canon and Creativity: Modern Writing and the Authority of Scripture*. New Haven: Yale University Press, 2000.

– 'Literary Criticism, A to Z.' Rev. of *Ferocious Alphabets*, by Denis Donoghue. *New Republic* (25 July 1981): 34–6.

– 'Outside the Academy.' Rev. of books by Patrick Parrinder and René Wellek. *London Review of Books* (13 February 1992): 15–16.

Altieri, Charles. *Canons and Consequences: Reflections on the Ethical Force of Imaginative Ideals*. Evanston, IL: Northwestern University Press, 1990.

Applebome, Peter. '[George Steiner,] A Classical Humanist and Elitist? Well, Perhaps.' *New York Times* (18 April 1998): B7+.

Arac, Jonathan. 'Frank Kermode and Normal Criticism: History and Mystery.' *Critical Genealogies: Historical Situations for Postmodern Literary Studies*. New York: Columbia University Press, 1987.

Arnold, Matthew. *The Portable Matthew Arnold*, ed. Lionel Trilling. New York: Viking Press, 1965.

Atlas, James. 'The Changing World of New York Intellectuals.' *New York Times Magazine* (25 August 1985): 22+.

Attridge, Derek. 'Literary Form and the Demands of Politics.' In Levine, ed., *Aesthetics and Ideology*, 243–63.

Auerbach, Nina. 'Roasting the Academics.' Rev. of *An Appetite for Poetry*, by Frank Kermode. *New York Times Book Review* (1 October 1989): 12.

Baker, Houston. 'Literature,' in 'Major Trends in Research: 22 Leading Scholars Report on Their Field.' *Chronicle of Higher Education* (4 September 1985): 12–14.

Banville, John. 'Portrait of the Critic as a Young Man.' Rev. of *Warrenpoint*, by Denis Donoghue. *New York Review of Books* (25 October 1990): 48–50.

Barthes, Roland. *Camera Lucida: Reflections on Photography*. Trans. Richard Howard. New York: Hill and Wang, 1983.

Bawer, Bruce. 'Public Intellectuals: An Endangered Species?' *Chronicle of Higher Education* (24 April 1998): A 72.

Bayley, John. 'The Greatest!' Rev. of *Shakespeare's Language*, by Frank Kermode. *New York Review of Books* (10 August 2000): 35–7.

Baym, Nina. 'The Agony of Feminism: Why Feminist Theory Is Necessary After All.' In Eddins, ed., *The Emperor Redressed*, 101–17.

Bellow, Saul. 'Summations.' In *The Ordering Mirror: Readers and Contexts (The Ben Belitt Lectures at Bennington College)*, ed. Phillip Lopate, 164–81. New York: Fordham University Press, 1993.

Benjamin, Andrew. 'A Place of Refuge.' Rev. of *Errata: An Examined Life*, by George Steiner. *Times Literary Supplement* (10 October 1997): 31–2.

Bennett, Tony. *Outside Literature*. London and New York: Routledge, 1990.

Bérubé, Michael. 'Defending Literary Studies Has Become a Lost Cause.' *Chronicle of Higher Education* (3 October 1999): B 6.

Beverley, John. *Against Literature*. Minneapolis: University of Minnesota Press, 1993.

Bloch, Ernst. *The Utopian Function of Art and Literature: Selected Essays*. Trans. Jack Zipes and Frank Mecklenburg. Cambridge: MIT Press, 1989.

Bloom, Harold. 'Literature as the Bible.' Rev. of *The Literary Guide to the Bible*, ed. Robert Alter and Frank Kermode. *New York Review of Books* (31 March 1988): 23–5.

– *The Western Canon: The Books and School of the Ages*. New York: Harcourt Brace, 1994.

Bonhoeffer, Dietrich. *The Cost of Discipleship*. 1937; repr. New York: Simon & Schuster, 1995.

Bourdieu, Pierre. *Distinction: A Social Critique of the Judgement of Taste.* Trans. Richard Nice. Cambridge: Harvard University Press, 1984.

Boyers, Robert, moderator. 'Discussion: Archives of Eden.' *Salmagundi,* no. 50–1 (Fall/Winter 1981): 115–18.

– moderator. 'The Responsibility of Intellectuals: A Discussion.' *Salmagundi,* no. 70–1 (Spring-Summer 1986): 164–95.

– 'Steiner As Cultural Critic: Confronting America.' In Scott and Sharp, eds., *Reading George Steiner,* 14–42.

Boyton, Robert S. 'The New Intellectuals.' *Atlantic Monthly* (March 1995): 53–70.

Bradbury, Malcolm. 'A Stern and Righteous Reader.' Rev. of *The Broken Estate,* by James Wood. *New Statesman* (12 February 1999): 52–3.

Bromwich, David. *Politics by Other Means: Higher Education and Group Thinking.* New Haven: Yale University Press, 1992.

– 'Slow Deconstruction.' *London Review of Books* (7 October 1993): 22–3.

– 'Titanic Humanism.' Rev. of *No Passion Spent,* by George Steiner. *New York Times Review of Books* (30 June 1996): 16–17.

Brooks, Peter. 'Aesthetics and Ideology: What Happened to Poetics?' In Levine, ed., *Aesthetics and Ideology,* 153–67.

Bruss, Elizabeth W. *Beautiful Theories: The Spectacle of Discourse in Contemporary Criticism.* Baltimore: Johns Hopkins University Press, 1982.

Burke, Kenneth. Rev. of *The Sovereign Ghost,* by Denis Donoghue. *New Republic* (10 September 1977): 29–31.

– 'Swift Now? Swift Then.' Rev. of *Jonathan Swift,* by Denis Donoghue. *New Republic* (9 May 1970): 30–3.

Burrow, Colin. 'Not for Horrid Profs.' Rev. of *Shakespeare's Language,* by Frank Kermode. *London Review of Books* (1 June 2000): 11–13.

Carey, John. 'A Way with Words.' Rev. of *Shakespeare's Language,* by Frank Kermode. *Sunday Times* (30 April 2000).

Carroll, Robert P. 'Toward a Grammar of Creation: On Steiner the Theologian.' In Scott and Sharp, eds., *Reading George Steiner,* 262–74.

Clayton, Jay. *The Pleasures of Babel: Contemporary American Literature and Theory.* Oxford: Oxford University Press, 1993.

Comnes, Gregory. *The Ethics of Indeterminacy in the Novels of William Gaddis.* Gainesville: University Press of Florida, 1994.

Conrad, Peter. 'In League with Iago and Satan.' Rev. of *Pleasing Myself,* by Frank Kermode. *Observer* (5 August 2001).

Culler, Jonathan. *Framing the Sign: Criticism and Its Institutions.* Oxford: Basil Blackwell, 1988.

Cunningham, Valentine. 'The Ethical Backlash.' Rev. of *Essays on Fiction,* by Frank Kermode. *Times Literary Supplement* (22 July 1983): 790.

– 'The Great Sublimator.' Rev. of *Walter Pater*, by Denis Donoghue. *New York Times Book Review* (14 May 1995): 15.

– *In the Reading Gaol: Postmodernity, Texts, and History*. Cambridge, MA: Basil Blackwell, 1994.

Damrosch, David. *We Scholars: Changing the Culture of the University*. Cambridge: Harvard University Press, 1995.

Davie, Donald. 'Certainties.' *London Review of Books* (20 May–2 June 1982): 6.

– 'The Clans and Their World-Pictures.' Rev. of *After Babel*, by George Steiner. *Times Literary Supplement* (31 January 1975): 98–100.

– 'Criticism and the Academy.' In *Criticism in the University*, ed. Gerald Graff and Reginald Gibbons, 170–6. Chicago: Northwestern Press, 1985.

– 'Reading and Believing.' Rev. of *The Literary Guide to the Bible*, ed. Robert Alter and Frank Kermode. *New Republic* (26 October 1987): 28–33.

Delbanco, Andrew. 'Night Vision.' Rev. of Lionel Trilling, *The Moral Obligation to Be Intelligent: Selected Essays*, ed. Leon Wieseltier. *New York Review of Books* (11 January 2001): 38–41.

De Man, Paul. *Allegories of Reading*. New Haven: Yale University Press, 1979.

– *Blindness and Insight*. Minneapolis: University of Minnesota Press, 1983.

– 'Blocking the Road: A Response to Frank Kermode.' In *Romanticism and Contemporary Criticism: The Gauss Seminar and Other Papers*, ed. E.S. Burt, Kevin Newmark, and Andrzej Warminski, 188–93. Baltimore: Johns Hopkins University Press, 1993.

– *Resistance to Theory*. Minneapolis: University of Minnesota Press, 1986.

– *The Rhetoric of Romanticism*. New York: Columbia University Press, 1984.

Derrida, Jacques. *The Archeology of the Frivolous: Reading Condillac*. Trans. John P. Leavey. Lincoln: University of Nebraska Press, 1987.

– 'Economimesis.' *Diacritics*, vol. 11 (1981): 3–25.

– *Positions*. Trans. Alan Bass. Chicago: University of Chicago Press, 1981.

– 'Psyche: Inventions of the Other.' Trans. Catherine Porter. In *Reading De Man Reading*, ed. Lindsay Waters and Wlad Godzich, 25–65. Minneapolis: University of Minnesota Press, 1989.

– *Writing and Difference*. Trans. Alan Bass. Chicago: University of Chicago Press, 1978.

Dickstein, Morris. 'Alive and 90 in the Jungles of Brazil.' Rev. of *The Portage to San Cristóbal of A.H.*, by George Steiner. *New York Times Book Review* (2 May 1982): 13, 21.

– *Double Agent: The Critic and Society*. Oxford: Oxford University Press, 1992.

– Letter. *PMLA* 115, no. 7 (2000): 1999.

Donoghue, Denis. 'Aboriginal Poet.' Rev. of *Collected Poems*, by Theodore
   Roethke; and *Theodore Roethke: An Introduction to the Poetry*, by Karl Malkoff.
   New York Review of Books (22 September 1966): 14–16.
– 'Absolute Pitch.' Rev. of *Nabokov: His Life in Art – A Critical Narrative*, by
   Andrew Field. *New York Review of Books* (3 August 1967): 4–6.
– *Adam's Curse: Reflections on Religion and Literature*. Notre Dame, IN: University
   of Notre Dame Press, 2001.
– 'The American Style of Failure.' *Sewanee Review* 82 (1974): 407–32.
– 'Ammons and the Lesser Celandine.' *Parnassus* 3, no. 2 (1975): 19–26.
– 'Anger and Dismay.' Omnibus rev. of books by, or edited by, James Gribble,
   Laurence Lerner and Geoffrey Thurley. *London Review of Books* (19 July–
   1 August 1984): 16.
– 'Another Country.' Omnibus review of books by Roddy Doyle. *New York Review
   of Books* (3 February 1994): 3+.
– *The Arts without Mystery*. Boston: Little, Brown and Co., 1983.
– 'Attitudes toward History: A Preface to The Sense of the Past.' *Salmagundi*
   (Fall–Winter 1985–6): 68–9, 107–24.
– 'Balloons.' Rev. of *Nil: Episodes in the Literary Conquest of Void during the Nine-
   teenth Century*, by Robert Martin Adams; *A World Elsewhere: The Place of Style in
   American Literature*, by Richard Poirier; and *In the Human Grain: Technological
   Culture and Its Effects on Man, Literature and Religion*, by Walter J. Ong. *New York
   Review of Books* (9 March 1967): 16–19.
– 'Beginning.' *Southern Review* 4, no. 3 (1998): 532–49.
– 'Being Irish Together.' *Sewanee Review* 84 (1976): 129–33.
– *Being Modern Together*. Atlanta: Scholar's Press, 1991.
– 'Bewitched, Bothered, and Bewildered.' Omnibus rev. of books by J. Hillis
   Miller, Frederick Crews, Morris Dickstein, and Giles Gunn. *New York Review of
   Books* (25 March 1993): 46–53.
– 'The Black Ox.' Rev. of *Forms of Discovery*, by Yvor Winters. *New York Review of
   Books* (29 February 1968): 22–4.
– 'Blues for Mr. Baldwin.' Rev. of *Going to Meet the Man*, by James Baldwin. *New
   York Review of Books* (9 December 1965): 6–7.
– 'Book of Books Books.' Omnibus rev. of books by Robert Alter, Burton L.
   Visotzky, Leslie Brisman, and Ricardo J. Quinones. *New York Review of Books*
   (5 November 1992): 46–50.
– 'The Book of Genius.' Rev. of *The Western Canon*, by Harold Bloom. *Times Liter-
   ary Supplement* (6 January 1995): 3–4.
– 'The Brainwashing of Lemuel Gulliver.' *Southern Review* 32, no. 1 (Winter
   1996): 128–46.
– 'Bright and Silly.' Rev. of *The Enemy: A Biography of Wyndham Lewis*, by Jeffrey

Meyers; and *Fables of Aggression: Wyndham Lewis, the Modernist as Fascist,* by
Fredric Jameson. *New York Review of Books* (29 April 1982): 28–30.

– 'Confidence Men.' Rev. of *The Adventures of Baron Munchausen,* by R.E. Raspe;
and *Selected Writings of E.T.A. Hoffmann,* ed. Leonard J. Kent and Elizabeth C.
Knight. *New York Review of Books* (4 December 1969): 24–8.

– *Connoisseurs of Chaos: Ideas of Order in Modern American Poetry.* 1964. New York:
Columbia University Press, 1984.

– 'Couples.' Rev. of *Going Places,* by Leonard Michaels; *Mirrors,* by Lucy Warner;
What I'm Going to Do, I Think, by L. Woiwode; and *A Nest of Ninnies,* by John
Ashbery and James Schuyler. *New York Review of Books* (10 July 1969): 17–20.

– 'A Criticism of One's Own.' *New Republic* (10 March 1986): 30–4.

– 'Critics at the Top.' Omnibus rev. of books by Irving Howe, Geoffrey H. Hartman, Frank Kermode, and J. Hillis Miller. *New York Review of Books* (15 August
1991): 53–6.

– 'Cummings and Goings.' Rev. of *Selected Letters of E.E. Cummings,* ed. F.W.
Dupee and George Stade. *New York Review of Books* (9 October 1969): 48–50.

– 'Darling, They're Quoting Our Poem.' Rev. of *The New Cambridge Bibliography
of English Literature.* Volume 4. *1900–1950,* ed. I.R. Willison; *The New Oxford
Book of English Verse, 1250–1950,* ed. Helen Gardner; and *The Oxford Book of
Twentieth-Century English Verse,* ed. Philip Larkin. *New York Review of Books*
(19 April 1973): 26–9.

– 'Deconstructing Deconstruction.' Rev. of *Deconstruction and Criticism,* by
Harold Bloom, Paul de Man, Jacques Derrida, Geoffrey H. Hartman, and
J. Hillis Miller; and *Allegories of Reading,* by Paul de Man. *New York Review of
Books* (12 June 1980): 37–41.

– 'The Delirium of the Brave.' Rev. of *In a Time of Violence,* by Eavan Boland. *New
York Review of Books* (26 May 1994): 25–7.

– 'Doing Things with Words: Criticism and the Attack on the Subject.' *Times
Literary Supplement* (15 July 1994): 4–5.

– 'Dream Work.' Rev. of *All the Pretty Horses.* Volume 1. *The Border Trilogy,* by
Cormac McCarthy. *New York Review of Books* (24 June 1993): 5+.

– 'Drums under the Window.' Rev. of *The Damnable Question,* by George Danger-
field; and *Mother Ireland,* by Edna O'Brien. *New York Review of Books* (14 October 1976): 12–15.

– 'Dry Dreams.' Omnibus review of books by Henry Miller. *New York Review of
Books* (14 October 1965): 5–7.

– 'Eliot's "Marina" and Closure.' *Hudson Review* 49 (Autumn 1996): 367–88.

– *Emily Dickinson.* Minneapolis: University of Minnesota Press, 1969.

– *England, Their England: Commentaries on English Language and Literature.* New
York: Knopf, 1988.

- 'The English Dickens and *Dombrey and Son.*' *Nineteenth-Century Fiction* 24 (1970): 383–404.
- 'The Englishness of English Poetry.' In *The Shelia Carmel Lectures, 1988–1993,* ed. Hana Wirth-Nescher. Tel Aviv: Tel Aviv University, 1995: 35–56.
- 'Enigma Variations.' Omnibus review of books by Kenneth Burke. *New York Review of Books* (11 July 1968): 39–41.
- 'Experiments in Folly.' Rev. of *The Doctor Is Sick,* by Anthony Burgess; *The Secret Swinger,* by Alan Harrington; and *A Season in the Life of Emmanuel,* by Maric-Claire Blais. *New York Review of Books* (9 June 1966): 20+.
- 'Fabulous Salad.' Rev. of *Wallace Stevens: The Making of Harmonium,* by Robert Buttel; and *Wallace Stevens: Musing the Obscure,* by Ronald Sukenick. *New York Review of Books* (1 February 1968): 23–6.
- 'The Fabulous Yeats Boys.' Rev. of *Jack Yeats,* by Bruce Arnold; *The Life of W.B. Yeats,* by Terence Brown; and *Yeats's Ghosts: The Secret Life of W.B. Yeats,* by Brenda Maddox. *New York Review of Books* (11 May 2000): 32–6.
- *Ferocious Alphabets.* 1981. New York: Columbia University Press, 1984.
- 'Five Hundred Years of the King's English.' Rev. of *The Oxford University Press and the Spread of Learning: An Illustrated History,* by Nicolas Barker; *A History of Oxford University Press,* Volume 1, by Harry Carter; *The Oxford University Press: An Informal History,* by Peter Sutcliffe; *Caught in the Web of Word: James Murray and the Oxford English Dictionary,* by K.M. Elisabeth Murray; and *The Coming of the Book: The Impact of Printing, 1450–1800,* by Lucien Febvre and Henri-Jean Martin. *New York Review of Books* (1 June 1978): 30–2.
- 'Fretting in the Other's Shadow.' Rev. of *The Penguin Book of Irish Fiction,* ed. Colm Tóibín. *Times Literary Supplement* (19 November 1999): 21.
- 'From the Country of the Blue.' Rev. of *The Poems of George Meredith,* ed. Phyllis B. Barlett. *New York Review of Books* (22 February 1979): 37–9.
- 'Frost: The Icon and the Man.' Rev. of *Robert Frost: A Life,* by Jay Parini; and *Robert Frost and the Challenge of Darwin,* by Robert Faggen. *New York Review of Books* (21 October 1999).
- 'The Gay Science.' Rev. of *A History of Modern Criticism 1750–1950,* by René Wellek. *Encounter* 28, no. 6 (June 1967): 80–4.
- 'Ghosts and Others.' Rev. of *Adam and the Train: Two Novels,* by Heinrich Böll; *Whitewater,* by Paul Horgan; *The Dick,* by Bruce Jay Friedman; and *The Ghost of Henry James,* by David Plante. *New York Review of Books* (5 November 1970): 22–4.
- 'God with Thunder.' *Times Literary Supplement* (3 November 1972): 1339–41.
- 'Good Grief.' Omnibus review of books by and about W.H. Auden. *New York Review of Books* (19 July 1973): 17–18.
- 'The Good Old Complex Fate.' *Hudson Review* 17 (1964): 267–78.

– 'Grand Old Opry.' Rev. of *Giles Goat-Boy*, by John Barth. *New York Review of Books* (18 August 1966): 30+.
– 'A Guide to the Revolution.' Rev. of *Literary Theory: An Introduction*, by Terry Eagleton. *New York Review of Books* (8 December 1983): 43–5.
– 'The Habits of the Poet.' *Times Literary Supplement* (25 April 1975): 442–3.
– 'The Hard Case of Yeats.' Rev. of *Yeats*, by Frank Tuohy; *Maude Gonne*, by Samuel Levenson; *W.B. Yeats and the Idea of a Theatre*, by James W. Flannery; and *The Cuchulain Plays of W.B. Yeats*, by Reg Skene. *New York Review of Books* (26 May 1977): 3–8.
– 'The Heart in Hiding.' Rev. of *Gerard Manley Hopkins: A Biography*, by Paddy Kitchen. *New York Review of Books* (27 September 1979): 51–3.
– 'Henry Adams' Novels.' *Nineteenth-Century Literature* 39, no. 2 (1984): 186–201.
– 'Henry James, at a Theater Near You.' *New York Times* (3 January 1997).
– 'The Heroism of Despair.' Omnibus review of books on or by Henry Adams. *New York Review of Books* (23 September 1993): 58+.
– 'Hide and Seek.' Rev. of *The Renaissance: Studies in Art and Poetry*, by Walter Pater; and *Walter Pater's Art of Autobiography*, by Gerald Monsman. *New York Review of Books* (14 May 1981): 40–3.
– 'Huston's Joyce.' Rev. of *The Dead*, directed by John Huston. *New York Review of Books* (3 March 1988): 18–19.
– 'I Have Never Been Able to Tell a Story.' *New York Times Book Review* (2 September 1990): 2+.
– 'The Idea of a Christian Society.' *Yale Review* 78, no. 2 (1989): 218–34.
– *Imagination*. Glasgow: University of Glasgow Press, 1974.
– 'Ireland: Race, Nation, State (Part One).' *Partisan Review* (Spring 1999): 223–34.
– 'Ireland: Race, Nation, State (Part Two).' *Partisan Review* (Summer 1999): 363–74.
– 'James's *The Awkward Age* and Pound's "Mauberley."' *Notes and Queries* 17 (1970): 49–50.
– *Jonathan Swift: A Critical Introduction*. 1969. Cambridge: Cambridge University Press, 1971.
– 'The Joy of Texts.' Rev. of *The Pleasure of Reading in an Ideological Age*, by Robert Alter. *New Republic* (26 June 1989): 36–8.
– 'Joyce's Many Lives.' Omnibus rev. of books on James Joyce. *New York Review of Books* (21 October 1993): 28–35.
– 'Kenneth Burke's Dangling Novel.' *Encounter* 29, no. 4 (1967): 78–84.
– 'Kicking the Air.' Rev. of *How Late It Was, How Late*, by James Kelman; *The Dead School*, by Patrick McCabe; and *Walking the Dog and Other Stories*, by Bernard MacLaverty. *New York Review of Books* (8 June 1995): 45+.

– 'Language Barriers.' Rev. of *The Best and the Last of Edwin O'Connor*, ed. Arthur Schlesinger, Jr; and *Max Jamison*, by Wilfrid Sheed. *New York Review of Books* (18 June 1970): 21–2.

– 'Leases of Lifelessness.' *London Review of Books* (7 October 1993): 16–17.

– 'Leavis and Eliot.' *Raritan* 1, no. 1 (1981): 68–87.

– 'Life Sentence.' Rev. of *Meet Me in the Green Glen*, by Robert Penn Warren; *The Condor Passes*, by Shirley Ann Grau; and *Edsel*, by Karl Shapiro. *New York Review of Books* (2 December 1971): 28–30.

– 'The Limits of Language.' Rev. of *The Resistance to Theory*, by Paul de Man; and *The Lesson of Paul de Man*, by Peter Brooks, Shoshana Felman, and J. Hillis Miller. *New Republic* (7 July 1986): 40–4.

– 'Listening to the Saddest Story.' *Sewanee Review* 88 (1980): 557–71.

– 'Lives of a Poet.' Rev. of *Crux: The Letters of James Dickey*, ed. Matthew J. Bruccoli and Judith S. Baughman; *James Dickey: The Selected Poems*, ed. Robert Kirschten; and *The James Dickey Reader*, ed. Henry Hart. *New York Review of Books* (18 November 1999): 55–7.

– 'The Long Poem.' Rev. of *Wildtrack*, by John Wain; *Rivers and Mountains*, by John Ashbery; *The War of the Secret Agents, and Other Poems*, by Henri Coulette; and *Nights and Days*, by James Merrill. *New York Review of Books* (14 April 1966): 18+.

– 'Lover of Lost Causes.' Rev. of *Canaan* and *The Triumph of Love*, by Geoffrey Hill. *New York Review of Books* (20 May 1999): 53–7.

– 'The Luck of the Irish.' Rev. of *The New Oxford Book of Irish Verse*, ed. Thomas Kinsella; and *The Faber Book of Contemporary Irish Poetry*, ed. Paul Muldoon. *New York Review of Books* (26 February 1987): 25–6.

– 'Magic Defeated.' Rev. of *The Time of the Angels*, by Iris Murdoch; *The Birds Fall Down*, by Rebecca West; and *The Animal Hotel*, by Jean Garrigue. *New York Review of Books* (17 November 1966): 22–5.

– 'The Magic of W.B. Yeats.' Omnibus review. *New York Review of Books* (21 April 1994): 49+.

– 'Man of Letters.' Omnibus review of books by and on Bernard Shaw. *New York Review of Books* (3 February 1966): 10+.

– 'A Man of Words.' Rev. of *James, Seumas and Jacques: Unpublished Writings of James Stephens*, ed. Lloyd Frankenberg; and *James Stephens: His Work and an Account of His Life*, by Hilary Pyle. *New York Review of Books* (26 August 1965): 17–18.

– 'Man without Art.' Rev. of *Death on the Installment Plan*, by Louis-Ferdinand Céline; and *Céline and His Vision*, by Erika Ostrovsky. *New York Review of Books* (15 June 1967): 20–2.

– 'Mediterranean Man.' *Partisan Review* 44 (1977): 452–7.

– 'Miracle Plays.' Rev. of *Miracles*, ed. Richard Lewis; *Bertha, and Other Plays*, by

Kenneth Koch; *Reason of the Heart*, by Edward Dahlberg; and *Cipango's Hinder Door*, by Edward Dahlberg. *New York Review of Books* (20 October 1966): 25–7.

- 'Mister Myth.' Omnibus rev. of books by Northrop Frye. *New York Review of Books* (9 April 1992): 25–8.
- 'Moidores for Hart Crane.' Rev. of *The Poetry of Hart Crane*, by R.W.B. Lewis. *New York Review of Books* (9 November 1967): 16–19.
- 'Moorish Gorgeousness.' Rev. of *Tell Me, Tell Me*, by Marianne Moore. *New York Review of Books* (12 January 1967): 3–4.
- 'Moravia's Vulgarity.' Rev. of *Man As an End* and *The Lie*, by Alberto Moravia. *New York Review of Books* (28 July 1966): 26–8.
- 'Musil.' Rev. of *Five Women*, by Robert Musil. *New York Review of Books* (26 May 1966): 24+.
- 'My Only Memoir.' *Partisan Review* 68, no. 1 (2001): 143–50.
- 'The Myth of Robert Graves.' Rev. of *Robert Graves and the White Goddess, 1940–1985*, by Richard Perceval Graves; *Robert Graves: His Life on the Edge*, by Miranda Seymour; *Robert Graves: His Life and Work*, by Martin Seymour-Smith. *New York Review of Books* (4 April 1996): 27–31.
- 'The Myth of W.B. Yeats.' Rev. of *W.B. Yeats: A Life*, Volume 1, by R.F. Foster; and *The Collected Letters of W.B. Yeats*, Volume 2, ed. Warwick Gould, John Kelly, and Deidre Toomey. *New York Review of Books* (19 February 1998): 17–19.
- 'New York Poets.' Rev. of *The Burning Mystery of Anna in 1951*, by Kenneth Koch; *The Morning of the Poem*, by James Schuyler; *Sunrise*, by Frederick Seidel; and *Trader*, by Robert Mazzocco. *New York Review of Books* (14 August 1980): 49–50.
- 'Newton's Other Law: Glory IS the Real Reward.' *New York Times Book Review* (21 April 1985): 34.
- 'Nuances of a Theme by Allen Tate.' *Southern Review* 12 (1976): 698–713.
- 'Oasis Poetry.' Omnibus review of poetry collections by Robert Duncan, James Wright, Alan Dugan, Adrienne Rich and Saint Geraud. *New York Review of Books* (7 May 1970): 35–8.
- 'Objects Solitary and Terrible.' Rev. of *Live or Die*, by Anne Sexton; *The Lice*, by W.S. Merwin; *Reasons for Moving*, by Mark Strand; and *Love Letters from Asia*, by Sandra Hochman. *New York Review of Books* (6 June 1968): 21–4.
- *The Old Moderns: Essays on Literature and Theory*. New York: Alfred K. Knopf, 1994.
- 'On the White Strand.' Rev. of *The Selected Letters of Jack B. Yeats*, ed. Robin Skelton. *London Review of Books* (4 April 1991): 17–18.
- 'Only Disconnect.' Rev. of *Daniel Martin*, by John Fowles; and *The Sun and the Moon*, by Niccolò Tucci. *New York Review of Books* (8 December 1977): 45–6.

– 'Orality, Literacy, and Their Discontents.' *New Literary History* 27, no. 1 (1996): 145–59.
– 'The Ordinary Universe.' Rev. of *The Pyramid*, by William Golding; *William Golding: A Critical Study*, by Mark Kinkead-Weekes and Ian Gregor; *The Art of William Golding*, by Bernard S. Oldsey and Stanley Weintraub; and *Imaginary Friends*, by Alison Lurie. *New York Review of Books* (7 December 1967): 21–4.
– *The Ordinary Universe: Soundings in Modern Literature.* 1968. New York: Ecco Press, 1987.
– 'An Organic Intellectual.' Rev. of *The World, The Text, and The Critic*, by Edward Said. *New Republic* (18 April 1983): 30–3.
– 'The Other Country.' Rev. of *The Golden Key*, by George MacDonald. *New York Review of Books* (21 December 1967): 34–6.
– 'Owning Literature.' Rev. of *The Force of Poetry*, by Christopher Ricks. *Raritan* 4, no. 4 (1985): 97–116.
– 'Parts of Speech.' Rev. of *The Counterfeiters*, by Hugh Kenner; *The Literature of Silence*, by Ihab Hassan; and *Yeats's Blessings on Von Hügel*, by Martin Green. *New York Review of Books* (13 February 1969): 2–25.
– 'The Philosopher of Selfless Love.' Omnibus rev. of books by Emmanuel Levinas. *New York Review of Books* (21 March 1996): 37–40.
– 'Play It Again, Sam.' Rev. of Samuel Beckett, *Waiting for Godot*, directed by Mike Nichols. *New York Review of Books* (8 December 1988): 30–5.
– 'The Poet in Limbo.' Rev. of *Conrad Aiken: Poet of White Horse Vale*, by Edward Butscher. *New York Review of Books* (22 December 1988): 45+.
– 'A Poet of the Self and the Weather.' *Times Literary Supplement* (25 April 1986): 435–6.
– 'The Political Turn in Criticism.' *Salmagundi* 81 (Winter 1988): 104–22.
– 'The Politics of Homosexuality.' Rev. of *Virtually Normal*, by Andrew Sullivan. *New York Times Book Review* (20 August 1995): 3+.
– *The Politics of Modern Criticism.* Bennington, VT: Bennington Chapbooks in Literature, 1981. Reprinted in *The Ordering Mirror: Readers and Contexts (The Ben Belitt Lectures at Bennington College)*, ed. Phillip Lopate. New York: Fordham University Press, 1993: 72–92.
– 'The Politics of Poetry.' Rev. of *W.B. Yeats and Georgian Ireland*, by Donald T. Torchiana; and *The Letters of John Gay*, by C.F. Burgess. *New York Review of Books* (6 April 1967): 2–25.
– 'Pound's Book of Beasts.' Omnibus review of books on Ezra Pound. *New York Review of Books* (2 June 1988): 14–16.
– *The Practice of Reading.* New Haven: Yale University Press, 1998.
– 'The Problems of Being Irish.' *Times Literary Supplement* (17 March 1972): 291–2.

- 'The Promiscuous Cool of Postmodernism.' *New York Times Review of Books* (22 June 1986): 1+.
- 'Provincialism.' Rev. of *The Penguin Book of Victorian Verse*, ed. Daniel Karlin. *London Review of Books* (4 June 1998): 24–5.
- *The Pure Good of Theory*. Cambridge, MA: Basil Blackwell, 1992.
- 'The Question of Voice,' in *Who Says What: A Lecture Given at the Princess Grace Irish Library*. Gerrards Cross: Colin Smythe, 1992.
- 'R.P. Blackmur and The Double Agent.' *Sewanee Review* 91, no. 4 (1983): 634–43.
- *Reading America: Essays on American Literature*. New York: Knopf, 1987.
- 'Reading Bakhtin.' *Raritan* 5, no. 2 (1985): 107–19.
- 'The Real McCoy.' Rev. of *Essays on Realism*, by Georg Lukács; and *The Realistic Imagination: English Fiction from Frankenstein to Lady Chatterley*, by George Levine. *New York Review of Books* (19 November 1981): 44–7.
- 'Reconsidering Katherine Anne Porter.' Rev. of *Collected Stories*, by Katherine Anne Porter. *New York Review of Books* (11 November 1965): 18–19.
- 'A Reply to Frank Kermode.' *Critical Inquiry* (December 1974): 447–52.
- 'The Return of the Native.' Rev. of *An American Procession*, by Alfred Kazin. *New York Review of Books* (19 July 1984): 32–4.
- 'The Revel's Ended.' Rev. of *Any Old Irony*, by Anthony Burgess. *New York Review of Books* (30 March 1989): 35–6.
- 'The Revolt against Tradition: Readers, Writers, and Critics.' *Partisan Review* 58, no. 2 (1991): 282–314.
- 'The Sad Captain of Criticism.' Rev. of *Ruin the Sacred Truths*, by Harold Bloom. *New York Review of Books* (2 March 1989): 22–4.
- 'Second Thoughts.' Rev. of *The World's Body*, by John Crowe Ransom; *John Crowe Ransom: Critical Essays and a Bibliography*, ed. Thomas Daniel Young; *Essays of Four Decades*, by Allen Tate; *The Fugitive Group: A Literary History*, by Louise Cowan; and *The Burden of Time: The Fugitives and Agrarians*, by John L. Stewart. *New York Review of Books* (22 May 1969): 41–4.
- 'Secret Sharer.' Rev. of *Ways of Escape*, by Graham Greene. *New York Review of Books* (19 February 1981): 15–17.
- 'She's Got Rhythm.' Rev. of *The Complete Prose of Marianne Moore*, ed. Patricia C. Willis. *New York Review of Books* (4 December 1986): 40–4.
- 'Sign Language.' Rev. of *As We Know*, by John Ashbery. *New York Review of Books* (24 January 1980): 36–9.
- 'The Snow Man.' Rev. of *Souvenirs and Prophecies: The Young Wallace Stevens*, by Holly Stevens. *New York Review of Books* (3 March 1977): 21–4.
- '"Some Day I'll Be In Out of the Rain."' Rev. of *Angela's Ashes*, by Frank McCourt. *New York Times Book Review* (15 September 1996): 13.

- 'Some Versions of Empson.' *Times Literary Supplement* (7 June 1974): 597–8.
- *The Sovereign Ghost: Studies in Imagination.* 1976; New York: Ecco Press, 1990.
- 'The Speculations of T.E. Hulme.' Rev. of *The Collected Writings of T.E. Hulme*, ed. Karen Csengeri. *Partisan Review* 65, no. 4 (1998): 648–52.
- 'The Stains of Ireland.' Rev. of *The Year of the French*, by Thomas Flanagan. *New York Review of Books* (14 July 1979): 21–3.
- 'Stevens at the Crossing.' Rev. of *Wallace Stevens: The Poems of Our Climate*, by Harold Bloom. *New York Review of Books* (15 September 1977): 39–42.
- 'The Storyteller.' *New York Times Book Review* (26 March 2000): 35.
- 'The Strange Case of Paul de Man.' *New York Review of Books* (29 June 1989): 32–7.
- 'The Supreme Fiction.' Rev. of *Soul Says: On Recent Poetry*; *The Breaking of Style: Hopkins, Heaney, Graham*; and *The Given and the Made: Strategies of Poetic Redefinition*, by Helen Vendler. *New York Review of Books* (28 November 1996): 59–63.
- 'Svevo's Comedy.' Rev. of *Short Sentimental Journey, and Other Stories*, by Italo Svevo; and *Italo Svevo: The Man and the Writer*, by P.N. Furbank. *New York Review of Books* (4 May 1967): 29–31.
- 'Sweepstakes.' Rev. of *Why Are We In Vietnam?*, by Norman Mailer; *Death Kit*, by Susan Sontag; and *The Puzzleheaded Girl*, by Christina Stead. *New York Review of Books* (28 September 1967): 5–8.
- 'T.S. Eliot and the Poem Itself.' *Partisan Review* 67, no. 1 (2000): 10–37.
- 'Teaching Literature: The Force of Form.' *New Literary History* 30, no. 1 (1999): 5–24.
- 'Textual Abuse.' Rev. of *Topographies*, by J. Hillis Miller. *Times Literary Supplement* (14 July 1995): 24–5.
- 'That Old Eloquence.' Rev. of *Not This Pig*, by Philip Levine; *A 1–12*, by Louis Zukofsky; and *After Experience*, by W.D. Snodgrass. *New York Review of Books* (25 April 1968): 16–18.
- 'Their Masters' Steps.' *Times Literary Supplement* (16–22 December 1988): 1399–1400.
- 'Themes from Derek Walcott.' *Parnassus* 6, no. 1 (1977): 88–100.
- *Thieves of Fire.* London: Faber and Faber, 1973.
- 'Three Ways of Reading.' *Southern Review* 34, no. 2 (1998): 383–401.
- 'Two Notes on Stevens.' *Wallace Stevens Journal* 4 (1980): 40–5.
- 'The Uncomplete Dossier.' Rev. of *Travels with My Aunt*, by Graham Greene; and *Blind Love, and Other Stories*, by V.S. Pritchett. *New York Review of Books* (4 December 1969): 24–8.
- 'The Use and Abuse of Theory.' *Modern Language Review* (October 1992): xxx–xxxviii; reprinted in *The Old Moderns*: 77–90.

– 'Ultra Writer.' Rev. of *Selected Letters of Malcolm Lowry*, ed. Harvey Breit and
  Margerie Bonner Lowry; and *Under the Volcano*, by Malcolm Lowry. *New York
  Review of Books* (3 March 1966): 16+.
– 'Untouched by Eliot.' Rev. of *Rounding the Horn: Collected Poems* and *Singing
  School: The Making of a Poet*, by John Stallworthy. *London Review of Books*
  (4 March 1999): 23–4.
– 'The Values of Moll Flanders.' *Sewanee Review* 71 (1963): 287–303.
– 'A Very Special Case.' Rev. of *Jonathan Swift: A Critical Biography*, by John Mid-
  dleton Murry; *Swift, The Man, His Works, and the Age*. Volume 2. *Dr. Swift*, by
  Irvin Ehrenpreis; *Jonathan Swift*, by Nigel Dennis; and *Protean Shape: A Study in
  18th-Century Vocabulary and Usage*, by Susie I. Tucker. *New York Review of Books*
  (16 January 1969): 10–12.
– 'W.B. Yeats.' *Times Literary Supplement* (9 February 1973): 153.
– 'Waiting for the End.' Omnibus review of poetry collections by Derek Walcott,
  W.S. Merwin, Mark Strand, James Merrill, C. Day-Lewis, Hugh Seidman, and
  Anne Waldman. *New York Review of Books* (6 May 1971): 27–31.
– 'Wallace Stevens, Imperator.' Rev. of *The Letters of Wallace Stevens*, ed. Holly
  Stevens. *New York Review of Books* (1 December 1966): 6–10.
– *Walter Pater: Lover of Strange Souls*. New York: Alfred A. Knopf, 1995.
– *Warrenpoint*. New York: Alfred A. Knopf, 1990.
– *We Irish: Essays on Irish Literature and Society*. Berkeley: University of California
  Press, 1986.
– 'What Fiction Is For.' *Sewanee Review* 107, no. 4 (1999): 527–54.
– 'What Makes Life Worth Writing?' *New York Times Review of Books* (29 March
  1987): 11–12.
– 'What's Really Wrong with the University.' Rev. of *Three Rival Versions of
  Moral Enquiry*, by Alasdair MacIntyre. *Wilson Quarterly* (Winter 1992):
  97–101.
– 'What's Your Inner Reality.' Rev. of *The Eighth Day*, by Thorton Wilder; and
  Snow White, by Donald Barthelme. *New York Review of Books* (24 August 1967):
  12–13.
– 'Who Says What' and 'The Question of Voice.' *The Princess Grace Irish Library
  Lectures: 9*. Gerard Cross, Buckinghamshire: Colin Smythe, 1992.
– 'Whose Trope Is It Anyway?' Rev. of *The Renewal of Literature*, by Richard Poir-
  ier. *New York Review of Books* (25 June 1987): 50–2.
– 'The Will to Certitude.' *Times Literary Supplement* (30 August 1974): 917–18.
– *William Butler Yeats*. 1971; New York: Ecco Press, 1988.
– 'William Wetmore Story and His Friends: The Enclosing Fact of Rome.' In
  The Sweetest Impression of Life: The James Family, ed. James W. Tuttleton and
  Augostino Lombardo. New York: New York University Press, 1990.

- 'Wonder Woman.' Rev. of *A Bloodsmoor Romance*, by Joyce Carol Oates. *New York Review of Books* (21 October 1982): 12–17.
- *Words Alone: The Poet T.S. Eliot*. New Haven: Yale University Press, 2000.
- 'The World Seen and Half-Seen.' Rev. of *The Hill Bachelors*, by William Trevor. *New York Review of Books* (22 February 2001): 41–3.
- 'Worlding.' Omnibus review of books by or on W.H. Auden. *New York Review of Books* (19 June 1969): 19–24.
- *Yeats*. London: Fontana, 1971.
- 'Yeats, Eliot, and the Mythical Method.' *Sewanee Review* 105, no. 3 (1997): 206–26.
- 'You Better Believe It.' Rev. of *The Middle Ground*, by Margaret Drabble; and *Setting the World on Fire*, by Angus Wilson. *New York Review of Books* (20 November 1980): 20–2.
- 'The Young Yeats.' Rev. of *The Collected Letters of W.B. Yeats*, Volume 1, *1865–1895*, ed. John Kelly. *New York Review of Books* (14 August 1986): 14–16.
- ed. *An Honoured Guest: New Essays on W.B. Yeats*. London: Edward Arnold Ltd, 1965.
- Eagleton, Terry. *Against the Grain: Essays, 1975–1985*. London: Verso, 1986.
- *The Function of Criticism: From the Spectator to Post-Structuralism*. London: Verso, 1984.
- *The Significance of Theory*. Cambridge, MA: Basil Blackwell, 1990.
- Early, Gerald. 'Blacks Like Them.' Rev. of *The Future of the Race*, by Henry Louis Gates, Jr. and Cornel West. *New York Times Book Review* (21 April 1996): 7+.
- Eddins, Dwight, ed. *The Emperor Redressed: Critiquing Critical Theory*. Tuscaloosa: University of Alabama Press, 1995.
- Edmundson, Mark. *Literature against Philosophy, Plato to Derrida: A Defence of Poetry*. Cambridge: Cambridge University Press, 1995.
- Eliot, T.S. *Selected Prose of T.S. Eliot*, ed. Frank Kermode. New York: Harcourt Brace Jovanovich/Farrar Straus Giroux, 1975.
- *The Use of Poetry and The Use of Criticism*. Cambridge: Harvard University Press, 1986.
- Emerson, Caryl. 'Tolstoy and Dostoevsky: Seductions of the Old Criticism.' In Scott and Sharp, eds., *Reading George Steiner*, 74–98.
- Empson, William. 'Advanced Thought.' Rev. of *The Genesis of Secrecy*, by Frank Kermode. In *Argufying*, ed. John Haffenden. Iowa City: University of Iowa Press, 1987: 516–21.
- *Seven Types of Ambiguity*. London: Chatto and Windus, 1947.
- Enright, D.J. 'Speak Up!' Rev. of *Language and Silence*, by George Steiner. *New York Review of Books* (12 October 1967): 26–8.

Felski, Rita. *Beyond Feminist Aesthetics: Feminist Literature and Social Change.* Cambridge: Harvard University Press, 1989.

Fender, Stephen. Letter ['The London Review of Books']. *London Review of Books* (8 November 1979): 2.

Fish, Stanley. 'Commentary: The Young and the Restless.' In Veeser, ed., *The New Historicism*: 303–16.

– *Professional Correctness: Literary Studies and Political Change.* Oxford: Oxford University Press, 1995.

Foucault, Michel. *The Order of Things: An Archaeology of the Human Sciences.* New York: Random House–Vintage, 1973.

Frank, Joseph. 'Spatial Form: An Answer to Critics.' *Critical Inquiry* 4 (Winter 1977): 231–52.

Freud, Sigmund. *Moses and Monotheism.* Trans. Katherine Jones. New York: Vintage Books, 1962.

Fromm, Harold. 'One Type of Ambiguity.' *American Scholar* (Autumn 1990): 622–5.

– Rev. of *Real Presences*, by George Steiner. *Georgia Review* (Summer 1991): 398–403.

Gagnier, Regenia. 'A Critique of Practical Aesthetics.' In Levine, ed., *Aesthetics and Ideology*, 264–82.

Gallagher, Catherine. 'Fighting for the Common Reader.' Rev. of *An Appetite for Poetry*, by Frank Kermode, and *Authors*, by Karl Miller. *Times Literary Supplement* (26 January–1 February 1990): 84.

Gallop, Jane. *Around 1981: Academic Feminist Literary Theory.* New York and London: Routledge, 1992.

Garber, Marjorie. Letter. *New York Times Book Review* (30 July 1995): 23.

– *Vice Versa: Bisexuality and the Eroticism of Everyday Life.* New York: Simon and Schuster, 1995.

Gardner, Helen. *In Defence of the Imagination.* Cambridge: Harvard University Press, 1982.

Gasché, Rudolphe. *Inventions of Difference.* Cambridge: Harvard University Press, 1994.

Gates, Henry Louis, Jr. 'The Charmer.' *New Yorker* (29 April–6 May 1996): 116–31.

Gilbert, Sandra M., and Susan Gubar, eds. *The Norton Anthology of Literature By Women.* New York: W.W. Norton & Co., 1985.

Girard, René. 'Violence, Difference, Sacrifice: A Conversation with René Girard.' Interviewed by Rebecca Adams. *Religion and Literature* 25, no. 2 (1993): 9–34.

Gorak, Jan. *Critic of Crisis: A Study of Frank Kermode.* Columbia, MS: University of Missouri Press, 1987.

Gottlieb, Anthony. 'Idea Man.' Rev. of *Errata: An Examined Life*, by George
Steiner. *New York Times Review of Books* (12 April 1998): 18.

Graff, Gerald. *Professing Literature: An Institutional History*. Chicago: University of
Chicago Press, 1987.

– Rev. of *The Genesis of Secrecy*, by Frank Kermode. *New Republic* (9 June 1979):
27–32.

Gray, John. 'Is the Writing on the Wall for Reading?' Rev. of *No Passion Spent*, by
George Steiner. *Times Higher Education Supplement* (1 March 1996): 28.

Greenblatt, Stephen. *Learning to Curse: Essays in Early Modern Culture*. New York:
Routledge, 1992.

Greenblatt, Stephen, and Giles Gunn, eds. *Redrawing the Boundaries: The Transformation of English and American Literary Studies*. New York: Modern Language
Association of America, 1992.

Gross, John. 'The Man of Letters in a Closed Shop.' *Times Literary Supplement*
(15 November 1991): 15–16.

– *The Rise and Fall of the Man of Letters: A Study of the Idiosyncratic and the Humane
in Modern Literature*. New York: Macmillan Company, 1969.

Guillory, John. *Cultural Capital: The Problem of Literary Canon Formation*. Chicago:
University of Chicago Press, 1993.

– 'The Ideology of Canon-Formation: T.S. Eliot and Cleanth Brooks.' In Robert
von Halberg, ed., *Canons*. Chicago: University of Chicago Press, 1984.

Gunn, Giles. *The Culture of Criticism and the Criticism of Culture*. Oxford: Oxford
University Press, 1988.

– *Thinking across the American Grain: Ideology, Intellect, and the New Pragmatism*.
Chicago: University of Chicago Press, 1992.

Guppy, Shusha. 'A Knight Recalls His Days.' Rev. of *Not Entitled: A Memoir*,
by Frank Kermode. *Times Higher Education Supplement* (20 September 1996):
20.

Handelman, Susan A. *The Slayers of Moses: The Emergence of Rabbinic Interpretation
in Modern Literary Theory*. Albany: State University of New York Press, 1982.

Hardison, O.B. 'Keeping the Canon Rolling.' Rev. of *Forms of Attention*, by Frank
Kermode. *New York Times Book Review* (14 July 1985): 7.

Harman, Claire. 'Big Talk about Shakespeare.' Rev. of *Shakespeare's Language*, by
Frank Kermode. *Evening Standard* (17 April 2000).

Hartman, Geoffrey H. *Minor Prophecies: The Literary Essay in the Culture Wars*.
Cambridge: Harvard University Press, 1991.

– Rev. of *After Babel*, by George Steiner. *New York Times Book Review* (8 June
1975): 21–3.

Hartman, Geoffrey H., and Sanford Budick, eds. *Midrash and Literature*. New
Haven: Yale University Press, 1986.

Hassan, Ihab. 'Confessions of a Reluctant Critic or, The Resistance to Literature.' *New Literary History* (Winter 1993): 1–15.

– *The Postmodern Turn: Essays in Postmodern Theory and Culture.* Columbus: Ohio State University Press, 1987.

– *Rumors of Change: Essays of Five Decades.* Tuscaloosa: University of Alabama Press, 1995.

– 'The Whole Mystery of Babel: On George Steiner.' *Salmagundi*, no. 70–1 (Spring/Summer 1986): 316–33.

Hawkes, Terence. 'Word of Mouth.' Rev. of *Shakespeare's Language*, by Frank Kermode. *New Statesman* (12 June 2000).

Hegel, G.W.F., *Phenomenology of Spirit.* Trans. A.V. Miller. Oxford: Oxford University Press, 1977.

Hensher, Philip. 'Wild and Whirling Words.' Rev. of *Shakespeare's Language*, by Frank Kermode. *The Spectator* (29 April 2000): 28–9.

Hirsch, Jr, E.D. 'Carnal Knowledge.' Rev. of *The Genesis of Secrecy*, by Frank Kermode. *New York Review of Books* (14 June 1979): 18–20.

Hough, Graham. 'Life and Substance.' Rev. of *The Ordinary Universe*, by Denis Donoghue. *New Statesman* (5 July 1968): 18.

Howe, Irving. 'The Common Reader.' In *A Critic's Notebook*, ed. Nicholas Howe. New York: Harcourt, Brace, 1994.

Hunter, George. 'The History of Styles As a Style of History.' In Tudeau-Clayton and Warner, eds., *Addressing Frank Kermode*, 74–88.

Jacoby, Russell. *The Last Intellectuals: American Culture in the Age of Academe.* New York: Basic Books, 1987.

James, Clive. 'The Whispering Critic.' Rev. of *Pleasing Myself*, by Frank Kermode. *Times Literary Supplement* (10 August 2001): 21.

James, William. *The Varieties of Religious Experience.* New York: Penguin, 1982.

Jameson, Fredric. *The Political Unconscious.* Ithaca: Cornell University Press, 1981.

Jardine, Lisa. Interview. In Tredell, *Conversations with Critics*, 365–80.

Jardine, Lisa, and Paul Smith, eds. *Men in Feminism.* New York and London: Methuen, 1987.

Julius, Anthony. *T.S. Eliot, Anti-Semitism and Literary Form.* Cambridge: Cambridge University Press, 1996.

Kant, Immanuel. *The Critique of Judgement.* Trans. James Creed Meredith. Oxford: Oxford University Press, 1986.

Kaplan, Carey, and Ellen Cronan Rose. *The Canon and the Common Reader.* Knoxville: University of Tennessee Press, 1990.

Katz, Steven. *The Holocaust in Historical Context.* Oxford: Oxford University Press, 1994.

Kazin, Alfred. 'Habits of Home.' Rev. of *Warrenpoint*, by Denis Donoghue. *New Republic* (24 September 1990): 44–6.

Kennedy, Paul. *Preparing for the Twentieth-First Century.* New York: Random House, 1993.

Kenner, Hugh. *A Sinking Island: The Modern English Writers.* Baltimore: Johns Hopkins University Press, 1989.

'Kermode and Donoghue: Editors' Comments.' *Critical Inquiry* 1 (March 1975): 700–4.

Kermode, Frank. 'The Academy vs. the Humanities.' Rev. of *Literature Lost: Social Agendas and the Corruption of the Humanities,* by John M. Ellis. *Atlantic Monthly* (August 1997): 93–6.

– 'Advertisement for Himself.' Rev. of *The Gospel According to the Son,* by Norman Mailer. *New York Review of Books* (15 May 1997): 4–8.

– 'Alien Sages.' Rev. of *Under the Sign of Saturn,* by Susan Sontag. *New York Review of Books* (6 November 1980): 42–3.

– 'American Miltonists and English Reviewers.' Rev. of *Ikon: John Milton and the Modern Critics,* by Robert Adams; and *Milton and Forbidden Knowledge,* by Howard Schultz. *Essays in Criticism* 7, no. 2 (1957): 196–207.

– 'Another Mother.' Rev. of *Morgan: A Biography of E.M. Forster,* by Nicola Beauman. *London Review of Books* (13 May 1993): 3–5.

– 'Apocalypse Now and Then.' Rev. of *The Second Coming: Popular Millenarianism 1780–1850,* by J.F.C. Harrison. *London Review of Books* (25 October 1979): 10–11.

– 'Apocalyptic Opacity.' Rev. of *The End of the Century at the End of the World,* by C.K. Stead. *London Review of Books* (24 September 1992): 17.

– *An Appetite for Poetry.* Cambridge: Harvard University Press, 1989.

– 'Art among the Ruins.' Rev. of *Practicing New Historicism,* by Catherine Gallagher and Stephen Greenblatt; and *Shakespeare after Theory,* by David Scott Kastan. *New York Review of Books* (5 July 2001): 59–63.

– *The Art of Telling: Essays on Fiction.* Cambridge: Harvard University Press, 1983.

– 'Asyah and Saif.' Rev. of *In the Eye of the Sun,* by Ahdaf Soueif. *London Review of Books* (25 June 1992): 19–20.

– 'At Tate Britain.' *London Review of Books* (14 December 2000): 27.

– 'The Attack on Leavis.' Letter. *Essays in Criticism* 13, no. 3 (1963): 305.

– 'Attracting, Taking, Holding: Tony Tanner and Henry James.' *Critical Quarterly* 42, no. 2 (1999): 60–2.

– 'Beckett Country.' Rev. of *How It Is,* by Samuel Beckett. *New York Review of Books* (19 March 1964): 9–11.

– 'Beethoven at Home.' Rev. of *Beethoven,* by Maynard Solomon. *New York Review of Books* (6 April 1978): 6–10.

– 'Beyond Category.' Rev. of *Vice Versa,* by Marjorie Garber. *New York Times Book Review* (9 July 1995): 6–7.

– 'Big Fish.' Rev. of *Tell Them I'm on My Way*, by Arnold Goodman; and *Not an Englishman: Conversations with Lord Goodman*, by David Selbourne. *London Review of Books* (9 September 1993): 10–11.

– 'The Bliss of the Big City.' Rev. of *Walking in the Shade: Volume Two of My Autobiography, 1949–1962*, by Doris Lessing. *New York Times Book Review* (14 September 1997): 16+.

– 'Bonjour Sagesse.' Rev. of *The Last Life*, by Claire Messud. *London Review of Books* (30 September 1999): 32.

– 'Booker Books.' *London Review of Books* (22 November 1979): 12–13.

– 'Breeding.' Rev. of *The Diaries of Sylvia Townsend Warner*, ed. Claire Harman; and *Sylvia and David: The Townsend Warner / Garnett Letters*, ed. Richard Garnett. *London Review of Books* (21 July 1994): 15–16.

– 'Bringing It Home to Uncle Willie.' Rev. of *Joseph Conrad: A Biography*, by Roger Tennant; *Edward Garnett: A Life in Literature*, by George Jefferson, *The Edwardian Novelists*, by John Batchelor; and *The Use of Obscurity: The Fiction of Early Modernism*, by Allon White. *London Review of Books* (6–19 May 1982): 13–14.

– 'Britten When Young.' Rev. of *Letters from a Life: The Selected Letters and Diaries of Benjamin Britten*, Volumes 1 and 2, ed. Donald Mitchell and Philip Reed. *London Review of Books* (29 August 1991): 3–5.

– 'Bumper Book of Death.' Rev. of *The Hour of Our Death*, by Philippe Ariès. *London Review of Books* (1–14 October 1981): 7–8.

– 'But Could She Cook?' Rev. of *Elizabeth I: Collected Works*, ed. Leah S. Marcus, Janel Mueller, and Mary Beth Rose. *New York Review of Books* (12 April 2001): 68–70.

– 'Buyer's Market.' Rev. of *George Gissing: The Born Exile*, by Gillian Tindall; *Arnold Bennett: A Biography*, by Margaret Drabble; and *Arnold Bennett: The Evening Standard Years*, ed. Andrew Mylett. *New York Review of Books* (31 October 1974): 3–4.

– 'Cad.' Rev. of *Bertrand Russell: The Spirit of Solitude*, by Ray Monk. *London Review of Books* (4 April 1996): 7–8.

– 'Canons.' Rev. of *Holy Scripture: Canon, Authority, Criticism*, by James Barr; and *Structuralist Interpretations of Biblical Myth*, by Edmund Leach and D. Alan Aycock. *London Review of Books* (2–15 February 1984): 3–4.

– 'A Canterbury Tale.' Rev. of T.S. Eliot, *Murder in the Cathedral*, Swan Theatre, Stratford-upon-Avon. *Times Literary Supplement* (28 May 1993): 19.

– 'The Cars of the Elect Will Be Driverless.' Rev. of *Omens of the Millennium*, by Harold Bloom. *London Review of Books* (31 October 1996): 10.

– 'The Case for William Golding.' Rev. of *The Spire*, by William Golding. *New York Review of Books* (30 April 1964): 3–4.

– 'Cities of Words: Professor Tony Tanner.' *Guardian* (8 December 1998): 18.

- *The Classic: Literary Images of Permanence and Change.* Cambridge: Harvard University Press, 1983.
- *Cleanth Brooks and the Art of Reading.* London: Institute of United States Studies, University of London, 1999.
- 'Cockaigne.' Rev. of *Orwell: The Authorised Biography*, by Michael Shelden. *London Review of Books* (24 October 1991): 8–9.
- 'Cold Feet.' Rev. of *Essays on Renaissance Literature*, Volume 1, *Donne and the New Philosophy*, by William Empson; and *William Empson: The Critical Achievement*, ed. Christopher Norris and Nigel Mapp. *London Review of Books* (22 July 1993): 15–17.
- 'Colette.' Rev. of *The Blue Lantern*, by Collete. *New York Review of Books* (12 December 1963).
- 'Coming Up for Air.' Rev. of *Sweet William*, by Beryl Bainbridge; and *Heat and Dust*, by Ruth Prawer Jhabvala. *New York Review of Books* (15 July 1976): 42–4.
- 'Complicated Detours.' Rev. of *Darwin's Worms*, by Adam Phillips. *London Review of Books* (11 November 1999): 7.
- *Continuities.* New York: Random House, 1968.
- 'Crisis Critic.' Rev. of *The Archaeology of Knowledge and the Discourse on Language*, by Michel Foucault. *New York Review of Books* (17 May 1973): 37–9.
- 'Critical List.' Rev. of *Literature and the Sixth Sense*, by Philip Rahv; and *The Writing on the Wall*, by Mary McCarthy. *New York Review of Books* (13 August 1970): 31–3.
- 'A Critical Vocation: Tony Tanner.' *Stand* (June 2000): 11–16.
- 'Criticism without Machinery.' Rev. of *Literary Reflections*, by R.W. Lewis. *New York Times Book Review* (11 July 1993): 16.
- 'Cross-Examining Milton.' Rev. of *How Milton Works*, by Stanley Fish. *New York Times Book Review* (24 June 2001): 12.
- *D.H. Lawrence.* London: Fontana/Collins, 1973.
- 'Dangerous Faults.' Rev. of *Shear*, by Tim Parks. *London Review of Books* (4 November 1993): 24.
- 'Dangerous Liaisons.' Rev. of *Ford Madox Ford*, by Alan Judd. *London Review of Books* (28 June 1990): 7.
- 'Dark Fates.' Rev. of *The Blue Flower*, by Penelope Fitzgerald. *London Review of Books* (5 October 1995): 7.
- 'Deciphering the Big Book.' Rev. of *The Birth of the Messiah: A Commentary on the Infancy Narratives in Matthew and Luke*, by Raymond E. Brown; *A Palpable God: Thirty Stories Translated from the Bible with an Essay on the Origins and Life of Narrative*, by Reynolds Price; and *The Early Versions of the New Testament*, by Bruce M. Metzger. *New York Review of Books* (29 June 1978).
- 'The Decline and Fall of the Readable Literary Critic.' *Guardian* (10 October 1991).

- 'The Decline of the Man of Letters.' *Partisan Review* 52, no. 3 (1985): 195–209.
- 'Deep Frye.' Rev. of *A Natural Perspective: The Development of Shakespearian Comedy and Romance*, by Northrop Frye. *New York Review of Books* (22 April 1965): 10–12.
- 'Diary.' *London Review of Books* (16 September–6 October 1982): 21.
- 'Diary.' *London Review of Books* (7–20 October 1982): 21.
- 'Diary.' *London Review of Books* (1–20 April 1983): 21.
- 'Diary.' *London Review of Books* (7–20 July 1983): 25.
- 'Diary.' *London Review of Books* (21 July–3 August 1983): 21.
- 'Diary.' *London Review of Books*. (20 April 1989): 21.
- 'Differences.' Rev. of *The Jew's Body*, by Sander Gilman; *Shylock: Four Hundred Years in the Life of a Legend*, by John Gross; and *Faultlines: Cultural Materialism and the Politics of Dissident Reading*, by Alan Sinfield. *London Review of Books* (22 October 1992): 5–6.
- 'Dis-Grace.' Rev. of *In the Beauty of the Lilies*, by John Updike. *London Review of Books* (21 March 1996): 23.
- 'Disintegration.' Rev. of *The Varieties of Metaphysical Poetry*, by T.S. Eliot. *London Review of Books* (27 January 1994): 13–15.
- 'Down There on a Visit.' Rev. of *Decadence: The Strange Life of an Epithet*, by Richard Gilman. *New York Review of Books* (28 June 1979).
- 'Dryden: a "Poet's Poet."' *Listener* 57 (30 May 1957): 877–8.
- 'Easy, Easy.' Rev. of *The Liverpool Scene*, ed. Edward Lucie-Smith; and *The Incredible Liverpool Scene*. *New York Review of Books* (23 May 1968): 6–7.
- 'Edmund Wilson's Achievement.' *Encounter* 26, no. 5 (1966): 61–70.
- 'Educating the Planet.' *London Review of Books* (20 March 1980): 1–4.
- 'Elizabeth's Chamber.' Rev. of *The Infection of Thomas DeQuincey: A Psychopathology of Imperialism*, by John Barrell. *London Review of Books* (9 May 1991): 11–12.
- 'The Enduring Lear.' Rev. of *King Lear in Our Time*, by Maynard Mack; and *Conceptions of Shakespeare*, by Alfred Harbage. *New York Review of Books* (12 May 1966): 12–14.
- 'Enemy of the Enemies of Truth.' Rev. of *The Footnote: A Curious History*, by Anthony Grafton. *London Review of Books* (19 March 1998): 26–7.
- 'England's Troubles.' Rev. of *The Scent of Dried Roses*, by Tim Lott. *London Review of Books* (17 October 1996): 30.
- 'English Changing.' *London Review of Books* (7 February 1980): 1–3.
- 'The Essential Orwell.' Rev. of *George Orwell: A Life*, by Bernard Crick; *Class, Culture and Social Change: A New View of the 1930s*, ed. Frank Gloversmith; and *Culture and Crisis in Britain in the Thirties*, ed. Jon Clark, Margot Heinemann, David Margolies, and Carole Snee. *London Review of Books* (22 January–4 February 1981): 5–6.

– 'Even Paranoids Have Enemies.' Rev. of *F.R. Leavis: A Life in Criticism*, by Ian MacKillop. *London Review of Books* (24 August 1995): 7–8.

– 'The Extremist.' Rev. of *Selected Letters of Rebecca West*, ed. Bonnie Kime Scott. *New Republic* (20 March 2000): 28+.

– 'Feast of St. Thomas.' Rev. of *Eliot's New Life*, by Lyndall Gordon; *The Letters of T.S. Eliot*, ed. Valerie Eliot; *The Poetics of Impersonality*, by Maud Ellmann; *T.S. Eliot and the Philosophy of Criticism*, by Richard Shusterman; *'The Men of 1914': T.S. Eliot and Early Modernism*, by Erik Svarny; *Eliot, Joyce and Company*, by Stanley Sultan; *The Savage and the City in the Work of T.S. Eliot*, by Robert Crawford; and *T.S. Eliot: The Poems*, by Martin Scofield. *London Review of Books* (29 September 1988): 3–6.

– 'Fighting Freud.' Rev. of *Out of My System: Psychoanalysis, Ideology, and Critical Method*, by Frederick Crews. *New York Review of Books* (29 April 1976): 39–41.

– 'First Pitch.' Rev. of *The Selected Letters of Marianne Moore*, ed. Bonnie Costello, Celeste Goodridge, and Cristanne Miller. *London Review of Books* (16 April 1998): 15–16.

– 'Floating Hair v. Blue Pencil.' Rev. of *Revision and Romantic Authorship*, by Zachary Leader. *London Review of Books* (6 June 1996): 15–17.

– 'For a Few Dollars More.' Rev. of *Frozen Desire: An Inquiry into the Meaning of Money*, by James Buchan. *London Review of Books* (18 September 1997): 3–5.

– 'Foreword.' *The King and the Adultress: A Psychoanalytical and Literary Reinterpretation of Madame Bovary and King Lear*, by Speziale Bagliacca. Durham: Duke University Press, 1998.

– *Forms of Attention*. Chicago: University of Chicago Press, 1985.

– 'Frank Kermode on a Falling-Out of Literary Friends.' *London Review of Books* (6 December 1979): 3–4.

– 'Frank Kermode Writes about Granada Television's Version, Broadcast on 15 April, of Ford Madox Ford's *The Good Soldier*.' *London Review of Books* (21 May–3 June 1981): 15.

– 'Free Fall.' Rev. of *The Presence of the Word*, by Walter J. Ong, S.J. *New York Review of Books* (14 March 1968): 22–6.

– 'Freedom and Interpretation.' *Yale Review* 81, no. 1 (1993): 41–91.

– 'The Future of an Elite: What's Wrong with Oxford?' *Encounter* 27, no. 1 (July 1966): 23–7.

– 'The Future of the English Literary Canon.' In *English Studies in Transition: Papers from the ESSE Inaugural Conference*, ed. Robert Clark and Piero Boitani. London and New York: Routledge, 1993: 9–21.

– 'Gaiety.' Rev. of *Angus Wilson*, by Margaret Drabble. *London Review of Books* (8 June 1995): 3–5.

- 'The Geat of Geats.' Rev. of *Beowulf*, trans. Seamus Heaney; and *Beowulf*, trans. R.M. Liuzza. *New York Review of Books* (20 July 2000): 18–21.
- 'Georgians Eyes Are Smiling.' Rev. of *Bernard Shaw*, Vol. 1, by Michael Holroyd; *Bernard Shaw: Collected Letters*, Vol. 4, ed. Dan Laurence; *Shaw: The Annual of Bernard Shaw Studies*, Vol. 8, ed. Stanley Weintraub; *Shaw's Sense of History*, by J.L. Wisenthal; *Collected Letters of Joseph Conrad*, Vol. 3, ed. Frederick Karl and Laurence Davies; and *Joseph Conrad: 'Nostromo,'* by Ian Watt. *London Review of Books* (15 September 1988): 9–12.
- *The Genesis of Secrecy: On the Interpretation of Narrative.* Cambridge: Harvard University Press, 1979.
- 'Georgie Came, Harry Went.' Rev. of *A Very Close Conspiracy: Vanessa Bell and Virginia Woolf*, by Jane Dunn; and *A Passionate Apprentice: The Early Journals of Virginia Woolf, 1897–1909*, ed. Mitchell Leaska. *London Review of Books* (25 April 1991): 17–18.
- 'Getting Even.' Rev. of *Revenge Tragedy: Aeschylus to Armageddon*, by John Kerrigan. *New York Review of Books* (28 November 1996): 29–31.
- 'Getting It Right.' Rev. of *Interpretation: An Essay in the Philosophy of Literary Criticism*, by P.D. Juhl. *London Review of Books* (7–20 May 1981): 12–13.
- 'Gloom without Doom.' Rev. of *Letters of Leonard Woolf*, ed. Frederic Spotts. *London Review of Books* (19 April 1990): 11–12.
- 'Gossip.' Rev. of *The Untouchables*, by John Banville. *London Review of Books* (5 June 1997): 23.
- 'Grandeur and Filth.' Rev. of *The Victorian City: Images and Realities*, ed. H.J. Dyos and Michael Wolff; *The Victorian Working Class: Selections from the Morning Chronicle*, ed. P.E. Razzell and R.W. Wainwright; *The Real Foundations: Literature and Social Change*, by David Craig; *The Victorians by the Sea*, ed. Howard Grey and Graham Stuart; and *Engels, Manchester, and the Working Class*, by Steven Marcus. *New York Review of Books* (30 May 1974): 6–12.
- 'Grandiose Movements.' Rev. of *Ford Madox Ford: A Dual Life*, Vol. 2, by Max Saunders. *London Review of Books* (6 February 1997): 17–18.
- 'The Groves of 155th Street.' Rev. of *A Century of Arts and Letters*, ed. John Updike. *New York Times Book Review* (31 May 1998): 13.
- 'The Guilt Laureate.' Rev. of *The Double Tongue*, by William Golding. *London Review of Books* (6 July 1995): 14–15.
- 'Hail to the Chief.' Rev. of *Learning to Curse: Essays in Early Modern Culture*, by Stephen Greenblatt. *London Review of Books* (10 January 1991): 6.
- 'Harvard Cheer.' Rev. of *Harvard Advocate Centennial Anthology*, ed. Jonathan Culler. *Encounter* 26, no. 1 (1967): 60–4.
- 'Hawkesbiz.' Omnibus rev. of Shakespeare criticism, including Terence Hawkes, *Meaning by Shakespeare*. *London Review of Books* (11 February 1993): 9–10.

- 'The Heart of Standing Is You Cannot Fly.' Rev. of *The Complete Poems of William Empson*, ed. John Haffenden. *London Review of Books* (22 June 2000): 10–11.
- 'Heaven, They're in Heaven.' Rev. of *The Book of Heaven*, ed. Philip and Carol Zaleski. *New York Times Book Review* (23 April 2000): 27.
- 'Hemingway's Last Novel.' Rev. of *A Moveable Feast*, by Ernest Hemingway. *New York Review of Books* (11 June 1964): 4–6.
- 'The High Cost of New History.' Rev. of *Forms of Nationhood: The Elizabethan Writing of England*, by Richard Helgerson. *New York Review of Books* (25 June 1992): 43+.
- 'Hip Gnosis.' Rev. of *Genius: A Mosaic of One Hundred Exemplary Creative Minds*, by Harold Bloom. *Guardian* (12 October 2002): Review Section, 9.
- *History and Value*. Oxford: Clarendon Press, 1989.
- 'How Did We Decide What Christ Looked Like?' Rev. of 'Seeing Salvation,' National Gallery Exhibition; and *The Image of Christ*, ed. Gabriele Finaldi. *London Review of Books* (27 April 2000): 8–9.
- 'How Do You Spell Shakespeare?' Rev. of *William Shakespeare: The Complete Works: Original-Spelling Edition*, ed. Stanley Wells and Gary Taylor; and *William Shakespeare: The Complete Works*, ed. Stanley Wells and Gary Taylor. *London Review of Books* (21 May 1987): 3–5.
- 'Howl.' Rev. of *Sabbath's Theater*, by Philip Roth. *New York Review of Books* (16 November 1995): 20–3.
- 'The IBM Shakespeare.' Rev. of *A Complete and Systematic Concordance to the Works of William Shakespeare*, by Marvin Spevack. *New York Review of Books* (30 January 1969): 30–2.
- 'Improving the Plays.' Rev. of *Shakespeare at Work*, by John Jones. *London Review of Books* (7 March 1996): 6–7.
- 'The Incomparable Benjamin.' Rev. of *Illuminations*, by Walter Benjamin. *New York Review of Books* (18 December 1969): 30–3.
- 'In Reverse.' Rev. of *Time's Arrow*, by Martin Amis. *London Review of Books* (12 September 1991): 11.
- 'Intelligent Theory.' Omnibus rev. of books by Gerard Genette, Tzvetan Todorov, Harold Bloom, Peter Hohnendahl, and Ann Barfield. *London Review of Books* (7–20 October 1982): 8–9.
- Interview. With Jerry Brotton. *Amazon.co.uk: 'Words, Words, Words.'* http://www.amazon.co.uk/exec/obidos/tg/feature/-/45431/ ref=pd_d_ra_rab_1_1/qid=
- Interview. With Katie Donovan. http://www.ireland.com/dublin/ entertainment/books/features 2204.htm
- Interview. With Imre Salusinszky. *Criticism in Society*. New York and London: Methuen, 1987.

– Interview. With Nicholas Tredell. *Conversations with Critics.* Riverdale-on-Hudson, NY: Sheep Meadow Press, 1994: 16–38.
– 'Into the Wilderness.' Rev. of *Quarantine*, by Jim Crace. *New York Times Book Review* (12 April 1998): 8.
– 'Introduction.' *Writers at Work: The Paris Review Interviews.* 6th series. (New York: Viking Press, 1984).
– 'Isadora.' Rev. of *Isadora Duncan: Her Life, Her Art, Her Legacy*, by Walter Terry. *New York Review of Books* (5 March 1964): 7.
– 'I Shall Presently Be Extinguished.' Rev. of *The Sixties*, by Edmund Wilson. *New York Times Book Review* (8 August 1993): 11–12.
– 'Is Writing Bad for You?' Rev. of *Writer's Block*, by Zachary Leader. *London Review of Books* (21 February 1991): 8–9.
– 'J'Accuzi.' Rev. of *The Moronic Inferno and Other Visits to America*, by Martin Amis. *London Review of Books* (24 July 1986): 5.
– 'Joyce Center.' *New York Review of Books* (2 May 1974).
– 'A Keen Wind from the North.' Rev. of *The Book of Prefaces*, by Alasdair Gray. *Spectator* (20 May 2000): 48–50.
– 'Laboring Fabians.' *New York Review of Books* (17 March 1977): 35–7.
– 'The Lattimore Version.' Rev. of *The Four Gospels and the Revelation*, trans. Richard Lattimore. *New York Review of Books* (19 July 1979).
– 'Lawrence and the Apocalyptic Types.' *Critical Quarterly* 10, nos. 1 & 2 (1968): 14–38.
– 'Lear at Lincoln Center.' *New York Review of Books* (25 June 1964): 4–5.
– Letter [Reply to Morton Smith]. *New York Review of Books* (21 December 1978): 57–8.
– 'Life and Death of the Novel.' Rev. of *Henry Fielding: Mask and Fear*, by Andrew Wright; *The True Patriot*, by Henry Fielding; *Radical Dr. Smollett*, by Donald Bruce; and *Jane Austen: A Study of Her Artistic Development*, by A. Walton Litz. *New York Review of Books* (28 October 1965).
– 'A Likely Story.' Rev. of *Howard Hodgkins: Paintings*, by Michael Auping, John Elderfield, and Susan Sontag; and *Howard Hodgkins*, by Andrew Graham-Dixon. *London Review of Books* (25 January 1996): 11.
– *The Literary Guide to the Bible*, ed. with Robert Atler. Cambridge: Harvard University Press, 1987.
– 'Liveried.' Rev. of *John Gay: A Profession of Friendship. A Critical Biography*, by David Nokes. *London Review of Books* (11 May 1995): 7–8.
– '"Love and Do As You Please."' Rev. of *Man of Nazareth*, by Anthony Burgess; and *The Living End*, by Stanley Elkin. *New York Review of Books* (16 August 1979): 44–5.
– 'Made in Heaven.' Rev. of *Frieda Lawrence*, by Rosie Jackson; *The Married Man:*

A Life of D.H. Lawrence, by Brenda Maddox; *Kangaroo*, by D.H. Lawrence; *Twilight in Italy and Other Essays*, by D.H. Lawrence. *London Review of Books* (10 November 1994): 24–5.

– 'Making a Start.' Rev. of *Openings: Narrative Beginnings from the Epic to the Novel*, by A.D. Nuttall. *London Review of Books* (11 June 1992): 13.

– 'The Man in the Closet.' Rev. of *The Life of Drama*, by Eric Bentley. *New York Review of Books* (3 December 1964): 33–6.

– 'Marvell Transprosed.' *Encounter* 27, no. 5 (1966): 77–84.

– 'Maximum Assistance from Good Cooking, Good Clothes, Good Drink.' Rev. of W.H. Auden, *Lectures on Shakespeare*, ed. Arthur Kirsch. *London Review of Books* (22 February 2001): 10–11.

– 'Meaningless Legs.' Omnibus review of books on John Gielgud. *London Review of Books* (21 June 2001): 25–6.

– 'The Midrash Mishmash.' Rev. of *The Bible As It Was*, by James L. Kugel. *New York Review of Books* (23 April 1998): 45–8.

– 'Millions of Strange Shadows.' Rev. of *The Art of Shakespeare's Sonnets*, by Helen Vendler. *New Republic* (17 November 1997): 27–32.

– 'A Mode of Thinking Congenial to His Nature.' Rev. of *Shakespeare and His Comedies*, by J.R. Brown. *Essays in Criticism* 8, no. 3 (1958): 298–303.

– 'The Model of a Modern Modernist.' Omnibus review on Peter Handke and Richard Gilman. *New York Review of Books* (1 May 1975): 20–3.

– *Modern Essays*. London: Collins, 1971.

– 'A Modern Master.' Rev. of *Selected Stories*, by V.S. Pritchett. *New York Review of Books* (17 August 1978): 18–19.

– 'Modernism Again.' *Encounter* 26, no. 4 (1966): 65–74.

– 'Modernisms: Cyril Connolly and Others.' *Encounter* 26, no. 3 (1966): 53–8.

– 'Modern Masters.' Rev. of *Where I Fell to Earth: A Life in Four Places*, by Peter Conrad; and *May Week Was in June*, by Clive James. *London Review of Books* (24 May 1990): 12.

– 'Molly's Methuselah.' Rev. of *Bernard Shaw*, Vol. 3, by Michael Holroyd. *London Review of Books* (26 September 1991): 14–15.

– 'Motoring.' Rev. of *Deep Romantic Chasm: Diaries 1979–81; A Mingled Measure: Diaries, 1953–72; Ancient as the Hills: Diaries 1973–74*, by James Lee-Milne. *London Review of Books* (30 November 2000): 15–16.

– 'Mr. E.M. Forster As a Symbol.' *Listener* 59 (2 January 1958): 17–18.

– 'My Mad Captains: Frank Kermode's Final War Report.' *London Review of Books* (14 December 1995): 24–7.

– 'My Mad Captains: Frank Kermode Returns to the War.' *London Review of Books* (30 November 1995): 25–7.

- 'A New Era in Shakespeare Criticism?' Omnibus review of Shakespeare criticism. *New York Review of Books* (5 November 1970): 33–8.
- 'No Tricks.' Rev. of *Call If You Need Me: The Uncollected Fiction and Prose*, by Raymond Carver. *London Review of Books* (19 October 2000): 17–18.
- *Not Entitled: A Memoir.* New York: Farrar, Straus and Giroux, 1995.
- 'Not His Type.' Rev. of *About Modern Art: Critical Essays 1948–96*, by David Sylvester. *London Review of Books* (5 September 1996): 16.
- 'Novels about Adultery.' Rev. of *Love and Marriage*, by Laurence Lerner; and *Adultery in the Novel*, by Tony Tanner. *London Review of Books* (15 May 1980): 1–3.
- 'Novels: Recognition and Deception.' *Critical Inquiry* 1 (1974): 103–21.
- 'Off the Edge.' Rev. of *Musical Elaborations*, by Edward Said. *London Review of Books* (7 November 1991): 3–4.
- 'The Old Amalaki.' Rev. of *Ramakrishna and His Disciples*, by Christopher Isherwood. *New York Review of Books* (17 June 1965): 18–20.
- 'Old Modern.' Rev. of *On Modernism: The Prospects for Literature and Freedom*, by Louis Kampf; and *New American Review*, No. 1, ed. Theodore Solotaroff. *New York Review of Books* (26 October 1967): 27–30.
- 'The Old New Age.' Rev. of *The English Bible and the Seventeenth-Century Revolution*, by Christopher Hill; and *The Battle of the Frogs and Fairford's Flies: Miracles and the Pulp Press during the English Revolution*, by Jerome Friedman. *New York Review of Books* (24 March 1994): 49+.
- 'On a Chinese Mountain.' Rev. of *The Royal Beasts* and *Essays on Shakespeare*, by William Empson. *London Review of Books* (20 November 1996): 8–9.
- 'Opinion, Truth and Value.' *Essays in Criticism* 5 (1955): 181–7.
- 'Our Fault.' Rev. of *Our Age: Portrait of a Generation*, by Noel Annan. *London Review of Books* (11 October 1990): 3–5.
- 'Out of Sight, out of Mind.' Rev. of *A.J. Ayer: A Life*, by Ben Rogers. *London Review of Books* (15 July 1999): 9–10.
- 'Paint Run Amuch.' Rev. of *Jack Yeats*, by Bruce Arnold. *London Review of Books* (12 November 1998): 19–20.
- 'A Passage to Cambridge.' Letter. *New York Review of Books* (14 February 1985): 40.
- 'Pathetic Maundy Money.' *Encounter* 28, no. 3 (1967): 56–9.
- 'Paul de Man's Abyss.' Rev. of Paul de Man, *Wartime Journalism, 1939–1943*, ed. Werner Hamacher, Neil Hertz, and Thomas Keenan; Paul de Man, *Critical Writings*, ed. Lindsay Waters; Christopher Norris, *Paul de Man: Deconstruction and the Critique of Aesthetic Ideology*; *Reading Paul de Man*, ed. Lindsay Waters and Wlad Godzich. *London Review of Books* (16 March 1989): 3–7.
- 'Penguin Classics: Features.' http://www.penguinclassics.com/cgi-bin/ redirect. asp?url=features/body.html&index=new

– 'Persevering with the Metaphysicals.' Rev. of *Metaphysical to Augustan,* by Geoffrey Walton; and *The Poetry of Meditation,* by Louis L. Martz. *Essays in Criticism* 6 (1956): 205–14.

– 'Playing the Seraphine.' Rev. of *The Means of Escape,* by Penelope Fitzgerald. *London Review of Books* (25 January 2001): 15.

– 'The Pleasure of the Text.' Rev. of *Great Books: My Adventures with Homer, Rousseau, Woolf, and Other Indestructible Writers of the Western World,* by David Denby. *New York Review of Books* (19 September 1996): 31+.

– *Poetry, Narrative, History.* Cambridge, MA: Blackwell, 1990.

– 'Pooka.' Rev. of *Jack Maggs,* by Peter Carey. *London Review of Books* (16 October 1997): 8.

– 'Posterity.' Rev. of *God's Fifth Column: A Biography of the Age, 1890–1940* and *Futility,* by William Gerhardie. *London Review of Books* (2–16 April 1981): 3–5.

– 'The Power to Enchant.' Rev. of *Later Auden,* by Edward Mendelson; and *W.H. Auden: A Commentary,* by John Fuller. *New Republic* (26 April 1999): 108+.

– 'The Quest for the Magical Jesus.' Rev. of *Jesus the Magician,* by Morton Smith. *New York Review of Books* (26 October 1978): 9–10.

– 'Reading Shakespeare's Mind.' Rev. of *Hamlet and Revenge,* by Eleanor Posser; and *Fools of Time: Studies in Shakespearian Tragedy,* by Northrop Frye. *New York Review of Books* (12 October 1967): 14–17.

– 'Remembering the Movement, and Researching It.' Rev. of *The Movement: English Poetry and Fiction in the 1950s,* by Blake Morrison; and *The Oxford Book of Contemporary Verse, 1945–1980,* ed. D.J. Enright. *London Review of Books* (3 June–18 June 1980): 6–7.

– 'A Reply to Denis Donoghue.' *Critical Inquiry* 1 (March 1975): 699–700.

– 'Reply to Jonathan Arac.' *Salmagundi,* no. 55 (Winter 1982): 156–62.

– 'A Reply to Joseph Frank.' *Critical Inquiry* 4 (Spring 1978): 579–88.

– 'Return to the Totem.' Rev. of *William Shakespeare: A Textual Companion,* by Stanley Wells and Gary Taylor; *Disowning Knowledge in Six Plays of Shakespeare,* by Stanley Cavell; *A History of English Literature,* by Alastair Fowler. *London Review of Books* (21 April 1988): 8–9.

– Rev. of *Language and Silence,* by George Steiner. *Book Week* (26 March 1967): 3.

– *The Romantic Image.* London: Routledge and Kegan Paul, 1957.

– 'Sacred Space.' Rev. of *The New Oxford Book of Christian Verse,* ed. Donald Davie; *The Poems of William Cowper,* ed. John D. Baird and Charles Ryskamp; and *The Letters and Prose Writings of William Cowper,* ed. James King and Charles Ryskamp. *New York Review of Books* (21 October 1982): 39–41.

– 'Sacrifices.' Rev. of *The Gonne–Yeats Letters, 1893–1938,* ed. Anna MacBride White and A. Norman Jeffares. *London Review of Books* (14 May 1992): 11–12.

- 'St. Mark on Broadway.' Rev. of *St. Mark's Gospel.* Performed by Alec Mc-Cowen. *New York Review of Books* (9 November 1978).
- *The Sense of an Ending: Studies in the Theory of Fiction.* 1967. New York: Oxford University Press, 1981.
- 'Sensing Endings.' *Nineteenth-Century Fiction* 33 (1978): 144–58.
- *Shakespeare: The Final Plays.* London: Longmans, Green, 1963.
- 'Shakespeare for the Eighties.' Omnibus review of books on Shakespeare. *New York Review of Books* (28 April 1983): 30–3.
- 'Shakespeare in the Movies.' Rev. of *Antony and Cleopatra,* directed by Charlton Heston; *Macbeth,* directed by Roman Polanski; and *King Lear,* directed by Peter Brook. *New York Review of Books* (4 May 1972): 18–21.
- *Shakespeare's Language.* New York: Farrar, Straus and Giroux, 2000.
- *Shakespeare, Spenser, Donne.* London: Routledge and Kegan Paul, 1971.
- 'The Shakespearian Rag.' Rev. of *Shakespeare Our Contemporary,* by Jan Kott. *New York Review of Books* (24 September 1964): 9–10.
- 'Shrinking the Princess.' Rev. of *Diana,* by Sally Bedell Smith. *New York Times Book Review* (22 August 1999): 7.
- 'Simple Mysteries.' Rev. of *On Trust,* by Gabriel Josipovici. *Times Literary Supplement* (25 February 2000): 4–5.
- 'The Small Noise Upstairs.' Rev. of *The Body Artist,* by Don DeLillo. *London Review of Books* (8 March 2001): 29.
- 'Sound and Fury.' Rev. of *Witches and Jesuits: Shakespeare's 'Macbeth,'* by Gary Wills. *London Review of Books* (16 February 1995): 35–6.
- 'Southern Virtues.' Rev. of *A Turn in the South,* by V.S. Naipaul; *Allen Tate: A Recollection,* by Walter Sullivan; and *Self-Consciousness,* by John Updike. *London Review of Books* (4 May 1989): 11–12.
- 'The Spree.' Rev. of *The Feminization of American Culture* and *Terrible Honesty: Mongrel Manhattan in the Twenties,* by Ann Douglas. *London Review of Books* (22 February 1996): 10–11.
- 'Staggering.' Rev. of *Writer and Society,* by Roy Fuller. *London Review of Books* (2 November 1995): 12–13.
- 'The State of Criticism.' In *The Shelia Carmel Lectures, 1988–1993,* ed. Hana Wirth-Nescher. Tel Aviv: Tel Aviv University, 1995: 3–29.
- 'Stephen Spender: Grand Old Man of Letters.' *Guardian* (17 July 1995): 12.
- 'Stowaway Woodworm.' Rev. of *A History of the World in 10½ Chapters,* by Julian Barnes. *London Review of Books* (22 June 1989): 20.
- 'Strait Is the Gate.' Rev. of *Gorbals Boy at Oxford,* by Ralph Glasser. *London Review of Books* (2 June 1988): 22.
- 'Strange Contemporaries: Wallace Stevens and Hart Crane.' *Encounter* 28, no. 5 (1967): 65–70.

- 'Strange, Sublime, Uncanny, Anxious.' Rev. of *The Western Canon: The Books and Schools of the Ages*, by Harold Bloom. *London Review of Books* (22 December 1994): 8–9.
- 'Structuralism Domesticated.' Rev. of *Working with Structuralism*, by David Lodge. *London Review of Books* (20 August–2 September 1981): 17.
- 'A Successful Alchemist.' Rev. of *The Abyss*, by Marguerite Yourcenar. *New York Review of Books* (14 October 1976): 6–10.
- 'Talk about Doing.' Rev. of *Against Deconstruction*, by John Ellis; *The New Historicism*, by H. Aram Veeser; *Rethinking Historicism: Critical Essays in Romantic History*, by Majorie Levinson et al.; *Toward a Literature of Knowledge*, by Jerome McGann; *The Stoic in Love: Selected Essays on Literature and Ideas*, by A.D. Nutall. *London Review of Books* (26 October 1989): 21–3.
- '"Tell Me Lies about Viet Nam ...": Peter Brooks and "US."' *Encounter* 28, no. 1 (1967): 62–4.
- 'Tennyson's Nerves.' Rev. of *Tennyson: The Unquiet Heart*, by Robert Bernard Martin; and *Thro' the Vision of the Night: A Study of Source, Evolution and Structure in Tennyson's 'Idylls of the King,'* by J.M. Gray. *London Review of Books* (6 November–19 November 1980): 4–6.
- 'Theory and Truth.' Rev. of *Minor Prophecies: The Literary Essay in the Culture Wars*, by Geoffrey Hartman; *Spinoza and the Origins of Modern Critical Theory* and *What's Wrong with Postmodernism: Critical Theory and the Ends of Philosophy*, by Christopher Norris. *London Review of Books* (21 November 1991): 9–10.
- 'Third World.' *London Review of Books* (2 March 1989): 7.
- 'This Charming Man.' Rev. of *The Collected and Recollected Mare*, ed. Mark Amory. *London Review of Books* (24 February 1994): 27.
- 'A Thriller with Something on Its Mind.' Rev. of *Night Train*, by Martin Amis. *Atlantic Monthly* (February 1998): 100–4.
- 'Time of Your Life.' Rev. of *Man and Time*, by J.B. Priestley. *New York Review of Books* (28 January 1965): 15–16.
- 'Tohu Bohu.' Rev. of *Hebrews Myths: The Book of Genesis*, by Robert Graves and Raphael Patal. *Encounter* 23, no. 6 (1964): 69–70.
- 'Tragedy and Revolution.' Rev. of *Modern Tragedy*, by Raymond Williams, *Encounter* 27, no. 2 (1966): 83–5.
- 'A Translation That Has Both Perils and Rewards.' *New York Times Magazine* (22 October 1995): 67.
- 'The Trillings.' *Partisan Review* (Winter 1994): 160–7.
- 'A Turn of Events.' Rev. of *Reality and Dreams*, by Muriel Spark. *London Review of Books* (14 November 1996): 23–4.
- 'TV Dinner.' Rev. of *Understanding Media*, by Marshall McLuhan. *New York Review of Books* (20 August 1964): 15–16.

- 'The Uncommon Reader: Virginia Woolf's Brilliance and Industry as a Literary Journalist.' *Times Literary Supplement* (22 July 1994): 3–4.
- 'Under the Loincloth.' Rev. of *The Sexuality of Christ in Renaissance Art and Modern Oblivion*, by Leo Stenberg. *London Review of Books* (3 April 1997): 11–12.
- 'Under Threat.' *London Review of Books* (21 June–4 July 1984): 15.
- 'The Universe of Myth.' Rev. of *The Great Code: The Bible and Literature*, by Northrop Frye. *New Republic* (9 June 1982): 30–3.
- *The Uses of Error*. Cambridge: Harvard University Press, 1991.
- 'Vérités Bergères.' Rev. of *Lilac and Flag*, by John Berger. *London Review of Books* (7 March 1991): 18.
- 'Victorian Vocations.' Rev. of *Frederic Harrison: The Vocations of a Positivist*, by Martha Vogeler; and *Leslie Stephen: The Godless Victorian*, by Noel Annan. *London Review of Books* (6–19 December 1984): 15–17.
- 'The Viennese Muses.' Rev. of *The Letters of Mozart and Family*, ed. Emily Anderson. *New York Review of Books* (15 December 1966): 16–20.
- 'Waiting for the End.' In *Apocalypse Theory and the Ends of the World*, ed. Malcolm Bull, 250–63. Oxford: Blackwell, 1995.
- *Wallace Stevens*. 1960; London: Faber and Faber, 1989.
- 'Wannabee.' Rev. of *Sacred Country*, by Rose Tremain. *London Review of Books* (8 October 1992): 14.
- 'What He Did.' Rev. of *W.B. Yeats: A Life*, Vol. I, by R.F. Foster, *London Review of Books* (20 March 1997): 3–4.
- 'What Is Art?' Rev. of *Meditations on a Hobby Horse and Other Essays*, by E.H. Gombrich. *New York Review of Books* (20 February 1964): 1–2.
- 'What Nathalie Knew.' Rev. of *Childhood*, by Nathalie Sarraute. *New York Review of Books* (25 October 1984): 49+.
- 'Who Can Blame Him?' Rev. of *Critical Terms for Literary Study*, by Frank Lentricchia and Thomas McLaughlin; and *The Ideology of the Aesthetic*, by Terry Eagleton. *London Review of Books* (5 April 1990): 14–15.
- 'The Wild Goose Chase.' Rev. of *The Search for the Perfect Language*, by Umberto Eco. *New York Review of Books* (23 May 1996): 32–5.
- 'William Empson: A Most Noteworthy Poet.' *Guardian* (15 June 2000).
- 'Wilson and McCarthy: Still Entangled.' *New York Times Book Review* (23 November 1997): 51.
- 'With the Aid of a Lorgnette.' Rev. of *The Lure of the Sea* and *The Foul and the Fragrant: Odour and the French Social Imagination*, by Alain Corbin. *London Review of Books* (28 April 1994): 14–15.
- 'The Wonder of Mozart.' Rev. of *Mozart: A Life*, by Maynard Solomon; *Mozart and Posterity*, by Gernot Gruber; *Mozart: Portrait of a Genius*, by Norbert Elias; *On Mozart*, ed. James M. Morris; *Hayden, Mozart and the Viennese School, 1740–*

1780, by Daniel Heartz; *Wolfgant Amadé Mozart*, by George Knepler. *New York Review of Books* (19 October 1995): 32+.

– 'Working up Work.' Rev. of *Work and Play: Ideas and Experience of Work and Leisure*, by Alasdair Clayre. *New York Review of Books* (27 November 1975): 35–6.

– 'The World Turned Upside Down.' Rev. of *The Dictionary of Global Culture*, by Kwame Anthony Appiah and Henry Louis Gates, Jr. *New York Review of Books* (6 February 1997): 30–2.

– 'Writing about Shakespeare.' *London Review of Books* (9 December 1999): 3–8.

– 'Yes, Santa, There Is a Virginia.' Omnibus review of books on Virginia Woolf. *New York Review of Books* (21 December 1978): 31–2.

– 'Yesterday.' Rev. of *The Pleasure of Peace: Art and Imagination in Post-War Britain*, by Bryan Appleyard. *London Review of Books* (27 July 1989): 14.

– 'Yoked together.' Rev. of *History: The Home Movie*, by Craig Raine. *London Review of Books* (22 September 1994): 3.

– 'Yonder Shakespeare, Who Is He?' Rev. of *William Shakespeare*, by A.I. Rowse; *Shakespeare*, by Peter Quennell; and *The Sonnets of Shakespeare*, by J. Dover Wilson. *New York Review of Books* (9 January 1964): 1–3.

– 'Youth.' Rev. of *The Generation of 1914*, by Robert Wohl. *London Review of Books* (19 June–2 July 1980): 12–13.

– Stephen Fender, and Kenneth Palmer. *English Renaissance Literature: Introductory Lectures.* London: Gray-Mills Publishing, 1974.

– ed. *Collected Poetry and Prose of Wallace Stevens.* New York: Library of America, 1997.

– ed. *Discussions of John Donne.* Boston: D.C. Heath and Company, 1962.

– ed. *The Figure in the Carpet and Other Stories*, by Henry James. London: Penguin, 1986.

– ed. *Four Centuries of Shakespearian Criticism.* New York: Avon, 1965.

– ed. *He Knew He Was Right*, by Anthony Trollope. New York: Viking Penguin, 1996.

– ed. *The Living Milton: Essays by Various Hands.* London: Routledge and Kegan Paul, 1960.

– ed. *Selected Prose of T.S. Eliot*, by T.S. Eliot. New York: Harcourt Brace Jovanovich, 1975.

– ed. *The Tempest*, by William Shakespeare, 1954; London: Routledge, 1988.

– ed. *The Waste Land and Other Poems*, by T.S. Eliot. London: Penguin, 1997.

– ed. *The Way We Live Now*, by Anthony Trollope. New York: Viking Penguin, 1995.

Kerrigan, William. 'Shakespeare and Kermode.' *Raritan* 20, no. 3 (2001): 141–6.

Kimball, Roger. 'Is the Future Just a Tense?' Rev. of *Grammars of Creation*, by George Steiner. *New York Times Book Review* (2 September 2001): 12.

Kincaid, James R. Letter. *New York Times Book Review* (30 July 1995): 23.

Kirsch, Adam. 'So Elegant, So Intelligent.' Rev. of *Words Alone*, by Denis Donoghue. *New York Times Book Review* (26 November 2000): 17.

Knights, L.C. Rev. of *Shakespeare, Spenser, Donne: Renaissance Essays*, by Frank Kermode. *New York Review of Books* (5 October 1972): 3+.

Knox, Bernard. 'The Life of a Legend.' Rev. of *Antigones*, by George Steiner.
New Republic (19 March 1984): 32–5.

Kripke, Saul A. *Wittgenstein: On Rules and Private Language*. Cambridge: Harvard
University Press, 1982.

Krupnick, Mark. 'Steiner's Literary Journalism: "The Heart of the Maze."' In
Scott and Sharp, eds., *Reading George Steiner,* 43–57.

Kugel, James L. 'Two Introductions to Midrash.' In Hartman and Budick, eds.,
Midrash and Literature, 77–103.

Kundera, Milan. *Testaments Betrayed: An Essay in Nine Parts*. Trans. Linda Asher.
New York: HarperCollins, 1995.

Lauter, Paul. *Canons and Contexts*. Oxford: Oxford University Press, 1991.

Lee, Hermione. 'Will's Power.' Rev. of *Shakespeare's Language*, by Frank Kermode. *Observer* (23 April 2000).

Leithauser, Brad. 'Words, Words, Words.' Rev. of *Shakespeare's Language*, by Frank
Kermode. *New York Times Book Review* (25 June 2000): 8.

Lentricchia, Frank. *After the New Criticism*. Chicago: University of Chicago Press,
1980.

Levenson, Michael H. 'Let Us Advert, You and I.' Rev. of *England, Their England*,
by Denis Donoghue. *New York Times Book Review* (25 December 1988): 13.

Levin, Richard. 'The Current Polarization of Literary Studies.' In Eddins, ed.,
The Emperor Redressed, 62–80.

Levinas, Emmanuel. *The Levinas Reader,* ed. Seán Hand. Cambridge, MA: Basil
Blackwell, 1992.

Levine, George, ed. *Aesthetics and Ideology*. New Brunswick, NJ: Rutgers University Press, 1994.

Lodge, David. 'Confessions of a Literary Man.' Rev. of *Not Entitled*, by Frank
Kermode. *New York Review of Books* (9 May 1996): 32–4.

Logan, Stephen. 'The Don in Grub Street.' *Spectator* (23 February 1991): 28–9.

Lowell, Robert. 'Yeats's Vision' [Letter responding to Denis Donoghue]. *New
York Review of Books* (14 July 1977): 4.

MacCabe, Colin. 'Wild and Whirling Words.' Rev. of *Shakespeare's Language*, by
Frank Kermode. *The Independent* (5 May 2000).

MacIntyre, Alasdair. *After Virtue*. Notre Dame: University of Notre Dame Press,
1984.

MacKillop, Ian. *F.R. Leavis: A Life in Criticism*. New York: St Martin's Press, 1995.

McCrea, Brian. *Addison and Steele Are Dead: The English Department, Its Canon, and the Professionalization of Literary Criticism.* Newark: University of Delaware Press, 1990.

McLillen, Liz. '"Hip-Hop Intellectual": Cultural-Studies Scholar Michael Eric Dyson Is a Lightning Rod for Controversy.' *Chronicle of Higher Education* (26 January 1996): A6+.

Middlebrook, Diane. Letter. *New York Times Book Review* (30 July 1995): 23.

Miller, J. Hillis. *The Ethics of Reading.* New York: Columbia University Press, 1987.

– *Hawthorne and History: Defacing It.* Cambridge, MA: Basil Blackwell, 1990.

– *Topographies.* Stanford: Stanford University Press, 1995.

– *Versions of Pygmalion.* Cambridge: Harvard University Press, 1990.

Miller, Karl. 'London Review of Books: Separate Publication.' *London Review of Books* (15 May 1980): 3.

– 'The London Review of Books.' *London Review of Books* (25 October 1979): 2.

Miller, Nancy K. *Getting Personal: Feminist Occasions and Other Autobiographical Acts.* New York and London: Routledge, 1991.

– 'Man on Feminism: A Criticism of His Own.' In *Men in Feminism*, ed. Alice Jardine and Paul Smith, 137–45. New York and London: Methuen, 1987.

Mitchell, W.J.T. 'The Good, the Bad, and the Ugly: Three Theories of Value.' *Raritan* 2 (Fall 1986): 63–76.

– 'Postcolonial Culture, Postimperial Criticism.' In *The Post-Colonial Studies Reader*, ed. Bill Ashcroft, Gareth Griffiths, and Helen Tiffin. London and New York: Routledge, 1995: 475–9.

Moss, Stephen. 'Too, too Solid Flesh.' Interview with Frank Kermode. *Guardian* (20 April 2000).

Murdoch, Iris. *Metaphysics As a Guide to Morals.* New York: Penguin, 1993.

Murray, Oswyn. 'The Archetype of Conflict.' Rev. of *Antigones*, by George Steiner. *Times Literary Supplement* (24 August 1984): 947–8.

Nagel, Thomas. *Equality and Partiality.* New York: Oxford University Press, 1991.

Nelson, Cary, ed. *Anthology of Modern American Poetry.* New York: Oxford University Press, 1999.

Newton-De Molina, David. 'George Steiner's *Language of Silence.*' *Critical Quarterly* 11, no. 4 (1969): 365–74.

Norris, Christopher. 'Introduction: Empson as a Literary Theorist.' In *William Empson: The Critical Achievement*, ed. Christopher Norris and Nigel Mapp. Cambridge: Cambridge University Press, 1993.

– *Spinoza and the Origins of Modern Critical Theory.* Oxford, UK, and Cambridge, MA: Basil Blackwell, 1991.

Ozick, Cythia. 'George Steiner's Either/Or: A Response.' *Salmagundi*, nos. 50–1 (Fall/Winter 1981): 90–5.

Padel, Ruth. 'George Steiner and the Greekness of Tragedy.' In Scott and Sharp, eds., *Reading George Steiner*, 99–133.

Parini, Jay. 'The Question of George Steiner.' *Hudson Review* (Autumn 1985): 496–502.

Park, Clara Clairborne. 'Left-Handed Compliments: The Practicality of Frank Kermode.' *Hudson Review* (Winter 1992): 659–66.

Parrinder, Patrick. *Authors and Authority: English and American Criticism, 1750–1990*. New York: Columbia University Press, 1991.

– 'Civil Service.' Rev. of *The Uses of Error*, by Frank Kermode. *New Statesman and Society* (15 February 1991): 45.

– '"Secular Surrogates": Frank Kermode and the Idea of the Critic.' In Tudeau-Clayton and Warner, eds., *Addressing Frank Kermode*, 58–73.

Pascal, Blaise. *Pensées*. Trans. Alban J. Krailsheimer. New York: Penguin, 1980.

Patcher, Henry. 'In Response to George Steiner.' *Salmagundi*, nos. 50–1 (Fall/Winter 1981): 96–101.

Phillips, Adam. 'Bellow and *Ravelstein*.' *Raritan* 20, no. 2 (2000): 1–11.

– 'In the Beginning ...' Rev. of *Grammars of Creation*, by George Steiner. *Observer* (11 March 2001).

– 'Provocation.' Rev. of *Walter Pater*, by Denis Donoghue. *London Review of Books* (24 August 1995): 9–10.

Poirier, Richard. Rev. of *Puzzles and Epiphanies*, by Frank Kermode. *New York Review of Books* (February 1963): 40.

Porter, Roy. 'Original Bliss.' Rev. of *Grammars of Creation*, by George Steiner. *Guardian* (17 March 2001).

Pound, Ezra. *Selected Prose, 1909–1965*, ed. William Cookson. London: Faber and Faber, 1973.

Raine, Craig. 'Conrad and Prejudice.' *London Review of Books* (22 June 1989): 16–18.

Richards, I.A. *Principles of Literary Criticism*. New York: Harcourt, Brace, Jovanovich, 1975.

Ricks, Christopher. 'Playboy of the Western World.' Rev. of *In Bluebeard's Castle*, by George Steiner. *New York Review of Books* (18 November 1971): 27–9.

– *T.S. Eliot and Prejudice*. Berkeley and Los Angeles: University of California Press, 1988.

Ricoeur, Paul. *Figuring the Sacred: Religion, Narrative, and Imagination*. Trans. David Pellauer. Minneapolis: Fortress Press, 1995.

Robbins, Bruce. *Secular Vocations: Intellectuals, Professionalism, Culture*. London and New York: Verso, 1993.

Roitman, Betty. 'Sacred Language and Open Text.' In Hartman and Budick, eds., *Midrash and Literature*, 159–75.

Ross, Andrew. *No Respect: Intellectuals and Popular Culture*. New York and London: Routledge, 1989.

Rothstein, Edward. 'A Jewish Canon, Yes, But Not Set in Stone.' *New York Times* (24 February 2001).

– 'Musicologists Roll Over Beethoven.' *New York Times* (26 November 1995): sec. 4, 1+.

Said, Edward W. *Culture and Imperialism*. New York: Alfred A. Knopf, 1993.

– 'Himself Observed.' Rev. of *George Steiner: A Reader*, by George Steiner. *Nation* (2 March 1985): 244–8.

– *Representations of the Intellectual: The 1993 Reith Lectures*. New York: Pantheon, 1994.

– *The World, the Text, and the Critic*. Cambridge: Harvard University Press, 1983.

Salusinszky, Imre. *Criticism in Society*. New York and London: Methuen, 1987.

Schiller, Friedrich. *On the Aesthetic Education of Man: In a Series of Letters*. Trans. Reginald Snell. New Haven: Yale University Press, 1954.

Scholem, Gershom. *The Messianic Idea in Judaism, and Other Essays on Jewish Spirituality*. New York: Schocken Books, 1974.

– *On Jews and Judaism in Crisis: Selected Essays*, ed. Werner J. Dannhauser. New York: Schocken Books, 1976.

Scott, Nathan A., and Ronald A. Sharp, eds. *Reading George Steiner*. Baltimore: Johns Hopkins University Press, 1994.

Scruton, Roger. 'Making Up for the Broken Word.' Rev. of *Real Presences*, by George Steiner. *Times Literary Supplement* (19–25 May 1989): 533–4.

Sexton, David. 'Kermode As Compère.' Rev. of *The Uses of Error*, by Frank Kermode. *Times Literary Supplement* (8 February 1991): 19.

Sharp, Ronald A. 'Steiner's Fiction and the Hermeneutics of Transcendence.' In Scott and Sharp, eds., *Reading George Steiner*, 205–29.

Shattuck, Roger. *Candor and Perversion*. New York: W.W. Norton, 1999.

– Rev. of *Continuities*, by Frank Kermode. *New York Review of Books* (12 March 1970): 3+.

Showalter, Elaine. 'Critical Cross-Dressing; Male Feminists and the Woman of the Year.' In *Men in Feminism*, ed. Alice Jardine and Paul Smith, 116–32. New York and London: Methuen, 1987.

Smith, Barbara Herrnstein. *Contingencies of Value*. Cambridge: Harvard University Press, 1988.

Smith, Peter D. 'The Wingbeat of the Unknown.' Rev. of *Grammars of Creation*, by George Steiner. *Times Literary Supplement* (6 April 2001): 13.

Southam, Brian. 'The Silence of the Bertrams: Slavery and the Chronology of *Mansfield Park.*' *Times Literary Supplement* (17 February 1995): 13–14.

Stein, Gertrude. *Lectures in America.* 1935. New York: Random House–Vintage, 1962.

Steiner, George. 'Acids of Tiredness.' *Encounter* 69, no. 5 (December 1987): 4.

– 'Affinities.' Rev. of *Spinoza and Other Heretics*, Vol. 1, by Yirmiyahu Yovel. *London Review of Books* (19 April 1990): 13–14.

– *After Babel: Aspects of Language and Translation.* 1975. 2nd ed. Oxford: Oxford University Press, 1992.

– 'After the Panzers, the Plunderers.' Rev. of *The Faustian Bargain: The Art World in Nazi Germany*, by Jonathan Petropoulos. *Observer* (16 April 2000).

– 'And the Reds Go Marching In ...' Rev. of *November 1916*, by Alexander Solzhenitsyn. *Observer* (13 June 1999).

– 'Anglican Inadequacies.' Rev. of *The Church in Crisis*, by Charles Moore, A.N. Wilson, and Gavin Stamp. *Times Literary Supplement* (7 November 1986): 1238.

– *Antigones: How the Antigone Legend Has Endured in Western Literature, Art, and Thought.* 1984. Oxford: Oxford University Press, 1986.

– 'The Archives of Eden.' *Salmagundi*, nos. 50–1 (Fall/Winter 1981): 57–89.

– 'The Art of Criticism, II.' Interview. With Ronald A. Sharp. *Paris Review*, no. 137 (Winter 1995): 42–102.

– 'Black Danube.' *New Yorker* (21 July 1986): 90–3.

– 'Books of Knowledge.' Rev. of *Routledge Encyclopedia of Philosophy*, trans. Edward Craig. *New York Times Book Review* (5 July 1998): 12–13.

– 'But Is That Enough? Hans-Georg Gadamer and the "Summons to Astonishment."' *Times Literary Supplement* (21 January 2001): 11–12.

– 'Conrad and Eliot and Prejudice.' Letter. *London Review of Books* (27 July 1989): 4.

– 'A Conversation with Claude Lévi-Strauss.' *Encounter* 26, no. 4 (1966): 32–8.

– '"Critic"/"Reader."' *New Literary History* 10, no. 3 (Spring 1979): 423–52.

– 'A Cross to Bear.' Rev. of *Pilate: The Biography of an Invented Man*, by Ann Wroe. *Observer* (4 April 1999).

– *The Death of Tragedy.* Oxford: Oxford University Press, 1980.

– 'Do-It-Yourself.' Rev. of *The Modern Epic: The World System from Goethe to Garcia Márquez*, by Franco Moretti. *Times Literary Supplement* (23 May 1996): 14.

– 'A Don Juan of libraries.' Rev. of *Into the Looking-Glass*, by Alberto Manguel. *Observer* (28 February 1999).

– 'Don't Just Sit There – Mean Something.' Rev. of *Gainsborough's Vision*, by Amal Asfour and Paul Williamson. *Observer* (9 January 2000).

– 'Echo, Marble and the Sounds of Water.' Rev. of *Storia Di Venezia*, by Giovanni Distefano. *Times Literary Supplement* (9 May 1997): 9–10.

- 'The End of Bookishness?' *Times Literary Supplement* (8–14 July 1988): 754.
- *Errata: An Examined Life*. New Haven: Yale University Press, 1998.
- 'An Examined Life.' Rev. of *Unseasonable Truths*, by Harry S. Ashmore. *New Yorker* (23 October 1989): 142–6.
- *Extra-territorial: Papers on Literature and the Language Revolution*. New York: Atheneum, 1971.
- 'F.R. Leavis.' *Encounter* 18, no. 5 (1962): 37–45; reprinted in *Language and Silence*: 221–38.
- *Fields of Force: Fischer and Spassky at Reykjavik*. New York: Viking, 1974.
- 'Food of Love.' Rev. of *The Romantic Generation*, by Charles Rosen. *New Yorker* (24 July 1995): 85–8.
- 'Foursome: The Art of Fernando Pessoa.' Rev. of *A Centenary Pessoa*, ed. Eugénio Lisboa and L.C. Taylor. *New Yorker* (8 January 1996): 77–80.
- 'Franco's Game.' Rev. of *Franco: A Biography*, by Paul Preston. *New Yorker* (17 October 1994): 115–20.
- 'A Friend of a Friend.' Rev. of *The Correspondence of Walter Benjamin and Gershom Scholem. New Yorker* (22 January 1990): 133–6.
- 'From Caxton to *Omeros*: The Continuing Appeal of Homer to Anglo-Saxon Ideals and Experience.' *Times Literary Supplement* (27 August 1993): 13–15.
- 'The Genius of Small Things.' Rev. of *Vermeer and the Delft School*, by Axel Ruger; and *Vermeer and Painting in Delft*, by Walter Liedtke. *Observer* (5 August 2001).
- *George Steiner: A Reader*. New York: Oxford University Press, 1984.
- 'George Steiner Thinks!' Interview. *Maclean's* (20 November 1978): 13, 15.
- 'Go Forth and Multiply.' Rev. of *Uncle Petros and Goldbach's Conjecture*, by Apostolos Doxiadis. *Observer* (5 March 2000).
- 'The Good Books.' Rev. of *The Literary Guide to the Bible*, ed. Robert Alter and Frank Kermode. *New Yorker* (11 January 1988): 94–8.
- *Grammars of Creation*. New Haven: Yale University Press, 2001.
- 'Graven Images.' Rev. of *Aby Warburg*, by E.H. Gombrich. *New Yorker* (2 February 1987): 95–8.
- 'Greek Is the Word.' Rev. of *The Oresteia* ... trans. Ted Hughes. *Observer* (24 October 1999).
- 'The Heart of the Matter.' Rev. of *Chardin*, by Philip Conisbee. *New Yorker* (17 November 1986): 144–50.
- *In Bluebeard's Castle: Some Notes towards the Redefinition of Culture*. New Haven: Yale University Press, 1971.
- 'Inscrutable and Tragic: Leo Strauss's Vision of the Jewish Destiny.' Rev. of *Jewish Philosophy and the Crisis of Modernity*, by Leo Strauss. *Times Literary Supplement* (14 November 1997): 4–5.

– Interview. In Tredell, *Conversations with Critics*, 75–93.
– 'A Jew's Grief.' *Harper's Magazine* (October 1988): 18–20.
– 'Knights of Old.' Rev. of *William Marshal: The Flower of Chivalry*, by Georges Duby. *New Yorker* (26 May 1986): 103–6.
– 'A Lacerated Destiny.' Rev. of *Paul Celan*, by John Felstiner; and Paul Celan and Franz Wurm, *Briefwechsel*, ed. Barbara Wiedemann. *Times Literary Supplement* (2 June 1995): 3–4.
– *Language and Silence: Essays on Language, Literature and the Inhuman.* New York: Atheneum, 1972.
– 'Language under Surveillance: The Writer and the State.' *New York Times Book Review* (12 January 1986): 12, 36.
– 'The Last Philosopher?' Rev. of *Le Siècle de Sartre*, by Bernard-Henri Lévy, *Trois aventures extraordinaires de Jean-Paul Sartre*, by Olivier Wickers; *Le Cause de Sartre*, by Philippe Petit. *Times Literary Supplement* (19 May 2000): 3–4.
– 'Learning to Speak? It's Child's Play.' Rev. of *New Horizons in the Study of Language and Mind*, by Noam Chomsky. *Observer* (2 April 2000).
– 'Levinas.' *Cross Currents* (Summer 1991): 243–8.
– 'Literary Theory in the University: A Survey.' *New Literary History*, no. 2 (Winter 1983): 444–5.
– 'Little-Read Schoolhouse.' Rev. of *Cultural Literacy*, by E.D. Hirsch. *New Yorker* (1 June 1987): 106–10.
– 'Long Day's Journey into Light.' Rev. of *Goethe: The Poet and the Age*, by Nicholas Boyle. *New Yorker* (23 September 1991): 109–15.
– 'The Long Life of Metaphor: An Approach to the Shoah.' *Encounter* 68 (February 1987): 55–61.
– 'Making a Homeland for the Mind.' Rev. of *Eine Autobiographie im Dialog*, by Georg Lukács. *Times Literary Supplement* (22 January 1982): 67–8.
– *Martin Heidegger.* 1978; Chicago: University of Chicago Press, 1991.
– 'More Than Just an Old Romantic.' Rev. of *Goethe: The Poet and the Age*, Vol. 2, by Nicholas Boyle. *Observer* (30 January 2000).
– 'Nabokov Was Miserable and Poor. Then His Wife Made Him Publish Lolita ...' Rev. of *Vera*, by Stacy Schiff. *Observer* (1 August 1999).
– 'The New *Nouvelle Héloïse*?' Rev. of *Hannah Arendt / Martin Heidegger*, by Elzbieta Ettinger. *Times Literary Supplement* (13 October 1995): 3–4.
– 'Nietzsche When Young.' Rev. of Friedrich Nietzsche, *Frühe Schriften*, ed. Hans Joachim Mette, Karl Schlechta, and Carl Koch. *Times Literary Supplement* (2 December 1994): 25.
– 'Night Words: High Pornography and Human Privacy.' *Encounter* 25, no. 4 (1965): 14–19.
– *No Passion Spent: Essays, 1978–1995.* New Haven: Yale University Press, 1996.

– *On Difficulty and Other Essays.* 1978. New York: Oxford University Press, 1980.
– 'On the Edge of Hunger.' Rev. of *Hitler's Wien*, by Brigitte Hamann. *Times Literary Supplement* (31 January 1997): 3–4.
– 'Our Homeland, the Text.' *Salmagundi*, no. 66 (Winter/Spring 1985): 4–25.
– 'Out of Central Europe: Hans Mayer, the Last German Marxist?' *Encounter* 22, no. 4 (April 1964): 112–17.
– 'The Philosopher's Philosopher.' Rev. of *Hegel: A Biography*, by Terry Pinkard. *Observer* (16 July 2000).
– *The Portage to San Cristóbal of A.H.* New York: Simon and Schuster, 1981.
– 'Postscript to a Tragedy.' Rev. of *Scroll of Agony: The Warsaw Diary of Chaim A. Kaplan*; and *Treblinka*, by Jean-François Steiner. *Encounter* 28, no. 2 (1967): 33–9.
– 'Power Play.' Rev. of Michel Foucault, *The Use of Pleasure*. *New Yorker* (17 March 1986): 105–9.
– *Proofs and Three Parables.* London: Granta Books, 1992.
– 'Pushkin's Date with Death.' Rev. of *Pushkin's Button*, by Serena Vitale. *Observer* (14 March 1999).
– *Real Presences: Is There Anything in What We Say?* London: Faber and Faber, 1989.
– 'Rear Guard.' Rev. of *Politics, Logic, and Love: The Life of Jean van Heijenoort*, by Anita Burdman Federman. *New Yorker* (20 December 1990): 139–42.
– 'Red Octobers.' Rev. of *Russian Studies*, by Leonard Shapiro. *New Yorker* (4 May 1987): 152–6.
– 'The Remembrancer.' Omnibus rev. of books on Walter Benjamin by Max Pensky, Margaret Cohen and Jeffrey Mehlman. *Times Literary Supplement* (8 October 1993): 37–8.
– 'Requiem for a Genius.' Rev. of *Berlioz: Servitude and Greatness*, by David Cairns. *Observer* (14 November 1999).
– 'The Retreat from the Word [Part I].' *Listener* 64 (14 July 1960): 56+.
– 'The Retreat from the Word [Part II].' *Listener* 64 (21 July 1960): 100–1.
– 'Sainte Simone: The Jewish Bases of Simone Weil's *Via Negativa* to the Philosophic Peaks.' Rev. of *Simone Weil's Philosophy of Culture*, ed. Richard H. Bell. *Times Literary Supplement* (4 June 1993): 3–4.
– 'The Scandal of Revelation.' *Salmagundi*, no. 98–9 (Spring/Summer 1993): 42–70.
– 'Seen the New Shakespeare Yet?' Rev. of William Shakespeare et al., *King Edward III*, ed. Giorgio Melchiori. *Observer* (10 May 1998).
– 'She's Scared to Blink in Case Her Man Turns into Somebody Else.' Rev. of *Identity*, by Milan Kundera. *Observer* (19 April 1998).
– 'Something Lurking at the Bottom of the Gene Pool ...' Rev. of *Brave New*

Worlds: Genetics of the Human Experience, by Bryan Appleyard. *Observer* (24 January 1999).

- 'Song of the Would-Be Executioner's Son.' Rev. of *Cahiers 1957–1972*, by E.M. Ciorcan. *Times Literary Supplement* (16 January 1998): 9.
- 'Stones of Light.' *New Yorker* (13 January 1997): 76–8.
- 'Stranglehold.' Rev. of *The Future Lasts Forever*, by Louis Althusser. *New Yorker* (21 February 1994): 115–18.
- 'Supreme Fiction.' Rev. of *In the Beauty of the Lilies*, by John Updike. *New Yorker* (11 March 1996): 105–6.
- 'The Thinking Eye: Gombrich on Norms and Forms.' *Encounter* 28, no. 5 (May 1967): 61–4.
- 'Through That Glass Darkly.' *Salmagundi*, no. 93 (Winter 1992): 32–50.
- *Tolstoy or Dostoevsky: An Essay in the Old Criticism.* New York: Knopf, 1959.
- 'To Speak of God.' Rev. of *Karl Barth's Critically Realistic Dialectical Theology*, by Bruce L. McCormack. *Times Literary Supplement* (19 May 1995): 7.
- 'The Total Experience: Hegel's Dogged Quest for the Meaning Beyond Representation.' Rev. of *Und die heroischen Jahre der Philosophie: Eine Biographie*, by Horst Althaus. *Times Literary Supplement* (8 May 1992): 3–5.
- 'Totem or Taboo.' *Salmagundi*, no. 88–9 (Fall 1990–Winter 1991): 385–98.
- 'Troubled Walter.' Rev. of *Walter Benjamin's Selected Writings*, Vol. 2, *Observer* (26 September 1999).
- 'True Leninist: The Apologia for Georg Lukács. *Times Literary Supplement* (13 October 2000): 7–8.
- 'Trusting in Reason: Husserl's "Trance-Like" Labours and the Drama of Betrayed Inheritance.' Rev. of Edmund Husserl, *Briefwechsel*, ed. Karl Schuhmann and Elisabeth Schuhmann. *Times Literary Supplement* (24 June 1994): 3–4.
- 'Two Suppers.' *Salmagundi*, no. 108 (Fall 1995): 33–61.
- *The Uncommon Reader.* Bennington Chapbooks in Literature. Bennington, VT, 1978. Reprinted in *The Ordering Mirror: Readers and Contexts (The Ben Belitt Lectures at Bennington College)*, ed. Phillip Lopate. New York: Fordham University Press, 1993: 1–20.
- 'The Unfinished.' Rev. of *The Man without Qualities*, by Robert Musil. *New Yorker* (17 April 1995): 101–7.
- 'Unfinished voyage.' Rev. of *Sulle Orme Di Ulisse*, by Pietro Boitani; *Ulisse*, ed. Pietro Boitani and Richard Ambrosini. *Times Literary Supplement* (15 October 1999): 15.
- 'Whereof One Cannot Speak.' Rev. of *Wittgenstein: A Life*, by Brian McGuinness. *London Review of Books* (23 June 1988): 15–16.
- 'With Wittgenstein at the End of the World.' Rev. of *Philosophical Investigations*, by Richard Wall. *Observer* (28 January 2001).

- 'Wives, not readers.' Rev. of *The Alphabet v. The Goddess*, by Leonard Schlain. *Observer* (2 May 1999).
- 'Wording Our World.' Rev. of *In Quest of the Ordinary*, by Stanley Cavell. *New Yorker* (19 June 1989): 97–9.
- 'Work in Progress.' Rev. of *The Arcades Project*, by Walter Benjamin. *Times Literary Supplement* (3 December 1999): 3–4.
- 'Yehudi Menuhin: A Magnificent Talent to Communicate.' *Observer* (13 June 1999).
- ed. *Homer in English*. London: Penguin, 1996.
Steiner, Wendy. *The Scandal of Pleasure*. Chicago: University of Chicago Press, 1995.
- 'Silence.' Rev. of *Real Presences*, by George Steiner. *London Review of Books* (1 June 1989): 10–11.
Stern, David. 'Midrash and the Language of Exegesis: A Study of Vayikra Rabbah, Chapter 1.' In Hartman and Budick, eds., *Midrash and Literature*, 105–24.
Stevens, Wallace. *The Necessary Angel*. New York: Vintage, 1951.
Sutherland, John, and Michael Billington, 'From Bard to Worse.' *Guardian* (3 May 2000).
Swift, Graham. *Ever After*. New York: Alfred A. Knopf, 1962.
Taplin, Oliver. 'Difficult Daughter.' Rev. of *Antigones*, by George Steiner. *New York Review of Books* (6 December 1984): 13–15.
Tate, Allen. 'Is Literary Criticism Possible?' In *Literary Criticism: An Introductory Reader*, ed. and introduced by Lionel Trilling, 419–29. New York: Holt, Rinehart and Winston, 1970.
Taylor, Charles. *Sources of the Self: The Making of Modern Identity*. Cambridge: Harvard University Press, 1989.
Taylor, Mark C. *Nots*. Chicago: University of Chicago Press, 1993.
Tompkins, Jane. 'Me and My Shadow. *New Literary History* 19, no. 1 (1987): 169–78.
Tredell, Nicholas. *Conversations with Critics*. Riverdale-on-Hudson: Sheep Meadow Press, 1994.
Trilling, Lionel, *Beyond Culture: Essays on Literature and Learning*. 1965; New York: Harcourt Brace Jovanovich, 1978.
- *The Liberal Imagination: Essays on Literature and Society*. 1965; New York: Viking, 1950.
- ed. *Literary Criticism: An Introductory Reader*. New York: Holt, Rinehart and Winston, Inc., 1970.
- *Mind in the Modern World*. New York: Viking Press, 1973.
Tudeau-Clayton, Margaret, and Martin Warner, eds. *Addressing Frank Kermode: Essays in Criticism and Interpretation*. Urbana: University of Illinois Press, 1991.

Veeser, H. Aram, ed. *Confessions of the Critics: North American Critics' Autobiographical Moves.* New York: Routledge, 1995.
– ed. *The New Historicism.* New York: Routledge, 1989.
Vermes, Geza. *The Religion of Jesus the Jew.* Minneapolis: Fortress Press, 1993.
Ward, Graham. 'Heidegger in Steiner.' In Scott and Sharp, eds., *Reading George Steiner,* 180–204.
White, Hayden. 'Kermode and Theory.' Rev. of *An Appetite for Poetry,* by Frank Kermode. *London Review of Books* (11 October 1990): 14–15.
Williams, William Carlos. *Spring and All.* In *The Collected Poems of William Carlos Williams,* Volume 1: *1909–1939,* ed. A. Walton Litz and Christopher MacGowan. New York: New Directions, 1986.
Winkler, Karen J. 'Scholars Mark the Beginning of the Age of "Post-Theory."' *Chronicle of Higher Education* (13 October 1993): A9, A16–17.
Wittgenstein, Ludwig. *Philosophical Investigations,* 3rd ed. Trans. G.E.M. Anscombe. New York: Macmillan, 1989.
– *Tractatus Logico-Philosophicus.* Trans. C.K. Ogden. London: Routledge, 1988.
Wolfe, Gregory. 'A Stay against Anarchy.' Rev. of *Words Alone,* by Denis Donoghue. *Commonweal* 128, no. 7 (6 April 2001): 24–5.
Wood, James. *The Broken Estate: Essays on Literature and Belief.* New York: Random House, 1999.
– 'George Steiner and the Mystically Unsayable.' Letter. *Times Literary Supplement* (31 October 1997): 21.
– 'Wild and Whirling Words.' Rev. of *Shakespeare's Language,* Frank Kermode. *Guardian* (6 May 2000).
Wood, Michael. 'A Fine Romance.' Rev. of *The Sovereign Ghost,* by Denis Donoghue. *New York Review of Books* (14 April 1977): 33–5.
– 'The Struggles of T.S. Eliot.' Rev. of *The Classic: Literary Images of Permanence and Change,* by Frank Kermode; and *Selected Prose of T.S. Eliot,* ed. Frank Kermode. *New York Review of Books* (13 May 1976).
Wyschogrod, Edith. 'The Mind of a Critical Moralist: Steiner as Jew.' In Scott and Sharp, eds., *Reading George Steiner,* 151–79.

INDEX

STUDIES IN BOOK AND PRINT CULTURE

General editor: Leslie Howsam